The Nature of Code

by Daniel Shiffman

The publisher would go here, but there isn't one; it's only me.

version 1.0, generated December 6, 2012

Dedication

For my grandmother, Bella Manel Greenfield (October 13, 1915 - April 3, 2010)

Bella Manel was born in New York City. A pioneering woman in mathematics, she earned her PhD in 1939 from New York University under the supervision of Richard Courant. She worked for Ramo-Wooldridge (now TRW) and at the Rand Corporation with Richard Bellman. Later, she taught mathematics at the College of Notre Dame (now Notre Dame de Namur University) in Belmont, California, and at UCLA. The Bella Manel Prize for outstanding graduate work by a woman or minority was established at NYU's Courant Institute in 1995.

ISBN-13: 978-0985930806
ISBN-10: 0985930802

This book was generated by the Magic Book Project (http://magicbookproject.com).

Editor	Shannon Fry
Illustrations	Zannah Marsh
Cover Design	David Wilson
Interior Design	David Wilson
Web Site Design	Steve Klise
Editorial and Design Assistant	Evan Emolo
Magic Book Lead Developers	Rune Madsen, Steve Klise
Magic Book Researchers	Evan Emolo, Miguel Bermudez, Luisa Peirera Hors
Index	WordCo Indexing Services

Acknowledgments

"The world around us moves in complicated and wonderful ways. We spend the earlier parts of our lives learning about our environment through perception and interaction. We expect the physical world around us to behave consistently with our perceptual memory, e.g. if we drop a rock it will fall due to gravity, if a gust of wind blows, lighter objects will be tossed by the wind further. This class focuses on understanding, simulating, and incorporating motion-based elements of our physical world into the digital worlds that we create. Our hope is to create intuitive, rich, and more satisfying experiences by drawing from the perceptual memories of our users."

— James Tu, Dynamic Bodies course description, Spring 2003, ITP

A.1 A little bit of history

In 2003, as a graduate student at the Interactive Telecommunications Program (ITP) in the Tisch School of the Arts at New York University, I enrolled in a course called Dynamic Bodies. The course was taught by interaction designer and ITP adjunct professor James Tu. At the time, my work was focused on a series of software experiments that generated real-time "non-photorealistic" imagery. The applications involved capturing images from a live source and "painting" the colors with elements that moved about the screen according to various rules. The Dynamic Bodies course—which covered vectors, forces, oscillations, particle systems, recursion, steering, and springs—aligned perfectly with my work.

I had been using these concepts informally in my own projects, but had never taken the time to closely examine the science behind the algorithms or learn object-oriented techniques to formalize their implementation. That very semester, I also enrolled in Foundations of Generative Art Systems, a course taught by Philip Galanter, that focused on the theory and practice of generative art, covering topics such as chaos, cellular automata, genetic algorithms, neural networks, and fractals. Both Tu's course and Galanter's course opened my eyes to a world of simulation algorithms and techniques that carried me through the next several years of work and teaching, and served as the foundation and inspiration for this book.

But there's another piece of the puzzle missing from this story.

Galanter's course was mostly theory-based, while Tu's was taught using Macromedia Director and the Lingo programming language. That semester, I learned many of the algorithms by translating them into C++ (the language I was using quite awkwardly at the time, well before C++ creative coding environments like openFrameworks and Cinder had arrived). Towards the end of the semester, I discovered something called Processing (http://www.processing.org). Processing was in alpha then (version 0055) and, having had some experience with Java, it intrigued me enough to ask the question: Could this open-source, artist-friendly programming language and environment be the right place to develop a suite of tutorials and examples about programming and simulation? With the support of the ITP and Processing communities, I embarked on what has now been an almost eight-year journey of teaching a variety of programming concepts and their applications using Processing.

I'd like to first thank Red Burns, ITP's founder, who has supported and encouraged me in my work for over ten years. Dan O'Sullivan, the chair of ITP, has been my teaching mentor and was the first to suggest that I try teaching a course on Processing, giving me a reason to start assembling programming tutorials in the first place. Shawn Van Every, developer extraordinaire and author of *Pro Android Media*, has also been a rich source of help and inspiration at ITP over the years. ITP faculty members Clay Shirky, Danny Rozin, Katherine Dillon, Marianne Petit, Marina Zurkow, and Tom Igoe have provided a great deal of support and feedback throughout the writing of this book. The rest of the faculty and staff at ITP have also made this possible: Brian Kim, Edward Gordon, George Agudow, John Duane, Marlon Evans, Matt Berger, Megan Demarest, Midori Yasuda, and Rob Ryan.

The students of ITP, too numerous to mention, have been an amazing source of feedback throughout this process. Much of the material in this book comes from my course of the same title, which I've now taught for five years. I have stacks of draft printouts of the book with notes scrawled along the margins as well as a vast archive of student emails with corrections, comments, and generous words of encouragement.

I am also indebted to the energetic and supportive community of Processing programmers and artists. I wouldn't be writing this book if it weren't for Casey Reas and Ben Fry, who created Processing. I've learned half of what I know simply from reading through the Processing source code; the elegant simplicity of the Processing language, website, and IDE has made programming accessible and fun for all of my students. I've received advice and inspiration from many Processing programmers including Andrés Colubri, Jer Thorp, Marius Watz, Karsten Schmidt, Robert Hodgin, Seb-Lee Delisle, and Ira Greenberg. Heather Dewey-Hagborg provided a great deal of excellent feedback on Chapter 10 (Neural Networks) and Philip Galanter helped to clarify the definitions of complexity and complex systems. Scott Murray provided some really helpful advice about inline SVGs over e-mail. Many of the titles in the Further Reading section were suggested by Golan Levin.

I am indebted to Shannon Fry, who edited this book every step of the way. The knowledge that I would always have her careful and thoughtful feedback on my writing allowed me to plow ahead, aware that everything would come out sounding better after she got her hands on my chapters.

A special mention goes to Zannah Marsh who worked tirelessly to create over a hundred illustrations for this book, developing a friendly and informal look. I especially want to thank her for her patience and willingness to go with the flow as we changed the illustration requirements several times. I also want to thank David Wilson, who came to my rescue at the last minute and designed the interior layout and cover for the book. I am particularly grateful to Steve Klise, who designed and built the book's website, helping me to develop a "pay what you want" model for the digital PDF.

As I'll explain a bit more in the preface, this book was generated with a new open-source system for publishing called "The Magic Book." A crack team of ITP programmers, designers, and artists worked over the course of more than a year to develop this system, which generates a book in a variety of formats (PDF, HTML, and more) from one single ASCIIDOC file, all designed with CSS layout. Rune Madsen began the project and developed the original Ruby / Sinatra framework. I am pretty sure I'd still be struggling with putting the book together well into 2013 if it weren't for Rune's dedication to seeing the project through to the end. Steve Klise contributed countless bug fixes and engineered the system that allows us to restyle code comments to the side of the code blocks themselves. Miguel Bermudez, Evan Emolo, and Luisa Pereira Hors contributed in many ways, learning the ins and outs of ASCIIDOC as well as CSS Paged Media. ITP researcher Greg Borenstein provided a tremendous amount of advice and support along the way regarding the areas of publishing for the Web and print. Prince (http://princexml.com) is the engine the Magic Book uses to generate a PDF from an HTML document, and I'd like to thank Michael Day, CEO of PrinceXML, who answered many of our questions (at lightning speed) along the way.

Finally I'd like to thank my family: my wife, Aliki Caloyeras, who supported this project throughout while having her own giant tome to write, and my children, Elias and Olympia, motivation for finishing this up so that I could spend more time hanging out with them. I'd also like to thank my father, Bernard Shiffman, who generously lent his mathematical expertise and provided feedback along the way, as well as my mother, Doris Yaffe Shiffman, and brother, Jonathan Shiffman, who were always tremendously supportive in asking the question: "How is the book coming along?"

A.2 Kickstarter

There is another organization and community that has made this book possible: Kickstarter.

In 2008, I completed work on my first book, *Learning Processing*, published by Morgan Kaufmann/Elsevier. *Learning Processing* took almost three years to finish. I didn't take a lot of care in choosing a publisher or thinking about the terms. I just thought — "Really? You want to publish a book by me? OK, I'll do it." Unfortunately, my experience was not entirely positive. I had five different editors assigned to me throughout the process, and I received little to no feedback on the content itself. The publisher outsourced the typesetting, which resulted in a great deal of mistakes and inconsistencies in production. In addition, I found the pricing of the book to be off the mark. My goal was to write a friendly, inexpensive (black and white), paperback introduction to programming in Processing, and the book ended up retailing for a "textbook" price of $50.

Now, I want to emphasize that my publisher had good intentions. They honestly wanted to produce the best book possible, one that I would be happy with, that they would be happy with, and that readers would enjoy. And they worked hard to make this happen. Unfortunately, they had to work within a very tight budget, and as a result were stretched extremely thin. In addition, I don't think they were terribly familiar with the world of open-source "creative" coding environments like Processing; their world is computer science textbooks.

As a result, for this Nature of Code book, I felt it was important to try self-publishing. Since I didn't get editing support from the publisher, why not hire an editor? I wasn't happy with the pricing, so why not set the price myself (or, in the case of the PDF, let the buyer set the price)? Then there's the question of marketing — does a publisher add value and help you reach an audience? In some cases, the answer is yes. The O'Reilly "Make" series, for example, does a wonderful job of creating a community around their books and products. Still, in the case of learning to program in Processing, reaching the audience is as simple as one URL — processing.org.

Unfortunately, I quickly discovered that there is one thing a publisher offers that I was not getting from my self-publishing path. One very important, highly crucial detail — a deadline. On my own, I floundered for two years, saying I was going to write the Nature of Code book but only drafting a little bit here and there. On my list of things I needed to do, it was always at the bottom. Then along came Kickstarter, and with an audience sitting and waiting (and having spent cash money), I lived in fear of not meeting my deadline. And the fact that you are reading this now is an indication that it worked.

Most importantly, self-publishing the book has allowed me a great deal of flexibility in how I price and distribute the content. On Elsevier's website, you can purchase *Learning Processing* as an e-book for $53.95. That's right, fifty-three dollars and ninety-five cents. Incidentally, for each e-book sold I get a royalty of 5%, which is $2.70. That's right, two dollars and seventy cents. If I self-publish, I can make the book massively cheaper. Selling a digital copy for $10, I'm reducing the cost to the reader by over eighty percent and tripling the money paid to me. I'm taking this even further with the PDF and allowing buyers to set the price themselves.

In addition, by owning all the content, I am able to release the entire book online for free as well as experiment with new digital formats. The raw text of the book, as well as all the code and illustrations, is licensed under a Creative Commons Attribution-NonCommercial license and is available on GitHub, where readers can submit issues (not to mention pull requests!) with corrections and comments. Finally, by using more flexible print-on-demand services, I can more easily make changes and keep the book current, releasing new editions as often as I like. (A one-time purchase of a digital copy of the book includes lifetime upgrades for free.)

So thank you to Kickstarter, both the company (especially Fred Benenson, who convinced me to take the plunge in the first place and advised me on how to license the book) as well as all the backers who took a chance on this book. Some of these backers, through generosity beyond the call of duty, earned an extra thank-you as part of their reward:

- Alexandre B.
- Robert Hodgin
- JooYoun Paek
- Angela McNamee (Boyhan)
- Bob Ippolito

All of the backers directly contributed to the finishing of this book. Just the sheer act of signing up to contribute money for draft and final versions lit a fire in me to finish, not to mention provided me with the resources to pay for design and editing work (and some babysitting during Saturday morning writing sessions).

In addition to contributing funds, Kickstarter backers read pre-release versions of the chapters and provided tons of feedback, catching many errors and pointing out confusing sections of the book. Two such readers that I'd like to thank are Frederik Vanhoutte and Hans de Wolf, whose expert knowledge of Newtonian physics was enormously helpful in the revising of Chapters 2 and 3.

Preface

P.1 What is this book?

At ITP (http://itp.nyu.edu), I teach a course entitled Introduction to Computational Media. In this course, the students learn the basics of programming (variables, conditionals, loops, objects, arrays) as well as a survey of applications related to making interactive projects (images, pixels, computer vision, networking, data, 3D). The course mostly follows the material found in my intro book *Learning Processing*; in many ways, *The Nature of Code* serves as a follow-up. Once you've learned the basics and seen an array of applications, your next step might be to delve deeply into a particular area. For example, you could focus on computer vision (and read a book like Greg Borenstein's *Making Things See*). In the most basic sense, this book is one possible next step in a world of many. It picks up exactly where *Learning Processing* leaves off, demonstrating more advanced programming techniques with Processing that focus on algorithms and simulation.

The goal of this book is simple. We want to take a look at something that naturally occurs in our physical world, then determine how we can write code to simulate that occurrence.

So then what is this book exactly? Is it a science book? The answer is a resounding no. True, we might examine topics that come from physics or biology, but it won't be our job to investigate these topics with a particularly high level of academic rigor. Instead, we're going to glance at scientific concepts and grab the parts that we need in the service of building a particular software example.

Is this an art or design book? I would also say no; after all, we are going to focus on algorithms and their affiliated programming techniques. Sure, the results will all be visual in nature (manifested as animated Processing sketches), but they will exist more as demonstrations of the algorithms and programming techniques themselves, drawn only with simple shapes and grayscale. It is my hope, however, that designers and artists can incorporate all of the material here into their practice to make new, engaging work.

In the end, if this book is anything, it is really just a good old-fashioned programming book. While a scientific topic may seed a chapter (Newtonian physics, cellular growth, evolution) or the results might inspire an artistic project, the content itself will always boil down to the code implementation, with a particular focus on object-oriented programming.

P.2 A word about Processing

I am using Processing in this book for a number of reasons. For one, it's the language and environment with which I am most comfortable, and it's what I enjoy using for my personal work. Two, it's free, open-source, and well suited to beginners. There is an active, energetic community of people who program with Processing; for many, it's the first programming language they've learned. In this sense, I hope that I can reach a wide audience and demonstrate the concepts in a friendly manner by using Processing.

All that said, there is nothing that ties what we are doing in this book strictly to Processing. This book could have been written using ActionScript, JavaScript, Java (without Processing), or any number of other open-source "creative coding" environments like openFrameworks, Cinder, or the newly released pocode. It is my hope that after I've completed this book, I'll be able to release versions of the examples that run in other environments. If anyone is interested in helping to port the examples, please feel free to contact me (daniel@shiffman.net).

All of the examples in this book have been tested with Processing 2.0b6, but for the most part, they should also work with earlier versions of Processing. I'll be keeping them up-to-date with whatever the latest version is. The most recent code can always be found on GitHub (http://github.com/shiffman/The-Nature-of-Code-Examples).

P.3 What do you need to know?

The prerequisite for understanding the material in this book could be stated as: "one semester of programming instruction with Processing (including familiarity with object-oriented programming)." That said, there's no reason why you couldn't read this book having learned programming using a different language or development environment. The key here is that you have experience with programming.

If you've never written any code before, you are going to struggle, because this book assumes knowledge of all the basics. I would suggest picking up an introductory book on Processing, a number of which are listed on the Processing website (http://processing.org/learning/books/).

If you are an experienced programmer, but haven't worked with Processing, you can probably pick it up by downloading Processing (http://processing.org/download/), poking through the examples, and reading through the Getting Started (http://processing.org/learning/gettingstarted/) page.

I should also point out that experience with object-oriented programming is crucial. We'll review some of the basics in the book's introduction, but I would suggest reading the Processing tutorial on objects (http://processing.org/learning/objects) first.

P.4 What are you using to read this book?

Are you reading this book on a Kindle? Printed paper? On your laptop in PDF form? On a tablet showing an animated HTML5 version? Are you strapped to a chair, absorbing the content directly into your brain via a series of electrodes, tubes, and cartridges?

The book you are reading right now was generated with the Magic Book project (http://www.magicbookproject.com). The Magic Book is an open-source framework for self-publishing developed at ITP (http://itp.nyu.edu). The idea here is that you only need to write the book once as a simple text file. Once you've written your content, you press a magic button, and out comes your book in a variety of formats—PDF, HTML5, printed hardcopy, Kindle, etc. Everything is designed and styled using CSS. As of the first release, the only versions available will be digital PDF, printed hardcopy, and HTML5 (which will include animated versions of the examples using Processing.js). Hopefully over the course of the next year, the book will be available in additional formats. If you'd like to help with this, please contact me (daniel@shiffman.net).

P.5 The "story" of this book

If you glance over the book's table of contents, you'll notice there are ten chapters, each one covering a different topic. And in one sense, this book is just that—a survey of ten concepts and associated code examples. Nevertheless, in putting together the material, I had always imagined something of a linear narrative. Before you begin reading the chapters, I'd like to walk you through this story.

Part I: Inanimate objects

A soccer ball lies in the grass. A kick launches it into the air. Gravity pulls it back down. A heavy gust of wind keeps it afloat a moment longer until it falls and bounces off the head of a jumping player. The soccer ball is not alive; it makes no choices as to how it will move throughout the world. Rather, it is an inanimate object waiting to be pushed and pulled by the forces of its environment.

How would we model a soccer ball moving in Processing? If you've ever programmed a circle moving across a window, then you've probably written the following line of code.

```
x = x + 1;
```

You draw some shape at location x. With each frame of animation, you increment the value of x, redraw the shape and voila—the illusion of motion! Maybe you took it a step or two further, and included a y location, as well as variables for speed along the *x* and *y* axes.

```
x = x + xspeed;
y = y + yspeed;
```

Part I of this story will take us one step further. We're going to take these variables `xspeed` and `yspeed` and learn how together they form a vector (**Chapter 1**), the building block of motion. We won't get any new functionality out of this, but it will build a solid foundation for the rest of the book.

Once we know a little something about vectors, we're going to quickly realize that a force (**Chapter 2**) is a vector. Kick a soccer ball and you are applying a force. What does a force cause an object to do? According to Isaac Newton, force equals mass times acceleration. That force causes an object to accelerate. Modeling forces will allow us to create systems with dynamic motion where objects move according to a variety of rules.

Now, that soccer ball to which you applied a force might have also been spinning. If an object moves according to its acceleration, it can spin according to its angular acceleration (**Chapter 3**). Understanding the basics of angles and trigonometry will allow us to model rotating objects as well as grasp the principles behind oscillating motion, like a pendulum swinging or a spring bouncing.

Once we've tackled the basics of motion and forces for an individual inanimate object, we'll learn how to make thousands upon thousands of those objects and manage them in a single system called a particle system (**Chapter 4**). Particle systems will allow us to look at some advanced features of object-oriented programming, namely inheritance and polymorphism.

In Chapters 1 through 4, all of the examples will be written from "scratch"—meaning the code for the algorithms driving the motion of the objects will be written directly in Processing. We're certainly not the first programmers ever to consider the idea of simulating physics in animation, so next we'll examine how physics libraries (**Chapter 5**) can be used to model more advanced and sophisticated behaviors. We'll look at Box2D (http://www.box2d.org) and toxiclibs' Verlet Physics package (http://toxiclibs.org/).

Part II: It's alive!

What does it mean to model life? Not an easy question to answer, but we can begin by building objects that have an ability to perceive their environment. Let's think about this for a moment. A block that falls off a table moves according to forces, as does a dolphin swimming through the water. But there is a key difference. The block cannot decide to leap off that table. The dolphin can decide to leap out of the water. The dolphin can have dreams and desires. It can feel hunger or fear, and those feelings can inform its movements. By examining techniques behind modeling autonomous agents (**Chapter 6**), we will breathe life into our inanimate objects, allowing them to make decisions about their movements according to their understanding of their environment.

Through combining the concept of autonomous agents with what we learned about modeling systems in Chapter 4, we'll look at models of group behavior that exhibit the properties of complexity. A complex system is typically defined as a system that is "more than the sum of its parts." While the individual elements of the system may be incredibly simple and easily understood, the behavior of the system as a whole can be highly complex, intelligent, and difficult to predict. This will lead us away from thinking purely about modeling motion and into the realm of rule-based systems. What can we model with cellular automata (**Chapter 7**), a system of cells living on a grid? What types of patterns can we generate with fractals (**Chapter 8**), the geometry of nature?

Part III: Intelligence

We made things move. Then we gave those things hopes and dreams and fears, along with rules to live by. The last step in this book will be to make our creations even smarter. Can we apply the biological process of evolution to computational systems (**Chapter 9**) in order to evolve our objects? Taking inspiration from the human brain, can we program an artificial neural network (**Chapter 10**) that can learn from its mistakes and allow our objects to adapt to their environment?

P.6 This book as a syllabus

While the content in this book certainly makes for an intense and highly compressed semester, I have designed it to fit into a fourteen-week course. Nevertheless, it's worth mentioning that I find that the book chapters sometimes work better expanded across multiple weeks. For example, the syllabus for my course generally works out as follows:

Week 1	Introduction and Vectors (Chapter 1)
Week 2	Forces (Chapter 2)
Week 3	Oscillations (Chapter 3)
Week 4	Particle Systems (Chapter 4)
Week 5	Physics Libraries Part I (Chapter 5)
Week 6	Physics Libraries Part II & Steering (Chapters 5-6)
Week 7	Present midterm projects about motion
Week 8	Complex Systems: Flocking and 1D Cellular Automata (Chapters 6-7)
Week 9	Complex Systems: 2D Cellular Automata and Fractals (Chapters 7-8)
Week 10	Genetic Algorithms (Chapter 9)
Week 11	Neural Networks (Chapter 10)
Weeks 12-13	Final project workshop
Week 14	Final project presentation

If you are considering using this text for a course or workshop, please feel free to contact me. I hope to eventually release a companion set of videos and slide presentations as supplementary educational materials.

P.7 The Ecosystem Project

As much as I'd like to pretend you could learn everything by curling up in a comfy chair and reading some prose about programming, to learn programming, you're really going to have to do some programming. You might find it helpful to keep in mind a project idea (or two) to develop as a set of exercises while going from chapter to chapter. In fact, when teaching the Nature of Code course at ITP, I have often found that students enjoy building a single project, step by step, week by week, over the course of a semester.

At the end of each chapter, you'll find a series of exercises for one such project—exercises that build on each other, one topic at a time. Consider the following scenario. You've been asked by a science museum to develop the software for a new exhibit—The Digital Ecosystem, a world of animated, procedural creatures that live on a projection screen for visitors to enjoy as they enter the museum. I don't mean to suggest that this is a particularly innovative or creative concept. Rather, we'll use this example project idea as a literal representation of the content in the book, demonstrating how the elements fit together in a single software project. I encourage you to develop your own idea, one that is more abstract and creative in its thinking.

P.8 Where do I find the code online and submit feedback?

For all things book-related, please visit the Nature of Code website (http://www.natureofcode.com). The raw source text of the book and all of the illustrations are on GitHub (http://github.com/shiffman/The-Nature-of-Code). Please leave feedback and submit corrections using GitHub issues.

The source code for all of the examples (and exercises) is also available on GitHub (http://github.com/shiffman/The-Nature-of-Code-Examples). The chapters themselves include code snippets in-line with the text. However, I want to mention that in many cases, I have shortened or simplified the code snippets in order to illustrate a specific point. In all cases, the full code with comments can be found via GitHub.

If you have questions about the code itself, I would suggest posting them on the Processing forum (http://forum.processing.org).

Table of Contents

Acknowledgments iv

A.1 A little bit of history v

A.2 Kickstarter vii

Preface ix

P.1 What is this book? ix

P.2 A word about Processing x

P.3 What do you need to know? x

P.4 What are you using to read this book? xi

P.5 The “story” of this book xi

P.6 This book as a syllabus xiii

P.7 The Ecosystem Project xiv

P.8 Where do I find the code online and submit feedback? xv

Introduction 1

I.1 Random Walks 1

I.2 The Random Walker Class 2

I.3 Probability and Non-Uniform Distributions 7

I.4 A Normal Distribution of Random Numbers 11
I.5 A Custom Distribution of Random Numbers 14
I.6 Perlin Noise (A Smoother Approach) 17
I.7 Onward 26

Chapter 1. Vectors 27

1.1 Vectors, You Complete Me 28
1.2 Vectors for Processing Programmers 30
1.3 Vector Addition 33
1.4 More Vector Math 37
1.5 Vector Magnitude 42
1.6 Normalizing Vectors 43
1.7 Vector Motion: Velocity 45
1.8 Vector Motion: Acceleration 49
1.9 Static vs. Non-Static Functions 54
1.10 Interactivity with Acceleration 57

Chapter 2. Forces 63

2.1 Forces and Newton's Laws of Motion 63
2.2 Forces and Processing—Newton's Second Law as a Function 67
2.3 Force Accumulation 68
2.4 Dealing with Mass 70
2.5 Creating Forces 73
2.6 Gravity on Earth and Modeling a Force 77
2.7 Friction 80
2.8 Air and Fluid Resistance 83
2.9 Gravitational Attraction 88
2.10 Everything Attracts (or Repels) Everything 97

Chapter 3. Oscillation 101

3.1 Angles 101
3.2 Angular Motion 104
3.3 Trigonometry 108
3.4 Pointing in the Direction of Movement 109
3.5 Polar vs. Cartesian Coordinates 112
3.6 Oscillation Amplitude and Period 116
3.7 Oscillation with Angular Velocity 119
3.8 Waves 122
3.9 Trigonometry and Forces: The Pendulum 127
3.10 Spring Forces 134

Chapter 4. Particle Systems 143

4.1 Why We Need Particle Systems 144
4.2 A Single Particle 145
4.3 The ArrayList 149
4.4 The Particle System Class 155
4.5 A System of Systems 157
4.6 Inheritance and Polymorphism: An Introduction 160
4.7 Inheritance Basics 162
4.8 Particles with Inheritance 166
4.9 Polymorphism Basics 168
4.10 Particle Systems with Polymorphism 170
4.11 Particle Systems with Forces 173
4.12 Particle Systems with Repellers 178
4.13 Image Textures and Additive Blending 183

Chapter 5. Physics Libraries 189

5.1 What Is Box2D and When Is It Useful? 190
5.2 Getting Box2D in Processing 192
5.3 Box2D Basics 192

5.4 Living in a Box2D World 196

5.5 Building a Box2D Body 198

5.6 Three's Company: Bodies and Shapes and Fixtures 200

5.7 Box2D and Processing: Reunited and It Feels So Good 203

5.8 Fixed Box2D Objects 209

5.9 A Curvy Boundary 211

5.10 Complex Forms 215

5.11 Feeling Attached—Box2D Joints 222

5.12 Bringing It All Back Home to Forces 232

5.13 Collision Events 234

5.14 A Brief Interlude—Integration Methods 238

5.15 Verlet Physics with toxiclibs 241

5.16 Particles and Springs in toxiclibs 244

5.17 Putting It All Together: A Simple Interactive Spring 247

5.18 Connected Systems, Part I: String 249

5.19 Connected Systems, Part II: Force-Directed Graph 253

5.20 Attraction and Repulsion Behaviors 256

Chapter 6. Autonomous Agents 260

6.1 Forces from Within 260

6.2 Vehicles and Steering 262

6.3 The Steering Force 263

6.4 Arriving Behavior 270

6.5 Your Own Desires: Desired Velocity 274

6.6 Flow Fields 276

6.7 The Dot Product 282

6.8 Path Following 286

6.9 Path Following with Multiple Segments 294

6.10 Complex Systems 298

6.11 Group Behaviors (or: Let's not run into each other) 300

6.12 Combinations 306

6.13 Flocking 308

6.14 Algorithmic Efficiency (or: Why does my $@(*%! run so slowly?) 315

6.15 A Few Last Notes: Optimization Tricks 317

Chapter 7. Cellular Automata 323

7.1 What Is a Cellular Automaton? 324

7.2 Elementary Cellular Automata 325

7.3 How to Program an Elementary CA 330

7.4 Drawing an Elementary CA 336

7.5 Wolfram Classification 340

7.6 The Game of Life 342

7.7 Programming the Game of Life 345

7.8 Object-Oriented Cells 349

7.9 Variations of Traditional CA 351

Chapter 8. Fractals 355

8.1 What Is a Fractal? 356

8.2 Recursion 358

8.3 The Cantor Set with a Recursive Function 363

8.4 The Koch Curve and the ArrayList Technique 366

8.5 Trees 374

8.6 L-systems 382

Chapter 9. The Evolution of Code 390

9.1 Genetic Algorithms: Inspired by Actual Events 391

9.2 Why Use Genetic Algorithms? 392

9.3 Darwinian Natural Selection 394

9.4 The Genetic Algorithm, Part I: Creating a Population 395

9.5 The Genetic Algorithm, Part II: Selection 397
9.6 The Genetic Algorithm, Part III: Reproduction 399
9.7 Code for Creating the Population 402
9.8 Genetic Algorithms: Putting It All Together 409
9.9 Genetic Algorithms: Make Them Your Own 413
9.10 Evolving Forces: Smart Rockets 420
9.11 Smart Rockets: Putting It All Together 425
9.12 Interactive Selection 431
9.13 Ecosystem Simulation 435

Chapter 10. Neural Networks 444

10.1 Artificial Neural Networks: Introduction and Application 445
10.2 The Perceptron 448
10.3 Simple Pattern Recognition Using a Perceptron 450
10.4 Coding the Perceptron 452
10.5 A Steering Perceptron 460
10.6 It's a "Network," Remember? 466
10.7 Neural Network Diagrams 468
10.8 Animating Feed Forward 473

Further Reading 481

Books 481
Papers and Articles 482

Index 484

Introduction

"I am two with nature."

— Woody Allen

Here we are: the beginning. Well, almost the beginning. If it's been a while since you've done any programming in Processing (or any math, for that matter), this introduction will get your mind back into computational thinking before we approach some of the more difficult and complex material.

In Chapter 1, we're going to talk about the concept of a vector and how it will serve as the building block for simulating motion throughout this book. But before we take that step, let's think about what it means for something to simply move around the screen. Let's begin with one of the best-known and simplest simulations of motion—the random walk.

I.1 Random Walks

Imagine you are standing in the middle of a balance beam. Every ten seconds, you flip a coin. Heads, take a step forward. Tails, take a step backward. This is a random walk—a path defined as a series of random steps. Stepping off that balance beam and onto the floor, you could perform a random walk in two dimensions by flipping that same coin twice with the following results:

Flip 1	Flip 2	Result
Heads	Heads	Step forward.
Heads	Tails	Step right.
Tails	Heads	Step left.
Tails	Tails	Step backward.

Yes, this may seem like a particularly unsophisticated algorithm. Nevertheless, random walks can be used to model phenomena that occur in the real world, from the movements of molecules in a gas to the behavior of a gambler spending a day at the casino. As for us, we begin this book studying a random walk with three goals in mind.

1. We need to review a programming concept central to this book—object-oriented programming. The random walker will serve as a template for how we will use object-oriented design to make things that move around a Processing window.

2. The random walk instigates the two questions that we will ask over and over again throughout this book: "How do we define the rules that govern the behavior of our objects?" and then, "How do we implement these rules in Processing?"

3. Throughout the book, we'll periodically need a basic understanding of randomness, probability, and Perlin noise. The random walk will allow us to demonstrate a few key points that will come in handy later.

I.2 The Random Walker Class

Let's review a bit of object-oriented programming (OOP) first by building a `Walker` object. This will be only a cursory review. If you have never worked with OOP before, you may want something more comprehensive; I'd suggest stopping here and reviewing the basics on the Processing website (http://processing.org/learning/objects/) before continuing.

An ***object*** in Processing is an entity that has both data and functionality. We are looking to design a `Walker` object that both keeps track of its data (where it exists on the screen) and has the capability to perform certain actions (such as draw itself or take a step).

A ***class*** is the template for building actual instances of objects. Think of a class as the cookie cutter; the objects are the cookies themselves.

Let's begin by defining the `Walker` class—what it means to be a `Walker` object. The `Walker` only needs two pieces of data—a number for its x-location and one for its y-location.

```
class Walker {
```

```
int x;                                   Objects have data.
int y;
```

Every class must have a constructor, a special function that is called when the object is first created. You can think of it as the object's `setup()`. There, we'll initialize the `Walker`'s starting location (in this case, the center of the window).

```
Walker() {                               Objects have a constructor where they are
  x = width/2;                           initialized.
  y = height/2;
}
```

Finally, in addition to data, classes can be defined with functionality. In this example, a `Walker` has two functions. We first write a function that allows the object to display itself (as a white dot).

```
void display() {                         Objects have functions.
  stroke(0);
  point(x,y);
}
```

The second function directs the `Walker` object to take a step. Now, this is where things get a bit more interesting. Remember that floor on which we were taking random steps? Well, now we can use a Processing window in that same capacity. There are four possible steps. A step to the right can be simulated by incrementing x (x++); to the left by decrementing x (x--); forward by going down a pixel (y++); and backward by going up a pixel (y--). How do we pick from these four choices? Earlier we stated that we could flip two coins. In Processing, however, when we want to randomly choose from a list of options, we can pick a random number using `random()`.

```
void step() {
  int choice = int(random(4));           0, 1, 2, or 3
```

The above line of code picks a random floating point number between 0 and 4 and converts it to an integer, with a result of 0, 1, 2, or 3. Technically speaking, the highest number will never be 4.0, but rather 3.999999999 (with as many 9s as there are decimal places); since the process of converting to an integer lops off the decimal place, the highest `int` we can get is 3. Next, we take the appropriate step (left, right, up, or down) depending on which random number was picked.

```
    if (choice == 0) {                The random "choice" determines our step.
      x++;
    } else if (choice == 1) {
      x--;
    } else if (choice == 2) {
      y++;
    } else {
      y--;
    }
  }
}
```

Now that we've written the class, it's time to make an actual `Walker` object in the main part of our sketch—`setup()` and `draw()`. Assuming we are looking to model a single random walk, we declare one global variable of type `Walker`.

```
Walker w;                A Walker object
```

Then we create the object in `setup()` by calling the constructor with the new operator.

Example I.1: Traditional random walk

Each time you see the above Example heading in this book, it means there is a corresponding code example available on GitHub (http://github.com/shiffman/The-Nature-of-Code-Examples).

```
void setup() {
  size(640,360);
  w = new Walker();            Create the Walker.
  background(255);
}
```

Finally, during each cycle through `draw()`, we ask the `Walker` to take a step and draw a dot.

```
void draw() {
  w.step();                    Call functions on the Walker.
  w.display();
}
```

Since we only draw the background once in `setup()`, rather than clearing it continually each time through `draw()`, we see the trail of the random walk in our Processing window.

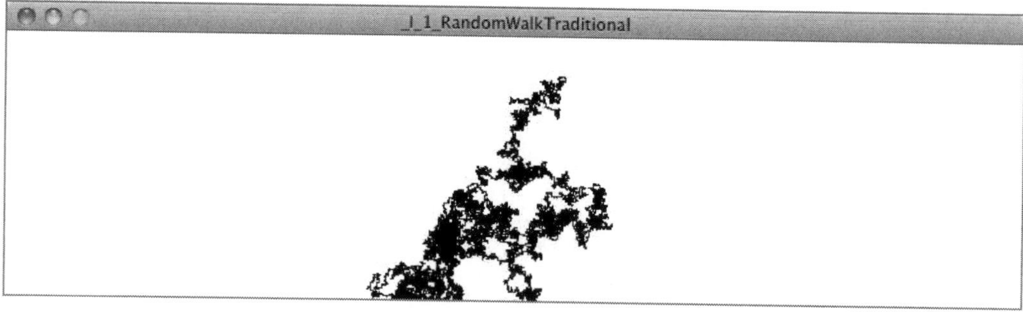

There are a couple improvements we could make to the random walker. For one, this `Walker`'s step choices are limited to four options—up, down, left, and right. But any given pixel in the window has eight possible neighbors, and a ninth possibility is to stay in the same place.

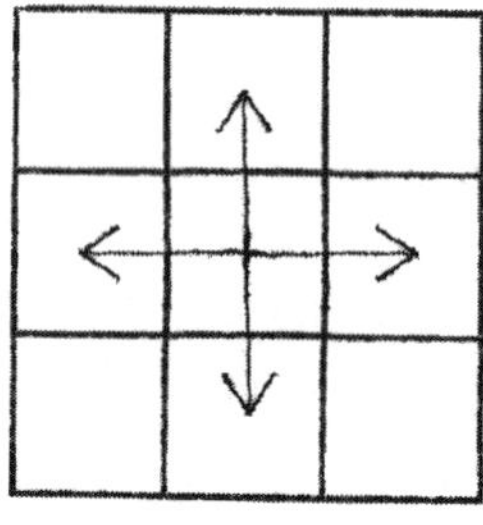

4 possible steps

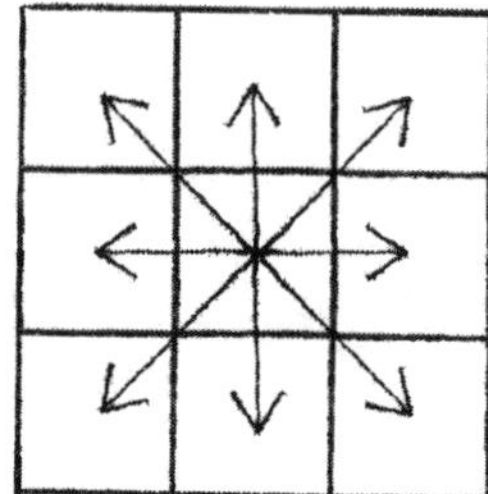

8 possible steps

Figure I.1

To implement a `Walker` object that can step to any neighboring pixel (or stay put), we could pick a number between 0 and 8 (nine possible choices). However, a more efficient way to write the code would be to simply pick from three possible steps along the x-axis (-1, 0, or 1) and three possible steps along the y-axis.

```
void step() {
  int stepx = int(random(3))-1;        // Yields -1, 0, or 1
  int stepy = int(random(3))-1;
  x += stepx;
  y += stepy;
}
```

Taking this further, we could use floating point numbers (i.e. decimal numbers) for x and y instead and move according to an arbitrary random value between -1 and 1.

```
void step() {
  float stepx = random(-1, 1);        // Yields any floating point number between -1.0 and 1.0
  float stepy = random(-1, 1);
```

```
    x += stepx;
    y += stepy;
  }
```

All of these variations on the "traditional" random walk have one thing in common: at any moment in time, the probability that the `Walker` will take a step in a given direction is equal to the probability that the `Walker` will take a step in any direction. In other words, if there are four possible steps, there is a 1 in 4 (or 25%) chance the `Walker` will take any given step. With nine possible steps, it's a 1 in 9 (or 11.1%) chance.

Conveniently, this is how the `random()` function works. Processing's random number generator (which operates behind the scenes) produces what is known as a "uniform" distribution of numbers. We can test this distribution with a Processing sketch that counts each time a random number is picked and graphs it as the height of a rectangle.

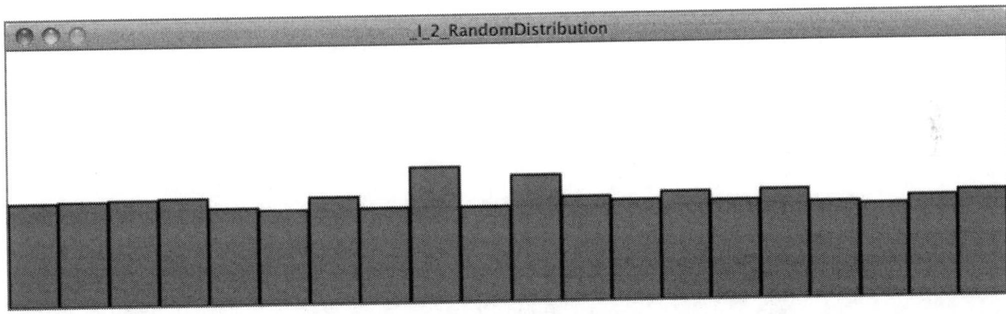

Example I.2: Random number distribution

```
int[] randomCounts;
```

An array to keep track of how often random numbers are picked

```
void setup() {
  size(640,240);
  randomCounts = new int[20];
}

void draw() {
  background(255);

  int index = int(random(randomCounts.length));
```

Pick a random number and increase the count.

```
  randomCounts[index]++;

  stroke(0);
  fill(175);
  int w = width/randomCounts.length;
```

```
  for (int x = 0; x < randomCounts.length; x++) {      Graphing the results
    rect(x*w,height-randomCounts[x],w-1,randomCounts[x]);
  }
}
```

The above screenshot shows the result of the sketch running for a few minutes. Notice how each bar of the graph differs in height. Our sample size (i.e. the number of random numbers we've picked) is rather small and there are some occasional discrepancies, where certain numbers are picked more often. Over time, with a good random number generator, this would even out.

Pseudo-Random Numbers

The random numbers we get from the `random()` function are not truly random; therefore they are known as "pseudo-random." They are the result of a mathematical function that simulates randomness. This function would yield a pattern over time, but that time period is so long that for us, it's just as good as pure randomness!

Exercise I.1

Create a random walker that has a tendency to move down and to the right. (We'll see the solution to this in the next section.)

I.3 Probability and Non-Uniform Distributions

Remember when you first started programming in Processing? Perhaps you wanted to draw a lot of circles on the screen. So you said to yourself: "Oh, I know. I'll draw all these circles at random locations, with random sizes and random colors." In a computer graphics system, it's often easiest to seed a system with randomness. In this book, however, we're looking to build systems modeled on what we see in nature. Defaulting to randomness is not a particularly thoughtful solution to a design problem—in particular, the kind of problem that involves creating an organic or natural-looking simulation.

With a few tricks, we can change the way we use `random()` to produce "non-uniform" distributions of random numbers. This will come in handy throughout the book as we look at a number of different scenarios. When we examine genetic algorithms, for example, we'll need a methodology for performing "selection"—which members of our population should be selected to pass their DNA to the next generation? Remember the concept of survival of the fittest? Let's say we have a population of monkeys evolving. Not every monkey will have a equal chance of reproducing. To simulate Darwinian evolution, we can't simply pick two random monkeys to be parents. We need the more "fit" ones to be more likely to be chosen. We need to define the "probability of the fittest." For example, a particularly fast and strong monkey might have a 90% chance of procreating, while a weaker one has only a 10% chance.

Let's pause here and take a look at probability's basic principles. First we'll examine single event probability, i.e. the likelihood that a given event will occur.

If you have a system with a certain number of possible outcomes, the probability of the occurrence of a given event equals the number of outcomes that qualify as that event divided by the total number of all possible outcomes. A coin toss is a simple example—it has only two possible outcomes, heads or tails. There is only one way to flip heads. The probability that the coin will turn up heads, therefore, is one divided by two: 1/2 or 50%.

Take a deck of fifty-two cards. The probability of drawing an ace from that deck is:

number of aces / number of cards = 4 / 52 = 0.077 = ~ 8%

The probability of drawing a diamond is:

number of diamonds / number of cards = 13 / 52 = 0.25 = 25%

We can also calculate the probability of multiple events occurring in sequence. To do this, we simply multiply the individual probabilities of each event.

The probability of a coin turning up heads three times in a row is:

(1/2) * (1/2) * (1/2) = 1/8 (or 0.125)

...meaning that a coin will turn up heads three times in a row one out of eight times (each "time" being three tosses).

Exercise I.2

What is the probability of drawing two aces in a row from a deck of fifty-two cards?

There are a couple of ways in which we can use the `random()` function with probability in code. One technique is to fill an array with a selection of numbers—some of which are repeated—then choose random numbers from that array and generate events based on those choices.

```
int[] stuff = new int[5]
stuff[0] = 1;
stuff[1] = 1;
```

1 is stored in the array twice, making it more likely to be picked.

```
stuff[2] = 2;
stuff[3] = 3;
stuff[4] = 3;
int index = int(random(stuff.length));
```

Picking a random element from an array

Running this code will produce a 40% chance of printing the value 1, a 20% chance of printing 2, and a 40% chance of printing 3.

We can also ask for a random number (let's make it simple and just consider random floating point values between 0 and 1) and allow an event to occur only if our random number is within a certain range. For example:

```
float prob = 0.10;
```

A probability of 10%

```
float r = random(1);
```

A random floating point value between 0 and 1

```
if (r < prob) {
   // try again!
}
```

If our random number is less than 0.1, try again!

This method can also be applied to multiple outcomes. Let's say that Outcome A has a 60% chance of happening, Outcome B, a 10% chance, and Outcome C, a 30% chance. We implement this in code by picking a random float and seeing into what range it falls.

- *between 0.00 and 0.60 (60%) –> Outcome A*
- *between 0.60 and 0.70 (10%) –> Outcome B*
- *between 0.70 and 1.00 (30%) –> Outcome C*

```
float num = random(1);
```

```
if (num < 0.6) {
```

If random number is less than 0.6

```
  println("Outcome A");
} else if (num < 0.7) {
```

Between 0.6 and 0.7

```
  println("Outcome B");
} else {
```

Greater than 0.7

```
  println("Outcome C");
}
```

We could use the above methodology to create a random walker that tends to move to the right. Here is an example of a `Walker` with the following probabilities:

- *chance of moving up: 20%*

- *chance of moving down: 20%*
- *chance of moving left: 20%*
- *chance of moving right: 40%*

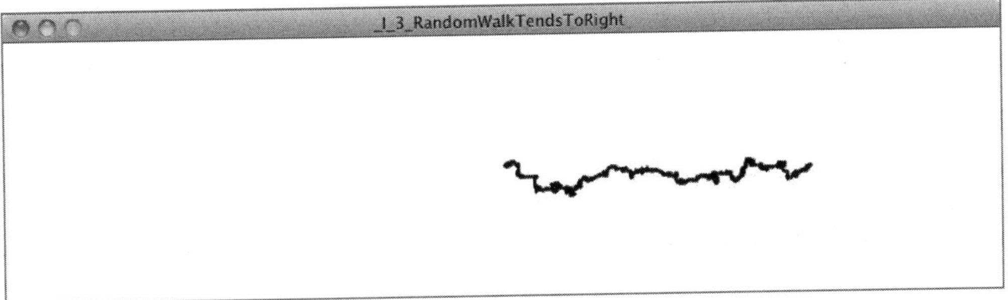

Example I.3: Walker that tends to move to the right

```
void step() {

  float r = random(1);
  if (r < 0.4) {                A 40% chance of moving to the right!
    x++;
  } else if (r < 0.6) {
    x--;
  } else if (r < 0.8) {
    y++;
  } else {
    y--;
  }
}
```

Exercise I.3

Create a random walker with dynamic probabilities. For example, can you give it a 50% chance of moving in the direction of the mouse?

I.4 A Normal Distribution of Random Numbers

Let's go back to that population of simulated Processing monkeys. Your program generates a thousand Monkey objects, each with a height value between 200 and 300 (as this is a world of monkeys that have heights between 200 and 300 pixels).

```
float h = random(200,300);
```

Does this accurately depict the heights of real-world beings? Think of a crowded sidewalk in New York City. Pick any person off the street and it may appear that their height is random. Nevertheless, it's not the kind of random that `random()` produces. People's heights are not uniformly distributed; there are a great deal more people of average height than there are very tall or very short ones. To simulate nature, we may want it to be more likely that our monkeys are of average height (250 pixels), yet still allow them to be, on occasion, very short or very tall.

A distribution of values that cluster around an average (referred to as the "mean") is known as a "normal" distribution. It is also called the Gaussian distribution (named for mathematician Carl Friedrich Gauss) or, if you are French, the Laplacian distribution (named for Pierre-Simon Laplace). Both mathematicians were working concurrently in the early nineteenth century on defining such a distribution.

When you graph the distribution, you get something that looks like the following, informally known as a bell curve:

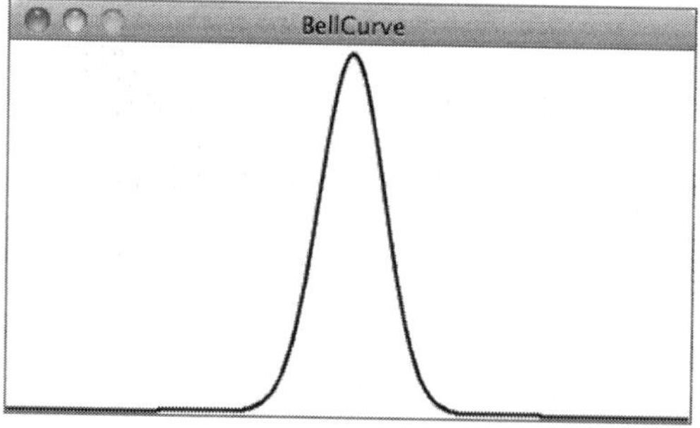

Figure I.2

Figure I.3

The curve is generated by a mathematical function that defines the probability of any given value occurring as a function of the mean (often written as μ, the Greek letter *mu*) and standard deviation (σ, the Greek letter *sigma*).

The mean is pretty easy to understand. In the case of our height values between 200 and 300, you probably have an intuitive sense of the mean (i.e. average) as 250. However, what if I were to say that the standard deviation is 3 or 15? What does this mean for the numbers? The graphs above should give us a hint. The graph on the left shows us the distribution with a very low standard deviation, where the majority of the values cluster closely around the mean. The graph on the right shows us a higher standard deviation, where the values are more evenly spread out from the average.

The numbers work out as follows: Given a population, 68% of the members of that population will have values in the range of one standard deviation from the mean, 98% within two standard deviations, and 99.7% within three standard deviations. Given a standard deviation of 5 pixels, only 0.3% of the monkey heights will be less than 235 pixels (three standard deviations below the mean of 250) or greater than 265 pixels (three standard deviations above the mean of 250).

Calculating Mean and Standard Deviation

Consider a class of ten students who receive the following scores (out of 100) on a test:

85, 82, 88, 86, 85, 93, 98, 40, 73, 83

The mean is the average: 81.3

The standard deviation is calculated as the square root of the average of the squares of deviations around the mean. In other words, take the difference from the mean for each person and square it (variance). Calculate the average of all these values and take the square root as the standard deviation.

Score	Difference from Mean	Variance
85	85-81.3 = 3.7	$(3.7)^2 = 13.69$
40	40-81.3 = -41.3	$(-41.3)^2 = 1705.69$
etc.		
	Average Variance:	**254.23**

The standard deviation is the square root of the average variance: 15.13

Luckily for us, to use a normal distribution of random numbers in a Processing sketch, we don't have to do any of these calculations ourselves. Instead, we can make use of a class known as `Random`, which we get for free as part of the default Java libraries imported into

Processing (see the JavaDocs (http://docs.oracle.com/javase/6/docs/api/java/util/Random.html) for more information).

To use the `Random` class, we must first declare a variable of type `Random` and create the `Random` object in `setup()`.

```
Random generator;

void setup() {
  size(640,360);
  generator = new Random();
}
```

We use the variable name "generator" because what we have here can be thought of as a random number generator.

If we want to produce a random number with a normal (or Gaussian) distribution each time we run through `draw()`, it's as easy as calling the function `nextGaussian()`.

```
void draw() {
  float num = (float) generator.nextGaussian();
}
```

Asking for a Gaussian random number. (Note nextGaussian() returns a double and must be converted to float.)

Here's the thing. What are we supposed to do with this value? What if we wanted to use it, for example, to assign the x-position of a shape we draw on screen?

The `nextGaussian()` function returns a normal distribution of random numbers with the following parameters: *a mean of zero* and *a standard deviation of one*. Let's say we want a mean of 320 (the center horizontal pixel in a window of width 640) and a standard deviation of 60 pixels. We can adjust the value to our parameters by multiplying it by the standard deviation and adding the mean.

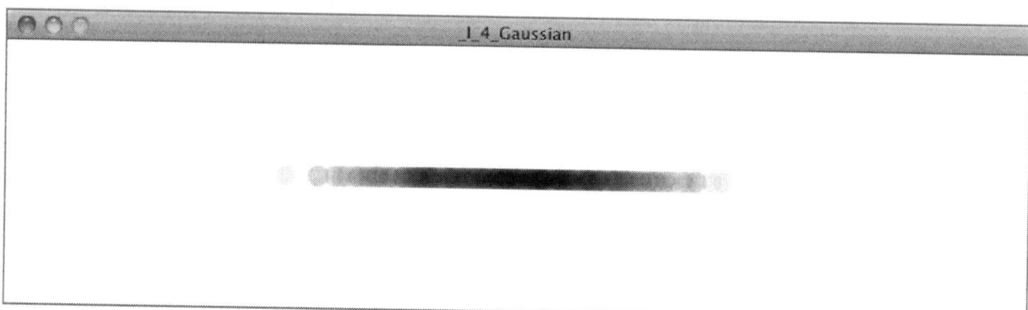

Example I.4: Gaussian distribution

```
void draw() {
```

```
  float num = (float) generator.nextGaussian();     Note that nextGaussian() returns a double.

  float sd = 60;
  float mean = 320;

  float x = sd * num + mean;                        Multiply by the standard deviation and add
                                                    the mean.

  noStroke();
  fill(255,10);
  ellipse(x,180,16,16);
}
```

By drawing the ellipses on top of each other with some transparency, we can actually see the distribution. The brightest spot is near the center, where most of the values cluster, but every so often circles are drawn farther to the right or left of the center.

Exercise I.4

Consider a simulation of paint splatter drawn as a collection of colored dots. Most of the paint clusters around a central location, but some dots do splatter out towards the edges. Can you use a normal distribution of random numbers to generate the locations of the dots? Can you also use a normal distribution of random numbers to generate a color palette?

Exercise I.5

A Gaussian random walk is defined as one in which the step size (how far the object moves in a given direction) is generated with a normal distribution. Implement this variation of our random walk.

I.5 A Custom Distribution of Random Numbers

There will come a time in your life when you do not want a uniform distribution of random values, or a Gaussian one. Let's imagine for a moment that you are a random walker in search of food. Moving randomly around a space seems like a reasonable strategy for finding something to eat. After all, you don't know where the food is, so you might as well search randomly until you find it. The problem, as you may have noticed, is that random walkers return to previously visited locations many times (this is known as "oversampling"). One strategy to avoid such a problem is to, every so often, take a very large step. This allows the walker to forage randomly around a specific location while periodically jumping very far away to reduce the amount of oversampling. This variation on the random walk (known as a Lévy flight) requires a custom set of probabilities. Though not an exact implementation of a Lévy flight, we could state the probability distribution as follows: the longer the step, the less likely it is to be picked; the shorter the step, the more likely.

Earlier in this prologue, we saw that we could generate custom probability distributions by filling an array with values (some duplicated so that they would be picked more frequently) or by testing the result of `random()`. We could implement a Lévy flight by saying that there is a 1% chance of the walker taking a large step.

```
float r = random(1);
if (r < 0.01) {                    // A 1% chance of taking a large step
  xstep = random(-100,100);
  ystep = random(-100,100);
} else {
  xstep = random(-1,1);
  ystep = random(-1,1);
}
```

However, this reduces the probabilities to a fixed number of options. What if we wanted to make a more general rule—the higher a number, the more likely it is to be picked? 3.145 would be more likely to be picked than 3.144, even if that likelihood is just a tiny bit greater. In other words, if x is the random number, we could map the likelihood on the y-axis with y = x.

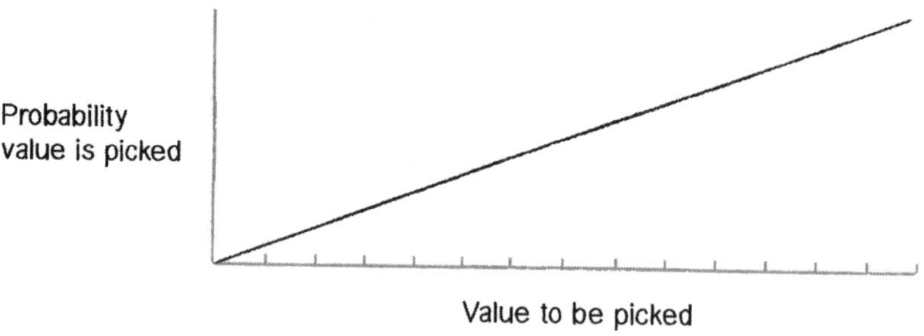

Figure I.4

If we can figure out how to generate a distribution of random numbers according to the above graph, then we will be able to apply the same methodology to any curve for which we have a formula.

One solution is to pick two random numbers instead of one. The first random number is just that, a random number. The second one, however, is what we'll call a "qualifying random value." It will tell us whether to use the first one or throw it away and pick another one. Numbers that have an easier time qualifying will be picked more often, and numbers that rarely qualify will be picked infrequently. Here are the steps (for now, let's consider only random values between 0 and 1):

1. Pick a random number: R1
2. Compute a probability P that R1 should qualify. Let's try: P = R1.
3. Pick another random number: R2
4. If R2 is less than P, then we have found our number—R1!
5. If R2 is not less than P, go back to step 1 and start over.

Here we are saying that the likelihood that a random value will qualify is equal to the random number itself. Let's say we pick 0.1 for R1. This means that R1 will have a 10% chance of qualifying. If we pick 0.83 for R1 then it will have a 83% chance of qualifying. The higher the number, the greater the likelihood that we will actually use it.

Here is a function (named for the Monte Carlo method, which was named for the Monte Carlo casino) that implements the above algorithm, returning a random value between 0 and 1.

```
float montecarlo() {
  while (true) {                          // We do this "forever" until we find a qualifying random value.

    float r1 = random(1);                 // Pick a random value.
    float probability = r1;               // Assign a probability.
    float r2 = random(1);                 // Pick a second random value.

    if (r2 < probability) {               // Does it qualify? If so, we're done!
      return r1;
    }
  }
}
```

Exercise I.6

Use a custom probability distribution to vary the size of a step taken by the random walker. The step size can be determined by influencing the range of values picked. Can you map the probability exponentially—i.e. making the likelihood that a value is picked equal to the value squared?

```
float stepsize = random(0,10);
```

A uniform distribution of step sizes. Change this!

```
float stepx = random(-stepsize,stepsize);
float stepy = random(-stepsize,stepsize);

x += stepx;
y += stepy;
```

(Later we'll see how to do this more efficiently using vectors.)

I.6 Perlin Noise (A Smoother Approach)

A good random number generator produces numbers that have no relationship and show no discernible pattern. As we are beginning to see, a little bit of randomness can be a good thing when programming organic, lifelike behaviors. However, randomness as the single guiding principle is not necessarily natural. An algorithm known as "Perlin noise," named for its inventor Ken Perlin, takes this concept into account. Perlin developed the noise function while working on the original *Tron* movie in the early 1980s; it was designed to create procedural textures for computer-generated effects. In 1997 Perlin won an Academy Award in technical achievement for this work. Perlin noise can be used to generate various effects with natural qualities, such as clouds, landscapes, and patterned textures like marble.

Perlin noise has a more organic appearance because it produces a naturally ordered ("smooth") sequence of pseudo-random numbers. The graph on the left below shows Perlin noise over time, with the x-axis representing time; note the smoothness of the curve. The graph on the right shows pure random numbers over time. (The code for generating these graphs is available in the accompanying book downloads.)

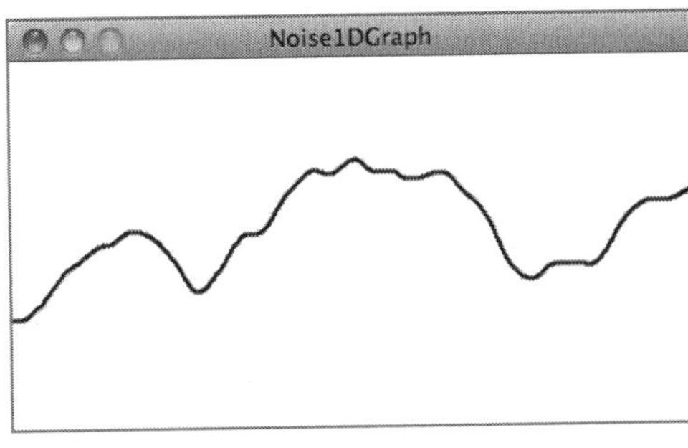

Figure I.5: Noise

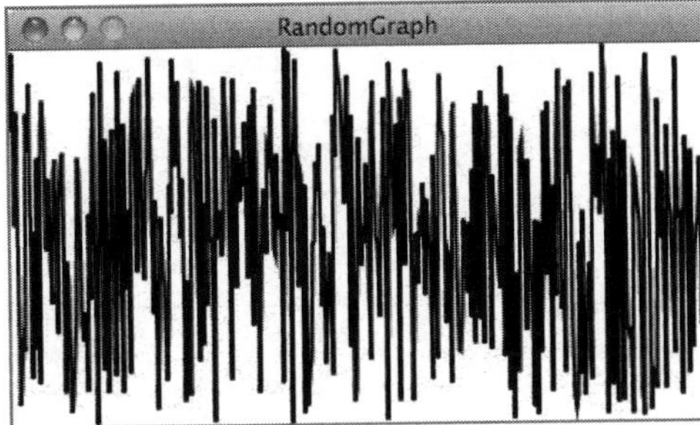

Figure I.6: Random

Processing has a built-in implementation of the Perlin noise algorithm: the function `noise()`. The `noise()` function takes one, two, or three arguments, as noise is computed in one, two, or three dimensions. Let's start by looking at one-dimensional noise.

Noise Detail

The Processing noise reference (http://processing.org/reference/noise_.html) tells us that noise is calculated over several "octaves." Calling the `noiseDetail()` (http://processing.org/reference/noiseDetail_.html) function will change both the number of octaves and their importance relative to one another. This in turn changes how the noise function behaves.

An online lecture by Ken Perlin lets you learn more about how noise works from Perlin himself (http://www.noisemachine.com/talk1/).

Consider drawing a circle in our Processing window at a random x-location.

```
float x = random(0,width);          A random x-location
ellipse(x,180,16,16);
```

Now, instead of a random x-location, we want a Perlin noise x-location that is "smoother." You might think that all you need to do is replace `random()` with `noise()`, i.e.

```
float x = noise(0,width);          A noise x-location?
```

While conceptually this is exactly what we want to do—calculate an x-value that ranges between 0 and the width according to Perlin noise—this is not the correct implementation. While the arguments to the `random()` function specify a range of values between a minimum and a maximum, `noise()` does not work this way. Instead, the output range is fixed—it always returns a value between 0 and 1. We'll see in a moment that we can get around this easily with Processing's `map()` function, but first we must examine what exactly `noise()` expects us to pass in as an argument.

We can think of one-dimensional Perlin noise as a linear sequence of values over time. For example:

Time	Noise Value
0	0.365
1	0.363
2	0.363
3	0.364
4	0.366

Now, in order to access a particular noise value in Processing, we have to pass a specific "moment in time" to the `noise()` function. For example:

```
float n = noise(3);
```

According to the above table, `noise(3)` will return 0.364 at time equals 3. We could improve this by using a variable for time and asking for a noise value continuously in `draw()`.

```
float t = 3;

void draw() {
  float n = noise(t);
  println(n);
}
```

We need the noise value for a specific moment in time.

The above code results in the same value printed over and over. This happens because we are asking for the result of the `noise()` function at the same point in time—3—over and over. If we increment the time variable `t`, however, we'll get a different result.

```
float t = 0;

void draw() {
  float n = noise(t);
  println(n);
```

Typically we would start at time = 0, though this is arbitrary.

```
    t += 0.01;                                  Now, we move forward in time!
}
```

How quickly we increment t also affects the smoothness of the noise. If we make large jumps in time, then we are skipping ahead and the values will be more random.

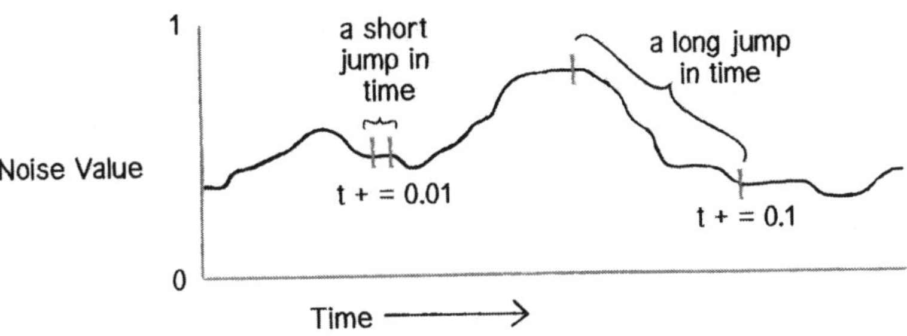

Figure I.7

Try running the code several times, incrementing t by 0.01, 0.02, 0.05, 0.1, 0.0001, and you will see different results.

Mapping Noise

Now we're ready to answer the question of what to do with the noise value. Once we have the value with a range between 0 and 1, it's up to us to map that range to what we want. The easiest way to do this is with Processing's `map()` function. The `map()` function takes five arguments. First up is the value we want to map, in this case n. Then we have to give it the value's current range (minimum and maximum), followed by our desired range.

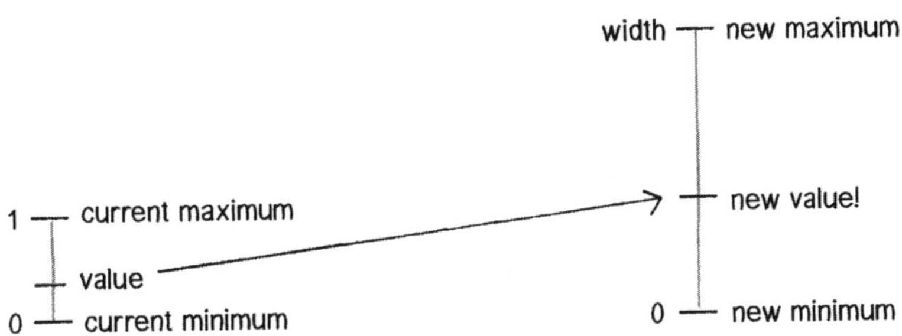

Figure I.8

In this case, we know that noise has a range between 0 and 1, but we'd like to draw our circle with a range between 0 and the window's width.

```
float t = 0;

void draw() {
  float n = noise(t);
  float x = map(n,0,1,0,width);
  ellipse(x,180,16,16);

  t += 0.01;
}
```

Using map() to customize the range of Perlin noise

We can apply the exact same logic to our random walker, and assign both its x- and y-values according to Perlin noise.

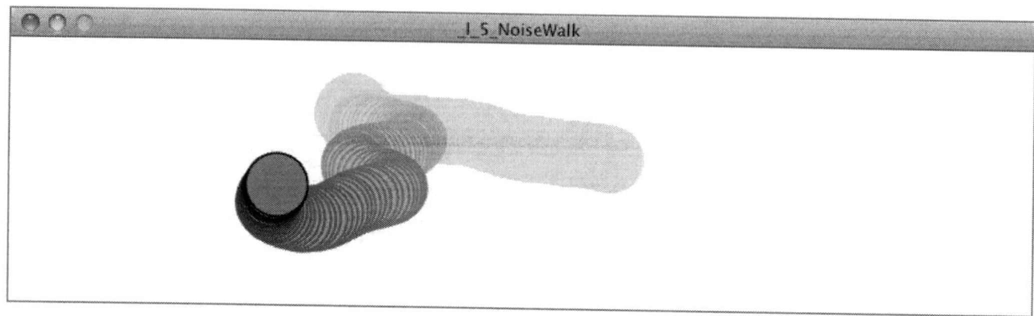

Example I.5: Perlin noise walker

```
class Walker {
  float x,y;

  float tx,ty;

  Walker() {
    tx = 0;
    ty = 10000;
  }

  void step() {
    x = map(noise(tx), 0, 1, 0, width);
    y = map(noise(ty), 0, 1, 0, height);

    tx += 0.01;
    ty += 0.01;
  }
}
```

x- and y-location mapped from noise

Move forward through "time."

Notice how the above example requires an additional pair of variables: `tx` and `ty`. This is because we need to keep track of two time variables, one for the x-location of the `Walker` object and one for the y-location. But there is something a bit odd about these variables. Why does `tx` start at 0 and `ty` at 10,000? While these numbers are arbitrary choices, we have very specifically initialized our two time variables with different values. This is because the noise function is deterministic: it gives you the same result for a specific time `t` each and every time. If we asked for the noise value at the same time `t` for both x and y, then x and y would always be equal, meaning that the `Walker` object would only move along a diagonal. Instead, we simply use two different parts of the noise space, starting at 0 for x and 10,000 for y so that x and y can appear to act independently of each other.

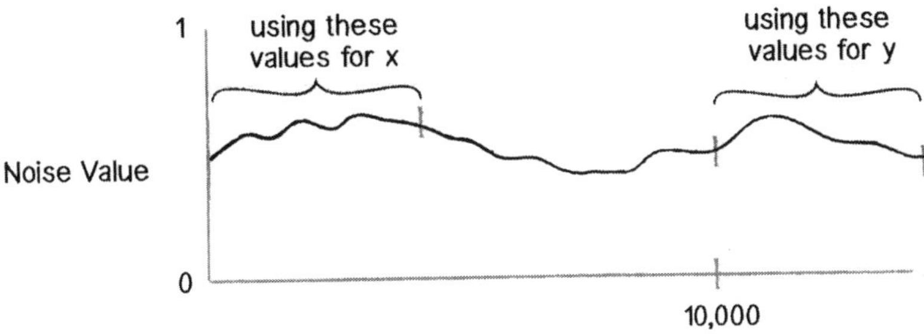

Figure I.9

In truth, there is no actual concept of time at play here. It's a useful metaphor to help us understand how the noise function works, but really what we have is space, rather than time. The graph above depicts a linear sequence of noise values in a one-dimensional space, and we can ask for a value at a specific x-location whenever we want. In examples, you will often see a variable named `xoff` to indicate the x-offset along the noise graph, rather than `t` for time (as noted in the diagram).

Exercise I.7

In the above random walker, the result of the noise function is mapped directly to the `Walker`'s location. Create a random walker where you instead map the result of the `noise()` function to a `Walker`'s step size.

Two-Dimensional Noise

This idea of noise values living in a one-dimensional space is important because it leads us right into a discussion of two-dimensional space. Let's think about this for a moment. With one-dimensional noise, we have a sequence of values in which any given value is similar to its neighbor. Because the value is in one dimension, it only has two neighbors: a value that comes before it (to the left on the graph) and one that comes after it (to the right).

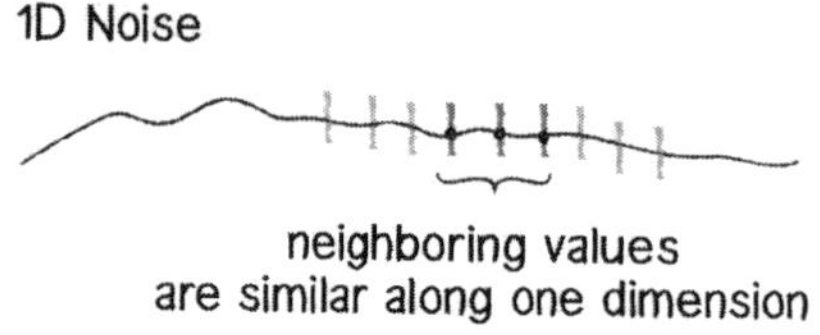
1D Noise
neighboring values
are similar along one dimension

Figure I.10: 1D Noise

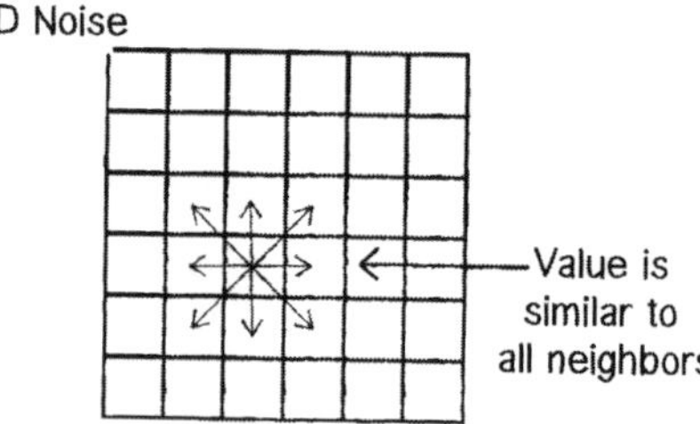
2D Noise
Value is
similar to
all neighbors

Figure I.11: 2D Noise

Two-dimensional noise works exactly the same way conceptually. The difference of course is that we aren't looking at values along a linear path, but values that are sitting on a grid. Think of a piece of graph paper with numbers written into each cell. A given value will be similar to all of its neighbors: above, below, to the right, to the left, and along any diagonal.

If you were to visualize this graph paper with each value mapped to the brightness of a color, you would get something that looks like clouds. White sits next to light gray, which sits next to gray, which sits next to dark gray, which sits next to black, which sits next to dark gray, etc.

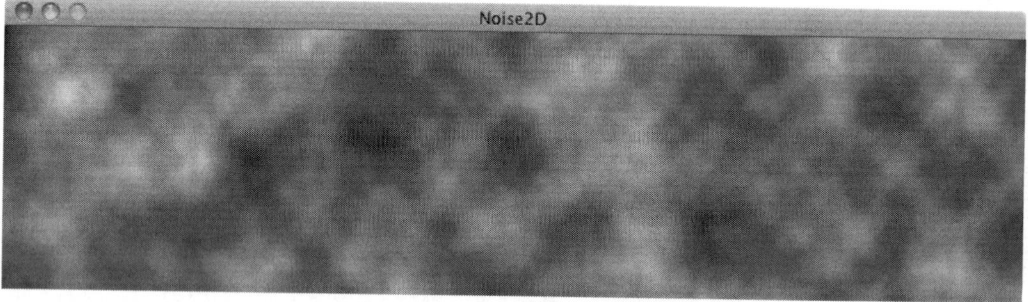
Noise2D

This is why noise was originally invented. You tweak the parameters a bit or play with color to make the resulting image look more like marble or wood or any other organic texture.

Let's take a quick look at how to implement two-dimensional noise in Processing. If you wanted to color every pixel of a window randomly, you would need a nested loop, one that accessed each pixel and picked a random brightness.

```
loadPixels();
for (int x = 0; x < width; x++) {
  for (int y = 0; y < height; y++) {
    float bright = random(255);                    A random brightness!
    pixels[x+y*width] = color(bright);
  }
}
updatePixels();
```

To color each pixel according to the `noise()` function, we'll do exactly the same thing, only instead of calling `random()` we'll call `noise()`.

```
float bright = map(noise(x,y),0,1,0,255);    A Perlin noise brightness!
```

This is a nice start conceptually—it gives you a noise value for every (x,y) location in our two-dimensional space. The problem is that this won't have the cloudy quality we want. Jumping from pixel 200 to pixel 201 is too large of a jump through noise. Remember, when we worked with one-dimensional noise, we incremented our time variable by 0.01 each frame, not by 1! A pretty good solution to this problem is to just use different variables for the noise arguments. For example, we could increment a variable called `xoff` each time we move horizontally, and a `yoff` variable each time we move vertically through the nested loops.

Example I.6: 2D Perlin noise

```
float xoff = 0.0;                              Start xoff at 0.

for (int x = 0; x < width; x++) {
  float yoff = 0.0;                            For every xoff, start yoff at 0.

  for (int y = 0; y < height; y++) {
    float bright =
map(noise(xoff,yoff),0,1,0,255);               Use xoff and yoff for noise().
    pixels[x+y*width] = color(bright);         Use x and y for pixel location.
    yoff += 0.01;                              Increment yoff.
  }
  xoff += 0.01;                                Increment xoff.
}
```

Exercise I.8

Play with color, `noiseDetail()`, and the rate at which `xoff` and `yoff` are incremented to achieve different visual effects.

Exercise I.9

Add a third argument to noise that increments once per cycle through `draw()` to animate the two-dimensional noise.

Exercise I.10

Use the noise values as the elevations of a landscape. See the screenshot below as a reference.

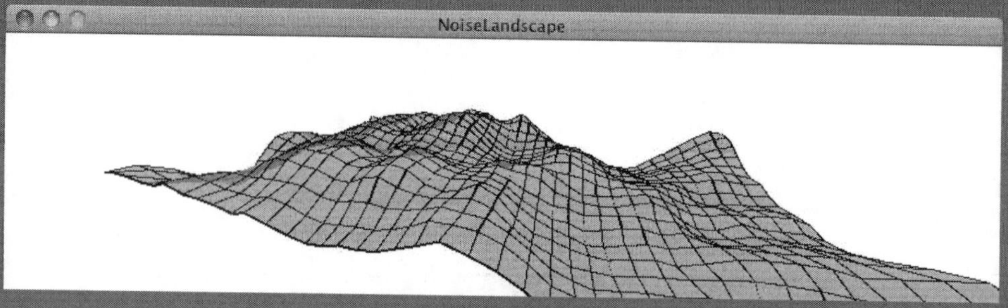

NoiseLandscape

We've examined several traditional uses of Perlin noise in this section. With one-dimensional noise, we used smooth values to assign the location of an object to give the appearance of wandering. With two-dimensional noise, we created a cloudy pattern with smoothed values on a plane of pixels. It's important to remember, however, that Perlin noise values are just that—values. They aren't inherently tied to pixel locations or color. Any example in this book that has a variable could be controlled via Perlin noise. When we model a wind force, its strength could be controlled by Perlin noise. Same goes for the angles between the branches in a fractal tree pattern, or the speed and direction of objects moving along a grid in a flow field simulation.

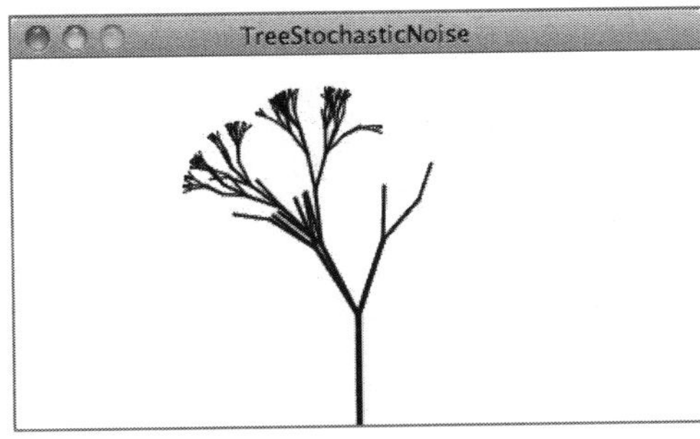

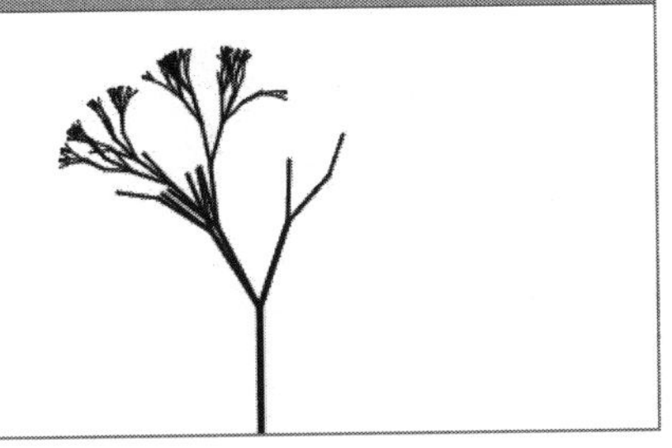

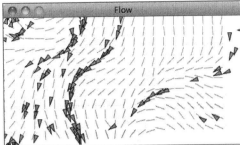

Figure I.12: Tree with Perlin noise

Figure I.13: Flow field with Perlin noise

I.7 Onward

We began this chapter by talking about how randomness can be a crutch. In many ways, it's the most obvious answer to the kinds of questions we ask continuously—how should this object move? What color should it be? This obvious answer, however, can also be a lazy one.

As we finish off the introduction, it's also worth noting that we could just as easily fall into the trap of using Perlin noise as a crutch. How should this object move? Perlin noise! What color should it be? Perlin noise! How fast should it grow? Perlin noise!

The point of all of this is not to say that you should or shouldn't use randomness. Or that you should or shouldn't use Perlin noise. The point is that the rules of your system are defined by you, and the larger your toolbox, the more choices you'll have as you implement those rules. The goal of this book is to fill your toolbox. If all you know is random, then your design thinking is limited. Sure, Perlin noise helps, but you'll need more. A lot more.

I think we're ready to begin.

Chapter 1. Vectors

"Roger, Roger. What's our vector, Victor?"
— Captain Oveur (Airplane)

This book is all about looking at the world around us and coming up with clever ways to simulate that world with code. Divided into three parts, the book will start by looking at basic physics—how an apple falls from a tree, a pendulum swings in the air, the earth revolves around the sun, etc. Absolutely everything contained within the first five chapters of this book requires the use of the most basic building block for programming motion—the ***vector***. And so this is where we begin our story.

Now, the word vector can mean a lot of different things. Vector is the name of a New Wave rock band formed in Sacramento, CA in the early 1980s. It's the name of a breakfast cereal manufactured by Kellogg's Canada. In the field of epidemiology, a vector is used to describe an organism that transmits infection from one host to another. In the C++ programming language, a vector (std::vector) is an implementation of a dynamically resizable array data structure. While all these definitions are interesting, they're not what we're looking for. What we want is called a ***Euclidean vector*** (named for the Greek mathematician Euclid and also known as a geometric vector). When you see the term "vector" in this book, you can assume it refers to a Euclidean vector, defined as *an entity that has both magnitude and direction*.

A vector is typically drawn as a arrow; the direction is indicated by where the arrow is pointing, and the magnitude by the length of the arrow itself.

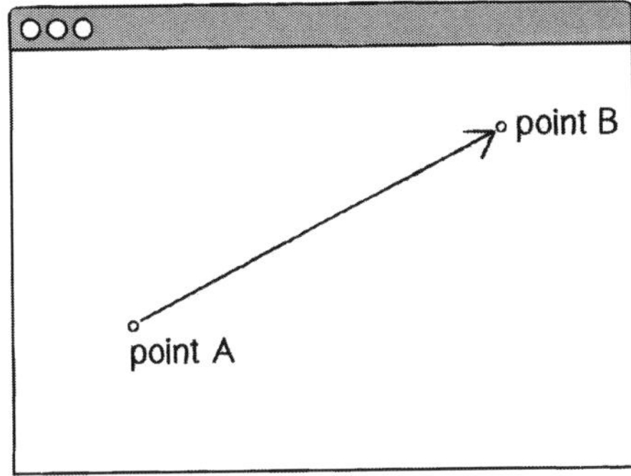

Figure 1.1: A vector (drawn as an arrow) has magnitude (length of arrow) and direction (which way it is pointing).

In the above illustration, the vector is drawn as an arrow from point A to point B and serves as an instruction for how to travel from A to B.

1.1 Vectors, You Complete Me

Before we dive into more of the details about vectors, let's look at a basic Processing example that demonstrates why we should care about vectors in the first place. If you've read any of the introductory Processing textbooks or taken a class on programming with Processing (and hopefully you've done one of these things to help prepare you for this book), you probably, at one point or another, learned how to write a simple bouncing ball sketch.

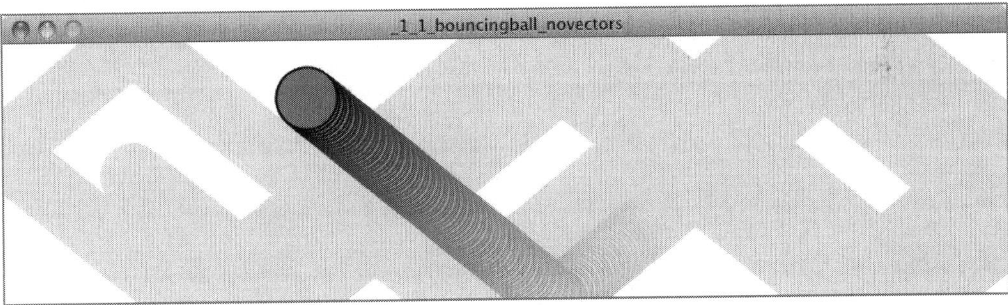

If you are reading this book as a PDF or in print, then you will only see screenshots of the code. Motion, of course, is a key element of our discussion, so to the extent possible, the static screenshots will include trails to give a sense of the behavior. For more about how to draw trails, see the code examples available for download.

Example 1.1: Bouncing ball with no vectors

```
float x = 100;
float y = 100;
float xspeed = 1;
float yspeed = 3.3;
```

Variables for location and speed of ball.

```
void setup() {
  size(640,360);
  background(255);
}
```

Remember how Processing works? setup() is executed once when the sketch starts and draw() loops forever and ever (until you quit).

```
void draw() {
  background(255);

  x = x + xspeed;
  y = y + yspeed;
```

Move the ball according to its speed.

```
  if ((x > width) || (x < 0)) {
    xspeed = xspeed * -1;
  }
  if ((y > height) || (y < 0)) {
    yspeed = yspeed * -1;
  }
```

Check for bouncing.

```
  stroke(0);
  fill(175);
  ellipse(x,y,16,16);
}
```

Display the ball at the location (x,y).

In the above example, we have a very simple world—a blank canvas with a circular shape (a "ball") traveling around. This ball has some properties, which are represented in the code as variables.

Location	*x and y*
Speed	*xspeed and yspeed*

In a more advanced sketch, we could imagine having many more variables:

Acceleration	*xacceleration and yacceleration*
Target location	*xtarget and ytarget*
Wind	*xwind and ywind*
Friction	*xfriction and yfriction*

It's becoming clearer that for every concept in this world (wind, location, acceleration, etc.), we'll need two variables. And this is only a two-dimensional world. In a 3D world, we'll need `x`, `y`, `z`, `xspeed`, `yspeed`, `zspeed`, and so on.

Wouldn't it be nice if we could simplify our code and use fewer variables?

Instead of:

```
float x;
float y;
float xspeed;
float yspeed;
```

We could simply have…

```
Vector location;
Vector speed;
```

Taking this first step in using vectors won't allow us to do anything new. Just adding vectors won't magically make your Processing sketches simulate physics. However, they will simplify your code and provide a set of functions for common mathematical operations that happen over and over and over again while programming motion.

As an introduction to vectors, we're going to live in two dimensions for quite some time (at least until we get through the first several chapters). All of these examples can be fairly easily extended to three dimensions (and the class we will use—`PVector`—allows for three dimensions.) However, it's easier to start with just two.

1.2 Vectors for Processing Programmers

One way to think of a vector is the difference between two points. Consider how you might go about providing instructions to walk from one point to another.

Here are some vectors and possible translations:

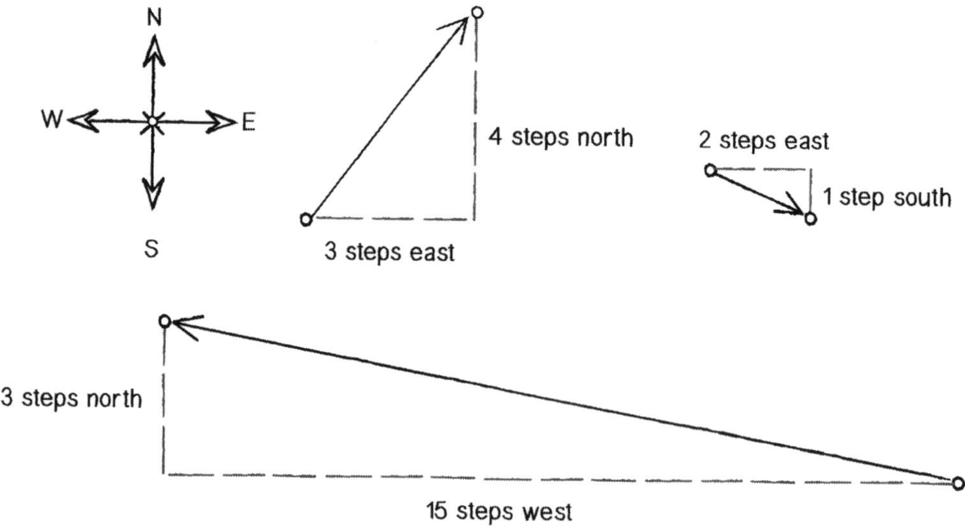

Figure 1.2

(-15, 3)	*Walk fifteen steps west; turn and walk three steps north.*
(3, 4)	*Walk three steps east; turn and walk five steps north.*
(2, -1)	*Walk two steps east; turn and walk one step south.*

You've probably done this before when programming motion. For every frame of animation (i.e. a single cycle through Processing's `draw()` loop), you instruct each object on the screen to move a certain number of pixels horizontally and a certain number of pixels vertically.

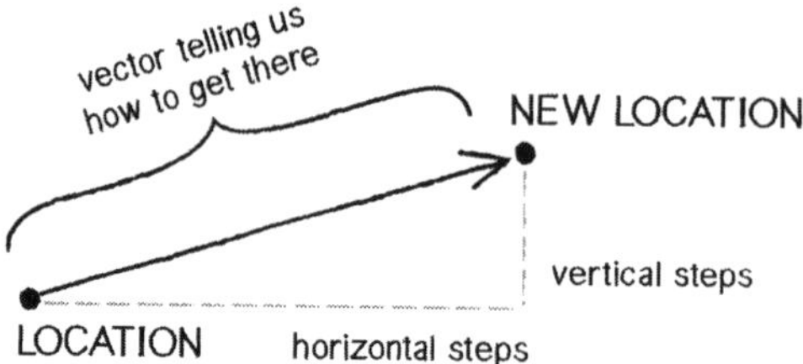

Figure 1.3

For every frame:

new location** = **velocity applied to current location

If velocity is a vector (the difference between two points), what is location? Is it a vector too? Technically, one might argue that location is not a vector, since it's not describing how to move from one point to another—it's simply describing a singular point in space.

Nevertheless, another way to describe a location is the path taken from the origin to reach that location. Hence, a location can be the vector representing the difference between location and origin.

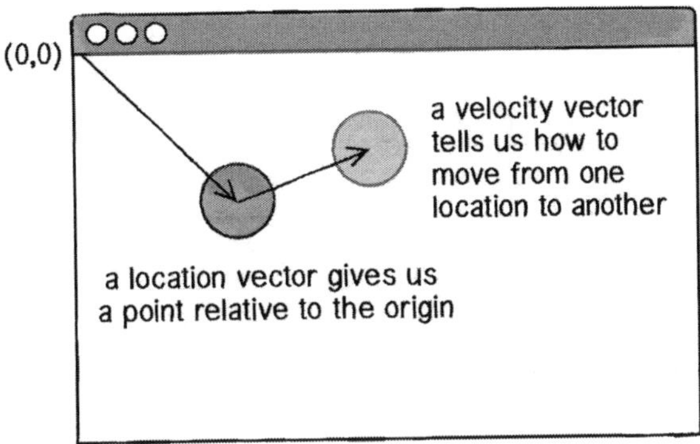

Figure 1.4

Let's examine the underlying data for both location and velocity. In the bouncing ball example, we had the following:

location	*x,y*
velocity	*xspeed,yspeed*

Notice how we are storing the same data for both—two floating point numbers, an x and a y. If we were to write a vector class ourselves, we'd start with something rather basic:

```
class PVector {

  float x;
  float y;

  PVector(float x_, float y_) {
    x = x_;
    y = y_;
  }

}
```

At its core, a `PVector` is just a convenient way to store two values (or three, as we'll see in 3D examples).

And so this ...

```
float x = 100;
float y = 100;
float xspeed = 1;
float yspeed = 3.3;
```

becomes ...

```
PVector location = new PVector(100,100);
PVector velocity = new PVector(1,3.3);
```

Now that we have two vector objects (location and velocity), we're ready to implement the algorithm for motion—***location = location + velocity***. In Example 1.1, without vectors, we had:

```
x = x + xspeed;    // Add each speed to each location.
y = y + yspeed;
```

In an ideal world, we would be able to rewrite the above as:

```
location = location + velocity;    // Add the velocity vector to the location vector.
```

However, in Processing, the addition operator + is reserved for primitive values (integers, floats, etc.) only. Processing doesn't know how to add two `PVector` objects together any more than it knows how to add two `PFont` objects or `PImage` objects. Fortunately for us, the `PVector` class includes functions for common mathematical operations.

1.3 Vector Addition

Before we continue looking at the `PVector` class and its `add()` method (purely for the sake of learning since it's already implemented for us in Processing itself), let's examine vector addition using the notation found in math and physics textbooks.

Vectors are typically written either in boldface type or with an arrow on top. For the purposes of this book, to distinguish a ***vector*** from a ***scalar*** (*scalar* refers to a single value, such as an integer or a floating point number), we'll use the arrow notation:

- Vector: $\vec{u}$
- Scalar: x

Let's say I have the following two vectors:

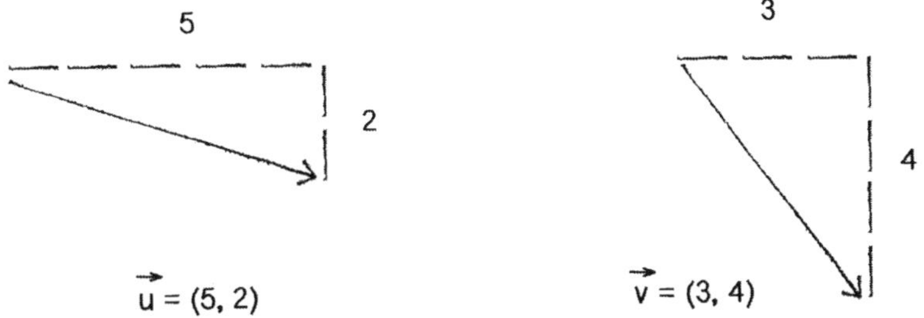

Figure 1.5

Each vector has two components, an x and a y. To add two vectors together, we simply add both x's and both y's.

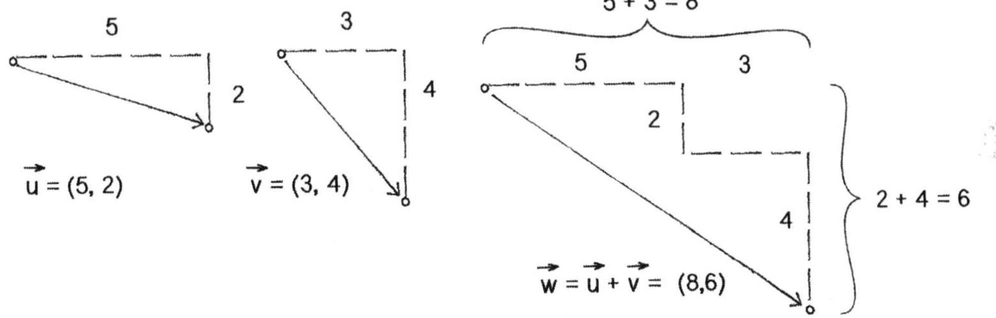

Figure 1.6

In other words:

$$\vec{w} = \vec{u} + \vec{v}$$

can be written as:

$$w_x = u_x + v_x$$
$$w_y = u_y + v_y$$

Then, replacing u and v with their values from Figure 1.6, we get:

$$w_x = 5 + 3$$

which means that:

Finally, we write that as a vector:

$$\vec{w} = (8,\ 6)$$

Now that we understand how to add two vectors together, we can look at how addition is implemented in the `PVector` class itself. Let's write a function called `add()` that takes another `PVector` object as its argument.

```
class PVector {

  float x;
  float y;

  PVector(float x_, float y_) {
    x = x_;
    y = y_;
  }

  void add(PVector v) {
    y = y + v.y;
    x = x + v.x;
  }
}
```

New! A function to add another PVector to this PVector. Simply add the *x* components and the *y* components together.

Now that we see how `add()` is written inside of `PVector`, we can return to our bouncing ball example with its ***location + velocity*** algorithm and implement vector addition:

```
location = location + velocity;
location.add(velocity);
```

Add the current velocity to the location.

And here we are, ready to rewrite the bouncing ball example using `PVector`.

Example 1.2: Bouncing ball with PVectors!

```
PVector location;
PVector velocity;
```

Instead of a bunch of floats, we now just have two PVector variables.

```
void setup() {
  size(640,360);
  location = new PVector(100,100);
  velocity = new PVector(2.5,5);
}

void draw() {
  background(255);

  location.add(velocity);
```

```
  if ((location.x > width) || (location.x < 0)) {
    velocity.x = velocity.x * -1;
  }
  if ((location.y > height) || (location.y < 0)) {
    velocity.y = velocity.y * -1;
  }
```

We still sometimes need to refer to the individual components of a PVector and can do so using the dot syntax: location.x, velocity.y, etc.

```
  stroke(0);
  fill(175);
  ellipse(location.x,location.y,16,16);
}
```

Now, you might feel somewhat disappointed. After all, this may initially appear to have made the code more complicated than the original version. While this is a perfectly reasonable and valid critique, it's important to understand that we haven't fully realized the power of programming with vectors just yet. Looking at a simple bouncing ball and only implementing vector addition is just the first step. As we move forward into a more complex world of multiple objects and multiple ***forces*** (which we'll introduce in Chapter 2), the benefits of `PVector` will become more apparent.

We should, however, note an important aspect of the above transition to programming with vectors. Even though we are using `PVector` objects to describe two values—the x and y of location and the x and y of velocity—we still often need to refer to the *x* and *y* components of each `PVector` individually. When we go to draw an object in Processing, there's no means for us to say:

```
ellipse(location,16,16);
```

The `ellipse()` function does not allow for a `PVector` as an argument. An ellipse can only be drawn with two scalar values, an x-coordinate and a y-coordinate. And so we must dig into the `PVector` object and pull out the *x* and *y* components using object-oriented dot syntax.

```
ellipse(location.x,location.y,16,16);
```

The same issue arises when testing if the circle has reached the edge of the window, and we need to access the individual components of both vectors: `location` and `velocity`.

```
if ((location.x > width) || (location.x < 0)) {
  velocity.x = velocity.x * -1;
}
```

Exercise 1.1

Find something you've previously made in Processing using separate x and y variables and use `PVector`s instead.

Exercise 1.2

Take one of the walker examples from the introduction and convert it to use `PVector`s.

Exercise 1.3

Extend the bouncing ball with vectors example into 3D. Can you get a sphere to bounce around a box?

1.4 More Vector Math

Addition was really just the first step. There are many mathematical operations that are commonly used with vectors. Below is a comprehensive list of the operations available as functions in the `PVector` class. We'll go through a few of the key ones now. As our examples get more sophisticated in later chapters, we'll continue to reveal the details of more functions.

- `add()` — add vectors
- `sub()` — subtract vectors
- `mult()` — scale the vector with multiplication
- `div()` — scale the vector with division
- `mag()` — calculate the magnitude of a vector
- `setMag()` - set the magnitude of a vector
- `normalize()` — normalize the vector to a unit length of 1
- `limit()` — limit the magnitude of a vector
- `heading()` — the 2D heading of a vector expressed as an angle
- `rotate()` — rotate a 2D vector by an angle

- `lerp()` — linear interpolate to another vector
- `dist()` — the Euclidean distance between two vectors (considered as points)
- `angleBetween()` — find the angle between two vectors
- `dot()` — the dot product of two vectors
- `cross()` — the cross product of two vectors (only relevant in three dimensions)
- `random2D()` - make a random 2D vector
- `random3D()` - make a random 3D vector

Having already covered addition, let's start with subtraction. This one's not so bad; just take the plus sign and replace it with a minus!

Vector subtraction

$\vec{w} = \vec{u} - \vec{v}$

can be written as:

$w_x = u_x - v_x$
$w_y = u_y - v_y$

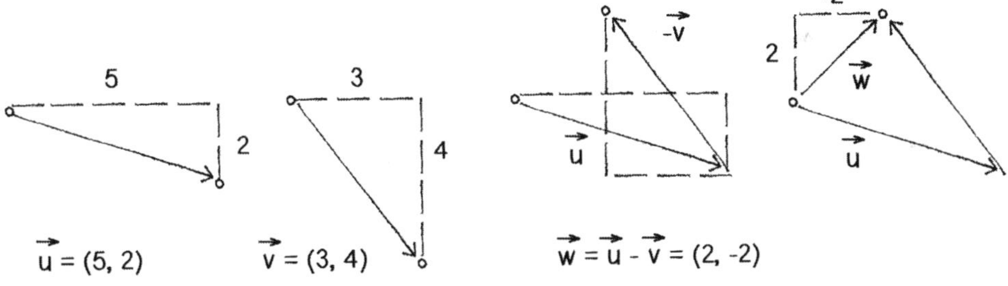

Figure 1.7: Vector Subtraction

and so the function inside `PVector` looks like:

```
void sub(PVector v) {
  x = x - v.x;
  y = y - v.y;
}
```

The following example demonstrates vector subtraction by taking the difference between two points—the mouse location and the center of the window.

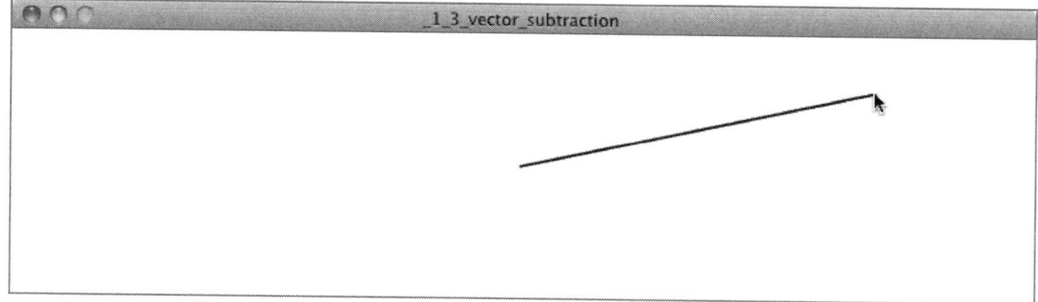

Example 1.3: Vector subtraction

```
void setup() {
  size(640,360);
}

void draw() {
  background(255);

  PVector mouse  = new PVector(mouseX,mouseY);
  PVector center = new PVector(width/2,height/2);

  mouse.sub(center);

  translate(width/2,height/2);

  line(0,0,mouse.x,mouse.y);
}
```

Two PVectors, one for the mouse location and one for the center of the window

PVector subtraction!

Draw a line to represent the vector.

Basic Number Properties with Vectors

Addition with vectors follow the same algebraic rules as with real numbers.

The commutative rule: $\vec{u} + \vec{v} = \vec{v} + \vec{u}$
The associative rule: $\vec{u} + (\vec{v} + \vec{w}) = (\vec{u} + \vec{v}) + \vec{w}$

Fancy terminology and symbols aside, this is really quite a simple concept. We're just saying that common sense properties of addition apply to vectors as well.

$3 + 2 = 2 + 3$
$(3 + 2) + 1 = 3 + (2 + 1)$

Vector multiplication

Moving on to multiplication, we have to think a little bit differently. When we talk about multiplying a vector, what we typically mean is ***scaling*** a vector. If we wanted to scale a vector to twice its size or one-third of its size (leaving its direction the same), we would say: "Multiply the vector by 2" or "Multiply the vector by 1/3." Note that we are multiplying a vector by a scalar, a single number, not another vector.

To scale a vector, we multiply each component (x and y) by a scalar.

$\vec{w} = \vec{u} * n$

can be written as:

$w_x = u_x * n$
$w_y = u_y * n$

Let's look at an example with vector notation.

$\vec{u} = (-3, 7)$
$n = 3$

$\vec{w} = \vec{u} * n$
$w_x = -3 * 3$
$w_y = 7 * 3$

$\vec{w} = (-9, 21)$

Therefore, the function inside the PVector class is written as:

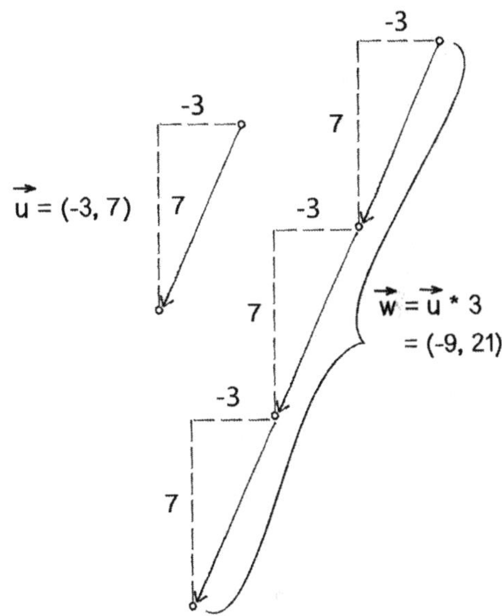

Figure 1.8: Scaling a vector

```
void mult(float n) {
   x = x * n;
   y = y * n;
 }
```

With multiplication, the components of the vector are multiplied by a number.

And implementing multiplication in code is as simple as:

```
PVector u = new PVector(-3,7);
u.mult(3);
```

This PVector is now three times the size and is equal to (-9,21).

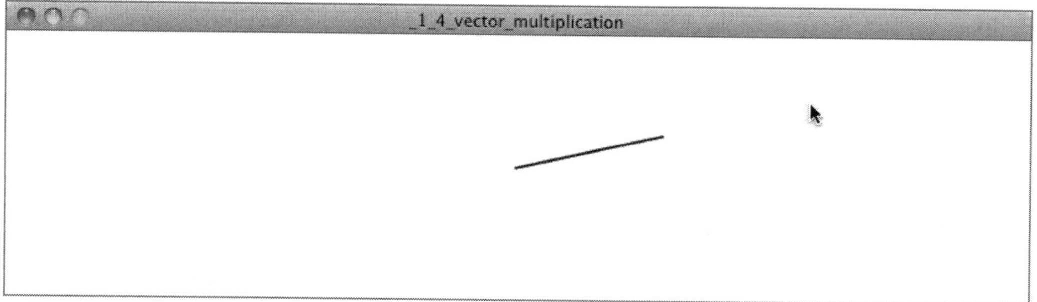

Example 1.4: Multiplying a vector

```
void setup() {
  size(640,360);
}

void draw() {
  background(255);

  PVector mouse = new PVector(mouseX,mouseY);
  PVector center = new PVector(width/2,height/2);
  mouse.sub(center);

  mouse.mult(0.5);

  translate(width/2,height/2);
  line(0,0,mouse.x,mouse.y);

}
```

Multiplying a vector! The vector is now half its original size (multiplied by 0.5).

Division works just like multiplication—we simply replace the multiplication sign (asterisk) with the division sign (forward slash).

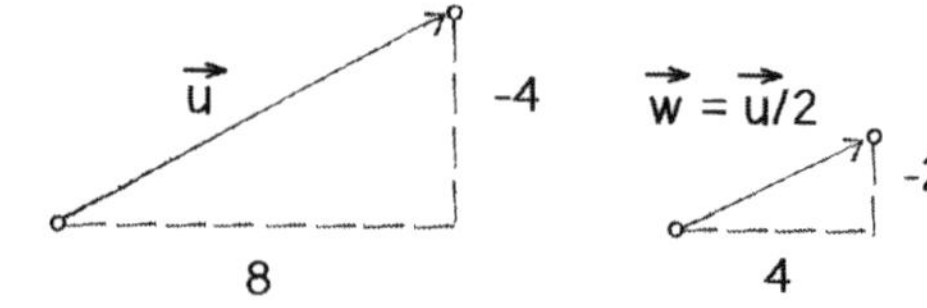

Figure 1.9

```
void div(float n) {
  x = x / n;
  y = y / n;
}

PVector u = new PVector(8,-4);
u.div(2);
```

Dividing a vector! The vector is now half its original size (divided by 2).

More Number Properties with Vectors

As with addition, basic algebraic rules of multiplication apply to vectors.

The associative rule: $(n * m) * \vec{v} = n * (m * \vec{v})$
The distributive rule with 2 scalars, 1 vector: $(n * m) * \vec{v} = n * \vec{v} + m * \vec{v}$
The distributive rule with 2 vectors, 1 scalar: $(\vec{u} + \vec{v}) * n = \vec{u} * n + \vec{v} * n$

1.5 Vector Magnitude

Multiplication and division, as we just saw, are means by which the length of the vector can be changed without affecting direction. Perhaps you're wondering: "OK, so how do I know what the length of a vector is? I know the components (x and y), but how long (in pixels) is the actual arrow?" Understanding how to calculate the length (also known as ***magnitude***) of a vector is incredibly useful and important.

Notice in the above diagram how the vector, drawn as an arrow and two components (x and y), creates a right triangle. The sides are the components and the hypotenuse is the arrow itself. We're very lucky to have this right triangle, because once upon a time, a Greek mathematician named Pythagoras developed a lovely formula to describe the relationship between the sides and hypotenuse of a right triangle.

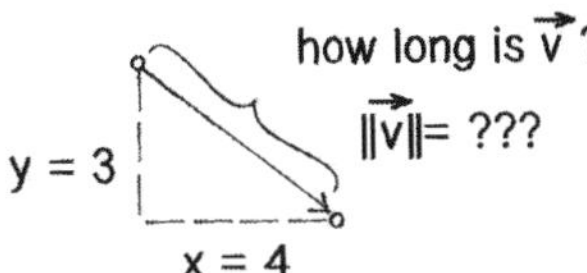

Figure 1.10: The length or "magnitude" of a vector v→ is often written as: ‖v→ ‖

The Pythagorean theorem is *a* squared plus *b* squared equals *c* squared.

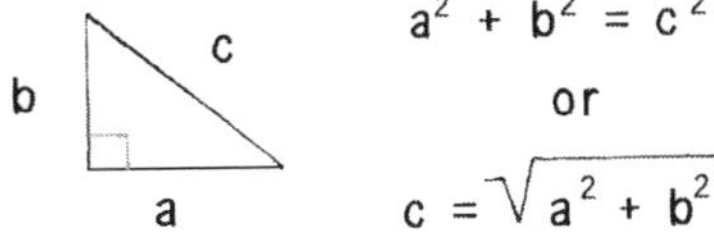

Figure 1.11: The Pythagorean Theorem

Armed with this formula, we can now compute the magnitude of $\vec{v}$ as follows:

$$\| \vec{v} \| = \sqrt{v_x * v_x + v_y * v_y}$$

or in `PVector`:

```
float mag() {
  return sqrt(x*x + y*y);
}
```

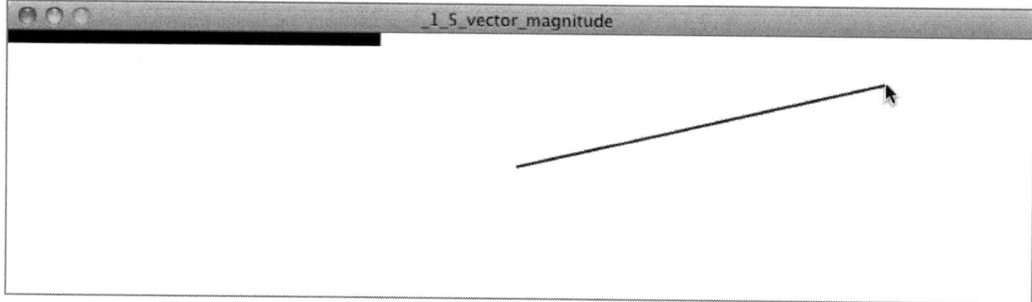

Example 1.5: Vector magnitude

```
void setup() {
  size(640,360);
}

void draw() {
  background(255);

  PVector mouse = new PVector(mouseX,mouseY);
  PVector center = new PVector(width/2,height/2);
  mouse.sub(center);

  float m = mouse.mag();
  fill(0);
  rect(0,0,m,10);

  translate(width/2,height/2);
  line(0,0,mouse.x,mouse.y);

}
```

The magnitude (i.e. length) of a vector can be accessed via the mag() function. Here it is used as the width of a rectangle drawn at the top of the window.

1.6 Normalizing Vectors

Calculating the magnitude of a vector is only the beginning. The magnitude function opens the door to many possibilities, the first of which is ***normalization***. Normalizing refers to the process of making something "standard" or, well, "normal." In the case of vectors, let's assume for the moment that a standard vector has a length of 1. To normalize a vector, therefore, is to take a vector of any length and, keeping it pointing in the same direction, change its length to 1, turning it into what is called a ***unit vector***.

Since it describes a vector's direction without regard to its length, it's useful to have the unit vector readily accessible. We'll see this come in handy once we start to work with forces in Chapter 2.

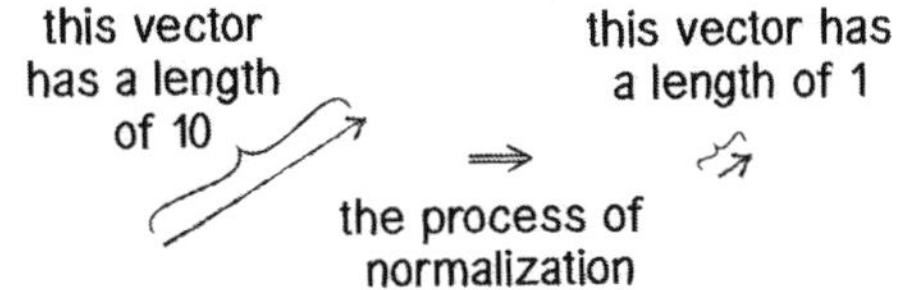

Figure 1.12

For any given vector $\vec{u}$, its unit vector (written as $\hat{u}$) is calculated as follows:

$$\hat{u} = \frac{\vec{u}}{\|\vec{u}\|}$$

In other words, to normalize a vector, simply divide each component by its magnitude. This is pretty intuitive. Say a vector is of length 5. Well, 5 divided by 5 is 1. So, looking at our right triangle, we then need to scale the hypotenuse down by dividing by 5. In that process the sides shrink, divided by 5 as well.

In the `PVector` class, we therefore write our normalization function as follows:

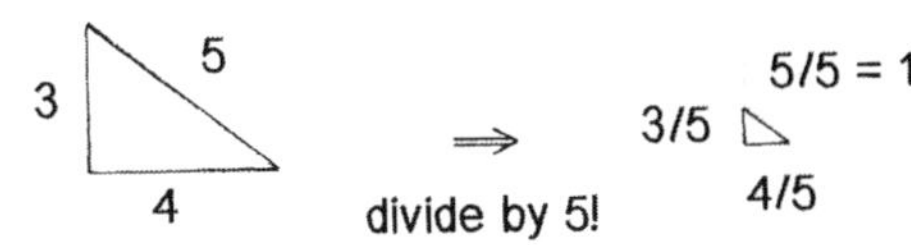

Figure 1.13

```
void normalize() {
  float m = mag();
  div(m);
}
```

Of course, there's one small issue. What if the magnitude of the vector is 0? We can't divide by 0! Some quick error checking will fix that right up:

```
void normalize() {
 float m = mag();
 if (m != 0) {
   div(m);
 }
}
```

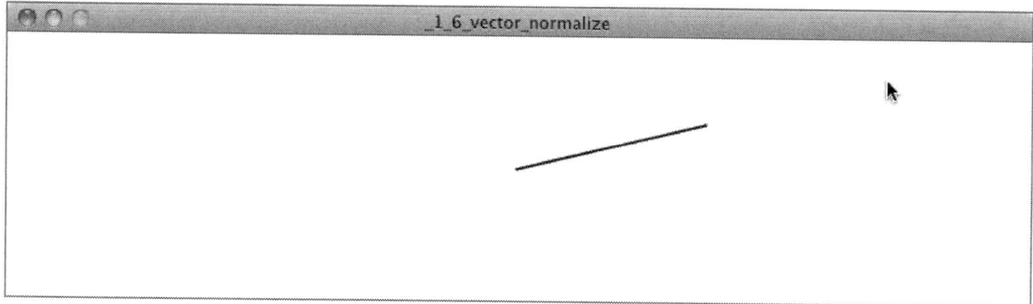

Example 1.6: Normalizing a vector

```
void draw() {
  background(255);

  PVector mouse = new PVector(mouseX,mouseY);
  PVector center = new PVector(width/2,height/2);
  mouse.sub(center);

  mouse.normalize();

  mouse.mult(50);
  translate(width/2,height/2);
  line(0,0,mouse.x,mouse.y);

}
```

In this example, after the vector is normalized, it is multiplied by 50 so that it is viewable onscreen. Note that no matter where the mouse is, the vector will have the same length (50) due to the normalization process.

1.7 Vector Motion: Velocity

All this vector math stuff sounds like something we should know about, but why? How will it actually help us write code? The truth of the matter is that we need to have some patience. It will take some time before the awesomeness of using the `PVector` class fully comes to light. This is actually a common occurrence when first learning a new data structure. For example, when you first learn about an array, it might seem like much more work to use an array than to just have several variables stand for multiple things. But that plan quickly breaks down when you need a hundred, or a thousand, or ten thousand things. The same can be true for `PVector`. What might seem like more work now will pay off later, and pay off quite nicely. And you don't have to wait too long, as your reward will come in the next chapter.

For now, however, we want to focus on simplicity. What does it mean to program motion using vectors? We've seen the beginning of this in Example 1.2 (see page 35): the bouncing ball. An object on screen has a location (where it is at any given moment) as well as a velocity (instructions for how it should move from one moment to the next). Velocity is added to location:

```
location.add(velocity);
```

And then we draw the object at that location:

```
ellipse(location.x,location.y,16,16);
```

This is Motion 101.

1. ***Add velocity to location***

2. ***Draw object at location***

In the bouncing ball example, all of this code happened in Processing's main tab, within `setup()` and `draw()`. What we want to do now is move towards encapsulating all of the logic for motion inside of a ***class***. This way, we can create a foundation for programming moving objects in Processing. In section I.2 of the introduction (see page 2), "The Random Walker Class," we briefly reviewed the basics of object-oriented-programming ("OOP"). Beyond that short introduction, this book assumes experience with objects and classes in Processing. If you need a refresher, I encourage you to check out the Processing objects tutorial (http://processing.org/learning/objects/).

In this case, we're going to create a generic `Mover` class that will describe a thing moving around the screen. And so we must consider the following two questions:

1. ***What data does a mover have?***

2. ***What functionality does a mover have?***

Our Motion 101 algorithm tells us the answers to these questions. A `Mover` object has two pieces of data: `location` and `velocity`, which are both `PVector` objects.

```
class Mover {

  PVector location;
  PVector velocity;
```

Its functionality is just about as simple. The `Mover` needs to move and it needs to be seen. We'll implement these needs as functions named `update()` and `display()`. We'll put all of our motion logic code in `update()` and draw the object in `display()`.

```
  void update() {
    location.add(velocity);          The Mover moves.
  }

  void display() {
    stroke(0);
    fill(175);
```

```
    ellipse(location.x,location.y,16,16);         The Mover is displayed.
  }

}
```

We've forgotten one crucial item, however: the object's ***constructor***. The constructor is a special function inside of a class that creates the instance of the object itself. It is where you give instructions on how to set up the object. It always has the same name as the class and is called by invoking the ***new*** operator:

```
Mover m = new Mover();
```

In our case, let's arbitrarily decide to initialize our `Mover` object by giving it a random location and a random velocity.

```
Mover() {
  location = new PVector(random(width),random(height));
  velocity = new PVector(random(-2,2),random(-2,2));
}
```

If object-oriented programming is at all new to you, one aspect here may seem a bit confusing. After all, we spent the beginning of this chapter discussing the `PVector` class. The `PVector` class is the template for making the `location` object and the `velocity` object. So what are they doing inside of yet another object, the `Mover` object? In fact, this is just about the most normal thing ever. An object is simply something that holds data (and functionality). That data can be numbers (integers, floats, etc.) or other objects! We'll see this over and over again in this book. For example, in Chapter 4 (see page 144) we'll write a class to describe a system of particles. That `ParticleSystem` object will have as its data a list of `Particle` objects…and each `Particle` object will have as its data several `PVector` objects!

Let's finish off the `Mover` class by incorporating a function to determine what the object should do when it reaches the edge of the window. For now let's do something simple, and just have it wrap around the edges.

```
void checkEdges() {

  if (location.x > width) {                When it reaches one edge, set location to
    location.x = 0;                        the other.
  } else if (location.x < 0) {
    location.x = width;
  }

  if (location.y > height) {
    location.y = 0;
  } else if (location.y < 0) {
    location.y = height;
  }
```

```
}
```

Now that the `Mover` class is finished, we can look at what we need to do in our main program. We first declare a `Mover` object:

```
Mover mover;
```

Then initialize the mover in `setup()`:

```
mover = new Mover();
```

and call the appropriate functions in `draw()`:

```
mover.update();
mover.checkEdges();
mover.display();
```

Here is the entire example for reference:

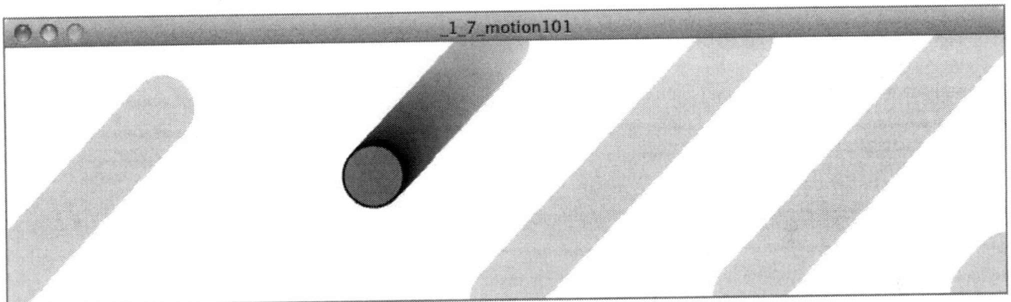

Example 1.7: Motion 101 (velocity)

```
Mover mover;                        // Declare Mover object.

void setup() {
  size(640,360);
  mover = new Mover();              // Create Mover object.
}

void draw() {
  background(255);
```

```
    mover.update();                          Call functions on Mover object.
    mover.checkEdges();
    mover.display();
}

class Mover {

  PVector location;                          Our object has two PVectors: location and
  PVector velocity;                          velocity.

  Mover() {
    location = new PVector(random(width),random(height));
    velocity = new PVector(random(-2,2),random(-2,2));
  }

  void update() {
    location.add(velocity);                  Motion 101: Location changes by velocity.
  }

  void display() {
    stroke(0);
    fill(175);
    ellipse(location.x,location.y,16,16);
  }

  void checkEdges() {
    if (location.x > width) {
      location.x = 0;
    } else if (location.x < 0) {
      location.x = width;
    }

    if (location.y > height) {
      location.y = 0;
    } else if (location.y < 0) {
      location.y = height;
    }
  }
}
```

1.8 Vector Motion: Acceleration

OK. At this point, we should feel comfortable with two things: (1) what a `PVector` is and (2) how we use `PVector`s inside of an object to keep track of its location and movement. This is an excellent first step and deserves a mild round of applause. Before standing ovations and screaming fans, however, we need to make one more, somewhat bigger step forward. After all, watching the Motion 101 example is fairly boring—the circle never speeds up, never slows down, and never turns. For more interesting motion, for motion that appears in the real world around us, we need to add one more `PVector` to our class—`acceleration`.

The strict definition of ***acceleration*** we're using here is: *the rate of change of velocity*. Let's think about that definition for a moment. Is this a new concept? Not really. Velocity is defined as *the rate of change of location*. In essence, we are developing a "trickle-down" effect. Acceleration affects velocity, which in turn affects location (for some brief foreshadowing, this point will become even more crucial in the next chapter, when we see how forces affect acceleration, which affects velocity, which affects location). In code, this reads:

```
velocity.add(acceleration);
location.add(velocity);
```

As an exercise, from this point forward, let's make a rule for ourselves. Let's write every example in the rest of this book without ever touching the value of velocity and location (except to initialize them). In other words, our goal now for programming motion is: Come up with an algorithm for how we calculate acceleration and let the trickle-down effect work its magic. (In truth, you'll find reasons to break this rule, but it's important to illustrate the principles behind our motion algorithm.) And so we need to come up with some ways to calculate acceleration:

Acceleration Algorithms!

1. *A constant acceleration*
2. *A totally random acceleration*
3. *Acceleration towards the mouse*

Algorithm #1, *a constant acceleration*, is not particularly interesting, but it is the simplest and will help us begin incorporating acceleration into our code. The first thing we need to do is add another `PVector` to the `Mover` class:

```
class Mover {

  PVector location;
  PVector velocity;
  PVector acceleration;        // A new PVector for acceleration
```

And incorporate acceleration into the `update()` function:

```
void update() {
    velocity.add(acceleration);    // Our motion algorithm is now two lines of code!
    location.add(velocity);
}
```

We're almost done. The only missing piece is initialization in the constructor.

```
  Mover() {
```

Let's start the `Mover` object in the middle of the window...

```
    location = new PVector(width/2,height/2);
```

...with an initial velocity of zero.

```
    velocity = new PVector(0,0);
```

This means that when the sketch starts, the object is at rest. We don't have to worry about velocity anymore, as we are controlling the object's motion entirely with acceleration. Speaking of which, according to Algorithm #1, our first sketch involves constant acceleration. So let's pick a value.

```
    acceleration = new PVector(-0.001,0.01);
  }
```

Maybe you're thinking, "Gosh, those values seem awfully small!" That's right, they are quite tiny. It's important to realize that our acceleration values (measured in pixels) accumulate over time in the velocity, about thirty times per second depending on our sketch's frame rate. And so to keep the magnitude of the velocity vector within a reasonable range, our acceleration values should remain quite small. We can also help this cause by incorporating the `PVector` function `limit()`.

```
velocity.limit(10);
```

The limit() function constrains the magnitude of a vector.

This translates to the following:

What is the magnitude of velocity? If it's less than 10, no worries; just leave it as is. If it's more than 10, however, reduce it to 10!

Exercise 1.4

Write the `limit()` function for the `PVector` class.

```
void limit(float max) {
  if (_______ > _______) {
    _________();
    ____(max);
  }
}
```

Let's take a look at the changes to the `Mover` class, complete with `acceleration` and `limit()`.

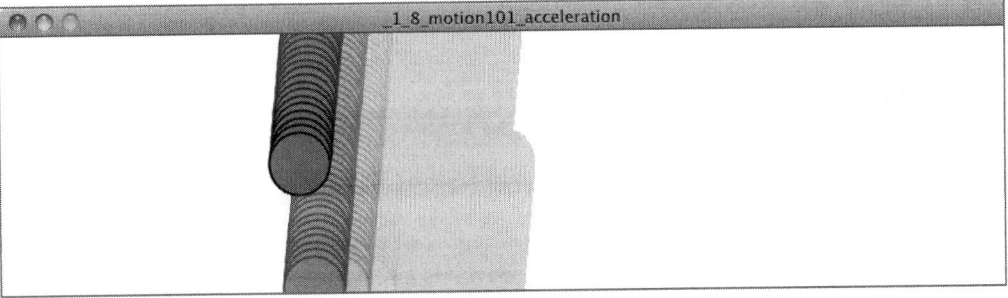

Example 1.8: Motion 101 (velocity and constant acceleration)

```
class Mover {

  PVector location;
  PVector velocity;
  PVector acceleration;
  float topspeed;

  Mover() {
    location = new PVector(width/2,height/2);
    velocity = new PVector(0,0);
    acceleration = new PVector(-0.001,0.01);
    topspeed = 10;
  }

  void update() {
    velocity.add(acceleration);
    velocity.limit(topspeed);
```

Acceleration is the key!

The variable topspeed will limit the magnitude of velocity.

Velocity changes by acceleration and is limited by topspeed.

```
    location.add(velocity);
  }

  void display() {}
  void checkEdges() {}
}
```

display() is the same.

checkEdges() is the same.

Exercise 1.5

Create a simulation of a car (or runner) that accelerates when you press the up key and brakes when you press the down key.

Now on to Algorithm #2, *a totally random acceleration*. In this case, instead of initializing acceleration in the object's constructor, we want to pick a new acceleration each cycle, i.e. each time `update()` is called.

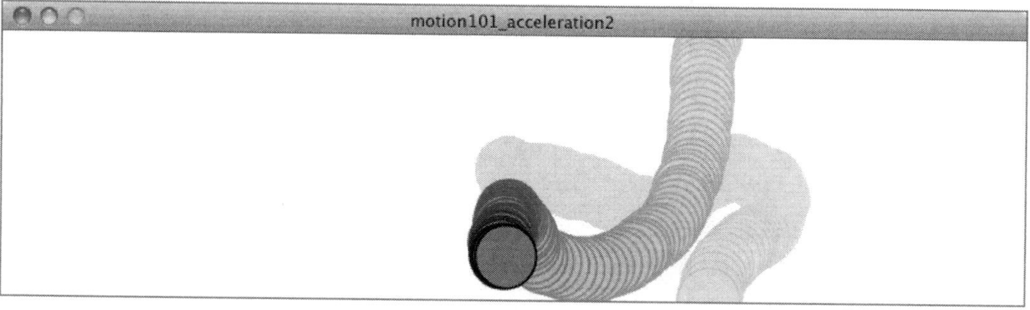

Example 1.9: Motion 101 (velocity and random acceleration)

```
  void update() {

    acceleration = PVector.random2D();

    velocity.add(acceleration);
    velocity.limit(topspeed);
    location.add(velocity);
  }
```

The random2D() function will give us a PVector of length 1 pointing in a random direction.

Because the random vector is a normalized one, we can try scaling it:

(a) scaling the acceleration to a constant value

```
acceleration = PVector.random2D();
```

```
acceleration.mult(0.5);                    Constant
```

(b) scaling the acceleration to a random value

```
acceleration = PVector.random2D();
acceleration.mult(random(2));              Random
```

While this may seem like an obvious point, it's crucial to understand that acceleration does not merely refer to the *speeding up* or *slowing down* of a moving object, but rather *any change* in velocity in either magnitude or direction. Acceleration is used to steer an object, and we'll see this again and again in future chapters as we begin to program objects that make decisions about how to move about the screen.

Exercise 1.6

Referring back to the Introduction (see page 17), implement acceleration according to Perlin noise.

1.9 Static vs. Non-Static Functions

Before we get to Algorithm #3 (*accelerate towards the mouse*), we need to cover one more rather important aspect of working with vectors and the PVector class: the difference between using ***static*** methods and ***non-static*** methods.

Forgetting about vectors for a moment, take a look at the following code:

```
float x = 0;
float y = 5;

x = x + y;
```

Pretty simple, right? x has the value of 0, we add y to it, and now x is equal to 5. We could write the corresponding code pretty easily based on what we've learned about PVector.

```
PVector v = new PVector(0,0);
PVector u = new PVector(4,5);
v.add(u);
```

The vector v has the value of (0,0), we add u to it, and now v is equal to (4,5). Easy, right?

Let's take a look at another example of some simple floating point math:

```
float x = 0;
float y = 5;

float z = x + y;
```

x has the value of 0, we add y to it, and store the result in a new variable z. The value of x does not change in this example (neither does y)! This may seem like a trivial point, and one that is quite intuitive when it comes to mathematical operations with floats. However, it's not so obvious with mathematical operations in `PVector`. Let's try to write the code based on what we know so far.

```
PVector v = new PVector(0,0);
PVector u = new PVector(4,5);
PVector w = v.add(u);          Don't be fooled; this is incorrect!!!
```

The above might seem like a good guess, but it's just not the way the `PVector` class works. If we look at the definition of `add()` . . .

```
void add(PVector v) {
    x = x + v.x;
    y = y + v.y;
 }
```

we see that this code does not accomplish our goal. First, it does not return a new `PVector` (the return type is "void") and second, it changes the value of the `PVector` upon which it is called. In order to add two `PVector` objects together and return the result as a new `PVector`, we must use the static `add()` function.

Functions that we call from the class name itself (rather than from a specific object instance) are known as ***static functions***. Here are two examples of function calls that assume two `PVector` objects, v and u:

```
PVector.add(v,u);          Static: called from the class name.
v.add(u);                  Not static: called from an object instance.
```

Since you can't write static functions yourself in Processing, you might not have encountered them before. `PVector`'s static functions allow us to perform generic mathematical operations on `PVector` objects without having to adjust the value of one of the input `PVector`s. Let's look at how we might write the static version of `add()`:

```
static PVector add(PVector v1, PVector v2) {
```

The static version of add allows us to add two PVectors together and assign the result to a new PVector while leaving the original PVectors (v and u above) intact.

```
    PVector v3 = new PVector(v1.x + v2.x, v1.y + v2.y);
    return v3;
}
```

There are several differences here:

- The function is labeled as ***static***.
- The function does not have a ***void*** return type, but rather returns a `PVector`.
- The function creates a new `PVector` (v3) and returns the sum of the components of v1 and v2 in that new `PVector`.

When you call a static function, instead of referencing an actual object instance, you simply reference the name of the class itself.

```
PVector v = new PVector(0,0);
PVector u = new PVector(4,5);
PVector w = v.add(u);
PVector w = PVector.add(v,u);
```

The `PVector` class has static versions of `add()`, `sub()`, `mult()`, and `div()`.

Exercise 1.7

Translate the following pseudocode to code using static or non-static functions where appropriate.

- The `PVector` v equals (1,5).
- The `PVector` u equals v multiplied by 2.
- The `PVector` w equals v minus u.
- Divide the `PVector` w by 3.

```
PVector v = new PVector(1,5);
PVector u = ________.______(__,__);
PVector w = ________.______(__,__);
___________;
```

1.10 Interactivity with Acceleration

To finish out this chapter, let's try something a bit more complex and a great deal more useful. We'll dynamically calculate an object's acceleration according to a rule stated in Algorithm #3 — *the object accelerates towards the mouse.*

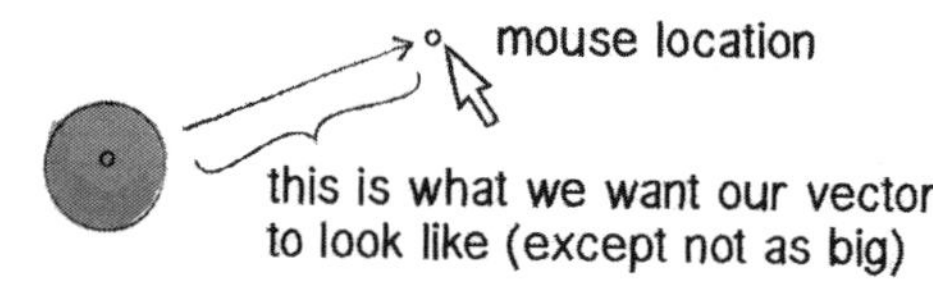

Figure 1.14

Anytime we want to calculate a vector based on a rule or a formula, we need to compute two things: ***magnitude*** and ***direction***. Let's start with direction. We know the acceleration vector should point from the object's location towards the mouse location. Let's say the object is located at the point (x,y) and the mouse at (`mouseX`,`mouseY`).

In Figure 1.15, we see that we can get a vector (dx,dy) by subtracting the object's location from the mouse's location.

- **`dx = mouseX - x`**
- **`dy = mouseY - y`**

Figure 1.15

Let's rewrite the above using `PVector` syntax. Assuming we are in the `Mover` class and thus have access to the object's `PVector location`, we then have:

```
PVector mouse = new PVector(mouseX,mouseY);
PVector dir = PVector.sub(mouse,location);
```

Look! We're using the static reference to sub() because we want a new PVector pointing from one point to another.

We now have a `PVector` that points from the mover's location all the way to the mouse. If the object were to actually accelerate using that vector, it would appear instantaneously at the mouse location. This does not make for good animation, of course, and what we want to do now is decide how quickly that object should accelerate toward the mouse.

In order to set the magnitude (whatever it may be) of our acceleration `PVector`, we must first ___ that direction vector. That's right, you said it. *Normalize*. If we can shrink the vector down to its unit vector (of length one) then we have a vector that tells us the direction and can easily be scaled to any value. One multiplied by anything equals anything.

```
float anything = ?????
dir.normalize();
dir.mult(anything);
```

To summarize, we take the following steps:

1. Calculate a vector that points from the object to the target location (mouse)
2. Normalize that vector (reducing its length to 1)
3. Scale that vector to an appropriate value (by multiplying it by some value)
4. Assign that vector to acceleration

And here are those steps in the `update()` function itself:

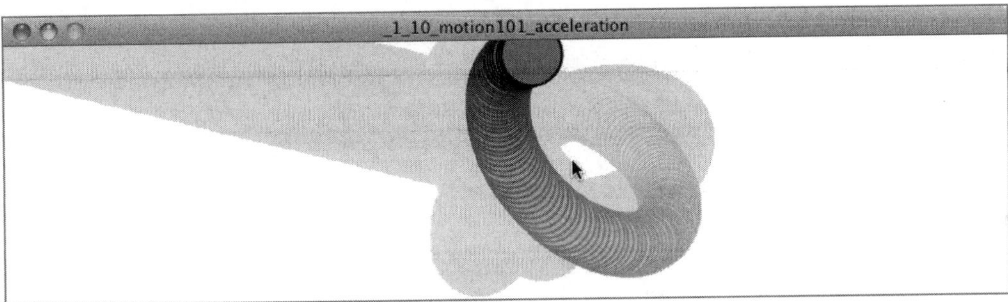

Example 1.10: Accelerating towards the mouse

```
void update() {

  PVector mouse = new PVector(mouseX,mouseY);
  PVector dir = PVector.sub(mouse,location);     Step 1: Compute direction

  dir.normalize();                               Step 2: Normalize

  dir.mult(0.5);                                 Step 3: Scale

  acceleration = dir;                            Step 4: Accelerate

  velocity.add(acceleration);
  velocity.limit(topspeed);
  location.add(velocity);

}
```

You may be wondering why the circle doesn't stop when it reaches the target. It's important to note that the object moving has no knowledge about trying to stop at a destination; it only knows where the destination is and tries to go there as quickly as possible. Going as quickly as possible means it will inevitably overshoot the location and have to turn around, again going as quickly as possible towards the destination, overshooting it again, and so on and so forth. Stay tuned; in later chapters we'll learn how to program an object to ***arrive*** at a location (slow down on approach).

This example is remarkably close to the concept of gravitational attraction (in which the object is attracted to the mouse location). Gravitational attraction will be covered in more detail in the next chapter. However, one thing missing here is that the strength of gravity (magnitude of acceleration) is inversely proportional to distance. This means that the closer the object is to the mouse, the faster it accelerates.

Exercise 1.8

Try implementing the above example with a variable magnitude of acceleration, stronger when it is either closer or farther away.

Let's see what this example would look like with an array of movers (rather than just one).

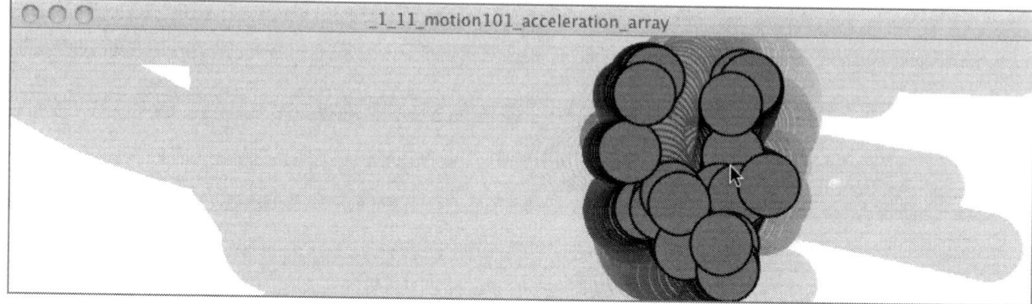

Example 1.11: Array of movers accelerating towards the mouse

```
Mover[] movers = new Mover[20];                    An array of objects

void setup() {
  size(640,360);
  background(255);
  for (int i = 0; i < movers.length; i++) {
```

```
      movers[i] = new Mover();          Initialize each object in the array.
  }
}

void draw() {
  background(255);

  for (int i = 0; i < movers.length; i++) {
    movers[i].update();                 Calling functions on all the objects in the
    movers[i].checkEdges();             array
    movers[i].display();
  }
}

class Mover {

  PVector location;
  PVector velocity;
  PVector acceleration;
  float topspeed;

  Mover() {
    location = new PVector(random(width),random(height));
    velocity = new PVector(0,0);
    topspeed = 4;
  }

  void update() {
```

<u>Our algorithm for calculating acceleration</u>:

```
    PVector mouse = new PVector(mouseX,mouseY);     Find the vector pointing towards the
    PVector dir = PVector.sub(mouse,location);      mouse.
    dir.normalize();                                Normalize.
    dir.mult(0.5);                                  Scale.
    acceleration = dir;                             Set to acceleration.

    velocity.add(acceleration);                     Motion 101! Velocity changes by
    velocity.limit(topspeed);                       acceleration. Location changes by velocity.
    location.add(velocity);
  }
```

```
  void display() {                                    Display the Mover
    stroke(0);
    fill(175);
    ellipse(location.x,location.y,16,16);
  }

  void checkEdges() {                                 What to do at the edges

    if (location.x > width) {
      location.x = 0;
    } else if (location.x < 0) {
      location.x = width;
    }

    if (location.y > height) {
      location.y = 0;
    }  else if (location.y < 0) {
      location.y = height;
    }
  }
}
```

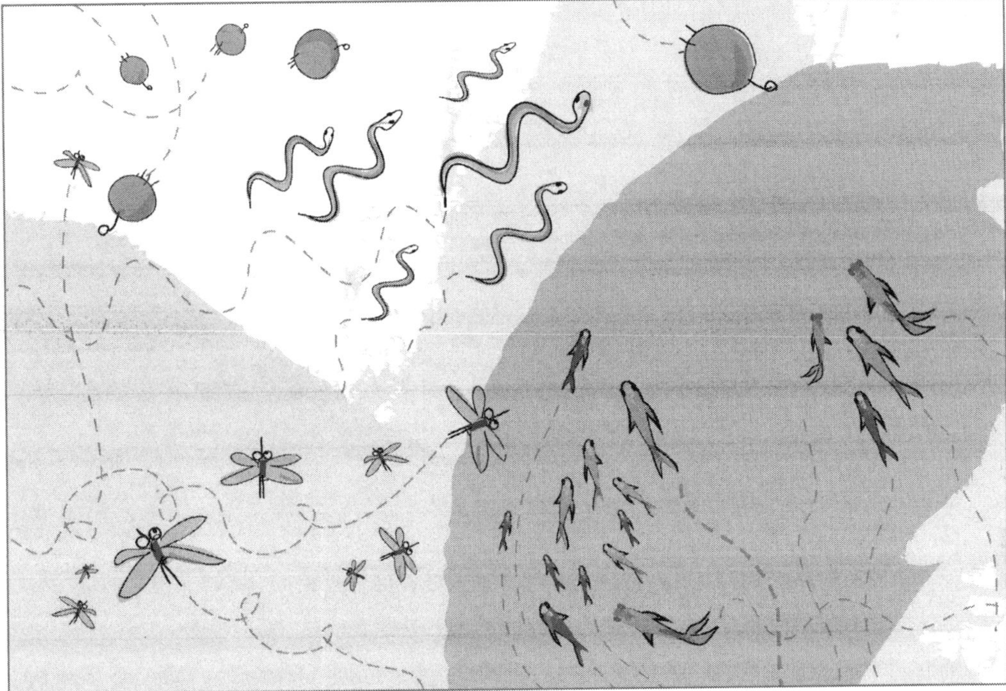

Figure 1.16: The Ecosystem Project

The Ecosystem Project

As mentioned in the preface, one way to use this book is to build a single project over the course of reading it, incorporating elements from each chapter one step at a time. We'll follow the development of an example project throughout this book—a simulation of an ecosystem. Imagine a population of computational creatures swimming around a digital pond, interacting with each other according to various rules.

Step 1 Exercise:

Develop a set of rules for simulating the real-world behavior of a creature, such as a nervous fly, swimming fish, hopping bunny, slithering snake, etc. Can you control the object's motion by only manipulating the acceleration? Try to give the creature a personality through its behavior (rather than through its visual design).

Chapter 2. Forces

"Don't underestimate the Force."

— Darth Vader

In the final example of Chapter 1, we saw how we could calculate a dynamic acceleration based on a vector pointing from a circle on the screen to the mouse location. The resulting motion resembled a magnetic attraction between circle and mouse, as if some *force* were pulling the circle in towards the mouse. In this chapter we will formalize our understanding of the concept of a force and its relationship to acceleration. Our goal, by the end of this chapter, is to understand how to make multiple objects move around the screen and respond to a variety of environmental forces.

2.1 Forces and Newton's Laws of Motion

Before we begin examining the practical realities of simulating forces in code, let's take a conceptual look at what it means to be a force in the real world. Just like the word "vector," "force" is often used to mean a variety of things. It can indicate a powerful intensity, as in "She pushed the boulder with great force" or "He spoke forcefully." The definition of ***force*** that we care about is much more formal and comes from Isaac Newton's laws of motion:

> A force is a vector that causes an object with mass to accelerate.

The good news here is that we recognize the first part of the definition: *a force is a vector*. Thank goodness we just spent a whole chapter learning what a vector is and how to program with `PVectors`!

Let's look at Newton's three laws of motion in relation to the concept of a force.

Newton's First Law

Newton's first law is commonly stated as:

> An object at rest stays at rest and an object in motion stays in motion.

However, this is missing an important element related to forces. We could expand it by stating:

> An object at rest stays at rest and an object in motion stays in motion at a constant speed and direction unless acted upon by an unbalanced force.

By the time Newton came along, the prevailing theory of motion—formulated by Aristotle—was nearly two thousand years old. It stated that if an object is moving, some sort of force is required to keep it moving. Unless that moving thing is being pushed or pulled, it will simply slow down or stop. Right?

This, of course, is not true. In the absence of any forces, no force is required to keep an object moving. An object (such as a ball) tossed in the earth's atmosphere slows down because of air resistance (a force). An object's velocity will only remain constant in the absence of any forces or if the forces that act on it cancel each other out, i.e. the net force adds up to zero. This is often referred to as ***equilibrium***. The falling ball will reach a terminal velocity (that stays constant) once the force of air resistance equals the force of gravity.

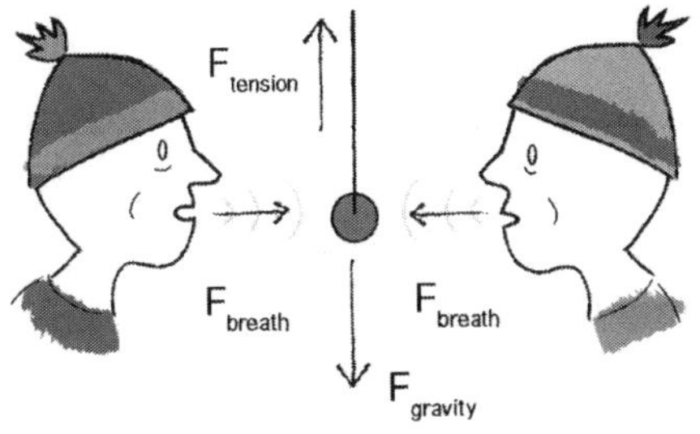

Figure 2.1: The pendulum doesn't move because all the forces cancel each other out (add up to a net force of zero).

In our Processing world, we could restate Newton's first law as follows:

> An object's PVector velocity will remain constant if it is in a state of equilibrium.

Skipping Newton's second law (arguably the most important law for our purposes) for a moment, let's move on to the third law.

Newton's Third Law

This law is often stated as:

> For every action there is an equal and opposite reaction.

This law frequently causes some confusion in the way that it is stated. For one, it sounds like one force causes another. Yes, if you push someone, that someone may *actively* decide to push you back. But this is not the action and reaction we are talking about with Newton's third law.

Let's say you push against a wall. The wall doesn't actively decide to push back on you. There is no "origin" force. Your push simply includes both forces, referred to as an "action/reaction pair."

A better way of stating the law might be:

> Forces always occur in pairs. The two forces are of equal strength, but in opposite directions.

Now, this still causes confusion because it sounds like these forces would always cancel each other out. This is not the case. Remember, the forces act on different objects. And just because the two forces are equal, it doesn't mean that the movements are equal (or that the objects will stop moving).

Try pushing on a stationary truck. Although the truck is far more powerful than you, unlike a moving one, a stationary truck will never overpower you and send you flying backwards. The force you exert on it is equal and opposite to the force exerted on your hands. The outcome depends on a variety of other factors. If the truck is a small truck on an icy downhill, you'll probably be able to get it to move. On the other hand, if it's a very large truck on a dirt road and you push hard enough (maybe even take a running start), you could injure your hand.

And if you are wearing roller skates when you push on that truck?

Figure 2.2

You'll accelerate away from the truck, sliding along the road while the truck stays put. Why do you slide but not the truck? For one, the truck has a much larger mass (which we'll get into with Newton's second law). There are other forces at work too, namely the friction of the truck's tires and your roller skates against the road.

Newton's Third Law (as seen through the eyes of Processing)

> If we calculate a PVector f that is a force of object A on object B, we must also apply the force—PVector.mult(f,-1);—that B exerts on object A.

We'll see that in the world of Processing programming, we don't always have to stay true to the above. Sometimes, such as in the case of see gravitational attraction between bodies (see page 94), we'll want to model equal and opposite forces. Other times, such as when we're simply saying, "Hey, there's some wind in the environment," we're not going to bother to model the force that a body exerts back on the air. In fact, we're not modeling the air at all! Remember, we are simply taking inspiration from the physics of the natural world, not simulating everything with perfect precision.

2.2 Forces and Processing—Newton's Second Law as a Function

And here we are at the most important law for the Processing programmer.

Newton's Second Law

This law is stated as:

> Force equals mass times acceleration.

Or:

$$\vec{F} = M \times \vec{A}$$

Why is this the most important law for us? Well, let's write it a different way.

$$\vec{A} = \vec{F} / M$$

Acceleration is directly proportional to force and inversely proportional to mass. This means that if you get pushed, the harder you are pushed, the faster you'll move (accelerate). The bigger you are, the slower you'll move.

Weight vs. Mass

- The ***mass*** of an object is a measure of the amount of matter in the object (measured in kilograms).
- ***Weight***, though often mistaken for mass, is technically the force of gravity on an object. From Newton's second law, we can calculate it as mass times the acceleration of gravity (`w = m * g`). Weight is measured in newtons.
- ***Density*** is defined as the amount of mass per unit of volume (grams per cubic centimeter, for example).

Note that an object that has a mass of one kilogram on earth would have a mass of one kilogram on the moon. However, it would weigh only one-sixth as much.

Now, in the world of Processing, what is mass anyway? Aren't we dealing with pixels? To start in a simpler place, let's say that in our pretend pixel world, all of our objects have a mass equal to 1. F/ 1 = F. And so:

$$\vec{A} = \vec{F}$$

The acceleration of an object is equal to force. This is great news. After all, we saw in Chapter 1 that acceleration was the key to controlling the movement of our objects on screen. Location is adjusted by velocity, and velocity by acceleration. Acceleration was where it all began. Now we learn that *force* is truly where it all begins.

Let's take our `Mover` class, with location, velocity, and acceleration.

```
class Mover {
  PVector location;
  PVector velocity;
  PVector acceleration;
}
```

Now our goal is to be able to add forces to this object, perhaps saying:

```
mover.applyForce(wind);
```

or:

```
mover.applyForce(gravity);
```

where wind and gravity are `PVector`s. According to Newton's second law, we could implement this function as follows.

```
void applyForce(PVector force) {
  acceleration = force;          Newton's second law at its simplest.
}
```

2.3 Force Accumulation

This looks pretty good. After all, *acceleration = force* is a literal translation of Newton's second law (without mass). Nevertheless, there's a pretty big problem here. Let's return to what we are trying to accomplish: creating a moving object on the screen that responds to wind and gravity.

```
mover.applyForce(wind);
mover.applyForce(gravity);
mover.update();
mover.display();
```

Ok, let's *be* the computer for a moment. First, we call `applyForce()` with wind. And so the `Mover` object's acceleration is now assigned the `PVector` `wind`. Second, we call `applyForce()` with gravity. Now the `Mover` object's acceleration is set to the gravity `PVector`. Third, we call `update()`. What happens in `update()`? Acceleration is added to velocity.

```
velocity.add(acceleration);
```

We're not going to see any error in Processing, but zoinks! We've got a major problem. What is the value of acceleration when it is added to velocity? It is equal to the gravity force. Wind has been left out! If we call `applyForce()` more than once, it overrides each previous call. How are we going to handle more than one force?

The truth of the matter here is that we started with a simplified statement of Newton's second law. Here's a more accurate way to put it:

> Net Force equals mass times acceleration.

Or, acceleration is equal to the *sum of all forces* divided by mass. This makes perfect sense. After all, as we saw in Newton's first law, if all the forces add up to zero, an object experiences an equilibrium state (i.e. no acceleration). Our implementation of this is through a process known as ***force accumulation***. It's actually very simple; all we need to do is add all of the forces together. At any given moment, there might be 1, 2, 6, 12, or 303 forces. As long as our object knows how to accumulate them, it doesn't matter how many forces act on it.

```
void applyForce(PVector force) {
  acceleration.add(force);
}
```

Newton's second law, but with force accumulation. We now add each force to acceleration, one at a time.

Now, we're not finished just yet. Force accumulation has one more piece. Since we're adding all the forces together at any given moment, we have to make sure that we clear acceleration (i.e. set it to zero) before each time `update()` is called. Let's think about wind for a moment. Sometimes the wind is very strong, sometimes it's weak, and sometimes there's no wind at all. At any given moment, there might be a huge gust of wind, say, when the user holds down the mouse.

```
if (mousePressed) {
  PVector wind = new PVector(0.5,0);
  mover.applyForce(wind);
}
```

When the user releases the mouse, the wind will stop, and according to Newton's first law, the object will continue to move at a constant velocity. However, if we had forgotten to reset acceleration to zero, the gust of wind would still be in effect. Even worse, it would add onto itself from the previous frame, since we are accumulating forces! Acceleration, in our simulation, has no memory; it is simply calculated based on the environmental forces present at a moment in time. This is different than, say, location, which must remember where the object was in the previous frame in order to move properly to the next.

The easiest way to implement clearing the acceleration for each frame is to multiply the `PVector` by 0 at the end of `update()`.

```
void update() {
  velocity.add(acceleration);
  location.add(velocity);
  acceleration.mult(0);
}
```

Exercise 2.1

Using forces, simulate a helium-filled balloon floating upward and bouncing off the top of a window. Can you add a wind force that changes over time, perhaps according to Perlin noise?

2.4 Dealing with Mass

OK. We've got one tiny little addition to make before we are done with integrating forces into our `Mover` class and are ready to look at examples. After all, Newton's second law is really $\vec{F} = M \times \vec{A}$, not $\vec{A} = \vec{F}$. Incorporating mass is as easy as adding an instance variable to our class, but we need to spend a little more time here because a slight complication will emerge.

First we just need to add mass.

```
class Mover {
  PVector location;
  PVector velocity;
  PVector acceleration;
  float mass;            // Adding mass as a float
```

Units of Measurement

Now that we are introducing mass, it's important to make a quick note about units of measurement. In the real world, things are measured in specific units. We say that two objects are 3 meters apart, the baseball is moving at a rate of 90 miles per hour, or this bowling ball has a mass of 6 kilograms. As we'll see later in this book, sometimes we will want to take real-world units into consideration. However, in this chapter, we're going to ignore them for the most part. Our units of measurement are in pixels ("These two circles are 100 pixels apart") and frames of animation ("This circle is moving at a rate of 2 pixels per frame"). In the case of mass, there isn't any unit of measurement for us to use. We're just going to make something up. In this example, we're arbitrarily picking the number 10. There is no unit of measurement, though you might enjoy inventing a unit of your own, like "1 moog" or "1 yurkle." It should also be noted that, for demonstration purposes, we'll tie mass to pixels (drawing, say, a circle with a radius of 10). This will allow us to visualize the mass of an object. In the real world, however, size does not definitely indicate mass. A small metal ball could have a much higher mass than a large balloon due to its higher density.

Mass is a scalar (float), not a vector, as it's just one number describing the amount of matter in an object. We could be fancy about things and compute the area of a shape as its mass, but it's simpler to begin by saying, "Hey, the mass of this object is...um, I dunno...how about 10?"

```
Mover() {
   location = new PVector(random(width),random(height));
   velocity = new PVector(0,0);
   acceleration = new PVector(0,0);
   mass = 10.0;
 }
```

This isn't so great since things only become interesting once we have objects with varying mass, but it'll get us started. Where does mass come in? We use it while applying Newton's second law to our object.

```
void applyForce(PVector force) {
  force.div(mass);                Newton's second law (with force
  acceleration.add(force);        accumulation and mass)
}
```

Yet again, even though our code looks quite reasonable, we have a fairly major problem here. Consider the following scenario with two `Mover` objects, both being blown away by a wind force.

```
Mover m1 = new Mover();
Mover m2 = new Mover();

PVector wind = new PVector(1,0);

m1.applyForce(wind);
m2.applyForce(wind);
```

Again, let's *be* the computer. Object `m1` receives the wind force—(1,0)—divides it by mass (10), and adds it to acceleration.

```
m1 equals wind force:      (1,0)
Divided by mass of 10:     (0.1,0)
```

OK. Moving on to object `m2`. It also receives the wind force—(1,0). Wait. Hold on a second. What is the value of the wind force? Taking a closer look, the wind force is actually now—(0.1,0)!! Do you remember this little tidbit about working with objects? When you pass an object (in this case a `PVector`) into a function, you are passing a reference to that object. It's not a copy! So if a function makes a change to that object (which, in this case, it does by dividing by mass) then that object is permanently changed! But we don't want `m2` to receive a force divided by the mass of object `m1`. We want it to receive that force in its original state—(1,0). And so we must protect ourselves and make a copy of the `PVector` f before dividing it by mass. Fortunately, the `PVector` class has a convenient method for making a copy—`get()`. `get()` returns a new `PVector` object with the same data. And so we can revise `applyForce()` as follows:

```
void applyForce(PVector force) {
  PVector f = force.get();        // Making a copy of the PVector before using it!
  f.div(mass);
  acceleration.add(f);
}
```

There's another way we could write the above function, using the static method `div()`. For help with this exercise, review static methods in Chapter 1 (see page 54).

Exercise 2.2

Rewrite the `applyForce()` method using the static method `div()` instead of `get()`.

```
void applyForce(PVector force) {
  PVector f = _______.___(______,____);
  acceleration.add(f);
}
```

2.5 Creating Forces

Let's take a moment to remind ourselves where we are. We know what a force is (a vector), and we know how to apply a force to an object (divide it by mass and add it to the object's acceleration vector). What are we missing? Well, we have yet to figure out how we get a force in the first place. Where do forces come from?

In this chapter, we'll look at two methods for creating forces in our Processing world.

1. **Make up a force!** After all, you are the programmer, the creator of your world. There's no reason why you can't just make up a force and apply it.

2. **Model a force!** Yes, forces exist in the real world. And physics textbooks often contain formulas for these forces. We can take these formulas, translate them into source code, and model real-world forces in Processing.

The easiest way to make up a force is to just pick a number. Let's start with the idea of simulating wind. How about a wind force that points to the right and is fairly weak? Assuming a `Mover` object m, our code would look like:

```
PVector wind = new PVector(0.01,0);
m.applyForce(wind);
```

The result isn't terribly interesting, but it is a good place to start. We create a `PVector` object, initialize it, and pass it into an object (which in turn will apply it to its own acceleration). If we wanted to have two forces, perhaps wind and gravity (a bit stronger, pointing down), we might write the following:

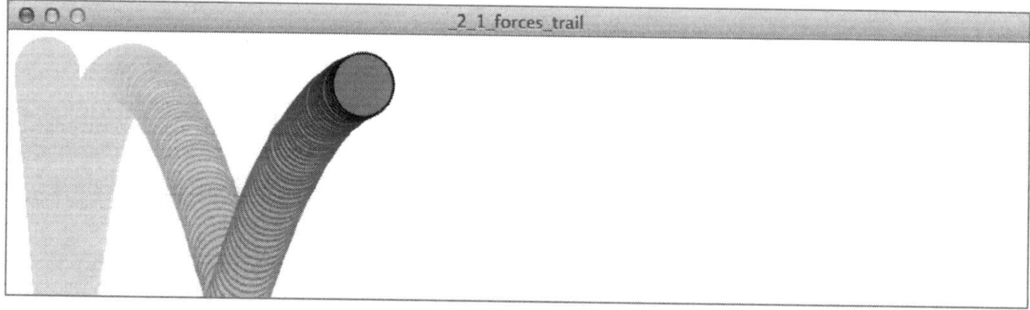

Example 2.1: Forces

```
PVector wind = new PVector(0.01,0);
PVector gravity = new PVector(0,0.1);
m.applyForce(wind);
m.applyForce(gravity);
```

Now we have two forces, pointing in different directions with different magnitudes, both applied to object `m`. We're beginning to get somewhere. We've now built a world for our objects in Processing, an environment to which they can actually respond.

Let's look at how we could make this example a bit more exciting with many objects of varying mass. To do this, we'll need a quick review of object-oriented programming. Again, we're not covering all the basics of programming here (for that you can check out any of the intro Processing books listed in the introduction). However, since the idea of creating a world filled with objects is pretty fundamental to all the examples in this book, it's worth taking a moment to walk through the steps of going from one object to many.

This is where we are with the `Mover` class as a whole. Notice how it is identical to the `Mover` class created in Chapter 1, with two additions—`mass` and a new `applyForce()` function.

```
class Mover {

  PVector location;
  PVector velocity;
  PVector acceleration;
  float mass;                                  // The object now has mass!

  Mover() {
    mass = 1;                                  // And for now, we'll just set the mass equal to 1 for simplicity.
    location = new PVector(30,30);
    velocity = new PVector(0,0);
    acceleration = new PVector(0,0);
  }

  void applyForce(PVector force) {             // Newton's second law.
    PVector f = PVector.div(force,mass);       // Receive a force, divide by mass, and add to acceleration.
    acceleration.add(f);
  }

  void update() {
    velocity.add(acceleration);                // Motion 101 from Chapter 1
    location.add(velocity);
    acceleration.mult(0);                      // Now add clearing the acceleration each time!
  }

  void display() {
    stroke(0);
    fill(175);
    ellipse(location.x,location.y,mass*16,mass*16);   // Scaling the size according to mass.
  }
```

```
void checkEdges() {

  if (location.x > width) {
    location.x = width;
    velocity.x *= -1;
  } else if (location.x < 0) {
    velocity.x *= -1;
    location.x = 0;
  }

  if (location.y > height) {
    velocity.y *= -1;
    location.y = height;
  }
 }
}
```

Somewhat arbitrarily, we are deciding that an object bounces when it hits the edges of a window.

Even though we said we shouldn't touch location and velocity directly, there are some exceptions. Here we are doing so as a quick and easy way to reverse the direction of our object when it reaches the edge.

Now that our class is set, we can choose to create, say, one hundred `Mover` objects with an array.

```
Mover[] movers = new Mover[100];
```

And then we can initialize all of those `Mover` objects in `setup()` with a loop.

```
void setup() {
  for (int i = 0; i < movers.length; i++) {
    movers[i] = new Mover();
  }
}
```

But now we have a small issue. If we refer back to the `Mover` object's constructor…

```
Mover() {
  mass = 1;
  location = new PVector(30,30);
  velocity = new PVector(0,0);
  acceleration = new PVector(0,0);
}
```

Every object has a mass of 1 and a location of (30,30).

…we discover that every `Mover` object is made exactly the same way. What we want are `Mover` objects of varying mass that start at varying locations. Here is where we need to increase the sophistication of our constructor by adding arguments.

```
Mover(float m, float x , float y) {
  mass = m;
  location = new PVector(x,y);
```

Now setting these variables with arguments

```
    velocity = new PVector(0,0);
    acceleration = new PVector(0,0);
  }
```

Notice how the mass and location are no longer set to hardcoded numbers, but rather initialized via arguments passed through the constructor. This means we can create a variety of `Mover` objects: big ones, small ones, ones that start on the left side of the screen, ones that start on the right, etc.

```
Mover m1 = new Mover(10,0,height/2);
```

A big Mover on the left side of the window

```
Mover m1 = new Mover(0.1,width,height/2);
```

A small Mover on the right side of the window

With an array, however, we want to initialize all of the objects with a loop.

```
void setup() {
  for (int i = 0; i < movers.length; i++) {
    movers[i] = new Mover(random(0.1,5),0,0);
  }
}
```

Initializing many Mover objects, all with random mass (and all starting at 0,0)

For each mover created, the mass is set to a random value between 0.1 and 5, the starting x-location is set to 0, and the starting y-location is set to 0. Certainly, there are all sorts of ways we might choose to initialize the objects; this is just a demonstration of one possibility.

Once the array of objects is declared, created, and initialized, the rest of the code is simple. We run through every object, hand them each the forces in the environment, and enjoy the show.

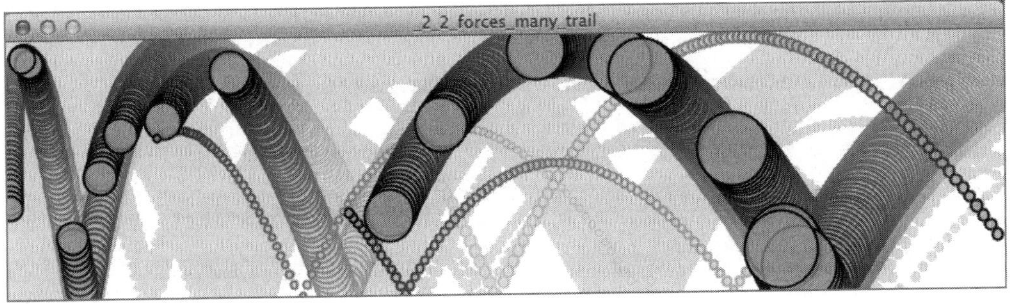

Example 2.2: Forces acting on many objects

```
void draw() {
  background(255);

  PVector wind = new PVector(0.01,0);
  PVector gravity = new PVector(0,0.1);          // Make up two forces.

  for (int i = 0; i < movers.length; i++) {      // Loop through all objects and apply both
    movers[i].applyForce(wind);                  // forces to each object.
    movers[i].applyForce(gravity);

    movers[i].update();
    movers[i].display();
    movers[i].checkEdges();
  }
}
```

Note how in the above image, the smaller circles reach the right of the window faster than the larger ones. This is because of our formula: *acceleration = force divided by mass*. The larger the mass, the smaller the acceleration.

Exercise 2.3

Instead of objects bouncing off the edge of the wall, create an example in which an invisible force pushes back on the objects to keep them in the window. Can you weight the force according to how far the object is from an edge—i.e., the closer it is, the stronger the force?

2.6 Gravity on Earth and Modeling a Force

You may have noticed something woefully inaccurate about this last example. The smaller the circle, the faster it falls. There is a logic to this; after all, we just stated (according to Newton's second law) that the smaller the mass, the higher the acceleration. But this is not what happens in the real world. If you were to climb to the top of the Leaning Tower of Pisa and drop two balls of different masses, which one will hit the ground first? According to legend, Galileo performed this exact test in 1589, discovering that they fell with the same acceleration, hitting the ground at the same time. Why is this? As we will see later in this chapter, the force of gravity is calculated relative to an object's mass. The bigger the object, the stronger the force. So if the force is scaled according to mass, it is canceled out when acceleration is divided by mass. We can implement this in our sketch rather easily by multiplying our made-up gravity force by mass.

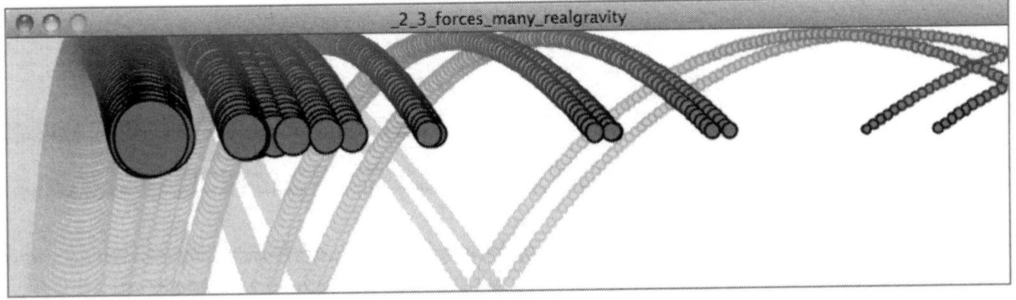

Example 2.3: Gravity scaled by mass

```
for (int i = 0; i < movers.length; i++) {

    PVector wind = new PVector(0.001,0);
    float m = movers[i].mass;
    PVector gravity = new PVector(0,0.1*m);      Scaling gravity by mass to be more accurate
    movers[i].applyForce(wind);
    movers[i].applyForce(gravity);

    movers[i].update();
    movers[i].display();
    movers[i].checkEdges();
  }
```

While the objects now fall at the same rate, because the strength of the wind force is independent of mass, the smaller objects still accelerate to the right more quickly.

Making up forces will actually get us quite far. The world of Processing is a pretend world of pixels and you are its master. So whatever you deem appropriate to be a force, well by golly, that's the force it should be. Nevertheless, there may come a time where you find yourself wondering: "But how does it really all work?"

Open up any high school physics textbook and you will find some diagrams and formulas describing many different forces—gravity, electromagnetism, friction, tension, elasticity, and more. In this chapter we're going to look at two forces—friction and gravity. The point we're making here is not that friction and gravity are fundamental forces that you always need to have in your Processing sketches. Rather, we want to evaluate these two forces as case studies for the following process:

- Understanding the concept behind a force
- Deconstructing the force's formula into two parts:
    - How do we compute the force's direction?

- How do we compute the force's magnitude?

- Translating that formula into Processing code that calculates a `PVector` to be sent through our `Mover`'s `applyForce()` function

If we can follow the above steps with two forces, then hopefully if you ever find yourself Googling "atomic nuclei weak nuclear force" at 3 a.m., you will have the skills to take what you find and adapt it for Processing.

Dealing with formulae

OK, in a moment we're going to write out the formula for friction. This isn't the first time we've seen a formula in this book; we just finished up our discussion of Newton's second law, $\vec{F} = M \times \vec{A}$ (or force = mass * acceleration). We didn't spend a lot of time worrying about this formula because it's a nice and simple one. Nevertheless, it's a scary world out there. Just take a look at the equation for a "normal" distribution, which we covered (without looking at the formula) in the Introduction (see page 10).

$$f(x;\,\mu,\,\sigma^2) = \frac{1}{\sigma\sqrt{2\pi}}e^{-\frac{(x-\mu)^2}{2\sigma^2}}$$

What we're seeing here is that formulas like to use a lot of symbols (quite often letters from the Greek alphabet). Let's take a look at the formula for friction.

$$\overrightarrow{Friction} = -\mu N \hat{v}$$

If it's been a while since you've looked at a formula from a math or physics textbook, there are three key points that are important to cover before we move on.

- ***Evaluate the right side, assign to the left side.*** This is just like in code! What we're doing here is evaluating the right side of the equation and assigning it to the left. In the case above, we want to calculate the force of friction—the left side tells us what we want to calculate and the right side tells us how to do it.
- ***Are we talking about a vector or a scalar?*** It's important for us to realize that in some cases, we'll be looking at a vector; in others, a scalar. For example, in this case the force of friction is a vector. We can see that by the arrow above the word "friction." It has a magnitude and direction. The right side of the equation also has a vector, as indicated by the symbol $\hat{v}$, which in this case stands for the velocity unit vector.
- ***When symbols are placed next to each other, we mean for them to be multiplied.*** The formula above actually has four elements: -1, μ, N, and $\hat{v}$. We want to multiply them together and read the formula as: $\overrightarrow{Friction} = -1 * \mu * N * \hat{v}$

2.7 Friction

Let's begin with friction and follow our steps.

Friction is a ***dissipative force***. A dissipative force is one in which the total energy of a system decreases when an object is in motion. Let's say you are driving a car. When you press your foot down on the brake pedal, the car's brakes use friction to slow down the motion of the tires. Kinetic energy (motion) is converted into thermal energy (heat). Whenever two surfaces come into contact, they experience friction. A complete model of friction would include separate cases for static friction (a body at rest against a surface) and kinetic friction (a body in motion against a surface), but for our purposes, we are only going to look at the kinetic case.

Here's the formula for friction:

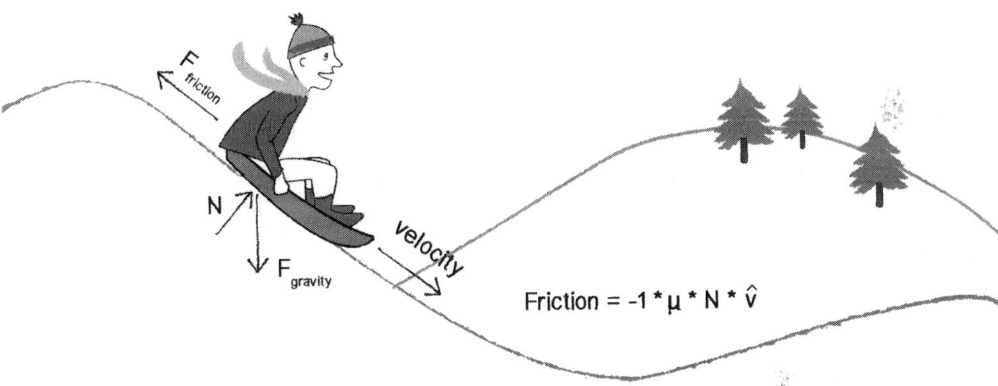

Figure 2.3

It's now up to us to separate this formula into two components that determine the direction of friction as well as the magnitude. Based on the diagram above, we can see that *friction points in the opposite direction of velocity.* In fact, that's the part of the formula that says -1 * $\hat{v}$, or -1 times the velocity unit vector. In Processing, this would mean taking the velocity vector, normalizing it, and multiplying by -1.

```
PVector friction = velocity.get();
friction.normalize();
friction.mult(-1);
```

Let's figure out the direction of the friction force (a unit vector in the opposite direction of velocity).

Notice two additional steps here. First, it's important to make a copy of the velocity vector, as we don't want to reverse the object's direction by accident. Second, we normalize the vector. This is because the magnitude of friction is not associated with how fast it is moving, and we want to start with a friction vector of magnitude 1 so that it can easily be scaled.

According to the formula, the magnitude is μ * N. μ, the Greek letter *mu* (pronounced "mew"), is used here to describe the ***coefficient of friction***. The coefficient of friction establishes the strength of a friction force for a particular surface. The higher it is, the stronger the friction; the lower, the weaker. A block of ice, for example, will have a much lower coefficient of friction than, say, sandpaper. Since we're in a pretend Processing world, we can arbitrarily set the coefficient based on how much friction we want to simulate.

```
float c = 0.01;
```

Now for the second part: N. N refers to the ***normal force***, the force perpendicular to the object's motion along a surface. Think of a vehicle driving along a road. The vehicle pushes down against the road with gravity, and Newton's third law tells us that the road in turn pushes back against the vehicle. That's the normal force. The greater the gravitational force, the greater the normal force. As we'll see in the next section, gravity is associated with mass, and so a lightweight sports car would experience less friction than a massive tractor trailer truck. With the diagram above, however, where the object is moving along a surface at an angle, computing the normal force is a bit more complicated because it doesn't point in the same direction as gravity. We'll need to know something about angles and trigonometry.

All of these specifics are important; however, in Processing, a "good enough" simulation can be achieved without them. We can, for example, make friction work with the assumption that the normal force will always have a magnitude of 1. When we get into trigonometry in the next chapter, we'll remember to return to this question and make our friction example a bit more sophisticated. Therefore:

```
float normal = 1;
```

Now that we have both the magnitude and direction for friction, we can put it all together…

```
float c = 0.01;
float normal = 1;
float frictionMag = c*normal;
```

Let's figure out the magnitude of friction (really just an arbitrary constant).

```
PVector friction = velocity.get();
friction.mult(-1);
friction.normalize();

friction.mult(frictionMag);
```

Take the unit vector and multiply it by magnitude and we have our force vector!

…and add it to our "forces" example, where many objects experience wind, gravity, and now friction:

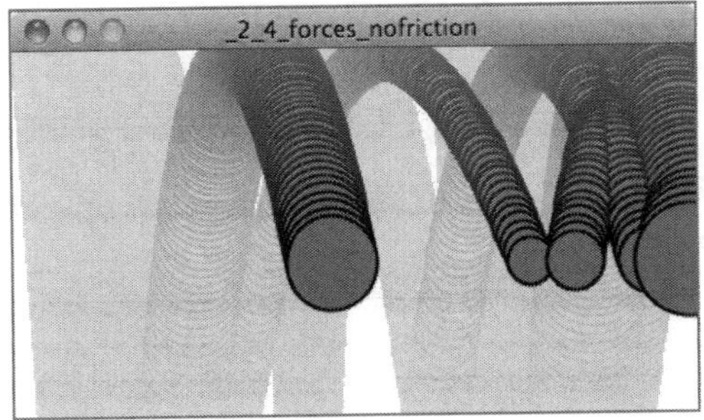

No friction

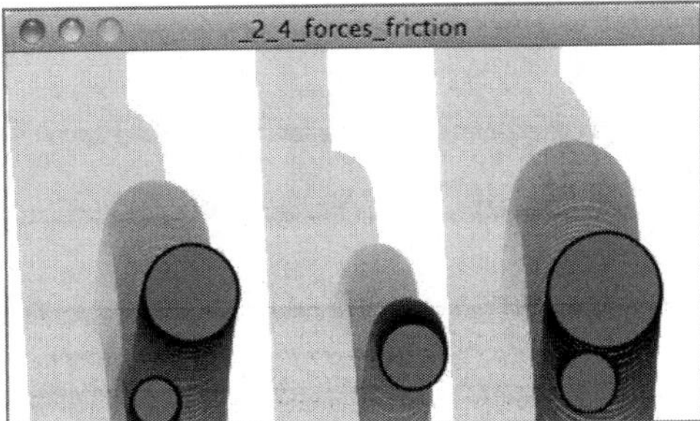

With friction

Example 2.4: Including friction

```
void draw() {
  background(255);

  PVector wind = new PVector(0.001,0);
  PVector gravity = new PVector(0,0.1);      // We could scale by mass to be more accurate.

  for (int i = 0; i < movers.length; i++) {

    float c = 0.01;
    PVector friction = movers[i].velocity.get();
    friction.mult(-1);
    friction.normalize();
    friction.mult(c);

    movers[i].applyForce(friction);          // Apply the friction force vector to the object.
    movers[i].applyForce(wind);
    movers[i].applyForce(gravity);

    movers[i].update();
    movers[i].display();
    movers[i].checkEdges();
  }

}
```

Running this example, you'll notice that the circles don't even make it to the right side of the window. Since friction continuously pushes against the object in the opposite direction of its movement, the object continuously slows down. This can be a useful technique or a problem depending on the goals of your visualization.

Exercise 2.4

Create pockets of friction in a Processing sketch so that objects only experience friction when crossing over those pockets. What if you vary the strength (friction coefficient) of each area? What if you make some pockets feature the opposite of friction—i.e., when you enter a given pocket you actually speed up instead of slowing down?

2.8 Air and Fluid Resistance

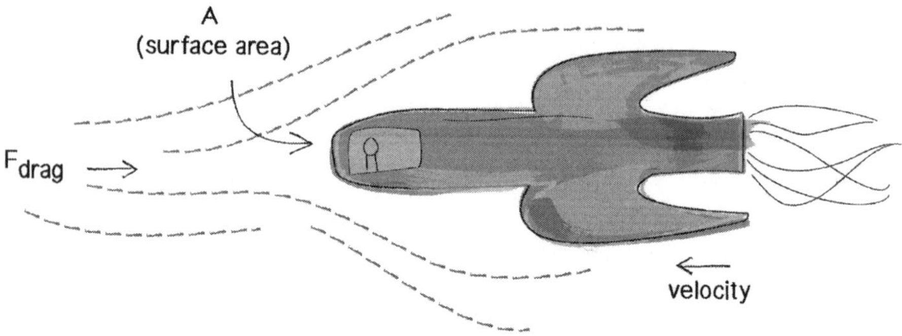

Figure 2.4

Friction also occurs when a body passes through a liquid or gas. This force has many different names, all really meaning the same thing: *viscous force*, *drag force*, *fluid resistance*. While the result is ultimately the same as our previous friction examples (the object slows down), the way in which we calculate a drag force will be slightly different. Let's look at the formula:

$$F_d = -\frac{1}{2}\rho v^2 A C_d \hat{v}$$

Now let's break this down and see what we really need for an effective simulation in Processing, making ourselves a much simpler formula in the process.

- F_d refers to *drag force*, the vector we ultimately want to compute and pass into our `applyForce()` function.
- - 1/2 is a constant: -0.5. This is fairly irrelevant in terms of our Processing world, as we will be making up values for other constants anyway. However, the fact that it is negative is important, as it tells us that the force is in the opposite direction of velocity (just as with friction).

- ρ is the Greek letter *rho*, and refers to the density of the liquid, something we don't need to worry about. We can simplify the problem and consider this to have a constant value of 1.
- v refers to the speed of the object moving. OK, we've got this one! The object's speed is the magnitude of the velocity vector: `velocity.magnitude()`. And v^2 just means v squared or $v * v$.
- A refers to the frontal area of the object that is pushing through the liquid (or gas). An aerodynamic Lamborghini, for example, will experience less air resistance than a boxy Volvo. Nevertheless, for a basic simulation, we can consider our object to be spherical and ignore this element.
- C_d is the coefficient of drag, exactly the same as the coefficient of friction (ρ). This is a constant we'll determine based on whether we want the drag force to be strong or weak.
- $\hat{v}$ Look familiar? It should. This refers to the velocity unit vector, i.e. `velocity.normalize()`. Just like with friction, drag is a force that points in the opposite direction of velocity.

Now that we've analyzed each of these components and determined what we need for a simple simulation, we can reduce our formula to:

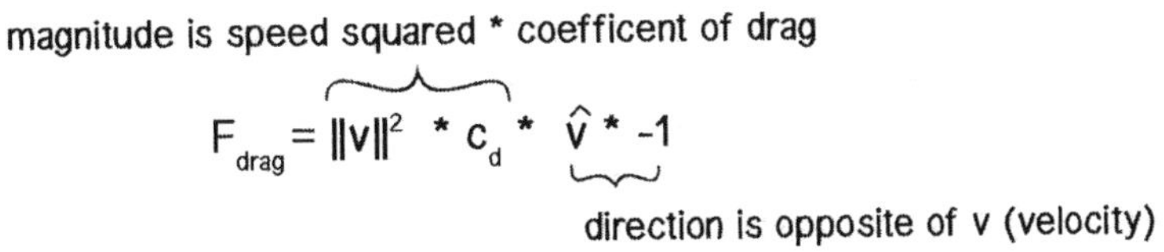

magnitude is speed squared * coefficent of drag

$$F_{drag} = \|v\|^2 * c_d * \hat{v} * -1$$

direction is opposite of v (velocity)

Figure 2.5: Our simplified drag force formula

or:

```
float c = 0.1;
float speed = v.mag();
float dragMagnitude = c * speed * speed;     // Part 1 of our formula (magnitude): Cd * v2
PVector drag = velocity.get();
drag.mult(-1);                               // Part 2 of our formula (direction): -1 * velocity
drag.normalize();
drag.mult(dragMagnitude);                    // Magnitude and direction together!
```

Let's implement this force in our `Mover` class example with one addition. When we wrote our friction example, the force of friction was always present. Whenever an object was moving, friction would slow it down. Here, let's introduce an element to the environment—a "liquid" that the `Mover` objects pass through. The `Liquid` object will be a rectangle and will know about its location, width, height, and "coefficient of drag"—i.e., is it easy for objects to move through it (like air) or difficult (like molasses)? In addition, it should include a function to draw itself on the screen (and two more functions, which we'll see in a moment).

```
class Liquid {
  float x,y,w,h;
  float c;

  Liquid(float x_, float y_, float w_, float h_, float c_) {
    x = x_;
    y = y_;
    w = w_;
    h = h_;
    c = c_;
  }

  void display() {
    noStroke();
    fill(175);
    rect(x,y,w,h);
  }

}
```

The liquid object includes a variable defining its coefficient of drag.

The main program will now include a Liquid object reference as well as a line of code that initializes that object.

```
Liquid liquid;

void setup() {
  liquid = new Liquid(0, height/2, width, height/2, 0.1);
}
```

Initialize a Liquid object. Note the coefficient is low (0.1), otherwise the object would come to a halt fairly quickly (which may someday be the effect you want).

Now comes an interesting question: how do we get the Mover object to talk to the Liquid object? In other words, we want to execute the following:

When a mover passes through a liquid it experiences a drag force.

...or in object-oriented speak (assuming we are looping through an array of Mover objects with index i):

```
if (movers[i].isInside(liquid)) {
  movers[i].drag(liquid);
}
```

If a Mover is inside a Liquid, apply the drag force.

The above code tells us that we need to add two functions to the `Mover` class: (1) a function that determines if a `Mover` object is inside the `Liquid` object, and (2) a function that computes and applies a drag force on the `Mover` object.

The first is easy; we can simply use a conditional statement to determine if the location vector rests inside the rectangle defined by the liquid.

```
boolean isInside(Liquid l) {
  if (location.x>l.x && location.x<l.x+l.w && location.y>l.y && location.y<l.y+l.h)
  {
    return true;
  } else {
    return false;
  }
}
```

This conditional statement determines if the PVector location is inside the rectangle defined by the Liquid class.

The `drag()` function is a bit more complicated; however, we've written the code for it already. This is simply an implementation of our formula. The drag force is equal to *the coefficient of drag multiplied by the speed of the* `Mover` *squared in the opposite direction of velocity!*

```
void drag(Liquid l) {

  float speed = velocity.mag();
  float dragMagnitude = l.c * speed * speed;

  PVector drag = velocity.get();
  drag.mult(-1);
  drag.normalize();

  drag.mult(dragMagnitude);

  applyForce(drag);
}
```

The force's magnitude: Cd * v~2~

The force's direction: -1 * velocity

Finalize the force: magnitude and direction together.

Apply the force.

And with these two functions added to the `Mover` class, we're ready to put it all together in the main tab:

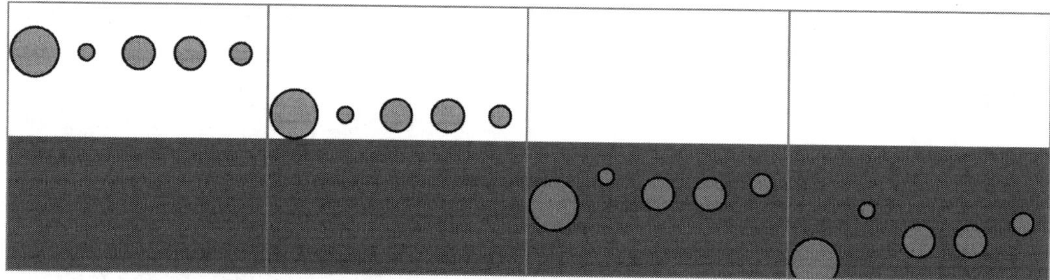

Example 2.5: Fluid Resistance

```
Mover[] movers = new Mover[100];

Liquid liquid;

void setup() {
  size(360, 640);
  for (int i = 0; i < movers.length; i++) {
    movers[i] = new Mover(random(0.1,5),0,0);
  }
  liquid = new Liquid(0, height/2, width, height/2, 0.1);
}

void draw() {
  background(255);

  liquid.display();

  for (int i = 0; i < movers.length; i++) {

    if (movers[i].isInside(liquid)) {
      movers[i].drag(liquid);
    }

    float m = 0.1*movers[i].mass;
    PVector gravity = new PVector(0, m);
    movers[i].applyForce(gravity);

    movers[i].update();
    movers[i].display();
    movers[i].checkEdges();
  }
}
```

Note that we are scaling gravity according to mass.

Running the example, you should notice that we are simulating balls falling into water. The objects only slow down when crossing through the gray area at the bottom of the window (representing the liquid). You'll also notice that the smaller objects slow down a great deal more than the larger objects. Remember Newton's second law? `A = F / M`. Acceleration equals force *divided* by mass. A massive object will accelerate less. A smaller object will accelerate more. In this case, the acceleration we're talking about is the "slowing down" due to drag. The smaller objects will slow down at a greater rate than the larger ones.

Exercise 2.5

Take a look at our formula for drag again: ***drag force = coefficient * speed * speed***. The faster an object moves, the greater the drag force against it. In fact, an object not moving in water experiences no drag at all. Expand the example to drop the balls from different heights. How does this affect the drag as they hit the water?

Exercise 2.6

The formula for drag also included surface area. Can you create a simulation of boxes falling into water with a drag force dependent on the length of the side hitting the water?

Exercise 2.7

Fluid resistance does not only work opposite to the velocity vector, but also perpendicular to it. This is known as "lift-induced drag" and will cause an airplane with an angled wing to rise in altitude. Try creating a simulation of lift.

2.9 Gravitational Attraction

Probably the most famous force of all is gravity. We humans on earth think of gravity as an apple hitting Isaac Newton on the head. Gravity means that stuff falls down. But this is only *our* experience of gravity. In truth, just as the earth pulls the apple towards it due to a gravitational force, the apple pulls the earth as well. The thing is, the earth is just so freaking big that it overwhelms all the other gravity interactions. Every object with mass exerts a gravitational force on every other object. And there is a formula for calculating the strengths of these forces, as depicted in Figure 2.6.

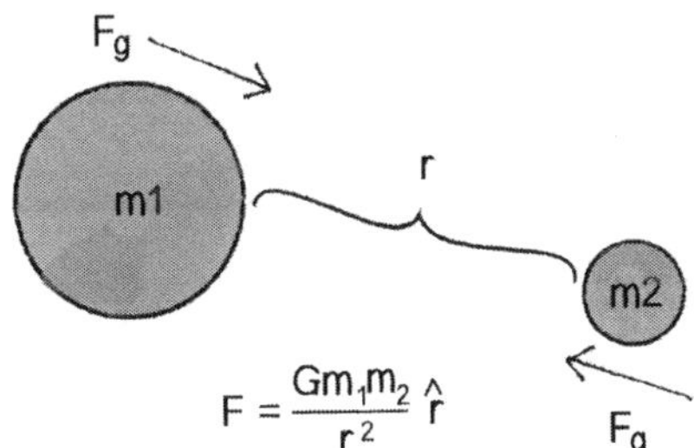

Figure 2.6

Let's examine this formula a bit more closely.

- F refers to the gravitational force, the vector we ultimately want to compute and pass into our `applyForce()` function.

- G is the *universal gravitational constant*, which in our world equals 6.67428 x 10^{-11} meters cubed per kilogram per second squared. This is a pretty important number if your name is Isaac Newton or Albert Einstein. It's not an important number if you are a Processing programmer. Again, it's a constant that we can use to make the forces in our world weaker or stronger. Just making it equal to one and ignoring it isn't such a terrible choice either.

- m_1 and m_2 are the masses of objects 1 and 2. As we saw with Newton's second law ($\vec{F} = M \times \vec{A}$), mass is also something we could choose to ignore. After all, shapes drawn on the screen don't actually have a physical mass. However, if we keep these values, we can create more interesting simulations in which "bigger" objects exert a stronger gravitational force than smaller ones.

- $\hat{r}$ refers to the unit vector pointing from object 1 to object 2. As we'll see in a moment, we can compute this direction vector by subtracting the location of one object from the other.

- r^2 refers to the distance between the two objects squared. Let's take a moment to think about this a bit more. With everything on the top of the formula—G, m_1, m_2—the bigger its value, the stronger the force. Big mass, big force. Big G, big force. Now, when we divide by something, we have the opposite. The strength of the force is inversely proportional to the distance squared. The *farther away* an object is, the *weaker* the force; the *closer*, the *stronger*.

Hopefully by now the formula makes some sense to us. We've looked at a diagram and dissected the individual components of the formula. Now it's time to figure out how we translate the math into Processing code. Let's make the following assumptions.

We have two objects, and:

1. Each object has a location: `PVector location1` and `PVector location2`.

2. Each object has a mass: `float mass1` and `float mass2`.

3. There is a variable `float G` for the universal gravitational constant.

Given these assumptions, we want to compute `PVector force`, the force of gravity. We'll do it in two parts. First, we'll compute the direction of the force $\hat{r}$ in the formula above. Second, we'll calculate the strength of the force according to the masses and distance.

Remember in Chapter 1 (see page 56), when we figured out how to have an object accelerate towards the mouse? (See Figure 2.7.)

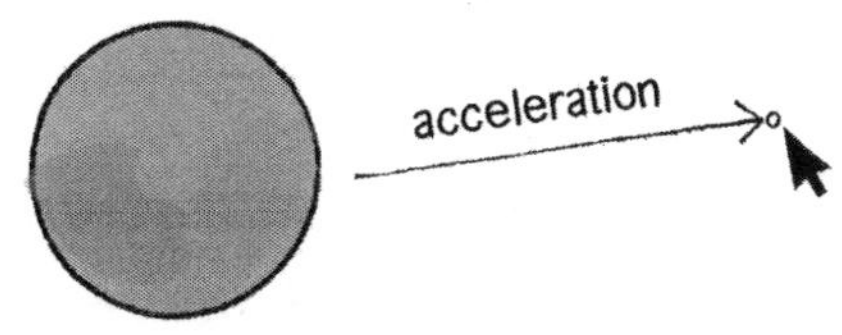

Figure 2.7

A vector is the difference between two points. To make a vector that points from the circle to the mouse, we simply subtract one point from another:

```
PVector dir = PVector.sub(mouse,location);
```

In our case, the direction of the attraction force that object 1 exerts on object 2 is equal to:

```
PVector dir = PVector.sub(location1,location2);
dir.normalize();
```

Don't forget that since we want a unit vector, a vector that tells us about direction only, we'll need to *normalize* the vector after subtracting the locations.

OK, we've got the direction of the force. Now we just need to compute the magnitude and scale the vector accordingly.

```
float m = (G * mass1 * mass2) / (distance * distance);
dir.mult(m);
```

The only problem is that we don't know the distance. `G`, `mass1`, and `mass2` were all givens, but we'll need to actually compute distance before the above code will work. Didn't we just make a vector that points all the way from one location to another? Wouldn't the length of that vector be the distance between two objects?

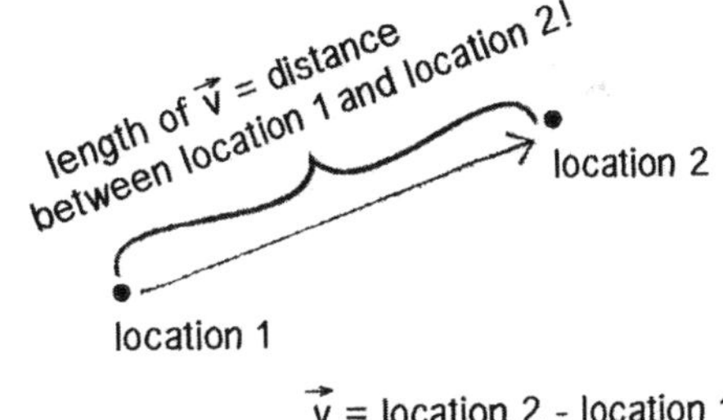

Figure 2.8

Well, if we add just one line of code and grab the magnitude of that vector before normalizing it, then we'll have the distance.

```
PVector force = PVector.sub(location1,location2);
```
The vector that points from one object to another

```
float distance = force.magnitude();
```
The length (magnitude) of that vector is the distance between the two objects.

```
float m = (G * mass1 * mass2) / (distance * distance);
```
Use the formula for gravity to compute the strength of the force.

```
force.normalize();
force.mult(m);
```

Normalize and scale the force vector to the appropriate magnitude.

Note that I also renamed the PVector "dir" as "force." After all, when we're finished with the calculations, the PVector we started with ends up being the actual force vector we wanted all along.

Now that we've worked out the math and the code for calculating an attractive force (emulating gravity), we need to turn our attention to applying this technique in the context of an actual Processing sketch. In Example 2.1, you may recall how we created a simple Mover object—a class with PVector's location, velocity, and acceleration as well as an applyForce(). Let's take this exact class and put it in a sketch with:

- A single Mover object.
- A single Attractor object (a new class that will have a fixed location).

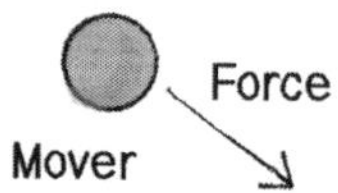

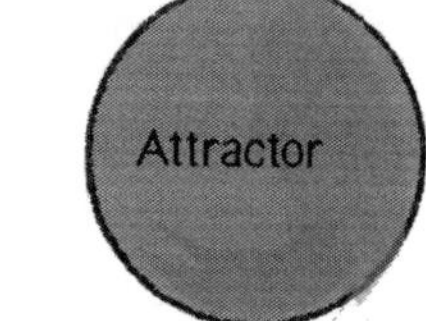

Figure 2.9

The Mover object will experience a gravitational pull towards the Attractor object, as illustrated in Figure 2.9.

We can start by making the new Attractor class very simple—giving it a location and a mass, along with a function to display itself (tying mass to size).

```
class Attractor {
  float mass;
  PVector location;

  Attractor() {
    location = new PVector(width/2,height/2);
    mass = 20;
  }

  void display() {
    stroke(0);
    fill(175,200);
    ellipse(location.x,location.y,mass*2,mass*2);
  }
}
```

Our Attractor is a simple object that doesn't move. We just need a mass and a location.

And in our main program, we can add an instance of the Attractor class.

```
Mover m;
Attractor a;

void setup() {
  size(640,360);
  m = new Mover();
  a = new Attractor();                    Initialize Attractor object.
}

void draw() {
  background(255);

  a.display();                            Display Attractor object.

  m.update();
  m.display();
}
```

This is a good structure: a main program with a `Mover` and an `Attractor` object, and a class to handle the variables and behaviors of movers and attractors. The last piece of the puzzle is how to get one object to attract the other. How do we get these two objects to talk to each other?

There are a number of ways we could do this. Here are just a few possibilities.

Task	Function
1. A function that receives both an Attractor and a Mover:	`attraction(a,m);`
2. A function in the Attractor class that receives a Mover:	`a.attract(m);`
3. A function in the Mover class that receives an Attractor:	`m.attractedTo(a);`
4. A function in the Attractor class that receives a Mover and returns a PVector, which is the attraction force. That attraction force is then passed into the Mover's applyForce() function:	`PVector f = a.attract(m);` `m.applyForce(f);`

and so on. . .

It's good to look at a range of options for making objects talk to each other, and you could probably make arguments for each of the above possibilities. I'd like to at least discard the first one, since an object-oriented approach is really a much better choice over an arbitrary function not tied to either the `Mover` or `Attractor` class. Whether you pick option 2 or option 3 is the difference between saying "The attractor attracts the mover" or "The mover is attracted to the attractor." Number 4 is really my favorite, at least in terms of where we are in this book. After all, we spent a lot of time working out the `applyForce()` function, and I think our examples will be clearer if we continue with the same methodology.

In other words, where we once had:

```
PVector f = new PVector(0.1,0);      Made-up force
m.applyForce(f);
```

We now have:

```
PVector f = a.attract(m);      Attraction force between two objects
m.applyForce(f);
```

And so our `draw()` function can now be written as:

```
void draw() {
  background(255);

  PVector f = a.attract(m);      Calculate attraction force and apply it.
  m.applyForce(f);

  m.update();

  a.display();
  m.display();

}
```

We're almost there. Since we decided to put the `attract()` function inside of the `Attractor` class, we'll need to actually write that function. The function needs to receive a `Mover` object and return a `PVector`, i.e.:

```
PVector attract(Mover m) {

}
```

And what goes inside that function? All of that nice math we worked out for gravitational attraction!

```
PVector attract(Mover m) {

  PVector force = PVector.sub(location,m.location);   What's the force's direction?
  float distance = force.mag();
  force.normalize();
```

```
    float strength = (G * mass * m.mass) / (distance * distance);
    force.mult(strength);                  What's the force's magnitude?

    return force;                          Return the force so that it can be applied!
  }
```

And we're done. Sort of. Almost. There's one small kink we need to work out. Let's look at the above code again. See that symbol for divide, the slash? Whenever we have one of these, we need to ask ourselves the question: What would happen if the distance happened to be a really, really small number or (even worse!) zero??! Well, we know we can't divide a number by 0, and if we were to divide a number by something like 0.0001, that is the equivalent of multiplying that number by 10,000! Yes, this is the real-world formula for the strength of gravity, but we don't live in the real world. We live in the *Processing* world. And in the Processing world, the mover could end up being very, very close to the attractor and the force could become so strong the mover would just fly way off the screen. And so with this formula, it's good for us to be practical and constrain the range of what `distance` can actually be. Maybe, no matter where the `Mover` actually is, we should never consider it less than 5 pixels or more than 25 pixels away from the attractor.

```
distance = constrain(distance,5,25);
```

For the same reason that we need to constrain the minimum distance, it's useful for us to do the same with the maximum. After all, if the mover were to be, say, 500 pixels from the attractor (not unreasonable), we'd be dividing the force by 250,000. That force might end up being so weak that it's almost as if we're not applying it at all.

Now, it's really up to you to decide what behaviors you want. But in the case of, "I want reasonable-looking attraction that is never absurdly weak or strong," then constraining the distance is a good technique.

Our `Mover` class hasn't changed at all, so let's just look at the main program and the `Attractor` class as a whole, adding a variable `G` for the universal gravitational constant. (On the website, you'll find that this example also has code that allows you to move the `Attractor` object with the mouse.)

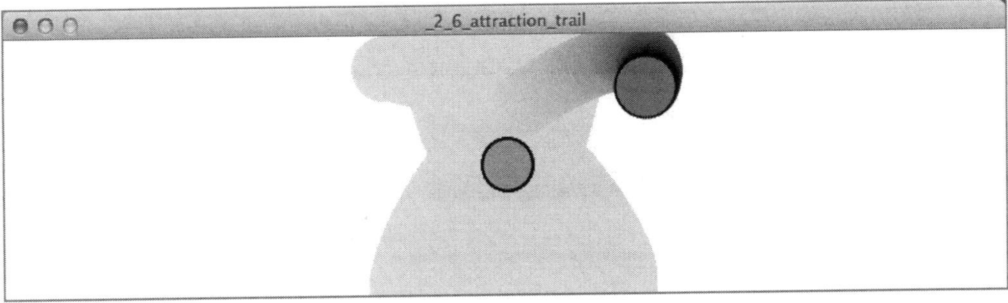

Example 2.6: Attraction

```
Mover m;                                          A Mover and an Attractor
Attractor a;

void setup() {
  size(640,360);
  m = new Mover();
  a = new Attractor();
}

void draw() {
  background(255);

  PVector force = a.attract(m);                   Apply the attraction force from the Attractor
                                                  on the Mover.
  m.applyForce(force);
  m.update();

  a.display();
  m.display();
}

class Attractor {
  float mass;
  PVector location;
  float G;

  Attractor() {
    location = new PVector(width/2,height/2);
    mass = 20;
    G = 0.4;
  }

  PVector attract(Mover m) {
    PVector force = PVector.sub(location,m.location);
    float distance = force.mag();
    distance = constrain(distance,5.0,25.0);      Remember, we need to constrain the
                                                  distance so that our circle doesn't spin out of
                                                  control.

    force.normalize();
    float strength = (G * mass * m.mass) / (distance * distance);
    force.mult(strength);
    return force;
  }

  void display() {
    stroke(0);
    fill(175,200);
    ellipse(location.x,location.y,mass*2,mass*2);
  }
}
```

And we could, of course, expand this example using an array to include many `Mover` objects, just as we did with friction and drag:

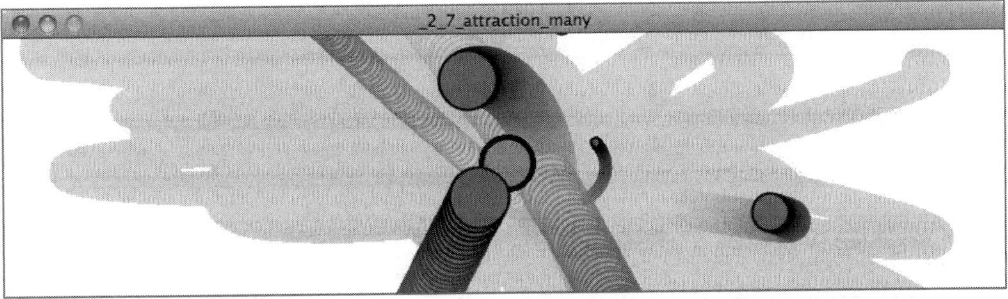

Example 2.7: Attraction with many Movers

```
Mover[] movers = new Mover[10];
```

Now we have 10 Movers!

```
Attractor a;

void setup() {
  size(400,400);
  for (int i = 0; i < movers.length; i++) {
    movers[i] = new Mover(random(0.1,2),random(width),random(height));
  }
  a = new Attractor();
}
```

Each Mover is initialized randomly.

```
void draw() {
  background(255);

  a.display();

  for (int i = 0; i < movers.length; i++) {
    PVector force = a.attract(movers[i]);
    movers[i].applyForce(force);

    movers[i].update();
    movers[i].display();
  }

}
```

We calculate an attraction force for each Mover object.

Exercise 2.8

In the example above, we have a system (i.e. array) of `Mover` objects and one `Attractor` object. Build an example that has systems of both movers and attractors. What if you make the attractors invisible? Can you create a pattern/design from the trails of objects moving around attractors? See the Metropop Denim project by Clayton Cubitt and Tom Carden (http://processing.org/exhibition/works/metropop/) for an example.

Exercise 2.9

It's worth noting that gravitational attraction is a model we can follow to develop our own forces. This chapter isn't suggesting that you should exclusively create sketches that use gravitational attraction. Rather, you should be thinking creatively about how to design your own rules to drive the behavior of objects. For example, what happens if you design a force that is weaker the closer it gets and stronger the farther it gets? Or what if you design your attractor to attract faraway objects, but repel close ones?

2.10 Everything Attracts (or Repels) Everything

Hopefully, you found it helpful that we started with a simple scenario—*one object attracts another object*—and moved on to *one object attracts many objects*. However, it's likely that you are going to find yourself in a slightly more complex situation: *many objects attract each other*. In other words, every object in a given system attracts every other object in that system (except for itself).

We've really done almost all of the work for this already. Let's consider a Processing sketch with an array of `Mover` objects:

```
Mover[] movers = new Mover[10];

void setup() {
  size(400,400);
  for (int i = 0; i < movers.length; i++) {
    movers[i] = new Mover(random(0.1,2),random(width),random(height));
  }
}

void draw() {
  background(255);
  for (int i = 0; i < movers.length; i++) {
    movers[i].update();
    movers[i].display();
  }
}
```

The `draw()` function is where we need to work some magic. Currently, we're saying: "for every mover `i`, update and display yourself." Now what we need to say is: "for every mover `i`, be attracted to every other mover `j`, and update and display yourself."

To do this, we need to nest a second loop.

```
for (int i = 0; i < movers.length; i++) {
  for (int j = 0; j < movers.length; j++) {        For every Mover, check every Mover!
    PVector force = movers[j].attract(movers[i]);
    movers[i].applyForce(force);
  }
  movers[i].update();
  movers[i].display();
}
```

In the previous example, we had an `Attractor` object with a function named `attract()`. Now, since we have movers attracting movers, all we need to do is copy the `attract()` function into the `Mover` class.

```
class Mover {

  // All the other stuff we had before plus. . .
```

```
  PVector attract(Mover m) {
```

The Mover now knows how to attract another Mover.

```
    PVector force = PVector.sub(location,m.location);
    float distance = force.mag();
    distance = constrain(distance,5.0,25.0);
    force.normalize();

    float strength = (G * mass * m.mass) / (distance * distance);
    force.mult(strength);
    return force;
  }
}
```

Of course, there's one small problem. When we are looking at every mover `i` and every mover `j`, are we OK with the times that `i` equals `j`? For example, should mover #3 attract mover #3? The answer, of course, is no. If there are five objects, we only want mover #3 to attract 0, 1, 2, and 4, skipping itself. And so, we finish this example by adding a simple conditional statement to skip applying the force when i equals j.

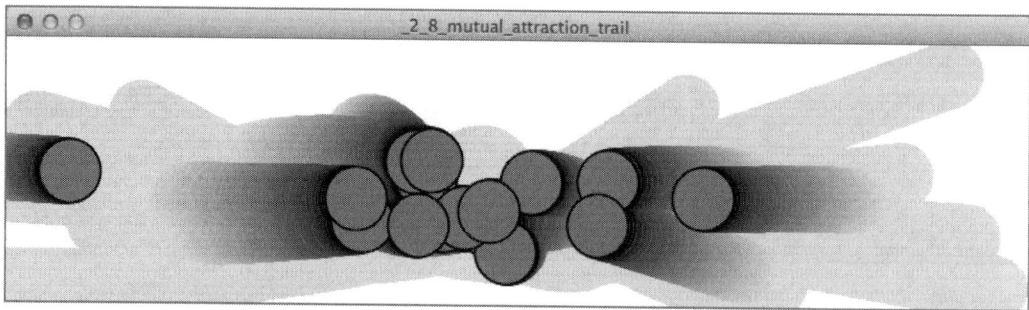

Example 2.8: Mutual attraction

```
Mover[] movers = new Mover[20];

float g = 0.4;

void setup() {
  size(400,400);
  for (int i = 0; i < movers.length; i++) {
    movers[i] = new Mover(random(0.1,2),random(width),random(height));
  }
}

void draw() {
  background(255);

  for (int i = 0; i < movers.length; i++) {
    for (int j = 0; j < movers.length; j++) {
```

```
      if (i != j) {                              Don't attract yourself!
        PVector force = movers[j].attract(movers[i]);
        movers[i].applyForce(force);
      }
    }
    movers[i].update();
    movers[i].display();
  }
}
```

Exercise 2.10

Change the attraction force in Example 2.8 to a repulsion force. Can you create an example in which all of the `Mover` objects are attracted to the mouse, but repel each other? Think about how you need to balance the relative strength of the forces and how to most effectively use distance in your force calculations.

The Ecosystem Project

Step 2 Exercise:

Incorporate the concept of forces into your ecosystem. Try introducing other elements into the environment (food, a predator) for the creature to interact with. Does the creature experience attraction or repulsion to things in its world? Can you think more abstractly and design forces based on the creature's desires or goals?

Chapter 3. Oscillation

"Trigonometry is a sine of the times."

— Anonymous

In Chapters 1 and 2, we carefully worked out an object-oriented structure to make something move on the screen, using the concept of a vector to represent location, velocity, and acceleration driven by forces in the environment. We could move straight from here into topics such as particle systems, steering forces, group behaviors, etc. If we did that, however, we'd skip an important area of mathematics that we're going to need: ***trigonometry***, or the mathematics of triangles, specifically right triangles.

Trigonometry is going to give us a lot of tools. We'll get to think about angles and angular velocity and acceleration. Trig will teach us about the sine and cosine functions, which when used properly can yield an nice ease-in, ease-out wave pattern. It's going to allow us to calculate more complex forces in an environment that involves angles, such as a pendulum swinging or a box sliding down an incline.

So this chapter is a bit of a mishmash. We'll start with the basics of angles in Processing and cover many trigonometric topics, tying it all into forces at the end. And by taking this break now, we'll also pave the way for more advanced examples that require trig later in this book.

3.1 Angles

OK. Before we can do any of this stuff, we need to make sure we understand what it means to be an angle in Processing. If you have experience with Processing, you've undoubtedly encountered this issue while using the `rotate()` function to rotate and spin objects.

The first order of business is to cover ***radians*** and ***degrees***. You're probably familiar with the concept of an angle in ***degrees***. A full rotation goes from 0 to 360 degrees. 90 degrees (a right angle) is 1/4th of 360, shown below as two perpendicular lines.

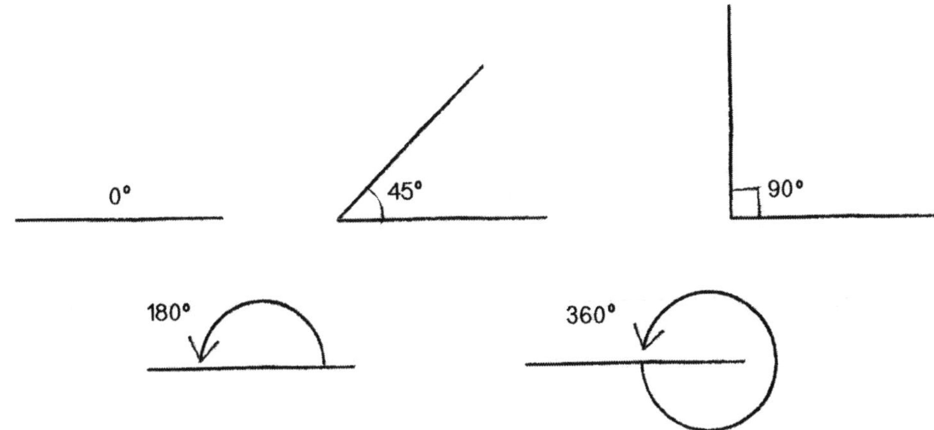

Figure 3.1

It's fairly intuitive for us to think of angles in terms of degrees. For example, the square in Figure 3.2 is rotated 45 degrees around its center.

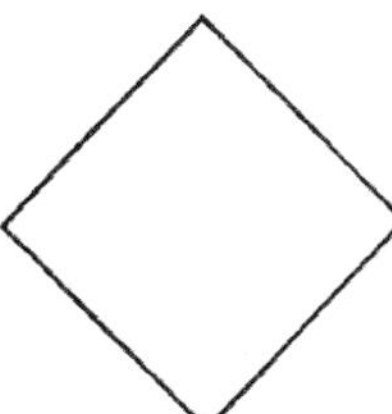

Figure 3.3

Processing, however, requires angles to be specified in ***radians***. A radian is a unit of measurement for angles defined by the ratio of the length of the arc of a circle to the radius of that circle. One radian is the angle at which that ratio equals one (see Figure 3.1). 180 degrees = PI radians, 360 degrees = 2*PI radians, 90 degrees = PI/2 radians, etc.

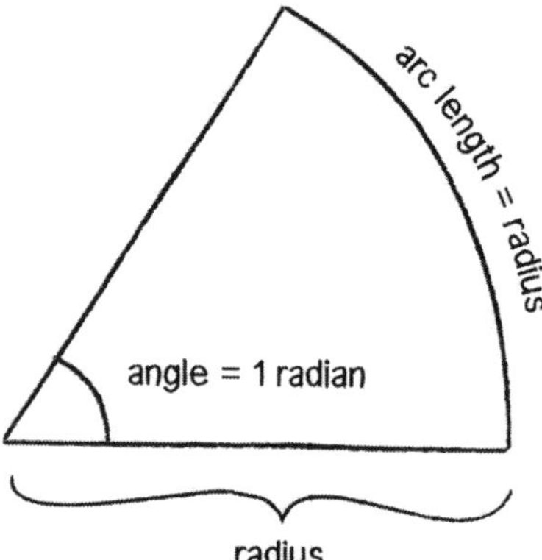

Figure 3.3

The formula to convert from degrees to radians is:

radians = 2 * PI * (degrees / 360)

Thankfully, if we prefer to think in degrees but code with radians, Processing makes this easy. The `radians()` function will automatically convert values from degrees to radians, and the constants `PI` and `TWO_PI` provide convenient access to these commonly used numbers (equivalent to 180 and 360 degrees, respectively). The following code, for example, will rotate shapes by 60 degrees.

```
float angle = radians(60);
rotate(angle);
```

If you are not familiar with how rotation is implemented in Processing, I would suggest this tutorial: Processing - Transform 2D (http://www.processing.org/learning/transform2d/).

What is PI?

The mathematical constant pi (or π) is a real number defined as the ratio of a circle's circumference (the distance around the perimeter) to its diameter (a straight line that passes through the circle's center). It is equal to approximately 3.14159 and can be accessed in Processing with the built-in variable `PI`.

Exercise 3.1

Rotate a baton-like object (see below) around its center using `translate()` and `rotate()`.

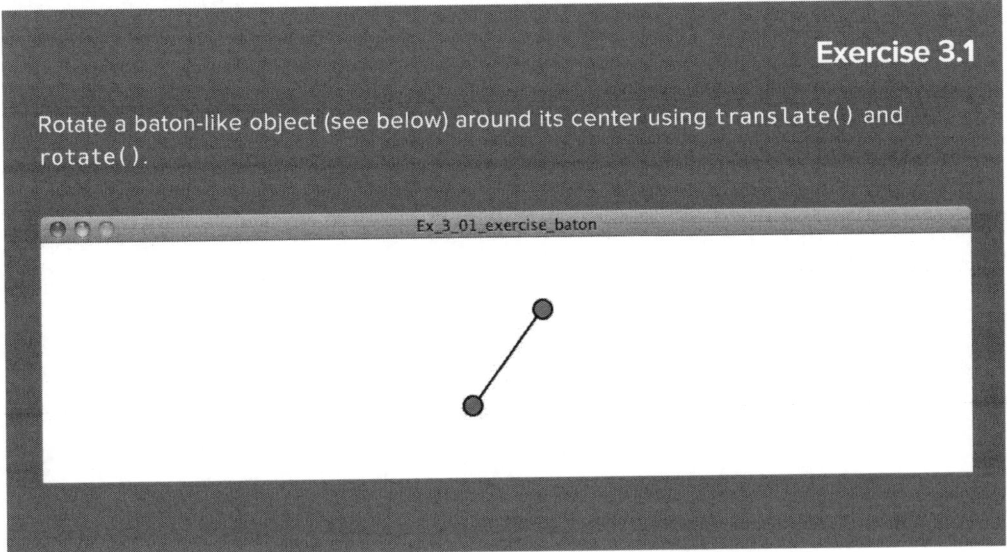

3.2 Angular Motion

Remember all this stuff?

```
location = location + velocity
velocity = velocity + acceleration
```

The stuff we dedicated almost all of Chapters 1 and 2 to? Well, we can apply exactly the same logic to a rotating object.

```
angle = angle + angular velocity
angular velocity = angular velocity + angular acceleration
```

In fact, the above is actually simpler than what we started with because an angle is a *scalar* quantity—a single number, not a vector!

Using the answer from Exercise 3.1 above, let's say we wanted to rotate a baton in Processing by some angle. We would have code like:

```
translate(width/2,height/2);
rotate(angle);
line(-50,0,50,0);
ellipse(50,0,8,8);
ellipse(-50,0,8,8);
```

Adding in our principles of motion brings us to the following example.

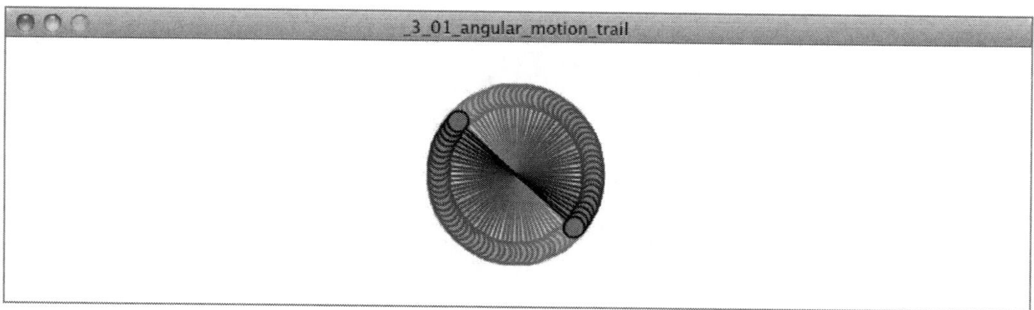

Example 3.1: Angular motion using rotate()

```
float angle = 0;                         // Location
float aVelocity = 0;                     // Velocity
float aAcceleration = 0.001;             // Acceleration

void setup() {
  size(640,360);
}

void draw() {
  background(255);

  fill(175);
  stroke(0);
  rectMode(CENTER);
  translate(width/2,height/2);
  rotate(angle);
  line(-50,0,50,0);
  ellipse(50,0,8,8);
  ellipse(-50,0,8,8);

  aVelocity += aAcceleration;            // Angular equivalent of velocity.add(acceleration);
  angle += aVelocity;                    // Angular equivalent of location.add(velocity);
}
```

The baton starts onscreen with no rotation and then spins faster and faster as the angle of rotation accelerates.

This idea can be incorporated into our `Mover` object. For example, we can add the variables related to angular motion to our `Mover`.

```
class Mover {

  PVector location;
  PVector velocity;
  PVector acceleration;
  float mass;

  float angle = 0;
  float aVelocity = 0;
  float aAcceleration = 0;
```

And then in `update()`, we update both location and angle according to the same algorithm!

```
void update() {

    velocity.add(acceleration);       // Regular old-fashioned motion
    location.add(velocity);

    aVelocity += aAcceleration;       // Newfangled angular motion
    angle += aVelocity;

    acceleration.mult(0);
  }
```

Of course, for any of this to matter, we also would need to rotate the object when displaying it.

```
void display() {
    stroke(0);
    fill(175,200);
    rectMode(CENTER);
    pushMatrix();                       // pushMatrix() and popMatrix() are necessary so that the rotation of this shape doesn't affect the rest of our world.

    translate(location.x,location.y);  // Set the origin at the shape's location.

    rotate(angle);                      // Rotate by the angle.

    rect(0,0,mass*16,mass*16);
    popMatrix();
  }
```

Now, if we were to actually go ahead and run the above code, we wouldn't see anything new. This is because the angular acceleration (`float aAcceleration = 0;`) is initialized to zero. For the object to rotate, we need to give it an acceleration! Certainly, we could hard-code in a different number.

```
float aAcceleration = 0.01;
```

However, we can produce a more interesting result by dynamically assigning an angular acceleration according to forces in the environment. Now, we could head far down this road, trying to model the physics of angular acceleration using the concepts of torque (http://en.wikipedia.org/wiki/Torque) and moment of inertia (http://en.wikipedia.org/wiki/Moment_of_inertia). Nevertheless, this level of simulation is beyond the scope of this book. (We will see more about modeling angular acceleration with a pendulum later in this chapter, as well as look at how Box2D realistically models rotational motion in Chapter 5.)

For now, a quick and dirty solution will do. We can produce reasonable results by simply calculating angular acceleration as a function of the object's acceleration vector. Here's one such example:

```
aAcceleration = acceleration.x;
```

Yes, this is completely arbitrary. But it does do something. If the object is accelerating to the right, its angular rotation accelerates in a clockwise direction; acceleration to the left results in a counterclockwise rotation. Of course, it's important to think about scale in this case. The *x* component of the acceleration vector might be a quantity that's too large, causing the object to spin in a way that looks ridiculous or unrealistic. So dividing the *x* component by some value, or perhaps constraining the angular velocity to a reasonable range, could really help. Here's the entire `update()` function with these tweaks added.

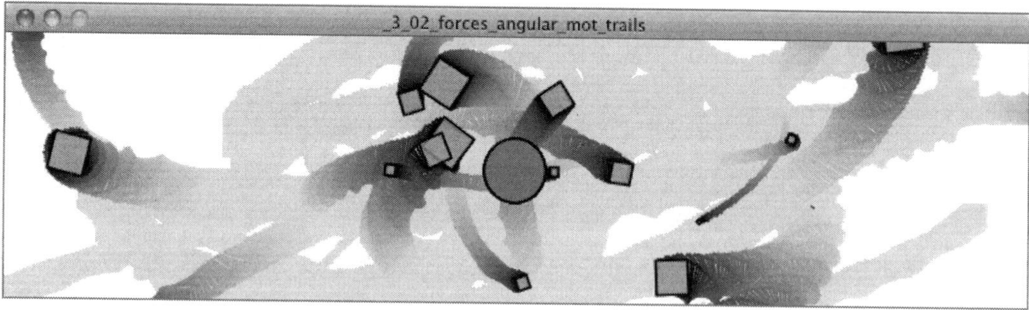

Example 3.2: Forces with (arbitrary) angular motion

```
void update() {

  velocity.add(acceleration);
  location.add(velocity);

  aAcceleration = acceleration.x / 10.0;
  aVelocity += aAcceleration;
```

Calculate angular acceleration according to acceleration's horizontal direction and magnitude.

```
    aVelocity = constrain(aVelocity,-0.1,0.1);
    angle += aVelocity;

    acceleration.mult(0);
  }
```

Use constrain() to ensure that angular velocity doesn't spin out of control.

Exercise 3.2

Step 1: Create a simulation where objects are shot out of a cannon. Each object should experience a sudden force when shot (just once) as well as gravity (always present).

Step 2: Add rotation to the object to model its spin as it is shot from the cannon. How realistic can you make it look?

3.3 Trigonometry

I think it may be time. We've looked at angles, we've spun an object. It's time for: *sohcahtoa*. Yes, *sohcahtoa*. This seemingly nonsensical word is actually the foundation for a lot of computer graphics work. A basic understanding of trigonometry is essential if you want to calculate an angle, figure out the distance between points, work with circles, arcs, or lines. And *sohcahtoa* is a mnemonic device (albeit a somewhat absurd one) for what the trigonometric functions sine, cosine, and tangent mean.

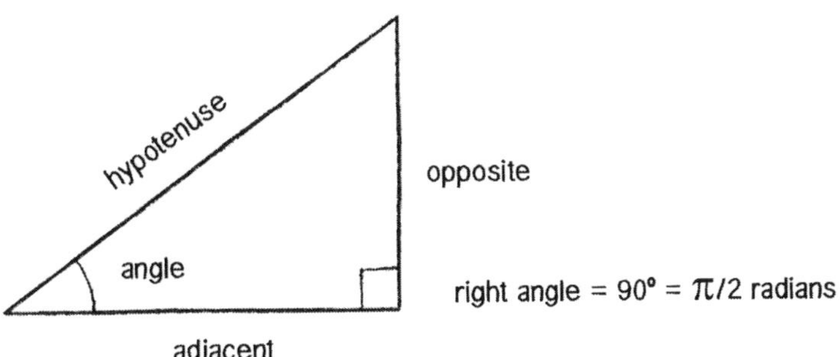

Figure 3.4

- ***soh***: sine = opposite / hypotenuse
- ***cah***: cosine = adjacent / hypotenuse
- ***toa***: tangent = opposite / adjacent

Take a look at Figure 3.4 again. There's no need to memorize it, but make sure you feel comfortable with it. Draw it again yourself. Now let's draw it a slightly different way (Figure 3.5).

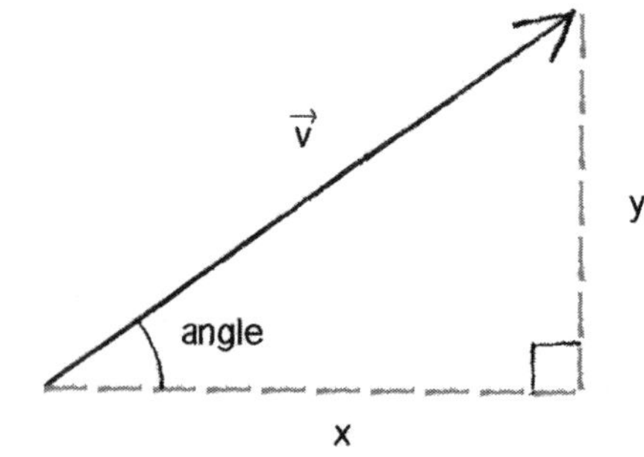

Figure 3.5

See how we create a right triangle out of a vector? The vector arrow itself is the hypotenuse and the components of the vector (x and y) are the sides of the triangle. The angle is an additional means for specifying the vector's direction (or "heading").

Because the trigonometric functions allow us to establish a relationship between the components of a vector and its direction + magnitude, they will prove very useful throughout this book. We'll begin by looking at an example that requires the tangent function.

3.4 Pointing in the Direction of Movement

Let's go all the way back to Example 1.10, which features a `Mover` object accelerating towards the mouse.

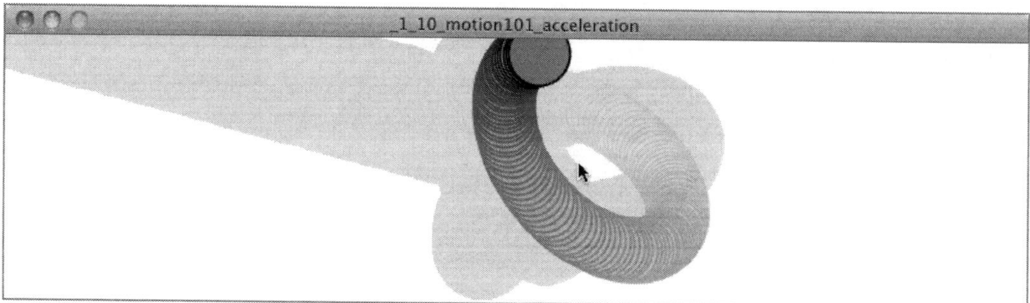

You might notice that almost all of the shapes we've been drawing so far are circles. This is convenient for a number of reasons, one of which is that we don't have to consider the question of rotation. Rotate a circle and, well, it looks exactly the same. However, there comes a time in all motion programmers' lives when they want to draw something on the screen that points in the direction of movement. Perhaps you are drawing an ant, or a car, or a spaceship. And when we say "point in the direction of movement," what we are really saying is "rotate according to the velocity vector." Velocity is a vector, with an x and a y component, but to rotate in Processing we need an angle, in radians. Let's draw our trigonometry diagram one more time, with an object's velocity vector (Figure 3.6).

OK. We know that the definition of tangent is:

$$tangent(angle) = \frac{velocity_y}{velocity_x}$$

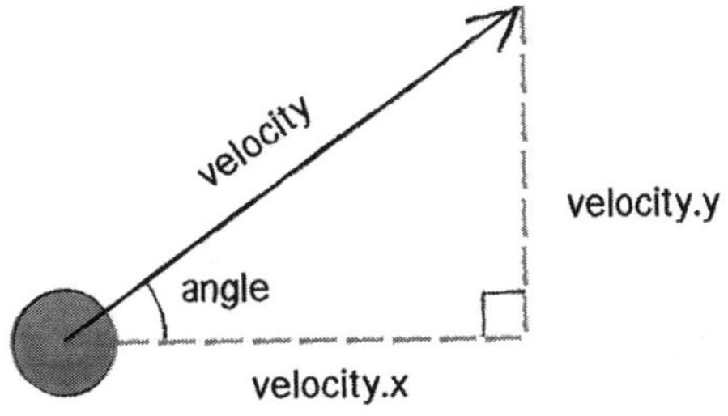

Figure 3.6

The problem with the above is that we know velocity, but we don't know the angle. We have to solve for the angle. This is where a special function known as *inverse tangent* comes in, sometimes referred to as *arctangent* or *tan*$^{-1}$. (There is also an *inverse sine* and an *inverse cosine*.)

If the tangent of some value a equals some value b, then the inverse tangent of b equals a. For example:

if	*tangent(a) = b*
then	*a = arctangent(b)*

See how that is the inverse? The above now allows us to solve for the angle:

if	$tangent(angle) = velocity_y / velocity_x$
then	$angle = arctangent(velocity_y / velocity_x)$

Now that we have the formula, let's see where it should go in our mover's `display()` function. Notice that in Processing, the function for arctangent is called `atan()`.

```
void display() {
  float angle = atan(velocity.y/velocity.x);        Solve for angle by using atan().

  stroke(0);
  fill(175);
  pushMatrix();
  rectMode(CENTER);
  translate(location.x,location.y);
  rotate(angle);                                    Rotate according to that angle.
  rect(0,0,30,10);
  popMatrix();
}
```

Now the above code is pretty darn close, and almost works. We still have a big problem, though. Let's consider the two velocity vectors depicted below.

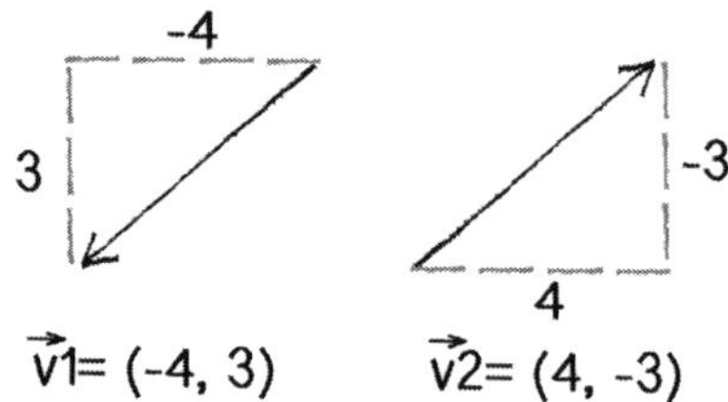

Figure 3.7

Though superficially similar, the two vectors point in quite different directions—opposite directions, in fact! However, if we were to apply our formula to solve for the angle to each vector...

```
V1 ⇒ angle = atan(-4/3) = atan(-1.25) = -0.9272952 radians = -53 degrees
V2 ⇒ angle = atan(4/-3) = atan(-1.25) = -0.9272952 radians = -53 degrees
```

...we get the same angle for each vector. This can't be right for both; the vectors point in opposite directions! The thing is, this is a pretty common problem in computer graphics. Rather than simply using `atan()` along with a bunch of conditional statements to account for positive/negative scenarios, Processing (along with pretty much all programming environments) has a nice function called `atan2()` that does it for you.

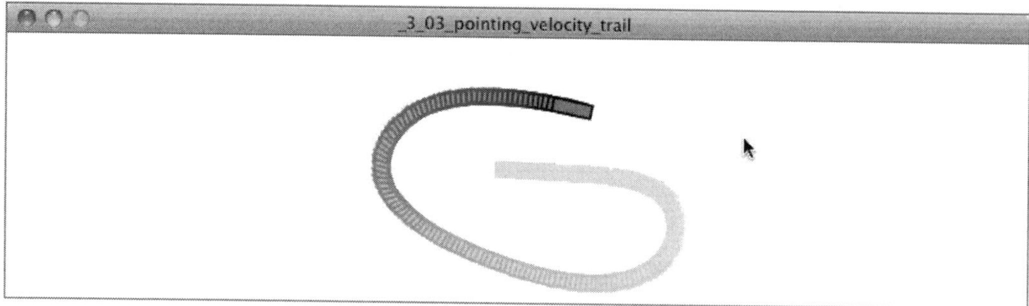

Example 3.3: Pointing in the direction of motion

```
void display() {
  float angle = atan2(velocity.y,velocity.x);
```

Using atan2() to account for all possible directions

```
  stroke(0);
  fill(175);
  pushMatrix();
  rectMode(CENTER);
  translate(location.x,location.y);
```

```
    rotate(angle);                              Rotate according to that angle.

    rect(0,0,30,10);
    popMatrix();
  }
```

To simplify this even further, the `PVector` class itself provides a function called `heading()`, which takes care of calling `atan2()` for you so you can get the 2D direction angle, in radians, for any Processing `PVector`.

```
  float angle = velocity.heading();             The easiest way to do this!
```

Exercise 3.3

Create a simulation of a vehicle that you can drive around the screen using the arrow keys: left arrow accelerates the car to the left, right to the right. The car should point in the direction in which it is currently moving.

3.5 Polar vs. Cartesian Coordinates

Any time we display a shape in Processing, we have to specify a pixel location, a set of x and y coordinates. These coordinates are known as ***Cartesian coordinates***, named for René Descartes, the French mathematician who developed the ideas behind Cartesian space.

Another useful coordinate system known as ***polar coordinates*** describes a point in space as an angle of rotation around the origin and a radius from the origin. Thinking about this in terms of a vector:

Cartesian coordinate—the *x,y* components of a vector
Polar coordinate—the magnitude (length) and direction (angle) of a vector

Processing's drawing functions, however, don't understand polar coordinates. Whenever we want to display something in Processing, we have to specify locations as *(x,y)* Cartesian coordinates. However, sometimes it is a great deal more convenient for us to think in polar coordinates when designing. Happily for us, with trigonometry we can convert back and forth between polar and Cartesian, which allows us to design with whatever coordinate system we have in mind but always draw with Cartesian coordinates.

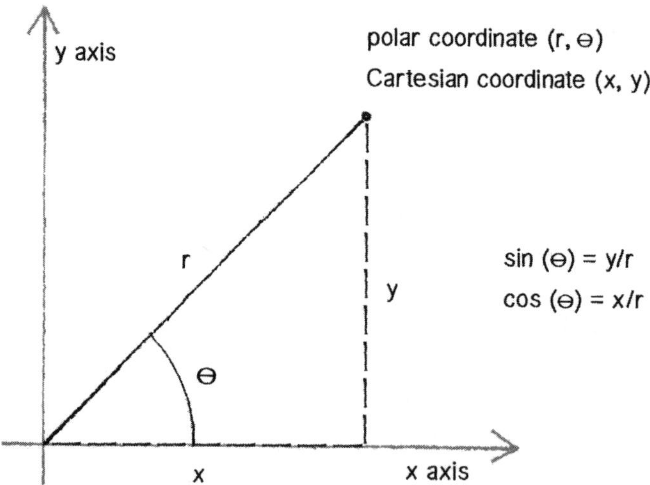

Figure 3.8: The Greek letter θ (theta) is often used to denote an angle. Since a polar coordinate is conventionally referred to as (r, θ), we'll use theta as a variable name when referring to an angle.

```
sine(theta)   = y/r   →   y = r * sine(theta)
cosine(theta) = x/r   →   x = r * cosine(theta)
```

For example, if `r` is 75 and `theta` is 45 degrees (or PI/4 radians), we can calculate `x` and `y` as below. The functions for sine and cosine in Processing are `sin()` and `cos()`, respectively. They each take one argument, an angle measured in radians.

```
float r = 75;
float theta = PI / 4;
float x = r * cos(theta);
float y = r * sin(theta);
```

Converting from polar (r,theta) to Cartesian (x,y)

This type of conversion can be useful in certain applications. For example, to move a shape along a circular path using Cartesian coordinates is not so easy. With polar coordinates, on the other hand, it's simple: increment the angle!

Here's how it is done with global variables `r` and `theta`.

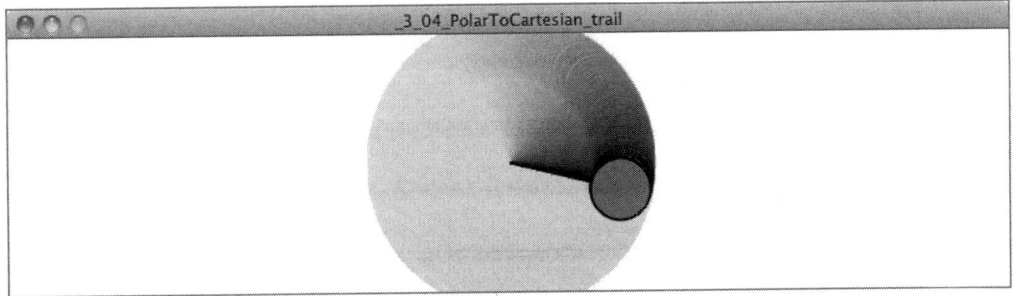

Example 3.4: Polar to Cartesian

```
float r = 75;
float theta = 0;

void setup() {
  size(640,360);
  background(255);
}

void draw() {

  float x = r * cos(theta);
  float y = r * sin(theta);
```

Polar coordinates (r,theta) are converted to Cartesian (x,y) for use in the ellipse() function.

```
  noStroke();
  fill(0);
  ellipse(x+width/2, y+height/2, 16, 16);

  theta += 0.01;
}
```

Exercise 3.4

Using Example 3.4 as a basis, draw a spiral path. Start in the center and move outwards. Note that this can be done by only changing one line of code and adding one line of code!

Ex_3_04_spiral

Exercise 3.5

Simulate the spaceship in the game Asteroids. In case you aren't familiar with Asteroids, here is a brief description: A spaceship (represented as a triangle) floats in two dimensional space. The left arrow key turns the spaceship counterclockwise, the right arrow key, clockwise. The *z* key applies a "thrust" force in the direction the spaceship is pointing.

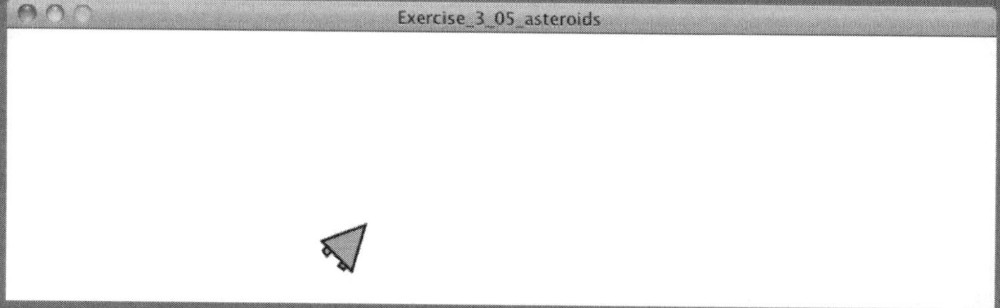

Exercise_3_05_asteroids

3.6 Oscillation Amplitude and Period

Are you amazed yet? We've seen some pretty great uses of tangent (for finding the angle of a vector) and sine and cosine (for converting from polar to Cartesian coordinates). We could stop right here and be satisfied. But we're not going to. This is only the beginning. What sine and cosine can do for you goes beyond mathematical formulas and right triangles.

Let's take a look at a graph of the sine function, where *y = sine(x)*.

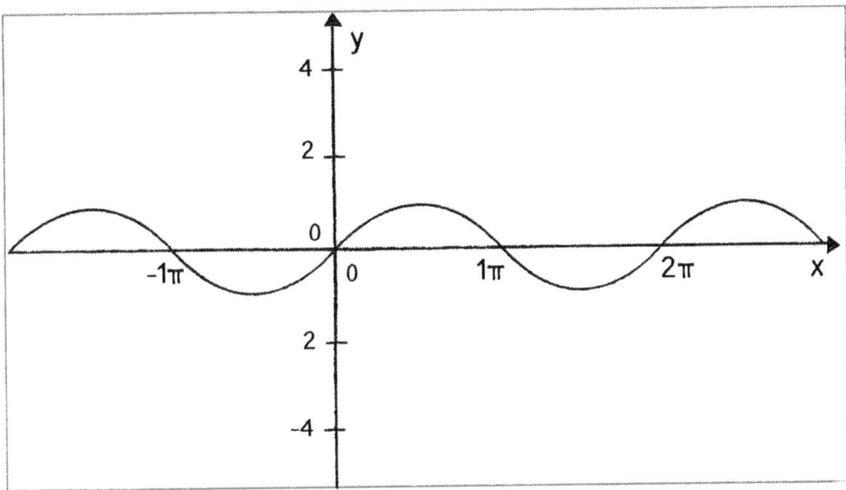

Figure 3.9: y = sine(x)

You'll notice that the output of the sine function is a smooth curve alternating between –1 and 1. This type of a behavior is known as ***oscillation***, a periodic movement between two points. Plucking a guitar string, swinging a pendulum, bouncing on a pogo stick—these are all examples of oscillating motion.

And so we happily discover that we can simulate oscillation in a Processing sketch by assigning the output of the sine function to an object's location. Note that this will follow the same methodology we applied to Perlin noise in the Introduction (see page 17).

Let's begin with a really basic scenario. We want a circle to oscillate from the left side to the right side of a Processing window.

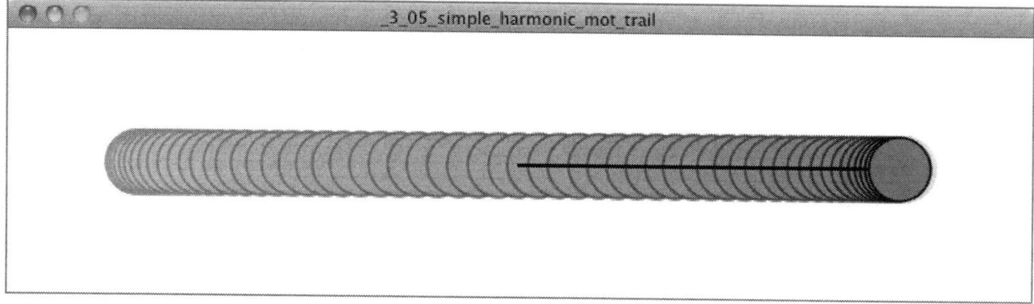

This is what is known as ***simple harmonic motion*** (or, to be fancier, "the periodic sinusoidal oscillation of an object"). It's going to be a simple program to write, but before we get into the code, let's familiarize ourselves with some of the terminology of oscillation (and waves).

Simple harmonic motion can be expressed as any location (in our case, the x location) as a function of time, with the following two elements:

- ***Amplitude***: The distance from the center of motion to either extreme
- ***Period***: The amount of time it takes for one complete cycle of motion

Looking at the graph of sine (Figure 3.9), we can see that the amplitude is 1 and the period is `TWO_PI`; the output of sine never rises above 1 or below -1; and every `TWO_PI` radians (or 360 degrees) the wave pattern repeats.

Now, in the Processing world we live in, what is amplitude and what is period? Amplitude can be measured rather easily in pixels. In the case of a window 200 pixels wide, we would oscillate from the center 100 pixels to the right and 100 pixels to the left. Therefore:

```
float amplitude = 100;
```

Our amplitude is measured in pixels.

Period is the amount of time it takes for one cycle, but what is time in our Processing world? I mean, certainly we could say we want the circle to oscillate every three seconds. And we could track the milliseconds—using `millis()` —in Processing and come up with an elaborate algorithm for oscillating an object according to real-world time. But for us, real-world time doesn't really matter. The real measure of time in Processing is in frames. The oscillating motion should repeat every 30 frames, or 50 frames, or 1000 frames, etc.

```
float period = 120;
```

Our period is measured in frames (our unit of time for animation).

Once we have the amplitude and period, it's time to write a formula to calculate x as a function of time, which we now know is the current frame count.

```
float x = amplitude * cos(TWO_PI * frameCount / period);
```

Let's dissect the formula a bit more and try to understand each component. The first is probably the easiest. Whatever comes out of the cosine function we multiply by amplitude. We know that cosine will oscillate between -1 and 1. If we take that value and multiply it by amplitude then we'll get the desired result: a value oscillating between -amplitude and amplitude. (Note: this is also a place where we could use Processing's `map()` function to map the output of cosine to a custom range.)

Now, let's look at what is inside the cosine function:

```
TWO_PI * frameCount / period
```

What's going on here? Let's start with what we know. We know that cosine will repeat every 2*PI radians—i.e. it will start at 0 and repeat at 2*PI, 4*PI, 6*PI, etc. If the period is 120, then we want the oscillating motion to repeat when the `frameCount` is at 120 frames, 240 frames, 360 frames, etc. `frameCount` is really the only variable; it starts at 0 and counts upward. Let's take a look at what the formula yields with those values.

frameCount	frameCount / period	TWO_PI * frameCount / period
0	0	0
60	0.5	PI
120	1	TWO_PI
240	2	2 * TWO_PI (or 4* PI)
etc.		

`frameCount` divided by `period` tells us how many cycles we've completed—are we halfway through the first cycle? Have we completed two cycles? By multiplying that number by `TWO_PI`, we get the result we want, since `TWO_PI` is the number of radians required for one cosine (or sine) to complete one cycle.

Wrapping this all up, here's the Processing example that oscillates the x location of a circle with an amplitude of 100 pixels and a period of 120 frames.

Example 3.5: Simple Harmonic Motion

```
void setup() {
  size(640,360);
}

void draw() {
  background(255);

  float period = 120;
  float amplitude = 100;
  float x = amplitude * cos(TWO_PI * frameCount / period);
  stroke(0);
  fill(175);
  translate(width/2,height/2);
  line(0,0,x,0);
  ellipse(x,0,20,20);
}
```

Calculating horizontal location according to the formula for simple harmonic motion

It's also worth mentioning the term ***frequency***: the number of cycles per time unit. Frequency is equal to 1 divided by `period`. If the period is 120 frames, then only 1/120th of a cycle is completed in one frame, and so frequency = 1/120. In the above example, we simply chose to define the rate of oscillation in terms of period and therefore did not need a variable for frequency.

Exercise 3.6

Using the sine function, create a simulation of a weight (sometimes referred to as a "bob") that hangs from a spring from the top of the window. Use the `map()` function to calculate the vertical location of the bob. Later in this chapter, we'll see how to recreate this same simulation by modeling the forces of a spring according to Hooke's law.

3.7 Oscillation with Angular Velocity

An understanding of the concepts of oscillation, amplitude, and frequency/period is often required in the course of simulating real-world behaviors. However, there is a slightly easier way to rewrite the above example with the same result. Let's take one more look at our oscillation formula:

```
float x = amplitude * cos(TWO_PI * frameCount / period);
```

And let's rewrite it a slightly different way:

```
float x = amplitude * cos ( some value that increments slowly );
```

If we care about precisely defining the period of oscillation in terms of frames of animation, we might need the formula the way we first wrote it, but we can just as easily rewrite our example using the concept of angular velocity (and acceleration) from section 3.2 (see page 104). Assuming:

```
float angle = 0;
float aVelocity = 0.05;
```

in `draw()`, we can simply say:

```
angle += aVelocity;
float x = amplitude * cos(angle);
```

`angle` is our "some value that increments slowly."

Example 3.6: Simple Harmonic Motion II

```
float angle = 0;
float aVelocity = 0.05;

void setup() {
  size(640,360);
}

void draw() {
  background(255);

  float amplitude = 100;
  float x = amplitude * cos(angle);
  angle += aVelocity;        // Using the concept of angular velocity to increment an angle variable

  ellipseMode(CENTER);
  stroke(0);
  fill(175);
  translate(width/2,height/2);
  line(0,0,x,0);
  ellipse(x,0,20,20);
}
```

Just because we're not referencing it directly doesn't mean that we've eliminated the concept of `period`. After all, the greater the angular velocity, the faster the circle will oscillate (therefore lowering the period). In fact, the number of times it takes to add up the angular velocity to get to `TWO_PI` is the period or:

```
period = TWO_PI / angular velocity
```

Let's expand this example a bit more and create an `Oscillator` class. And let's assume we want the oscillation to happen along both the x-axis (as above) and the y-axis. To do this, we'll need two angles, two angular velocities, and two amplitudes (one for each axis). Another perfect opportunity for `PVector`!

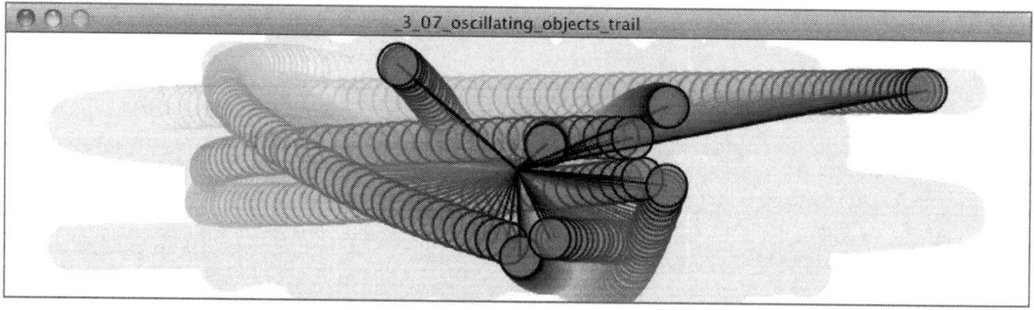

Example 3.7: Oscillator objects

```
class Oscillator  {

  PVector angle;                                  Using a PVector to track two angles!
  PVector velocity;
  PVector amplitude;

  Oscillator()  {
    angle = new PVector();
    velocity = new PVector(random(-0.05,0.05),random(-0.05,0.05));
    amplitude = new PVector(random(width/2),random(height/2));
  }                                               Random velocities and amplitudes

  void oscillate()  {
    angle.add(velocity);
  }

  void display()  {
    float x = sin(angle.x)*amplitude.x;           Oscillating on the x-axis
    float y = sin(angle.y)*amplitude.y;           Oscillating on the y-axis

    pushMatrix();
    translate(width/2,height/2);
    stroke(0);
    fill(175);
```

```
    line(0,0,x,y);
    ellipse(x,y,16,16);
    popMatrix();
  }
}
```

Drawing the Oscillator as a line connecting a circle

Exercise 3.7

Try initializing each `Oscillator` object with velocities and amplitudes that are not random to create some sort of regular pattern. Can you make the oscillators appear to be the legs of a insect-like creature?

Exercise 3.8

Incorporate angular acceleration into the `Oscillator` object.

3.8 Waves

If you're saying to yourself, "Um, this is all great and everything, but what I really want is to draw a wave onscreen," well, then, the time has come. The thing is, we're about 90% there. When we oscillate a single circle up and down according to the sine function, what we are doing is looking at a single point along the x-axis of a wave pattern. With a little panache and a `for` loop, we can place a whole bunch of these oscillating circles next to each other.

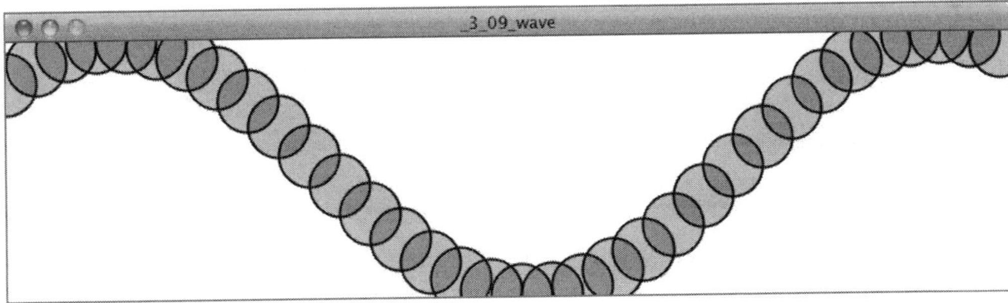

This wavy pattern could be used in the design of the body or appendages of a creature, as well as to simulate a soft surface (such as water).

Here, we're going to encounter the same questions of amplitude (height of pattern) and period. Instead of period referring to time, however, since we're looking at the full wave, we can talk about period as the width (in pixels) of a full wave cycle. And just as with simple oscillation, we have the option of computing the wave pattern according to a precise period or simply following the model of angular velocity.

Let's go with the simpler case, angular velocity. We know we need to start with an angle, an angular velocity, and an amplitude:

```
float angle = 0;
float angleVel = 0.2;
float amplitude = 100;
```

Then we're going to loop through all of the x values where we want to draw a point of the wave. Let's say every 24 pixels for now. In that loop, we're going to want to do three things:

1. Calculate the y location according to amplitude and sine of the angle.
2. Draw a circle at the *(x,y)* location.
3. Increment the angle according to angular velocity.

```
for (int x = 0; x <= width; x += 24) {
  float y = amplitude*sin(angle);    // 1) Calculate the y location according to amplitude and sine of the angle.
  ellipse(x,y+height/2,48,48);       // 2) Draw a circle at the (x,y) location.
  angle += angleVel;                 // 3) Increment the angle according to angular velocity.
}
```

Let's look at the results with different values for `angleVel`:

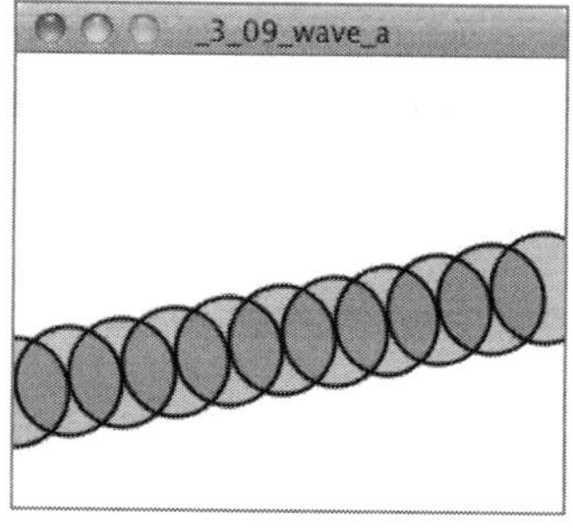

angleVel = 0.05

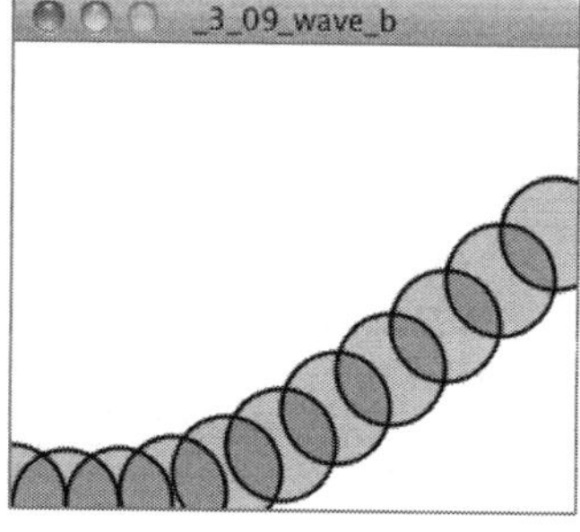

angleVel = 0.2

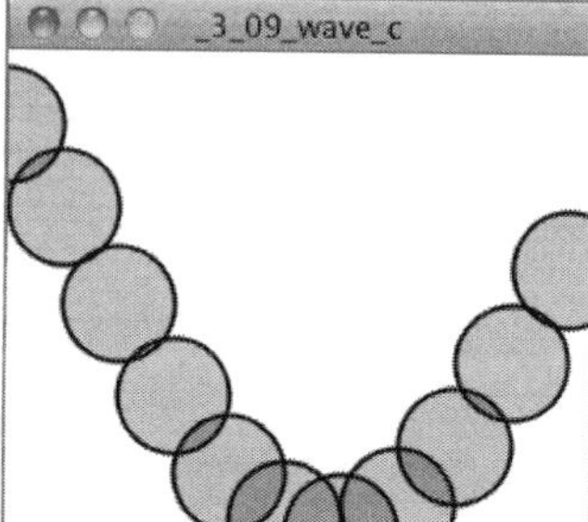

angleVel = 0.4

Notice how, although we're not precisely computing the period of the wave, the higher the angular velocity, the shorter the period. It's also worth noting that as the period becomes shorter, it becomes more and more difficult to make out the wave itself as the distance between the individual points increases. One option we have is to use `beginShape()` and `endShape()` to connect the points with a line.

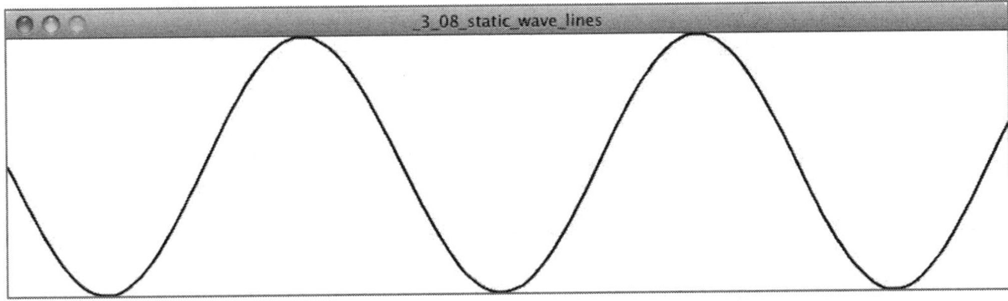

Example 3.8: Static wave drawn as a continuous line

```
float angle = 0;
float angleVel = 0.2;
float amplitude = 100;

size(400,200);
background(255);

stroke(0);
strokeWeight(2);
noFill();

beginShape();
for (int x = 0; x <= width; x += 5) {
  float y = map(sin(angle),-1,1,0,height);
  vertex(x,y);
  angle +=angleVel;
}
endShape();
```

Here's an example of using the map() function instead.

With beginShape() and endShape(), you call vertex() to set all the vertices of your shape.

You may have noticed that the above example is static. The wave never changes, never undulates. This additional step is a bit tricky. Your first instinct might be to say: "Hey, no problem, we'll just let theta be a global variable and let it increment from one cycle through `draw()` to another."

While it's a nice thought, it doesn't work. If you look at the wave, the righthand edge doesn't match the lefthand; where it ends in one cycle of `draw()` can't be where it starts in the next. Instead, what we need to do is have a variable dedicated entirely to tracking what value of angle the wave should start with. This angle (which we'll call `startAngle`) increments with its own angular velocity.

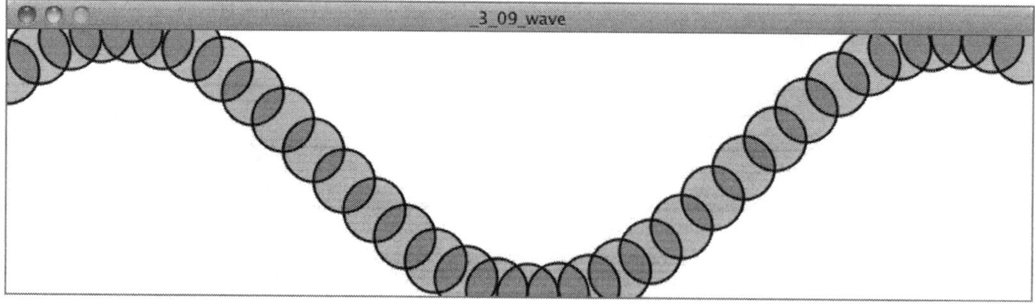

Example 3.9: The Wave

```
float startAngle = 0;
float angleVel = 0.1;

void setup() {
  size(400,200);
}

void draw() {
  background(255);
```

```
float angle = startAngle;
```

In order to move the wave, we start at a different theta value each frame. startAngle += 0.02;

```
  for (int x = 0; x <= width; x += 24) {
    float y = map(sin(angle),-1,1,0,height);
    stroke(0);
    fill(0,50);
    ellipse(x,y,48,48);
    angle += angleVel;
  }
}
```

Exercise 3.9

Try using the Perlin noise function instead of sine or cosine with the above example.

Exercise 3.10

Encapsulate the above examples into a `Wave` class and create a sketch that displays two waves (with different amplitudes/periods) as in the screenshot below. Move beyond plain circles and lines and try visualizing the wave in a more creative way.

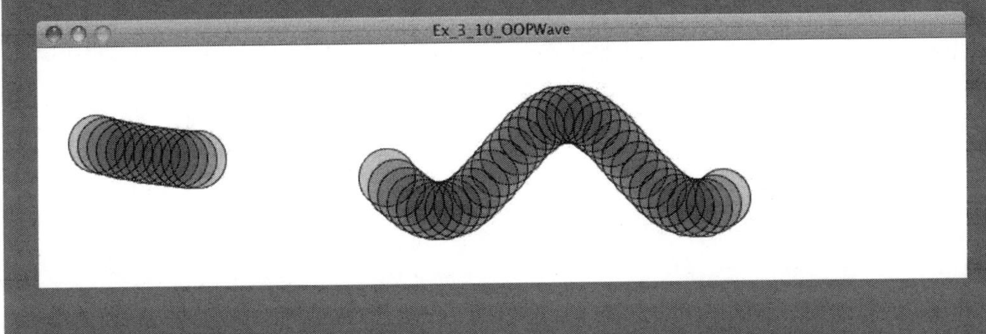

Exercise 3.11

More complex waves can be produced by the values of multiple waves together. Create a sketch that implements this, as in the screenshot below.

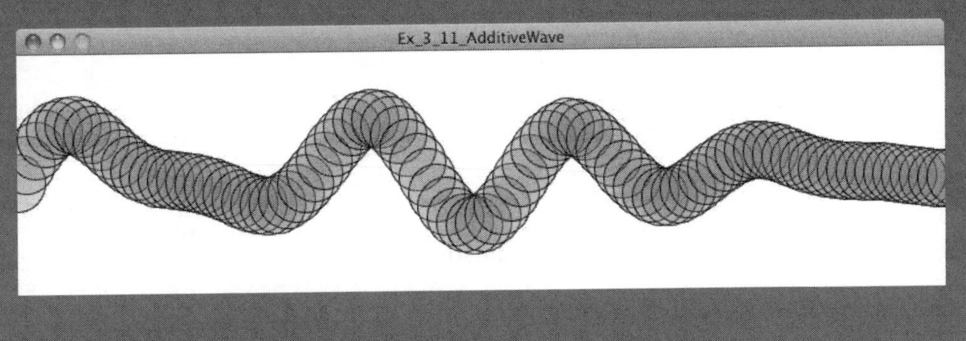

3.9 Trigonometry and Forces: The Pendulum

Do you miss Newton's laws of motion? I know I sure do. Well, lucky for you, it's time to bring it all back home. After all, it's been nice learning about triangles and tangents and waves, but really, the core of this book is about simulating the physics of moving bodies. Let's take a look at how trigonometry can help us with this pursuit.

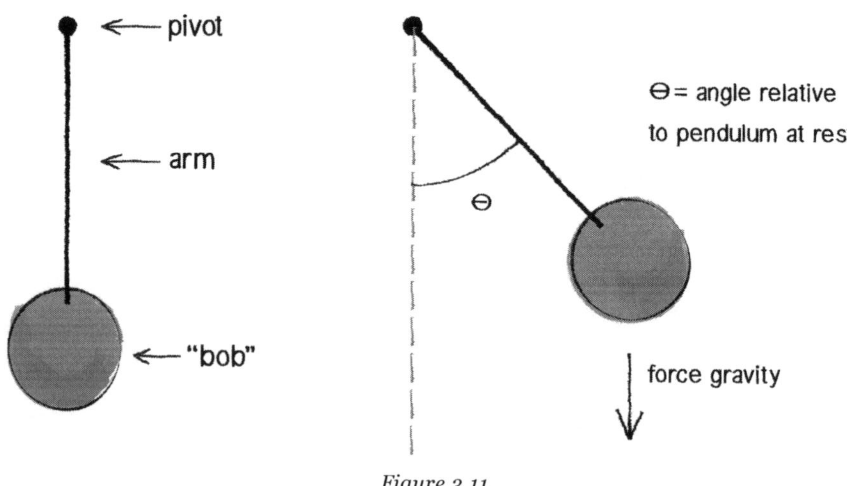

Figure 3.10

Figure 3.11

A pendulum is a bob suspended from a pivot. Obviously a real-world pendulum would live in a 3D space, but we're going to look at a simpler scenario, a pendulum in a 2D space—a Processing window (see Figure 3.10).

In Chapter 2, we learned how a force (such as the force of gravity in Figure 3.11) causes an object to accelerate. `F = M * A` or `A = F / M`. In this case, however, the pendulum bob doesn't simply fall to the ground because it is attached by an arm to the pivot point. And so, in order to determine its *angular* acceleration, we not only need to look at the force of gravity, but also the force at the angle of the pendulum's arm (relative to a pendulum at rest with an angle of 0).

In the above case, since the pendulum's arm is of fixed length, the only variable in the scenario is the angle. We are going to simulate the pendulum's motion through the use of angular velocity and acceleration. The angular acceleration will be calculated using Newton's second law with a little trigonometry twist.

Let's zoom in on the right triangle from the pendulum diagram.

We can see that the force of the pendulum (F_p) should point perpendicular to the arm of the pendulum in the direction that the pendulum is swinging. After all, if there were no arm, the bob would just fall straight down. It's the tension force of the arm that keeps the bob accelerating towards the pendulum's rest state. Since the force of gravity (F_p) points downward, by making a right triangle out of these two vectors, we've accomplished something quite magnificent. We've made the force of gravity the hypotenuse of a right triangle and separated the vector into two components, one of which represents the force of the pendulum. Since sine equals opposite over hypotenuse, we have:

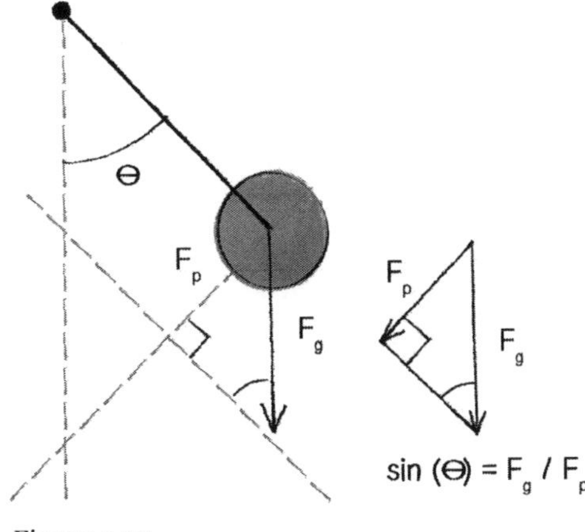

Figure 3.12

```
sine(θ) = Fp / Fg
```

Therefore:

```
Fp = Fg * sine(θ)
```

Lest we forget, we've been doing all of this with a single question in mind: What is the angular acceleration of the pendulum? Once we have the angular acceleration, we'll be able to apply our rules of motion to find the new angle for the pendulum.

```
angular velocity = angular velocity + angular acceleration
angle = angle + angular velocity
```

The good news is that with Newton's second law, we know that there is a relationship between force and acceleration, namely F = M * A, or A = F / M. So if the force of the pendulum is equal to the force of gravity times sine of the angle, then:

```
pendulum angular acceleration = acceleration due to gravity * sine (θ)
```

This is a good time to remind ourselves that we're Processing programmers and not physicists. Yes, we know that the acceleration due to gravity on earth is 9.8 meters per second squared. But this number isn't relevant to us. What we have here is just an arbitrary constant (we'll call it `gravity`), one that we can use to scale the acceleration to something that feels right.

```
angular acceleration = gravity * sine(θ)
```

Amazing. After all that, the formula is so simple. You might be wondering, why bother going through the derivation at all? I mean, learning is great and all, but we could have easily just said, "Hey, the angular acceleration of a pendulum is some constant times the sine of the angle." This is just another moment in which we remind ourselves that the purpose of the book is not to learn how pendulums swing or gravity works. The point is to think creatively about how things can move about the screen in a computationally based graphics system. The pendulum is just a case study. If you can understand the approach to programming a pendulum, then however you choose to design your onscreen world, you can apply the same techniques.

Of course, we're not finished yet. We may be happy with our simple, elegant formula, but we still have to apply it in code. This is most definitely a good time to practice our object-oriented programming skills and create a `Pendulum` class. Let's think about all the properties we've encountered in our pendulum discussion that the class will need:

- arm length
- angle
- angular velocity
- angular acceleration

```
class Pendulum  {

  float r;                  // Length of arm
  float angle;              // Pendulum arm angle
  float aVelocity;          // Angular velocity
  float aAcceleration;      // Angular acceleration
```

We'll also need to write a function `update()` to update the pendulum's angle according to our formula…

```
  void update() {
    float gravity = 0.4;                              // Arbitrary constant
    aAcceleration = -1 * gravity * sin(angle);        // Calculate acceleration according to our formula.
    aVelocity += aAcceleration;                       // Increment velocity.
    angle += aVelocity;                               // Increment angle.
  }
```

…as well as a function `display()` to draw the pendulum in the window. This begs the question: "Um, where do we draw the pendulum?" We know the angle and the arm length, but how do we know the *x,y* (Cartesian!) coordinates for both the pendulum's pivot point (let's call it origin) and bob location (let's call it location)? This may be getting a little tiring, but the answer, yet again, is trigonometry.

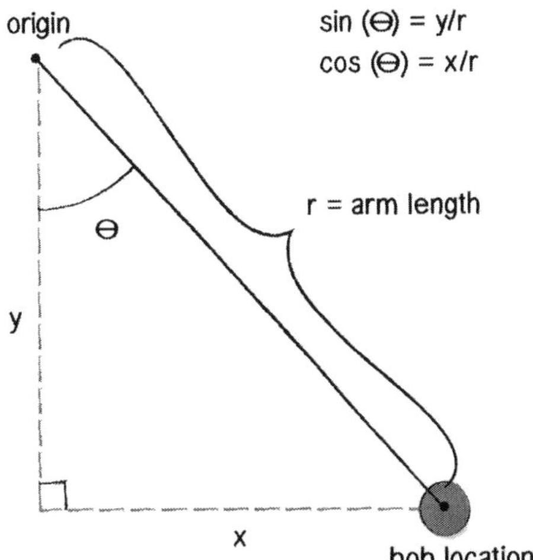

Figure 3.13

The origin is just something we make up, as is the arm length. Let's say:

```
PVector origin = new PVector(100,10);
float r = 125;
```

We've got the current angle stored in our variable `angle`. So relative to the origin, the pendulum's location is a polar coordinate: *(r,angle)*. And we need it to be Cartesian. Luckily for us, we just spent some time (section 3.5) deriving the formula for converting from polar to Cartesian. And so:

```
PVector location = new PVector(r*sin(angle),r*cos(angle));
```

Since the location is relative to wherever the origin happens to be, we can just add origin to the location `PVector`:

```
location.add(origin);
```

And all that remains is the little matter of drawing a line and ellipse (you should be more creative, of course).

```
stroke(0);
fill(175);
line(origin.x,origin.y,location.x,location.y);
ellipse(location.x,location.y,16,16);
```

Before we put everything together, there's one last little detail I neglected to mention. Let's think about the pendulum arm for a moment. Is it a metal rod? A string? A rubber band? How is it attached to the pivot point? How long is it? What is its mass? Is it a windy day? There are a lot of questions that we could continue to ask that would affect the simulation. We're living, of course, in a fantasy world, one where the pendulum's arm is some idealized rod that never bends and the mass of the bob is concentrated in a single, infinitesimally small point. Nevertheless, even though we don't want to worry ourselves with all of the questions, we should add one more variable to our calculation of angular acceleration. To keep things simple, in our derivation of the pendulum's acceleration, we assumed that the length of the pendulum's arm is 1. In fact, the length of the pendulum's arm affects the acceleration greatly: the longer the arm, the slower the acceleration. To simulate a pendulum more accurately, we divide by that length, in this case `r`. For a more involved explanation, visit The Simple Pendulum website (http://calculuslab.deltacollege.edu/ODE/7-A-2/7-A-2-h.html).

```
aAcceleration = (-1 * G * sin(angle)) / r;
```

Finally, a real-world pendulum is going to experience some amount of friction (at the pivot point) and air resistance. With our code as is, the pendulum would swing forever, so to make it more realistic we can use a "damping" trick. I say *trick* because rather than model the resistance forces with some degree of accuracy (as we did in Chapter 2), we can achieve a similar result by simply reducing the angular velocity during each cycle. The following code reduces the velocity by 1% (or multiplies it by 99%) during each frame of animation:

```
aVelocity *= 0.99;
```

Putting everything together, we have the following example (with the pendulum beginning at a 45-degree angle).

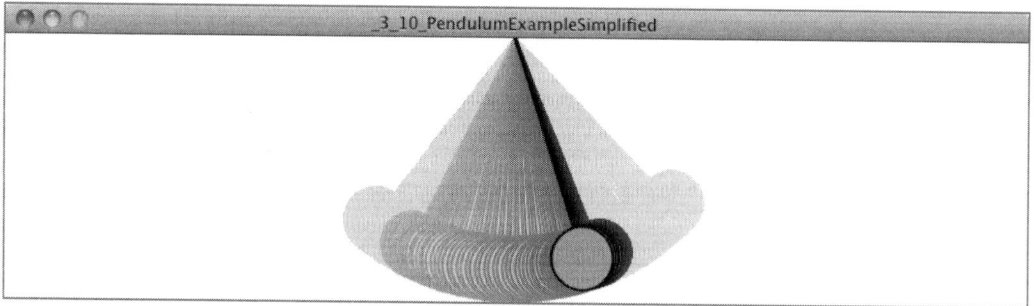

Example 3.10: Swinging pendulum

```
Pendulum p;

void setup() {
  size(640,360);
```

```
  p = new Pendulum(new PVector(width/2,10),125);
}

void draw() {
  background(255);
  p.go();
}

class Pendulum  {
  PVector location;    // Location of bob
  PVector origin;      // Location of arm origin
  float r;             // Length of arm
  float angle;         // Pendulum arm angle
  float aVelocity;     // Angle velocity
  float aAcceleration; // Angle acceleration
  float damping;       // Arbitrary damping amount

  Pendulum(PVector origin_, float r_) {
    origin = origin_.get();
    location = new PVector();
    r = r_;
    angle = PI/4;

    aVelocity = 0.0;
    aAcceleration = 0.0;
    damping = 0.995;
  }

  void go() {
    update();
    display();
  }

  void update() {
    float gravity = 0.4;
    aAcceleration = (-1 * gravity / r) * sin(angle);

    aVelocity += aAcceleration;
    angle += aVelocity;

    aVelocity *= damping;
  }

  void display() {
    location.set(r*sin(angle),r*cos(angle),0);
    location.add(origin);

    stroke(0);
```

We make a new Pendulum object with an origin location and arm length.

Many, many variables to keep track of the Pendulum's various properties

An arbitrary damping so that the Pendulum slows over time

Formula we worked out for angular acceleration

Standard angular motion algorithm

Apply some damping.

Where is the bob relative to the origin? Polar to Cartesian coordinates will tell us!

```
    line(origin.x,origin.y,location.x,location.y);      The arm
    fill(175);
    ellipse(location.x,location.y,16,16);               The bob
  }
}
```

(Note that the version of the example posted on the website has additional code to allow the user to grab the pendulum and swing it with the mouse.)

Exercise 3.12

String together a series of pendulums so that the endpoint of one is the origin point of another. Note that doing this may produce intriguing results but will be wildly inaccurate physically. Simulating an actual double pendulum involves sophisticated equations, which you can read about here: http://scienceworld.wolfram.com/physics/DoublePendulum.html (http://scienceworld.wolfram.com/physics/DoublePendulum.html).

Exercise 3.13

Using trigonometry, what is the magnitude of the normal force in the illustration on the right (the force perpendicular to the incline on which the sled rests)? Note that, as indicated, the "normal" force is a component of the force of gravity.

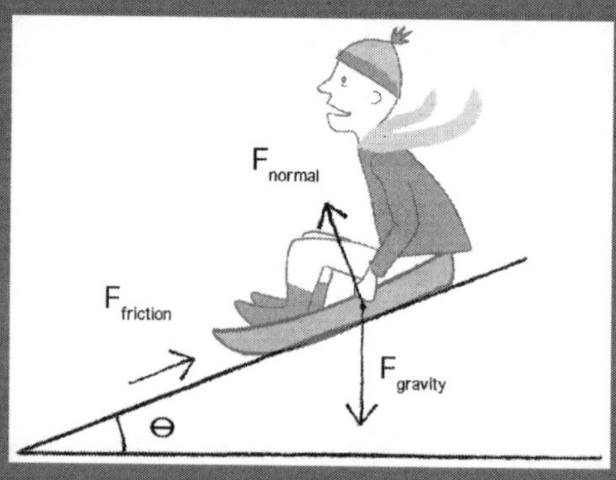

Exercise 3.14

Create an example that simulates a box sliding down the incline with friction. Note that the magnitude of the friction force is equal to the normal force.

3.10 Spring Forces

In section 3.6 (see page 115), we looked at modeling simple harmonic motion by mapping the sine wave to a pixel range. Exercise 3.6 (see page 119) asked you to use this technique to create a simulation of a bob hanging from a spring. While using the `sin()` function is a quick-and-dirty, one-line-of-code way of getting something up and running, it won't do if what we really want is to have a bob hanging from a spring in a two-dimensional space that responds to other forces in the environment (wind, gravity, etc.) To accomplish a simulation like this (one that is identical to the pendulum example, only now the arm is a springy connection), we need to model the forces of a spring using `PVector`.

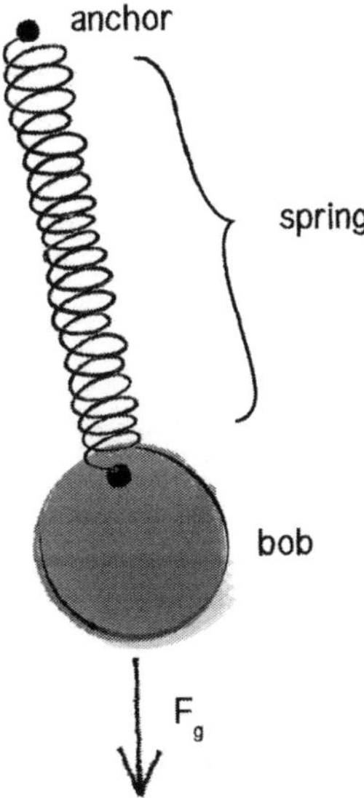

Figure 3.14

The force of a spring is calculated according to Hooke's law, named for Robert Hooke, a British physicist who developed the formula in 1660. Hooke originally stated the law in Latin: "*Ut tensio, sic vis*," or "As the extension, so the force." Let's think of it this way:

> The force of the spring is directly proportional to the extension of the spring.

In other words, if you pull on the bob a lot, the force will be strong; if you pull on the bob a little, the force will be weak. Mathematically, the law is stated as follows:

$$F_{spring} = - k * x$$

- k is constant and its value will ultimately scale the force. Is the spring highly elastic or quite rigid?
- x refers to the displacement of the spring, i.e. the difference between the current length and the rest length. The rest length is defined as the length of the spring in a state of equilibrium.

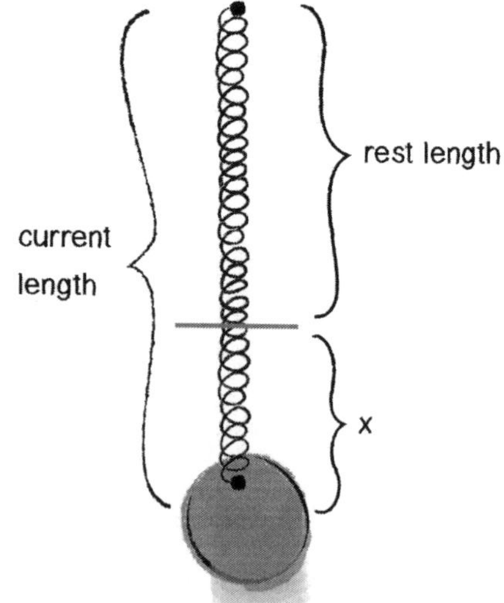

Figure 3.15: x = current length - rest length

Now remember, force is a vector, so we need to calculate both magnitude and direction. Let's look at one more diagram of the spring and label all the givens we might have in a Processing sketch.

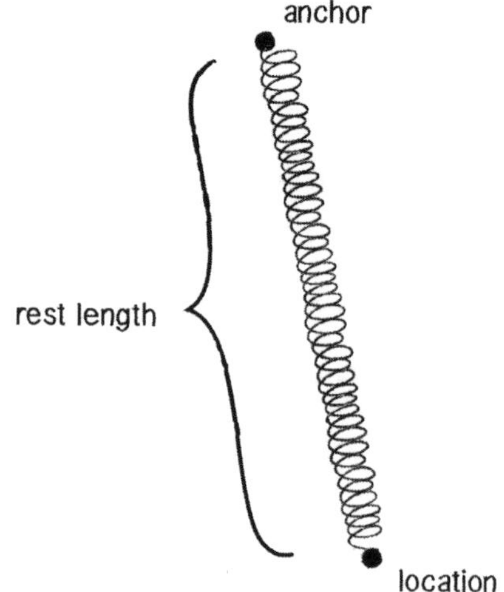

Figure 3.16

Let's establish the following three variables as shown in Figure 3.16.

```
PVector anchor;
PVector location;
float restLength;
```

First, let's use Hooke's law to calculate the magnitude of the force. We need to know k and x. k is easy; it's just a constant, so let's make something up.

```
float k = 0.1;
```

x is perhaps a bit more difficult. We need to know the "difference between the current length and the rest length." The rest length is defined as the variable `restLength`. What's the current length? The distance between the anchor and the bob. And how can we calculate that distance? How about the magnitude of a vector that points from the anchor to the bob? (Note that this is exactly the same process we employed when calculating distance in Example 2.9: gravitational attraction.)

```
PVector dir = PVector.sub(bob,anchor);
float currentLength = dir.mag();
float x = restLength - currentLength;
```

A vector pointing from anchor to bob gives us the current length of the spring.

Now that we've sorted out the elements necessary for the magnitude of the force (-1 * k * x), we need to figure out the direction, a unit vector pointing in the direction of the force. The good news is that we already have this vector. Right? Just a moment ago we thought to ourselves: "How we can calculate that distance? How about the magnitude of a vector that points from the anchor to the bob?" Well, that is the direction of the force!

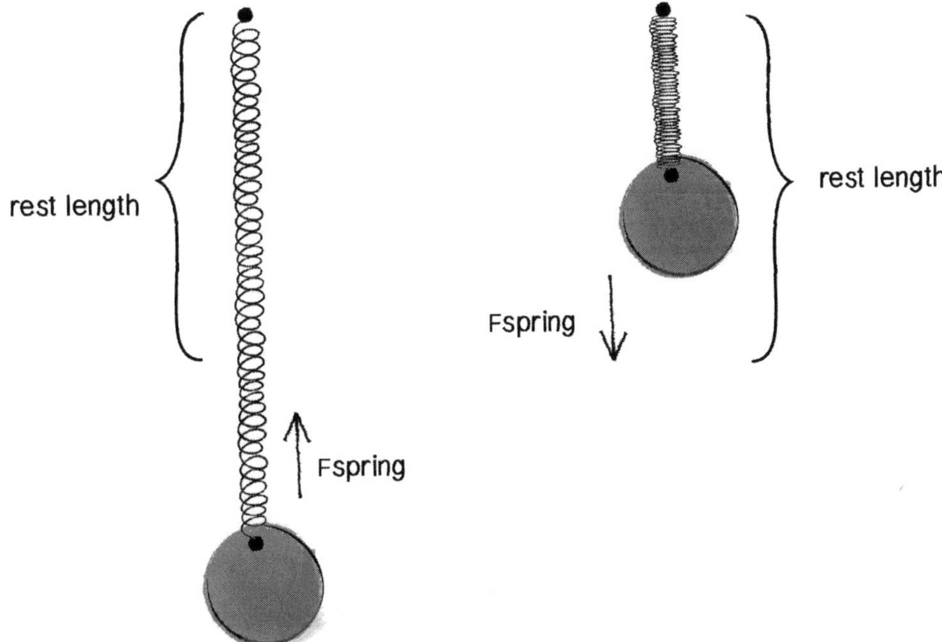

Figure 3.17

In Figure 3.17, we can see that if we stretch the spring beyond its rest length, there should be a force pulling it back towards the anchor. And if it shrinks below its rest length, the force should push it away from the anchor. This reversal of direction is accounted for in the formula with the -1. And so all we need to do is normalize the `PVector` we used for the distance calculation! Let's take a look at the code and rename that `PVector` variable as "force."

```
float k = 0.1;                                          // Magnitude of spring force according to Hooke's law

PVector force = PVector.sub(bob,anchor);
float currentLength = dir.mag();
float x = restLength - currentLength;

force.normalize();                                      // Direction of spring force (unit vector)

force.mult(-1 * k * x);                                 // Putting it together: direction and magnitude!
```

Now that we have the algorithm worked out for computing the spring force vector, the question remains: what object-oriented programming structure should we use? This, again, is one of those situations in which there is no "correct" answer. There are several possibilities; which one we choose depends on the program's goals and one's own personal coding style. Still, since we've been working all along with a `Mover` class, let's keep going with this same framework. Let's think of our `Mover` class as the spring's "bob." The bob needs `location`, `velocity`, and `acceleration` vectors to move about the screen. Perfect—we've got that already! And perhaps the bob experiences a gravity force via the `applyForce()` function. Just one more step—we need to apply the spring force:

```
Bob bob;

void setup() {
  bob = new Bob();
}

void draw()  {
  PVector gravity = new PVector(0,1);                   // Our Chapter 2 "make-up-a-gravity force"
  bob.applyForce(gravity);
  PVector springForce = _______________????             // We need to also calculate and apply a spring force!
  bob.applyForce(spring);

  bob.update();                                         // Our standard update() and display() functions
  bob.display();
}
```

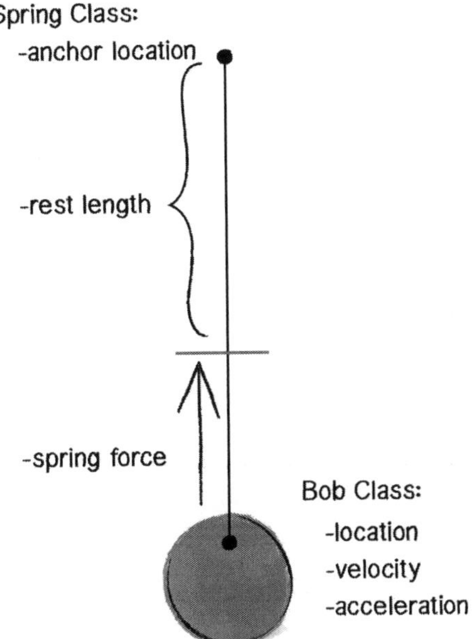

Figure 3.18

One option would be to write out all of the spring force code in the main `draw()` loop. But thinking ahead to when you might have multiple bobs and multiple spring connections, it makes a good deal of sense to write an additional class, a `Spring` class. As shown in Figure 3.18, the `Bob` class keeps track of the movements of the bob; the `Spring` class keeps track of the spring's anchor and its rest length and calculates the spring force on the bob.

This allows us to write a lovely main program as follows:

```
Bob bob;
Spring spring;                         // Adding a Spring object

void setup() {
  bob = new Bob();
  spring = new Spring();
}

void draw()  {
  PVector gravity = new PVector(0,1);
  bob.applyForce(gravity);

  spring.connect(bob);                 // This new function in the Spring class will
                                       // take care of computing the force of the
                                       // spring on the bob.

  bob.update();
  bob.display();
  spring.display();
}
```

You may notice here that this is quite similar to what we did in Example 2.6 (see page 94) with an attractor. There, we said something like:

```
PVector force = attractor.attract(mover);
mover.applyForce(force);
```

The analogous situation here with a spring would be:

```
PVector force = spring.connect(bob);
bob.applyForce(force);
```

Nevertheless, in this example all we said was:

```
spring.connect(bob);
```

What gives? Why don't we need to call `applyForce()` on the bob? The answer is, of course, that we do need to call `applyForce()` on the bob. Only instead of doing it in `draw()`, we're just demonstrating that a perfectly reasonable (and sometimes preferable) alternative is to ask the `connect()` function to internally handle calling `applyForce()` on the bob.

```
void connect(Bob b) {
  PVector force = some fancy calculations

  b.applyForce(force);
}
```

The function connect() takes care of calling applyForce() and therefore doesn't have to return a vector to the calling area.

Why do it one way with the `Attractor` class and another way with the `Spring` class? When we were first learning about forces, it was a bit clearer to show all the forces being applied in the main `draw()` loop, and hopefully this helped you learn about force accumulation. Now that we're more comfortable with that, perhaps it's simpler to embed some of the details inside the objects themselves.

Let's take a look at the rest of the elements in the `Spring` class.

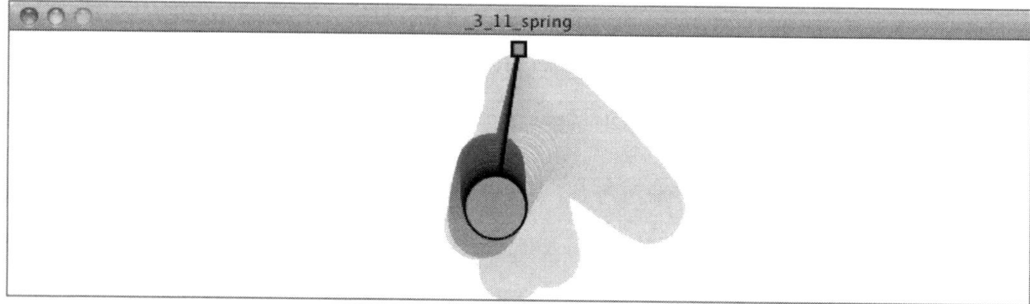

Example 3.11: A Spring connection

```
class Spring {

  PVector anchor;
```

We need to keep track of the spring's anchor location.

```
  float len;
  float k = 0.1;
```

Rest length and spring constant variables

```
  Spring(float x, float y, int l) {
    anchor = new PVector(x,y);
    len = l;
  }
```

The constructor initializes the anchor point and rest length.

```
  void connect(Bob b) {
```

Calculate spring force—our implementation of Hooke's Law.

```
    PVector force =
      PVector.sub(b.location,anchor);
```

Get a vector pointing from anchor to Bob location.

```
    float d = force.mag();
    float stretch = d - len;
```

Calculate the displacement between distance and rest length.

```
    force.normalize();
    force.mult(-1 * k * stretch);
```

Direction and magnitude together!

```
    b.applyForce(force);
  }
```

Call applyForce() right here!

```
  void display() {
    fill(100);
    rectMode(CENTER);
    rect(anchor.x,anchor.y,10,10);
  }
```

Draw the anchor.

```
  void displayLine(Bob b) {
    stroke(255);
    line(b.location.x,b.location.y,anchor.x,anchor.y);
  }

}
```

Draw the spring connection between Bob location and anchor.

The full code for this example is included on the book website, and the Web version also incorporates two additional features: (1) the `Bob` class includes functions for mouse interactivity so that the bob can be dragged around the window, and (2) the `Spring` object includes a function to constrain the connection's length between a minimum and a maximum.

Exercise 3.15

Before running to see the example online, take a look at this constrain function and see if you can fill in the blanks.

```
void constrainLength(Bob b, float minlen, float maxlen) {
  PVector dir = PVector.sub(______,______);       Vector pointing from Bob to Anchor
  float d = dir.mag();

  if (d < minlen) {                                Is it too short?
    dir.normalize();
    dir.mult(________);
    b.location = PVector.add(______,______);       Keep location within constraint.
    b.velocity.mult(0);
  } else if (___________) {                        Is it too long?
    dir.normalize();
    dir.mult(________);
    b.location = PVector.add(______,______);       Keep location within constraint.
    b.velocity.mult(0);
  }
}
```

Exercise 3.16

Create a system of multiple bobs and spring connections. How would you have a bob connected to a bob with no fixed anchor?

The Ecosystem Project

Step 3 Exercise:

Take one of your creatures and incorporate oscillation into its motion. You can use the `Oscillator` class from Example 3.7 as a model. The `Oscillator` object, however, oscillates around a single point (the middle of the window). Try oscillating around a moving point. In other words, design a creature that moves around the screen according to location, velocity, and acceleration. But that creature isn't just a static shape, it's an oscillating body. Consider tying the speed of oscillation to the speed of motion. Think of a butterfly's flapping wings or the legs of an insect. Can you make it appear that the creature's internal mechanics (oscillation) drive its locomotion? For a sample, check out the "AttractionArrayWithOscillation" example with the code download.

Chapter 4. Particle Systems

"That is wise. Were I to invoke logic, however, logic clearly dictates that the needs of the many outweigh the needs of the few."
— Spock

In 1982, William T. Reeves, a researcher at Lucasfilm Ltd., was working on the film *Star Trek II: The Wrath of Khan*. Much of the movie revolves around the Genesis Device, a torpedo that when shot at a barren, lifeless planet has the ability to reorganize matter and create a habitable world for colonization. During the sequence, a wall of fire ripples over the planet while it is being "terraformed." The term ***particle system***, an incredibly common and useful technique in computer graphics, was coined in the creation of this particular effect.

> *"A particle system is a collection of many many minute particles that together represent a fuzzy object. Over a period of time, particles are generated into a system, move and change from within the system, and die from the system."*
> *—William Reeves, "Particle Systems—A Technique for Modeling a Class of Fuzzy Objects,"* ACM Transactions on Graphics *2:2 (April 1983), 92.*

Since the early 1980s, particle systems have been used in countless video games, animations, digital art pieces, and installations to model various irregular types of natural phenomena, such as fire, smoke, waterfalls, fog, grass, bubbles, and so on.

This chapter will be dedicated to looking at implementation strategies for coding a particle system. How do we organize our code? Where do we store information related to individual particles versus information related to the system as a whole? The examples we'll look at will focus on managing the data associated with a particle system. They'll use simple shapes for the particles and apply only the most basic behaviors (such as gravity). However, by using this framework and building in more interesting ways to render the particles and compute behaviors, you can achieve a variety of effects.

4.1 Why We Need Particle Systems

We've defined a particle system to be a collection of independent objects, often represented by a simple shape or dot. Why does this matter? Certainly, the prospect of modeling some of the phenomena we listed (explosions!) is attractive and potentially useful. But really, there's an even better reason for us to concern ourselves with particle systems. If we want to get anywhere in this nature of code life, we're going to need to work with systems of *many* things. We're going to want to look at balls bouncing, birds flocking, ecosystems evolving, all sorts of things in plural.

Just about every chapter after this one is going to need to deal with a list of objects. Yes, we've done this with an array in some of our first vector and forces examples. But we need to go where no array has gone before.

First, we're going to want to deal with flexible quantities of elements. Sometimes we'll have zero things, sometimes one thing, sometimes ten things, and sometimes ten thousand things. Second, we're going to want to take a more sophisticated object-oriented approach. Instead of simply writing a class to describe a single particle, we're also going to want to write a class that describes the collection of particles—the particle system itself. The goal here is to be able to write a main program that looks like the following:

```
ParticleSystem ps;

void setup() {
  size(640,360);
  ps = new ParticleSystem();
}

void draw() {
  background(255);
  ps.run();
}
```

Ah, isn't this main program so simple and lovely?

No single particle is ever referenced in the above code, yet the result will be full of particles flying all over the screen. Getting used to writing Processing sketches with multiple classes, and classes that keep lists of instances of other classes, will prove very useful as we get to more advanced chapters in this book.

Finally, working with particle systems is also a good excuse for us to tackle two other advanced object-oriented programming techniques: inheritance and polymorphism. With the examples we've seen up until now, we've always had an array of a single type of object, like "movers" or "oscillators." With inheritance (and polymorphism), we'll learn a convenient way to store a single list that contains objects of different types. This way, a particle system need not only be a system of a single type of particle.

Though it may seem obvious to you, I'd also like to point out that there are typical implementations of particle systems, and that's where we will begin in this chapter. However, the fact that the particles in this chapter look or behave a certain way should not limit your imagination. Just because particle systems tend to look sparkly, fly forward, and fall with gravity doesn't mean that those are the characteristics yours should have.

The focus here is really just how to keep track of a system of many elements. What those elements do and how those elements look is up to you.

4.2 A Single Particle

Before we can get rolling on the system itself, we have to write the class that will describe a single particle. The good news: we've done this already. Our `Mover` class from Chapter 2 serves as the perfect template. For us, a particle is an independent body that moves about the screen. It has `location`, `velocity`, and `acceleration`, a constructor to initialize those variables, and functions to `display()` itself and `update()` its location.

```
class Particle {
  PVector location;
  PVector velocity;
  PVector acceleration;

  Particle(PVector l) {
    location = l.get();
    acceleration = new PVector();
    velocity = new PVector();
  }

  void update() {
    velocity.add(acceleration);
    location.add(velocity);
  }

  void display() {
    stroke(0);
    fill(175);
    ellipse(location.x,location.y,8,8);
  }
}
```

A "Particle" object is just another name for our "Mover." It has location, velocity, and acceleration.

This is about as simple as a particle can get. From here, we could take our particle in several directions. We could add an `applyForce()` function to affect the particle's behavior (we'll do precisely this in a future example). We could add variables to describe color and shape, or reference a `PImage` to draw the particle. For now, however, let's focus on adding just one additional detail: ***lifespan***.

Typical particle systems involve something called an ***emitter***. The emitter is the source of the particles and controls the initial settings for the particles, location, velocity, etc. An emitter might emit a single burst of particles, or a continuous stream of particles, or both. The point is that for a typical implementation such as this, a particle is born at the emitter but does not live forever. If it were to live forever, our Processing sketch would eventually grind to a halt as the number of particles increases to an unwieldy number over time. As new particles are born, we need old particles to die. This creates the illusion of an infinite stream of particles, and the performance of our program does not suffer. There are many different ways to decide when a particle dies. For example, it could come into contact with another object, or it could simply leave the screen. For our first `Particle` class, however, we're simply going to add a `lifespan` variable. The timer will start at 255 and count down to 0, when the particle will be considered "dead." And so we expand the `Particle` class as follows:

```
class Particle {
  PVector location;
  PVector velocity;
  PVector acceleration;
  float lifespan;            // A new variable to keep track of how long the particle has been "alive"

  Particle(PVector l) {
    location = l.get();
    acceleration = new PVector();
    velocity = new PVector();
    lifespan = 255;          // We start at 255 and count down for convenience
  }

  void update() {
    velocity.add(acceleration);
    location.add(velocity);
    lifespan -= 2.0;         // Lifespan decreases
  }

  void display() {
    stroke(0,lifespan);      // Since our life ranges from 255 to 0 we can use it for alpha
    fill(175,lifespan);
    ellipse(location.x,location.y,8,8);
  }
}
```

The reason we chose to start the lifespan at 255 and count down to 0 is for convenience. With those values, we can assign `lifespan` to act as the alpha transparency for the ellipse as well. When the particle is "dead" it will also have faded away onscreen.

With the addition of the `lifespan` variable, we'll also need one additional function—a function that can be queried (for a true or false answer) as to whether the particle is alive or dead. This will come in handy when we are writing the `ParticleSystem` class, whose task will be to manage the list of particles themselves. Writing this function is pretty easy; we just need to check and see if the value of `lifespan` is less than 0. If it is we `return true`, if not we `return false`.

```
boolean isDead() {
  if (lifespan < 0.0) {        Is the particle still alive?
    return true;
  } else {
    return false;
  }
}
```

Before we get to the next step of making many particles, it's worth taking a moment to make sure our particle works correctly and create a sketch with one single `Particle` object. Here is the full code below, with two small additions. We add a convenience function called `run()` that simply calls both `update()` and `display()` for us. In addition, we give the particle a random initial velocity as well as a downward acceleration (to simulate gravity).

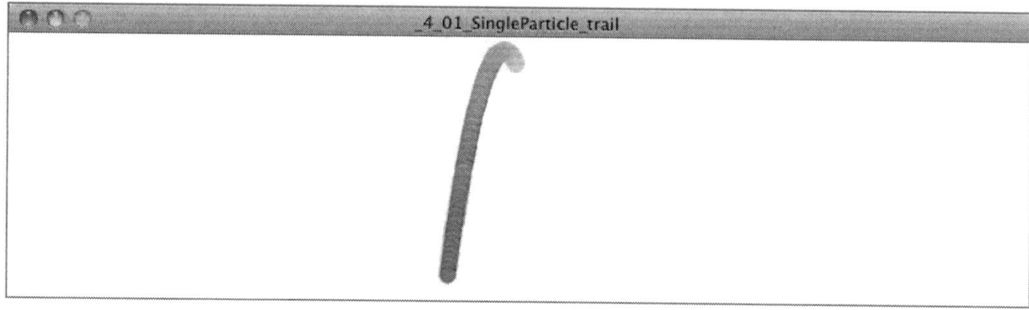

Example 4.1: A single particle

```
Particle p;

void setup() {
  size(640,360);
  p = new Particle(new PVector(width/2,10));
}

void draw() {
  background(255);
```

```
  p.run();                                   Operating the single Particle
  if (p.isDead()) {
    println("Particle dead!");
  }
}

class Particle {
  PVector location;
  PVector velocity;
  PVector acceleration;
  float lifespan;

  Particle(PVector l) {
    acceleration = new PVector(0,0.05);
    velocity = new PVector(random(-1,1),random(-2,0));
    location = l.get();
    lifespan = 255.0;
  }

  void run() {
    update();
    display();
  }

  void update() {
    velocity.add(acceleration);
    location.add(velocity);
    lifespan -= 2.0;
  }

  void display() {
    stroke(0,lifespan);
    fill(0,lifespan);
    ellipse(location.x,location.y,8,8);
  }

  boolean isDead() {
    if (lifespan < 0.0) {
      return true;
    } else {
      return false;
    }
  }
}
```

For demonstration purposes we assign the Particle an initial velocity and constant acceleration.

Sometimes it's convenient to have a "run" function that calls all the other functions we need.

Is the Particle alive or dead?

Exercise 4.1

Rewrite the example so that the particle can respond to force vectors via an `applyForce()` function.

Exercise 4.2

Add angular velocity (rotation) to the particle. Create your own non-circle particle design.

Now that we have a class to describe a single particle, we're ready for the next big step. How do we keep track of many particles, when we can't ensure exactly how many particles we might have at any given time?

4.3 The ArrayList

In truth, we could use a simple array to manage our `Particle` objects. Some particle systems might have a fixed number of particles, and arrays are magnificently efficient in those instances. Processing also offers `expand()`, `contract()`, `subset()`, `splice()`, and other methods for resizing arrays. However, for these examples, we're going to take a more sophisticated approach and use the Java class `ArrayList`, found in the java.util package ArrayList Documentation (http://download.oracle.com/javase/6/docs/api/java/util/ArrayList.html).

Using an `ArrayList` follows the same idea as using a standard array, but with different syntax. The following two code examples (which assume the existence of a generic `Particle` class) produce the same result: first with an array, and second with an `ArrayList`.

The standard array way:

```
int total = 10;
Particle[] parray = new Particle[total];

void setup() {
  for (int i = 0; i < parray.length; i++) {
    parray[i] = new Particle();
  }
```

This is what we're used to, accessing elements on the array via an index and brackets—[ ].

```
}

void draw() {
  for (int i = 0; i < parray.length; i++) {
    Particle p = parray[i];
    p.run();
  }
}
```

The new ArrayList way:

Have you ever seen this syntax before? This is a new feature in Java 1.6 (called "generics") that Processing now supports. It allows us to specify in advance what type of object we intend to put in the ArrayList.

```
int total = 10;

ArrayList<Particle> plist = new ArrayList<Particle>();

void setup() {
  for (int i = 0; i < total; i++) {
    plist.add(new Particle());
  }
}
```

An object is added to an ArrayList with add().

```
void draw() {
  for (int i = 0; i < plist.size(); i++) {
    Particle p = plist.get(i);
    p.run();
  }
}
```

The size of the ArrayList is returned by size().

An object is accessed from the ArrayList with get(). Because we are using generics, we do not need to specify a type when we pull objects out of the ArrayList.

This last `for` loop looks pretty similar to our code that looped through a regular array by accessing each index. We initialize a variable called `i` to 0 and count up by 1, accessing each element of the `ArrayList` until we get to the end. However, this is a good time to mention the "enhanced `for` loop" available in Java (and Processing), which is a bit more concise. The enhanced loop works with both `ArrayList`s and regular arrays and looks like this:

```
ArrayList<Particle> plist = new ArrayList<Particle>();

for (Particle p: particles) {
  p.run();
}
```

Let's translate that. Say "for each" instead of "for" and say "in" instead of ":". Now you have:

"For each Particle p in particles, run that Particle p!"

I know. You cannot contain your excitement. I can't. I know it's not necessary, but I just have to type that again.

```
for (Particle p : particles) {
  p.run();
}
```

This enhanced loop also works for regular arrays!

Simple, elegant, concise, lovely. Take a moment. Breathe. I have some bad news. Yes, we love that enhanced loop and we will get to use it. But not right now. Our particle system examples will require a feature that makes using that loop impossible. Let's continue.

The code we've written above doesn't take advantage of the `ArrayList`'s resizability, and it uses a fixed size of 10. We need to design an example that fits with our particle system scenario, where we emit a continuous stream of `Particle` objects, adding one new particle with each cycle through `draw()`. We'll skip rehashing the `Particle` class code here, as it doesn't need to change.

```
ArrayList<Particle> particles;

void setup() {
  size(640,360);
  particles = new ArrayList<Particle>();
}

void draw() {
  background(255);
  particles.add(new Particle(new PVector(width/2,50)));

  for (int i = 0; i < particles.size(); i++) {
    Particle p = particles.get(i);
    p.run();
  }
}
```

A new Particle object is added to the ArrayList every cycle through draw().

Run the above code for a few minutes and you'll start to see the frame rate slow down further and further until the program grinds to a halt (my tests yielded horrific performance after fifteen minutes). The issue of course is that we are creating more and more particles without removing any.

Fortunately, the `ArrayList` class has a convenient `remove()` function that allows us to delete a particle (by referencing its index). This is why we cannot use the new enhanced `for` loop we just learned; the enhanced loop provides no means for deleting elements while iterating. Here, we want to call `remove()` when the particle's `isDead()` function returns true.

```
for (int i = 0; i < particles.size(); i++) {
  Particle p = particles.get(i);
  p.run();
  if (p.isDead()) {
    particles.remove(i);
  }
}
```

If the particle is "dead," we can go ahead and delete it from the list.

Although the above code will run just fine (and the program will never grind to a halt), we have opened up a medium-sized can of worms. Whenever we manipulate the contents of a list while iterating through that very list, we can get ourselves into trouble. Take, for example, the following code.

```
for (int i = 0; i < particles.size(); i++) {
  Particle p = particles.get(i);
  p.run();
  particles.add(new Particle(new PVector(width/2,50)));
}
```

Adding a new Particle to the list while iterating?

This is a somewhat extreme example (with flawed logic), but it proves the point. In the above case, for each particle in the list, we add a new particle to the list (manipulating the `size()` of the `ArrayList`). This will result in an infinite loop, as `i` can never increment past the size of the `ArrayList`.

While removing elements from the `ArrayList` during a loop doesn't cause the program to crash (as it does with adding), the problem is almost more insidious in that it leaves no evidence. To discover the problem we must first establish an important fact. When an object is removed from the `ArrayList`, all elements are shifted one spot to the left. Note the diagram below where particle C (index 2) is removed. Particles A and B keep the same index, while particles D and E shift from 3 and 4 to 2 and 3, respectively.

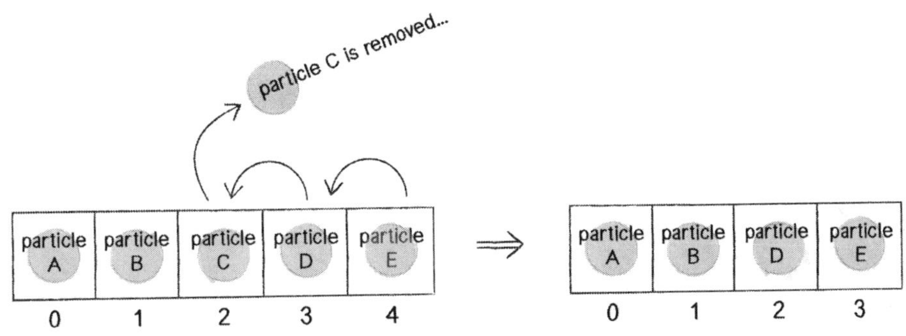

Figure 4.1

Let's pretend we are `i` looping through the `ArrayList`.

```
when i = 0 → Check particle A → Do not delete
when i = 1 → Check particle B → Do not delete
when i = 2 → Check particle C → Delete!
             Slide particles D and E back from slots 3 and 4 to 2 and 3
when i = 3 → Check particle E → Do not delete
```

Notice the problem? We never checked particle D! When C was deleted from slot #2, D moved into slot #2, but i has already moved on to slot # 3. This is not a disaster, since particle D will get checked the next time around. Still, the expectation is that we are writing code to iterate through every single element of the `ArrayList`. Skipping an element is unacceptable.

There are two solutions to this problem. The first solution is to simply iterate through the `ArrayList` backwards. If you are sliding elements from right to left as elements are removed, it's impossible to skip an element by accident. Here's how the code would look:

```
for (int i = particles.size()-1; i >= 0; i--) {      Looping through the list backwards
  Particle p = (Particle) particles.get(i);
  p.run();
  if (p.isDead()) {
    particles.remove(i);
  }
}
```

This is a perfectly fine solution in ninety-nine cases out of a hundred. But sometimes, the order in which the elements are drawn could be important and you may not want to iterate backwards. Java provides a special class—`Iterator`—that takes care of all of the details of iteration for you. You get to say:

Hey, I'd like to iterate through this `ArrayList`*. Could you continue to give me the next element in the list one at a time until we get to the end? And if I remove elements or move them around in the list while we're iterating, will you make sure I don't look at any elements twice or skip any by accident?*

An `ArrayList` can produce an `Iterator` object for you.

```
Iterator<Particle> it = particles.iterator();
```

Note that with the Iterator object, we can also use the new <ClassName> generics syntax and specify the type that the Iterator will reference.

Once you've got the iterator, the `hasNext()` function will tell us whether there is a `Particle` for us to run and the `next()` function will grab that `Particle` object itself.

```
while (it.hasNext()) {
  Particle p = it.next();
  p.run();
```

An Iterator object doing the iterating for you

And if you call the `remove()` function on the `Iterator` object during the loop, it will delete the current `Particle` object (and not skip ahead past the next one, as we saw with counting forward through the `ArrayList`).

```
    if (p.isDead()) {
```

```
      it.remove();
    }
  }
```

An Iterator object doing the deleting for you

Putting it all together, we have:

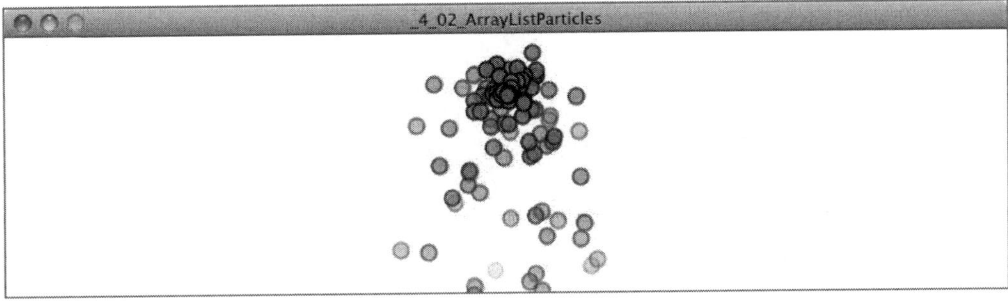

Example 4.2: ArrayList of particles with Iterator

```
ArrayList<Particle> particles;

void setup() {
  size(640,360);
  particles = new ArrayList<Particle>();
}

void draw() {
  background(255);

  particles.add(new Particle(new PVector(width/2,50)));

  Iterator<Particle> it = particles.iterator();
  while (it.hasNext()) {
    Particle p = it.next();
    p.run();
    if (p.isDead()) {
       it.remove();
    }
  }
}
```

Using an Iterator object instead of counting with int i

4.4 The Particle System Class

OK. Now we've done two things. We've written a class to describe an individual `Particle` object. We've conquered the `ArrayList` and used it to manage a list of many `Particle` objects (with the ability to add and delete at will).

We could stop here. However, one additional step we can and should take is to write a class to describe the list of `Particle` objects itself—the `ParticleSystem` class. This will allow us to remove the bulky logic of looping through all particles from the main tab, as well as open up the possibility of having more than one particle system.

If you recall the goal we set at the beginning of this chapter, we wanted our main tab to look like this:

```
ParticleSystem ps;                                  Just one wee ParticleSystem!

void setup() {
  size(640,360);
  ps = new ParticleSystem();
}

void draw() {
  background(255);
  ps.run();
}
```

Let's take the code from Example 4.2 and review a bit of object-oriented programming, looking at how each piece from the main tab can fit into the `ParticleSystem` class.

ArrayList in the main tab	ArrayList in the ParticleSystem class

`ArrayList<Particle> particles;`
 	
`void setup() {`
`  size(640,360);`
`  particles = new ArrayList<Particle>();`
`}`
 	
`void draw() {`
`  background(255);`
 	
`  particles.add(new Particle());`
 	
`  Iterator<Particle> it =`
`      particles.iterator();`
`  while (it.hasNext()) {`
`    Particle p = it.next();`
`    p.run();`
`    if (p.isDead()) {`
`      it.remove();`
`    }`
`  }`
`}`
	`class ParticleSystem {`
	`  ArrayList<Particle> particles;`
	
	`  ParticleSystem() {`
	`    particles = new ArrayList<Particle>();`
	`  }`
	
	`  void addParticle() {`
	`    particles.add(new Particle());`
	`  }`
	
	`  void run() {`
	`    Iterator<Particle> it =`
	`        particles.iterator();`
	`    while (it.hasNext()) {`
	`      Particle p = it.next();`
	`      p.run();`
	`      if (p.isDead()) {`
	`        it.remove();`
	`      }`
	`    }`
	`  }`
	`}`

We could also add some new features to the particle system itself. For example, it might be useful for the `ParticleSystem` class to keep track of an origin point where particles are made. This fits in with the idea of a particle system being an "emitter," a place where particles are born and sent out into the world. The origin point should be initialized in the constructor.

Example 4.3: Simple Single Particle System

```
class ParticleSystem {
  ArrayList particles;
  PVector origin;

  ParticleSystem(PVector location) {
    origin = location.get();
    particles = new ArrayList();
  }

  void addParticle() {
    particles.add(new Particle(origin));
  }
```

This particular ParticleSystem implementation includes an origin point where each Particle begins.

The origin is passed to each Particle when it is added.

Exercise 4.3

Make the origin point move dynamically. Have the particles emit from the mouse location or use the concepts of velocity and acceleration to make the system move autonomously.

Exercise 4.4

Building off Chapter 3's "Asteroids" example, use a particle system to emit particles from the ship's "thrusters" whenever a thrust force is applied. The particles' initial velocity should be related to the ship's current direction.

4.5 A System of Systems

Let's review for a moment where we are. We know how to talk about an individual `Particle` object. We also know how to talk about a system of `Particle` objects, and this we call a "particle system." And we've defined a particle system as a collection of independent objects. But isn't a particle system itself an object? If that's the case (which it is), there's no reason why we couldn't also have a collection of many particle systems, i.e. a system of systems.

This line of thinking could of course take us even further, and you might lock yourself in a basement for days sketching out a diagram of a system of systems of systems of systems of systems of systems. Of systems. After all, this is how the world works. An organ is a system of cells, a human body is a system of organs, a neighborhood is a system of human bodies, a city is a system of neighborhoods, and so on and so forth. While this is an interesting road to travel down, it's a bit beyond where we need to be right now. It is, however, quite useful to know how to write a Processing sketch that keeps track of many particle systems, each of which keep track of many particles. Let's take the following scenario.

You start with a blank screen.

_4_04_SystemofSystems

You click the mouse and generate a particle system at the mouse's location.

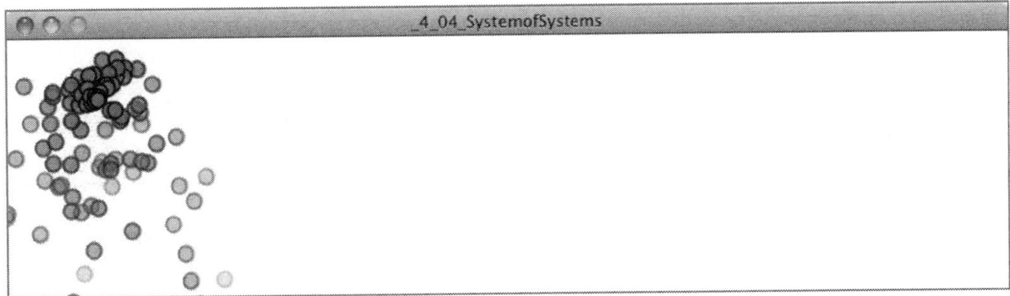

Each time you click the mouse, a new particle system is created at the mouse's location.

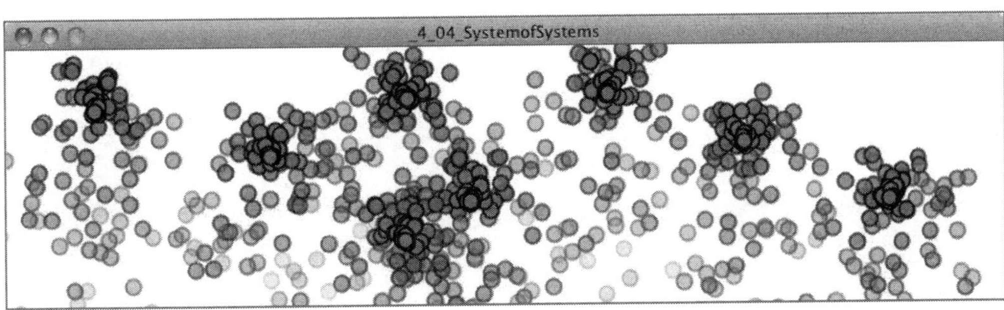

In Example 4.3 (see page 156), we stored a single reference to a `ParticleSystem` object in the variable `ps`.

```
ParticleSystem ps;

void setup() {
  size(640,360);
  ps = new ParticleSystem(1,new PVector(width/2,50));
}

void draw() {
  background(255);
  ps.run();
  ps.addParticle();
}
```

For this new example, what we want to do instead is create an `ArrayList` to keep track of multiple instances of particle systems. When the program starts, i.e. in `setup()`, the `ArrayList` is empty.

Example 4.4: System of systems

```
ArrayList<ParticleSystem> systems;

void setup() {
  size(600,200);
  systems = new ArrayList<ParticleSystem>();
}
```

This time, the type of thing we are putting in the ArrayList is a ParticleSystem itself!

Whenever the mouse is pressed, a new `ParticleSystem` object is created and placed into the `ArrayList`.

```
void mousePressed() {
  systems.add(new ParticleSystem(new PVector(mouseX,mouseY)));
}
```

And in `draw()`, instead of referencing a single `ParticleSystem` object, we now look through all the systems in the `ArrayList` and call `run()` on each of them.

```
void draw() {
  background(255);
  for (ParticleSystem ps: systems) {
    ps.run();
    ps.addParticle();
  }
}
```

Since we aren't deleting elements, we can use our enhanced loop!

Exercise 4.5

Rewrite Example 4.4 so that each particle system doesn't live forever. When a particle system is empty (i.e. has no particles left in its `ArrayList`), remove it from the `ArrayList systems`.

Exercise 4.6

Create a simulation of an object shattering into many pieces. How can you turn one large shape into many small particles? What if there are several large shapes on the screen and they shatter when you click on them?

4.6 Inheritance and Polymorphism: An Introduction

You may have encountered the terms *inheritance* and *polymorphism* in your programming life before this book. After all, they are two of the three fundamental principles behind the theory of object-oriented programming (the other being *encapsulation*). If you've read other Processing or Java programming books, chances are it's been covered. My beginner text, *Learning Processing*, has close to an entire chapter (#22) dedicated to these two topics.

Still, perhaps you've only learned about it in the abstract sense and never had a reason to really use inheritance and polymorphism. If this is true, you've come to the right place. Without these two topics, your ability to program a variety of particles and particle systems is extremely limited. (In the next chapter, we'll also see how understanding these topics will help us to use physics libraries.)

Imagine the following. It's a Saturday morning, you've just gone out for a lovely jog, had a delicious bowl of cereal, and are sitting quietly at your computer with a cup of warm chamomile tea. It's your old friend So and So's birthday and you've decided you'd like to make a greeting card in Processing. How about some confetti for a birthday? Purple confetti, pink confetti, star-shaped confetti, square confetti, fast confetti, fluttery confetti, etc. All of these pieces of confetti with different appearances and different behaviors explode onto the screen at once.

What we've got here is clearly a particle system—a collection of individual pieces of confetti (i.e. particles). We might be able to cleverly design our `Particle` class to have variables that store its color, shape, behavior, etc. And perhaps we initialize the values of these variables randomly. But what if your particles are drastically different? This could become very messy, having all sorts of code for different ways of being a particle in the same class. Well, you might consider doing the following:

```
class HappyConfetti {

}

class FunConfetti {

}

class WackyConfetti {

}
```

This is a nice solution: we have three different classes to describe the different kinds of pieces of confetti that could be part of our particle system. The `ParticleSystem` constructor could then have some code to pick randomly from the three classes when filling the `ArrayList`. Note that this probabilistic method is the same one we employed in our random walk examples in the Introduction (see page 2).

```
class ParticleSystem {
  ParticleSystem(int num) {
    particles = new ArrayList();
    for (int i = 0; i < num; i++) {
      float r = random(1);
```

Randomly picking a "kind" of particle

```
      if      (r < 0.33) { particles.add(new HappyConfetti()); }
      else if (r < 0.67) { particles.add(new FunConfetti());   }
      else               { particles.add(new WackyConfetti()); }
    }
  }
```

OK, we now need to pause for a moment. We've done nothing wrong. All we wanted to do was wish our friend a happy birthday and enjoy writing some code. But while the reasoning behind the above approach is quite sound, we've opened up two major problems.

Problem #1: Aren't we going to be copying/pasting a lot of code between the different "confetti" classes?

Yes. Even though our kinds of particles are different enough to merit our breaking them out into separate classes, there is still a ton of code that they will likely share. They'll all have `PVector`s to keep track of location, velocity, and acceleration; an `update()` function that implements our motion algorithm; etc.

This is where ***inheritance*** comes in. Inheritance allows us to write a class that *inherits* variables and functions from another class, all the while implementing its own custom features.

Problem #2: How will the ArrayList know which objects are which type?

This is a pretty serious problem. Remember, we were using generics to tell the `ArrayList` what type of objects we're going to put inside it. Are we suddenly going to need three different `ArrayList`s?

```
ArrayList<HappyConfetti> a1 = new ArrayList<HappyConfetti>();
ArrayList<FunConfetti>   a2 = new ArrayList<FunConfetti>();
ArrayList<WackyConfetti> a3 = new ArrayList<WackyConfetti>();
```

This seems awfully inconvenient, given that we really just want one list to keep track of all the stuff in the particle system. That can be made possible with polymorphism. Polymorphism will allow us to consider objects of different types as the same type and store them in a single `ArrayList`.

Now that we understand the problem, let's look at these two concepts in a bit more detail and then create a particle system example that implements both inheritance and polymorphism.

4.7 Inheritance Basics

Let's take a different example, the world of animals: dogs, cats, monkeys, pandas, wombats, and sea nettles. We'll start by programming a **Dog** class. A **Dog** object will have an age variable (an integer), as well as `eat()`, `sleep()`, and `bark()` functions.

```
class Dog {
  int age;

  Dog() {
    age = 0;
  }

  void eat() {
    println("Yum!");
  }

  void sleep() {
    println("Zzzzzz");
  }

  void bark() {
    println("WOOF!");
  }
}
```

Dogs and cats have the same variables (age) and functions (eat, sleep).

A unique function for barking.

Now, let's move on to cats.

```
class Cat {
  int age;

  Cat() {
    age = 0;
  }

  void eat() {
    println("Yum!");
  }

  void sleep() {
    println("Zzzzzz");
  }

  void meow() {
    println("MEOW!");
  }
}
```

As we rewrite the same code for fish, horses, koalas, and lemurs, this process will become rather tedious. Instead, let's develop a generic `Animal` class that can describe any type of animal. All animals eat and sleep, after all. We could then say:

- A dog is an animal and has all the properties of animals and can do all the things animals do. Also, a dog can bark.
- A cat is an animal and has all the properties of animals and can do all the things animals do. Also, a cat can meow.

Inheritance makes this all possible. With inheritance, classes can inherit properties (variables) and functionality (methods) from other classes. A `Dog` class is a child (***subclass***) of an `Animal` class. Children will automatically inherit all variables and functions from the parent (***superclass***), but can also include functions and variables not found in the parent. Like a phylogenetic "tree of life," inheritance follows a tree structure. Dogs inherit from canines, which inherit from mammals, which inherit from animals, etc.

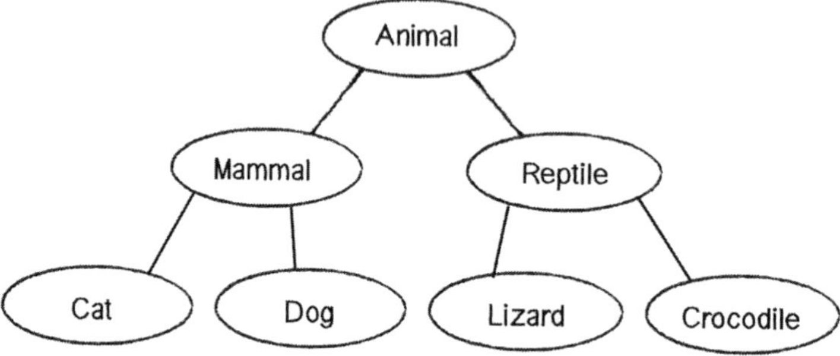

Figure 4.2

Here is how the syntax works with inheritance.

```
class Animal {
```

The Animal class is the parent (or super) class.

```
  int age;
```

Dog and Cat inherit the variable age.

```
  Animal() {
    age = 0;
  }

  void eat() {
    println("Yum!");
  }

  void sleep() {
    println("Zzzzzz");
  }
}
```

Dog and Cat inherit the functions eat() and sleep().

```
class Dog extends Animal {
```

The Dog class is the child (or sub) class, indicated by the code "extends Animal".

```
  Dog() {
    super();
```

super() executes code found in the parent class.

```
  }
  void bark() {
```

We define bark() in the child class, since it isn't part of the parent class.

```
    println("WOOF!");
  }
}

class Cat extends Animal {
  Cat() {
    super();
  }
  void meow() {
    println("MEOW!");
  }
}
```

This brings up two new terms:

- ***extends*** – This keyword is used to indicate a parent for the class being defined. Note that classes can only extend *one* class. However, classes can extend classes that extend other classes, i.e. `Dog extends Animal`, `Terrier extends Dog`. Everything is inherited all the way down the line.
- ***super()*** – This calls the constructor in the parent class. In other words, whatever you do in the parent constructor, do so in the child constructor as well. Other code can be written into the constructor in addition to `super()`. `super()` can also

receive arguments if there is a parent constructor defined with matching arguments.

A subclass can be expanded to include additional functions and properties beyond what is contained in the superclass. For example, let's assume that a `Dog` object has a haircolor variable in addition to age, which is set randomly in the constructor. The class would now look like this:

```
class Dog extends Animal {
  color haircolor;

  Dog() {
    super();
    haircolor = color(random(255));
  }

  void bark() {
    println("WOOF!");
  }
}
```

A child class can introduce new variables not included in the parent.

Note how the parent constructor is called via `super()`, which sets the age to 0, but the haircolor is set inside the `Dog` constructor itself. If a `Dog` object eats differently than a generic `Animal` object, parent functions can be *overridden* by rewriting the function inside the subclass.

```
class Dog extends Animal {
  color haircolor;

  Dog() {
     super();
     haircolor = color(random(255));
  }

  void eat() {
    println("Woof! Woof! Slurp.")
  }

  void bark() {
    println("WOOF!");
  }
}
```

A child can override a parent function if necessary.

A Dog's specific eating characteristics

But what if a dog eats the same way as a generic animal, just with some extra functionality? A subclass can both run the code from a parent class and incorporate custom code.

```
class Dog extends Animal {
  color haircolor;

  Dog() {
    super();
    haircolor = color(random(255));
  }

  void eat() {
    super.eat();
    println("Woof!!!");
  }

  void bark() {
   println("WOOF!");
  }
}
```

Call eat() from Animal. A child can execute a function from the parent while adding its own code.

Add some additional code for a Dog's specific eating characteristics.

4.8 Particles with Inheritance

Now that we've had an introduction to the theory of inheritance and its syntax, we can develop a working example in Processing based on our `Particle` class.

Let's review a simple `Particle` implementation, further simplified from Example 4.1 (see page 147):

```
class Particle {
  PVector location;
  PVector velocity;
  PVector acceleration;

  Particle(PVector l) {
    acceleration = new PVector(0,0.05);
    velocity = new PVector(random(-1,1),random(-2,0));
    location = l.get();
  }

  void run() {
    update();
    display();
  }

  void update() {
    velocity.add(acceleration);
    location.add(velocity);
  }

  void display() {
    fill(0);
    ellipse(location.x,location.y,8,8);
  }
}
```

Next, we create a subclass from `Particle` (let's call it `Confetti`). It will inherit all the instance variables and methods from `Particle`. We write a new constructor with the name `Confetti` and execute the code from the parent class by calling `super()`.

```
class Confetti extends Particle {

  // We could add variables for only Confetti here.

  Confetti(PVector l) {
    super(l);
  }

  // There is no code here because we inherit update() from parent.

  // Override the display method.
  void display() {
    rectMode(CENTER);
    fill(175);
    stroke(0);
    rect(location.x,location.y,8,8);
  }
}
```

Let's make this a bit more sophisticated. Let's say we want to have the `Confetti` particle rotate as it flies through the air. We could, of course, model angular velocity and acceleration as we did in Chapter 3. Instead, we'll try a quick and dirty solution.

We know a particle has an *x* location somewhere between 0 and the width of the window. What if we said: when the particle's *x* location is 0, its rotation should be 0; when its *x* location is equal to the width, its rotation should be equal to `TWO_PI`? Does this ring a bell? Whenever we have a value with one range that we want to map to another range, we can use Processing's `map()` function, which we learned about in the Introduction (see page 17)!

```
float angle = map(location.x,0,width,0,TWO_PI);
```

And just to give it a bit more spin, we can actually map the angle's range from 0 to TWO_PI*2. Let's look at how this code fits into the `display()` function.

```
void display() {
  float theta = map(location.x,0,width,0,TWO_PI*2);

  rectMode(CENTER);
  fill(0,lifespan);
  stroke(0,lifespan);
  pushMatrix();
  translate(location.x,location.y);
  rotate(theta);
  rect(0,0,8,8);
  popMatrix();
}
```

If we rotate() a shape in Processing, we need to familiarize ourselves with transformations. For more, visit: http://processing.org/learning/transform2d/

Exercise 4.7

Instead of using `map()` to calculate theta, how would you model angular velocity and acceleration?

Now that we have a `Confetti` class that extends our base `Particle` class, we need to figure out how our `ParticleSystem` class can manage particles of different types within the same system. To accomplish this goal, let's return to the animal kingdom inheritance example and see how the concept extends into the world of polymorphism.

4.9 Polymorphism Basics

With the concept of inheritance under our belts, we can imagine how we would program a diverse animal kingdom using `ArrayLists`—an array of dogs, an array of cats, of turtles, of kiwis, etc. frolicking about.

```
ArrayList<Dog> dogs = new ArrayList<Dog>();              Separate ArrayLists for each animal
ArrayList<Cat> cats = new ArrayList<Cat>();
ArrayList<Turtle> turtles = new ArrayList<Turtle>();
ArrayList<Kiwi> kiwis = new ArrayList<Kiwi>();
```

```
for (int i = 0; i < 10; i++) {
  dogs.add(new Dog());
}
for (int i = 0; i < 15; i++) {
  cats.add(new Cat());
}
for (int i = 0; i < 6; i++) {
  turtles.add(new Turtle());
}
for (int i = 0; i < 98; i++) {
  kiwis.add(new Kiwi());
}
```

As the day begins, the animals are all pretty hungry and are looking to eat. So it's off to looping time (enhanced looping time!)...

```
for (Dog d: dogs) {                                      Separate loops for each animal
  d.eat();
}
for (Cat c: cats) {
  c.eat();
}
for (Turtle t: turtles) {
  t.eat();
}
for (Kiwi k: kiwis) {
  k.eat();
}
```

This works well, but as our world expands to include many more animal species, we're going to get stuck writing a lot of individual loops. Is this really necessary? After all, the creatures are all animals, and they all like to eat. Why not just have one `ArrayList` of `Animal` objects and fill it with all different *kinds* of animals?

```
ArrayList<Animal> kingdom = new ArrayList<Animal>();
```

Just one ArrayList for all the animals!

```
for (int i = 0; i < 1000; i++) {
  if (i < 100) kingdom.add(new Dog());
  else if (i < 400) kingdom.add(new Cat());
  else if (i < 900) kingdom.add(new Turtle());
  else kingdom.add(new Kiwi());
}

for (Animal a: kingdom) {
  a.eat();
}
```

The ability to treat a `Dog` object as either a member of the `Dog` class or the `Animal` class (its parent) is an example of polymorphism. ***Polymorphism*** (from the Greek *polymorphos*, meaning many forms) refers to the treatment of a single instance of an object in multiple forms. A dog is certainly a dog, but since `Dog extends Animal`, it can also be considered an animal. In code, we can refer to it both ways.

```
Dog rover = new Dog();
Animal spot = new Dog();
```

Although the second line of code might initially seem to violate syntax rules, both ways of declaring a `Dog` object are legal. Even though we declare `spot` as an `Animal` object, we're really making a `Dog` object and storing it in the `spot` variable. And we can safely call all of the `Animal` class methods on spot because the rules of inheritance dictate that a dog can do anything an animal can.

What if the `Dog` class, however, overrides the `eat()` function in the `Animal` class? Even if spot is declared as an `Animal`, Java will determine that its true identity is that of a `Dog` and run the appropriate version of the `eat()` function.

This is particularly useful when we have an array or `ArrayList`.

4.10 Particle Systems with Polymorphism

Let's pretend for a moment that polymorphism doesn't exist and rewrite a `ParticleSystem` class to include many `Particle` objects and many `Confetti` objects.

```
class ParticleSystem {
  ArrayList<Particle> particles;
  ArrayList<Confetti> confetti;
```

We're stuck doing everything twice with two lists!

```
  PVector origin;

  ParticleSystem(PVector location) {
    origin = location.get();
    particles = new ArrayList<Particle>();
    confetti = new ArrayList<Confetti>();
  }

  void addParticle() {
    particles.add(new Particle(origin));
    particles.add(new Confetti(origin));
  }

  void run() {
    Iterator<Particle> it = particles.iterator();
    while (it.hasNext()) {
      Particle p = it.next();
      p.run();
      if (p.isDead()) {
        it.remove();
      }
    }
    it = confetti.iterator();
    while (it.hasNext()) {
      Confetti c = it.next();
      c.run();
      if (c.isDead()) {
        it.remove();
      }
    }
  }
}
```

We're stuck doing everything twice with two lists!

We're stuck doing everything twice with two lists!

We're stuck doing everything twice with two lists!

Notice how we have two separate lists, one for particles and one for confetti. Every action we want to perform we have to do twice! Polymorphism allows us to simplify the above by just making one `ArrayList` of particles that contains both standard `Particle` objects as well as `Confetti` objects. We don't have to worry about which are which; this will all be taken care of for us! (Also, note that the code for the main program and the classes has not changed, so we aren't including it here. See the website for the full example.)

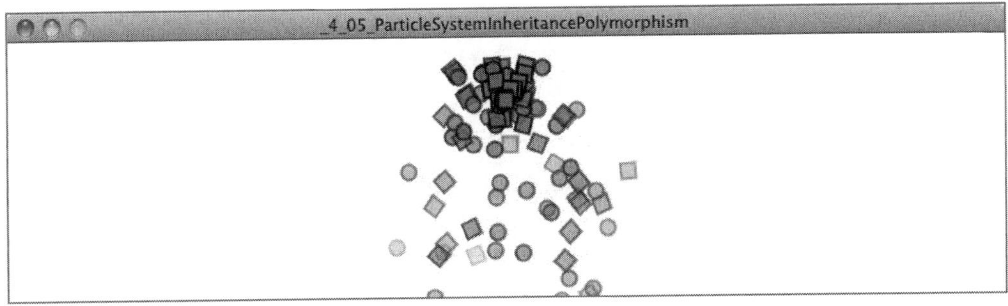

Example 4.5: Particle system inheritance and polymorphism

```
class ParticleSystem {
  ArrayList<Particle> particles;
  PVector origin;

  ParticleSystem(PVector location) {
    origin = location.get();
    particles = new ArrayList<Particle>();
  }

  void addParticle() {
    float r = random(1);
    if (r < 0.5) {
      particles.add(new Particle(origin));
    } else {
      particles.add(new Confetti(origin));
    }
  }

  void run() {
    Iterator<Particle> it = particles.iterator();
    while (it.hasNext()) {
      Particle p = it.next();
      p.run();
      if (p.isDead()) {
        it.remove();
      }
    }
  }
}
```

One list, for anything that is a Particle or extends Particle

We have a 50% chance of adding each kind of Particle.

Polymorphism allows us to treat everything as a Particle, whether it is a Particle or a Confetti.

Exercise 4.8

Create a particle system with different "kinds" of particles in the same system. Try varying more than just the look of the particles. How do you deal with different behaviors using inheritance?

4.11 Particle Systems with Forces

So far in this chapter, we've been focusing on structuring our code in an object-oriented way to manage a collection of particles. Maybe you noticed, or maybe you didn't, but during this process we unwittingly took a couple steps backward from where we were in previous chapters. Let's examine the constructor of our simple `Particle` class.

```
Particle(PVector l) {
  acceleration = new PVector(0,0.05);
  velocity = new PVector(random(-1,1),random(-2,0));
  location = l.get();
  lifespan = 255.0;
}
```

We're setting acceleration to a constant value!

And now let's look at the `update()` function.

```
void update() {
  velocity.add(acceleration);
  location.add(velocity);

  // Where is the line of code to clear acceleration?

  lifespan -= 2.0;
}
```

Our `Particle` class is structured to have a constant acceleration, one that never changes. A much better framework would be to follow Newton's second law (F = M* A) and incorporate the force accumulation algorithm we worked so hard on in Chapter 2 (see page 68).

Step 1 would be to add in the `applyForce()` function. (Remember, we need to make a copy of the `PVector` before we divide it by mass.)

```
void applyForce(PVector force) {
  PVector f = force.get();
  f.div(mass);
  acceleration.add(f);
}
```

Once we have this, we can add in one more line of code to clear the acceleration at the end of `update()`.

```
void update() {
  velocity.add(acceleration);
  location.add(velocity);
  acceleration.mult(0);        There it is!
  lifespan -= 2.0;
}
```

And our `Particle` class is complete!

```
class Particle {
  PVector location;
  PVector velocity;
  PVector acceleration;
  float lifespan;

  float mass = 1;        We could vary mass for more interesting results.

  Particle(PVector l) {
    acceleration = new PVector(0,0);        We now start with acceleration of 0.
    velocity = new PVector(random(-1,1),random(-2,0));
    location = l.get();
    lifespan = 255.0;
  }

  void run() {
    update();
    display();
  }

  void applyForce(PVector force) {        Newton's second law & force accumulation
    PVector f = force.get();
    f.div(mass);
    acceleration.add(f);
  }

  void update() {        Standard update
    velocity.add(acceleration);
    location.add(velocity);
    acceleration.mult(0);
    lifespan -= 2.0;
  }
```

```
  void display() {                                  Our Particle is a circle.
    stroke(255,lifespan);
    fill(255,lifespan);
    ellipse(location.x,location.y,8,8);
  }

  boolean isDead() {                                Should the Particle be deleted?
    if (lifespan < 0.0) {
      return true;
    } else {
      return false;
    }
  }
}
```

Now that the `Particle` class is completed, we have a very important question to ask. Where do we call the `applyForce()` function? Where in the code is it appropriate to apply a force to a particle? The truth of the matter is that there's no right or wrong answer; it really depends on the exact functionality and goals of a particular Processing sketch. Still, we can create a generic situation that would likely apply to most cases and craft a model for applying forces to individual particles in a system.

Let's consider the following goal: Apply a force globally every time through `draw()` to all particles. We'll pick an easy one for now: a force pointing down, like gravity.

```
PVector gravity = new PVector(0,0.1);
```

We said it should always be applied, i.e. in `draw()`, so let's take a look at our `draw()` function as it stands.

```
void draw() {
  background(100);
  ps.addParticle();
  ps.run();
}
```

Well, it seems that we have a small problem. `applyForce()` is a method written inside the `Particle` class, but we don't have any reference to the individual particles themselves, only the `ParticleSystem` object: the variable `ps`.

Since we want all particles to receive the force, however, we can decide to apply the force to the particle system and let it manage applying the force to all the individual particles:

```
void draw() {
  background(100);

  PVector gravity = new PVector(0,0.1);
```

```
    ps.applyForce(gravity);                    Applying a force to the system as a whole

    ps.addParticle();
    ps.run();
}
```

Of course, if we call a new function on the `ParticleSystem` object in `draw()`, well, we have to write that function in the `ParticleSystem` class. Let's describe the job that function needs to perform: receive a force as a `PVector` and apply that force to all the particles.

Now in code:

```
void applyForce(PVector f) {
  for (Particle p: particles) {
    p.applyForce(f);
  }
}
```

It almost seems silly to write this function. What we're saying is "apply a force to a particle system so that the system can apply that force to all of the individual particles." Nevertheless, it's really quite reasonable. After all, the `ParticleSystem` object is in charge of managing the particles, so if we want to talk to the particles, we've got to talk to them through their manager. (Also, here's a chance for the enhanced loop since we aren't deleting particles!)

Here is the full example (assuming the existence of the `Particle` class written above; no need to include it again since nothing has changed):

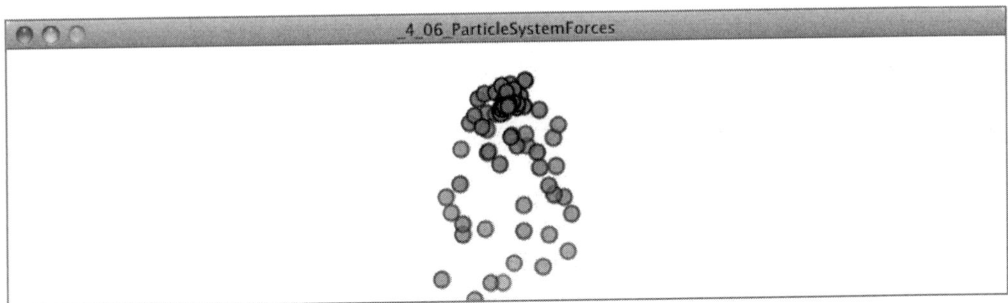

Example 4.6: Particle system with forces

```
ParticleSystem ps;

void setup() {
  size(640,360);
  ps = new ParticleSystem(new PVector(width/2,50));
}

void draw() {
  background(100);

  PVector gravity = new PVector(0,0.1);      // Apply a force to all particles.
  ps.applyForce(gravity);

  ps.addParticle();
  ps.run();
}


class ParticleSystem {
  ArrayList<Particle> particles;
  PVector origin;

  ParticleSystem(PVector location) {
    origin = location.get();
    particles = new ArrayList<Particle>();
  }

  void addParticle() {
    particles.add(new Particle(origin));
  }

  void applyForce(PVector f) {
    for (Particle p: particles) {            // Using an enhanced loop to apply the force
      p.applyForce(f);                       // to all particles
    }
  }

  void run() {
    Iterator<Particle> it = particles.iterator();   // Can't use the enhanced loop because we
    while (it.hasNext()) {                          // want to check for particles to delete.
      Particle p = (Particle) it.next();
      p.run();
      if (p.isDead()) {
        it.remove();
      }
    }
  }
}
```

4.12 Particle Systems with Repellers

What if we wanted to take this example one step further and add a `Repeller` object—the inverse of the `Attractor` object we covered in Chapter 2 (see page 88) that pushes any particles away that get close? This requires a bit more sophistication because, unlike the gravity force, each force an attractor or repeller exerts on a particle must be calculated for each particle.

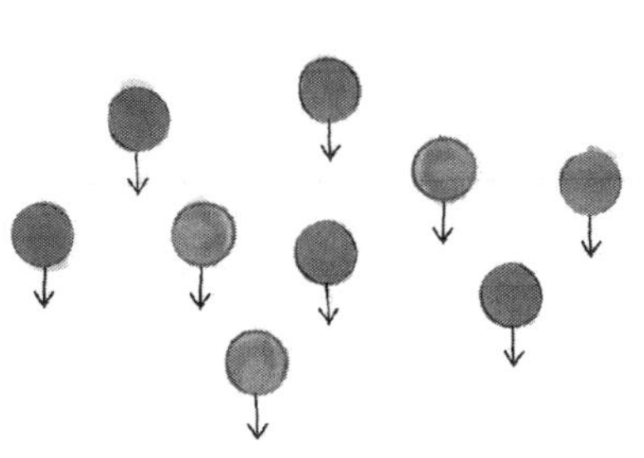

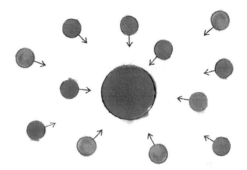

Figure 4.3: Gravity force—vectors are all identical

Figure 4.4: Attractor force—vectors are all different

Let's start solving this problem by examining how we would incorporate a new `Repeller` object into our simple particle system plus forces example. We're going to need two major additions to our code:

1. A `Repeller` object (declared, initialized, and displayed).
2. A function that passes the `Repeller` object into the `ParticleSystem` so that it can apply a force to each particle object.

```
ParticleSystem ps;
Repeller repeller;
```

New thing: we declare a Repeller object.

```
void setup() {
  size(640,360);
  ps = new ParticleSystem(new PVector(width/2,50));
```

```
  repeller = new Repeller(width/2-20,height/2);      New thing: we initialize a Repeller object.
}

void draw() {
  background(100);
  ps.addParticle();

  PVector gravity = new PVector(0,0.1);
  ps.applyForce(gravity);

  ps.applyRepeller(repeller);                        New thing: we need a function to apply a
                                                     force from a repeller.
  ps.run();
  repeller.display();                                New thing: we display the Repeller object.
}
```

Making a `Repeller` object is quite easy; it's a duplicate of the `Attractor` class from Chapter 2, Example 2.6 .

```
class Repeller {
  PVector location;                                  A Repeller doesn't move, so you just need
  float r = 10;                                      location.

  Repeller(float x, float y)  {
    location = new PVector(x,y);
  }

  void display() {
    stroke(255);
    fill(255);
    ellipse(location.x,location.y,r*2,r*2);
  }
}
```

The more difficult question is, how do we write the `applyRepeller()` function? Instead of passing a `PVector` into a function like we do with `applyForce()`, we're going to instead pass a `Repeller` object into `applyRepeller()` and ask that function to do the work of calculating the force between the repeller and all particles. Let's look at both of these functions side by side.

applyForce()	applyRepeller

`void applyForce(PVector f) {`
`  for (Particle p: particles) {`
`    p.applyForce(f);`
`  }`
`}`
	`void applyRepeller(Repeller r) {`
	`  for (Particle p: particles) {`
	`    PVector force = r.repel(p);`
	`    p.applyForce(force);`
	`  }`
	`}`

The functions are almost identical. There are only two differences. One we mentioned before—a `Repeller` object is the argument, not a `PVector`. The second difference is the important one. We must calculate a custom `PVector` force for each and every particle and apply that force. How is that force calculated? In a function called `repel()`, which is the inverse of the `attract()` function we wrote for the `Attractor` class.

```
PVector repel(Particle p) {
```

All the same steps we had to calculate an attractive force, only pointing in the opposite direction.

```
  PVector dir =
    PVector.sub(location,p.location);
```

1) Get force direction.

```
  float d = dir.mag();
  d = constrain(d,5,100);
```

2) Get distance (constrain distance).

```
  dir.normalize();
  float force = -1 * G / (d * d);
```

3) Calculate magnitude.

```
  dir.mult(force);
```

4) Make a vector out of direction and magnitude.

```
  return dir;
}
```

Notice how throughout this entire process of adding a repeller to the environment, we've never once considered editing the `Particle` class itself. A particle doesn't actually have to know anything about the details of its environment; it simply needs to manage its location, velocity, and acceleration, as well as have the ability to receive an external force and act on it.

So we can now look at this example in its entirety, again leaving out the `Particle` class, which hasn't changed.

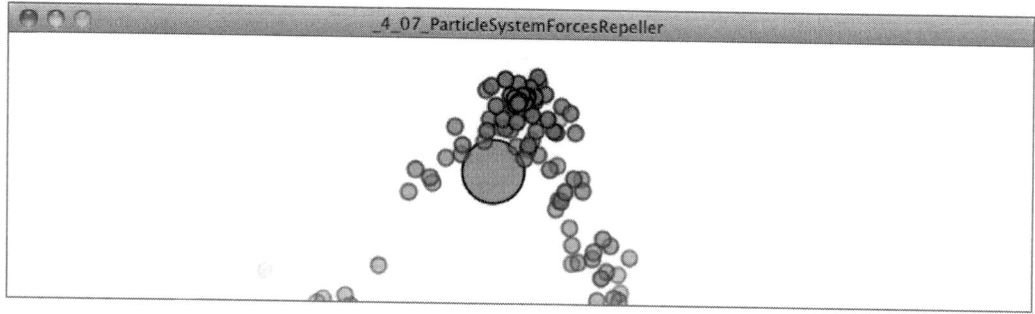

Example 4.7: ParticleSystem with repeller

```
ParticleSystem ps;                          // One ParticleSystem
Repeller repeller;                          // One repeller

void setup() {
  size(640,360);
  ps = new ParticleSystem(new PVector(width/2,50));
  repeller = new Repeller(width/2-20,height/2);
}

void draw() {
  background(100);
  ps.addParticle();
  PVector gravity = new PVector(0,0.1);     // We're applying a universal gravity.
  ps.applyForce(gravity);
  ps.applyRepeller(repeller);               // Applying the repeller

  ps.run();
  repeller.display();
}


class ParticleSystem {                      // The ParticleSystem manages all the Particles.
  ArrayList<Particle> particles;
  PVector origin;

  ParticleSystem(PVector location) {
    origin = location.get();
    particles = new ArrayList<Particle>();
  }

  void addParticle() {
    particles.add(new Particle(origin));
  }
```

```
  void applyForce(PVector f) {
    for (Particle p: particles) {
      p.applyForce(f);
    }
  }

  void applyRepeller(Repeller r) {
    for (Particle p: particles) {
      PVector force = r.repel(p);
      p.applyForce(force);
    }
  }

  void run() {
    Iterator<Particle> it = particles.iterator();
    while (it.hasNext()) {
      Particle p = (Particle) it.next();
      p.run();
      if (p.isDead()) {
        it.remove();
      }
    }
  }
}

class Repeller {

  float strength = 100;
  PVector location;
  float r = 10;

  Repeller(float x, float y)  {
    location = new PVector(x,y);
  }

  void display() {
    stroke(255);
    fill(255);
    ellipse(location.x,location.y,r*2,r*2);
  }

  PVector repel(Particle p) {
    PVector dir =
PVector.sub(location,p.location);
    float d = dir.mag();
    dir.normalize();
    d = constrain(d,5,100);
    float force = -1 * strength / (d * d);
    dir.mult(force);
    return dir;
```

Applying a force as a PVector

Calculating a force for each Particle based on a Repeller

How strong is the repeller?

This is the same repel algorithm we used in Chapter 2: forces based on gravitational attraction.

```
    }
  }
```

Exercise 4.9

Expand the above example to include many repellers (using an array or `ArrayList`).

Exercise 4.10

Create a particle system in which each particle responds to every other particle. (Note that we'll be going through this in detail in Chapter 6.)

4.13 Image Textures and Additive Blending

Even though this book is really about behaviors and algorithms rather than computer graphics and design, I don't think we would be able to live with ourselves if we went through a discussion of particle systems and never once looked at an example that involves texturing each particle with an image. The way you choose to draw a particle is a big part of the puzzle in terms of designing certain types of visual effects.

Let's try to create a smoke simulation in Processing. Take a look at the following two images:

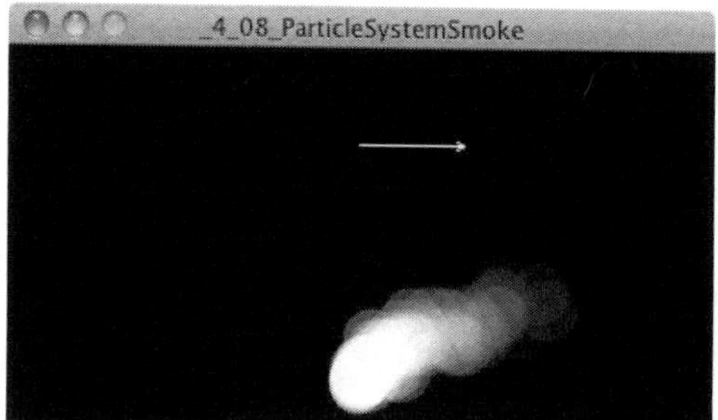

White circles

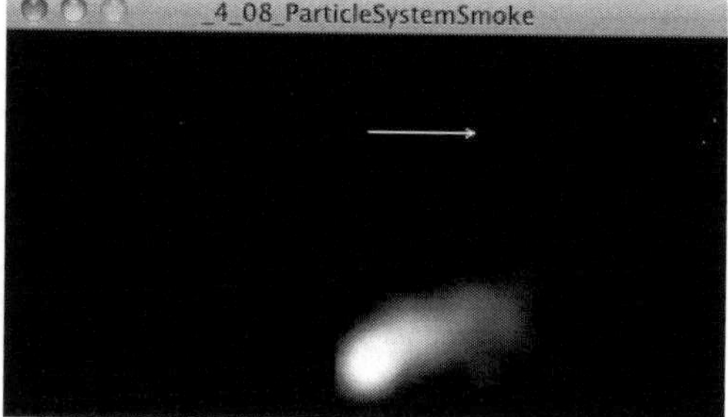

Fuzzy images with transparency

Both of these images were generated from identical algorithms. The only difference is that a white circle is drawn in image A for each particle and a "fuzzy" blob is drawn for each in B.

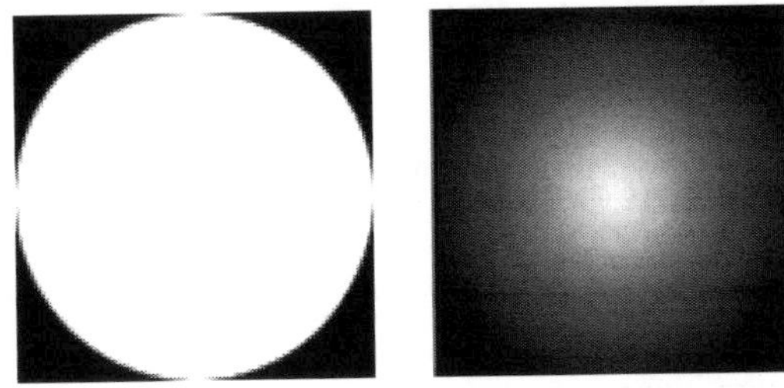

Figure 4.5

The good news here is that you get a lot of bang for very little buck. Before you write any code, however, you've got to make your image texture! I recommend using PNG format, as Processing will retain the alpha channel (i.e. transparency) when drawing the image, which is needed for blending the texture as particles layer on top of each other. Once you've made your PNG and deposited it in your sketch's "data" folder, you are on your way with just a few lines of code.

First, we'll need to declare a `PImage` object.

Example 4.8: Image texture particle system

```
PImage img;
```

Load the image in `setup()`.

```
void setup() {
  img = loadImage("texture.png");      // Loading the PNG
}
```

And when it comes time to draw the particle, we'll use the image reference instead of drawing an ellipse or rectangle.

```
void render() {
  imageMode(CENTER);
  tint(255,lifespan);       // Note how tint() is the image equivalent of shape's fill().
  image(img,loc.x,loc.y);
}
```

Incidentally, this smoke example is a nice excuse to revisit the Gaussian number distributions from the Introduction (see page 10). To make the smoke appear a bit more realistic, we don't want to launch all the particles in a purely random direction. Instead, by creating initial velocity vectors mostly around a mean value (with a lower probability of outliers), we'll get an effect that appears less fountain-like and more like smoke (or fire).

Assuming a Random object called "generator", we could create initial velocities as follows:

```
float vx = (float) generator.nextGaussian()*0.3;
float vy = (float) generator.nextGaussian()*0.3 - 1.0;
vel = new PVector(vx,vy);
```

Finally, in this example, a wind force is applied to the smoke mapped from the mouse's horizontal location.

```
void draw() {
  background(0);

  float dx = map(mouseX,0,width,-0.2,0.2);
  PVector wind = new PVector(dx,0);          // Wind force points towards mouseX.
  ps.applyForce(wind);
  ps.run();
  for (int i = 0; i < 2; i++) {              // Two particles are added each cycle through draw().
    ps.addParticle();
  }
}
```

Exercise 4.11

Try creating your own textures for different types of effects. Can you make it look like fire, instead of smoke?

Exercise 4.12

Use an array of images and assign each `Particle` object a different image. Even though single images are drawn by multiple particles, make sure you don't call `loadImage()` any more than you need to, i.e. once for each image file.

Finally, it's worth noting that there are many different algorithms for blending colors in computer graphics. These are often referred to as "blend modes." By default, when we draw something on top of something else in Processing, we only see the top layer—this is commonly referred to as a "normal" blend mode. When the pixels have alpha transparency (as they do in the smoke example), Processing uses an alpha compositing algorithm that combines a percentage of the background pixels with the new foreground pixels based on the alpha values.

However, it's possible to draw using other blend modes, and a much loved blend mode for particle systems is "additive." Additive blending in Processing was pioneered by Robert Hodgin (http://roberthodgin.com/) in his famous particle system and forces exploration,

Magnetosphere, which later became the iTunes visualizer. For more see: Magnetosphere (http://roberthodgin.com/magnetosphere-part-2/).

Additive blending is in fact one of the simplest blend algorithms and involves adding the pixel values of one layer to another (capping all values at 255 of course). This results in a space-age glow effect due to the colors getting brighter and brighter with more layers.

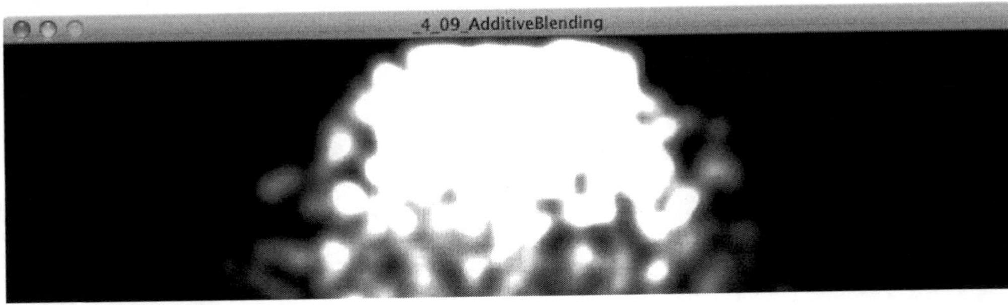

To achieve additive blending in Processing, you'll need to use the P2D or P3D renderer.

Example 4.9: Additive blending

```
void setup() {
  size(640,360,P2D);            // Using the P2D renderer
}
```

Then, before you go to draw anything, you set the blend mode using `blendMode()`:

```
void draw() {
  blendMode(ADD);               // Additive blending

  background(0);                // Note that the "glowing" effect of additive
                                // blending will not work with a white (or very
                                // bright) background.

                                // All your other particle stuff would go here.
}
```

Exercise 4.13

Use `tint()` in combination with additive blending to create a rainbow effect.

Exercise 4.14

Try blending with other modes, such as `SUBTRACT`, `LIGHTEST`, `DARKEST`, `DIFFERENCE`, `EXCLUSION`,or `MULTIPLY`.

The Ecosystem Project

Step 4 Exercise:

Take your creature from Step 3 and build a system of creatures. How can they interact with each other? Can you use inheritance and polymorphism to create a variety of creatures, derived from the same code base? Develop a methodology for how they compete for resources (for example, food). Can you track a creature's "health" much like we tracked a particle's lifespan, removing creatures when appropriate? What rules can you incorporate to control how creatures are born?

(Also, you might consider using a particle system itself in the design of a creature. What happens if your emitter is tied to the creature's location?)

Chapter 5. Physics Libraries

"A library implies an act of faith/Which generations still in darkness hid/ Sign in their night in witness of the dawn."

— Victor Hugo

Before we move on to anything else, let's revisit some of the things we've done in the first four chapters. We have:

1. Learned about concepts from the world of physics — What is a vector? What is a force? What is a wave? etc.
2. Understood the math and algorithms behind such concepts.
3. Implemented the algorithms in Processing with an object-oriented approach.

These activities have yielded a set of motion simulation examples, allowing us to creatively define the physics of the worlds we build (whether realistic or fantastical). Of course, we aren't the first to try this. The world of computer graphics and programming is full of source code dedicated to simulation. Just try Googling "open-source physics engine" and you could spend the rest of your day pouring over rich and complex code. And so we must ask the question: If a code library will take care of physics simulation, why should we bother learning how to write any of the algorithms ourselves?

Here is where the philosophy behind this book comes into play. While many of the libraries out there give us physics (and super awesome advanced physics at that) for free, there are significant reasons for learning the fundamentals from scratch before diving into libraries. First, without an understanding of vectors, forces, and trigonometry, we'd be completely lost just reading the documentation of a library. Second, even though a library may take care of the math for us, it won't necessarily simplify our code. As we'll see in a moment, there can be a great deal of overhead in simply understanding how a library works and what it expects from you code-wise. Finally, as wonderful as a physics engine might be, if you look deep down into your hearts, it's likely that you seek to create worlds and visualizations that stretch the limits of imagination. A library is great, but it provides a limited set of features. It's important to know both when to live within limitations in the pursuit of a Processing project and when those limits prove to be confining.

This chapter is dedicated to examining two open-source physics libraries—Box2D and toxiclibs' VerletPhysics engine. With each library, we'll evaluate its pros and cons and look at reasons why you might choose one of these libraries for a given project.

5.1 What Is Box2D and When Is It Useful?

Box2D began as a set of physics tutorials written in C++ by Erin Catto for the Game Developer's Conference in 2006. Over the last five years it has evolved into an rich and elaborate open-source physics engine. It's been used for countless projects, most notably highly successful games such as the award-winning puzzle game Crayon Physics and the runaway mobile and tablet hit Angry Birds.

One of the key things to realize about Box2D is that it is a true physics engine. Box2D knows nothing about computer graphics and the world of pixels; it is simply a library that takes in numbers and spits out more numbers. And what are those numbers? Meters, kilograms, seconds, etc. All of Box2D's measurements and calculations are for real-world measurements—only its "world" is a two-dimensional plane with top, bottom, left, and right edges. You tell it things like: "The gravity of our world is 9.81 newtons per kilogram, and a circle with a radius of four meters and a mass of fifty kilograms is located ten meters above the world's bottom." Box2D will then tell you things like: "One second later, the rectangle is at five meters from the bottom; two seconds later, it is ten meters below," etc. While this provides for an amazing and realistic physics engine, it also necessitates lots of complicated code in order to translate back and forth between the physics "world" (a key term in Box2D) and the world we want to draw on —the "pixel" world of Processing.

So when is it worth it to have this additional overhead? If I just want to simulate a circle falling down a Processing window with gravity, do I really need to write all the extra Box2D code just to get that effect? Certainly, the answer is no. We saw how to do this rather easily in the first chapter of this book. Let's consider another scenario. What if I want to have a hundred of those circles falling? And what if those circles aren't circles at all, but irregularly shaped polygons? And what if I want these polygons to bounce off each other in a realistic manner when they collide?

You may have noticed that the first four chapters of this book, while covering motion and forces in detail, has skipped over a rather important aspect of physics simulation—*collisions*. Let's pretend for a moment that you aren't reading a chapter about libraries and that we decided right now to cover how to handle collisions in a particle system. We'd have to evaluate and learn two distinct algorithms that address these questions:

1. How do I determine if two shapes are colliding (i.e. intersecting)?
2. How do I determine the shapes' velocity after the collision?

If we're thinking about shapes like rectangles or circles, question #1 isn't too tough. You've likely encountered this before. For example, we know two circles are intersecting if the distance between them is less than the sum of their radii.

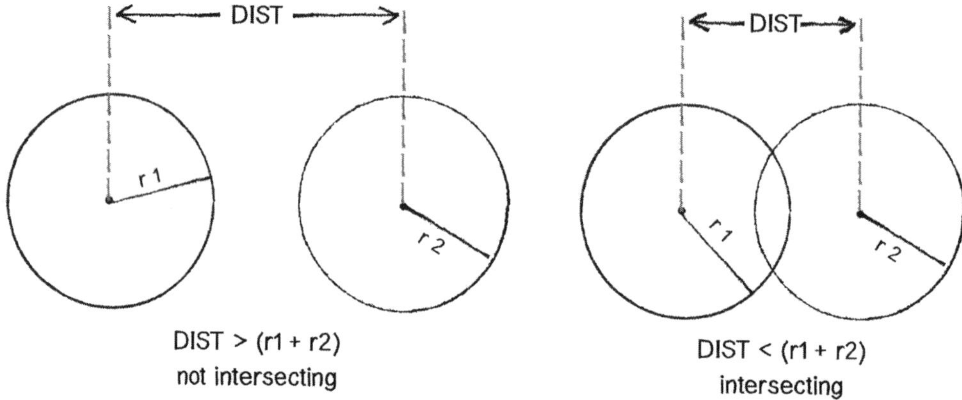

Figure 5.1

OK. Now that we know how to determine if two circles are colliding, how do we calculate their velocities after the collision? This is where we're going to stop our discussion. Why, you ask? It's not that understanding the math behind collisions isn't important or valuable. (In fact, I'm including additional examples on the website related to collisions without a physics library.) The reason for stopping is that life is short (let this also be a reason for you to consider going outside and frolicking instead of programming altogether). We can't expect to master every detail of physics simulation. And while we could continue this discussion for circles, it's only going to lead us to wanting to work with rectangles. And strangely shaped polygons. And curved surfaces. And swinging pendulums colliding with springy springs. And and and and and.

Working with collisions in our Processing sketch while still having time to spend with our friends and family—that's the reason for this chapter. Erin Catto spent years developing solutions to these kinds of problems so you don't need to engineer them yourselves, at least for now.

In conclusion, if you find yourself describing an idea for a Processing sketch and the word "collisions" comes up, then it's likely time to learn Box2D. (We'll also encounter other words that might lead you down this path to Box2D, such as "joint," "hinge," "pulley," "motor," etc.)

5.2 Getting Box2D in Processing

So, if Box2D is a physics engine that knows nothing about pixel-based computer graphics and is written in C++, how are we supposed to use it in Processing?

The good news is that Box2D is such an amazing and useful library that everyone wants to use it—Flash, Javascript, Python, Ruby programmers. Oh, and Java programmers. There is something called JBox2D, a Java port of Box2D. And because Processing is built on top of Java, JBox2D can be used directly in Processing!

So here's where we are so far.

- Box2D site (http://www.box2d.org/) for reference.
- JBox2D site (http://www.jbox2d.org/) for Processing compatibility.

This is all you need to get started writing Box2D code in Processing. However, as we are going to see in a moment, there are several pieces of functionality we'll repeatedly need in our Processing code, and so it's worth having one additional layer between our sketches and JBox2D. I'm calling this PBox2D—a Processing Box2D "helper" library included as part of this book's code example downloads.

- PBox2D GitHub repository (http://github.com/shiffman/PBox2D)

It's important to realize that PBox2D is not a Processing wrapper for all of Box2D. After all, Box2D is a thoughtfully organized and well-structured API and there's no reason to take it apart and re-implement it. However, it's useful to have a small set of functions that help you get your Box2D world set up, as well as help you figure out where to draw your Box2D shapes. And this is what PBox2D will provide.

I should also mention before we move forward that there are other Processing libraries that wrap Box2D for you. One I would recommend taking a look at is Fisica (http://www.ricardmarxer.com/fisica/) by Ricard Marxer.

5.3 Box2D Basics

Do not despair! We really are going to get to the code very soon, and in some ways we'll blow our previous work out of the water. But before we're ready to do that, it's important to walk through the overall process of using Box2D in Processing. Let's begin by writing a pseudocode generalization of all of our examples in Chapters 1 through 4.

SETUP:

1. Create all the objects in our world.

DRAW:

1. Calculate all the forces in our world.
2. Apply all the forces to our objects (F = M * A).
3. Update the locations of all the objects based on their acceleration.
4. Draw all of our objects.

Great. Let's rewrite this pseudocode as it will appear in our Box2D examples.

SETUP:

1. Create all the objects in our world.

DRAW:

1. Draw all of our objects.

This, of course, is the fantasy of Box2D. We've eliminated all of those painful steps of figuring out how the objects are moving according to velocity and acceleration. Box2D is going to take care of this for us! The good news is that this does accurately reflect the overall process. Let's imagine Box2D as a magic box.

In `setup()`, we're going to say to Box2D: "Hello there. Here are all of the things I want in my world." In `draw()`, we're going to politely ask Box2D: "Oh, hello again. If it's not too much trouble, I'd like to draw all of those things in my world. Could you tell me where they are?"

The bad news: it's not as simple as the above explanation would lead you to believe. For one, making the stuff that goes in the Box2D world involves wading through the documentation for how different kinds of shapes are built and configured. Second, we have to remember that we can't tell Box2D anything about pixels, as it will simply get confused and fall apart. Before we tell Box2D what we want in our world, we have to convert our pixel units to Box2D "world" units. And the same is true when it comes time to draw our stuff. Box2D is going to tell us the location of the things in its world, which we then have to translate for the pixel world.

SETUP

1. Create everything that lives in our pixel world.

2. Translate the pixel world into the Box2D world.

DRAW

1. Ask Box2D where everything is.
2. Translate Box2D's answer into the pixel world.
3. Draw everything.

Now that we understand that anything we create in our Processing sketch has to be placed into the Box2D world, let's look at an overview of the elements that make up that world.

Core elements of a Box2D world:

1. ***World***: Manages the physics simulation. It knows everything about the overall coordinate space and also stores lists of every element in the world (see 2-4 below).
2. ***Body***: Serves as the primary element in the Box2D world. It has a location. It has a velocity. Sound familiar? The `Body` is essentially the class we've been writing on our own in our vectors and forces examples.
3. ***Shape***: Keeps track of all the necessary collision geometry attached to a body.
4. ***Fixture***: Attaches a shape to a body and sets properties such as density, friction, and restitution.
5. ***Joint***: Acts as a connection between two bodies (or between one body and the world itself).

In the next four sections, we are going to walk through each of the above elements in detail, building several examples along the way. But first there is one other important element we should briefly discuss.

6. ***Vec2***: Describes a vector in the Box2D world.

And so here we are, arriving with trepidation at an unfortunate truth in the world of using physics libraries. Any physics simulation is going to involve the concept of a vector. This is the good part. After all, we just spent several chapters familiarizing ourselves with what it means to describe motion and forces with vectors. We don't have to learn anything new conceptually.

Now for the part that makes the single tear fall from my eye: we don't get to use `PVector`. It's nice that Processing has `PVector` for us, but anytime you use a physics library you will probably discover that the library includes its own vector implementation. This makes sense, after all; why should Box2D be expected to know about `PVector`? And in many cases, the physics engine will want to implement a vector class in a specific way so that it is especially compatible with the rest of the library's code. So while we don't have to learn anything new conceptually, we do have to get used to some new naming conventions and syntax. Let's quickly demonstrate a few of the basics in `Vec2` as compared to those in `PVector`.

Let's say we want to add two vectors together.

PVector	Vec2

`PVector a = new PVector(1,-1);`
`PVector b = new PVector(3,4);`
`a.add(b);`
	`Vec2 a = new Vec2(1,-1);`
	`Vec2 b = new Vec2(3,4);`
	`a.addLocal(b);`

`PVector a = new PVector(1,-1);`
`PVector b = new PVector(3,4);`
`PVector c = PVector.add(a,b);`
	`Vec2 a = new Vec2(1,-1);`
	`Vec2 b = new Vec2(3,4);`
	`Vec2 c = a.add(b);`

How about if we want to multiply and scale them?

PVector	Vec2

`PVector a = new PVector(1,-1);`
`float n = 5;`
`a.mult(n);`
	`Vec2 a = new Vec2(1,-1);`
	`float n = 5;`
	`a.mulLocal(n);`

`PVector a = new PVector(1,-1);`
`float n = 5;`
`PVector c = PVector.mult(a,n);`
	`Vec2 a = new Vec2(1,-1);`
	`float n = 5;`
	`Vec2 c = a.mul(n);`

Magnitude and normalize?

PVector	Vec2

`PVector a = new PVector(1,-1);`
`float m = a.mag();`
`a.normalize();`
	`Vec2 a = new Vec2(1,-1);`
	`float m = a.length();`
	`a.normalize();`

As you can see, the concepts are the same, but the function names and the arguments are slightly different. For example, instead of static and non-static `add()` and `mult()`, if a `Vec2` is altered, the word "local" is included in the function name—`addLocal()`, `multLocal()`.

We'll cover the basics of what you need to know here, but if you are looking for more, full documentation of Vec2 can be found by downloading the JBox2D source code (http://code.google.com/p/jbox2d/).

5.4 Living in a Box2D World

The Box2D World object is in charge of everything. It manages the coordinate space of the world, all of the stuff that lives in the world, and decides when time moves forward in the world.

In order to have Box2D as part of our Processing sketches, the World is the very first thing that needs to be set up. Here is where PBox2D comes in handy and takes care of making the world for us.

```
PBox2D box2d;

void setup() {
  box2d = new PBox2D(this);
  box2d.createWorld();
}
```

Initializes a Box2D world with default settings

When you call createWorld(), PBox2D will set up a default gravity for you (pointing down); however, you can always alter the gravity of your world by saying:

```
box2d.setGravity(0, -10);
```

It's worth noting that gravity doesn't have to be fixed, nor does it always have to point downwards; you can adjust the gravity vector while your program is running. Gravity can be turned off by setting it to a (0,0) vector.

So, what are those numbers 0 and -10? This should remind us of one of the most important details of using Box2D: the Box2D coordinate system is not your pixel coordinate system! Let's look at how Box2D and a Processing window think differently of their worlds.

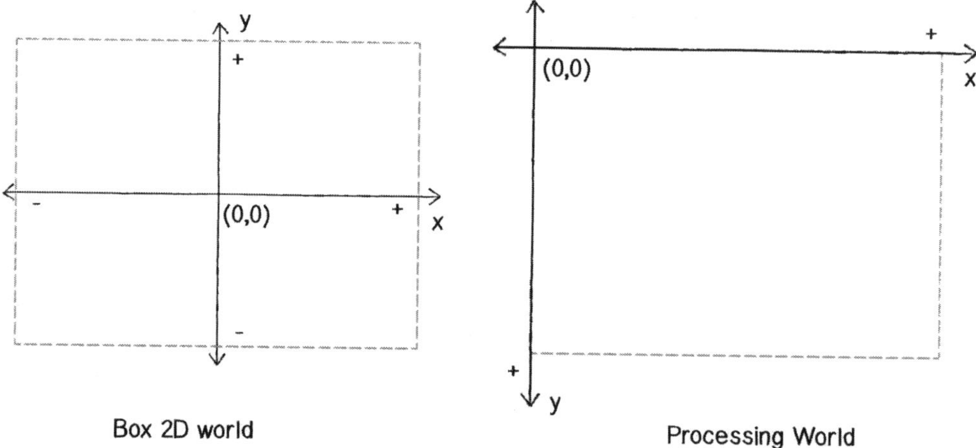

Figure 5.2

Notice how in Box2D *(0,0)* is in the center and *up* is the positive direction along the y-axis! Box2D's coordinate system is just like that lovely old-fashioned Cartesian one with *(0,0)* in the center and *up* pointing in a positive direction. Processing, on the other hand, uses a traditional computer graphics coordinate system where *(0,0)* is in the top left corner and *down* is the positive direction along the y-axis. This is why if we want objects to fall down with gravity, we need to give Box2D a gravity force with a negative y-value.

```
Vec2 gravity = new Vec2(0, -10);
```

Luckily for us, if we prefer to think in terms of pixel coordinates (which as Processing programmers, we are likely to do), PBox2D offers a series of helper functions that convert between pixel space and Box2D space. Before we move onto the next section and begin creating Box2D bodies, let's take a look at how these helper functions work.

Let's say we want to tell Box2D where the mouse is in its world. We know the mouse is located at `(mouseX,mouseY)` in Processing. To convert it, we say we want to convert a "coordinate" from "pixels" to "world"—`coordPixelsToWorld()`. Or:

```
Vec2 mouseWorld =
box2d.coordPixelsToWorld(mouseX,mouseY);
```

Convert mouseX,mouseY to coordinate in Box2D world.

What if we had a Box2D world coordinate and wanted to translate it to our pixel space?

```
Vec2 worldPos = new Vec2(-10,25);
```

To demonstrate, let's just make up a world position.

```
Vec2 pixelPos = box2d.coordWorldToPixels(worldPos);
ellipse(pixelPos.x, pixelPos.y,16,16);
```

Convert to pixel space. This is necessary because ultimately we are going to want to draw the elements in our window.

PBox2D has a set of functions to take care of translating back and forth between the Box2D world and pixels. It's probably easier to learn about all of these functions during the course of actually implementing our examples, but let's quickly look over the list of the possibilities.

Task	Function
Convert location from World to Pixels	`Vec2 coordWorldToPixels(Vec2 world)`
Convert location from World to Pixels	`Vec2 coordWorldToPixels(float worldX, float worldY)`
Convert location from Pixels to World	`Vec2 coordPixelsToWorld(Vec2 screen)`
Convert location from Pixels to World	`Vec2 coordPixelsToWorld(float pixelX, float pixelY)`
Scale a dimension (such as height, width, or radius) from Pixels to World	`float scalarPixelsToWorld(float val)`
Scale a dimension from World to Pixels	`float scalarWorldToPixels(float val)`

There are also additional functions that allow you to pass or receive a `PVector` when translating back and forth, but since we are only working with Box2D in the examples in this chapter, it's easiest to stick with the `Vec2` class for all vectors.

Once the world is initialized, we are ready to actually put stuff in the world—Box2D bodies.

5.5 Building a Box2D Body

A Box2D body is the primary element in the Box2D world. It's the equivalent to the `Mover` class we built on our own in previous chapters—the thing that moves around the space and experiences forces. It can also be static (meaning fixed and not moving). It's important to note, however, that a body has no geometry; it isn't anything physical. Rather, bodies have Box2D shapes attached to them. (This way, a body can be a single rectangle or a rectangle attached to a circle, etc.) We'll look at shapes in a moment; first, let's build a body.

Step 1: Define a body.

The first thing we have to do is create a "body definition." This will let us define the properties of the body we intend to make. This may seem a bit awkward at first, but it's how Box2D is structured. Anytime you want to make a "thing," you have to make a "thing definition" first. This will hold true for bodies, shapes, and joints.

```
BodyDef bd = new BodyDef();
```

Make a body definition before making a Body.

Step 2: Configure the body definition.

The body definition is where we can set specific properties or attributes of the body we intend to make. One attribute of a body, for example, is its starting location. Let's say we want to position the body in the center of the Processing window.

```
Vec2 center = new Vec2(width/2,height/2);
```

A Vec2 in the center of the Processing window

Danger, danger! I'm not going to address this with every single example, but it's important to at least point out the perilous path we are taking with the above line of code. Remember, if we are going to tell Box2D where we want the body to start, we must give Box2D a world coordinate! Yes, we want to think of its location in terms of pixels, but Box2D doesn't care. And so before we pass that position to the body definition, we must make sure to use one of our helper conversion functions.

```
Vec2 center =
box2d.coordPixelsToWorld(width/2,height/2));
```

A Vec2 in the center of the Processing window converted to Box2D World coordinates!

```
bd.position.set(center);
```

Setting the position attribute of the Box2D body definition

The body definition must also specify the "type" of body we want to make. There are three possibilities:

- ***Dynamic.*** This is what we will use most often—a "fully simulated" body. A dynamic body moves around the world, collides with other bodies, and responds to the forces in its environment.
- ***Static.*** A static body is one that cannot move (as if it had an infinite mass). We'll use static bodies for fixed platforms and boundaries.
- ***Kinematic.*** A kinematic body can be moved manually by setting its velocity directly. If you have a user-controlled object in your world, you can use a kinematic body. Note that kinematic bodies collide only with dynamic bodies and not with other static or kinematic ones.

There are several other properties you can set in the body definition. For example, if you want your body to have a fixed rotation (i.e. never rotate), you can say:

```
bd.fixedRotation = true;
```

You can also set a value for linear or angular damping, so that the object continuously slows as if there is friction.

```
bd.linearDamping = 0.8;
bd.angularDamping = 0.9;
```

In addition, fast-moving objects in Box2D should be set as bullets. This tells the Box2D engine that the object may move very quickly and to check its collisions more carefully so that it doesn't accidentally jump over another body.

```
bd.bullet = true;
```

Step 3: Create the body.

Once we're done with the definition (`BodyDef`), we can create the `Body` object itself. PBox2D provides a helper function for this—`createBody()`.

```
Body body = box2d.createBody(bd);
```

The Body object is created by passing in the Body Definition. (This allows for making multiple bodies from one definition.)

Step 4: Set any other conditions for the body's starting state.

Finally, though not required, if you want to set any other initial conditions for the body, such as linear or angular velocity, you can do so with the newly created `Body` object.

```
body.setLinearVelocity(new Vec2(0,3));
```

Setting an arbitrary initial velocity

```
body.setAngularVelocity(1.2);
```

Setting an arbitrary initial angular velocity

5.6 Three's Company: Bodies and Shapes and Fixtures

A body on its own doesn't physically exist in the world. It's like a soul with no human form to inhabit. For a body to have mass, we must first define a shape and attach that shape to the body with something known as a fixture.

The job of the Box2D `Shape` class is to keep track of all the necessary collision geometry attached to a body. A shape also has several important properties that affect the body's motion. There is density, which ultimately determines that body's mass. Shapes also have *friction* and *restitution* ("bounciness") which will be defined through a fixture. One of the nice things about Box2D's methodology, which separates the concepts of bodies and shapes into two separate objects, is that you can attach multiple shapes to a single body in order to create more complex forms. We'll see this in a future example.

To create a shape, we need to first decide what kind of shape we want to make. For most non-circular shapes, a `PolygonShape` object will work just fine. For example, let's look at how we define a rectangle.

Step 1: Define a shape.

```
PolygonShape ps = new PolygonShape();
```

Define the shape: a polygon.

Next up, we have to define the width and height of the rectangle. Let's say we want our rectangle to be 150×100 pixels. Remember, pixel units are no good for Box2D shapes! So we have to use our helper functions to convert them first.

```
float box2Dw = box2d.scalarPixelsToWorld(150);
float box2Dh = box2d.scalarPixelsToWorld(100);
```

Scale dimensions from pixels to Box2D world.

```
ps.setAsBox(box2Dw, box2Dh);
```

Use setAsBox() function to define shape as a rectangle.

Step 2: Create a fixture.

The shape and body are made as two separate entities. In order to attach a shape to a body, we must make a fixture. A fixture is created, just as with the body, via a fixture definition (i.e. `FixtureDef` class) and assigned a shape.

```
FixtureDef fd = new FixtureDef();
fd.shape = ps;
```

The fixture is assigned the PolygonShape we just made.

Once we have the fixture definition, we can set parameters that affect the physics for the shape being attached.

```
fd.friction = 0.3;
```

The coefficient of friction for the shape, typically between 0 and 1

```
fd.restitution = 0.5;
```

The Shape's restitution (i.e. elasticity), typically between 0 and 1

```
fd.density = 1.0;
```

The Shape's density, measured in kilograms per meter squared

Step 3: Attach the shape to the body with the fixture.

Once the fixture is defined, all we have left to do is attach the shape to the body with the fixture by calling the `createFixture()` function.

```
body.createFixture(fd);
```

Creates the Fixture and attaches the Shape to the Body object

I should note that Step 2 can be skipped if you do not need to set the physics properties. (Box2D will use default values.) You can create a fixture and attach the shape all in one step by saying:

```
body.createFixture(ps,1);
```

Creates the Fixture and attaches the Shape with a density of 1

While most of our examples will take care of attaching shapes only once when the body is first built, this is not a limitation of Box2D. Box2D allows for shapes to be created and destroyed on the fly.

Before we put any of this code we've been writing into a Processing sketch, let's review all the steps we took to construct a Body.

1. Define a body using a `BodyDef` object (set any properties, such as location).
2. Create the `Body` object from the body definition.
3. Define a `Shape` object using `PolygonShape`, `CircleShape`, or any other shape class.
4. Define a fixture using `FixtureDef` and assign the fixture a shape (set any properties, such as friction, density, and restitution).
5. Attach the shape to the body.

```
BodyDef bd = new BodyDef();
bd.position.set(box2d.coordPixelsToWorld(width/2,height/2));
```

Step 1. Define the body.

```
Body body = box2d.createBody(bd);
```

Step 2. Create the body.

```
PolygonShape ps = new PolygonShape();
float w = box2d.scalarPixelsToWorld(150);
float h = box2d.scalarPixelsToWorld(100);
ps.setAsBox(w, h);
```

Step 3. Define the shape.

```
FixtureDef fd = new FixtureDef();
```

Step 4. Define the fixture.

```
fd.shape = ps;
fd.density = 1;
fd.friction = 0.3;
fd.restitution = 0.5;
```

```
body.createFixture(fd);
```

Step 5. Attach the shape to the body with the Fixture.

Exercise 5.1

Knowing what you know about Box2D so far, fill in the blank in the code below that demonstrates how to make a circular shape in Box2D.

```
CircleShape cs = new CircleShape();
float radius = 10;
cs.m_radius = ____________________;
FixtureDef fd = new FixtureDef();
fd.shape = cs;
fd.density = 1;
fd.friction = 0.1;
fd.restitution = 0.3;

body.createFixture(fd);
```

5.7 Box2D and Processing: Reunited and It Feels So Good

Once a body is made, it lives in the Box2D physics world. Box2D will always know it's there, check it for collisions, move it appropriately according to the forces, etc. It'll do all that for you without you having to lift a finger! What it won't do, however, is display the body for you. This is a good thing. This is your time to shine. When working with Box2D, what we're essentially saying is, "I want to be the designer of my world, and I want you, Box2D, to compute all the physics."

Now, Box2D will keep a list of all the bodies that exist in the world. This can be accessed by calling the World object's `getBodyList()` function. Nevertheless, what I'm going to demonstrate here is a technique for keeping your own body lists. Yes, this may be a bit redundant and we perhaps sacrifice a bit of efficiency. But we more than make up for that with ease of use. This methodology will allow us to program like we're used to in Processing, and we can easily keep track of which bodies are which and render them appropriately. Let's consider the structure of the following Processing sketch:

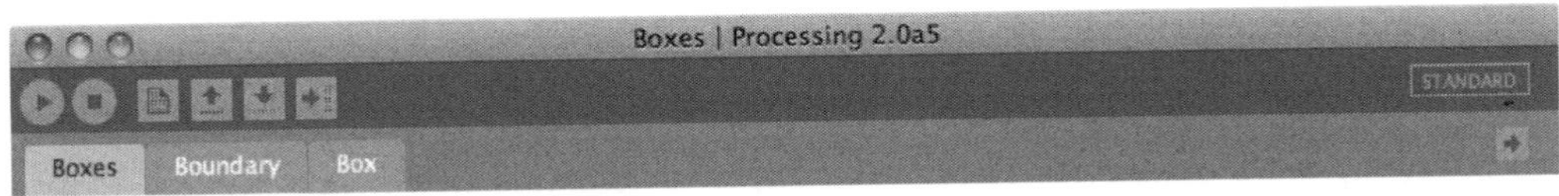

Figure 5.3

This looks like any ol' Processing sketch. We have a main tab called "Boxes" and a "Boundary" and a "Box" tab. Let's think about the Box tab for a moment. The Box tab is where we will write a simple class to describe a Box object, a rectangular body in our world.

```
class Box  {

  float x,y;
  float w,h;

  Box(float x_, float y_) {
    x = x_;
    y = y_;
    w = 16;
    h = 16;
  }

  void display() {
    fill(175);
    stroke(0);
    rectMode(CENTER);
    rect(x,y,w,h);
  }
}
```

Our Box object has an x,y location and a width and a height.

The location is initalized in the constructor via arguments

We draw the Box object using Processing's rect() function.

Let's write a main tab that creates a new Box whenever the mouse is pressed and stores all the Box objects in an ArrayList. (This is very similar to our approach in the particle system examples from Chapter 4.)

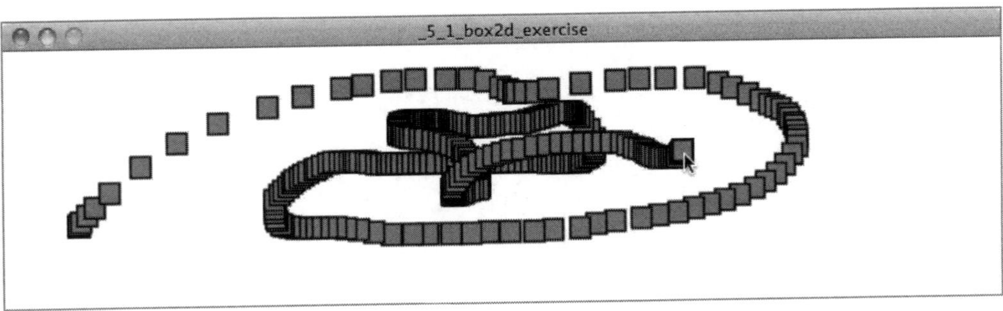

Example 5.1: A comfortable and cozy Processing sketch that needs a little Box2D

```
ArrayList<Box> boxes;
```

A list to store all Box objects

```
void setup() {
  size(400,300);
  boxes = new ArrayList<Box>();
}

void draw() {
  background(255);

  if (mousePressed) {
    Box p = new Box(mouseX,mouseY);
    boxes.add(p);
  }
```

When the mouse is pressed, add a new Box object.

```
  for (Box b: boxes) {
    b.display();
  }
}
```

Display all the Box objects.

Now, here's our assignment. Take the above example verbatim, but instead of drawing fixed boxes on the screen, draw boxes that experience physics (via Box2D) as soon as they appear.

We'll need two major steps to accomplish our goal.

Step 1: Add Box2D to our main program (i.e. setup() and draw()).

This part is not too tough. We saw this already in our discussion of building a Box2D world. This is taken care of for us by the PBox2D helper class. We can create a PBox2D object and initialize it in `setup()`.

```
PBox2D box2d;

void setup() {
  box2d = new PBox2D(this);
  box2d.createWorld();
}
```

Initialize and create the Box2D world.

Then in `draw()`, we need to make sure we call one very important function: `step()`. Without this function, nothing would ever happen! `step()` advances the Box2D world a step further in time. Internally, Box2D sweeps through and looks at all of the Bodies and figures out what to do with them. Just calling `step()` on its own moves the Box2D world forward with default settings; however, it is customizable (and this is documented in the PBox2D source).

```
void draw() {
  box2d.step();
}
```

We must always step through time!

Step 2: Link every Processing Box object with a Box2D Body object.

As of this moment, the Box class includes variables for location and width and height. What we now want to say is:

"I hereby relinquish the command of this object's position to Box2D. I no longer need to keep track of anything related to location, velocity, and acceleration. Instead, I only need to keep track of a Box2D body and have faith that Box2D will do the rest."

```
class Box  {

  Body body;

  float w;
  float h;
```

Instead of any of the usual variables, we will store a reference to a Box2D body.

We don't need *(x,y)* anymore since, as we'll see, the body itself will keep track of its location. The body technically could also keep track of the width and height for us, but since Box2D isn't going to do anything to alter those values over the life of the Box object, we might as well just hold onto them ourselves until it's time to draw the Box.

Then, in our constructor, in addition to initializing the width and height, we can go ahead and include all of the body and shape code we learned in the previous two sections!

```
  Box() {
    w = 16;
    h = 16;

    BodyDef bd = new BodyDef();
    bd.type = BodyType.DYNAMIC;
    bd.position.set(box2d.coordPixelsToWorld(mouseX,mouseY));
    body = box2d.createBody(bd);

    PolygonShape ps = new PolygonShape();

    float box2dW = box2d.scalarPixelsToWorld(w/2);
    float box2dH = box2d.scalarPixelsToWorld(h/2);
```

Build body.

Build shape.

Box2D considers the width and height of a rectangle to be the distance from the center to the edge (so half of what we normally think of as width or height).

```
    ps.setAsBox(box2dW, box2dH);

    FixtureDef fd = new FixtureDef();
    fd.shape = ps;
    fd.density = 1;
    fd.friction = 0.3;                         Set physics parameters.
    fd.restitution = 0.5;

    body.createFixture(fd);                    Attach the Shape to the Body with the
  }                                            Fixture.
```

OK, we're almost there. Before we introduced Box2D, it was easy to draw the Box. The object's location was stored in variables x and y.

```
  void display() {                             Drawing the object using rect()
    fill(175);
    stroke(0);
    rectMode(CENTER);
    rect(x,y,w,h);
  }
```

But now Box2D manages the object's motion, so we can no longer use our own variables to display the shape. Not to fear! Our Box object has a reference to the Box2D body associated with it. So all we need to do is politely ask the body, "Pardon me, where are you located?" Since this is a task we'll need to do quite often, PBox2D includes a helper function: `getBodyPixelCoord()`.

```
Vec2 pos = box2d.getBodyPixelCoord(body);
```

Just knowing the location of a body isn't enough; we also need to know its angle of rotation.

```
float a = body.getAngle();
```

Once we have the location and angle, it's easy to display the object using `translate()` and `rotate()`. Note, however, that the Box2D coordinate system considers rotation in the opposite direction from Processing, so we need to multiply the angle by -1.

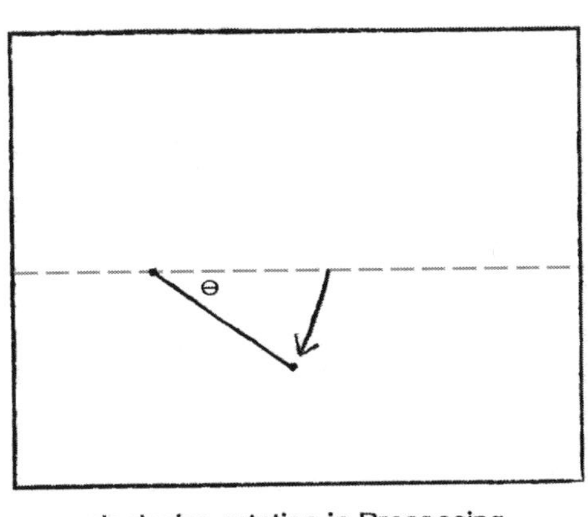

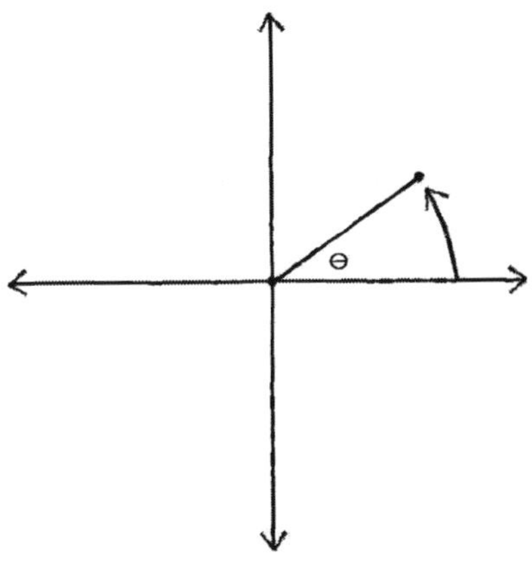

Figure 5.4

```
void display() {
  Vec2 pos = box2d.getBodyPixelCoord(body);
  float a = body.getAngle();

  pushMatrix();
  translate(pos.x,pos.y);
  rotate(-a);
  fill(175);
  stroke(0);
  rectMode(CENTER);
  rect(0,0,w,h);
  popMatrix();
}
```

We need the Body's location and angle.

Using the Vec2 position and float angle to translate and rotate the rectangle

In case we want to have objects that can be removed from the Box2D world, it's also useful to include a function to destroy a body, such as:

```
void killBody() {
  box2d.destroyBody(body);
}
```

This function removes a body from the Box2D world.

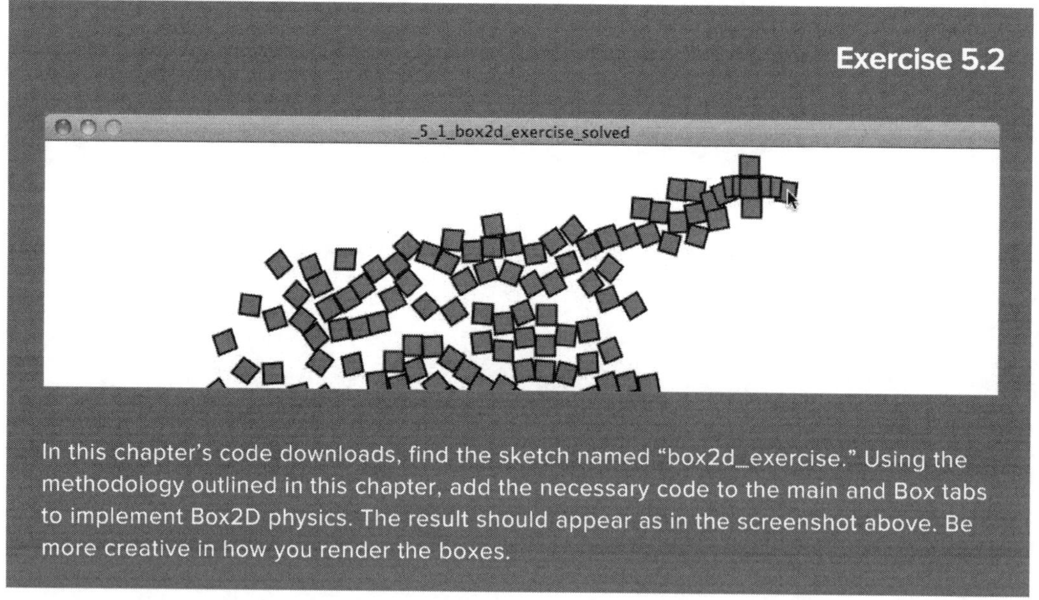

Exercise 5.2

In this chapter's code downloads, find the sketch named "box2d_exercise." Using the methodology outlined in this chapter, add the necessary code to the main and Box tabs to implement Box2D physics. The result should appear as in the screenshot above. Be more creative in how you render the boxes.

5.8 Fixed Box2D Objects

In the example we just created, the `Box` objects appear at the mouse location and fall downwards due to Box2D's default gravity force. What if we wanted to install some immovable boundaries in the Box2D world that would block the path of the `Box` objects (as in the illustration below)?

Box2D makes this easy for us by providing a means to lock a body (and any associated shapes) in place. Just set the `BodyDef` object's type to `STATIC`.

```
BodyDef bd = new BodyDef();
bd.type = BodyType.STATIC;
```

When BodyDef type = STATIC, the Body is locked in place.

We can add this feature to our Boxes example by writing a `Boundary` class and having each boundary create a fixed Box2D body.

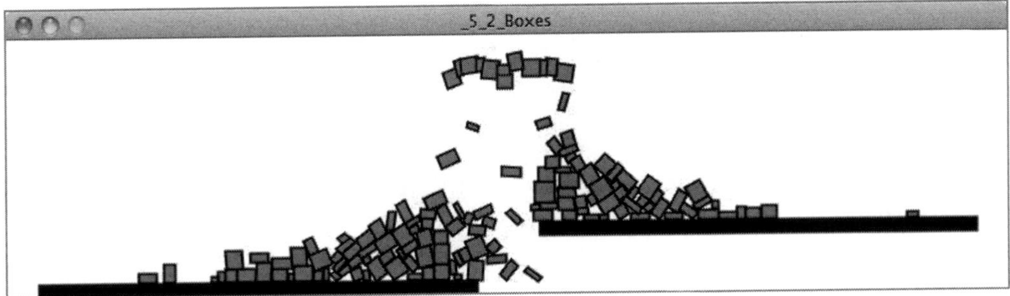

Example 5.2: Falling boxes hitting boundaries

```
class Boundary {

  float x,y;
  float w,h;
```
A boundary is a simple rectangle with x, y, width, and height.

```
  Body b;

  Boundary(float x_,float y_, float w_, float h_) {
    x = x_;
    y = y_;
    w = w_;
    h = h_;

    BodyDef bd = new BodyDef();
```
Build the Box2D Body and Shape.

```
    bd.position.set(box2d.coordPixelsToWorld(x,y));
    bd.type = BodyType.STATIC;
```
Make it fixed by setting type to STATIC!

```
    b = box2d.createBody(bd);

    float box2dW = box2d.scalarPixelsToWorld(w/2);
    float box2dH = box2d.scalarPixelsToWorld(h/2);
    PolygonShape ps = new PolygonShape();
    ps.setAsBox(box2dW, box2dH);
```
The PolygonShape is just a box.

```
    b.createFixture(ps,1);
```
Using the createFixture() shortcut

```
  }

  void display() {
```
Since we know it can never move, we can just draw it the old-fashioned way, using our original variables. No need to query Box2D.

```
    fill(0);
    stroke(0);
    rectMode(CENTER);
    rect(x,y,w,h);
  }

}
```

5.9 A Curvy Boundary

If you want a fixed boundary that is a curved surface (as opposed to a polygon), this can be achieved with the shape `ChainShape`.

The `ChainShape` class is another shape like `PolygonShape` or `CircleShape`, so to include one in our system, we follow the same steps.

Step 1: Define a body.

```
BodyDef bd = new BodyDef();
Body body = box2d.world.createBody(bd);
```

The body does not need a position; the EdgeShape will take care of that for us. It also does not need a type, as it is STATIC by default.

Step 2: Define the Shape.

```
ChainShape chain = new ChainShape();
```

Step 3: Configure the Shape.

The `ChainShape` object is a series of connected vertices. To create the chain, we must first specify an array of vertices (each as a `Vec2` object). For example, if we wanted a straight line from the left-hand side of our window to the right-hand side, we would just need an array of two vertices: (0,150) and (width,150). (Note that if you want to create a loop where the first vertex connects to the last vertex in a loop, you can use the `ChainLoop` class instead.)

```
Vec2[] vertices = new Vec2[2];
vertices[0] = box2d.coordPixelsToWorld(0,150);      // Adding a vertex on the right side of window
vertices[1] = box2d.coordPixelsToWorld(width,150);  // Adding a vertex on the left side of window
```

To create the chain with the vertices, the array is then passed into a function called `createChain()`.

```
chain.createChain(vertices, vertices.length);
```

If you don't want to use the entire array, you can specify a value less than length.

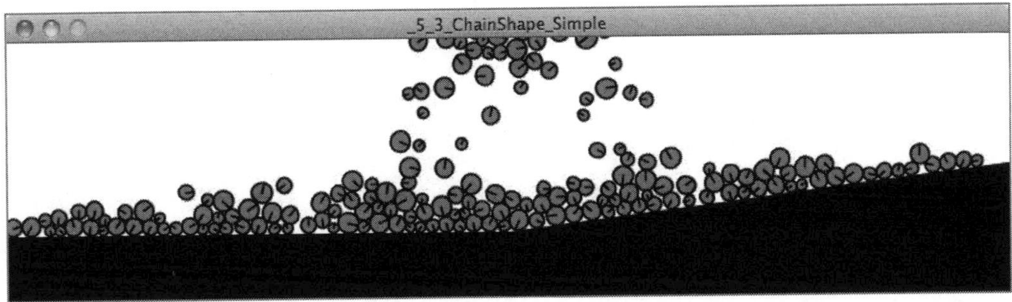

Step 4: Attach the Shape to the body with a Fixture.

A Shape is not part of Box2D unless it is attached to a body. Even if it is a fixed boundary and never moves, it must still be attached. Just as with other shapes, a ChainShape object can be given properties like restitution and friction with a Fixture.

```
FixtureDef fd = new FixtureDef();
fd.shape = chain;                    A fixture assigned to the ChainShape
fd.density = 1;
fd.friction = 0.3;
fd.restitution = 0.5;

body.createFixture(fd);
```

Now, if we want to include a ChainShape object in our sketch, we can follow the same strategy as we did with a fixed boundary. Let's write a class called Surface:

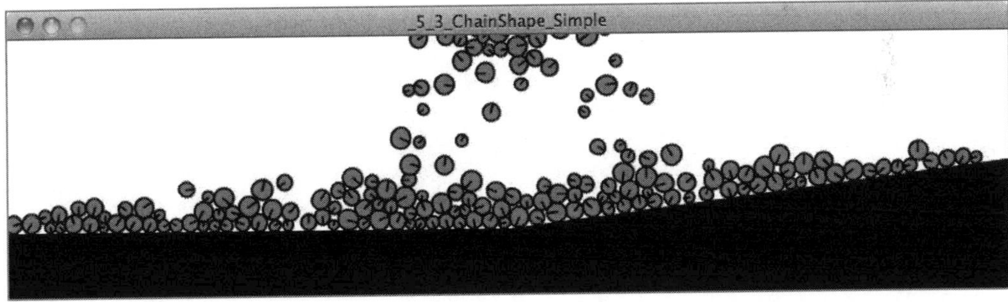

Example 5.3: ChainShape with three hard-coded vertices

```
class Surface {
  ArrayList<Vec2> surface;

  Surface() {

    surface = new ArrayList<Vec2>();
    surface.add(new Vec2(0, height/2+50));           // 3 vertices in pixel coordinates
    surface.add(new Vec2(width/2, height/2+50));
    surface.add(new Vec2(width, height/2));

    ChainShape chain = new ChainShape();

    Vec2[] vertices = new Vec2[surface.size()];      // Make an array of Vec2 for the ChainShape.

    for (int i = 0; i < vertices.length; i++) {      // Convert each vertex to Box2D World coordinates.
      vertices[i] = box2d.coordPixelsToWorld(surface.get(i));
    }

    chain.createChain(vertices, vertices.length);    // Create the ChainShape with array of Vec2.

    BodyDef bd = new BodyDef();                      // Attach the Shape to the Body.
    Body body = box2d.world.createBody(bd);
    body.createFixture(chain, 1);
  }
```

Notice how the above class includes an `ArrayList` to store a series of `Vec2` objects. Even though we fully intend to store the coordinates of the chain in the chain shape itself, we are choosing the ease of redundancy and keeping our own list of those points as well. Later, when we go to draw the `Surface` object, we don't have to ask Box2D for the locations of the chain shape's vertices.

```
  void display() {
    strokeWeight(1);
    stroke(0);
    noFill();
    beginShape();                  // Draw the ChainShape as a series of vertices.
    for (Vec2 v: surface) {
      vertex(v.x,v.y);
    }
    endShape();
  }
}
```

What we need in `setup()` and `draw()` for the `Surface` object is quite simple, given that Box2D takes care of all of the physics for us.

```
PBox2D box2d;

Surface surface;

void setup() {
  size(500,300);
  box2d = new PBox2D(this);
  box2d.createWorld();

  surface = new Surface();                  // Make a Surface object.
}

void draw() {
  box2d.step();

  background(255);
  surface.display();                        // Draw the Surface.
}
```

Exercise 5.3

Review how we learned to draw a wave pattern in Chapter 3. Create a `ChainShape` object out of a sine wave. Try using Perlin noise (see page 17) as well.

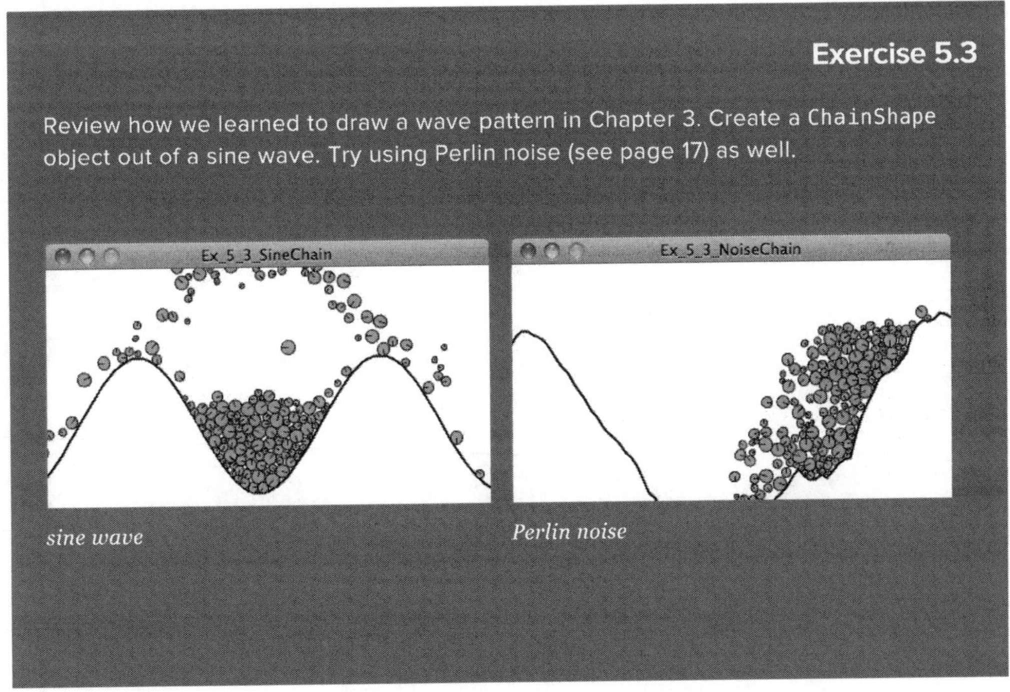

sine wave

Perlin noise

5.10 Complex Forms

Now that we've seen how easy it is to make simple geometric forms in Box2D, let's imagine that you want to have a more complex form, such as a little alien stick figure.

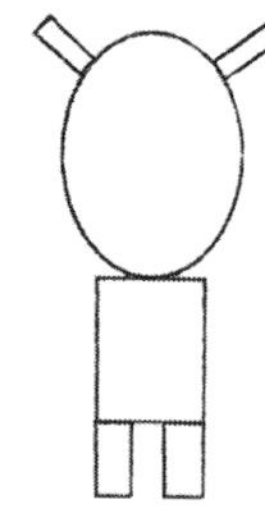

Figure 5.5

There are two strategies in Box2D for making forms that are more advanced than a basic circle or square. One is to use a `PolygonShape` in a different way. In our previous examples, we used `PolygonShape` to generate a rectangular shape with the `setAsBox()` function.

```
PolygonShape ps = new PolygonShape();
ps.setAsBox(box2dW, box2dH);
```

This was a good way to start because of the inherent simplicity of working with rectangles. However, a `PolygonShape` object can also be generated from an array of vectors, which allows you to build a completely custom shape as a series of connected vertices. This works very similarly to the `ChainShape` class.

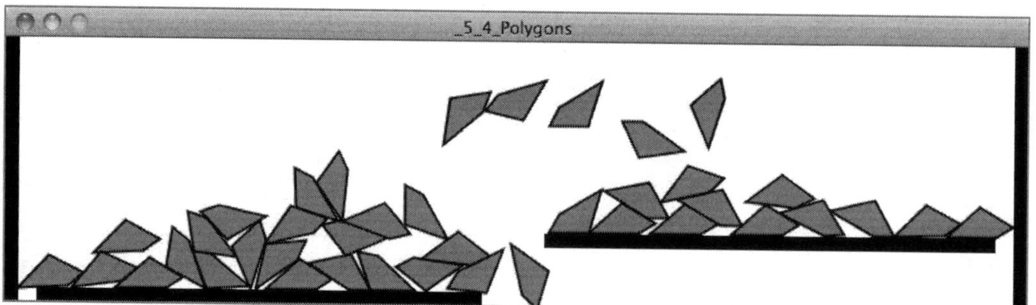

Example 5.4: Polygon shapes

```
Vec2[] vertices = new Vec2[4];  // An array of 4 vectors
vertices[0] = box2d.vectorPixelsToWorld(new Vec2(-15, 25));
vertices[1] = box2d.vectorPixelsToWorld(new Vec2(15, 0));
vertices[2] = box2d.vectorPixelsToWorld(new Vec2(20, -15));
vertices[3] = box2d.vectorPixelsToWorld(new Vec2(-10, -10));
```

```
PolygonShape ps = new PolygonShape();
ps.set(vertices, vertices.length);
```
Making a polygon from that array

When building your own polygon in Box2D, you must remember two important details.

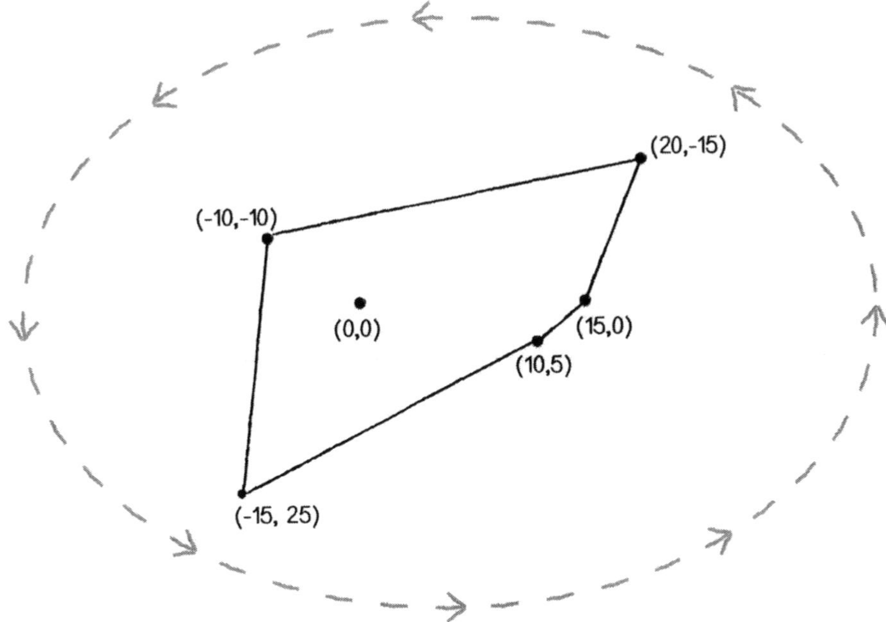

Figure 5.6

1. **Order of vertices!** If you are thinking in terms of pixels (as above) the vertices should be defined in counterclockwise order. (When they are translated to Box2D World vectors, they will actually be in clockwise order since the vertical axis is flipped.)

2. **Convex shapes only!** A concave shape is one where the surface curves inward. Convex is the opposite (see illustration below). Note how in a concave shape every internal angle must be 180 degrees or less. Box2D is not capable of handling collisions for concave shapes. If you need a concave shape, you will have to build one out of multiple convex shapes (more about that in a moment).

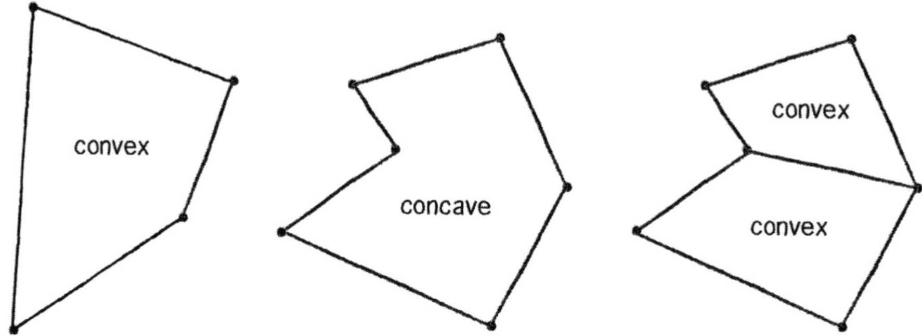

Figure 5.7: A concave shape can be drawn with multiple convex shapes.

Now, when it comes time to display the shape in Processing, we can no longer just use `rect()` or `ellipse()`. Since the shape is built out of custom vertices, we'll want to use Processing's `beginShape()`, `endShape()`, and `vertex()` functions. As we saw with the `ChainShape`, we could choose to store the pixel locations of the vertices in our own `ArrayList` for drawing. However, it's also useful to see how we can ask Box2D to report back to use the vertex locations.

```
void display() {
  Vec2 pos = box2d.getBodyPixelCoord(body);
  float a = body.getAngle();

  Fixture f = body.getFixtureList();
```

First we get the Fixture attached to the body...

```
  PolygonShape ps = (PolygonShape) f.getShape();
```

...then the Shape attached to the Fixture.

```
  rectMode(CENTER);
  pushMatrix();
  translate(pos.x,pos.y);
  rotate(-a);
  fill(175);
  stroke(0);
  beginShape();
  for (int i = 0; i < ps.getVertexCount(); i++) {
    Vec2 v = box2d.vectorWorldToPixels(ps.getVertex(i));
    vertex(v.x,v.y);
  }
  endShape(CLOSE);
  popMatrix();
}
```

We can loop through that array and convert each vertex from Box2D space to pixels.

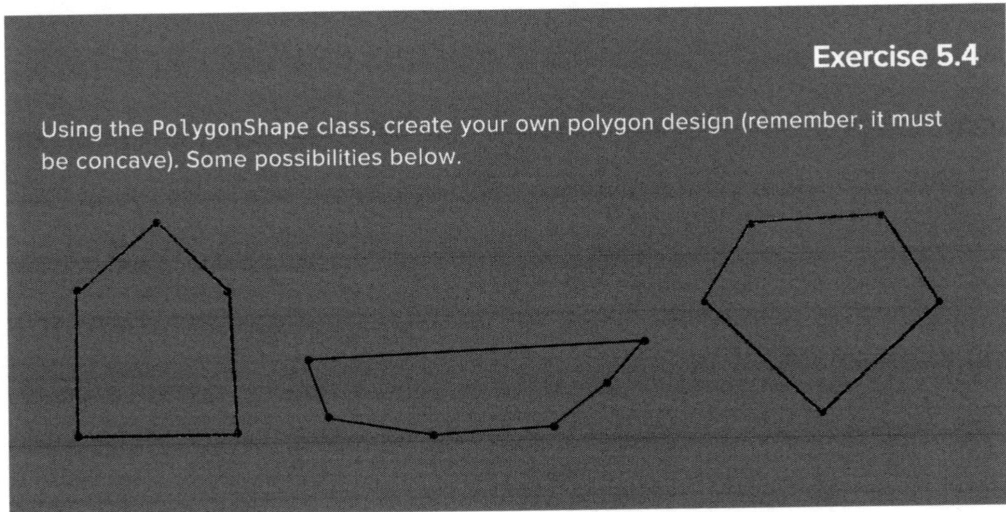

Exercise 5.4

Using the `PolygonShape` class, create your own polygon design (remember, it must be concave). Some possibilities below.

A polygon shape will get us pretty far in Box2D. Nevertheless, the convex shape requirement will severely limit the range of possibilities. The good news is that we can completely eliminate this restriction by creating a single Box2D body out of multiple shapes! Let's return to our little alien creature and simplify the shape to be a thin rectangle with a circle on top.

How can we build a single body with two shapes? Let's first review how we built a single body with one shape.

Step 1: Define the body.
Step 2: Create the body.
Step 3: Define the shape.
Step 4: Attach the shape to the body.
Step 5: Finalize the body's mass.

Attaching more than one shape to a body is as simple as repeating steps 3 and 4 over and over again.

Step 3a: Define shape 1.
Step 4a: Attach shape 1 to the body.
Step 3b: Define shape 2.
Step 4b: Attach shape 2 to the body.
etc. etc. etc.

Let's see what this would look like with actual Box2D code.

```
BodyDef bd = new BodyDef();
bd.type = BodyType.DYNAMIC;
bd.position.set(box2d.coordPixelsToWorld(center));
body = box2d.createBody(bd);
```

Making the body

```
PolygonShape ps = new PolygonShape();
float box2dW = box2d.scalarPixelsToWorld(w/2);
float box2dH = box2d.scalarPixelsToWorld(h/2);
sd.setAsBox(box2dW, box2dH);
```

Making shape 1 (the rectangle)

```
CircleShape cs = new CircleShape();
cs.m_radius = box2d.scalarPixelsToWorld(r);
```

Making shape 2 (the circle)

```
body.createFixture(ps,1.0);
body.createFixture(cs, 1.0);
```

Attach both shapes with a fixture.

The above looks pretty good, but sadly, if we run it, we'll get the following result:

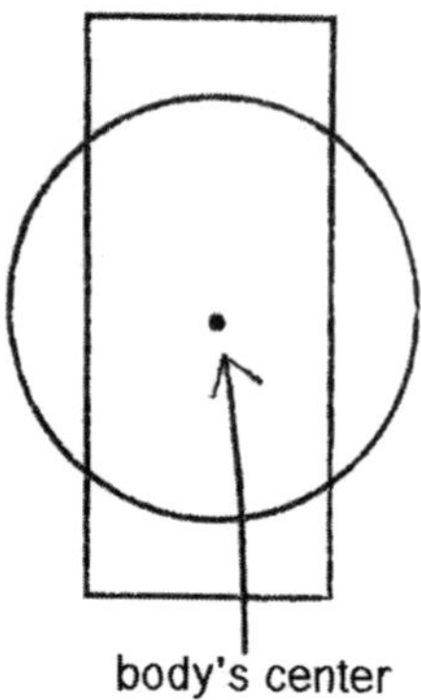

Figure 5.8

When you attach a shape to a body, by default, the center of the shape will be located at the center of the body. But in our case, if we take the center of the rectangle to be the center of the body, we want the center of the circle to be offset along the y-axis from the body's center.

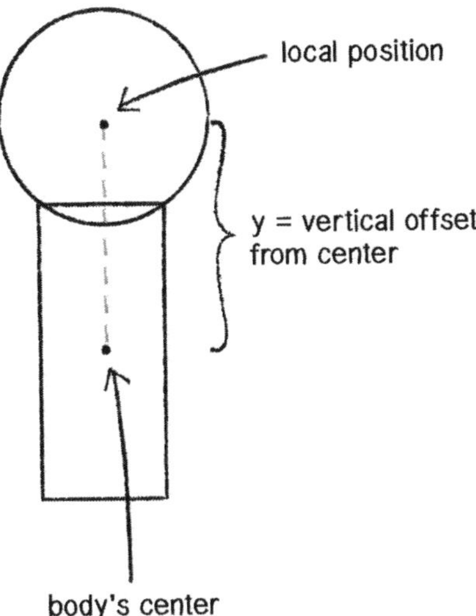

Figure 5.9

This is achieved by using the local position of a shape, accessed via a Vec2 variable called m_p.

```
Vec2 offset = new Vec2(0,-h/2);                  // Our offset in pixels
offset = box2d.vectorPixelsToWorld(offset);      // Converting the vector to Box2D world
circle.m_p.set(offset.x,offset.y);               // Setting the local position of the circle
```

Then, when we go to draw the body, we use both `rect()` and `ellipse()` with the circle offset the same way.

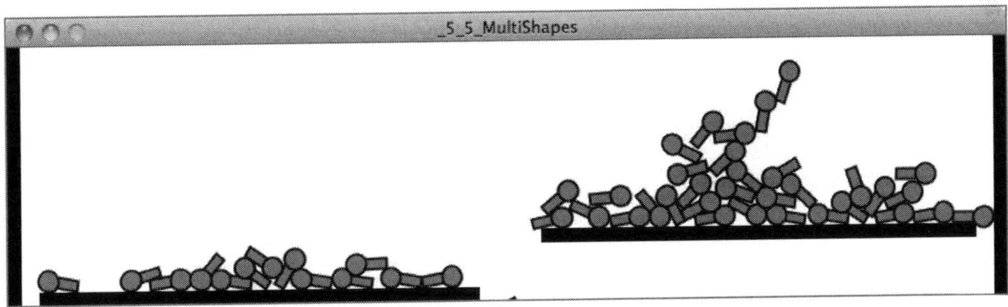

Example 5.5: Multiple shapes on one body

```
void display() {
  Vec2 pos = box2d.getBodyPixelCoord(body);
  float a = body.getAngle();

  rectMode(CENTER);
  pushMatrix();
  translate(pos.x,pos.y);
  rotate(-a);
  fill(175);
  stroke(0);
  rect(0,0,w,h);                       // First the rectangle at (0,0)
  ellipse(0,-h/2,r*2,r*2);             // Then the ellipse offset at (0,-h/2)
  popMatrix();
}
```

Finishing off this section, I want to stress the following: the stuff you draw in your Processing window doesn't magically experience physics simply because we created some Box2D bodies and shapes. These examples work because we very carefully matched how we draw our elements with how we defined the bodies and shapes we put into the Box2D world. If you accidentally draw your shape differently, you won't get an error, not from Processing or from Box2D. However, your sketch will look odd and the physics won't work correctly. For example, what if we had written:

```
Vec2 offset = new Vec2(0,-h/2);
```

when we created the shape, but:

```
ellipse(0,h/2,r*2,r*2);
```

when it came time to display the shape?

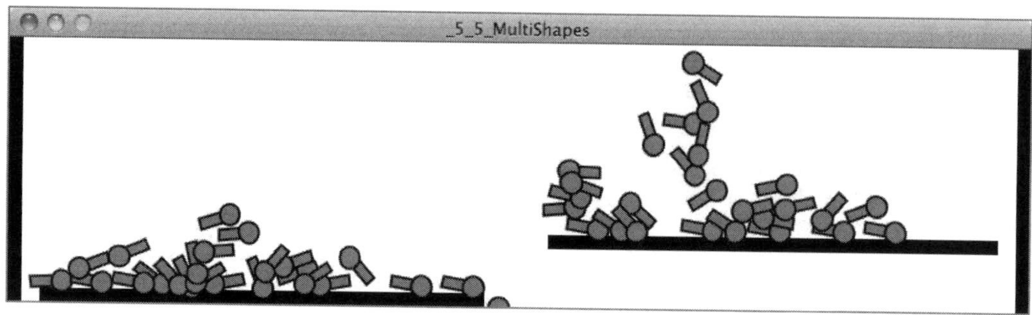

The results would look like the image above, where clearly, the collisions are not functioning as expected. This is not because the physics is broken; it's because we did not communicate properly with Box2D, either when we put stuff in the magic world or queried the world for locations.

Exercise 5.5

Make your own little alien being using multiple shapes attached to a single body. Try using more than one polygon to make a concave shape. Remember, you aren't limited to using the shape drawing functions in Processing; you can use images, colors, add hair with lines, etc. Think of the Box2D shapes only as skeletons for your creative and fantastical design!

5.11 Feeling Attached—Box2D Joints

Box2D joints allow you to connect one body to another, enabling more advanced simulations of swinging pendulums, elastic bridges, squishy characters, wheels spinning on an axle, etc. There are many different kinds of Box2D joints. In this chapter we're going to look at three: distance joints, revolute joints, and "mouse" joints.

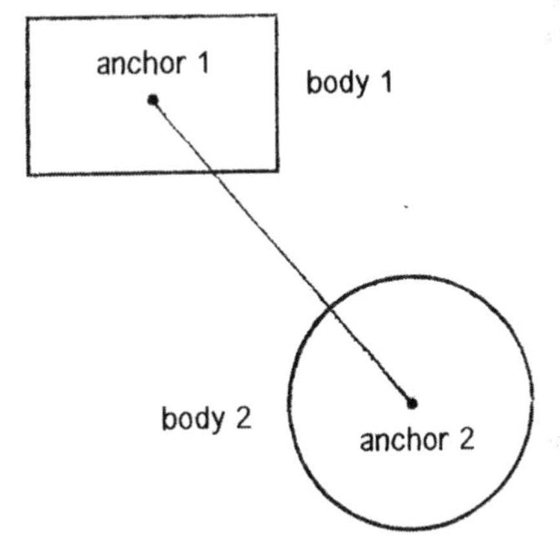

Figure 5.10

Let's begin with a distance joint, a joint that connects two bodies with a fixed length. The joint is attached to each body at a specified anchor point (a point relative to the body's center). For any Box2D joint, we need to follow these steps. This, of course, is similar to the methodology we used to build bodies and shapes, with some quirks.

Step 1. Make sure you have two bodies ready to go.
Step 2. Define the joint.
Step 3. Configure the joint's properties (What are the bodies? Where are the anchors? What is its rest length? Is it elastic or rigid?)
Step 4. Create the joint.

Let's assume we have two `Particle` objects that each store a reference to a Box2D `Body` object. We'll call them particles `p1` and `p2`.

```
Particle p1 = new Particle();
Particle p2 = new Particle();
```

OK, onto Step 2. Let's define the joint.

```
DistanceJointDef djd = new DistanceJointDef();
```

Easy, right? Now it's time to configure the joint. First we tell the joint which two bodies it connects:

```
djd.bodyA = p1.body;
djd.bodyB = p2.body;
```

Then we set up a rest length. Remember, if our rest length is in pixels, we need to convert it!

```
djd.length = box2d.scalarPixelsToWorld(10);
```

A distance joint also includes two optional settings that can make the joint soft, like a spring connection: `frequencyHz` and `dampingRatio`.

```
djd.frequencyHz  = ___;
```

Measured in Hz, like the frequency of harmonic oscillation; try values between 1 and 5.

```
djd.dampingRatio = ___;
```

Dampens the spring; typically a number between 0 and 1.

Finally, we create the joint.

```
DistanceJoint dj = (DistanceJoint) box2d.world.createJoint(djd);
```

Box2D won't keep track of what kind of joint we are making, so we have to cast it as a `DistanceJoint` upon creation.

We can create Box2D joints anywhere in our Processing sketch. Here's an example of how we might write a class to describe two Box2D bodies connected with a single joint.

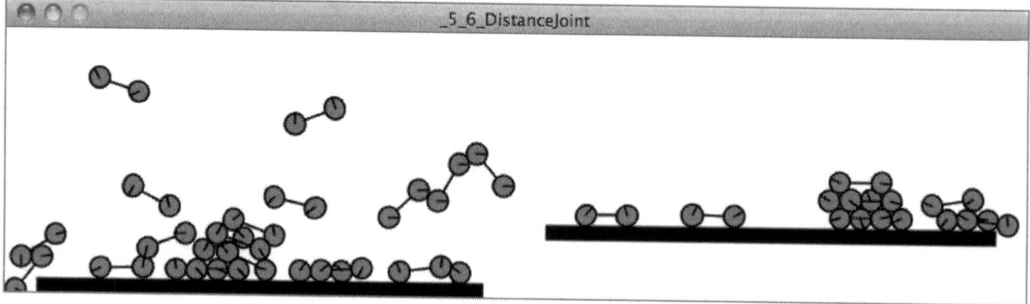

Example 5.6: DistanceJoint

```
class Pair {

  Particle p1;
  Particle p2;

  float len = 32;

  Pair(float x, float y) {

    p1 = new Particle(x,y);
    p2 = new Particle(x+random(-1,1),y+random(-1,1));

    DistanceJointDef djd = new DistanceJointDef();
    djd.bodyA = p1.body;
    djd.bodyB = p2.body;
    djd.length = box2d.scalarPixelsToWorld(len);
    djd.frequencyHz = 0;  // Try a value less than 5
    djd.dampingRatio = 0; // Ranges between 0 and 1

    DistanceJoint dj = (DistanceJoint) box2d.world.createJoint(djd);
  }

  void display() {
    Vec2 pos1 = box2d.getBodyPixelCoord(p1.body);
    Vec2 pos2 = box2d.getBodyPixelCoord(p2.body);
    stroke(0);
    line(pos1.x,pos1.y,pos2.x,pos2.y);

    p1.display();
    p2.display();
  }
}
```

Two objects that each have a Box2D body

Arbitrary rest length

Problems can result if the bodies are initialized at the same location.

Making the joint!

Make the joint. Note that we aren't storing a reference to the joint anywhere! We might need to someday, but for now it's OK.

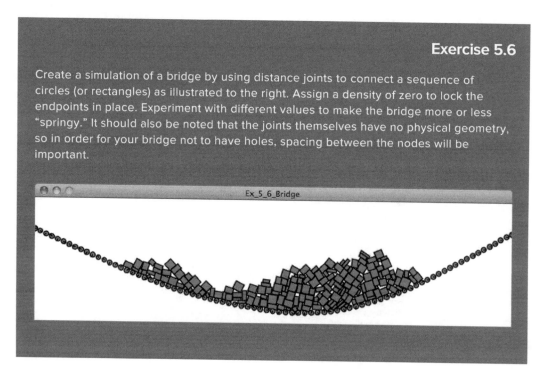

Exercise 5.6

Create a simulation of a bridge by using distance joints to connect a sequence of circles (or rectangles) as illustrated to the right. Assign a density of zero to lock the endpoints in place. Experiment with different values to make the bridge more or less "springy." It should also be noted that the joints themselves have no physical geometry, so in order for your bridge not to have holes, spacing between the nodes will be important.

Another joint you can create in Box2D is a *revolute joint*. A revolute joint connects two Box2D bodies at a common anchor point, which can also be referred to as a "hinge." The joint has an "angle" that describes the relative rotation of each body. To use a revolute joint, we follow the same steps we did with the distance joint.

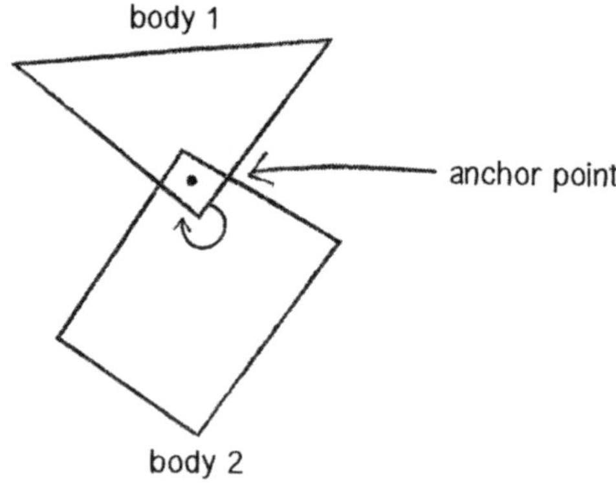

Figure 5.11

Step 1: Make sure you have two bodies ready to go.

Let's assume we have two Box objects, each of which stores a reference to a Box2D body.

```
Box box1 = new Box();
Box box2 = new Box();
```

Step 2: Define the joint.

Now we want a RevoluteJointDef object.

```
RevoluteJointDef rjd = new RevoluteJointDef();
```

Step 3: Configure the joint's properties.

The most important properties of a revolute joint are the two bodies it connects as well as their mutual anchor point (i.e. where they are connected). They are set with the function initialize().

```
rjd.initialize(box1.body, box2.body, box1.body.getWorldCenter());
```

Notice how the first two arguments specify the bodies and the second point specifies the anchor, which in this case is located at the center of the first body.

An exciting feature of a RevoluteJoint object is that you can motorize it so it spins autonomously. For example:

`rjd.enableMotor = true;`	Turn on the motor.
`rjd.motorSpeed = PI*2;`	How fast is the motor?
`rjd.maxMotorTorque = 1000.0;`	How powerful is the motor?

The motor can be enabled and disabled while the program is running.

Finally, the ability for a revolute joint to spin can be constrained between two angles. (By default, it can rotate a full 360 degrees, or TWO_PI radians.)

```
rjd.enableLimit = true;
rjd.lowerAngle = -PI/8;
rjd.upperAngle = PI/8;
```

Step 4: Create the joint.

```
RevoluteJoint joint = (RevoluteJoint) box2d.world.createJoint(rjd);
```

Let's take a look at all of these steps together in a class called Windmill, which connects two boxes with a revolute joint. In this case, box1 has a density of zero, so only box2 spins around a fixed point.

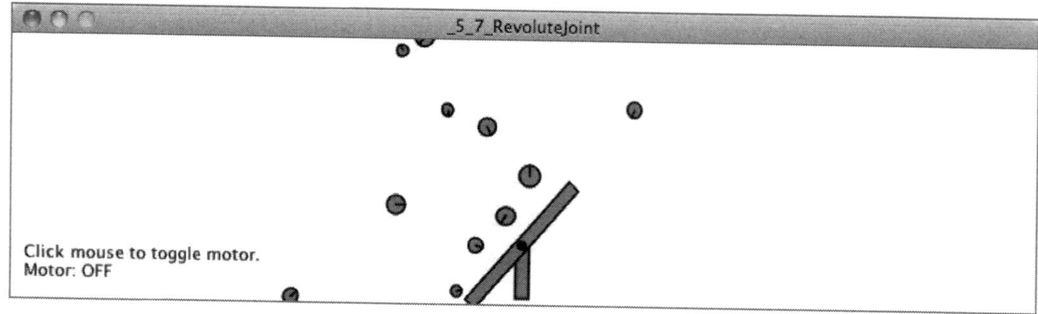

Example 5.7: Spinning Windmill

```
class Windmill {

  RevoluteJoint joint;
  Box box1;
  Box box2;

  Windmill(float x, float y) {

    box1 = new Box(x,y,120,10,false);
    box2 = new Box(x,y,10,40,true);

    RevoluteJointDef rjd = new RevoluteJointDef();
    rjd.initialize(box1.body, box2.body, box1.body.getWorldCenter());

    rjd.motorSpeed = PI*2;
    rjd.maxMotorTorque = 1000.0;
    rjd.enableMotor = true;

    joint = (RevoluteJoint) box2d.world.createJoint(rjd);
  }

  void toggleMotor() {
    boolean motorstatus = joint.isMotorEnabled();
    joint.enableMotor(!motorstatus);
  }
```

Our "Windmill" is two boxes and one joint.

In this example, the Box class expects a boolean argument that will be used to determine if the Box is fixed or not. See website for the Box class code.

The joint connects two bodies and is anchored at the center of the first body.

A motor!

Create the Joint.

Turning the motor on or off

```
  void display() {
    box1.display();
    box2.display();
  }
}
```

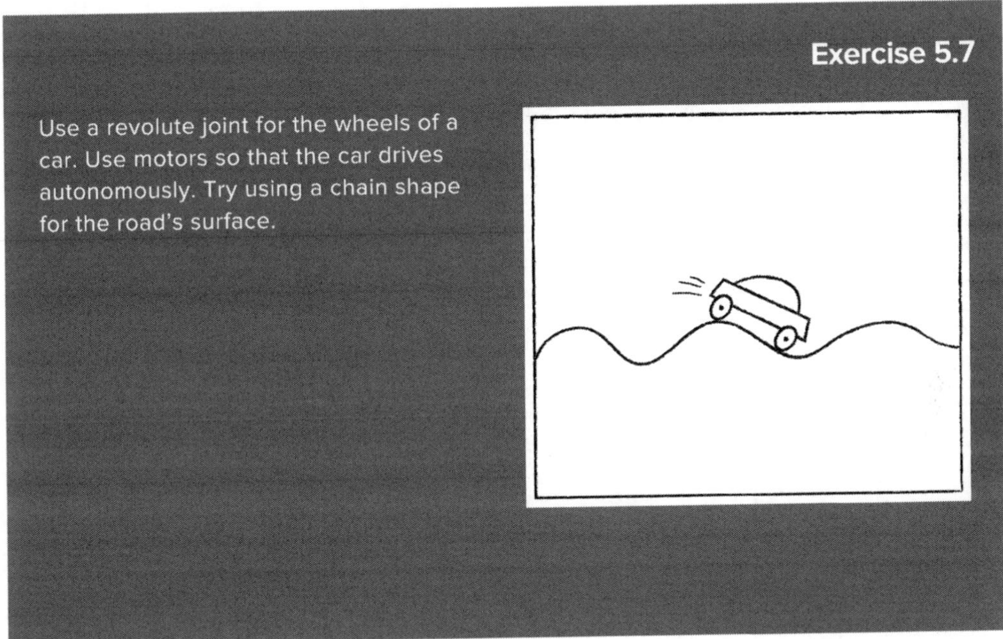

Exercise 5.7

Use a revolute joint for the wheels of a car. Use motors so that the car drives autonomously. Try using a chain shape for the road's surface.

The last joint we'll look at is a mouse joint. A mouse joint is typically used for moving a body with the mouse. However, it can also be used to drag an object around the screen according to some arbitrary *x* and *y*. The joint functions by pulling the body towards a "target" position.

Before we look at the `MouseJoint` object itself, let's ask ourselves why we even need it in the first place. If you look at the Box2D documentation, there is a function called `setTransform()` that specifically "sets the position of the body's origin and rotation (radians)." If a body has a position, can't we just assign the body's position to the mouse?

```
Vec2 mouse = box2d.screenToWorld(x,y);
body.setTransform(mouse,0);
```

While this will in fact move the body, it will also have the unfortunate result of breaking the physics. Let's imagine you built a teleportation machine that allows you to teleport from your bedroom to your kitchen (good for late-night snacking). Now, go ahead and rewrite Newton's laws of motion to account for the possibility of teleportation. Not so easy, right? Box2D has the same problem. If you manually assign the location of an body, it's like saying "teleport that body" and Box2D no longer knows how to compute the physics properly.

However, Box2D does allow you to tie a rope to yourself and get a friend of yours to stand in the kitchen and drag you there. This is what the `MouseJoint` does. It's like a string you attach to a body and pull towards a target.

Let's look at making this joint, assuming we have a `Box` object called `box`. This code will look identical to our distance joint with one small difference.

```
MouseJointDef md = new MouseJointDef();
```

Just like before, define the Joint.

```
md.bodyA = box2d.getGroundBody();
```

Whoa, this is new!

```
md.bodyB = box.body;
```

Attach the Box body.

```
md.maxForce = 5000.0;
md.frequencyHz = 5.0;
md.dampingRatio = 0.9;
```

Set properties.

```
MouseJoint mouseJoint = (MouseJoint)
box2d.world.createJoint(md);.
```

Create the joint.

So, what's this line of code all about?

```
md.bodyA = box2d.getGroundBody();
```

Well, as we've stated, a joint is a connection between *two* bodies. With a mouse joint, we're saying that the second body is, well, the ground. Hmm. What the heck is the *ground* in Box2D? One way to imagine it is to think of the screen as the ground. What we're doing is making a joint that connects a rectangle drawn on the window with the Processing window itself. And the point in the window to which the connection is tied is a moving target.

Once we have a mouse joint, we'll want to update the target location continually while the sketch is running.

```
Vec2 mouseWorld = box2d.coordPixelsToWorld(mouseX,mouseY);
mouseJoint.setTarget(mouseWorld);
```

To make this work in an actual Processing sketch, we'll want to have the following:

1. ***Box class***—An object that references a Box2D body.
2. ***Spring class***—An object that manages the mouse joint that drags the `Box` object around.

3. ***Main tab***—Whenever `mousePressed()` is called, the mouse joint is created; whenever `mouseReleased()` is called, the mouse joint is destroyed. This allows us to interact with a body only when the mouse is pressed.

Let's take a look at the main tab. You can find the rest of the code for the `Box` and `Spring` classes via the book website.

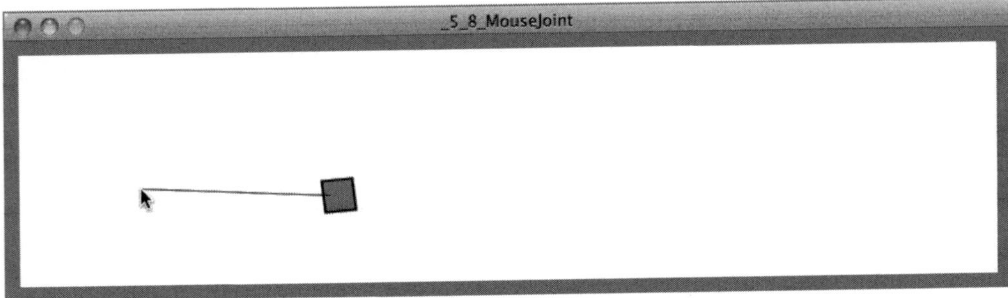

Example 5.8: MouseJoint demonstration

```
PBox2D box2d;

Box box;                                  // One Box
Spring spring;                            // Object to manage MouseJoint

void setup() {
  size(400,300);
  box2d = new PBox2D(this);
  box2d.createWorld();

  box = new Box(width/2,height/2);
  spring = new Spring();                  // The MouseJoint is really null until we click the mouse.
}

void mousePressed() {
  if (box.contains(mouseX, mouseY)) {     // Was the mouse clicked inside the Box?
    spring.bind(mouseX,mouseY,box);       // If so, attach the MouseJoint.
  }
}

void mouseReleased() {
```

```
    spring.destroy();
  }
```

When the mouse is released, we're done with the MouseJoint.

```
void draw() {
  background(255);

  box2d.step();

  spring.update(mouseX,mouseY);
```

We must always update the MouseJoint's target.

```
  box.display();
  spring.display();
}
```

Exercise 5.8

Use a mouse joint to move a Box2D body around the screen according to an algorithm or input other than the mouse. For example, assign it a location according to Perlin noise or key presses. Or build your own controller using an Arduino (http://www.arduino.cc/).

It's worth noting that while the technique for dragging an object around using a `MouseJoint` is useful, Box2D also allows a body to have a `KINEMATIC` type.

```
BodyDef bd = new BodyDef();
bd.type = BodyType.KINEMATIC;
```

Setting the body type to Kinematic

Kinematic bodies can be controlled by the user by setting their velocity directly. For example, let's say you want an object to follow a target (like your mouse). You could create a vector that points from a body's location to a target.

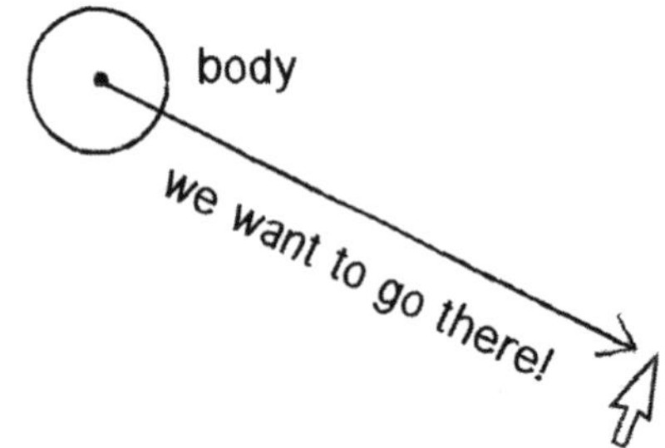

Figure 5.12

```
Vec2 pos = body.getWorldCenter();
Vec2 target = box2d.coordPixelsToWorld(mouseX,mouseY);
Vec2 v = target.sub(pos);
```

A vector pointing from the body position to the Mouse

Once you have that vector, you could assign it to the body's velocity so that it moves to the target.

```
body.setLinearVelocity(v);          Assigning a body's velocity directly, overriding physics!
```

You can also do the same with angular velocity (or leave it alone and allow the physics to take over).

It is important to note that kinematic bodies do not collide with other kinematic or static bodies. In these cases, the mouse joint strategy is preferable.

Exercise 5.9

Redo Exercise 5.8, but use a kinematic body instead.

5.12 Bringing It All Back Home to Forces

In Chapter 2, we spent a lot of time thinking about building environments with multiple forces. An object might respond to gravitational attraction, wind, air resistance, etc. Clearly there are forces at work in Box2D as we watch rectangles and circles spin and fly around the screen. But so far, we've only had the ability to manipulate a single global force—gravity.

```
box2d = new PBox2D(this);
box2d.createWorld();
box2d.setGravity(0, -20);          Setting the global gravity force
```

If we want to use any of our Chapter 2 techniques with Box2D, we need look no further than our trusty `applyForce()` function. In our `Mover` class we wrote a function called `applyForce()`, which received a vector, divided it by mass, and accumulated it into the mover's acceleration. With Box2D, the same function exists, but we don't need to write it ourselves. Instead, we can call the Box2D body's `applyForce()` function!

```
class Box {
  Body body;

  void applyForce(Vec2 force) {
    Vec2 pos = body.getWorldCenter();
    body.applyForce(force, pos);          Calling the Body's applyForce() function
  }
}
```

Here we are receiving a force vector and passing it along to the Box2D Body object. The key difference is that Box2D is a more sophisticated engine than our examples from Chapter 2. Our earlier forces examples assumed that the force was always applied at the mover's center. Here we get to specify exactly where on the body the force is applied. In the above code, we're just applying it to the center by asking the body for its center, but this could be adjusted.

Let's say we wanted to use a gravitational attraction force. Remember the code we wrote back in Chapter 2 in our `Attractor` class?

```
PVector attract(Mover m) {
  PVector force = PVector.sub(location,m.location);
  float distance = force.mag();
  distance = constrain(distance,5.0,25.0);
  force.normalize();
  float strength = (g * mass * m.mass) / (distance * distance);
  force.mult(strength);
  return force;
}
```

We can rewrite the exact same function using `Vec2` instead and use it in a Box2D example. Note how for our force calculation we can stay completely within the Box2D coordinate system and never think about pixels.

```
Vec2 attract(Mover m) {
  Vec2 pos = body.getWorldCenter();                 We have to ask Box2D for the locations first!
  Vec2 moverPos = m.body.getWorldCenter();
  Vec2 force = pos.sub(moverPos);
  float distance = force.length();
  distance = constrain(distance,1,5);
  force.normalize();
  float strength = (G * 1 * m.body.m_mass) / (distance * distance);
  force.mulLocal(strength);                         Remember, it's mulLocal() for Vec2.
  return force;
}
```

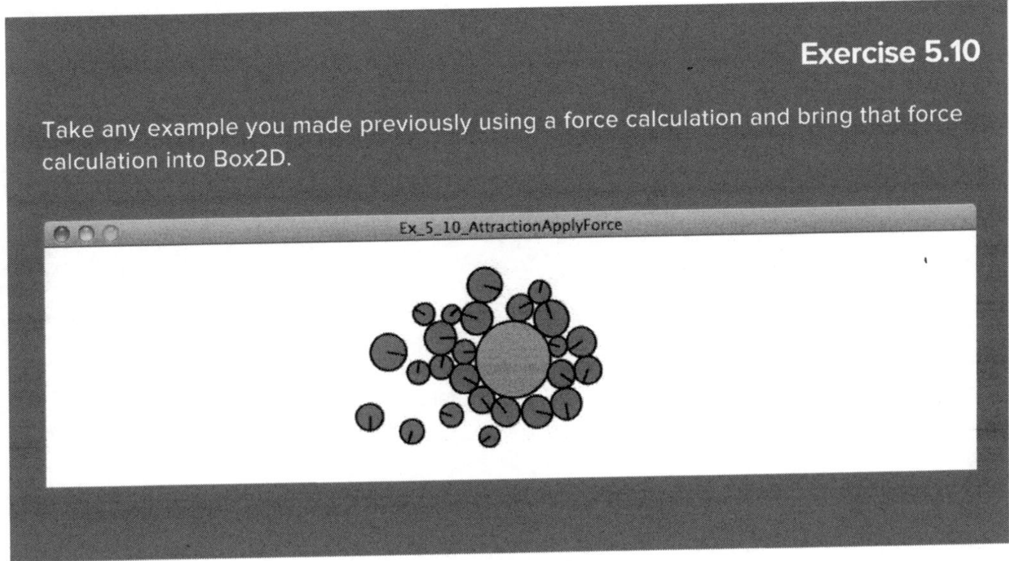

Exercise 5.10

Take any example you made previously using a force calculation and bring that force calculation into Box2D.

5.13 Collision Events

Now we've seen a survey of what can be done with Box2D. Since this book is not called "The Nature of Box2D," it's not my intention to cover every single possible feature of the Box2D engine. But hopefully by looking at the basics of building bodies, shapes, and joints, when it comes time to use an aspect of Box2D that we haven't covered, the skills we've gained here will make that process considerably less painful. There is one more feature of Box2D, however, that I do think is worth covering.

Let's ask a question you've likely been wondering about:

What if I want something to happen when two Box2D bodies collide? I mean, don't get me wrong—I'm thrilled that Box2D is handling all of the collisions for me. But if it takes care of everything for me, how am I supposed to know when things are happening?

Your first thoughts when considering an event during which two objects collide might be as follows: Well, if I know all the bodies in the system, and I know where they are all located, then I can just start comparing the locations, see which ones are intersecting, and determine that they've collided. That's a nice thought, but hello??!? The whole point of using Box2D is that Box2D will take care of that for us. If we are going to do the geometry to test for intersection ourselves, then all we're doing is re-implementing Box2D.

Of course, Box2D has thought of this problem before. It's a pretty common one. After all, if you intend to make a bajillion dollars selling some game called Angry Birds, you better well make something happen when an ill-tempered pigeon smashes into a cardboard box. Box2D alerts you to moments of collision with something called an "interface." It's worth learning about interfaces, an advanced feature of object-oriented programming. You can take a look at the Java Interface Tutorial (http://download.oracle.com/javase/tutorial/java/concepts/interface.html) as well as the JBox2D `ContactListener` class. (I have also included an example on the website that demonstrates using the interface directly.)

If you are using PBox2D, as we are here, you don't need to implement your own interface. Detecting collision events is done through a callback function. Much like `mousePressed()` is triggered when the mouse is pressed, `beginContact()` is triggered when two shapes collide.

```
void mousePressed() {
  println("The mouse was pressed!");
}
```

The mousePressed event with which we are comfortable.

```
void beginContact(Contact cp) {
  println("Something collided in the Box2D World!");
}
```

What our "beginContact" event looks like.

Before the above will work, you must first let PBox2D know you intend to listen for collisions. (This allows the library to reduce overhead by default; it won't bother listening if it doesn't have to.)

```
void setup() {
  box2d = new PBox2D(this);
  box2d.createWorld();
  box2d.listenForCollisions();
}
```

Add this line if you want to listen for collisions.

There are four collision event callbacks.

1. `beginContact()` —Triggered whenever two shapes first come into contact with each other.
2. `endContact()` —Triggered over and over again as long as shapes continue to be in contact.
3. `preSolve()` —Triggered before Box2D solves the outcome of the collision, i.e. before `beginContact()`. It can be used to disable a collision if necessary.
4. `postSolve()` —Triggered after the outcome of the collision is solved. It allows you to gather information about that "solution" (known as an "impulse").

The details behind `preSolve()` and `postSolve()` are beyond the scope of this book; however, we are going to take a close look at `beginContact()`, which will cover the majority of conventional cases in which you want to trigger an action when a collision occurs. `endContact()` works identically to `beginContact()`, the only difference being that it occurs the moment bodies separate.

`beginContact()` is written as follows:

```
void beginContact(Contact cp) {

}
```

Notice that the function above includes an argument of type `Contact`. A `Contact` object includes all the data associated with a collision—the geometry and the forces. Let's say we have a Processing sketch with `Particle` objects that store a reference to a Box2D body. Here is the process we are going to follow.

Step 1: Contact, could you tell me what two things collided?

Now, what has collided here? Is it the bodies? The shapes? The fixtures? Box2D detects collisions between shapes; after all, these are the entities that have geometry. However, because shapes are attached to bodies with fixtures, what we really want to ask Box2D is: "Could you tell me which two fixtures collided?"

```
Fixture f1 = cp.getFixtureA();
Fixture f2 = cp.getFixtureB();
```

The contact stores the fixtures as A and B.

Step 2: Fixtures, could you tell me which body you are attached to?

```
Body b1 = f1.getBody();
Body b2 = f2.getBody();
```

getBody() gives us the body to which the Fixture is attached.

Step 3: Bodies, could you tell me which Particles you are associated with?

OK, this is the harder part. After all, Box2D doesn't know anything about our code. Sure, it is doing all sorts of stuff to keep track of the relationships between shapes and bodies and joints, but it's up to us to manage our own objects and their associations with Box2D elements. Luckily for us, Box2D provides a function that allows us to attach our Processing object (a `Particle`) to a Box2D body via the `setUserData()` and `getUserData()` methods.

Let's take a look at the constructor in our `Particle` class where the body is made. We are expanding our body-making procedure by one line of code, noted below.

```
class Particle {
  Body body;

  Particle(float x, float y, float r) {
    BodyDef bd = new BodyDef();
    bd.position = box2d.coordPixelsToWorld(x, y);
    bd.type = BodyType.DYNAMIC;
    body = box2d.createBody(bd);
    CircleShape cs = new CircleShape();
    cs.m_radius = box2d.scalarPixelsToWorld(r);
    body.createFixture(fd,1);

    body.setUserData(this);
  }
```

"this" refers to this Particle object. We are telling the Box2D Body to store a reference to this Particle that we can access later.

Later, in our `addContact()` function, once we know the body, we can access the `Particle` object with `getUserData()`.

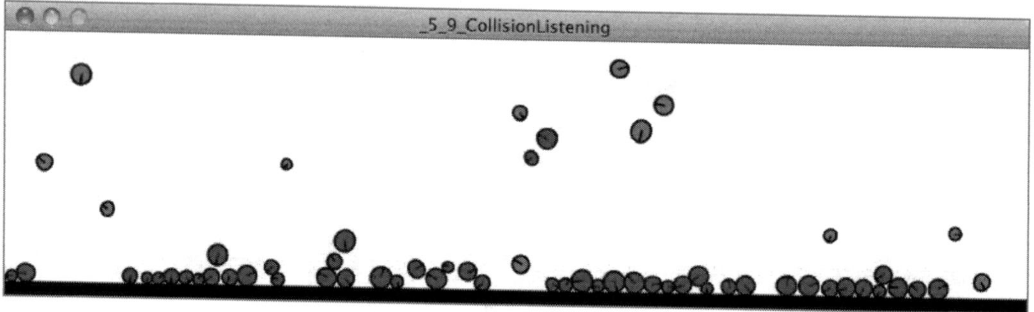

Example 5.9: CollisionListening

```
void beginContact(Contact cp) {

  Fixture f1 = cp.getFixtureA();
  Fixture f2 = cp.getFixtureB();

  Body b1 = f1.getBody();
  Body b2 = f2.getBody();

  Particle p1 = (Particle) b1.getUserData();
  Particle p2 = (Particle) b2.getUserData();

  p1.change();
  p2.change();
}
```

When we pull the "user data" object out of the Body object, we have to remind our program that it is a Particle object. Box2D doesn't know this.

Once we have the particles, we can do anything to them. Here we just call a function that changes their color.

Now, in many cases, we cannot assume that the objects that collided are all `Particle` objects. We might have a sketch with `Boundary` objects, `Particle` objects, `Box` objects, etc. So often we will have to query the "user data" and find out what kind of object it is before proceeding.

```
Object o1 = b1.getUserData();                 Getting a generic object

if (o1.getClass() == Particle.class) {        Asking that object if it's a Particle
  Particle p = (Particle) o1;
  p.change();
}
```

It should also be noted that due to how Box2D triggers these callbacks, you cannot create or destroy Box2D entities inside of `beginContact()`, `endContact()`, `preSolve()`, or `postSolve()`. If you want to do this, you'll need to set a variable inside an object (something like: `markForDeletion = true`), which you check during `draw()` and then delete objects.

Exercise 5.11

Consider how polymorphism could help in the above case. Build an example in which several classes extend one class and therefore eliminate the need for such testing.

Exercise 5.12

Create a simulation in which `Particle` objects disappear when they collide with one another. Use the methodology I just described.

5.14 A Brief Interlude—Integration Methods

Has the following ever happened to you? You're at a fancy cocktail party regaling your friends with tall tales of software physics simulations. Someone pipes up: "Enchanting! But what integration method are you using?" "What?!" you think to yourself. "Integration?"

Maybe you've heard the term before. Along with "differentiation," it's one of the two main operations in calculus. Right, calculus. The good news is, we've gotten through about 90% of the material in this book related to physics simulation and we haven't really needed to dive into calculus. But as we're coming close to finishing this topic, it's worth taking a moment to examine the calculus behind what we have been doing and how it relates to the methodology in certain physics libraries (like Box2D and the upcoming toxiclibs).

Let's begin by answering the question: "What does integration have to do with location, velocity, and acceleration?" Well, first let's define ***differentiation***, the process of finding a "derivative." The derivative of a function is a measure of how a function changes over time. Consider location and its derivative. Location is a point in space, while velocity is change in location over time. Therefore, velocity can be described as the "derivative" of location. What is acceleration? The change in velocity over time—i.e. the "derivative" of velocity.

Now that we understand the derivative (differentiation), we can define the integral (integration) as the inverse of the derivative. In other words, the integral of an object's velocity over time tells us the object's new location when that time period ends. Location is the integral of velocity, and velocity is the integral of acceleration. Since our physics simulation is founded upon the process of calculating acceleration based on forces, we need integration to figure out where the object is after a certain period of time (like one frame of animation!)

So we've been doing integration all along! It looks like this:

```
velocity.add(acceleration);
location.add(velocity);
```

The above methodology is known as Euler integration (named for the mathematician Leonhard Euler, pronounced "Oiler") or the Euler method. It's essentially the simplest form of integration and very easy to implement in our code (see the two lines above!) However, it is not necessarily the most efficient form, nor is it close to being the most accurate. Why is Euler inaccurate? Let's think about it this way. When you drive a car down the road pressing the gas pedal with your foot and accelerating, does the car sit in one location at time equals one second, then disappear and suddenly reappear in a new location at time equals two seconds, and do the same thing for three seconds, and four, and five? No, of course not. The car moves continuously down the road. But what's happening in our Processing sketch? A circle is at one location at frame 0, another at frame 1, another at frame 2. Sure, at thirty frames per second, we're seeing the illusion of motion. But we only calculate a new location every **N** units of time, whereas the real world is perfectly continuous. This results in some inaccuracies, as shown in the diagram below:

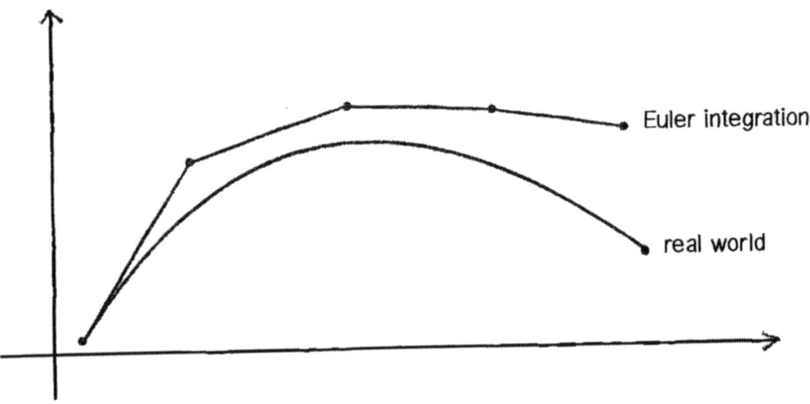

Figure 5.13

The “real world” is the curve; Euler simulation is the series of line segments.

One option to improve on Euler is to use smaller timesteps—instead of once per frame, we could recalculate an object’s location twenty times per frame. But this isn’t practical; our sketch would then run too slowly.

I still believe that Euler is the best method for learning the basics, and it’s also perfectly adequate for most of the projects we might make in Processing. Anything we lose in efficiency or inaccuracy we make up in ease of use and understandability. For better accuracy, Box2D uses something called symplectic Euler or semi-explicit Euler (http://en.wikipedia.org/wiki/Symplectic_Euler_method), a slight modification of Euler.

There is also an integration method called Runge-Kutta (named for German mathematicians C. Runge and M. W. Kutta), which is used in some physics engines.

A very popular integration method that our next physics library uses is known as “Verlet integration.” A simple way to describe Verlet integration is to think of our typical motion algorithm without velocity. After all, we don’t really need to store the velocity. If we always know where an object was at one point in time and where it is now, we can extrapolate its velocity. Verlet integration does precisely this, though instead of having a variable for velocity, it calculates velocity while the program is running. Verlet integration is particularly well suited for particle systems, especially particle systems with spring connections between the particles. We don’t need to worry about the details because toxiclibs, as we’ll see below, takes care of them for us. However, if you are interested, here is the seminal paper on Verlet physics, from which just about every Verlet computer graphics simulation is derived: "Advanced Character Physics" (http://www.gamasutra.com/resource_guide/20030121/jacobson_pfv.htm). And of course, you can find out more about Verlet integration from Wikipedia (http://en.wikipedia.org/wiki/Verlet_integration).

5.15 Verlet Physics with toxiclibs

From toxiclibs.org:

"toxiclibs is an independent, open source library collection for computational design tasks with Java & Processing developed by Karsten "toxi" Schmidt (thus far). The classes are purposefully kept fairly generic in order to maximize re-use in different contexts ranging from generative design, animation, interaction/interface design, data visualization to architecture and digital fabrication, use as teaching tool and more."

In other words, we should thank our lucky stars for toxiclibs. We are only going to focus on a few examples related to Verlet physics, but toxiclibs includes a suite of other wonderful packages that help with audio, color, geometry, and more. In particular, if you are looking to work with form and fabrication in Processing, take a look at the geometry package. Demos can be found at Open Processing (http://www.openprocessing.org/portal/?userID=4530).

We should note that toxiclibs was designed specifically for use with Processing. This is great news. The trouble we had with making Box2D work in Processing (multiple coordinate systems, Box2D vs. JBox2D vs. PBox2D) is not an issue here. toxiclibs is a library that you just download, stick in your libraries folder, and use. And the coordinate system that we'll use for the physics engine is the coordinate system of Processing, so no translating back and forth. In addition, toxiclibs is not limited to a 2D world; all of the physics simulations and functions work in both two and three dimensions. So how do you decide which library you should use? Box2D or toxiclibs? If you fall into one of the following two categories, your decision is a bit easier:

1. My project involves collisions. I have circles, squares, and other strangely shaped objects that knock each other around and bounce off each other.

In this case, you are going to need Box2D. toxiclibs does not handle collisions.

2. My project involves lots of particles flying around the screen. Sometimes they attract each other. Sometimes they repel each other. And sometimes they are connected with springs.

In this case, toxiclibs is likely your best choice. It is simpler to use than Box2D and particularly well suited to connected systems of particles. toxiclibs is also very high performance, due to the speed of the Verlet integration algorithm (not to mention the fact that the program gets to ignore all of the collision geometry).

Here is a little chart that covers some of the features for each physics library.

Feature	Box2D	toxiclibs VerletPhysics
Collision geometry	Yes	No
3D physics	No	Yes
Particle attraction / repulsion forces	No	Yes
Spring connections	Yes	Yes
Other connections: revolute, pulley, gear, prismatic	Yes	No
Motors	Yes	No
Friction	Yes	No

Getting toxiclibs

Everything you need to download and install toxiclibs can be found at:

toxiclibs (http://toxiclibs.org/)

When you download the library, you'll notice that it comes with eight modules (i.e. sub-folders), each a library in its own right. For the examples in this chapter, you will only need "verletphysics" and "toxiclibscore"; however, I recommend you take a look at and consider using all of the modules!

Once you have the library installed to your Processing library folder (http://wiki.processing.org/w/How_to_Install_a_Contributed_Library), you are ready to start looking at the following examples.

Core Elements of VerletPhysics

We spent a lot of time working through the core elements of a Box2D world: world, body, shape, joint. This gives us a head start on understanding toxiclibs, since it follows a similar structure.

Box2D	toxiclibs VerletPhysics
World	VerletPhysics
Body	VerletParticle
Shape	Nothing! toxiclibs does not handle shape geometry
Fixture	Nothing! toxiclibs does not handle shape geometry
Joint	VerletSpring

Vectors with toxiclibs

Here we go again. Remember all that time we spent learning the ins and outs of the `PVector` class? Then remember how when we got to Box2D, we had to translate all those concepts to a Box2D vector class: `Vec2`? Well, it's time to do it again. toxiclibs also includes its own vector classes, one for two dimensions and one for three: `Vec2D` and `Vec3D`.

Again, toxiclibs vectors are the same conceptually, but we need to learn a bit of new syntax. You can find all of the documentation for these vector classes here:

Vec2D (http://toxiclibs.org/docs/core/toxi/geom/Vec2D.html)
Vec3D (http://toxiclibs.org/docs/core/toxi/geom/Vec3D.html)

And let's just review some of the basic vector math operations with `PVector` translated to `Vec2D` (we're sticking with 2D for simplicity's sake).

PVector	Vec2D

`PVector a = new PVector(1,-1);`
`PVector b = new PVector(3,4);`
`a.add(b);`
	`Vec2D a = new Vec2D(1,-1);`
	`Vec2D b = new Vec2D(3,4);`
	`a.addSelf(b);`

`PVector a = new PVector(1,-1);`
`PVector b = new PVector(3,4);`
`PVector c = PVector.add(a,b);`
	`Vec2D a = new Vec2D(1,-1);`
	`Vec2D b = new Vec2D(3,4);`
	`Vec2D c = a.add(b);`

`PVector a = new PVector(1,-1);`
`float m = a.mag();`
`a.normalize();`
	`Vec2D a = new Vec2D(1,-1);`
	`float m = a.magnitude();`
	`a.normalize();`

Building the toxiclibs physics world

The first thing we need to do to create a toxiclibs physics world in our examples is import the library itself.

```
import toxi.physics2d.*;                      Importing the libraries
import toxi.physics2d.behaviors.*;
import toxi.geom.*;
```

Then we'll need a reference to our physics world, a `VerletPhysics` or `VerletPhysics2D` object (depending on whether we are working in two or three dimensions). The examples in this chapter will operate in 2D only for simplicity, but they could easily be extended into 3D (and 3D versions are available with the chapter download).

```
VerletPhysics2D physics;

void setup() {
  physics=new VerletPhysics2D();              Creating a toxiclibs Verlet physics world
```

Once you have your `VerletPhysics` object, you can set some global properties for your world. For example, if you want it to have hard boundaries past which objects cannot travel, you can set its limits:

```
  physics.setWorldBounds(new Rect(0,0,width,height));
```

In addition, you can add gravity to the physics world with a `GravityBehavior` object. A gravity behavior requires a vector—how strong and in what direction is the gravity?

```
  physics.addBehavior(new GravityBehavior(new Vec2D(0,0.5)));
}
```

Finally, in order to calculate the physics of the world and move the objects in the world, we have to call `update()`. Typically this would happen once per frame in `draw()`.

```
void draw() {
  physics.update();                           This is the same as Box2D's "step()"
                                              function
}
```

5.16 Particles and Springs in toxiclibs

In the Box2D examples, we saw how we can create our own class (called, say, `Particle`) and include a reference to a Box2D body.

```
class Particle {
  Body body;
```

This technique is somewhat redundant since Box2D itself keeps track of all of the bodies in its world. However, it allows us to manage which body is which (and therefore how each body is drawn) without having to rely on iterating through Box2D's internal lists.

Let's look at how we might take the same approach with the class `VerletParticle2D` in toxiclibs. We want to make our own `Particle` class so that we can draw our particles a certain way and include any custom properties. We'd probably write our code as follows:

```
class Particle {
  VerletParticle2D p;

  Particle(Vec2D pos) {
    p = new VerletParticle2D(pos);
  }

  void display() {
    fill(0,150);
    stroke(0);
    ellipse(p.x,p.y,16,16);
  }
}
```

Our Particle has a reference to a VerletParticle.

A VerletParticle needs an initial location (an x and y).

When it comes time to draw the Particle, we ask the VerletParticle for its x and y coordinates.

Looking at the above, we should first be thrilled to notice that drawing the particle is as simple as grabbing the *x* and *y* and using them. No awkward conversions between coordinate systems here since toxiclibs is designed to think in pixels. Second, you might notice that this `Particle` class's sole purpose is to store a reference to a `VerletParticle2D` object. This hints at something. Remember our discussion of inheritance back in Chapter 4: Particle Systems? What is a `Particle` object other than an "augmented" `VerletParticle`? Why bother making a Verlet particle inside a particle when we could simply `extend` `VerletParticle`?

```
class Particle extends VerletParticle2D {

  Particle(Vec2D loc) {
    super(loc);
  }

  void display() {
    fill(175);
    stroke(0);
```

Calling super() so that the object is initialized properly

We want this to be just like a VerletParticle, only with a display() method.

```
    ellipse(x,y,16,16);                We've inherited x and y from VerletParticle!
  }
}
```

Remember our multi-step process with the Box2D examples? We had to ask the body for its location, then convert that location to pixels, then use that location in a drawing function. Now, because we have inherited everything from the `VerletParticle` class, our only step is to draw the shape at x and y!

Incidentally, it's interesting to note that the `VerletParticle2D` class is a subclass of `Vec2D`. So in addition to inheriting everything from `VerletParticle2D`, our `Particle` class actually has all of the `Vec2D` functions available as well.

We can now create particles anywhere within our sketch.

```
Particle p1 = new Particle(new Vec2D(100,20));
Particle p2 = new Particle(new Vec2D(100,180));
```

Just making a particle isn't enough, however. We have to make sure we tell our physics world about them with the `addParticle()` function.

```
physics.addParticle(p1);
physics.addParticle(p2);
```

If you look at the toxiclibs documentation, you'll see that the `addParticle()` expects a `VerletParticle2D` object.

```
addParticle(VerletParticle2D particle)
```

And how can we then pass into the function our own `Particle` object? Remember that other tenet of object-oriented programming—polymorphism? Here, because our `Particle` class `extends VerletParticle2D`, we can choose to treat our particle in two different ways—as a `Particle` or as a `VerletParticle2D`. This is an incredibly powerful feature of object-oriented programming. If we build our custom classes based on classes from toxiclibs, we can use our objects in conjunction with all of the functions toxiclibs has to offer.

In addition to the `VerletParticle` class, toxiclibs has a set of classes that allow you to connect particles with spring forces. There are three types of springs in toxiclibs:

- `VerletSpring`: This class creates a springy connection between two particles in space. A spring's properties can be configured in such a way as to create a stiff stick-like connection or a highly elastic stretchy connection. A particle can also be locked so that only one end of the spring can move.

- `VerletConstrainedSpring`: A `VerletConstrainedSpring` object is a spring whose maximum distance can be limited. This can help the whole spring system achieve better stability.

- `VerletMinDistanceSpring`: A `VerletMinDistanceSpring` object is a spring that only enforces its rest length if the current distance is less than its rest length. This is handy if you want to ensure objects are at least a certain distance from each other, but don't care if the distance is bigger than the enforced minimum.

The inheritance and polymorphism technique we employed in the previous section also proves to be useful when creating springs. A spring expects two particles when it is created. And again, because our `Particle` class `extends VerletParticle`, a `VerletSpring` object will accept our `Particle` objects passed into the constructor. Let's take a look at some example code that assumes the existence of our two previous particles `p1` and `p2` and creates a connection between them with a given rest length and strength.

```
float len = 80;                          // What is the rest length of the spring?
float strength = 0.01;                   // How strong is the spring?
VerletSpring2D spring=new VerletSpring2D(p1,p2,len,strength);
```

Just as with particles, in order for the connection to actually be part of the physics world, we need to explicitly add it.

```
physics.addSpring(spring);
```

5.17 Putting It All Together: A Simple Interactive Spring

One thing we saw with Box2D is that the physics simulation broke down when we overrode it and manually set the location of a body. With toxiclibs, we don't have this problem. If we want to move the location of a particle, we can simply set its *x* and *y* location manually. However, before we do so, it's generally a good idea to call the `lock()` function.

`lock()` is typically used to lock a particle in place and is identical to setting a Box2D body's density to 0. However, here we are going to show how to lock a particle temporarily, move it, and then unlock it so that it continues to move according to the physics simulation. Let's say you want to move a given particle whenever you click the mouse.

```
if (mousePressed) {
```

```
    p2.lock();
    p2.x = mouseX;
    p2.y = mouseY;
    p2.unlock();
  }
```

First lock the particle, then set the x and y, then unlock() it.

And now we're ready to put all of these elements together in a simple example that connects two particles with a spring. One particle is locked in place, and the other can be moved by dragging the mouse. Note that this example is virtually identical to Example 3.11 (see page 139).

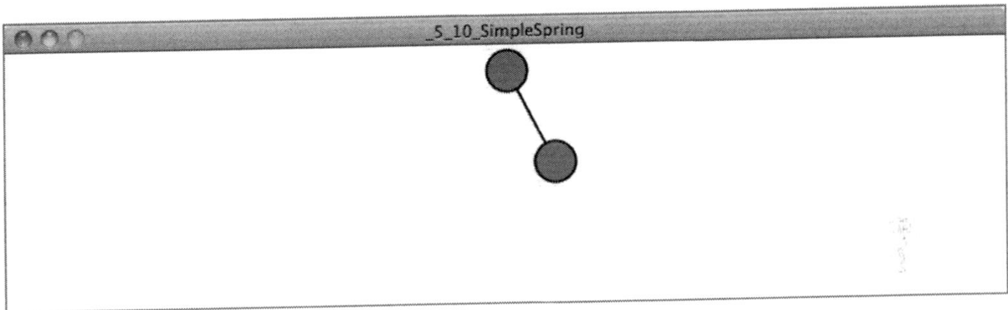

Example 5.10: Simple Spring with toxiclibs

```
import toxi.physics2d.*;
import toxi.physics2d.behaviors.*;
import toxi.geom.*;

VerletPhysics2D physics;
Particle p1;
Particle p2;

void setup() {
  size(640,360);

  physics=new VerletPhysics2D();
  physics.addBehavior(new GravityBehavior2D(new Vec2D(0,0.5)));
  physics.setWorldBounds(new Rect(0,0,width,height));

  p1 = new Particle(new Vec2D(100,20));
  p2 = new Particle(new Vec2D(100,180));
  p1.lock();

  VerletSpring2D spring=new VerletSpring2D(p1,p2,80,0.01);
```

Creating a physics world

Creating two Particles

Locking Particle 1 in place

Creating one Spring

```
  physics.addParticle(p1);                          Must add everything to the world
  physics.addParticle(p2);
  physics.addSpring(spring);
}

void draw() {
  physics.update();                                 Must update the physics

  background(255);

  line(p1.x,p1.y,p2.x,p2.y);                        Drawing everything
  p1.display();
  p2.display();

  if (mousePressed) {
    p2.lock();                                      Moving a Particle according to the mouse
    p2.x = mouseX;
    p2.y = mouseY;
    p2.unlock();
  }
}

class Particle extends VerletParticle2D {           How cute is our simple Particle class?!

  Particle(Vec2D loc) {
    super(loc);
  }

  void display() {
    fill(175);
    stroke(0);
    ellipse(x,y,16,16);
  }
}
```

5.18 Connected Systems, Part I: String

The above example, two particles connected with a single spring, is the core building block for what toxiclibs' physics is particularly well suited for: soft body simulations. For example, a string can be simulated by connecting a line of particles with springs. A blanket can be simulated by connecting a grid of particles with springs. And a cute, cuddly, squishy cartoon character can be simulated by a custom layout of particles connected with springs.

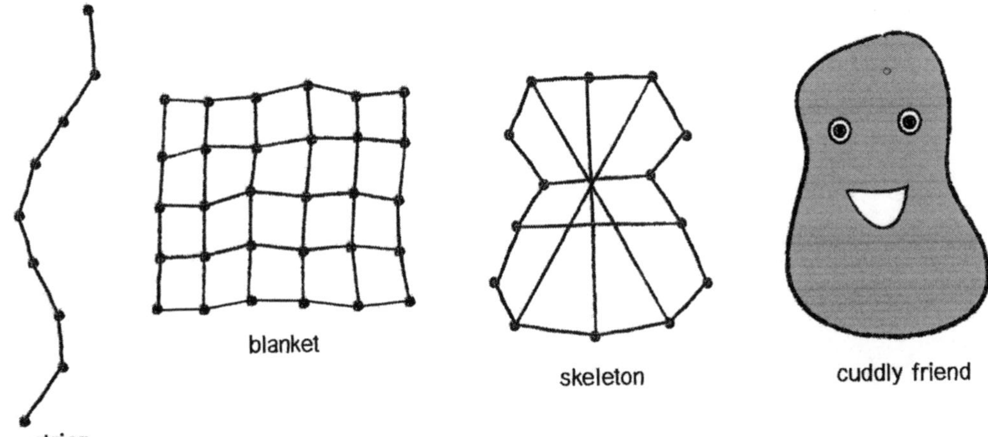

Figure 5.14

Let's begin by simulating a "soft pendulum"—a bob hanging from a string, instead of a rigid arm like we had in Chapter 3 (see page 131). Let's use the "string" in Figure 5.14 above as our model.

First, we'll need a list of particles (let's use the same `Particle` class we built in the previous example).

```
ArrayList<Particle> particles = new ArrayList<Particle>();
```

Now, let's say we want to have 20 particles, all spaced 10 pixels apart.

Figure 5.15

```
float len = 10;
float numParticles = 20;
```

We can loop from `i` equals 0 all the way up to 20, with each particle's *y* location set to `i * 10` so that the first particle is at *(0,10)*, the second at *(0,20)*, the third at *(0,30)*, etc.

```
for(int i=0; i < numPoints; i++) {
  Particle particle=new Particle(i*len,10);     // Spacing them out along the x-axis
  physics.addParticle(particle);                // Add the particle to our list.
```

```
  particles.add(particle);
}
```

Add the particle to the physics world.

Even though it's a bit redundant, we're going to add the particle to both the toxiclibs physics world and to our own list. In case we eventually have multiple strings, this will allow us to know which particles are connected to which strings.

Now for the fun part: It's time to connect all the particles. Particle 1 will be connected to particle 0, particle 2 to particle 1, 3 to 2, 4 to 3, etc.

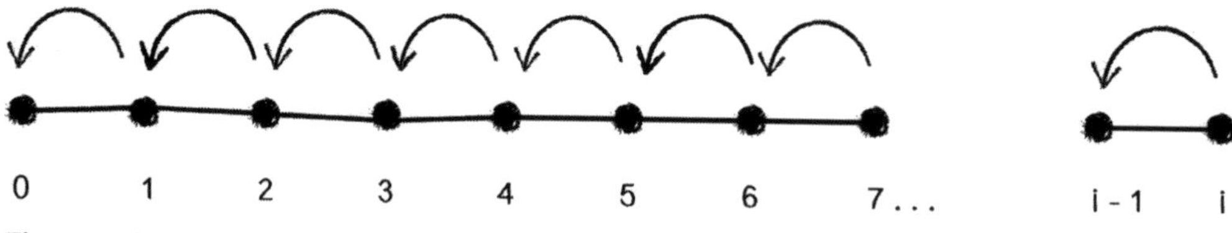

Figure 5.16

In other words, particle `i` needs to be connected to particle `i-1` (except for when `i` equals zero).

```
if (i != 0) {
  Particle previous = particles.get(i-1);
  VerletSpring2D spring = new VerletSpring2D(particle,previous,len,strength);
  physics.addSpring(spring);
}
```

First we need a reference to the previous particle.

Then we make a spring connection between the particle and the previous particle with a rest length and strength (both floats).

We must not forget to add the spring to the physics world.

Now, what if we want the string to hang from a fixed point? We can lock one of the particles—the first, the last, the middle one, etc. Here's how we would access the first particle (in the `ArrayList`) and lock it.

```
Particle head=particles.get(0);
head.lock();
```

And if we want to draw all the particles as being connected with a line, along with a circle for the last particle, we can use `beginShape()`, `endShape()`, and `vertex()`, accessing the particle locations from our `ArrayList`.

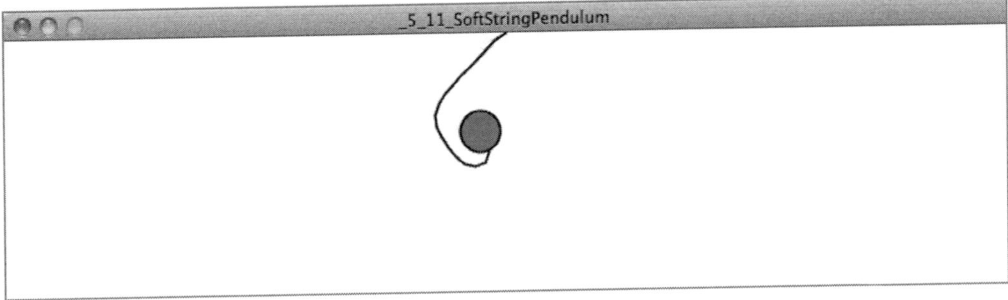

Example 5.11: Soft swinging pendulum

```
stroke(0);
noFill();
beginShape();
for (Particle p : particles) {
  vertex(p.x,p.y);                    // Each particle is one point in the line.
}
endShape();
Particle tail = particles.get(numPoints-1);
tail.display();                       // This draws the last particle as a circle.
```

The full code available with the chapter download also demonstrates how to drag the tail particle with the mouse.

Exercise 5.13

Create a hanging cloth simulation using the technique above, but connect all the particles with a grid as demonstrated in the screenshot below.

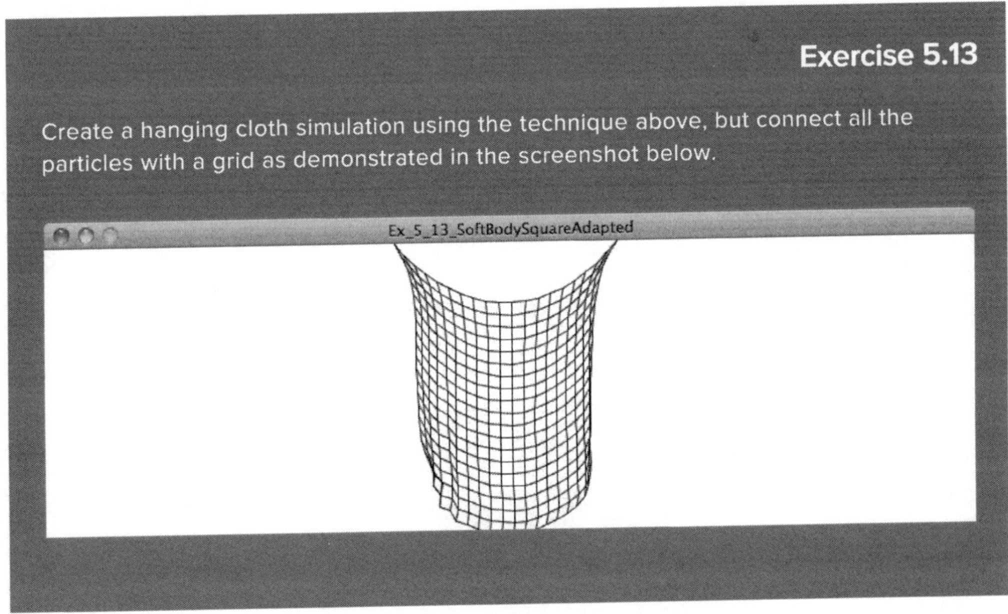

5.19 Connected Systems, Part II: Force-Directed Graph

Have you ever encountered the following scenario?

"I have a whole bunch of stuff I want to draw on the screen and I want all that stuff to be spaced out evenly in a nice, neat, organized manner. Otherwise I have trouble sleeping at night."

This is not an uncommon problem in computational design. One solution is typically referred to as a "force-directed graph." A force-directed graph is a visualization of elements—let's call them "nodes"—in which the positions of those nodes are not manually assigned. Rather, the nodes arrange themselves according to a set of forces. While any forces can be used, a typical example involves spring forces. And so toxiclibs is perfect for this scenario.

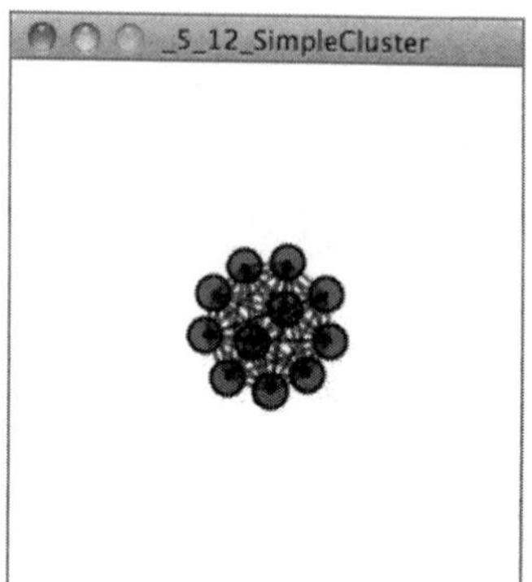

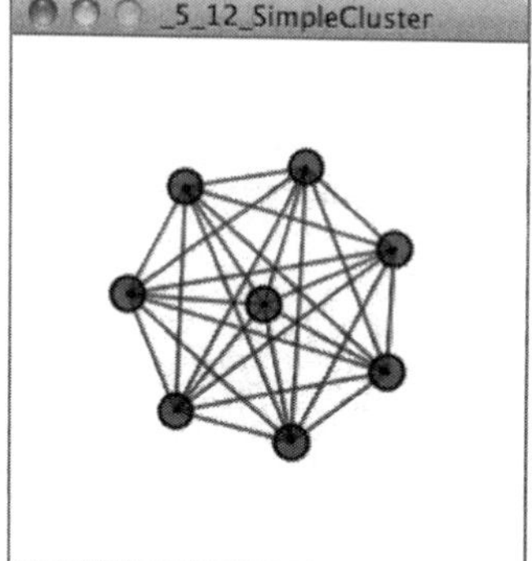

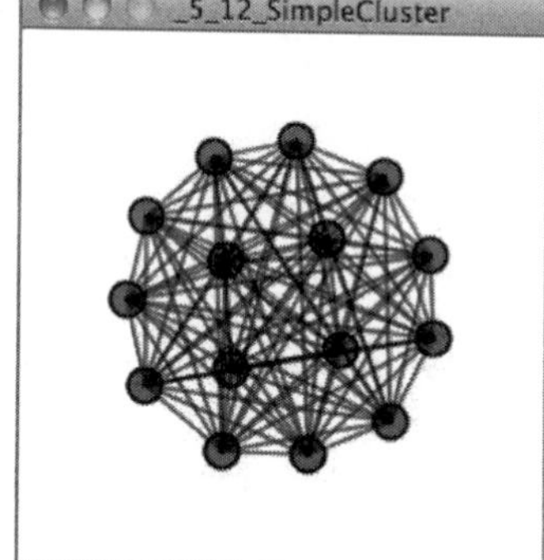

How do we implement the above?

First, we'll need a `Node` class. This is the easy part; it can `extend VerletParticle2D`. Really, this is just what we did before, only we're calling it `Node` now instead of `Particle`.

```
class Node extends VerletParticle2D {
  Node(Vec2D pos) {
    super(pos);
  }

  void display() {
    fill(0,150);
    stroke(0);
    ellipse(x,y,16,16);
  }
}
```

Next we can write a class called `Cluster`, which will describe a list of nodes.

```
class Cluster {

  ArrayList<Node> nodes;

  float diameter;
```

We'll use this variable for the rest length between all the nodes.

```
  Cluster(int n, float d, Vec2D center) {
    nodes = new ArrayList<Node>();
    diameter = d;

    for (int i = 0; i < n; i++) {
      nodes.add(new Node(center.add(Vec2D.randomVector())));
```

Here's a funny little detail. We're going to have a problem if all the Node objects start in exactly the same location. So we add a random vector to the center location so that each Node is slightly offset.

```
    }
  }
```

Let's assume we added a `display()` function to draw all the nodes in the cluster and created a `Cluster` object in `setup()` and displayed it in `draw()`. If we ran the sketch as is, nothing would happen. Why? Because we forgot the whole force-directed graph part! We need to connect every single node to every other node with a force. But what exactly do we mean by that? Let's assume we have four **`Node`** objects: 0, 1, 2 and 3. Here are our connections:

```
0 connected to 1
0 connected to 2
0 connected to 3
1 connected to 2
1 connected to 3
2 connected to 3
```

Notice two important details about our connection list.

- ***No node is connected to itself.*** We don't have 0 connected to 0 or 1 connected to 1.
- ***We don't need to repeat connections in reverse.*** In other words, if we've already said 0 is connected to 1, we don't need to say 1 is connected to 0 because, well, it already is!

So how do we write code to make these connections for *N* number of nodes?

Look at the left column. It reads: 000 11 22. So we know we need to access each node in the list from 0 to *N*-1.

```
for (int i = 0; i < nodes.size()-1; i++) {
  VerletParticle2D ni = nodes.get(i);
```

Now, we know we need to connect node 0 to nodes 1,2,3. For node 1: 2,3. For node 2: 3. So for every node i, we must loop from i+1 until the end of the list.

```
    for (int j = i+1; j < nodes.size(); j++) {
      VerletParticle2D nj = nodes.get(j);
```

Look how we start j at i + 1.

With every two Nodes we find, all we have to do then is make a spring.

```
      physics.addSpring(new
VerletSpring2D(ni,nj,diameter,0.01));
    }
  }
```

The Spring connects Nodes "ni" and "nj".

Assuming those connections are made in the `Cluster` constructor, we can now create a cluster in our main tab and see the results!

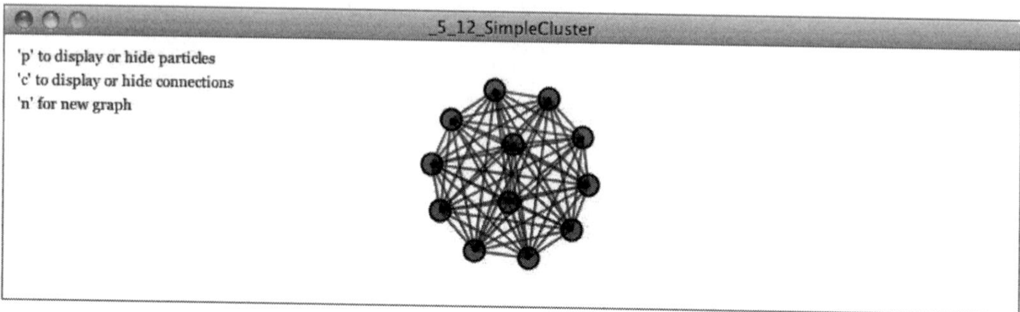
_5_12_SimpleCluster
'p' to display or hide particles
'c' to display or hide connections
'n' for new graph

Example 5.12: Cluster

```
import toxi.geom.*;
import toxi.physics2d.*;

VerletPhysics2D physics;
Cluster cluster;

void setup() {
  size(300,300);
  physics=new VerletPhysics2D();
  cluster = new Cluster(8,100,new Vec2D(width/2,height/2));
}

void draw() {
  physics.update();
  background(255);
```

Make a cluster.

```
  cluster.display();                Draw the cluster.
}
```

Exercise 5.14

Use the `Cluster` structure as a skeleton for a cute, cuddly, squishy creature (à la "Nokia Friends"). Add gravity and also allow the creature to be dragged with the mouse.

Exercise 5.15

Expand the force-directed graph to have more than one `Cluster` object. Use a `VerletMinDistanceSpring2D` object to connect cluster to cluster.

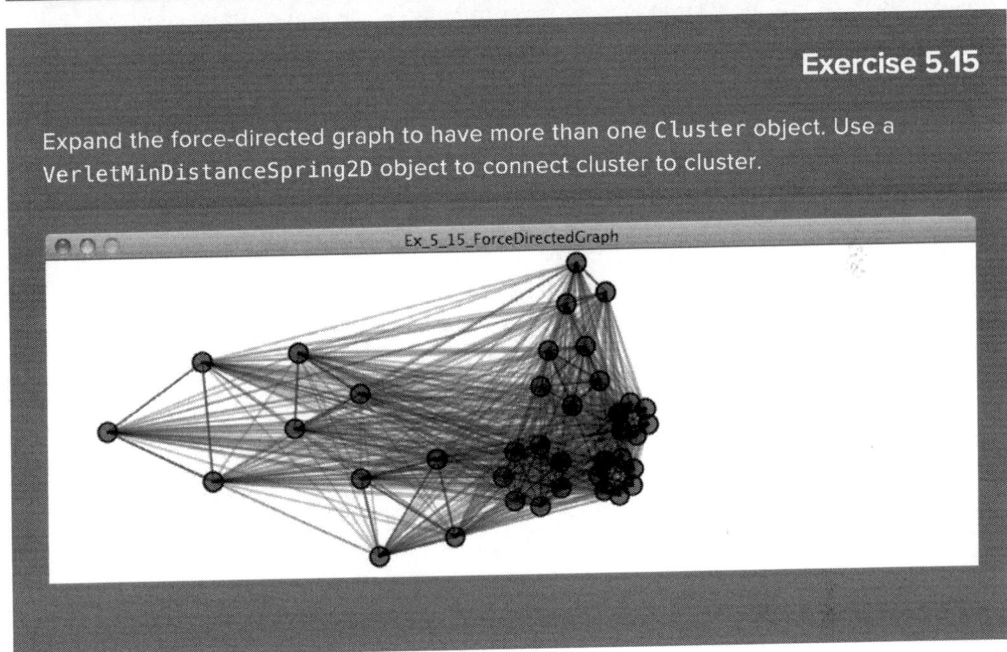

5.20 Attraction and Repulsion Behaviors

When we looked at adding an attraction force to Box2D, we found that the Box2D `Body` class included an `applyForce()` function. All we needed to do was calculate the attraction force (Force = G * mass1 * mass2 / distance squared) as a vector and apply it to the body. toxiclibs `VerletParticle` class also includes a function called `addForce()` that we can use to apply any calculated force to a particle.

However, toxiclibs also takes this idea one step further by allowing us to attach some common forces (let's call them "behaviors") to particles, calculating them and applying them for us! For example, if we attach an `AttractionBehavior` object to a particle, then all other particles in the physics world will be attracted to that particle.

Let's say we have a `Particle` class (that `extends VerletParticle`).

```
Particle p = new Particle(new Vec2D(200,200));
```

Once we've made a `Particle` object, we can create an `AttractionBehavior` object associated with that particle.

```
float distance = 20;
float strength = 0.1;
AttractionBehavior behavior = new AttractionBehavior(p, distance, strength);
```

Notice how the behavior is created with two parameters—`distance` and `strength`. The distance specifies the range within which the behavior will be applied. For example, in the above scenario, only other particles within twenty pixels will feel the attraction force. The strength, of course, specifies how strong the force is.

Finally, in order for the force to be activated, the behavior needs to be added to the physics world.

```
physics.addBehavior(behavior);
```

This means everything that lives in the physics simulation will always be attracted to that particle, as long as it is within the distance threshold.

Even though toxiclibs does not handle collisions, you can create a collision-like effect by adding a repulsive behavior to each and every particle (so that every particle repels every other particle). Let's look at how we might modify our `Particle` class to do this.

```
class Particle extends VerletParticle2D {

  float r;                                              // We've added a radius to every Particle.

  Particle (Vec2D loc) {
    super(loc);
    r = 4;
    physics.addBehavior(new AttractionBehavior(this, r*4, -1));
  }
  // Every time a Particle is made, an AttractionBehavior is generated and added
  // to the physics world. Note that when the strength is negative, it's a repulsive force!

  void display () {
    fill (255);
    stroke (255);
    ellipse (x, y, r*2, r*2);
  }
}
```

We could now recreate our attraction example by having a single `Attractor` object that exerts an attraction behavior over the entire window.

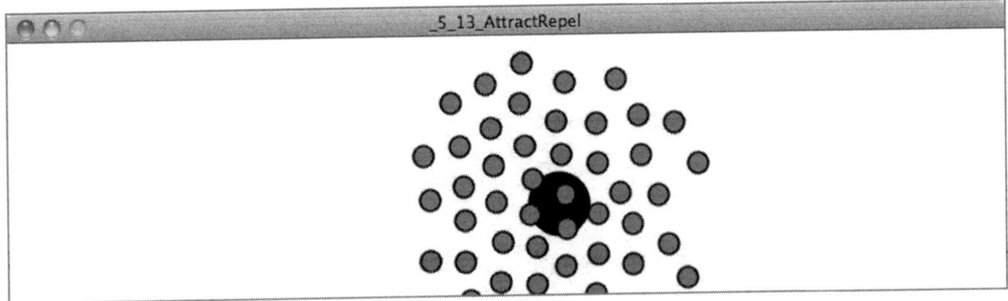

Example 5.13: Attraction/Repulsion

```
class Attractor extends VerletParticle2D {

  float r;

  Attractor (Vec2D loc) {
    super (loc);
    r = 24;
    physics.addBehavior(new AttractionBehavior(this, width, 0.1));
  }

  void display () {
    fill(0);
    ellipse (x, y, r*2, r*2);
  }
}
```

The AttractionBehavior "distance" equals the width so that it covers the entire window.

Exercise 5.16

Create an object that both attracts and repels. What if it attracts any particle that is far away but repels those particles at a short distance?

Exercise 5.17

Use `AttractionBehavior` in conjunction with spring forces.

The Ecosystem Project

Step 5 Exercise:

Take your system of creatures from Step 4 and use a physics engine to drive their motion and behaviors. Some possibilities:

- Use Box2D to allow collisions between creatures. Consider triggering events when creatures collide.
- Use Box2D to augment the design of your creatures. Build a skeleton with distance joints or make appendages with revolute joints.
- Use toxiclibs to augment the design of your creature. Use a chain of toxiclibs particles for tentacles or a mesh of springs as a skeleton.
- Use toxiclibs to add attraction and repulsion behaviors to your creatures.
- Use spring (or joint) connections between objects to control their interactions. Create and delete these springs on the fly. Consider making these connections visible or invisible to the viewer.

Chapter 6. Autonomous Agents

"This is an exercise in fictional science, or science fiction, if you like that better."

— Valentino Braitenberg

Believe it or not, there is a purpose. Well, at least there's a purpose to the first five chapters of this book. We could stop right here; after all, we've looked at several different ways of modeling motion and simulating physics. Angry Birds, here we come!

Still, let's think for a moment. Why are we here? The *nature* of code, right? What have we been designing so far? Inanimate objects. Lifeless shapes sitting on our screens that flop around when affected by forces in their environment. What if we could breathe life into those shapes? What if those shapes could live by their own rules? Can shapes have hopes and dreams and fears? This is what we are here in this chapter to do—develop *autonomous agents*.

6.1 Forces from Within

The term ***autonomous agent*** generally refers to an entity that makes its own choices about how to act in its environment without any influence from a leader or global plan. For us, "acting" will mean moving. This addition is a significant conceptual leap. Instead of a box sitting on a boundary waiting to be pushed by another falling box, we are now going to design a box that has the ability and "desire" to leap out of the way of that other falling box, if it so chooses. While the concept of forces that come from within is a major shift in our design thinking, our code base will barely change, as these desires and actions are simply that—*forces*.

Here are three key components of autonomous agents that we'll want to keep in mind as we build our examples.

- **An autonomous agent has a *limited* ability to perceive environment.** It makes sense that a living, breathing being should have an awareness of its environment. What does this mean for us, however? As we look at examples in this chapter, we will point out programming techniques for allowing objects to store references to other objects and therefore "perceive" their environment. It's also crucial that we consider the word *limited* here. Are we designing an all-knowing rectangle that flies around a Processing window, aware of everything else in that window? Or are we creating a shape that can only examine any other object within fifteen pixels of itself? Of course, there is no right answer to this question; it all depends. We'll explore some possibilities as we move forward. For a simulation to feel more "natural," however, limitations are a good thing. An insect, for example, may only be aware of the sights and smells that immediately surround it. For a real-world creature, we could study the exact science of these limitations. Luckily for us, we can just make stuff up and try it out.

- **An autonomous agent processes the information from its environment and calculates an action.** This will be the easy part for us, as the action is a force. The environment might tell the agent that there's a big scary-looking shark swimming right at it, and the action will be a powerful force in the opposite direction.

- **An autonomous agent has no leader.** This third principle is something we care a little less about. After all, if you are designing a system where it makes sense to have a leader barking commands at various entities, then that's what you'll want to implement. Nevertheless, many of these examples will have no leader for an important reason. As we get to the end of this chapter and examine group behaviors, we will look at designing collections of autonomous agents that exhibit the properties of complex systems— intelligent and structured group dynamics that emerge not from a leader, but from the local interactions of the elements themselves.

In the late 1980s, computer scientist Craig Reynolds (http://www.red3d.com/cwr/) developed algorithmic steering behaviors for animated characters. These behaviors allowed individual elements to navigate their digital environments in a "lifelike" manner with strategies for fleeing, wandering, arriving, pursuing, evading, etc. Used in the case of a single autonomous agent, these behaviors are fairly simple to understand and implement. In addition, by building a system of multiple characters that steer themselves according to simple, locally based rules, surprising levels of complexity emerge. The most famous example is Reynolds's "boids" model for "flocking/swarming" behavior.

6.2 Vehicles and Steering

Now that we understand the core concepts behind autonomous agents, we can begin writing the code. There are many places where we could start. Artificial simulations of ant and termite colonies are fantastic demonstrations of systems of autonomous agents. (For more on this topic, I encourage you to read *Turtles, Termites, and Traffic Jams* by Mitchel Resnick.) However, we want to begin by examining agent behaviors that build on the work we've done in the first five chapters of this book: modeling motion with vectors and driving motion with forces. And so it's time to rename our `Mover` class that became our `Particle` class once again. This time we are going to call it `Vehicle`.

```
class Vehicle {

  PVector location;
  PVector velocity;
  PVector acceleration;

  // What else do we need to add?
```

In his 1999 paper "Steering Behaviors for Autonomous Characters," Reynolds uses the word "vehicle" to describe his autonomous agents, so we will follow suit.

Why Vehicle?

In 1986, Italian neuroscientist and cyberneticist Valentino Braitenberg described a series of hypothetical vehicles with simple internal structures in his book *Vehicles: Experiments in Synthetic Psychology*. Braitenberg argues that his extraordinarily simple mechanical vehicles manifest behaviors such as fear, aggression, love, foresight, and optimism. Reynolds took his inspiration from Braitenberg, and we'll take ours from Reynolds.

Reynolds describes the motion of *idealized* vehicles (idealized because we are not concerned with the actual engineering of such vehicles, but simply assume that they exist and will respond to our rules) as a series of three layers—**Action Selection**, **Steering**, and **Locomotion**.

1. ***Action Selection.*** A vehicle has a goal (or goals) and can select an action (or a combination of actions) based on that goal. This is essentially where we left off with autonomous agents. The vehicle takes a look at its environment and calculates an action based on a desire: "I see a zombie marching towards me. Since I don't want my brains to be eaten, I'm going to flee from the zombie." The goal is to keep one's brains and the action is to flee. Reynolds's paper describes many goals and associated actions such as: seek a target, avoid an obstacle, and

follow a path. In a moment, we'll start building these examples out with Processing code.

2. ***Steering.*** Once an action has been selected, the vehicle has to calculate its next move. For us, the next move will be a force; more specifically, a steering force. Luckily, Reynolds has developed a simple steering force formula that we'll use throughout the examples in this chapter: ***steering force = desired velocity - current velocity***. We'll get into the details of this formula and why it works so effectively in the next section.

3. ***Locomotion.*** For the most part, we're going to ignore this third layer. In the case of fleeing zombies, the locomotion could be described as "left foot, right foot, left foot, right foot, as fast as you can." In our Processing world, however, a rectangle or circle or triangle's actual movement across a window is irrelevant given that it's all an illusion in the first place. Nevertheless, this isn't to say that you should ignore locomotion entirely. You will find great value in thinking about the locomotive design of your vehicle and how you choose to animate it. The examples in this chapter will remain visually bare, and a good exercise would be to elaborate on the animation style —could you add spinning wheels or oscillating paddles or shuffling legs?

Ultimately, the most important layer for you to consider is #1—*Action Selection*. What are the elements of your system and what are their goals? In this chapter, we are going to look at a series of steering behaviors (i.e. actions): seek, flee, follow a path, follow a flow field, flock with your neighbors, etc. It's important to realize, however, that the point of understanding how to write the code for these behaviors is not because you should use them in all of your projects. Rather, these are a set of building blocks, a foundation from which you can design and develop vehicles with creative goals and new and exciting behaviors. And even though we will think literally in this chapter (follow that pixel!), you should allow yourself to think more abstractly (like Braitenberg). What would it mean for your vehicle to have "love" or "fear" as its goal, its driving force? Finally (and we'll address this later in the chapter), you won't get very far by developing simulations with only one action. Yes, our first example will be "seek a target." But for you to be creative—to make these steering behaviors *your own*—it will all come down to mixing and matching multiple actions within the same vehicle. So view these examples not as singular behaviors to be emulated, but as pieces of a larger puzzle that you will eventually assemble.

6.3 The Steering Force

We can entertain ourselves by discussing the theoretical principles behind autonomous agents and steering as much as we like, but we can't get anywhere without first understanding the concept of a steering force. Consider the following scenario. A vehicle moving with velocity desires to seek a target.

Its goal and subsequent action is to seek the target in Figure 6.1. If you think back to Chapter 2, you might begin by making the target an attractor and apply a gravitational force that pulls the vehicle to the target. This would be a perfectly reasonable solution, but conceptually it's not what we're looking for here. We don't want to simply calculate a force that pushes the vehicle towards its target; rather, we are asking the vehicle to make an intelligent decision to steer towards the target based on its perception of its state and environment (i.e. how fast and in what direction is it currently moving). The vehicle should look at how it desires to move (a vector pointing to the target), compare that goal with how quickly it is currently moving (its velocity), and apply a force accordingly.

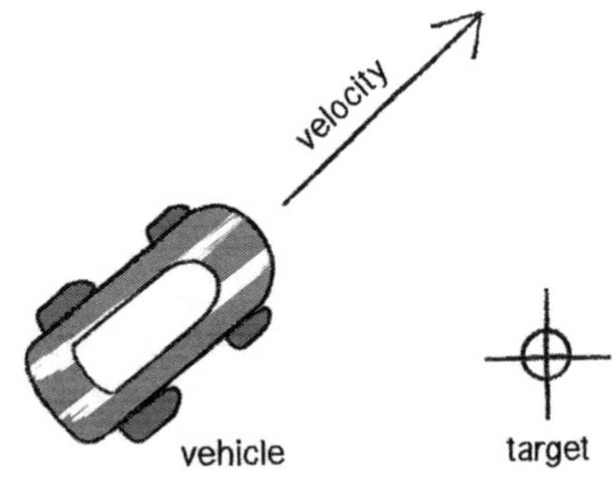

Figure 6.1

steering force = desired velocity - current velocity

Or as we might write in Processing:

```
PVector steer = PVector.sub(desired,velocity);
```

In the above formula, velocity is no problem. After all, we've got a variable for that. However, we don't have the *desired velocity*; this is something we have to calculate. Let's take a look at Figure 6.2. If we've defined the vehicle's goal as "seeking the target," then its desired velocity is a vector that points from its current location to the target location.

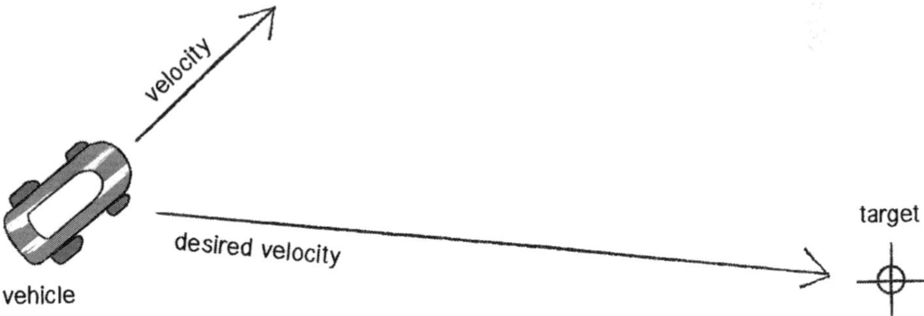

Figure 6.2

Assuming a `PVector` target, we then have:

```
PVector desired = PVector.sub(target,location);
```

But this isn't particularly realistic. What if we have a very high-resolution window and the target is thousands of pixels away? Sure, the vehicle might desire to teleport itself instantly to the target location with a massive velocity, but this won't make for an effective animation. What we really want to say is:

The vehicle desires to move towards the target at maximum speed.

In other words, the vector should point from location to target and with a magnitude equal to maximum speed (i.e. the fastest the vehicle can go). So first, we need to make sure we add a variable to our `Vehicle` class that stores maximum speed.

```
class Vehicle {
  PVector location;
  PVector velocity;
  PVector acceleration;
  float maxspeed;                 // Maximum speed
```

Then, in our desired velocity calculation, we scale according to maximum speed.

```
PVector desired = PVector.sub(target,location);
desired.normalize();
desired.mult(maxspeed);
```

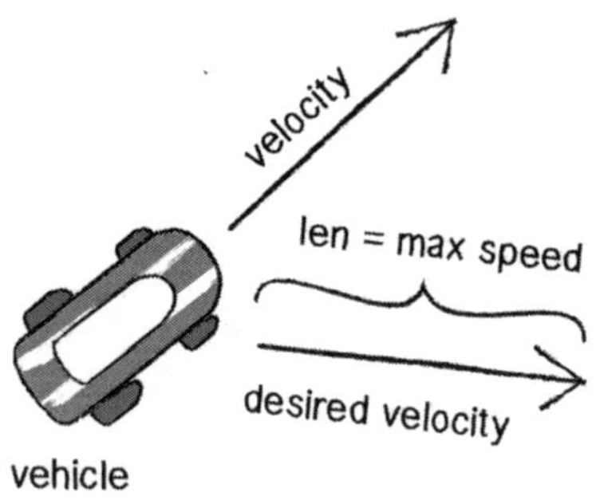

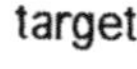

Figure 6.3

Putting this all together, we can write a function called `seek()` that receives a `PVector` target and calculates a steering force towards that target.

```
void seek(PVector target) {
  PVector desired = PVector.sub(target,location);
  desired.normalize();
  desired.mult(maxspeed);                             // Calculating the desired velocity to target at max speed

  PVector steer = PVector.sub(desired,velocity);      // Reynolds's formula for steering force
```

```
    applyForce(steer);
  }
```

Using our physics model and applying the force to the object's acceleration

Note how in the above function we finish by passing the steering force into `applyForce()`. This assumes that we are basing this example on the foundation we built in Chapter 2 (see page 66). However, you could just as easily use the steering force with Box2D's `applyForce()` function or toxiclibs' `addForce()` function.

So why does this all work so well? Let's see what the steering force looks like relative to the vehicle and target locations.

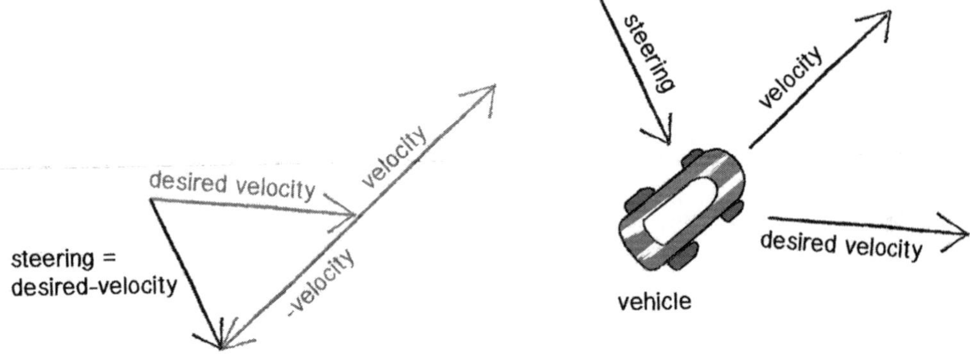

Figure 6.4

Again, notice how this is not at all the same force as gravitational attraction. Remember one of our principles of autonomous agents: An autonomous agent has a *limited* ability to perceive its environment. Here is that ability, subtly embedded into Reynolds's steering formula. If the vehicle weren't moving at all (zero velocity), desired minus velocity would be equal to desired. But this is not the case. The vehicle is aware of its own velocity and its steering force compensates accordingly. This creates a more active simulation, as the way in which the vehicle moves towards the targets depends on the way it is moving in the first place.

In all of this excitement, however, we've missed one last step. What sort of vehicle is this? Is it a super sleek race car with amazing handling? Or a giant Mack truck that needs a lot of advance notice to turn? A graceful panda, or a lumbering elephant? Our example code, as it stands, has no feature to account for this variability in steering ability. Steering ability can be controlled by limiting the magnitude of the steering force. Let's call that limit the "maximum force" (or `maxforce` for short). And so finally, we have:

```
class Vehicle {
  PVector location;
  PVector velocity;
  PVector acceleration;
```

```
float maxspeed;           // Maximum speed
float maxforce;           // Now we also have maximum force.
```

followed by:

```
void seek(PVector target) {
  PVector desired = PVector.sub(target,location);
  desired.normalize();
  desired.mult(maxspeed);
  PVector steer = PVector.sub(desired,velocity);

  steer.limit(maxforce);     // Limit the magnitude of the steering force.

  applyForce(steer);
}
```

Limiting the steering force brings up an important point. We must always remember that it's not actually our goal to get the vehicle to the target as fast as possible. If that were the case, we would just say "location equals target" and there the vehicle would be. Our goal, as Reynolds puts it, is to move the vehicle in a "lifelike and improvisational manner." We're trying to make it appear as if the vehicle is steering its way to the target, and so it's up to us to play with the forces and variables of the system to simulate a given behavior. For example, a large maximum steering force would result in a very different path than a small one. One is not inherently better or worse than the other; it depends on your desired effect. (And of course, these values need not be fixed and could change based on other conditions. Perhaps a vehicle has health: the higher the health, the better it can steer.)

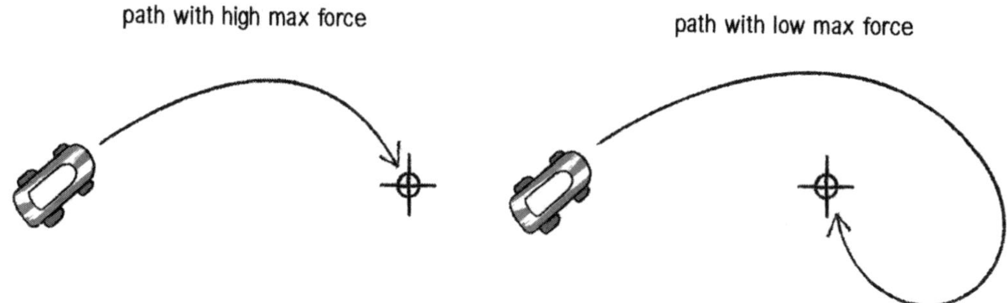

Figure 6.5

Here is the full `Vehicle` class, incorporating the rest of the elements from the Chapter 2 `Mover` object.

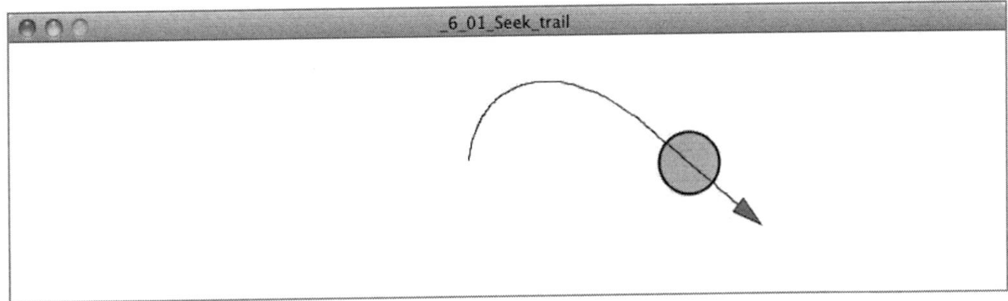

Example 6.1: Seeking a target

```
class Vehicle {

  PVector location;
  PVector velocity;
  PVector acceleration;
  float r;                          // Additional variable for size
  float maxforce;
  float maxspeed;

  Vehicle(float x, float y) {
    acceleration = new PVector(0,0);
    velocity = new PVector(0,0);
    location = new PVector(x,y);
    r = 3.0;
    maxspeed = 4;                   // Arbitrary values for maxspeed and force;
    maxforce = 0.1;                 // try varying these!
  }

  void update() {                   // Our standard "Euler integration" motion model
    velocity.add(acceleration);
    velocity.limit(maxspeed);
    location.add(velocity);
    acceleration.mult(0);
  }

  void applyForce(PVector force) {  // Newton's second law; we could divide by mass if we wanted.
    acceleration.add(force);
  }
```

```
void seek(PVector target) {                          Our seek steering force algorithm
  PVector desired = PVector.sub(target,location);
  desired.normalize();
  desired.mult(maxspeed);
  PVector steer = PVector.sub(desired,velocity);
  steer.limit(maxforce);
  applyForce(steer);
}

void display() {
  float theta = velocity.heading() + PI/2;           Vehicle is a triangle pointing in the direction
                                                     of velocity; since it is drawn pointing up, we
                                                     rotate it an additional 90 degrees.
  fill(175);
  stroke(0);
  pushMatrix();
  translate(location.x,location.y);
  rotate(theta);
  beginShape();
  vertex(0, -r*2);
  vertex(-r, r*2);
  vertex(r, r*2);
  endShape(CLOSE);
  popMatrix();
}
```

Exercise 6.1

Implement a “fleeing” steering behavior (desired vector is inverse of “seek”).

Exercise 6.2

Implement seeking a moving target, often referred to as “pursuit.” In this case, your desired vector won't point towards the object's current location, but rather its “future” location as extrapolated from its current velocity. We'll see this ability for a vehicle to “predict the future” in later examples.

Exercise 6.3

Create a sketch where a vehicle's maximum force and maximum speed do not remain constant, but rather vary according to environmental factors.

6.4 Arriving Behavior

After working for a bit with the seeking behavior, you probably are asking yourself, "What if I want my vehicle to slow down as it approaches the target?" Before we can even begin to answer this question, we should look at the reasons behind why the seek behavior causes the vehicle to fly past the target so that it has to turn around and go back. Let's consider the brain of a seeking vehicle. What is it thinking?

Frame 1: I want to go as fast as possible towards the target!
Frame 2: I want to go as fast as possible towards the target!
Frame 3: I want to go as fast as possible towards the target!
Frame 4: I want to go as fast as possible towards the target!
Frame 5: I want to go as fast as possible towards the target!
etc.

The vehicle is so gosh darn excited about getting to the target that it doesn't bother to make any intelligent decisions about its speed relative to the target's proximity. Whether it's far away or very close, it always wants to go as fast as possible.

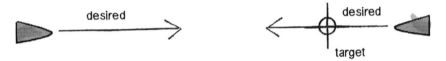

Figure 6.6

In some cases, this is the desired behavior (if a missile is flying at a target, it should always travel at maximum speed.) However, in many other cases (a car pulling into a parking spot, a bee landing on a flower), the vehicle's thought process needs to consider its speed relative to the distance from its target. For example:

Frame 1: I'm very far away. I want to go as fast as possible towards the target!
Frame 2: I'm very far away. I want to go as fast as possible towards the target!
Frame 3: I'm somewhat far away. I want to go as fast as possible towards the target!
Frame 4: I'm getting close. I want to go more slowly towards the target!
Frame 5: I'm almost there. I want to go very slowly towards the target!
Frame 6: I'm there. I want to stop!

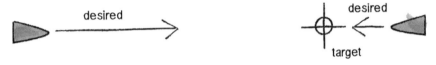

Figure 6.7

How can we implement this "arriving" behavior in code? Let's return to our `seek()` function and find the line of code where we set the magnitude of the desired velocity.

```
PVector desired = PVector.sub(target,location);
desired.normalize();
desired.mult(maxspeed);
```

In Example 6.1, the magnitude of the desired vector is always “maximum” speed.

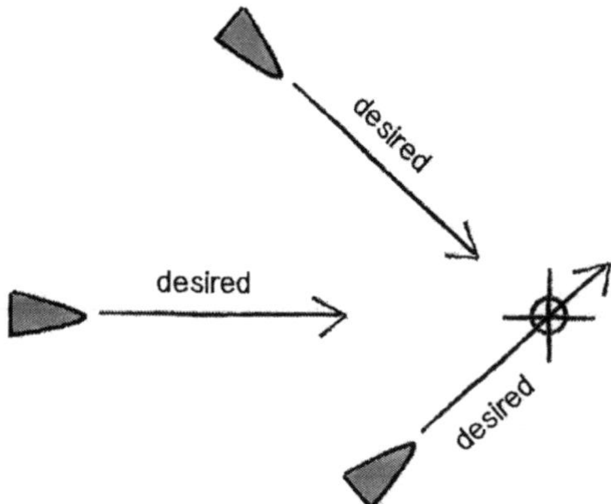

Figure 6.8

What if we instead said the desired velocity is equal to half the distance?

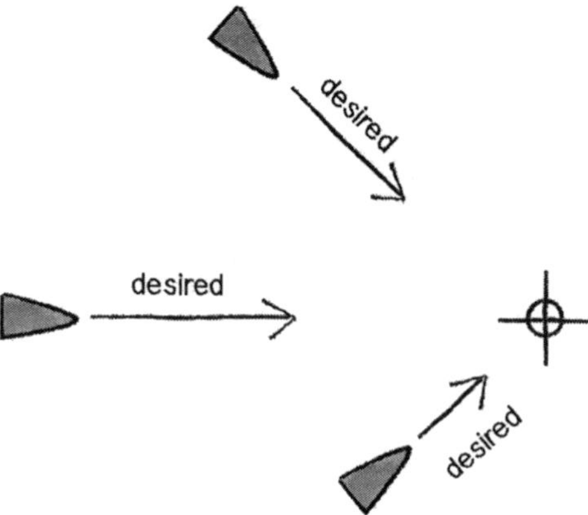

Figure 6.9

```
PVector desired = PVector.sub(target,location);
desired.div(2);
```

While this nicely demonstrates our goal of a desired speed tied to our distance from the target, it’s not particularly reasonable. After all, 10 pixels away is rather close and a desired speed of 5 is rather large. Something like a desired velocity with a magnitude of 5% of the distance would work much better.

```
PVector desired = PVector.sub(target,location);
desired.mult(0.05);
```

Reynolds describes a more sophisticated approach. Let's imagine a circle around the target with a given radius. If the vehicle is within that circle, it slows down—at the edge of the circle, its desired speed is maximum speed, and at the target itself, its desired speed is 0.

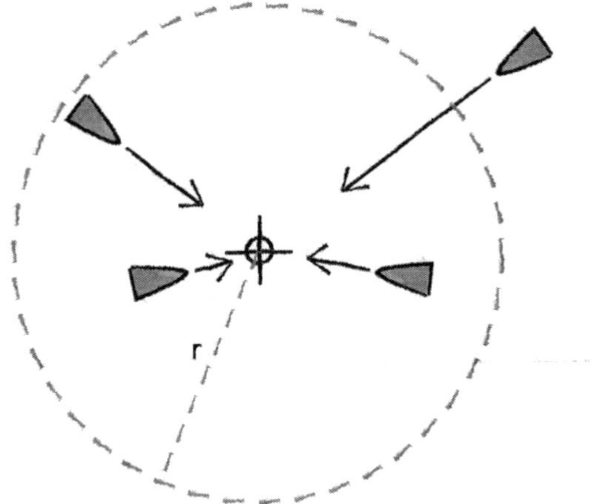

Figure 6.10

In other words, if the distance from the target is less than r, the desired speed is between 0 and maximum speed mapped according to that distance.

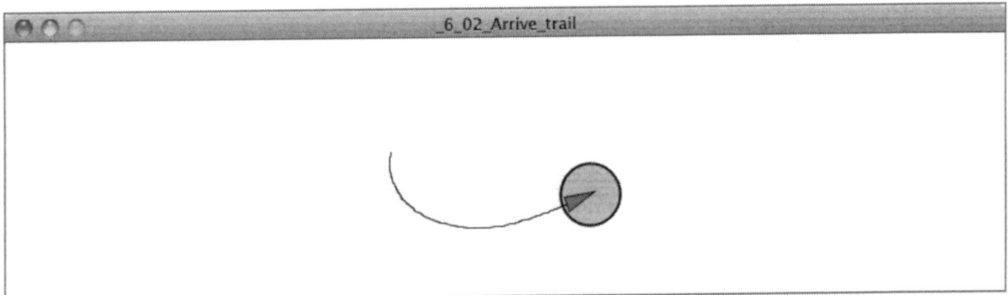

Example 6.2: Arrive steering behavior

```
void arrive(PVector target) {
  PVector desired = PVector.sub(target,location);

  float d = desired.mag();
  desired.normalize();
```

The distance is the magnitude of the vector pointing from location to target.

```
    if (d < 100) {                                      If we are closer than 100 pixels...
      float m = map(d,0,100,0,maxspeed);                ...set the magnitude according to how close
      desired.mult(m);                                  we are.
    } else {
      desired.mult(maxspeed);                           Otherwise, proceed at maximum speed.
    }

    PVector steer = PVector.sub(desired,velocity);      The usual steering = desired - velocity
    steer.limit(maxforce);
    applyForce(steer);
  }
```

The arrive behavior is a great demonstration of the magic of "desired minus velocity." Let's examine this model again relative to how we calculated forces in earlier chapters. In the "gravitational attraction" examples, the force always pointed directly from the object to the target (the exact direction of the desired velocity), whether the force was strong or weak.

The steering function, however, says: "I have the ability to perceive the environment." The force isn't based on just the desired velocity, but on the desired velocity relative to the current velocity. Only things that are alive can know their current velocity. A box falling off a table doesn't know it's falling. A cheetah chasing its prey, however, knows it is chasing.

The steering force, therefore, is essentially a manifestation of the current velocity's ***error***: "I'm supposed to be going this fast in this direction, but I'm actually going this fast in another direction. My error is the difference between where I want to go and where I am currently going." Taking that error and applying it as a steering force results in more dynamic, lifelike simulations. With gravitational attraction, you would never have a force pointing away from the target, no matter how close. But with arriving via steering, if you are moving too fast towards the target, the error would actually tell you to slow down!

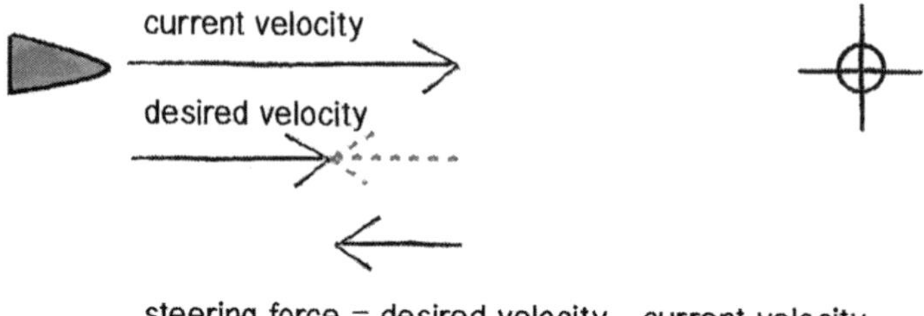

Figure 6.11

6.5 Your Own Desires: Desired Velocity

The first two examples we've covered—seek and arrive—boil down to calculating a single vector for each behavior: the *desired* velocity. And in fact, every single one of Reynolds's steering behaviors follows this same pattern. In this chapter, we're going to walk through several more of Reynolds's behaviors—flow field, path-following, flocking. First, however, I want to emphasize again that these are *examples*—demonstrations of common steering behaviors that are useful in procedural animation. They are not the be-all and end-all of what *you* can do. As long as you can come up with a vector that describes a vehicle's *desired* velocity, then you have created your own steering behavior.

Let's see how Reynolds defines the desired velocity for his wandering behavior.

> *"Wandering is a type of random steering which has some long term order: the steering direction on one frame is related to the steering direction on the next frame. This produces more interesting motion than, for example, simply generating a random steering direction each frame."*
>
> *—Craig Reynolds (http://www.red3d.com/cwr/steer/Wander.html)*

For Reynolds, the goal of wandering is not simply random motion, but rather a sense of moving in one direction for a little while, wandering off to the next for a little bit, and so on and so forth. So how does Reynolds calculate a desired vector to achieve such an effect?

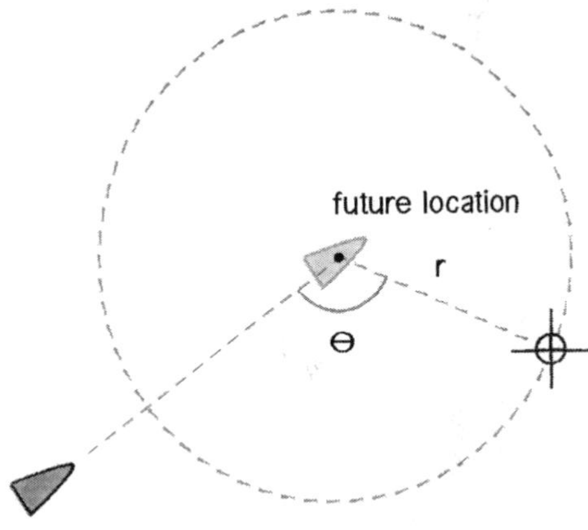

Figure 6.12

Figure 6.12 illustrates how the vehicle predicts its future location as a fixed distance in front of it (in the direction of its velocity), draws a circle with radius `r` at that location, and picks a random point along the circumference of the circle. That random point moves randomly around the circle in each frame of animation. And that random point is the vehicle's target, its desired vector pointing in that direction.

Sounds a bit absurd, right? Or, at the very least, rather arbitrary. In fact, this is a very clever and thoughtful solution—it uses randomness to drive a vehicle's steering, but constrains that randomness along the path of a circle to keep the vehicle's movement from appearing jittery, and, well, random.

But the seemingly random and arbitrary nature of this solution should drive home the point I'm trying to make—these are made-up behaviors inspired by real-life motion. You can just as easily concoct some elaborate scenario to compute a desired velocity yourself. And you should.

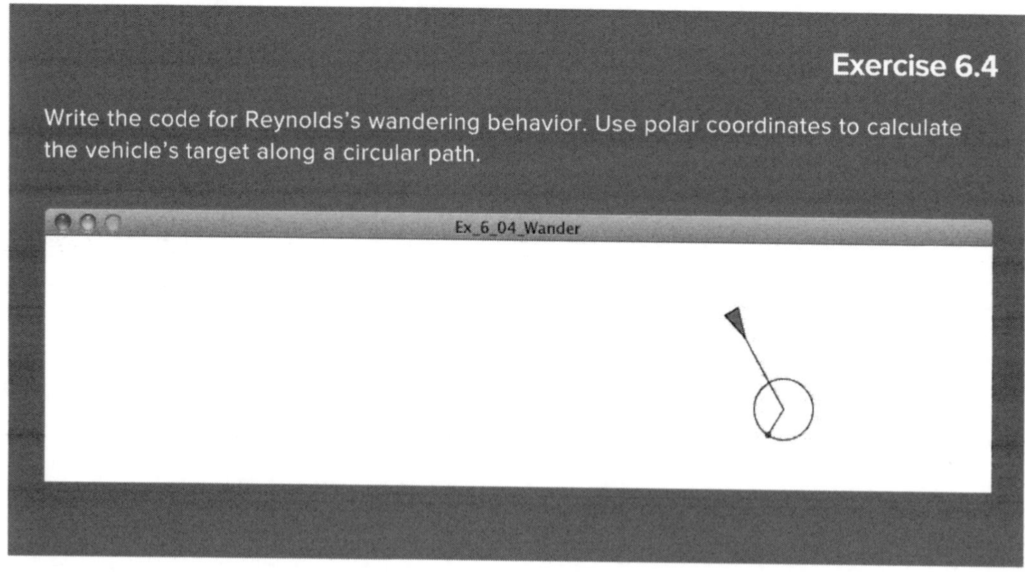

Exercise 6.4

Write the code for Reynolds's wandering behavior. Use polar coordinates to calculate the vehicle's target along a circular path.

Let's say we want to create a steering behavior called "stay within walls." We'll define the desired velocity as:

If a vehicle comes within a distance* d *of a wall, it desires to move at maximum speed in the opposite direction of the wall.

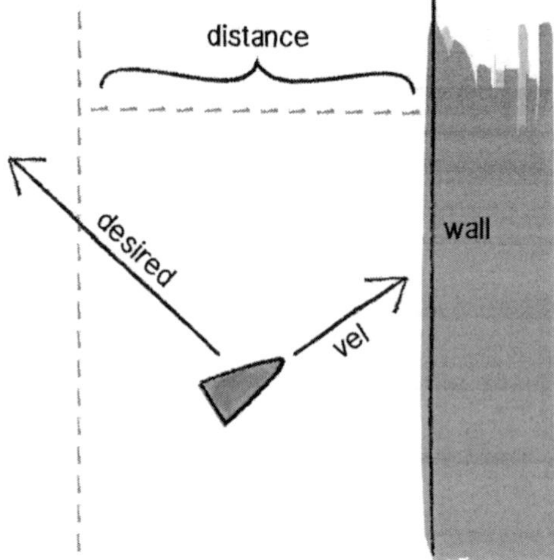

Figure 6.13

If we define the walls of the space as the edges of a Processing window and the distance d as 25, the code is rather simple.

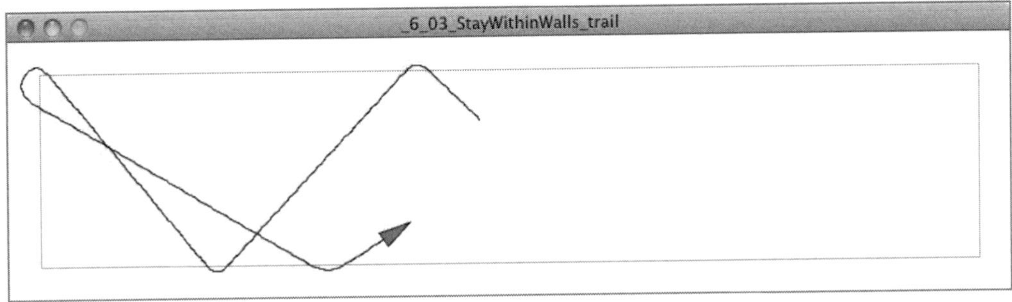

Example 6.3: "Stay within walls" steering behavior

```
if (location. x > 25) {
  PVector desired = new PVector(maxspeed,velocity.y);
  PVector steer = PVector.sub(desired, velocity);
  steer.limit(maxforce);
  applyForce(steer);
}
```

Make a desired vector that retains the y direction of the vehicle but points the x direction directly away from the window's left edge.

Exercise 6.5

Come up with your own arbitrary scheme for calculating a desired velocity.

6.6 Flow Fields

Now back to the task at hand. Let's examine a couple more of Reynolds's steering behaviors. First, ***flow field following***. What is a flow field? Think of your Processing window as a grid. In each cell of the grid lives an arrow pointing in some direction—you know, a vector. As a vehicle moves around the screen, it asks, "Hey, what arrow is beneath me? That's my desired velocity!"

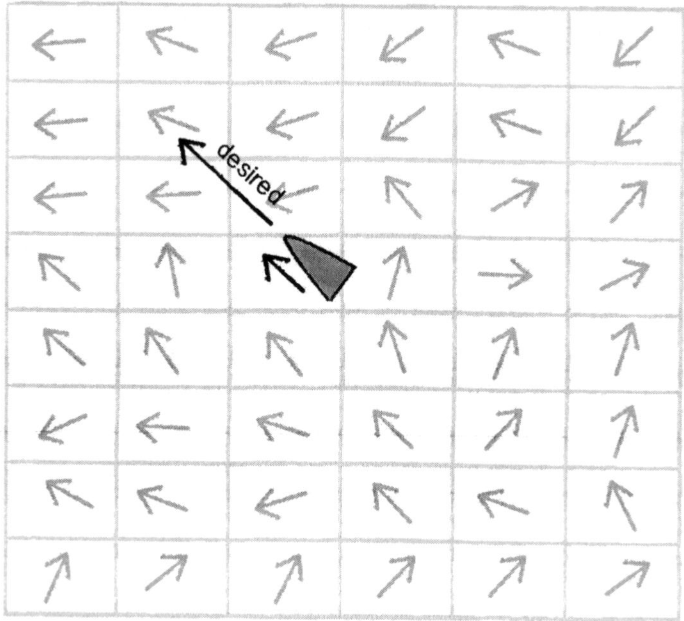

Figure 6.14

Reynolds's flow field following example has the vehicle predicting its future location and following the vector at that spot, but for simplicity's sake, we'll have the vehicle simply look to the vector at its current location.

Before we can write the additional code for our `Vehicle` class, we'll need to build a class that describes the flow field itself, the grid of vectors. A two-dimensional array is a convenient data structure in which to store a grid of information. If you are not familiar with 2D arrays, I suggest reviewing this online Processing tutorial: 2D array (http://processing.org/learning/2darray/). The 2D array is convenient because we reference each element with two indices, which we can think of as columns and rows.

```
class FlowField {

  PVector[][] field;        // Declaring a 2D array of PVectors

  int cols, rows;           // How many columns and how many rows in the grid?

  int resolution;           // Resolution of grid relative to window width and height in pixels
```

Notice how we are defining a third variable called `resolution` above. What is this variable? Let's say we have a Processing window that is 200 pixels wide by 200 pixels high. We could make a flow field that has a `PVector` object for every single pixel, or 40,000 `PVectors` (200 * 200). This isn't terribly unreasonable, but in our case, it's overkill. We don't need a `PVector` for every single pixel; we can achieve the same effect by having, say, one every ten pixels (20 * 20 = 400). We use this resolution to define the number of columns and rows based on the size of the window divided by resolution:

```
FlowField() {
  resolution = 10;
  cols = width/resolution;        // Total columns equals width divided by resolution.
  rows = height/resolution;       // Total rows equals height divided by resolution.
  field = new PVector[cols][rows];
}
```

Now that we've set up the flow field's data structures, it's time to compute the vectors in the flow field itself. How do we do that? However we feel like it! Perhaps we want to have every vector in the flow field pointing to the right.

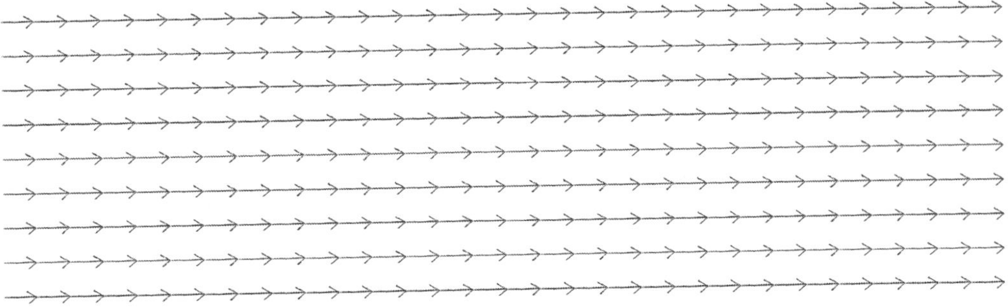

Figure 6.15

```
for (int i = 0; i < cols; i++) {       // Using a nested loop to hit every column and every row of the flow field
  for (int j = 0; j < rows; j++) {
    field[i][j] = new PVector(1,0);    // Arbitrary decision to make each vector point to the right
  }
}
```

Or perhaps we want the vectors to point in random directions.

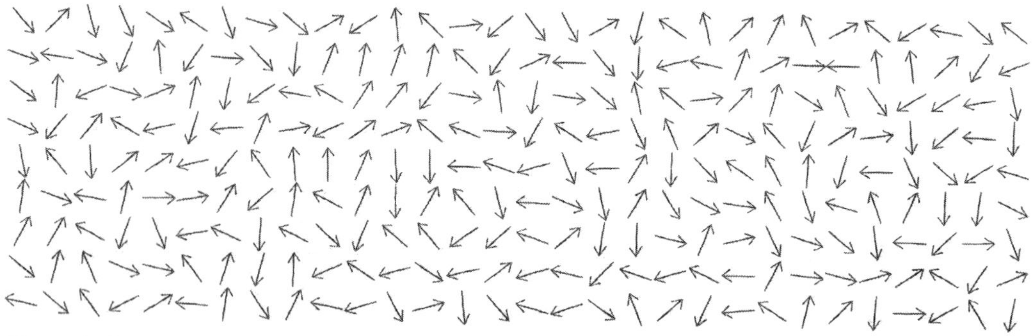

Figure 6.16

```
for (int i = 0; i < cols; i++) {
  for (int j = 0; j < rows; j++) {

    field[i][j] = PVector.2D();                    A random PVector

  }
}
```

What if we use 2D Perlin noise (mapped to an angle)?

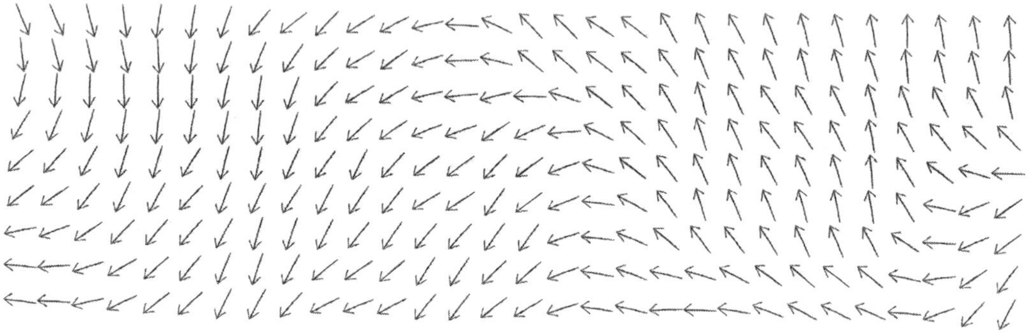

Figure 6.17

```
float xoff = 0;
for (int i = 0; i < cols; i++) {
  float yoff = 0;
  for (int j = 0; j < rows; j++) {                 Noise

    float theta = map(noise(xoff,yoff),0,1,0,TWO_PI);

    field[i][j] = new PVector(cos(theta),sin(theta));
    yoff += 0.1;
  }
  xoff += 0.1;
}
```

Now we're getting somewhere. Flow fields can be used for simulating various effects, such as an irregular gust of wind or the meandering path of a river. Calculating the direction of your vectors using Perlin noise is one way to achieve such an effect. Of course, there's no "correct" way to calculate the vectors of a flow field; it's really up to you to decide what you're looking to simulate.

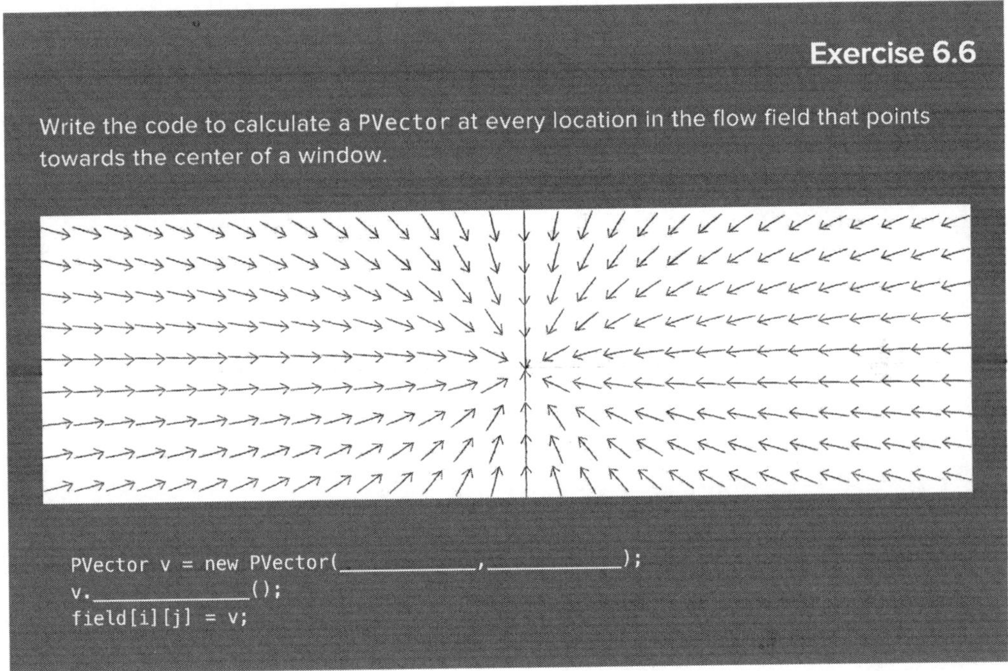

Exercise 6.6

Write the code to calculate a `PVector` at every location in the flow field that points towards the center of a window.

```
PVector v = new PVector(____________,____________);
v.____________();
field[i][j] = v;
```

Now that we have a two-dimensional array storing all of the flow field vectors, we need a way for a vehicle to look up its desired vector in the flow field. Let's say we have a vehicle that lives at a `PVector`: its location. We first need to divide by the resolution of the grid. For example, if the resolution is 10 and the vehicle is at *(100,50)*, we need to look up column 10 and row 5.

```
int column = int(location.x/resolution);
int row = int(location.y/resolution);
```

Because a vehicle could theoretically wander off the Processing window, it's also useful for us to employ the `constrain()` function to make sure we don't look outside of the flow field array. Here is a function we'll call `lookup()` that goes in the `FlowField` class—it receives a `PVector` (presumably the location of our vehicle) and returns the corresponding flow field `PVector` for that location.

Using constrain()

```
PVector lookup(PVector lookup) {
  int column = int(constrain(lookup.x/resolution,0,cols-1));
  int row = int(constrain(lookup.y/resolution,0,rows-1));
```

```
    return field[column][row].get();
  }
```

Note the use of get() to ensure we return a copy of the PVector.

Before we move on to the Vehicle class, let's take a look at the FlowField class all together.

```
class FlowField {

  PVector[][] field;
  int cols, rows;
  int resolution;

  FlowField(int r) {
    resolution = r;
    cols = width/resolution;
    rows = height/resolution;
    field = new PVector[cols][rows];
    init();
  }

  void init() {
    float xoff = 0;
    for (int i = 0; i < cols; i++) {
      float yoff = 0;
      for (int j = 0; j < rows; j++) {
        float theta = map(noise(xoff,yoff),0,1,0,TWO_PI);
        field[i][j] = new PVector(cos(theta),sin(theta));
        yoff += 0.1;
      }
      xoff += 0.1;
    }
  }

  PVector lookup(PVector lookup) {
    int column = int(constrain(lookup.x/resolution,0,cols-1));
    int row = int(constrain(lookup.y/resolution,0,rows-1));
    return field[column][row].get();
  }
}
```

A flow field is a two-dimensional array of PVectors.

Determine the number of columns and rows.

In this example, we use Perlin noise to seed the vectors.

Polar to Cartesian coordinate transformation to get x and y components of the vector

A function to return a PVector based on a location

So let's assume we have a FlowField object called "flow". Using the lookup() function above, our vehicle can then retrieve a desired vector from the flow field and use Reynolds's rules (steering = desired - velocity) to calculate a steering force.

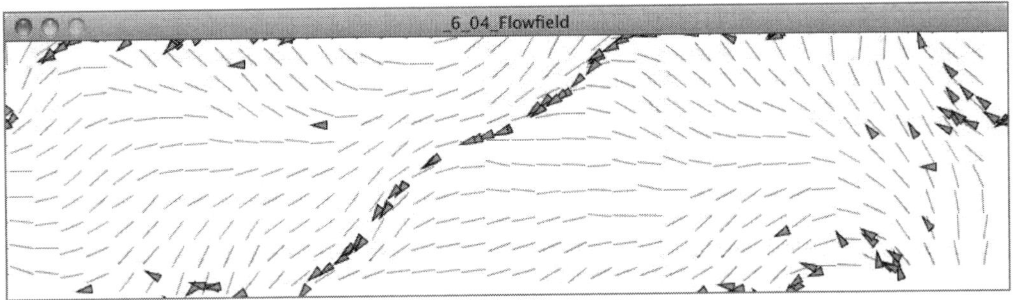

Example 6.4: Flow field following

```
class Vehicle {

  void follow(FlowField flow) {
    PVector desired = flow.lookup(location);
    desired.mult(maxspeed);

    PVector steer = PVector.sub(desired,
velocity);
    steer.limit(maxforce);
    applyForce(steer);
  }
```

What is the vector at that spot in the flow field?

Steering is desired minus velocity

Exercise 6.7

Adapt the flow field example so that the `PVectors` change over time. (Hint: try using the third dimension of Perlin noise!)

Exercise 6.8

Can you seed a flow field from a `PImage`? For example, try having the `PVectors` point from dark to light colors (or vice versa).

6.7 The Dot Product

In a moment, we're going to work through the algorithm (along with accompanying mathematics) and code for another of Craig Reynolds's steering behaviors: Path Following (http://www.red3d.com/cwr/steer/PathFollow.html). Before we can do this, however, we have to spend some time learning about another piece of vector math that we skipped in Chapter 1—the dot product. We haven't needed it yet, but it's likely going to prove quite useful for you (beyond just this path-following example), so we'll go over it in detail now.

Remember all the basic vector math we covered in Chapter 1? Add, subtract, multiply, and divide?

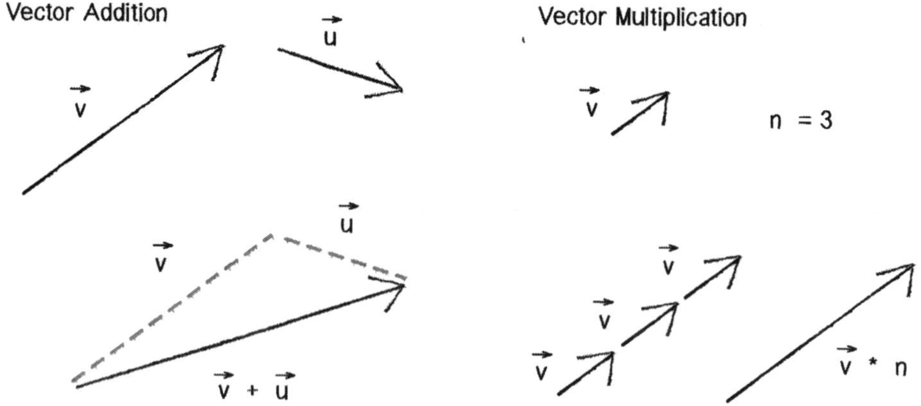

Figure 6.18

Notice how in the above diagram, vector multiplication involves multiplying a vector by a scalar value. This makes sense; when we want a vector to be twice as large (but facing the same direction), we multiply it by 2. When we want it to be half the size, we multiply it by 0.5.

However, there are two other *multiplication-like* operations with vectors that are useful in certain scenarios—the dot product and the cross product. For now we're going to focus on the dot product, which is defined as follows. Assume vectors $\vec{A}$ and $\vec{B}$:

$\vec{A} = (a_x, a_y)$
$\vec{B} = (b_x, b_y)$

THE DOT PRODUCT: $\vec{A} \cdot \vec{B} = a_x \times b_x + a_y \times b_y$

For example, if we have the following two vectors:

$\vec{A} = (-3, 5)$
$\vec{B} = (10, 1)$

$\vec{A} \cdot \vec{B} = -3 * 10 + 5 * 1 = -30 + 5 = 35$

Notice that the result of the dot product is a scalar value (a single number) and not a vector.

In Processing, this would translate to:

```
PVector a = new PVector(-3,5);
PVector b = new PVector(10,1);

float n = a.dot(b);
```

The PVector class includes a function to calculate the dot product.

And if we were to look in the guts of the `PVector` source, we'd find a pretty simple implementation of this function:

```
public float dot(PVector v) {
  return x*v.x + y*v.y + z*v.z;
}
```

This is simple enough, but why do we need the dot product, and when is it going to be useful for us in code?

One of the more common uses of the dot product is to find the angle between two vectors. Another way in which the dot product can be expressed is:

$$\vec{A} \cdot \vec{B} = \| \vec{A} \| \times \| \vec{B} \| \times \cos(\theta)$$

In other words, A dot B is equal to the magnitude of A times magnitude of B times cosine of theta (with theta defined as *the angle between the two vectors A and B*).

The two formulas for dot product can be derived from one another with trigonometry (http://mathworld.wolfram.com/DotProduct.html), but for our purposes we can be happy with operating on the assumption that:

$$\vec{A} \cdot \vec{B} = \| \vec{A} \| \times \| \vec{B} \| \times \cos(\theta)$$
$$\vec{A} \cdot \vec{B} = a_x \times b_x + a_y \times b_y$$

both hold true and therefore:

$$a_x \times b_x + a_y \times b_y = \| \vec{A} \| \times \| \vec{B} \| \times \cos(\theta)$$

Now, let's start with the following problem. We have the vectors A and B:

$$\vec{A} = (10,\ 2)$$
$$\vec{B} = (4,\ -3)$$

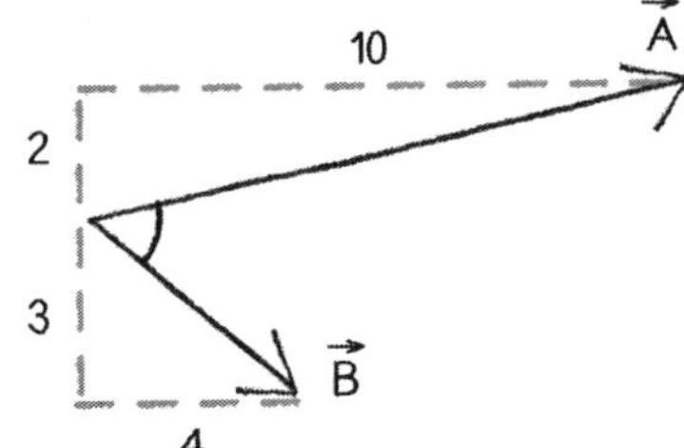

Figure 6.19

We now have a situation in which we know everything except for theta. We know the components of the vector and can calculate the magnitude of each vector. We can therefore solve for cosine of theta:

$$\cos(\theta) = (\ \vec{A} \cdot \vec{B}\ ) \,/\, (\ \| \vec{A} \| \times \| \vec{B} \|\ )$$

To solve for theta, we can take the inverse cosine (often expressed as *cosine*$^{-1}$ or *arccosine*).

$$\theta = \cos^{-1}((\vec{A} \cdot \vec{B}) / (\|\vec{A}\| \times \|\vec{B}\|))$$

Let's now do the math with actual numbers:

$$\|\vec{A}\| = 10.2$$
$$\|\vec{B}\| = 5$$

Therefore:

$$\theta = \cos^{-1}((10 \times 4 + 2 \times -3) / (10.2 \times 5))$$
$$\theta = \cos^{-1}(34 / 51)$$
$$\theta = \sim 48^{\circ}$$

The Processing version of this would be:

```
PVector a = new PVector(10,2);
PVector b = new PVector(4,-3);
float theta = acos(a.dot(b) / (a.mag() * b.mag()));
```

And, again, if we were to dig into the guts of the Processing source code, we would see a function that implements this exact algorithm.

```
static public float angleBetween(PVector v1, PVector v2) {
  float dot = v1.dot(v2);
  float theta = (float) Math.acos(dot / (v1.mag() * v2.mag()));
  return theta;
}
```

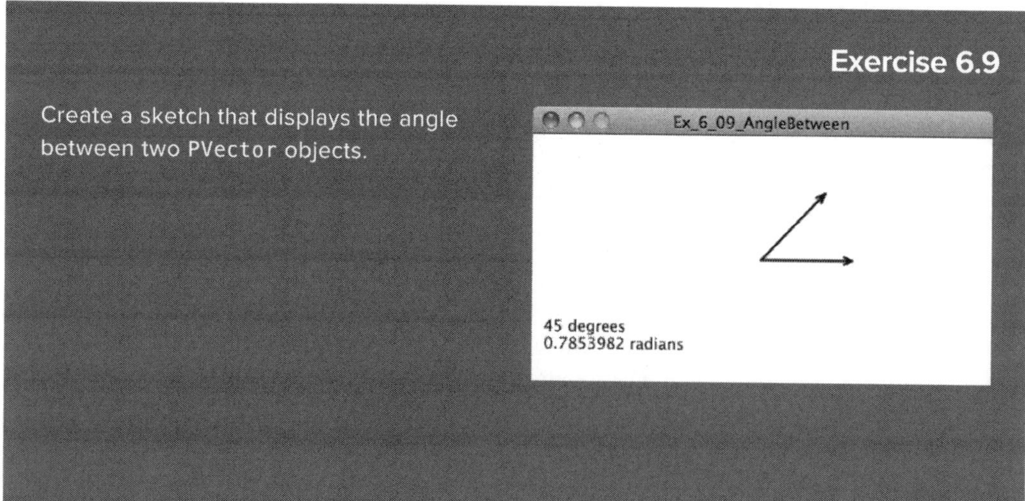

Exercise 6.9
Create a sketch that displays the angle between two PVector objects.
Ex_6_09_AngleBetween
45 degrees
0.7853982 radians

A couple things to note here:

1. If two vectors ($\vec{A}$ and $\vec{B}$) are orthogonal (i.e. perpendicular), the dot product ($\vec{A} \cdot \vec{B}$) is equal to 0.

2. If two vectors are unit vectors, then the dot product is simply equal to cosine of the angle between them, i.e. $\vec{A} \cdot \vec{B} = \cos(\theta)$ if $\vec{A}$ and $\vec{B}$ are of length 1.

6.8 Path Following

Now that we've got a basic understanding of the dot product under our belt, we can return to a discussion of Craig Reynolds's path-following algorithm. Let's quickly clarify something. We are talking about path *following*, not path *finding*. Pathfinding refers to a research topic (commonly studied in artificial intelligence) that involves solving for the shortest distance between two points, often in a maze. With ***path following***, the path already exists and we're asking a vehicle to follow that path.

Before we work out the individual pieces, let's take a look at the overall algorithm for path following, as defined by Reynolds.

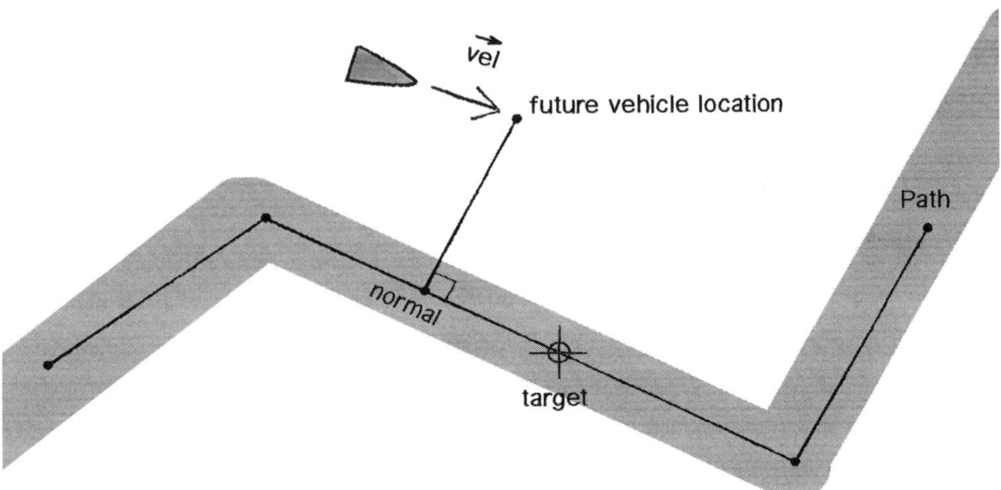

Figure 6.20

We'll first define what we mean by a path. There are many ways we could implement a path, but for us, a simple way will be to define a path as a series of connected points:

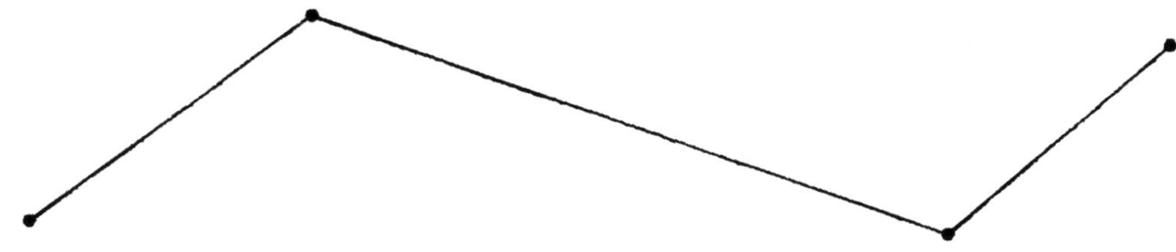

Figure 6.21: Path

An even simpler path would be a line between two points.

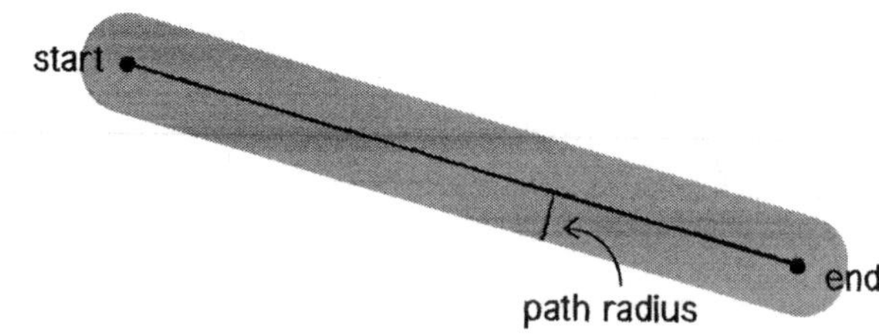

Figure 6.22: Simple path

We're also going to consider a path to have a radius. If we think of the path as a road, the radius determines the road's width. With a smaller radius, our vehicles will have to follow the path more closely; a wider radius will allow them to stray a bit more.

Putting this into a class, we have:

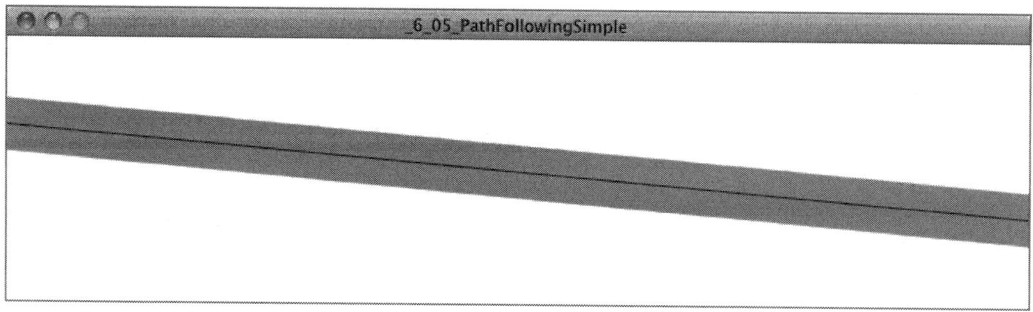


```
class Path {

  PVector start;
  PVector end;
```
A path is only two points, start and end.

```
  float radius;
```
A path has a radius, i.e. how wide it is.

```
  Path() {
```

```
    radius = 20;
    start = new PVector(0,height/3);
    end = new PVector(width,2*height/3);
  }

  void display() {  // Display the path.
    strokeWeight(radius*2);
    stroke(0,100);
    line(start.x,start.y,end.x,end.y);
    strokeWeight(1);
    stroke(0);
    line(start.x,start.y,end.x,end.y);
  }
}
```

Picking some arbitrary values to initialize the path

Now, let's assume we have a vehicle (as depicted below) outside of the path's radius, moving with a velocity.

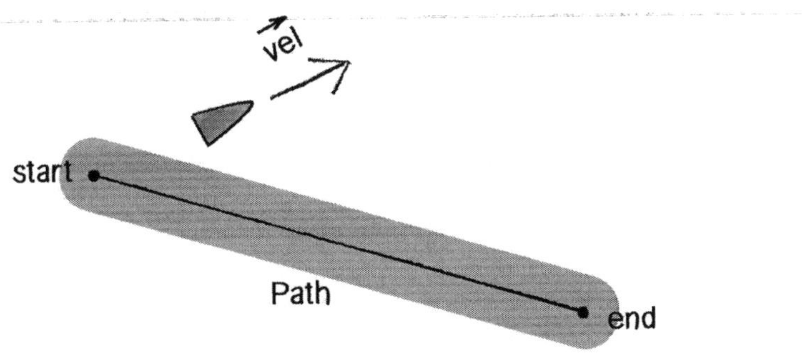

Figure 6.23

The first thing we want to do is predict, assuming a constant velocity, where that vehicle will be in the future.

```
PVector predict = vel.get();
```

Start by making a copy of the velocity.

```
predict.normalize();
predict.mult(25);
```

Normalize it and look 25 pixels ahead by scaling the vector up.

```
PVector predictLoc = PVector.add(loc, predict);
```

Add vector to location to find the predicted location.

Once we have that location, it's now our job to find out the vehicle's current distance from the path of that predicted location. If it's very far away, well, then, we've strayed from the path and need to steer back towards it. If it's close, then we're doing OK and are following the path nicely.

So, how do we find the distance between a point and a line? This concept is key. The distance between a point and a line is defined as the length of the normal between that point and line. The normal is a vector that extends from that point and is perpendicular to the line.

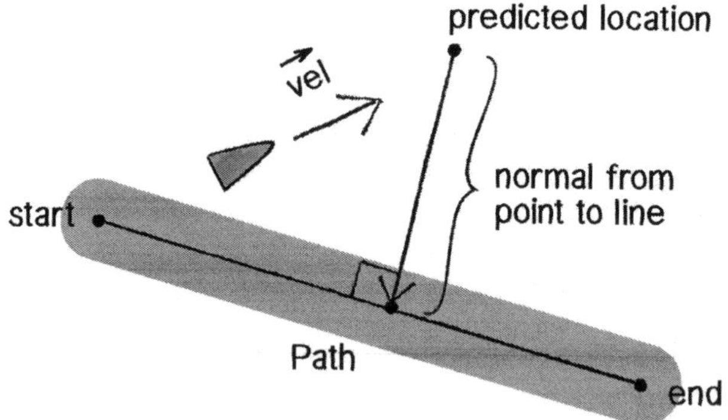

Figure 6.24

Let's figure out what we do know. We know we have a vector (call it $\vec{A}$) that extends from the path's starting point to the vehicle's predicted location.

```
PVector a = PVector.sub(predictLoc,path.start);
```

We also know that we can define a vector (call it $\vec{B}$) that points from the start of the path to the end.

```
PVector b = PVector.sub(path.end,path.start);
```

Now, with basic trigonometry, we know that the distance from the path's start to the normal point is: **|A| * cos(theta)**.

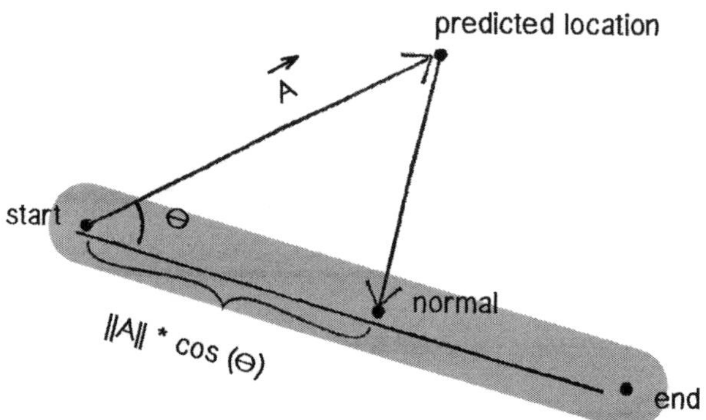

Figure 6.25

If we knew theta, we could easily define that normal point as follows:

```
float d = a.mag()*cos(theta);                      The distance from START to NORMAL
b.normalize();
b.mult(d);                                         Scale PVector b to that distance.
PVector normalPoint = PVector.add(path.start,b);   The normal point can be found by adding
                                                   the scaled version of b to the path's starting
                                                   point.
```

And if the dot product has taught us anything, it's that given two vectors, we can get theta, the angle between.

```
float theta = PVector.angleBetween(a,b);           What is theta? The angle between A and B
b.normalize();
b.mult(a.mag()*cos(theta));
PVector normalPoint = PVector.add(path.start,b);
```

While the above code will work, there's one more simplification we can make. If you'll notice, the desired magnitude for vector $\vec{B}$ is:

`a.mag()*cos(theta)`

which is the code translation of:

$\|\vec{A}\| \times \cos(\theta)$

And if you recall:

$\vec{A} \cdot \vec{B} = \|\vec{A}\| \times \|\vec{B}\| \times \cos(\theta)$

Now, what if vector $\vec{B}$ is a unit vector, i.e. length 1? Then:

$\vec{A} \cdot \vec{B} = \|\vec{A}\| \times 1 \times \cos(\theta)$

or

$\vec{A} \cdot \vec{B} = \|\vec{A}\| \times \cos(\theta)$

And what are we doing in our code? Normalizing b!

```
b.normalize();
```

Because of this fact, we can simplify our code as:

~~`float theta = PVector.angleBetween(a,b);`~~

```
b.normalize();
```

```
b.mult(a.dot(b));
```

We can use the dot product to scale b's length.

```
PVector normalPoint = PVector.add(path.start,b);
```

This process is commonly known as "scalar projection." ***|A| cos(θ) is the scalar projection of A onto B.***

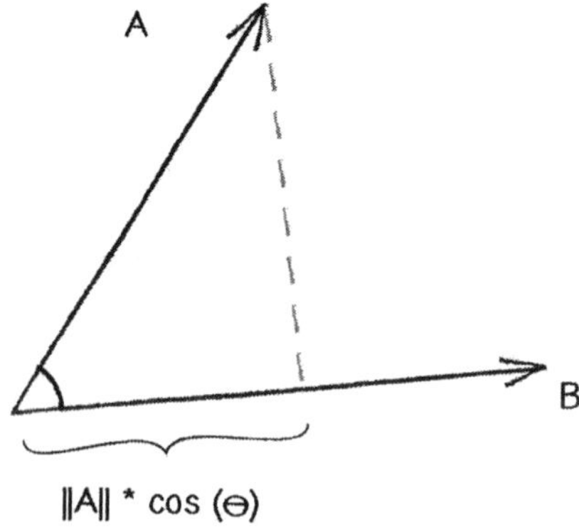

Figure 6.26

Once we have the normal point along the path, we have to decide whether the vehicle should steer towards the path and how. Reynolds's algorithm states that the vehicle should only steer towards the path if it strays beyond the path (i.e., if the distance between the normal point and the predicted future location is greater than the path radius).

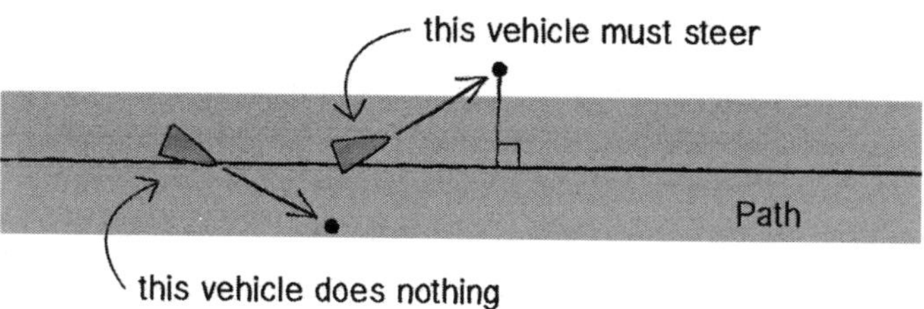

Figure 6.27

```
float distance = PVector.dist(predictLoc, normalPoint);
```

```
if (distance > path.radius) {
```

If the vehicle is outside the path, seek the target.

```
  seek(target);
}
```

We don't have to work out the desired velocity and steering force; all that is taken care of by seek(), which we already wrote in Example 6.1.

But what is the target?

Reynolds's algorithm involves picking a point ahead of the normal on the path (see step #3 above). But for simplicity, we could just say that the target is the normal itself. This will work fairly well:

```
float distance = PVector.dist(predictLoc, normalPoint);
if (distance > path.radius) {
  seek(normalPoint);                    // Seek the normal point on the path.
}
```

Since we know the vector that defines the path (we're calling it "B"), we can implement Reynolds's "point ahead on the path" without too much trouble.

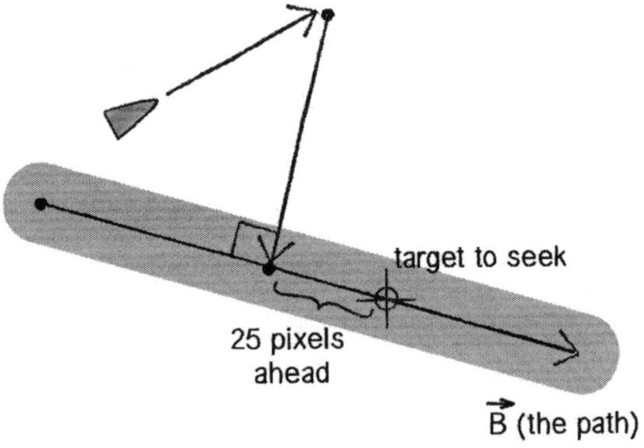

Figure 6.28

```
float distance = PVector.dist(predictLoc, normalPoint);
if (distance > path.radius) {
  b.normalize();                        // Normalize and scale b (pick 25 pixels
  b.mult(25);                           // arbitrarily).
  PVector target = PVector.add(normalPoint,b);   // By adding b to normalPoint, we now move
                                                 // 25 pixels ahead on the path.

  seek(target);
}
```

Putting it all together, we have the following steering function in our `Vehicle` class.

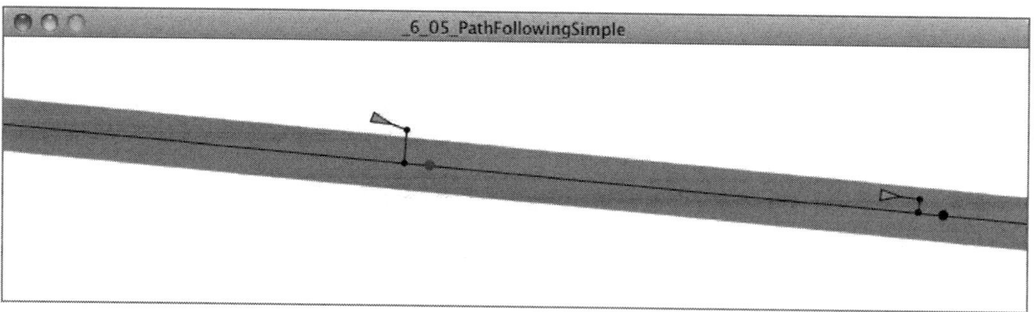

Example 6.5: Simple path following

```
void follow(Path p) {

  PVector predict = vel.get();
  predict.normalize();
  predict.mult(25);
  PVector predictLoc = PVector.add(loc, predict);
```

Step 1: Predict the vehicle's future location.

```
  PVector a = p.start;
  PVector b = p.end;
  PVector normalPoint = getNormalPoint(predictLoc, a, b);
```

Step 2: Find the normal point along the path.

```
  PVector dir = PVector.sub(b, a);
  dir.normalize();
  dir.mult(10);
  PVector target = PVector.add(normalPoint, dir);
```

Step 3: Move a little further along the path and set a target.

```
  float distance =
    PVector.dist(normalPoint, predictLoc);
  if (distance > p.radius) {
    seek(target);
  }
}
```

Step 4: If we are off the path, seek that target in order to stay on the path.

Now, you may notice above that instead of using all that dot product/scalar projection code to find the normal point, we instead call a function: `getNormalPoint()`. In cases like this, it's useful to break out the code that performs a specific task (finding a normal point) into a function that it can be used generically in any case where it is required. The function takes three `PVector`s: the first defines a point in Cartesian space and the second and third arguments define a line segment.

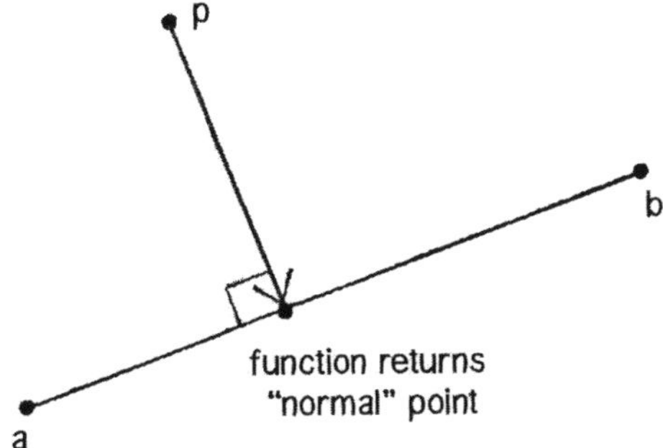

Figure 6.29

```
PVector getNormalPoint(PVector p, PVector a, PVector b) {
  PVector ap = PVector.sub(p, a);          // PVector that points from a to p
  PVector ab = PVector.sub(b, a);          // PVector that points from a to b

  ab.normalize();                          // Using the dot product for scalar projection
  ab.mult(ap.dot(ab));
  PVector normalPoint = PVector.add(a, ab);  // Finding the normal point along the line segment

  return normalPoint;
}
```

What do we have so far? We have a `Path` class that defines a path as a line between two points. We have a `Vehicle` class that defines a vehicle that can follow the path (using a steering behavior to seek a target along the path). What is missing?

Take a deep breath. We're almost there.

6.9 Path Following with Multiple Segments

Figure 6.30

We've built a great example so far, yes, but it's pretty darn limiting. After all, what if we want our path to be something that looks more like:

Figure 6.31

While it's true that we could make this example work for a curved path, we're much less likely to end up needing a cool compress on our forehead if we stick with line segments. In the end, we can always employ the same technique we discovered with Box2D—we can draw whatever fancy curved path we want and approximate it behind the scenes with simple geometric forms.

So, what's the problem? If we made path following work with one line segment, how do we make it work with a series of connected line segments? Let's take a look again at our vehicle driving along the screen. Say we arrive at Step 3.

Step 3: Find a target point on the path.

To find the target, we need to find the normal to the line segment. But now that we have a series of line segments, we have a series of normal points (see above)! Which one do we choose? The solution we'll employ is to pick the normal point that is (a) closest and (b) on the path itself.

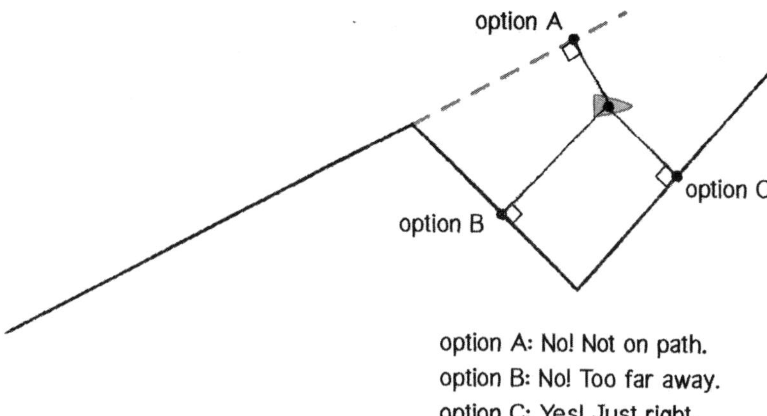
option A
option B
option C
option A: No! Not on path.
option B: No! Too far away.
option C: Yes! Just right.

Figure 6.32

If we have a point and an infinitely long line, we'll always have a normal. But, as in the path-following example, if we have a point and a line segment, we won't necessarily find a normal that is on the line segment itself. So if this happens for any of the segments, we can disqualify those normals. Once we are left with normals that are on the path itself (only two in the above diagram), we simply pick the one that is closest to our vehicle's location.

In order to write the code for this, we'll have to expand our `Path` class to have an `ArrayList` of points (rather than just two, a start and an end).

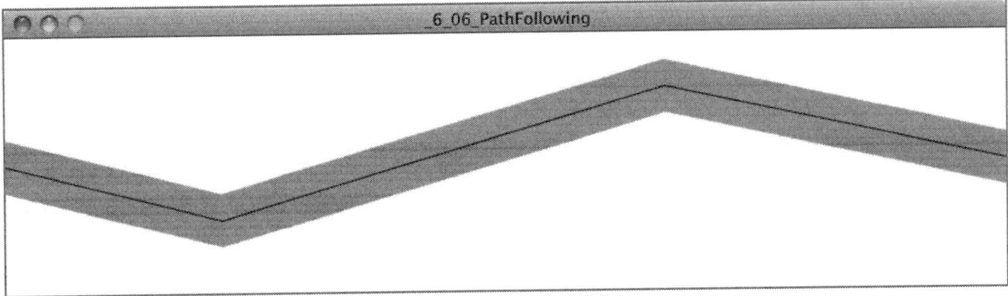


```
class Path {

  ArrayList<PVector> points;
  float radius;

  Path() {
    radius = 20;
    points = new ArrayList<PVector>();
  }

  void addPoint(float x, float y) {
    PVector point = new PVector(x,y);
    points.add(point);
  }

  void display() {
    stroke(0);
    noFill();
    beginShape();
    for (PVector v : points) {
      vertex(v.x,v.y);
    }
    endShape();
  }
}
```

A Path is now an ArrayList of points (PVector objects).

This function allows us to add points to the path.

Display the path as a series of points.

Now that we have the `Path` class defined, it's the vehicle's turn to deal with multiple line segments. All we did before was find the normal for one line segment. We can now find the normals for all the line segments in a loop.

```
for (int i = 0; i < p.points.size()-1; i++) {
  PVector a = p.points.get(i);
  PVector b = p.points.get(i+1);
```

```
PVector normalPoint = getNormalPoint(predictLoc, a, b);
```

Finding the normals for each line segment

Then we should make sure the normal point is actually between points a and b. Since we know our path goes from left to right in this example, we can test if the *x* component of `normalPoint` is outside the *x* components of a and b.

```
if (normalPoint.x < a.x || normalPoint.x > b.x) {
  normalPoint = b.get();
}
```

Use the end point of the segment as our normal point if we can't find one.

As a little trick, we'll say that if it's not within the line segment, let's just pretend the end point of that line segment is the normal. This will ensure that our vehicle always stays on the path, even if it strays out of the bounds of our line segments.

Finally, we'll need to make sure we find the normal point that is closest to our vehicle. To accomplish this, we start with a very high "world record" distance and iterate through each normal point to see if it beats the record (i.e. is less than). Each time a normal point beats the record, the world record is updated and the winning point is stored in a variable named `target`. At the end of the loop, we'll have the closest normal point in that variable.

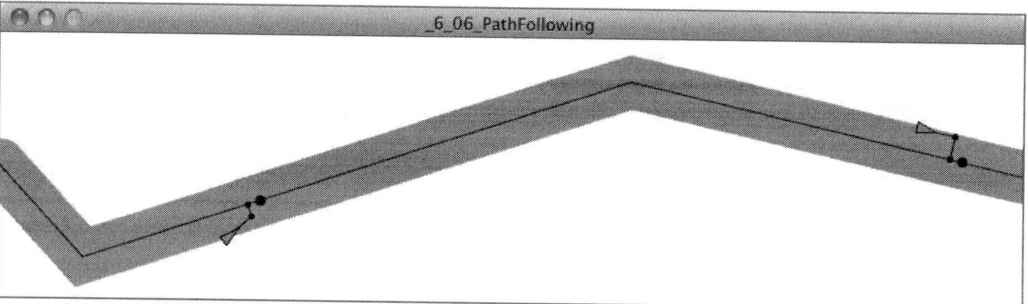

Example 6.6: Path following

```
PVector target = null;
```

```
float worldRecord = 1000000;
```

Start with a very high record that can easily be beaten.

```
for (int i = 0; i < p.points.size()-1; i++) {
  PVector a = p.points.get(i);
  PVector b = p.points.get(i+1);
  PVector normalPoint = getNormalPoint(predictLoc, a, b);
  if (normalPoint.x < a.x || normalPoint.x > b.x) {
    normalPoint = b.get();
  }

  float distance = PVector.dist(predictLoc, normalPoint);

  if (distance < worldRecord) {
    worldRecord = distance;
    target = normalPoint.get();
  }
}
```

If we beat the record, then this should be our target!

Exercise 6.10

Update the path-following example so that the path can go in any direction. (Hint: you'll need to use the `min()` and `max()` function when determining if the normal point is inside the line segment.)

```
if (normalPoint.x < ____(____,____) || normalPoint.x > ____(____,____)) {
  normalPoint = b.get();
}
```

Exercise 6.11

Create a path that changes over time. Can the points that define the path itself have their own steering behaviors?

6.10 Complex Systems

Remember our purpose? To breathe life into the things that move around our Processing windows? By learning to write the code for an autonomous agent and building a series of examples of individual behaviors, hopefully our souls feel a little more full. But this is no place to stop and rest on our laurels. We're just getting started. After all, there is a deeper purpose at work here. Yes, a vehicle is a simulated being that makes decisions about how to seek and flow and follow. But what is a life led alone, without the love and support of others? Our purpose here is not only to build individual behaviors for our vehicles, but to put our vehicles into systems of many vehicles and allow those vehicles to interact with each other.

Let's think about a tiny, crawling ant—one single ant. An ant is an autonomous agent; it can perceive its environment (using antennae to gather information about the direction and strength of chemical signals) and make decisions about how to move based on those signals. But can a single ant acting alone build a nest, gather food, defend its queen? An ant is a simple unit and can only perceive its immediate environment. A colony of ants, however, is a sophisticated complex system, a "superorganism" in which the components work together to accomplish difficult and complicated goals.

We want to take what we've learned during the process of building autonomous agents in Processing into simulations that involve many agents operating in parallel—agents that have an ability to perceive not only their physical environment but also the actions of their fellow agents, and then act accordingly. We want to create complex systems in Processing.

What is a complex system? A complex system is typically defined as a system that is "more than the sum of its parts." While the individual elements of the system may be incredibly simple and easily understood, the behavior of the system as a whole can be highly complex, intelligent, and difficult to predict. Here are three key principles of complex systems.

- ***Simple units with short-range relationships.*** This is what we've been building all along: vehicles that have a limited perception of their environment.

- ***Simple units operate in parallel.*** This is what we need to simulate in code. For every cycle through Processing's `draw()` loop, each unit will decide how to move (to create the appearance of them all working in parallel).

- ***System as a whole exhibits emergent phenomena.*** Out of the interactions between these simple units emerges complex behavior, patterns, and intelligence. Here we're talking about the result we are hoping for in our sketches. Yes, we know this happens in nature (ant colonies, termites, migration patterns, earthquakes, snowflakes, etc.), but can we achieve the same result in our Processing sketches?

Following are three additional features of complex systems that will help frame the discussion, as well as provide guidelines for features we will want to include in our software simulations. It's important to acknowledge that this is a fuzzy set of characteristics and not all complex systems have all of them.

- ***Non-linearity.*** This aspect of complex systems is often casually referred to as "the butterfly effect," coined by mathematician and meteorologist Edward Norton Lorenz, a pioneer in the study of chaos theory. In 1961, Lorenz was running a computer weather simulation for the second time and, perhaps to save a little time, typed in a starting value of 0.506 instead of 0.506127. The end result was completely different from the first result of the simulation. In other words, the theory is that a single butterfly flapping its wings on the other side of the world could cause a massive weather shift and ruin our weekend at the beach. We call it "non-linear" because there isn't a linear relationship between a change in initial conditions and a change in outcome. A small change in initial conditions can have a massive effect on the outcome. Non-linear systems are a superset of chaotic systems. In the next chapter, we'll see how even in a system of many zeros and ones, if we change just one bit, the result will be completely different.

- ***Competition and cooperation.*** One of the things that often makes a complex system tick is the presence of both competition and cooperation between the elements. In our upcoming flocking system, we will have three rules—alignment, cohesion, and separation. Alignment and cohesion will ask the elements to "cooperate"—i.e. work together to stay together and move together. Separation, however, will ask the elements to "compete" for space. As we get to the flocking system, try taking out the cooperation or the competition and you'll see how you are left without complexity. Competition and cooperation are found in living complex systems, but not in non-living complex systems like the weather.

- ***Feedback.*** Complex systems often include a feedback loop where the the output of the system is fed back into the system to influence its behavior in a positive or negative direction. Let's say you drive to work each day because the price of gas is low. In fact, everyone drives to work. The price of gas goes up as demand begins to exceed supply. You, and everyone else, decide to take the train to work because driving is too expensive. And the price of gas declines as the demand declines. The price of gas is both the input of the system (determining whether you choose to drive or ride the train) and the output (the demand that results from your choice). I should note that economic models (like supply/demand, the stock market) are one example of a human complex system. Others include fads and trends, elections, crowds, and traffic flow.

Complexity will serve as a theme for the remaining content in this book. In this chapter, we'll begin by adding one more feature to our `Vehicle` class: an ability to look at neighboring vehicles.

6.11 Group Behaviors (or: Let's not run into each other)

A group is certainly not a new concept. We've done this before—in Chapter 4, where we developed a framework for managing collections of particles in a `ParticleSystem` class. There, we stored a list of particles in an `ArrayList`. We'll do the same thing here: store a bunch of `Vehicle` objects in an `ArrayList`.

```
ArrayList<Vehicle> vehicles;
```

Declare an ArrayList of Vehicle objects.

```
void setup() {
  vehicles = new ArrayList<Vehicle>;
  for (int i = 0; i < 100; i++) {
    vehicles.add(new Vehicle(random(width),random(height)));
  }
}
```

Initialize and fill the ArrayList with a bunch of Vehicles.

Now when it comes time to deal with all the vehicles in `draw()`, we simply loop through all of them and call the necessary functions.

```
void draw(){
  for (Vehicle v : vehicles) {
    v.update();
    v.display();
  }
}
```

OK, so maybe we want to add a behavior, a force to be applied to all the vehicles. This could be seeking the mouse.

```
    v.seek(mouseX,mouseY);
```

But that's an individual behavior. We've already spent thirty-odd pages worrying about individual behaviors. We're here because we want to apply a group behavior. Let's begin with separation, a behavior that commands, "Avoid colliding with your neighbors!"

```
    v.separate();
```

Is that right? It sounds good, but it's not. What's missing? In the case of seek, we said, "Seek `mouseX` and `mouseY`." In the case of separate, we're saying "separate from *everyone else*." Who is everyone else? It's the list of all the other vehicles.

```
    v.separate(vehicles);
```

This is the big leap beyond what we did before with particle systems. Instead of having each element (particle or vehicle) operate on its own, we're now saying, "Hey you, the vehicle! When it comes time for you to operate, you need to operate with an awareness of everyone else. So I'm going to go ahead and pass you the `ArrayList` of everyone else."

This is how we've mapped out `setup()` and `draw()` to deal with a group behavior.

```
ArrayList<Vehicle> vehicles;

void setup() {
  size(320,240);
  vehicles = new ArrayList<Vehicle>();
  for (int i = 0; i < 100; i++) {
    vehicles.add(new Vehicle(random(width),random(height)));
  }
}

void draw() {
  background(255);

  for (Vehicle v : vehicles) {
    v.separate(vehicles);
    v.update();
    v.display();
  }
}
```

This is really the only new thing we're doing in this section. We're asking a Vehicle object to examine all the other vehicles in the process of calculating a separation force.

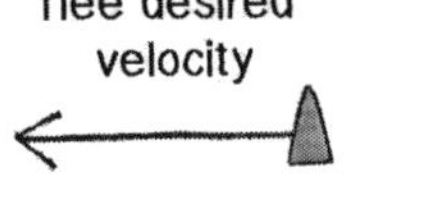

Figure 6.33

Of course, this is just the beginning. The real work happens inside the `separate()` function itself. Let's figure out how we want to define separation. Reynolds states: "Steer to avoid crowding." In other words, if a given vehicle is too close to you, steer away from that vehicle. Sound familiar? Remember the seek behavior where a vehicle steers towards a target? Reverse that force and we have the flee behavior.

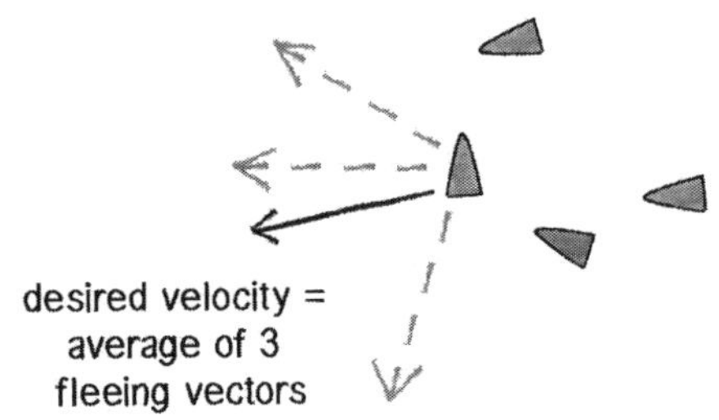

Figure 6.34

But what if more than one vehicle is too close? In this case, we'll define separation as the average of all the vectors pointing away from any close vehicles.

Let's begin to write the code. As we just worked out, we're writing a function called `separate()` that receives an `ArrayList` of Vehicle objects as an argument.

```
void separate (ArrayList<Vehicle> vehicles) {

}
```

Inside this function, we're going to loop through all of the vehicles and see if any are too close.

```
float desiredseparation = 20;
```

This variable specifies how close is too close.

```
for (Vehicle other : vehicles) {

  float d = PVector.dist(location, other.location);
```

What is the distance between me and another Vehicle?

```
  if ((d > 0) && (d < desiredseparation)) {

  }
}
```

Any code here will be executed if the Vehicle is within 20 pixels.

Notice how in the above code, we are not only checking if the distance is less than a desired separation (i.e. too close!), but also if the distance is greater than zero. This is a little trick that makes sure we don't ask a vehicle to separate from itself. Remember, all the vehicles are in the `ArrayList`, so if you aren't careful you'll be comparing each vehicle to itself!

Once we know that two vehicles are too close, we need to make a vector that points away from the offending vehicle.

```
  if ((d > 0) && (d < desiredseparation)) {
    PVector diff = PVector.sub(location, other.location);
    diff.normalize();
  }
```

A PVector pointing away from the other's location

This is not enough. We have that vector now, but we need to make sure we calculate the average of all vectors pointing away from close vehicles. How do we compute average? We add up all the vectors and divide by the total.

```
PVector sum = new PVector();
int count = 0;
for (Vehicle other : vehicles) {
```

Start with an empty PVector.

We have to keep track of how many Vehicles are too close.

```
  float d = PVector.dist(location, other.location);
  if ((d > 0) && (d < desiredseparation)) {
    PVector diff = PVector.sub(location, other.location);
    diff.normalize();
    sum.add(diff);
    count++;
  }
}
```

Add all the vectors together and increment the count.

```
if (count > 0) {
  sum.div(count);
}
```

We have to make sure we found at least one close vehicle. We don't want to bother doing anything if nothing is too close (not to mention we can't divide by zero!)

Once we have the average vector (stored in the `PVector` object "sum"), that `PVector` can be scaled to maximum speed and become our desired velocity—we *desire* to move in that direction at maximum speed! And once we have the desired velocity, it's the same old Reynolds story: steering equals desired minus velocity.

```
if (count > 0) {
  sum.div(count);

  sum.setMag(maxspeed);

  PVector steer = PVector.sub(sum,vel);

  steer.limit(maxforce);

  applyForce(steer);
}
```

Scale average to maxspeed (this becomes desired).

Reynolds's steering formula

Apply the force to the Vehicle's acceleration.

Let's see the function in its entirety. There are two additional improvements, noted in the code comments.

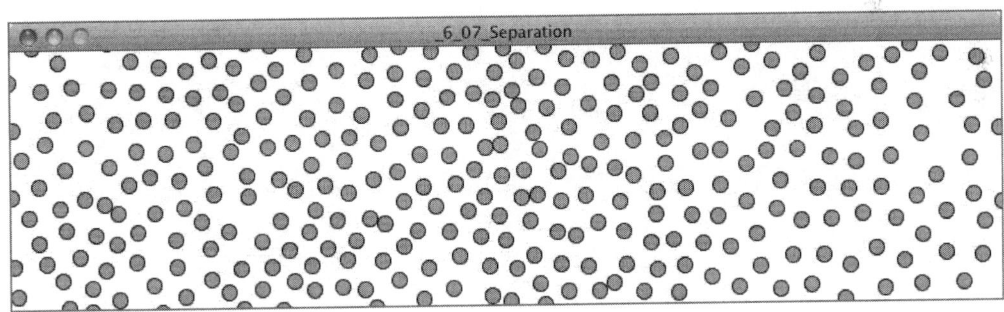

Example 6.7: Group behavior: Separation

```
void separate (ArrayList<Vehicle> vehicles) {
```

```
    float desiredseparation = r*2;

    PVector sum = new PVector();
    int count = 0;
    for (Vehicle other : vehicles) {
      float d = PVector.dist(location, other.location);
      if ((d > 0) && (d < desiredseparation)) {
        PVector diff = PVector.sub(location, other.location);
        diff.normalize();

        diff.div(d);

        sum.add(diff);
        count++;

      }
    }
    if (count > 0) {
      sum.div(count);
      sum.normalize();
      sum.mult(maxspeed);
      PVector steer = PVector.sub(sum, vel);
      steer.limit(maxforce);
      applyForce(steer);
    }

  }
```

Note how the desired separation is based on the Vehicle's size.

What is the magnitude of the PVector pointing away from the other vehicle? The closer it is, the more we should flee. The farther, the less. So we divide by the distance to weight it appropriately.

Exercise 6.12

Rewrite `separate()` to work in the opposite fashion ("cohesion"). If a vehicle is beyond a certain distance, steer towards that vehicle. This will keep the group together. (Note that in a moment, we're going to look at what happens when we have both cohesion and separation in the same simulation.)

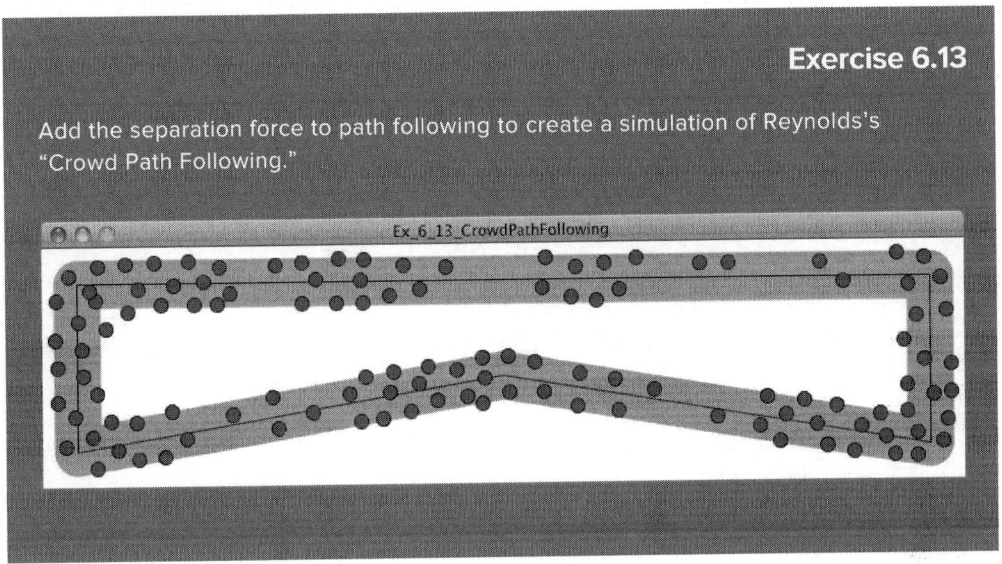

Exercise 6.13
Add the separation force to path following to create a simulation of Reynolds's "Crowd Path Following."
Ex_6_13_CrowdPathFollowing

6.12 Combinations

The previous two exercises hint at what is perhaps the most important aspect of this chapter. After all, what is a Processing sketch with one steering force compared to one with many? How could we even begin to simulate emergence in our sketches with only one rule? The most exciting and intriguing behaviors will come from mixing and matching multiple steering forces, and we'll need a mechanism for doing so.

You may be thinking, "Duh, this is nothing new. We do this all the time." You would be right. In fact, we did this as early as Chapter 2.

```
PVector wind = new PVector(0.001,0);
PVector gravity = new PVector(0,0.1);
mover.applyForce(wind);
mover.applyForce(gravity);
```

Here we have a mover that responds to two forces. This all works nicely because of the way we designed the `Mover` class to accumulate the force vectors into its acceleration vector. In this chapter, however, our forces stem from internal desires of the movers (now called vehicles). And those desires can be weighted. Let's consider a sketch where all vehicles have two desires:

- ***Seek the mouse location.***
- ***Separate from any vehicles that are too close.***

We might begin by adding a function to the `Vehicle` class that manages all of the behaviors. Let's call it `applyBehaviors()`.

```
void applyBehaviors(ArrayList<Vehicle> vehicles) {
  separate(vehicles);
  seek(new PVector(mouseX,mouseY));
}
```

Here we see how a single function takes care of calling the other functions that apply the forces—`separate()` and `seek()`. We could start mucking around with those functions and see if we can adjust the strength of the forces they are calculating. But it would be easier for us to ask those functions to return the forces so that we can adjust their strength before applying them to the vehicle's acceleration.

```
void applyBehaviors(ArrayList<Vehicle> vehicles) {
  PVector separate = separate(vehicles);
  PVector seek = seek(new PVector(mouseX,mouseY));
  applyForce(separate);
  applyForce(seek);
}
```

We have to apply the force here since seek() and separate() no longer do so.

Let's look at how the seek function changed.

```
PVector seek(PVector target) {
  PVector desired = PVector.sub(target,loc);
  desired.normalize();
  desired.mult(maxspeed);
  PVector steer = PVector.sub(desired,vel);
  steer.limit(maxforce);

  applyForce(steer);
  return steer;
}
```

Instead of applying the force we return the PVector.

This is a subtle change, but incredibly important for us: it allows us to alter the strength of these forces in one place.

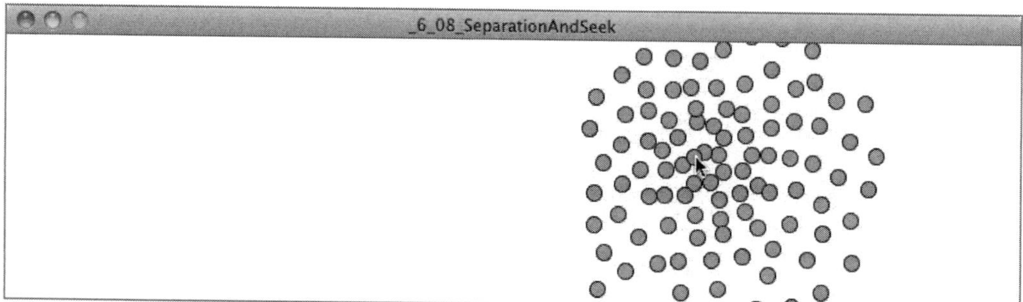

Example 6.8: Combining steering behaviors: Seek and separate

```
void applyBehaviors(ArrayList<Vehicle> vehicles) {
  PVector separate = separate(vehicles);
  PVector seek = seek(new PVector(mouseX,mouseY));

  separate.mult(1.5);
  seek.mult(0.5);

  applyForce(separate);
  applyForce(seek);
}
```

These values can be whatever you want them to be! They can be variables that are customized for each vehicle, or they can change over time.

Exercise 6.14

Redo Example 6.8 so that the behavior weights are not constants. What happens if they change over time (according to a sine wave or Perlin noise)? Or if some vehicles are more concerned with seeking and others more concerned with separating? Can you introduce other steering behaviors as well?

6.13 Flocking

Flocking is an group animal behavior that is characteristic of many living creatures, such as birds, fish, and insects. In 1986, Craig Reynolds created a computer simulation of flocking behavior and documented the algorithm in his paper, "Flocks, Herds, and Schools: A Distributed Behavioral Model." Recreating this simulation in Processing will bring together all the concepts in this chapter.

1. *We will use the steering force formula (steer = desired - velocity) to implement the rules of flocking.*
2. *These steering forces will be group behaviors and require each vehicle to look at all the other vehicles.*
3. *We will combine and weight multiple forces.*
4. *The result will be a complex system—intelligent group behavior will emerge from the simple rules of flocking without the presence of a centralized system or leader.*

The good news is, we've already done items 1 through 3 in this chapter, so this section will be about just putting it all together and seeing the result.

Before we begin, I should mention that we're going to change the name of our `Vehicle` class (yet again). Reynolds uses the term "boid" (a made-up word that refers to a bird-like object) to describe the elements of a flocking system and we will do the same.

Let's take an overview of the three rules of flocking.

1. ***Separation*** (also known as "avoidance"): Steer to avoid colliding with your neighbors.
2. ***Alignment*** (also known as "copy"): Steer in the same direction as your neighbors.
3. ***Cohesion*** (also known as "center"): Steer towards the center of your neighbors (stay with the group).

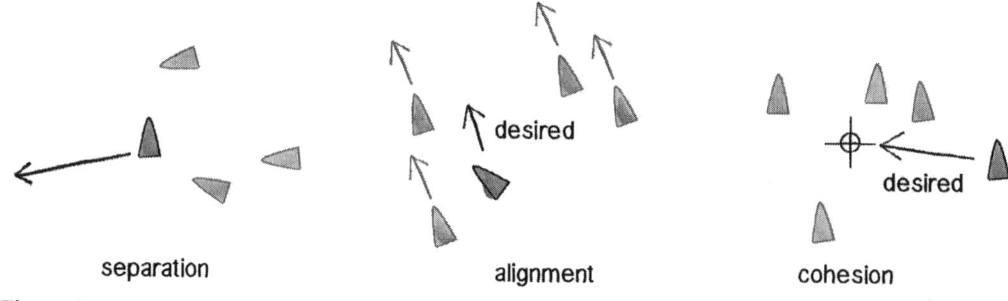

Figure 6.35

Just as we did with our separate and seek example, we'll want our `Boid` objects to have a single function that manages all the above behaviors. We'll call this function `flock()`.

```
void flock(ArrayList<Boid> boids) {
  PVector sep = separate(boids);    // The three flocking rules
  PVector ali = align(boids);
  PVector coh = cohesion(boids);

  sep.mult(1.5);                    // Arbitrary weights for these forces (Try different ones!)
  ali.mult(1.0);
  coh.mult(1.0);

  applyForce(sep);                  // Applying all the forces
  applyForce(ali);
  applyForce(coh);
}
```

Now, it's just a matter of implementing the three rules. We did separation before; it's identical to our previous example. Let's take a look at alignment, or steering in the same direction as your neighbors. As with all of our steering behaviors, we've got to boil down this concept into a desire: the boid's desired velocity is the average velocity of its neighbors.

So our algorithm is to calculate the average velocity of all the other boids and set that to desired.

```
PVector align (ArrayList<Boid> boids) {
  PVector sum = new PVector(0,0);          // Add up all the velocities and divide by the
  for (Boid other : boids) {               // total to calculate the average velocity.
    sum.add(other.velocity);
  }
  sum.div(boids.size());

  sum.setMag(maxspeed);                    // We desire to go in that direction at
                                           // maximum speed.

  PVector steer = PVector.sub(sum,velocity);  // Reynolds's steering force formula
  steer.limit(maxforce);
  return steer;
}
```

The above is pretty good, but it's missing one rather crucial detail. One of the key principles behind complex systems like flocking is that the elements (in this case, boids) have short-range relationships. Thinking about ants again, it's pretty easy to imagine an ant being able to sense its immediate environment, but less so an ant having an awareness of what another ant is doing hundreds of feet away. The fact that the ants can perform such complex collective behavior from only these neighboring relationships is what makes them so exciting in the first place.

In our alignment function, we're taking the average velocity of all the boids, whereas we should really only be looking at the boids within a certain distance. That distance threshold is up to you, of course. You could design boids that can see only twenty pixels away or boids that can see a hundred pixels away.

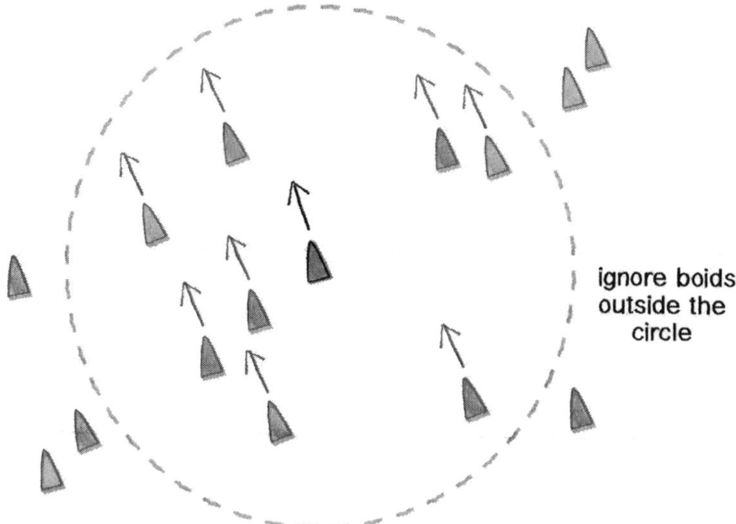
ignore boids
outside the
circle

Figure 6.36

Much like we did with separation (only calculating a force for others within a certain distance), we'll want to do the same with alignment (and cohesion).

```
PVector align (ArrayList<Boid> boids) {
  float neighbordist = 50;
  PVector sum = new PVector(0,0);
  int count = 0;
  for (Boid other : boids) {
    float d = PVector.dist(location,other.location);
    if ((d > 0) && (d < neighbordist)) {
      sum.add(other.velocity);
      count++;
    }
  }
  if (count > 0) {
    sum.div(count);
    sum.normalize();
    sum.mult(maxspeed);
    PVector steer = PVector.sub(sum,velocity);
    steer.limit(maxforce);
    return steer;
  } else {
    return new PVector(0,0);
  }
}
```

This is an arbitrary value and could vary from boid to boid.

For an average, we need to keep track of how many boids are within the distance.

If we don't find any close boids, the steering force is zero.

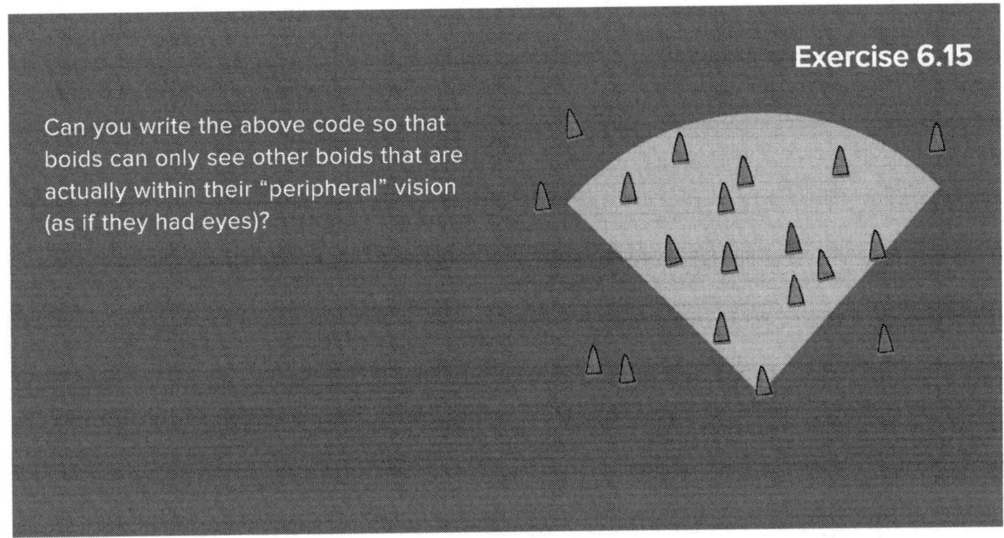

Exercise 6.15
Can you write the above code so that boids can only see other boids that are actually within their "peripheral" vision (as if they had eyes)?

Finally, we are ready for cohesion. Here our code is virtually identical to that for alignment—only instead of calculating the average velocity of the boid's neighbors, we want to calculate the average location of the boid's neighbors (and use that as a target to seek).

```
PVector cohesion (ArrayList<Boid> boids) {
  float neighbordist = 50;
  PVector sum = new PVector(0,0);
  int count = 0;
  for (Boid other : boids) {
    float d = PVector.dist(location,other.location);
    if ((d > 0) && (d < neighbordist)) {
      sum.add(other.location);          // Adding up all the others' locations
      count++;
    }
  }
  if (count > 0) {
    sum.div(count);
    return seek(sum);                   // Here we make use of the seek() function
                                        // we wrote in Example 6.8. The target we
                                        // seek is the average location of our
                                        // neighbors.
  } else {
    return new PVector(0,0);
  }
}
```

It's also worth taking the time to write a class called `Flock`, which will be virtually identical to the `ParticleSystem` class we wrote in Chapter 4 with only one tiny change: When we call `run()` on each `Boid` object (as we did to each `Particle` object), we'll pass in a reference to the entire `ArrayList` of boids.

```
class Flock {
  ArrayList<Boid> boids;

  Flock() {
    boids = new ArrayList<Boid>();
  }

  void run() {
    for (Boid b : boids) {
      b.run(boids);                    // Each Boid object must know about all the other Boids.
    }
  }

  void addBoid(Boid b) {
    boids.add(b);
  }
}
```

And our main program will look like:

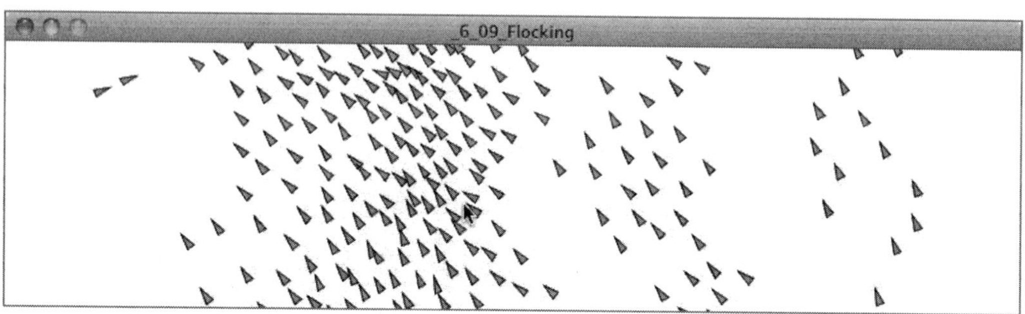

Example 6.9: Flocking

```
Flock flock;                           // A Flock object manages the entire group.

void setup() {
  size(300,200);
  flock = new Flock();
  for (int i = 0; i < 100; i++) {
    Boid b = new Boid(width/2,height/2);
    flock.addBoid(b);                  // The Flock starts out with 100 Boids.
  }
}

void draw() {
  background(255);
  flock.run();
}
```

Exercise 6.16

Combine flocking with some other steering behaviors.

Exercise 6.17

In his book The *Computational Beauty of Nature* (MIT Press, 2000), Gary Flake describes a fourth rule for flocking: "View: move laterally away from any boid that blocks the view." Have your boids follow this rule.

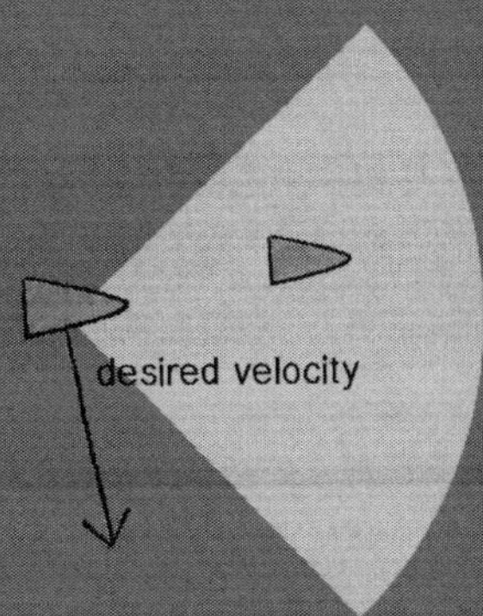

Exercise 6.18

Create a flocking simulation where all of the parameters (*separation weight*, *cohesion weight*, *alignment weight*, *maximum force*, *maximum speed*) change over time. They could be controlled by Perlin noise or by user interaction. (For example, you could use a library such as controlp5 (http://www.sojamo.de/libraries/controlP5/) to tie the values to slider positions.)

Exercise 6.19

Visualize the flock in an entirely different way.

6.14 Algorithmic Efficiency (or: Why does my $@(*%! run so slowly?)

I would like to hide the dark truth behind we've just done, because I would like you to be happy and live a fulfilling and meaningful life. But I also would like to be able to sleep at night without worrying about you so much. So it is with a heavy heart that I must bring up this topic. Group behaviors are wonderful. But they can be slow, and the more elements in the group, the slower they can be. Usually, when we talk about Processing sketches running slowly, it's because drawing to the screen can be slow—the more you draw, the slower your sketch runs. This is actually a case, however, where the slowness derives from the algorithm itself. Let's discuss.

Computer scientists classify algorithms with something called "Big O notation," which describes the efficiency of an algorithm: how many computational cycles does it require to complete? Let's consider a simple analog search problem. You have a basket containing one hundred chocolate treats, only one of which is pure dark chocolate. That's the one you want to eat. To find it, you pick the chocolates out of the basket one by one. Sure, you might be lucky and find it on the first try, but in the worst-case scenario you have to check all one hundred before you find the dark chocolate. To find one thing in one hundred, you have to check one hundred things (or to find one thing in N things, you have to check N times.) Your Big O Notation is N. This, incidentally, is the Big O Notation that describes our simple particle system. If we have N particles, we have to run and display those particles N times.

Now, let's think about a group behavior (such as flocking). For every `Boid` object, we have to check every other `Boid` object (for its velocity and location). Let's say we have one hundred boids. For boid #1, we need to check one hundred boids; for boid #2, we need to check one hundred boids, and so on and so forth. For one hundred boids, we need to perform one hundred times one hundred checks, or ten thousand. No problem: computers are fast and can do things ten thousand times pretty easily. Let's try one thousand.

1,000 x 1,000 = 1,000,000 cycles.

OK, this is rather slow, but still somewhat manageable. Let's try 10,000 elements:

10,000 x 10,000 elements = 100,000,000 cycles.

Now, we're really getting slow. Really, really, really slow.

Notice something odd? As the number of elements increases by a factor of 10, the number of required cycles increases by a factor of 100. Or as the number of elements increases by a factor of N, the cycles increase by a factor of N times N. This is known as Big O Notation N-Squared.

I know what you are thinking. You are thinking: "No problem; with flocking, we only need to consider the boids that are close to other boids. So even if we have 1,000 boids, we can just look at, say, the 5 closest boids and then we only have 5,000 cycles." You pause for a moment, and then start thinking: "So for each boid I just need to check all the boids and find the five closest ones and I'm good!" See the catch-22? Even if we only want to look at the close ones, the only way to know what the close ones are would be to check all of them.

Or is there another way?

Let's take a number that we might actually want to use, but would still run too slowly: 2,000 (4,000,000 cycles required).

What if we could divide the screen into a grid? We would take all 2,000 boids and assign each boid to a cell within that grid. We would then be able to look at each boid and compare it to its neighbors within that cell at any given moment. Imagine a 10 x 10 grid. In a system of 2,000 elements, on average, approximately 20 elements would be found in each cell (20 x 10 x 10 = 2,000). Each cell would then require 20 x 20 = 400 cycles. With 100 cells, we'd have 100 x 400 = 40,000 cycles, a massive savings over 4,000,000.

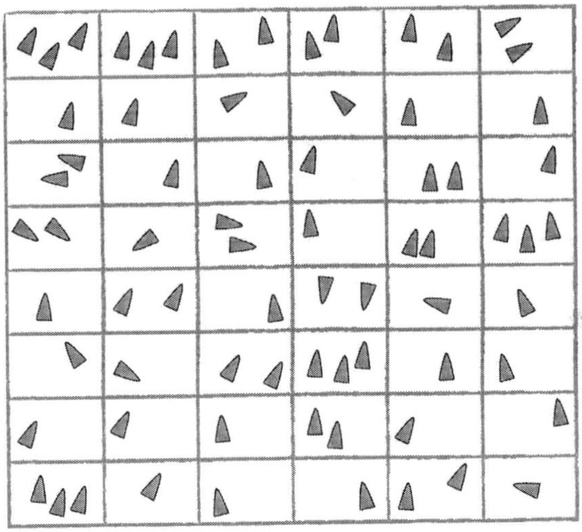

Figure 6.37

This technique is known as "bin-lattice spatial subdivision" and is outlined in more detail in (surprise, surprise) Reynolds's 2000 paper, "Interaction with Groups of Autonomous Characters" (http://www.red3d.com/cwr/papers/2000/pip.pdf). How do we implement such an algorithm in Processing? One way is to keep multiple `ArrayLists`. One `ArrayList` would keep track of all the boids, just like in our flocking example.

```
ArrayList<Boid> boids;
```

In addition to that `ArrayList`, we store an additional reference to each `Boid` object in a two-dimensional `ArrayList`. For each cell in the grid, there is an `ArrayList` that tracks the objects in that cell.

```
ArrayList<Boid>[][] grid;
```

In the main `draw()` loop, each `Boid` object then registers itself in the appropriate cell according to its location.

```
int column = int(boid.x) / resolution;
int row    = int(boid.y) /resolution;
grid[column][row].add(boid);
```

Then when it comes time to have the boids check for neighbors, they can look at only those in their particular cell (in truth, we also need to check neighboring cells to deal with border cases).

Example 6.10: Bin-lattice spatial subdivision

```
int column = int(boid.x) / resolution;
int row    = int(boid.y) /resolution;
boid.flock(boids);
boid.flock(grid[column][row]);
```

Instead of looking at all the boids, just this cell

We're only covering the basics here; for the full code, check the book's website.

Now, there are certainly flaws with this system. What if all the boids congregate in the corner and live in the same cell? Then don't we have to check all 2,000 against all 2,000?

The good news is that this need for optimization is a common one and there are a wide variety of similar techniques out there. For us, it's likely that a basic approach will be good enough (in most cases, you won't need one at all.) For another, more sophisticated approach, check out toxiclibs' Octree examples (http://toxiclibs.org/2010/02/new-package-simutils/).

6.15 A Few Last Notes: Optimization Tricks

This is something of a momentous occasion. The end of Chapter 6 marks the end of our story of motion (in the context of this book, that is). We started with the concept of a vector, moved on to forces, designed systems of many elements, examined physics libraries, built entities with hopes and dreams and fears, and simulated emergence. The story doesn't end here, but it does take a bit of a turn. The next two chapters won't focus on moving bodies, but rather on systems of rules. Before we get there, I have a few quick items I'd like to mention that are important when working with the examples in Chapters 1 through 6. They also relate to optimizing your code, which fits in with the previous section.

1) Magnitude squared (or sometimes distance squared)

What is magnitude squared and when should you use it? Let's revisit how the magnitude of a vector is calculated.

```
float mag() {
  return sqrt(x*x + y*y);
}
```

Magnitude requires the square root operation. And it should. After all, if you want the magnitude of a vector, then you've got to look up the Pythagorean theorem and compute it (we did this in Chapter 1). However, if you could somehow skip using the square root, your code would run faster. Let's consider a situation where you just want to know the relative magnitude of a vector. For example, is the magnitude greater than ten? (Assume a `PVector` v.)

```
if (v.mag() > 10) {
  // Do Something!
}
```

Well, this is equivalent to saying:

```
if (v.magSq() > 100) {
  // Do Something!
}
```

And how is magnitude squared calculated?

```
float magSq() {
  return x*x + y*y;
}
```

Same as magnitude, but without the square root. In the case of a single `PVector` object, this will never make a significant difference on a Processing sketch. However, if you are computing the magnitude of thousands of `PVector` objects each time through `draw()`, using `magSq()` instead of `mag()` could help your code run a wee bit faster. (Note: `magSq()` is only available in Processing 2.0a1 or later.)

2) Sine and cosine lookup tables

There's a pattern here. What kinds of functions are slow to compute? Square root. Sine. Cosine. Tangent. Again, if you just need a sine or cosine value here or there in your code, you are never going to run into a problem. But what if you had something like this?

```
void draw() {
  for (int i = 0; i < 10000; i++) {
     println(sin(PI));
  }
}
```

Sure, this is a totally ridiculous code snippet that you would never write. But it illustrates a certain point. If you are calculating the sine of pi ten thousand times, why not just calculate it once, save that value, and refer to it whenever necessary? This is the principle behind sine and cosine lookup tables. Instead of calling the sine and cosine functions in your code whenever you need them, you can build an array that stores the results of sine and cosine at angles between 0 and `TWO_PI` and just look up the values when you need them. For example, here are two arrays that store the sine and cosine values for every angle, 0 to 359 degrees.

```
float sinvalues[] = new float[360];
float cosvalues[] = new float[360];
for (int i = 0; i < 360; i++) {
  sinvalues[i] = sin(radians(i));
  cosvalues[i] = cos(radians(i));
}
```

Now, what if you need the value of sine of pi?

```
int angle = int(degrees(PI));
float answer = sinvalues[angle];
```

A more sophisticated example of this technique is available on the Processing wiki (http://wiki.processing.org/w/Sin/Cos_look-up_table).

3) Making gajillions of unnecessary PVector objects

I have to admit, I am perhaps the biggest culprit of this last note. In fact, in the interest of writing clear and understandable examples, I often choose to make extra `PVector` objects when I absolutely do not need to. For the most part, this is not a problem at all. But sometimes, it can be. Let's take a look at an example.

```
void draw() {
  for (Vehicle v : vehicles) {
   PVector mouse = new PVector(mouseX,mouseY);
   v.seek(mouse);
  }
}
```

Let's say our `ArrayList` of vehicles has one thousand vehicles in it. We just made one thousand new `PVector` objects every single time through `draw()`. Now, on any ol' laptop or desktop computer you've purchased in recent times, your sketch will likely not register a complaint, run slowly, or have any problems. After all, you've got tons of RAM, and Java will be able to handle making a thousand or so temporary objects and dispose of them without much of a problem.

If your numbers grow larger (and they easily could) or perhaps more likely, if you are working with Processing on Android, you will almost certainly run into a problem. In cases like this you want to look for ways to reduce the number of `PVector` objects you make. An obvious fix for the above code is:

```
void draw() {
  PVector mouse = new PVector(mouseX,mouseY);
  for (Vehicle v : vehicles) {
   v.seek(mouse);
  }
}
```

Now you've made just one `PVector` instead of one thousand. Even better, you could turn the `PVector` into a global variable and just assign the x and y value:

```
PVector mouse = new PVector();

void draw() {
  mouse.x = mouseX;
  mouse.y = mouseY;
  for (Vehicle v : vehicles) {
   v.seek(mouse);
  }
}
```

Now you never make a new `PVector`; you use just one over the length of your sketch!

Throughout the book's examples, you can find lots of opportunities to reduce the number of temporary objects. Let's look at one more. Here is a snippet from our `seek()` function.

```
PVector desired = PVector.sub(target,location);
desired.normalize();
desired.mult(maxspeed);

PVector steer = PVector.sub(desired,velocity);   // Create a new PVector to store the steering force.
steer.limit(maxforce);
return steer;
```

See how we've made two `PVector` objects? First, we figure out the desired vector, then we calculate the steering force. Notice how we could rewrite this to create only one `PVector`.

```
PVector desired = PVector.sub(target, location);
desired.normalize();
desired.mult(maxspeed);
```

```
    desired.sub(velocity);
    desired.limit(maxforce);
    return desired;
```

Calculate the steering force in the desired PVector.

We don't actually need a second `PVector` called `steer`. We could just use the desired `PVector` object and turn it into the steering force by subtracting velocity. I didn't do this in my example because it is more confusing to read. But in some cases, it may be greatly more efficient.

Exercise 6.20

Eliminate as many temporary `PVector` objects from the flocking example as possible. Also use `magSq()` where possible.

Exercise 6.21

Use steering behaviors with Box2D or toxiclibs.

The Ecosystem Project

Step 6 Exercise:

Use the concept of steering forces to drive the behavior of the creatures in your ecosystem. Some possibilities:

- Create "schools" or "flocks" of creatures.
- Use a seeking behavior for creatures to search for food (for chasing moving prey, consider "pursuit").
- Use a flow field for the ecosystem environment. For example, how does your system behave if the creatures live in a flowing river?
- Build a creature with countless steering behaviors (as many as you can reasonably add). Think about ways to vary the weights of these behaviors so that you can dial those behaviors up and down, mixing and matching on the fly. How are creatures' initial weights set? What rules drive how the weights change over time?
- Complex systems can be nested. Can you design a single creature out of a flock of boids? And can you then make a flock of those creatures?
- Complex systems can have memory (and be adaptive). Can the history of your ecosystem affect the behavior in its current state? (This could be the driving force behind how the creatures adjust their steering force weights.)

Chapter 7. Cellular Automata

"To play life you must have a fairly large checkerboard and a plentiful supply of flat counters of two colors. It is possible to work with pencil and graph paper but it is much easier, particularly for beginners, to use counters and a board."

— Martin Gardner, *Scientific American* (October 1970)

In this chapter, we're going to take a break from talking about vectors and motion. In fact, the rest of the book will mostly focus on systems and algorithms (albeit ones that we can, should, and will apply to moving bodies). In the previous chapter, we encountered our first Processing example of a complex system: flocking. We briefly stated the core principles behind complex systems: more than the sum of its parts, a complex system is a system of elements, operating in parallel, with short-range relationships that as a whole exhibit emergent behavior. This entire chapter is going to be dedicated to building another complex system simulation in Processing. Oddly, we are going to take some steps backward and simplify the elements of our system. No longer are the individual elements going to be members of a physics world; instead we will build a system out of the simplest digital element possible, a single bit. This bit is going to be called a cell and its value (0 or 1) will be called its state. Working with such simple elements will help us understand more of the details behind how complex systems work, and we'll also be able to elaborate on some programming techniques that we can apply to code-based projects.

7.1 What Is a Cellular Automaton?

First, let's get one thing straight. The term ***cellular automata*** is plural. Our code examples will simulate just one—a ***cellular automaton***, singular. To simplify our lives, we'll also refer to cellular automata as "CA."

In Chapters 1 through 6, our objects (mover, particle, vehicle, boid) generally existed in only one "state." They might have moved around with advanced behaviors and physics, but ultimately they remained the same type of object over the course of their digital lifetime. We've alluded to the possibility that these entities can change over time (for example, the weights of steering "desires" can vary), but we haven't fully put this into practice. In this context, cellular automata make a great first step in building a system of many objects that have varying states over time.

A cellular automaton is a model of a system of "cell" objects with the following characteristics.

- The cells live on a ***grid***. (We'll see examples in both one and two dimensions in this chapter, though a cellular automaton can exist in any finite number of dimensions.)
- Each cell has a ***state***. The number of state possibilities is typically finite. The simplest example has the two possibilities of 1 and 0 (otherwise referred to as "on" and "off" or "alive" and "dead").
- Each cell has a ***neighborhood***. This can be defined in any number of ways, but it is typically a list of adjacent cells.

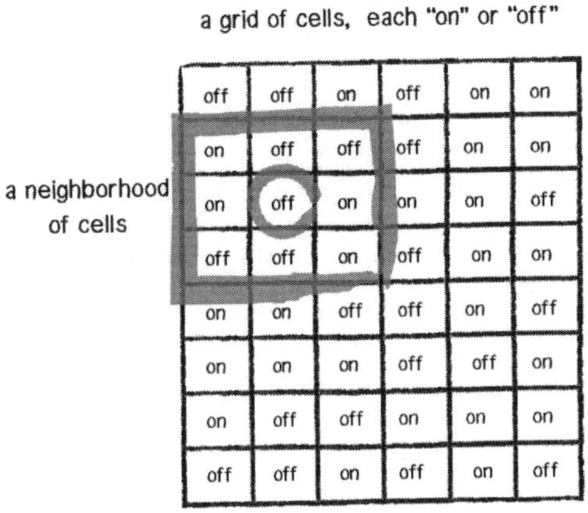

a grid of cells, each "on" or "off"

a neighborhood of cells

off	off	on	off	on	on
on	off	off	off	on	on
on	off	on	on	on	off
off	off	on	off	on	on
on	on	off	off	on	off
on	on	on	off	off	on
on	off	off	on	on	on
off	off	on	off	on	off

Figure 7.1

The development of cellular automata systems is typically attributed to Stanisław Ulam and John von Neumann, who were both researchers at the Los Alamos National Laboratory in

New Mexico in the 1940s. Ulam was studying the growth of crystals and von Neumann was imagining a world of self-replicating robots. That's right, robots that build copies of themselves. Once we see some examples of CA visualized, it'll be clear how one might imagine modeling crystal growth; the robots idea is perhaps less obvious. Consider the design of a robot as a pattern on a grid of cells (think of filling in some squares on a piece of graph paper). Now consider a set of simple rules that would allow that pattern to create copies of itself on that grid. This is essentially the process of a CA that exhibits behavior similar to biological reproduction and evolution. (Incidentally, von Neumann's cells had twenty-nine possible states.) Von Neumann's work in self-replication and CA is conceptually similar to what is probably the most famous cellular automaton: the "Game of Life," which we will discuss in detail in section 7.3.

Perhaps the most significant scientific (and lengthy) work studying cellular automata arrived in 2002: Stephen Wolfram's 1,280-page *A New Kind of Science* (http://www.wolframscience.com/nksonline/toc.html). Available in its entirety for free online, Wolfram's book discusses how CA are not simply neat tricks, but are relevant to the study of biology, chemistry, physics, and all branches of science. This chapter will barely scratch the surface of the theories Wolfram outlines (we will focus on the code implementation) so if the examples provided spark your curiosity, you'll find plenty more to read about in his book.

7.2 Elementary Cellular Automata

The examples in this chapter will begin with a simulation of Wolfram's work. To understand Wolfram's elementary CA, we should ask ourselves the question: "What is the simplest cellular automaton we can imagine?" What's exciting about this question and its answer is that even with the simplest CA imaginable, we will see the properties of complex systems at work.

Let's build Wolfram's elementary CA from scratch. Concepts first, then code. What are the three key elements of a CA?

1) ***Grid***. The simplest grid would be one-dimensional: a line of cells.

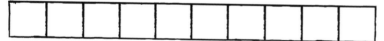

Figure 7.2

2) ***States***. The simplest set of states (beyond having only one state) would be two states: 0 or 1.

1	0	1	0	1	1	1	0	0	1

Figure 7.3

3) ***Neighborhood***. The simplest neighborhood in one dimension for any given cell would be the cell itself and its two adjacent neighbors: one to the left and one to the right.

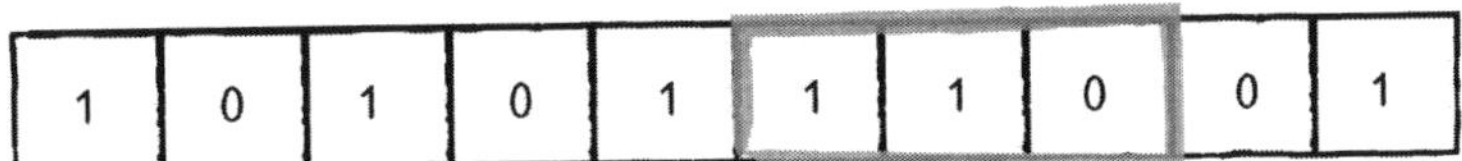

Figure 7.4: A neighborhood is three cells.

So we begin with a line of cells, each with an initial state (let's say it is random), and each with two neighbors. We'll have to figure out what we want to do with the cells on the edges (since those have only one neighbor each), but this is something we can sort out later.

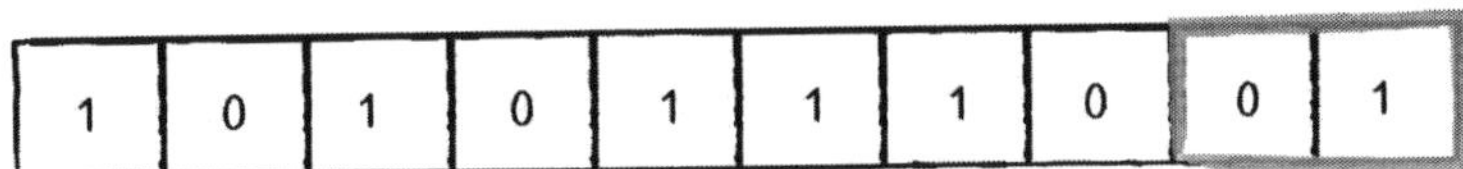

Figure 7.5: The edge cell only has a neighborhood of two.

We haven't yet discussed, however, what is perhaps the most important detail of how cellular automata work—*time*. We're not really talking about real-world time here, but about the CA living over a period of *time*, which could also be called a ***generation*** and, in our case, will likely refer to the ***frame count*** of an animation. The figures above show us the CA at time equals 0 or generation 0. The questions we have to ask ourselves are: *How do we compute the states for all cells at generation 1? And generation 2?* And so on and so forth.

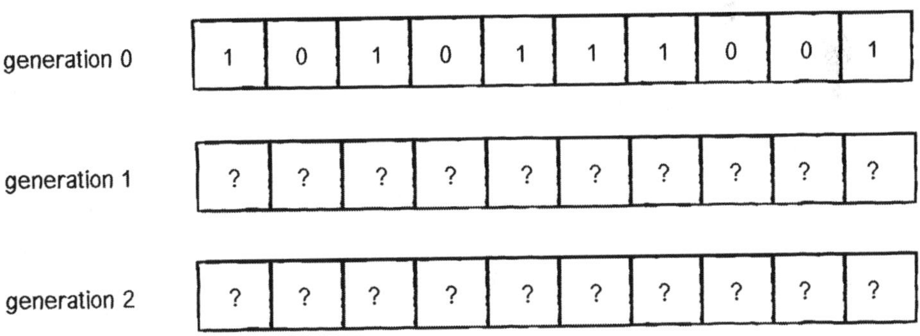

Figure 7.6

Let's say we have an individual cell in the CA, and let's call it CELL. The formula for calculating CELL's state at any given time t is as follows:

```
CELL state at time t = f(CELL neighborhood at time t - 1)
```

In other words, a cell's new state is a function of all the states in the cell's neighborhood at the previous moment in time (or during the previous generation). We calculate a new state value by looking at all the previous neighbor states.

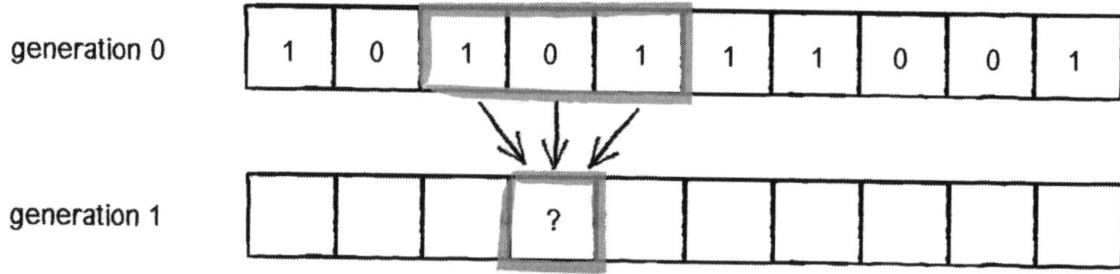

Figure 7.7

Now, in the world of cellular automata, there are many ways we could compute a cell's state from a group of cells. Consider blurring an image. (Guess what? Image processing works with CA-like rules.) A pixel's new state (i.e. its color) is the average of all of its neighbors' colors. We could also say that a cell's new state is the sum of all of its neighbors' states. With Wolfram's elementary CA, however, we can actually do something a bit simpler and seemingly absurd: We can look at all the possible configurations of a cell and its neighbor and define the state outcome for every possible configuration. It seems ridiculous—wouldn't there be way too many possibilities for this to be practical? Let's give it a try.

We have three cells, each with a state of 0 or 1. How many possible ways can we configure the states? If you love binary, you'll notice that three cells define a 3-bit number, and how high can you count with 3 bits? Up to 8. Let's have a look.

000 001 010 011 100 101 110 111

Figure 7.8

Once we have defined all the possible neighborhoods, we need to define an outcome (new state value: 0 or 1) for each neighborhood configuration.

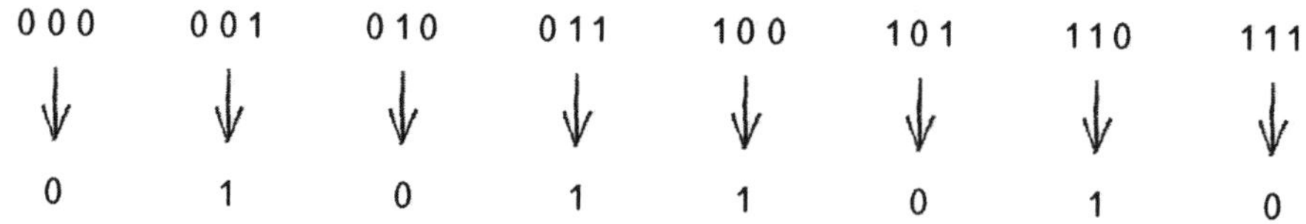

Figure 7.9

The standard Wolfram model is to start generation 0 with all cells having a state of 0 except for the middle cell, which should have a state of 1.

Figure 7.10

Referring to the ruleset above, let's see how a given cell (we'll pick the center one) would change from generation 0 to generation 1.

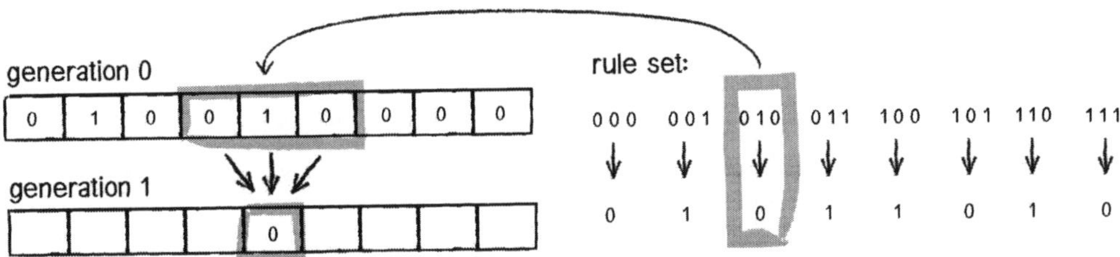

Figure 7.11

Try applying the same logic to all of the cells above and fill in the empty cells.

Now, let's go past just one generation and color the cells —0 means white, 1 means black—and stack the generations, with each new generation appearing below the previous one.

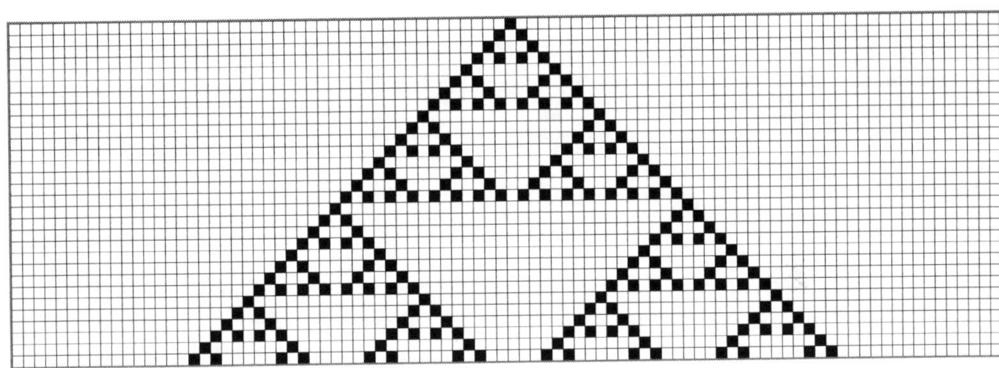

Figure 7.12: Rule 90

The low-resolution shape we're seeing above is the "Sierpiński triangle." Named after the Polish mathematician Wacław Sierpiński, it's a fractal pattern that we'll examine in the next chapter. That's right: this incredibly simple system of 0s and 1s, with little neighborhoods of three cells, can generate a shape as sophisticated and detailed as the Sierpiński triangle. Let's look at it again, only with each cell a single pixel wide so that the resolution is much higher.

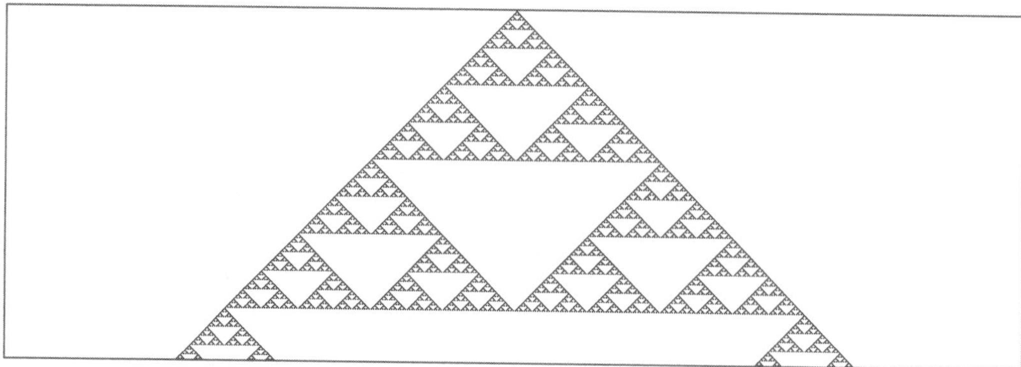

Figure 7.13: Rule 90

This particular result didn't happen by accident. I picked this set of rules because of the pattern it generates. Take a look at Figure 7.8 one more time. Notice how there are eight possible neighborhood configurations; we therefore define a "ruleset" as a list of 8 bits.

So this particular rule can be illustrated as follows:

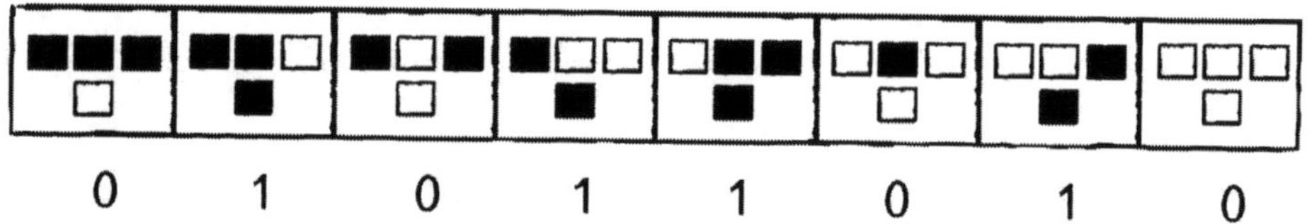

Figure 7.14: Rule 90

Eight 0s and 1s means an 8-bit number. How many combinations of eight 0s and 1s are there? 256. This is just like how we define the components of an RGB color. We get 8 bits for red, green, and blue, meaning we make colors with values from 0 to 255 (256 possibilities).

In terms of a Wolfram elementary CA, we have now discovered that there are 256 possible rulesets. The above ruleset is commonly referred to as "Rule 90" because if you convert the binary sequence—01011010—to a decimal number, you'll get the integer 90. Let's try looking at the results of another ruleset.

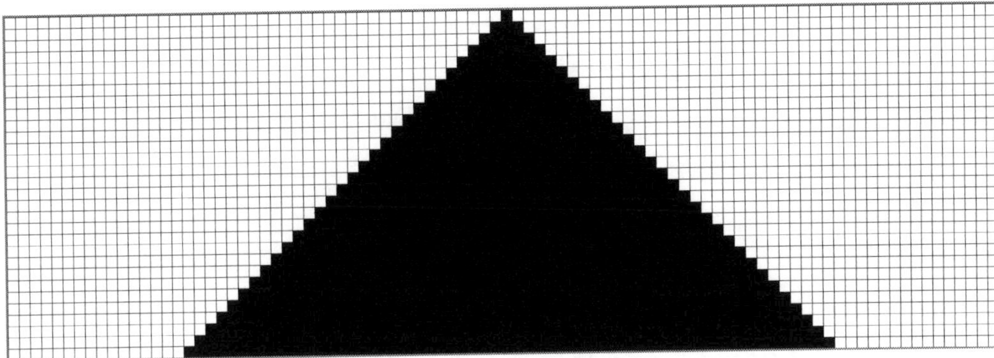

Figure 7.15: Rule 222

As we can now see, the simple act of creating a CA and defining a ruleset does not guarantee visually interesting results. Out of all 256 rulesets, only a handful produce compelling outcomes. However, it's quite incredible that even one of these rulesets for a one-dimensional CA with only two possible states can produce the patterns we see every day in nature (see Figure 7.16), and it demonstrates how valuable these systems can be in simulation and pattern generation.

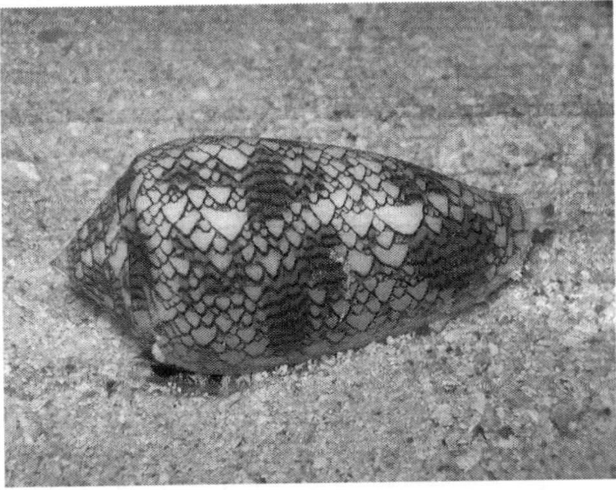

Figure 7.16: A Textile Cone Snail (Conus textile), Cod Hole, Great Barrier Reef, Australia, 7 August 2005. Photographer: Richard Ling richard@research.canon.com.au

Before we go too far down the road of how Wolfram classifies the results of varying rulesets, let's look at how we actually build a Processing sketch that generates the Wolfram CA and visualizes it onscreen.

7.3 How to Program an Elementary CA

You may be thinking: "OK, I've got this cell thing. And the cell thing has some properties, like a state, what generation it's on, who its neighbors are, where it lives pixel-wise on the screen. And maybe it has some functions: it can display itself, it can generate its new state, etc." This line of thinking is an excellent one and would likely lead you to write some code like this:

```
class Cell {

}
```

This line of thinking, however, is not the road we will first travel. Later in this chapter, we will discuss why an object-oriented approach could prove valuable in developing a CA simulation, but to begin, we can work with a more elementary data structure. After all, what is an elementary CA but a list of 0s and 1s? Certainly, we could describe the following CA generation using an array:

Figure 7.17

```
int[] cells = {1,0,1,0,0,0,0,1,0,1,1,1,0,0,0,1,1,1,0,0};
```

To draw that array, we simply check if we've got a 0 or a 1 and create a fill accordingly.

```
for (int i = 0; i < cells.length; i++) {        Loop through every cell.
  if (cells[i] == 0) fill(255);
  else fill(0);                                  Create a fill based on its state (0 or 1).
  stroke(0);
  rect(i*50,0,50,50);
}
```

Now that we have the array to describe the cell states of a given generation (which we'll ultimately consider the "current" generation), we need a mechanism by which to compute the next generation. Let's think about the pseudocode of what we are doing at the moment.

For every cell in the array:

- ***Take a look at the neighborhood states: left, middle, right.***
- ***Look up the new value for the cell state according to some ruleset.***
- ***Set the cell's state to that new value.***

This may lead you to write some code like this:

```
for (int i = 0; i < cells.length; i++) {        For every cell in the array...

  int left   = cell[i-1];                        ...take a look at the neighborhood.
  int middle = cell[i];
  int right  = cell[i+1];

  int newstate = rules(left,middle,right);       Look up the new value according to the rules.
```

```
  cell[i] = newstate;                    Set the cell's state to the new value.
}
```

We're fairly close to getting this right, but we've made one minor blunder and one major blunder in the above code. Let's talk about what we've done well so far.

Notice how easy it is to look at a cell's neighbors. Because an array is an ordered list of data, we can use the fact that the indices are numbered to know which cells are next to which cells. We know that cell number 15, for example, has cell 14 to its left and 16 to its right. More generally, we can say that for any cell `i`, its neighbors are `i-1` and `i+1`.

We're also farming out the calculation of a new state value to some function called `rules()`. Obviously, we're going to have to write this function ourselves, but the point we're making here is modularity. We have a basic framework for the CA in this function, and if we later want to change how the rules operate, we don't have to touch that framework; we can simply rewrite the `rules()` function to compute the new states differently.

So what have we done wrong? Let's talk through how the code will execute. First, we look at cell index `i` equals 0. Now let's look at 0's neighbors. Left is index -1. Middle is index 0. And right is index 1. However, our array by definition does not have an element with the index -1. It starts with 0. This is a problem we've alluded to before: the edge cases.

How do we deal with the cells on the edge who don't have a neighbor to both their left and their right? Here are three possible solutions to this problem:

1. ***Edges remain constant.*** This is perhaps the simplest solution. We never bother to evaluate the edges and always leave their state value constant (0 or 1).

2. ***Edges wrap around.*** Think of the CA as a strip of paper and turn that strip of paper into a ring. The cell on the left edge is a neighbor of the cell on the right and vice versa. This can create the appearance of an infinite grid and is probably the most used solution.

3. ***Edges have different neighborhoods and rules.*** If we wanted to, we could treat the edge cells differently and create rules for cells that have a neighborhood of two instead of three. You may want to do this in some circumstances, but in our case, it's going to be a lot of extra lines of code for little benefit.

To make the code easiest to read and understand right now, we'll go with option #1 and just skip the edge cases, leaving their values constant. This can be accomplished by starting the loop one cell later and ending one cell earlier:

```
for (int i = 1; i < cells.length-1; i++) {      A loop that ignores the first and last cell
  int left   = cell[i-1];
  int middle = cell[i];
  int right  = cell[i+1];
  int newstate = rules(left,middle,right);
  cell[i] = newstate;
}
```

There's one more problem we have to fix before we're done. It's subtle and you won't get a compilation error; the CA just won't perform correctly. However, identifying this problem is absolutely fundamental to the techniques behind programming CA simulations. It all lies in this line of code:

```
cell[i] = newstate;
```

This seems like a perfectly innocent line. After all, we've computed the new state value and we're simply giving the cell its new state. But in the next iteration, you'll discover a massive bug. Let's say we've just computed the new state for cell #5. What do we do next? We calculate the new state value for cell #6.

Cell #6, generation 0 = some state, 0 or 1
*Cell #6, generation 1 = a function of states for **cell #5**, cell #6, and cell #7 at *generation 0**

Notice how we need the value of cell #5 at generation 0 in order to calculate cell #6's new state at generation 1? A cell's new state is a function of the previous neighbor states. Do we know cell #5's value at generation 0? Remember, Processing just executes this line of code for *i = 5*.

```
cell[i] = newstate;
```

Once this happens, we no longer have access to cell #5's state at generation 0, and cell index 5 is storing the value for generation 1. We cannot overwrite the values in the array while we are processing the array, because we need those values to calculate the new values. A solution to this problem is to have two arrays, one to store the current generation states and one for the next generation states.

```
int[] newcells = new int[cells.length];      Another array to store the states for the next
                                              generation.
for (int i = 1; i < cells.length-1; i++) {
  int left   = cell[i-1];                     Look at the states from the current array.
  int middle = cell[i];
  int right  = cell[i+1];
  int newstate = rules(left,middle,right);
  newcells[i] = newstate;                     Saving the new state in the new array
}
```

Once the entire array of values is processed, we can then discard the old array and set it equal to the new array of states.

```
cells = newcells;
```

The new generation becomes the current generation.

We're almost done. The above code is complete except for the fact that we haven't yet written the `rules()` function that computes the new state value based on the neighborhood (left, middle, and right cells). We know that function needs to return an integer (0 or 1) as well as receive three arguments (for the three neighbors).

```
  int rules (int a, int b, int c) {
```

Function receives 3 ints and returns 1.

Now, there are many ways we could write this function, but I'd like to start with a long-winded one that will hopefully provide a clear illustration of what we are doing.

Let's first establish how we are storing the ruleset. The ruleset, if you remember from the previous section, is a series of 8 bits (0 or 1) that defines that outcome for every possible neighborhood configuration.

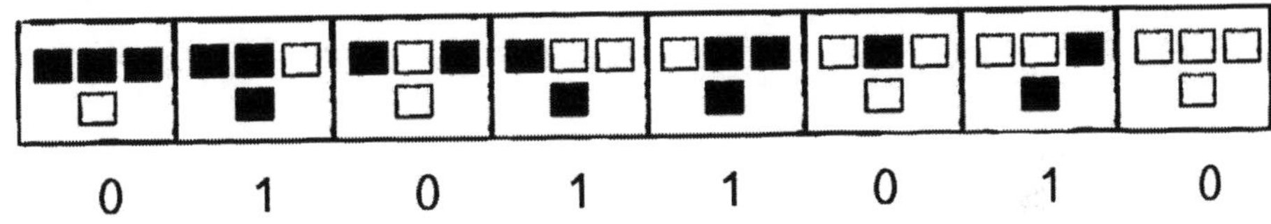

Figure 7.14 (repeated)

We can store this ruleset in Processing as an array.

```
int[] ruleset = {0,1,0,1,1,0,1,0};
```

And then say:

```
if (a == 1 && b == 1 && c == 1) return ruleset[0];
```

If left, middle, and right all have the state 1, then that matches the configuration 111 and the new state should be equal to the first value in the ruleset array. We can now duplicate this strategy for all eight possibilities.

```
int rules (int a, int b, int c) {
  if      (a == 1 && b == 1 && c == 1) return ruleset[0];
  else if (a == 1 && b == 1 && c == 0) return ruleset[1];
  else if (a == 1 && b == 0 && c == 1) return ruleset[2];
  else if (a == 1 && b == 0 && c == 0) return ruleset[3];
  else if (a == 0 && b == 1 && c == 1) return ruleset[4];
  else if (a == 0 && b == 1 && c == 0) return ruleset[5];
  else if (a == 0 && b == 0 && c == 1) return ruleset[6];
  else if (a == 0 && b == 0 && c == 0) return ruleset[7];
  return 0;
}
```

For this function to be valid, we have to make sure something is returned in cases where the states do not match one of the eight possibilities. We know this is impossible given the rest of our code, but Processing does not.

I like having the example written as above because it describes line by line exactly what is happening for each neighborhood configuration. However, it's not a great solution. After all, what if we design a CA that has 4 possible states (0-3) and suddenly we have 64 possible neighborhood configurations? With 10 possible states, we have 1,000 configurations. Certainly we don't want to type in 1,000 lines of code!

Another solution, though perhaps a bit more difficult to follow, is to convert the neighborhood configuration (a 3-bit number) into a regular integer and use that value as the index into the ruleset array. This can be done in Java like so.

```
int rules (int a, int b, int c) {
  String s = "" + a + b + c;
  int index = Integer.parseInt(s,2);
  return ruleset[index];
}
```

A quick way to join three bits into a String

The second argument '2' indicates that we intend to parse a binary number (base 2).

There's one tiny problem with this solution, however. Let's say we are implementing rule 222:

```
int[] ruleset = {1,1,0,1,1,1,1,0};
```

Rule 222

And we have the neighborhood "111". The resulting state is equal to ruleset index 0, as we see in the first way we wrote the function.

```
if (a == 1 && b == 1 && c == 1) return ruleset[0];
```

If we convert "111" to a decimal number, we get 7. But we don't want ruleset[7]; we want ruleset[0]. For this to work, we need to write the ruleset with the bits in reverse order, i.e.

```
int[] ruleset = {0,1,1,1,1,0,1,1};     Rule 222 in “reverse” order
```

So far in this section, we’ve written everything we need to compute the generations for a Wolfram elementary CA. Let’s take a moment to organize the above code into a class, which will ultimately help in the design of our overall sketch.

```
class CA {
  int[] cells;                         We need an array for the cells and one for
  int[] ruleset;                       the rules.

  CA() {
    cells = new int[width];
    ruleset = {0,1,0,1,1,0,1,0};       Arbitrarily starting with rule 90

    for (int i = 0; i < cells.length; i++) {
      cells[i] = 0;
    }
    cells[cells.length/2] = 1;         All cells start with state 0, except the center
  }                                    cell has state 1.

  void generate() {
    int[] nextgen = new int[cells.length];     Compute the next generation.
    for (int i = 1; i < cells.length-1; i++) {
      int left   = cells[i-1];
      int me     = cells[i];
      int right  = cells[i+1];
      nextgen[i] = rules(left, me, right);
    }
    cells = nextgen;
  }

  int rules (int a, int b, int c) {    Look up a new state from the ruleset.
    String s = "" + a + b + c;
    int index = Integer.parseInt(s,2);
    return ruleset[index];
  }
}
```

7.4 Drawing an Elementary CA

What’s missing? Presumably, it’s our intention to display cells and their states in visual form. As we saw earlier, the standard technique for doing this is to stack the generations one on top of each other and draw a rectangle that is black (for state 1) or white (for state 0).

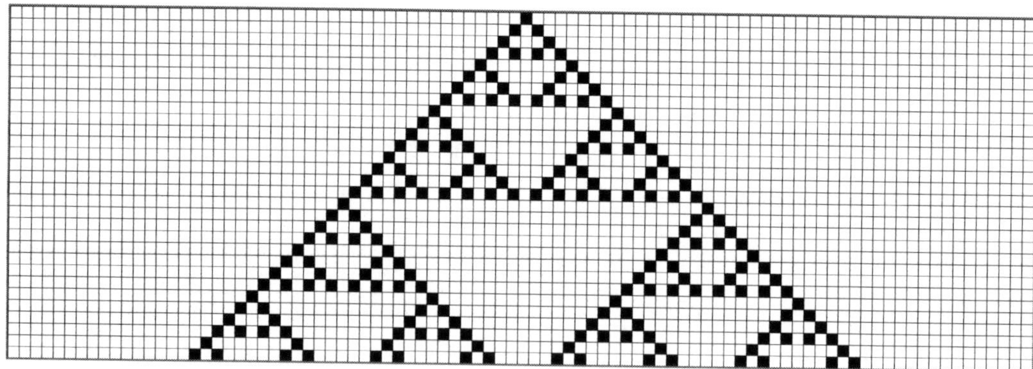

Figure 7.12 (repeated)

Before we implement this particular visualization, I'd like to point out two things.

One, this visual interpretation of the data is completely literal. It's useful for demonstrating the algorithms and results of Wolfram's elementary CA, but it shouldn't necessarily drive your own personal work. It's rather unlikely that you are building a project that needs precisely this algorithm with this visual style. So while learning to draw the CA in this way will help you understand and implement CA systems, this skill should exist only as a foundation.

Second, the fact that we are visualizing a one-dimensional CA with a two-dimensional image can be confusing. It's very important to remember that this is not a 2D CA. We are simply choosing to show a history of all the generations stacked vertically. This technique creates a two-dimensional image out of many instances of one-dimensional data. But the system itself is one-dimensional. Later, we are going to look at an actual 2D CA (the Game of Life) and discuss how we might choose to display such a system.

The good news is that drawing the CA is not particularly difficult. Let's begin by looking at how we would render a single generation. Assume we have a Processing window 600 pixels wide and we want each cell to be a 10x10 square. We therefore have a CA with 60 cells. Of course, we can calculate this value dynamically.

```
int w = 10;
int[] cells = new int[width/w];
```

How many cells fit across given a certain width

Assuming we've gone through the process of generating the cell states (which we did in the previous section), we can now loop through the entire array of cells, drawing a black cell when the state is 1 and a white one when the state is 0.

```
for (int i = 0; i < cells.length; i++) {
  if (cells[i] == 1) fill(0);
  else               fill(255);
```

Black or white fill?

```
    rect(i*w, 0, w, w);
  }
```

Notice how the x-location is the cell index times the cell width. In the above scenario, this would give us cells located at x equals 0, 10, 20, 30, all the way up to 600.

In truth, we could optimize the above by having a white background and only drawing when there is a black cell (saving us the work of drawing many white squares), but in most cases this solution is good enough (and necessary for other more sophisticated designs with varying colors, etc.) Also, if we wanted each cell to be represented as a single pixel, we would not want to use Processing's `rect()` function, but rather access the pixel array directly.

In the above code, you'll notice the y-location for each rectangle is 0. If we want the generations to be drawn next to each other, with each row of cells marking a new generation, we'll also need to compute a y-location based on how many iterations of the CA we've executed. We could accomplish this by adding a "generation" variable (an integer) to our CA class and incrementing it each time through `generate()`. With these additions, we can now look at the CA class with all the features for both computing and drawing the CA.

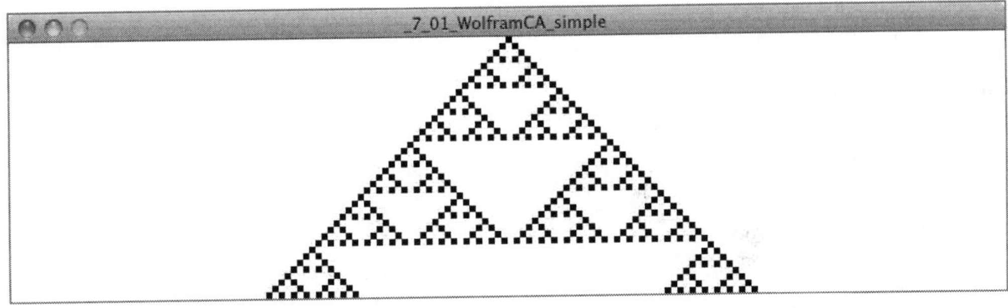

Example 7.1: Wolfram elementary cellular automata

```
class CA {
  int[] cells;
  int[] ruleset;
  int w = 10;
  int generation = 0;
  CA() {
    cells = new int[width/w];
    ruleset = {0,1,0,1,1,0,1,0};
    cells[cells.length/2] = 1;
  }
```

The CA should keep track of how many generations.

```
  void generate() {                          Function to compute the next generation
    int[] nextgen = new int[cells.length];
    for (int i = 1; i < cells.length-1; i++) {
      int left   = cells[i-1];
      int me     = cells[i];
      int right  = cells[i+1];
      nextgen[i] = rules(left, me, right);
    }
    cells = nextgen;
    generation++;                            Increment the generation counter.
  }

  int rules(int a, int b, int c) {
    String s = "" + a + b + c;
    int index = Integer.parseInt(s,2);
    return ruleset[index];
  }

  for (int i = 0; i < cells.length; i++) {
    if (cells[i] == 1) fill(0);
    else               fill(255);
    rect(i*w, generation*w, w, w);           Set the y-location according to the
  }                                          generation.
}
```

Exercise 7.1

Expand Example 7.1 to have the following feature: when the CA reaches the bottom of the Processing window, the CA starts over with a new, random ruleset.

Exercise 7.2

Examine what patterns occur if you initialize the first generation with each cell having a random state.

Exercise 7.3

Visualize the CA in a non-traditional way. Break all the rules you can; don't feel tied to using squares on a perfect grid with black and white.

Exercise 7.4

Create a visualization of the CA that scrolls upwards as the generations increase so that you can view the generations to "infinity." Hint: instead of keeping track of only one generation at a time, you'll need to store a history of generations, always adding a new one and deleting the oldest one in each frame.

7.5 Wolfram Classification

Before we move on to looking at CA in two dimensions, it's worth taking a brief look at Wolfram's classification for cellular automata. As we noted earlier, the vast majority of elementary CA rulesets produce uninspiring results, while some result in wondrously complex patterns like those found in nature. Wolfram has divided up the range of outcomes into four classes:

Figure 7.18: Rule 222

Class 1: Uniformity. Class 1 CAs end up, after some number of generations, with every cell constant. This is not terribly exciting to watch. Rule 222 (above) is a class 1 CA; if you run it for enough generations, every cell will eventually become and remain black.

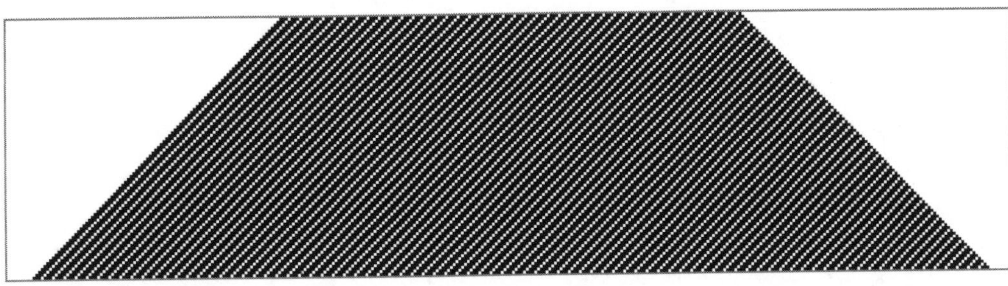

Figure 7.19: Rule 190

Class 2: Repetition. Like class 1 CAs, class 2 CAs remain stable, but the cell states are not constant. Rather, they oscillate in some regular pattern back and forth from 0 to 1 to 0 to 1 and so on. In rule 190 (above), each cell follows the sequence 11101110111011101110.

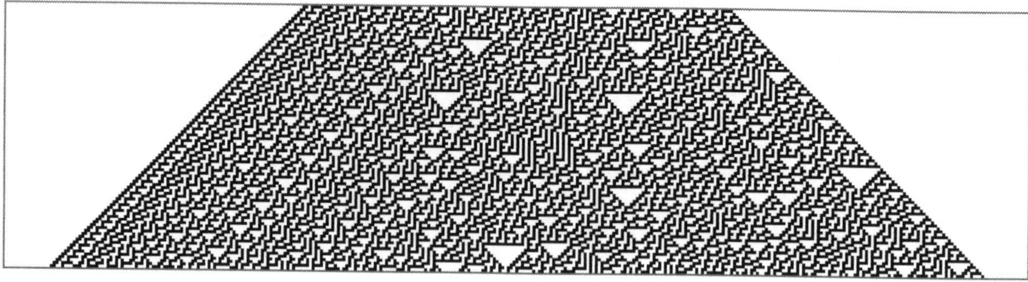

Figure 7.20: Rule 30

Class 3: Random. Class 3 CAs appear random and have no easily discernible pattern. In fact, rule 30 (above) is used as a random number generator in Wolfram's Mathematica software. Again, this is a moment where we can feel amazed that such a simple system with simple rules can descend into a chaotic and random pattern.

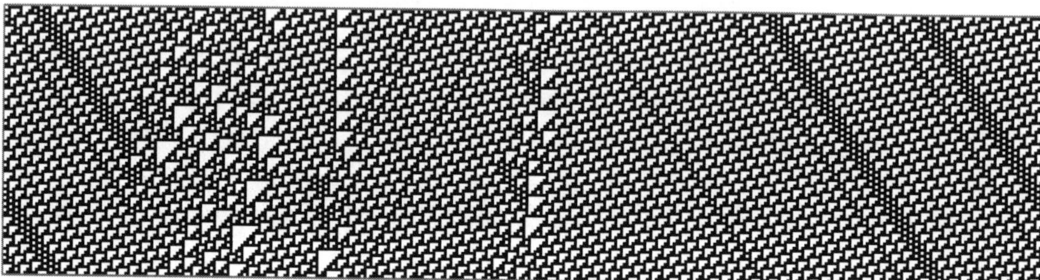

Figure 7.21: Rule 110

Class 4: Complexity. Class 4 CAs can be thought of as a mix between class 2 and class 3. One can find repetitive, oscillating patterns inside the CA, but where and when these patterns appear is unpredictable and seemingly random. Class 4 CAs exhibit the properties of complex systems that we described earlier in this chapter and in Chapter 6. If a class 3 CA wowed you, then a class 4 like Rule 110 above should really blow your mind.

Exercise 7.5

Create a Processing sketch that saves an image for every possible ruleset. Can you classify them?

7.6 The Game of Life

The next step we are going to take is to move from a one-dimensional CA to a two-dimensional one. This will introduce some additional complexity; each cell will have a bigger neighborhood, but that will open up the door to a range of possible applications. After all, most of what we do in computer graphics lives in two dimensions, and this chapter will demonstrate how to apply CA thinking to what we draw in our Processing sketches.

In 1970, Martin Gardner wrote an article in *Scientific American* that documented mathematician John Conway's new "Game of Life," describing it as "recreational" mathematics and suggesting that the reader get out a chessboard and some checkers and "play." While the Game of Life has become something of a computational cliché (make note of the myriad projects that display the Game of Life on LEDs, screens, projection surfaces, etc.), it is still important for us to build it from scratch. For one, it provides a good opportunity to practice our skills with two-dimensional arrays, object orientation, etc. But perhaps more importantly, its core principles are tied directly to our core goals—simulating the natural world with code. Though we may want to avoid simply duplicating it without a great deal of thought or care, the algorithm and its technical implementation will provide us with the inspiration and foundation to build simulations that exhibit the characteristics and behaviors of biological systems of reproduction.

Unlike von Neumann, who created an extraordinarily complex system of states and rules, Conway wanted to achieve a similar "lifelike" result with the simplest set of rules possible. Martin Gardner outlined Conway's goals as follows:

> *"1. There should be no initial pattern for which there is a simple proof that the population can grow without limit. 2. There should be initial patterns that apparently do grow without limit. 3. There should be simple initial patterns that grow and change for a considerable period of time before coming to an end in three possible ways: fading away completely (from overcrowding or becoming too sparse), settling into a stable configuration that remains unchanged thereafter, or entering an oscillating phase in which they repeat an endless cycle of two or more periods."*
>
> *—Martin Gardner,* Scientific American (http://www.ibiblio.org/lifepatterns/october1970.html) *223 (October 1970): 120-123.*

The above might sound a bit cryptic, but it essentially describes a Wolfram class 4 CA. The CA should be patterned but unpredictable over time, eventually settling into a uniform or oscillating state. In other words, though Conway didn't use this terminology, it should have all those properties of a *complex system* that we keep mentioning.

Let's look at how the Game of Life works. It won't take up too much time or space, since we've covered the basics of CA already.

First, instead of a line of cells, we now have a two-dimensional matrix of cells. As with the elementary CA, the possible states are 0 or 1. Only in this case, since we're talking about "life," 0 means dead and 1 means alive.

Two-dimensional cellular automata

1	0	1	0	1	0
0	0	1	0	1	1
1	1	1	0	1	1
1	0	1	0	1	0
0	0	0	1	1	0
1	1	0	0	1	0
1	1	1	0	0	0
1	0	1	1	1	1

a neighborhood of 9 cells

Figure 7.22

The cell's neighborhood has also expanded. If a neighbor is an adjacent cell, a neighborhood is now nine cells instead of three.

With three cells, we had a 3-bit number or eight possible configurations. With nine cells, we have 9 bits, or 512 possible neighborhoods. In most cases, it would be impractical to define an outcome for every single possibility. The Game of Life gets around this problem by defining a set of rules according to general characteristics of the neighborhood. In other words, is the neighborhood overpopulated with life? Surrounded by death? Or just right? Here are the rules of life.

1. ***Death.*** If a cell is alive (state = 1) it will die (state becomes 0) under the following circumstances.
    - ***Overpopulation:*** If the cell has four or more alive neighbors, it dies.
    - ***Loneliness:*** If the cell has one or fewer alive neighbors, it dies.
2. ***Birth.*** If a cell is dead (state = 0) it will come to life (state becomes 1) if it has exactly three alive neighbors (no more, no less).
3. ***Stasis.*** In all other cases, the cell state does not change. To be thorough, let's describe those scenarios.
    - ***Staying Alive:*** If a cell is alive and has exactly two or three live neighbors, it stays alive.
    - ***Staying Dead:*** If a cell is dead and has anything other than three live neighbors, it stays dead.

Let's look at a few examples.

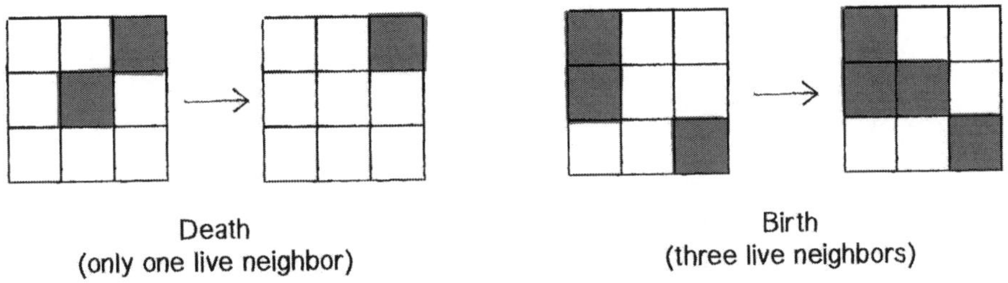

Figure 7.23

With the elementary CA, we were able to look at all the generations next to each other, stacked as rows in a 2D grid. With the Game of Life, however, the CA itself is in two dimensions. We could try creating an elaborate 3D visualization of the results and stack all the generations in a cube structure (and in fact, you might want to try this as an exercise). Nevertheless, the typical way the Game of Life is displayed is to treat each generation as a single frame in an animation. So instead of viewing all the generations at once, we see them one at a time, and the result resembles rapidly growing bacteria in a petri dish.

One of the exciting aspects of the Game of Life is that there are initial patterns that yield intriguing results. For example, some remain static and never change.

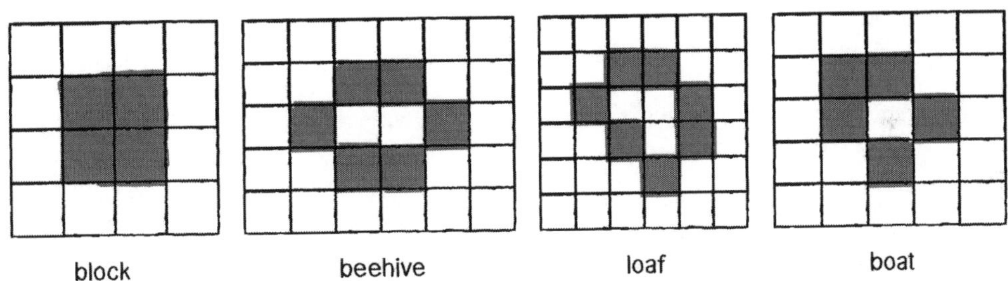

Figure 7.24

There are patterns that oscillate back and forth between two states.

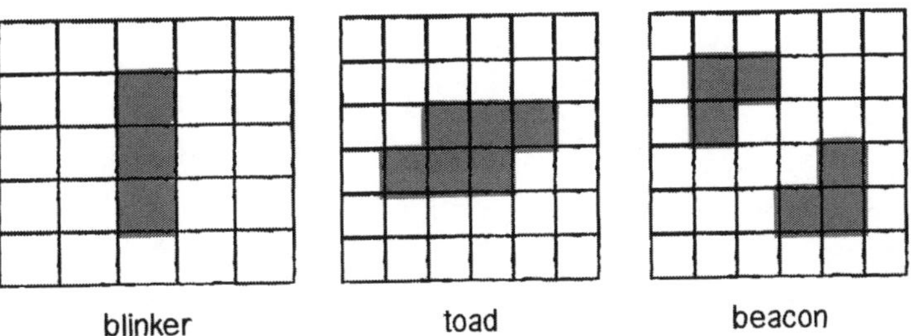

Figure 7.25

And there are also patterns that from generation to generation move about the grid. (It's important to note that the cells themselves aren't actually moving, although we see the appearance of motion in the result as the cells turn on and off.)

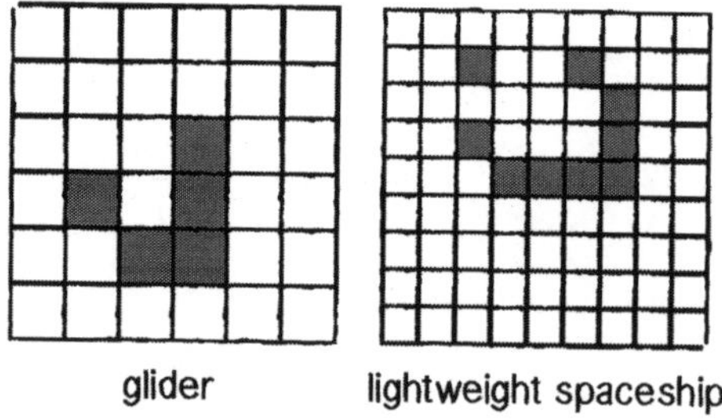

Figure 7.26

If you are interested in these patterns, there are several good "out of the box" Game of Life demonstrations online that allow you to configure the CA's initial state and watch it run at varying speeds. Two examples you might want to examine are:

- Exploring Emergence (http://llk.media.mit.edu/projects/emergence/) by Mitchel Resnick and Brian Silverman, Lifelong Kindergarten Group, MIT Media Laboratory
- Conway's Game of Life (http://stevenklise.github.com/ConwaysGameOfLife) by Steven Klise (uses Processing.js!)

For the example we'll build from scratch in the next section, it will be easier to simply randomly set the states for each cell.

7.7 Programming the Game of Life

Now we just need to extend our code from the Wolfram CA to two dimensions. We used a one-dimensional array to store the list of cell states before, and for the Game of Life, we can use a two-dimensional array (http://www.processing.org/learning/2darray/).

```
int[][] board = new int[columns][rows];
```

We'll begin by initializing each cell of the board with a random state: 0 or 1.

```
for (int x = 0; x < columns; x++) {
  for (int y = 0; y < rows; y++) {
    current[x][y] = int(random(2));          Initialize each cell with a 0 or 1.
  }
}
```

And to compute the next generation, just as before, we need a fresh 2D array to write to as we analyze each cell's neighborhood and calculate a new state.

```
int[][] next = new int[columns][rows];

for (int x = 0; x < columns; x++) {
  for (int y = 0; y < rows; y++) {

    next[x][y] = _____________?;

  }
}
```

We need a new state for each cell.

OK. Before we can sort out how to actually calculate the new state, we need to know how we can reference each cell's neighbor. In the case of the 1D CA, this was simple: if a cell index was `i`, its neighbors were i-1 and i+1. Here each cell doesn't have a single index, but rather a column and row index: x,y. As shown in Figure 7.27, we can see that its neighbors are: *(x-1,y-1) (x,y-1), (x+1,y-2), (x-1,y), (x+1,y), (x-1,y+1), (x,y+1),* and *(x+1,y+1).*

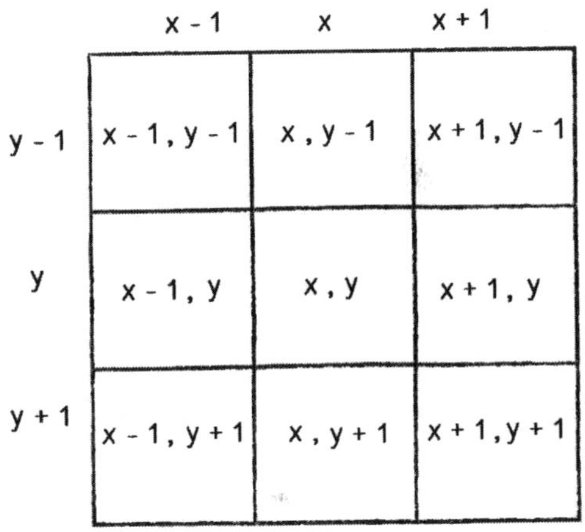

	x - 1	x	x + 1
y - 1	x - 1, y - 1	x , y - 1	x + 1, y - 1
y	x - 1, y	x , y	x + 1, y
y + 1	x - 1, y + 1	x , y + 1	x + 1, y + 1

Figure 7.27

All of the Game of Life rules operate by knowing how many neighbors are alive. So if we create a neighbor counter variable and increment it each time we find a neighbor with a state of 1, we'll have the total of live neighbors.

```
int neighbors = 0;

if (board[x-1][y-1] == 1) neighbors++;
if (board[x  ][y-1] == 1) neighbors++;
if (board[x+1][y-1] == 1) neighbors++;
```

Top row of neighbors

```
if (board[x-1][y]   == 1) neighbors++;
if (board[x+1][y]   == 1) neighbors++;
```

Middle row of neighbors (note we don't count self)

```
if (board[x-1][y+1] == 1) neighbors++;
if (board[x  ][y+1] == 1) neighbors++;
if (board[x+1][y+1] == 1) neighbors++;
```

Bottom row of neighbors

And again, just as with the Wolfram CA, we find ourselves in a situation where the above is a useful and clear way to write the code for teaching purposes, allowing us to see every step (each time we find a neighbor with a state of one, we increase a counter). Nevertheless, it's a bit silly to say, "If the cell state equals one, add one to a counter" when we could just say, "Add the cell state to a counter." After all, if the state is only a 0 or 1, the sum of all the neighbors' states will yield the total number of live cells. Since the neighbors are arranged in a mini 3x3 grid, we can add them all up with another loop.

```
for (int i = -1; i <= 1; i++) {
  for (int j = -1; j <= 1; j++) {
    neighbors += board[x+i][y+j];
  }
}
```

Add up all the neighbors' states.

Of course, we've made a mistake in the code above. In the Game of Life, the cell itself does not count as one of the neighbors. We could use a conditional to skip adding the state when both `i` and `j` equal 0, but another option would be to just subtract the cell state once we've finished the loop.

```
neighbors -= board[x][y];
```

Whoops! Subtract the cell's state, which we don't want in the total.

Finally, once we know the total number of live neighbors, we can decide what the cell's new state should be according to the rules: birth, death, or stasis.

```
if      ((board[x][y] == 1) && (neighbors <  2)) {
  next[x][y] = 0;
}
```

If it is alive and has less than 2 live neighbors, it dies from loneliness.

```
else if ((board[x][y] == 1) && (neighbors >  3)) {
  next[x][y] = 0;
}
```

If it is alive and has more than 3 live neighbors, it dies from overpopulation.

```
else if ((board[x][y] == 0) && (neighbors == 3)) {
  next[x][y] = 1;
}
```

If it is dead and has exactly 3 live neighbors, it is born!

```
else {
  next[x][y] = board[x][y];
}
```

In all other cases, its state remains the same.

Putting this all together, we have:

```
int[][] next = new int[columns][rows];
```

The next board

```
for (int x = 1; x < columns-1; x++) {
  for (int y = 1; y < rows-1; y++) {
```

Looping but skipping the edge cells

```
    int neighbors = 0;

    for (int i = -1; i <= 1; i++) {
      for (int j = -1; j <= 1; j++) {
        neighbors += board[x+i][y+j];
      }
    }
```

Add up all the neighbor states to calculate the number of live neighbors.

```
    neighbors -= board[x][y];
```

Correct by subtracting the cell state itself.

The rules of life!

```
    if      ((board[x][y] == 1) && (neighbors <  2)) next[x][y] = 0;
    else if ((board[x][y] == 1) && (neighbors >  3)) next[x][y] = 0;
    else if ((board[x][y] == 0) && (neighbors == 3)) next[x][y] = 1;
    else next[x][y] = board[x][y];
  }
}
```

```
board = next;
```

The 2D array "next" is now the current board.

Finally, once the next generation is calculated, we can employ the same method we used to draw the Wolfram CA—a square for each spot, white for off, black for on.

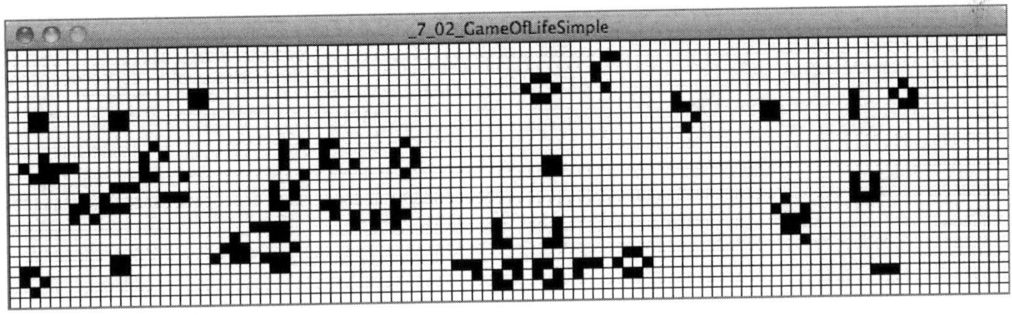

Example 7.2: Game of Life

```
for ( int i = 0; i < columns;i++) {
  for ( int j = 0; j < rows;j++) {
```

```
    if ((board[i][j] == 1)) fill(0);
```

Black when state = 1

```
      else fill(255);                    White when state = 0

      stroke(0);

      rect(i*w, j*w, w, w);
    }
  }
```

Exercise 7.6

Create a Game of Life simulation that allows you to manually configure the grid by drawing or with specific known patterns.

Exercise 7.7

Implement "wrap-around" for the Game of Life so that cells on the edges have neighbors on the opposite side of the grid.

Exercise 7.8

While the above solution (Example 7.2) is convenient, it is not particularly memory-efficient. It creates a new 2D array for every frame of animation! This matters very little for a Processing desktop application, but if you were implementing the Game of Life on a microcontroller or mobile device, you'd want to be more careful. One solution is to have only two arrays and constantly swap them, writing the next set of states into whichever one isn't the current array. Implement this particular solution.

7.8 Object-Oriented Cells

Over the course of the previous six chapters, we've slowly built examples of systems of *objects* with properties that move about the screen. And in this chapter, although we've been talking about a "cell" as if it were an object, we actually haven't been using any object orientation in our code (other than a class to describe the CA system as a whole). This has worked because a cell is such an enormously simple object (a single bit). However, in a moment, we are going to discuss some ideas for further developing CA systems, many of which involve keeping track of multiple properties for each cell. For example, what if a cell needed to remember its last ten states? Or what if we wanted to apply some of our motion and physics thinking to a CA and have the cells move about the window, dynamically changing their neighbors from frame to frame?

To accomplish any of these ideas (and more), it would be helpful to see how we might treat a cell as an object with multiple properties, rather than as a single 0 or 1. To show this, let's just recreate the Game of Life simulation. Only instead of:

```
int[][] board;
```

Let's have:

```
Cell[][] board;
```

where `Cell` is a class we will write. What are the properties of a `Cell` object? In our Game of Life example, each cell has a location and size, as well as a state.

```
class Cell {

  float x, y;        // Location and size
  float w;

  int state;         // What is the cell's state?
```

In the non-OOP version, we used a separate 2D array to keep track of the states for the current and next generation. By making a cell an object, however, each cell could keep track of both states. In this case, we'll think of the cell as remembering its previous state (for when new states need to be computed).

```
  int previous;      // What was its previous state?
```

This allows us to visualize more information about what the state is doing. For example, we could choose to color a cell differently if its state has changed. For example:

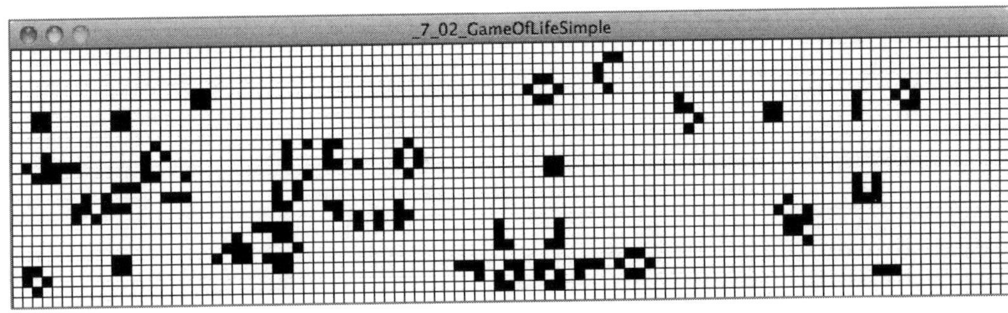

Example 7.3: Game of Life OOP

```
void display() {
```

```
  if (previous == 0 && state == 1) fill(0,0,255);     If the cell is born, color it blue!
  else if (state == 1) fill(0);

  else if (previous == 1 && state == 0) fill(255,0,0);
  else fill(255);                                      If the cell dies, color it red!

  rect(x, y, w, w);
}
```

Not much else about the code (at least for our purposes here) has to change. The neighbors can still be counted the same way; the difference is that we now need to refer to the object's state variables as we loop through the 2D array.

```
for (int x = 1; x < columns-1; x++) {
  for (int y = 1; y < rows-1; y++) {

    int neighbors = 0;
    for (int i = -1; i <= 1; i++) {
      for (int j = -1; j <= 1; j++) {
        neighbors += board[x+i][y+j].previous;    Use the previous state when tracking
      }                                           neighbors.
    }
    neighbors -= board[x][y].previous;

                                                  We are calling a function newState() to
                                                  assign a new state to each cell.
    if      ((board[x][y].state == 1) && (neighbors <  2)) board[x][y].newState(0);
    else if ((board[x][y].state == 1) && (neighbors >  3)) board[x][y].newState(0);
    else if ((board[x][y].state == 0) && (neighbors == 3)) board[x][y].newState(1);

  }                                               else do nothing!
}
```

7.9 Variations of Traditional CA

Now that we have covered the basic concepts, algorithms, and programming strategies behind the most famous 1D and 2D cellular automata, it's time to think about how you might take this foundation of code and build on it, developing creative applications of CAs in your own work. In this section, we'll talk through some ideas for expanding the features of the CA examples. Example answers to each of these exercises can be found on the book website.

1) Non-rectangular Grids. There's no particular reason why you should limit yourself to having your cells on a rectangular grid. What happens if you design a CA with another type of shape?

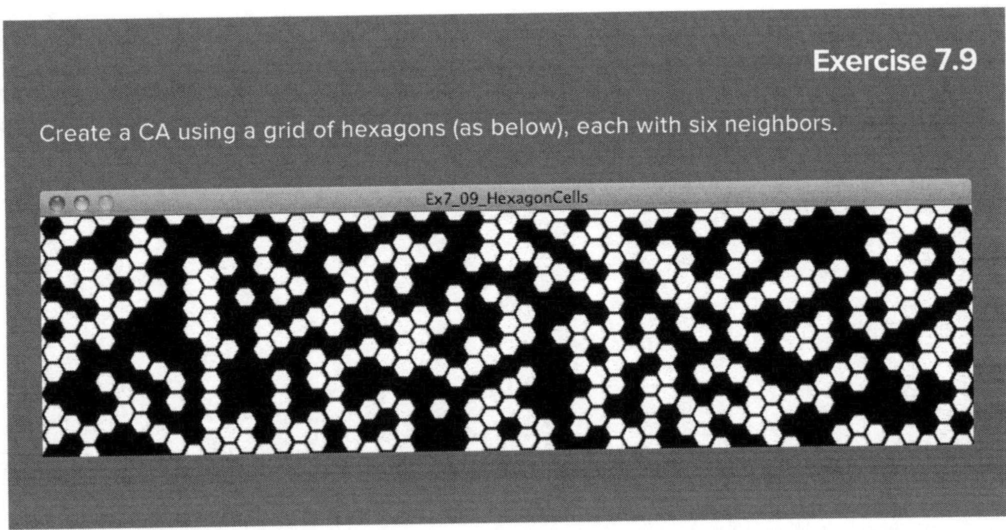

Exercise 7.9

Create a CA using a grid of hexagons (as below), each with six neighbors.

2) Probabilistic. The rules of a CA don't necessarily have to define an exact outcome.

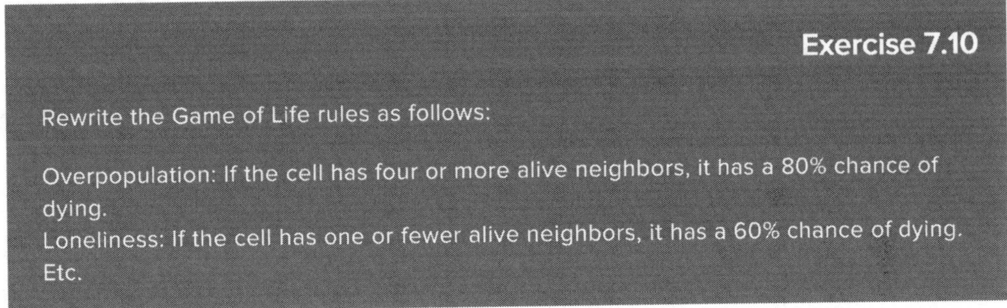

Exercise 7.10

Rewrite the Game of Life rules as follows:

Overpopulation: If the cell has four or more alive neighbors, it has a 80% chance of dying.
Loneliness: If the cell has one or fewer alive neighbors, it has a 60% chance of dying.
Etc.

3) Continuous. We've looked at examples where the cell's state can only be a 1 or a 0. But what if the cell's state was a floating point number between 0 and 1?

Exercise 7.11

Adapt Wolfram elementary CA to have the state be a float. You could define rules such as, "If the state is greater than 0.5" or "...less than 0.2."

4) Image Processing. We briefly touched on this earlier, but many image-processing algorithms operate on CA-like rules. Blurring an image is creating a new pixel out of the average of a neighborhood of pixels. Simulations of ink dispersing on paper or water rippling over an image can be achieved with CA rules.

Exercise 7.12

Create a CA in which a pixel is a cell and a color is its state.

5) Historical. In the Game of Life object-oriented example, we used two variables to keep track of its state: current and previous. What if you use an array to keep track of a cell's state history? This relates to the idea of a "complex adaptive system," one that has the ability to adapt and change its rules over time by learning from its history. We'll see an example of this in Chapter 10: Neural Networks.

Exercise 7.13

Visualize the Game of Life by coloring each cell according to how long it's been alive or dead. Can you also use the cell's history to inform the rules?

6) Moving cells. In these basic examples, cells have a fixed position on a grid, but you could build a CA with cells that have no fixed position and instead move about the screen.

Exercise 7.14

Use CA rules in a flocking system. What if each boid had a state (that perhaps informs its steering behaviors) and its neighborhood changed from frame to frame as it moved closer to or further from other boids?

7) Nesting. Another feature of complex systems is that they can be nested. Our world tends to work this way: a city is a complex system of people, a person is a complex system of organs, an organ is a complex system of cells, and so on and so forth.

Exercise 7.15

Design a CA in which each cell itself is a smaller CA or a system of boids.

The Ecosystem Project

Step 7 Exercise:

Incorporate cellular automata into your ecosystem. Some possibilities:

- Give each creature a state. How can that state drive their behavior? Taking inspiration from CA, how can that state change over time according to its neighbors' states?
- Consider the ecosystem's world to be a CA. The creatures move from tile to tile. Each tile has a state—is it land? water? food?
- Use a CA to generate a pattern for the design of a creature in your ecosystem.

Chapter 8. Fractals

"Pathological monsters! cried the terrified mathematician
Every one of them a splinter in my eye
I hate the Peano Space and the Koch Curve
I fear the Cantor Ternary Set
The Sierpinski Gasket makes me wanna cry
And a million miles away a butterfly flapped its wings
On a cold November day a man named Benoit Mandelbrot was born"

— Jonathan Coulton, lyrics from "Mandelbrot Set"

Once upon a time, I took a course in high school called "Geometry." Perhaps you did too. You learned about shapes in one dimension, two dimensions, and maybe even three. What is the circumference of a circle? The area of a rectangle? The distance between a point and a line? Come to think of it, we've been studying geometry all along in this book, using vectors to describe the motion of bodies in Cartesian space. This sort of geometry is generally referred to as Euclidean geometry, after the Greek mathematician Euclid.

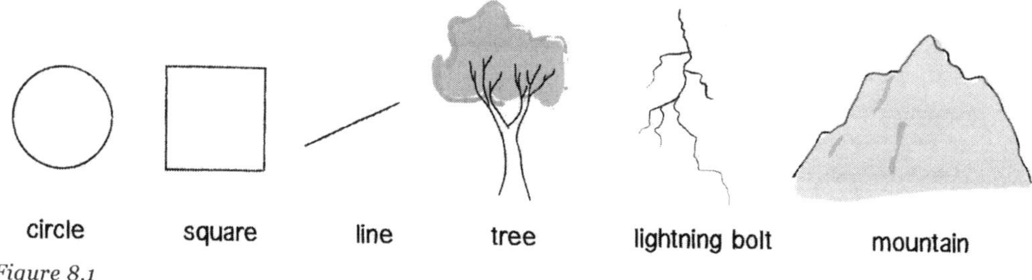

Figure 8.1

For us nature coders, we have to ask the question: Can we describe our world with Euclidean geometry? The LCD screen I'm staring at right now sure looks like a rectangle. And the plum I ate this morning is circular. But what if I were to look further, and consider the trees that line the street, the leaves that hang off those trees, the lightning from last night's thunderstorm, the cauliflower I ate for dinner, the blood vessels in my body, and the mountains and coastlines that cover land beyond New York City? Most of the stuff you find in nature cannot be described by the idealized geometrical forms of Euclidean geometry. So if we want to start building computational designs with patterns beyond the simple shapes `ellipse()`, `rect()`, and `line()`, it's time for us to learn about the concepts behind and techniques for simulating the geometry of nature: fractals.

8.1 What Is a Fractal?

The term ***fractal*** (from the Latin *fractus*, meaning "broken") was coined by the mathematician Benoit Mandelbrot in 1975. In his seminal work "The Fractal Geometry of Nature," he defines a fractal as "a rough or fragmented geometric shape that can be split into parts, each of which is (at least approximately) a reduced-size copy of the whole."

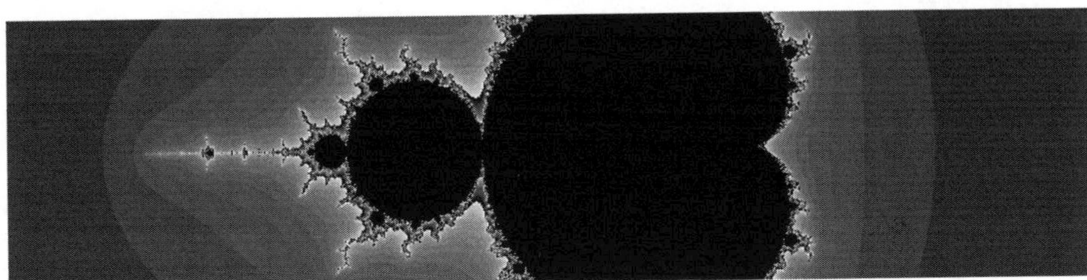

Figure 8.2: One of the most well-known and recognizable fractal patterns is named for Benoit Mandelbrot himself. Generating the Mandelbrot set involves testing the properties of complex numbers after they are passed through an iterative function. Do they tend to infinity? Do they stay bounded? While a fascinating mathematical discussion, this "escape-time" algorithm is a less practical method for generating fractals than the recursive techniques we'll examine in this chapter. However, an example for generating the Mandelbrot set is included in the code examples.

Let's illustrate this definition with two simple examples. First, let's think about a tree branching structure (for which we'll write the code later):

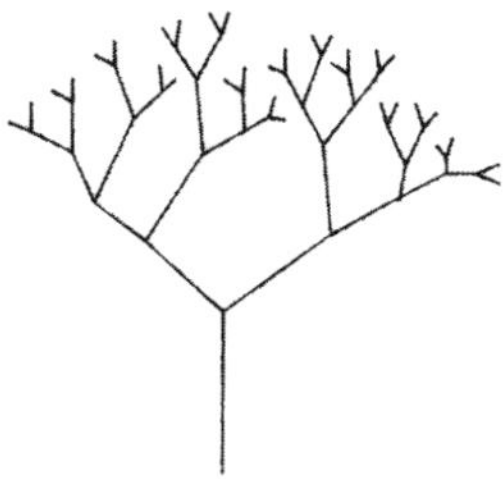

Figure 8.3

Notice how the tree in Figure 8.3 has a single root with two branches connected at its end. Each one of those branches has two branches at its end and those branches have two branches and so on and so forth. What if we were to pluck one branch from the tree and examine it on its own?

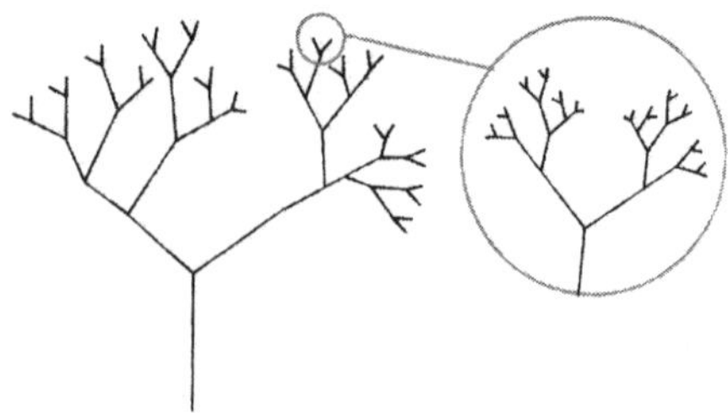

Figure 8.4

Looking closely at a given section of the tree, we find that the shape of this branch resembles the tree itself. This is known as ***self-similarity***; as Mandelbrot stated, each part is a "reduced-size copy of the whole."

The above tree is perfectly symmetrical and the parts are, in fact, exact replicas of the whole. However, fractals do not have to be perfectly self-similar. Let's take a look at a graph of the stock market (adapted from actual Apple stock data).

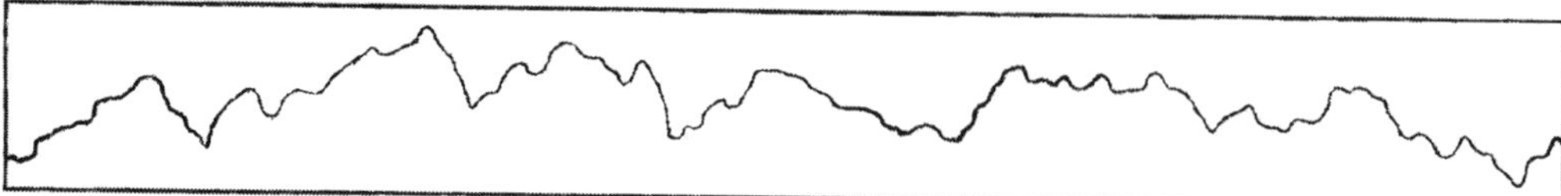

Figure 8.5: Graph A

And one more.

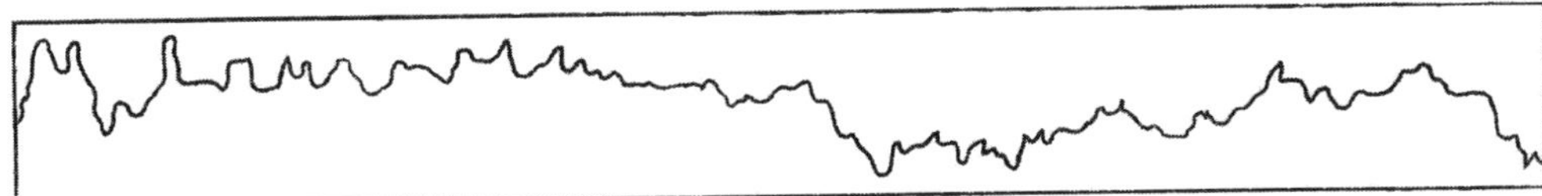

Figure 8.6: Graph B

In these graphs, the x-axis is time and the y-axis is the stock's value. It's not an accident that I omitted the labels, however. Graphs of stock market data are examples of fractals because they look the same at any scale. Are these graphs of the stock over one year? One day? One hour? There's no way for you to know without a label. (Incidentally, graph A shows six months' worth of data and graph B zooms into a tiny part of graph A, showing six hours.)

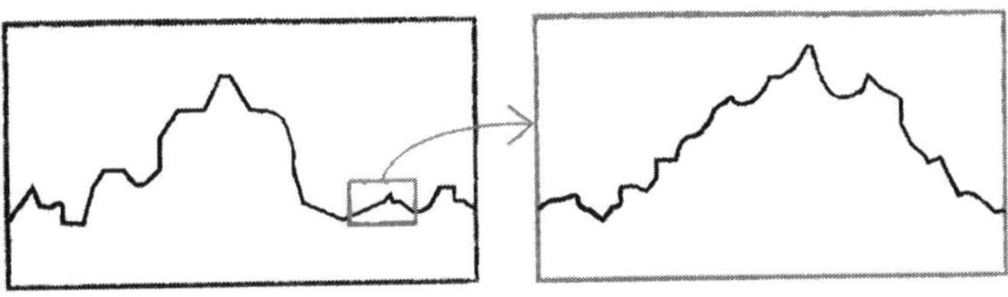

Figure 8.7

This is an example of a ***stochastic*** fractal, meaning that it is built out of probabilities and randomness. Unlike the deterministic tree-branching structure, it is statistically self-similar. As we go through the examples in this chapter, we will look at both deterministic and stochastic techniques for generating fractal patterns.

While self-similarity is a key trait of fractals, it's important to realize that self-similarity alone does not make a fractal. After all, a line is self-similar. A line looks the same at any scale, and can be thought of as comprising lots of little lines. But it's not a fractal. Fractals are characterized by having a fine structure at small scales (keep zooming into the stock market graph and you'll continue to find fluctuations) and cannot be described with Euclidean geometry. If you can say "It's a line!" then it's not a fractal.

Another fundamental component of fractal geometry is recursion. Fractals all have a recursive definition. We'll start with recursion before developing techniques and code examples for building fractal patterns in Processing.

8.2 Recursion

Let's begin our discussion of recursion by examining the first appearance of fractals in modern mathematics. In 1883, German mathematician George Cantor developed simple rules to generate an infinite set:

1. Start with a line.
2. Erase the middle third of that line
3. Repeat step 2 for the remaining lines, again and again and again.

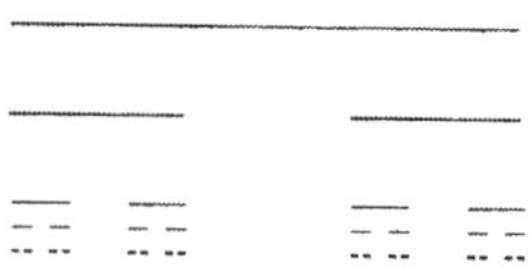

Figure 8.8: The Cantor set

There is a feedback loop at work here. Take a single line and break it into two. Then return to those two lines and apply the same rule, breaking each line into two, and now we're left with four. Then return to those four lines and apply the rule. Now you've got eight. This process is known as ***recursion***: the repeated application of a rule to successive results. Cantor was interested in what happens when you apply these rules an infinite number of times. We, however, are working in a finite pixel space and can mostly ignore the questions and paradoxes that arise from infinite recursion. We will instead construct our code in such a way that we do not apply the rules forever (which would cause our program to freeze).

Before we implement the Cantor set, let's take a look at what it means to have recursion in code. Here's something we're used to doing all the time—calling a function inside another function.

```
void someFunction() {
  background(0);
}
```

Calling the function background() in the definition of someFunction()

What would happen if we called the function we are defining within the function itself? Can `someFunction()` call `someFunction()`?

```
void someFunction() {
  someFunction();
}
```

In fact, this is not only allowed, but it's quite common (and essential to how we will implement the Cantor set). Functions that call themselves are *recursive* and good for solving certain problems. For example, certain mathematical calculations are implemented recursively; the most common example is *factorial*.

The factorial of any number n, usually written as n!, is defined as:

```
n! = n * n - 1 * . . . . * 3 * 2 * 1
0! = 1
```

Here we'll write a function in Processing that uses a `for` loop to calculate factorial:

```
int factorial(int n) {
  int f = 1;
```

```
  for (int i = 0; i < n; i++) {
    f = f * (i+1);
  }
```

Using a regular loop to compute factorial

```
  return f;
}
```

Upon close examination, you'll notice something interesting about how factorial works. Let's look at 4! and 3!

```
4! = 4 * 3 * 2 * 1
3! = 3 * 2 * 1
```

therefore. . .

```
4! = 4 * 3!
```

In more general terms, for any positive integer n:

```
n! = n * (n-1)!
1! = 1
```

Written out:

The *factorial* of n is defined as n times the *factorial* of n−1.

The definition of ***factorial*** includes ***factorial***?! It's kind of like defining "tired" as "the feeling you get when you are tired." This concept of self-reference in functions is an example of recursion. And we can use it to write a factorial function that calls itself.

```
int factorial(int n) {
  if (n == 1) {
    return 1;
  } else {
    return n * factorial(n-1);
  }
}
```

It may look crazy, but it works. Here are the steps that happen when `factorial(4)` is called.

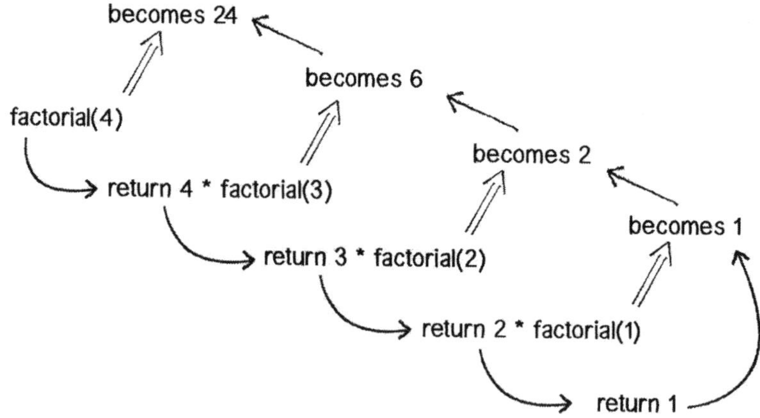

Figure 8.9

We can apply the same principle to graphics with interesting results, as we will see in many examples throughout this chapter. Take a look at this recursive function.

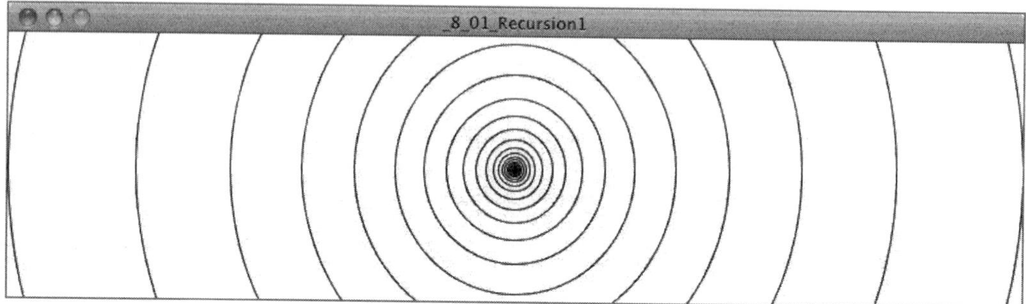

Example 8.1: Recursive Circles I

```
void drawCircle(int x, int y, float radius) {
  ellipse(x, y, radius, radius);
  if(radius > 2) {
    radius *= 0.75f;
    drawCircle(x, y, radius);
  }
}
```

The drawCircle() function is calling itself recursively.

`drawCircle()` draws an ellipse based on a set of parameters that it receives as arguments. It then calls itself with those same parameters, adjusting them slightly. The result is a series of circles, each of which is drawn inside the previous circle.

Notice that the above function only recursively calls itself if the radius is greater than 2. This is a crucial point. As with iteration, *all recursive functions must have an exit condition!* You likely are already aware that all `for` and `while` loops must include a boolean expression that eventually evaluates to false, thus exiting the loop. Without one, the program would crash, caught inside of an infinite loop. The same can be said about recursion. If a recursive function calls itself forever and ever, you'll be most likely be treated to a nice frozen screen.

This circles example is rather trivial; it could easily be achieved through simple iteration. However, for scenarios in which a function calls itself more than once, recursion becomes wonderfully elegant.

Let's make `drawCircle()` a bit more complex. For every circle displayed, draw a circle half its size to the left and right of that circle.

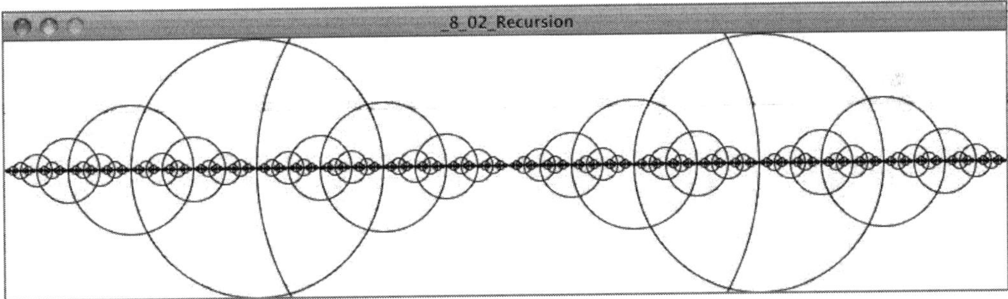

Example 8.2: Recursion twice

```
void setup() {
  size(640,360);
}

void draw() {
  background(255);
  drawCircle(width/2,height/2,200);
}

void drawCircle(float x, float y, float radius) {
  stroke(0);
  noFill();
  ellipse(x, y, radius, radius);
  if(radius > 2) {
    drawCircle(x + radius/2, y, radius/2);
    drawCircle(x - radius/2, y, radius/2);
  }
}
```

drawCircle() calls itself twice, creating a branching effect. For every circle, a smaller circle is drawn to the left and the right.

With just a little more code, we could also add a circle above and below each circle.

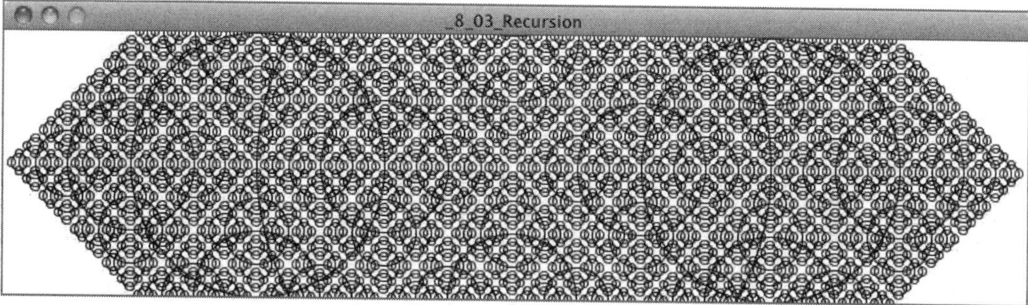

Example 8.3: Recursion four times

```
void drawCircle(float x, float y, float radius) {
  ellipse(x, y, radius, radius);
  if(radius > 8) {
    drawCircle(x + radius/2, y, radius/2);
    drawCircle(x - radius/2, y, radius/2);
    drawCircle(x, y + radius/2, radius/2);
    drawCircle(x, y - radius/2, radius/2);
  }
}
```

Try reproducing this sketch with iteration instead of recursion—I dare you!

8.3 The Cantor Set with a Recursive Function

Now we're ready to visualize the Cantor set in Processing using a recursive function. Where do we begin? Well, we know that the Cantor set begins with a line. So let's start there and write a function that draws a line.

```
void cantor(float x, float y, float len) {
  line(x,y,x+len,y);
}
```

The above `cantor()` function draws a line that starts at pixel coordinate *(x,y)* with a length of `len`. (The line is drawn horizontally here, but this is an arbitrary decision.) So if we called that function, saying:

```
cantor(10, 20, width-20);
```

we'd get the following:

Figure 8.10

Now, the Cantor rule tells us to erase the middle third of that line, which leaves us with two lines, one from the beginning of the line to the one-third mark, and one from the two-thirds mark to the end of the line.

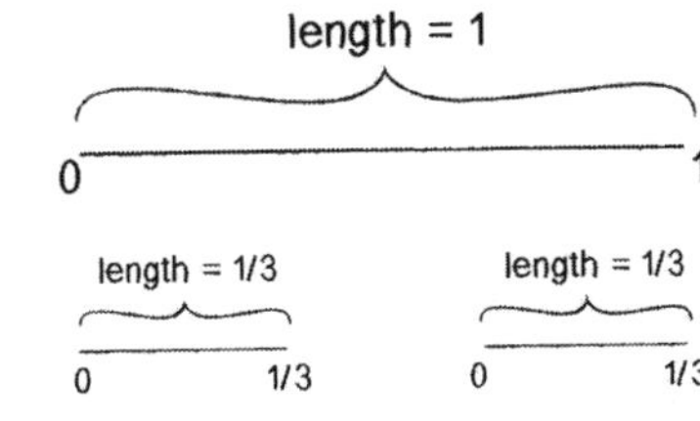

Figure 8.11

We can now add two more lines of code to draw the second pair of lines, moving the y-location down a bunch of pixels so that we can see the result below the original line.

```
void cantor(float x, float y, float len) {
  line(x,y,x+len,y);

  y += 20;
  line(x,y,x+len/3,y);            From start to 1/3rd

  line(x+len*2/3,y,x+len,y);      From 2/3rd to end
}
```

Figure 8.12

While this is a fine start, such a manual approach of calling `line()` for each line is not what we want. It will get unwieldy very quickly, as we'd need four, then eight, then sixteen calls to `line()`. Yes, a `for` loop is our usual way around such a problem, but give that a try and you'll see that working out the math for each iteration quickly proves inordinately complicated. Here is where recursion comes and rescues us.

Take a look at where we draw that first line from the start to the one-third mark.

```
line(x,y,x+len/3,y);
```

Instead of calling the `line()` function directly, we can simply call the `cantor()` function itself. After all, what does the `cantor()` function do? It draws a line at an *(x,y)* location with a given length! And so:

```
line(x,y,x+len/3,y);        becomes ------->  cantor(x,y,len/3);
```

And for the second line:

```
line(x+len*2/3,y,x+len,y);    becomes ------->  cantor(x+len*2/3,y,len/3);
```

Leaving us with:

```
void cantor(float x, float y, float len) {
  line(x,y,x+len,y);

  y += 20;

  cantor(x,y,len/3);
  cantor(x+len*2/3,y,len/3);
}
```

And since the `cantor()` function is called recursively, the same rule will be applied to the next lines and to the next and to the next as `cantor()` calls itself again and again! Now, don't go and run this code yet. We're missing that crucial element: an exit condition. We'll want to make sure we stop at some point—for example, if the length of the line ever is less than 1 pixel.

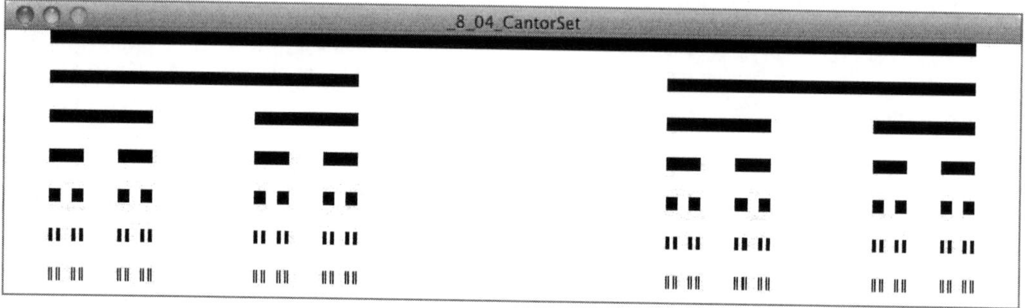

Example 8.4: Cantor set

```
void cantor(float x, float y, float len) {
  if (len >= 1) {                                   Stop at 1 pixel!
    line(x,y,x+len,y);
    y += 20;
    cantor(x,y,len/3);
    cantor(x+len*2/3,y,len/3);
  }
}
```

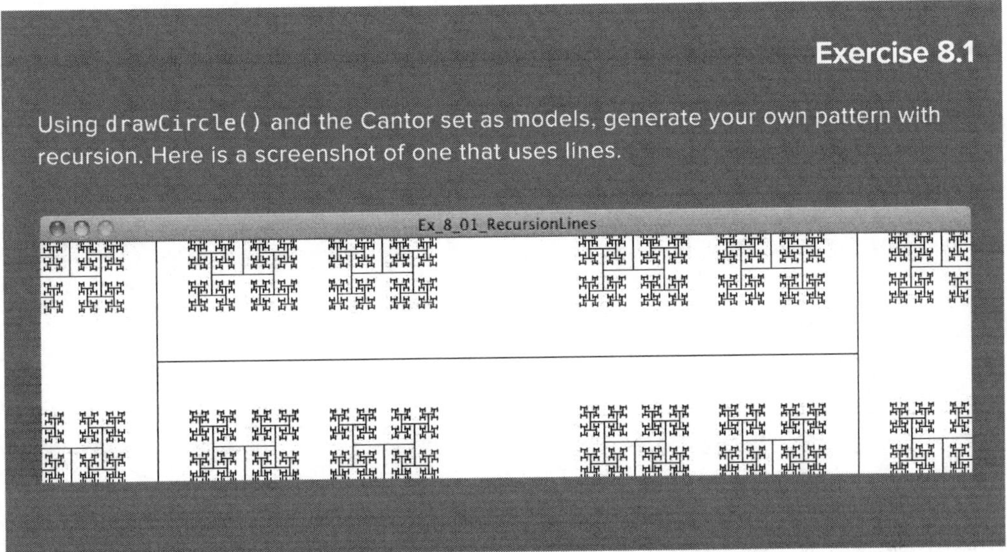

Exercise 8.1

Using `drawCircle()` and the Cantor set as models, generate your own pattern with recursion. Here is a screenshot of one that uses lines.

8.4 The Koch Curve and the ArrayList Technique

Writing a function that recursively calls itself is one technique for generating a fractal pattern on screen. However, what if you wanted the lines in the above Cantor set to exist as individual objects that could be moved independently? The recursive function is simple and elegant, but it does not allow you to do much besides simply generating the pattern itself. However, there is another way we can apply recursion in combination with an `ArrayList` that will allow us to not only generate a fractal pattern, but keep track of all its individual parts as objects.

To demonstrate this technique, let's look at another famous fractal pattern, discovered in 1904 by Swedish mathematician Helge von Koch. Here are the rules. (Note that it starts the same way as the Cantor set, with a single line.)

1. Start with a line.

2. Divide the line into three equal parts.

3. Draw an equilateral triangle (a triangle where all the sides are equal) using the middle segment as its base.

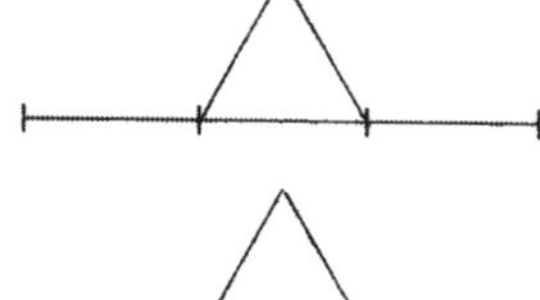

4. Erase the base of the equilateral triangle (the middle segment from step 2).

5. Repeat steps 2 through 4 for the remaining lines again and again and again.

Figure 8.13

The result looks like:

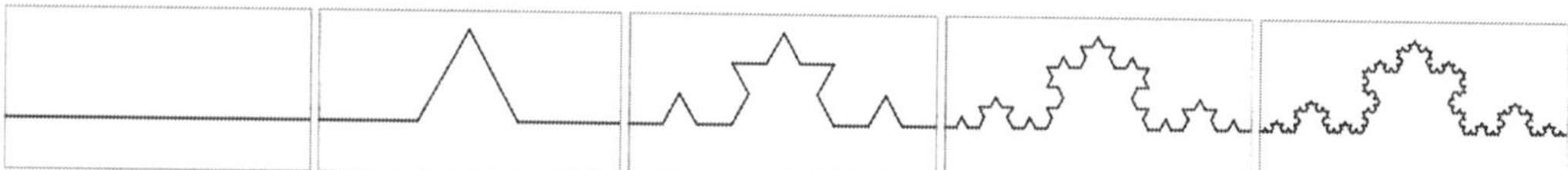

Figure 8.14

The "Monster" Curve

The Koch curve and other fractal patterns are often called "mathematical monsters." This is due to an odd paradox that emerges when you apply the recursive definition an infinite number of times. If the length of the original starting line is one, the first iteration of the Koch curve will yield a line of length four-thirds (each segment is one-third the length of the starting line). Do it again and you get a length of sixteen-ninths. As you iterate towards infinity, the length of the Koch curve approaches infinity. Yet it fits in the tiny finite space provided right here on this paper (or screen)!

Since we are working in the Processing land of finite pixels, this theoretical paradox won't be a factor for us. We'll have to limit the number of times we recursively apply the Koch rules so that our program won't run out of memory or crash.

We could proceed in the same manner as we did with the Cantor set, and write a recursive function that iteratively applies the Koch rules over and over. Nevertheless, we are going to tackle this problem in a different manner by treating each segment of the Koch curve as an individual object. This will open up some design possibilities. For example, if each segment is an object, we could allow each segment to move independently from its original location and participate in a physics simulation. In addition, we could use a random color, line thickness, etc. to display each segment differently.

In order to accomplish our goal of treating each segment as an individual object, we must first decide what this object should be in the first place. What data should it store? What functions should it have?

The Koch curve is a series of connected lines, and so we will think of each segment as a "KochLine." Each `KochLine` object has a start point ("a") and an end point ("b"). These points are `PVector` objects, and the line is drawn with Processing's `line()` function.

```
class KochLine {

  PVector start;                          A line between two points: start and end
  PVector end;

  KochLine(PVector a, PVector b) {
    start = a.get();
    end = b.get();
  }

  void display() {
    stroke(0);
    line(start.x, start.y, end.x, end.y);   Draw the line from PVector start to end.
  }
}
```

Now that we have our `KochLine` class, we can get started on the main program. We'll need a data structure to keep track of what will eventually become many `KochLine` objects, and an `ArrayList` (see Chapter 4 for a review of `ArrayLists`) will do just fine.

```
ArrayList<KochLine> lines;
```

In `setup()`, we'll want to create the `ArrayList` and add the first line segment to it, a line that stretches from 0 to the width of the sketch.

```
void setup() {
  size(600, 300);
  lines = new ArrayList<KochLine>();          Create the ArrayList.

  PVector start = new PVector(0, 200);        Left side of window

  PVector end   = new PVector(width, 200);    Right side of window
```

```
    lines.add(new KochLine(start, end));        The first KochLine object
  }
```

Then in `draw()`, all `KochLine` objects (just one right now) can be displayed in a loop.

```
void draw() {
  background(255);
  for (KochLine l : lines) {
    l.display();
  }
}
```

This is our foundation. Let's review what we have so far:

- ***KochLine class:*** A class to keep track of a line from point A to B.
- ***ArrayList:*** A list of all `KochLine` objects.

With the above elements, how and where do we apply Koch rules and principles of recursion?

Remember the Game of Life cellular automata? In that simulation, we always kept track of two generations: current and next. When we were finished computing the next generation, next became current and we moved on to computing the new next generation. We are going to apply a similar technique here. We have an `ArrayList` that keeps track of the current set of `KochLine` objects (at the start of the program, there is only one). We will need a second `ArrayList` (let's call it "next") where we will place all the new `KochLine` objects that are generated from applying the Koch rules. For every `KochLine` object in the current `ArrayList`, four new `KochLine` objects are added to the next `ArrayList`. When we're done, the next `ArrayList` becomes the current one.

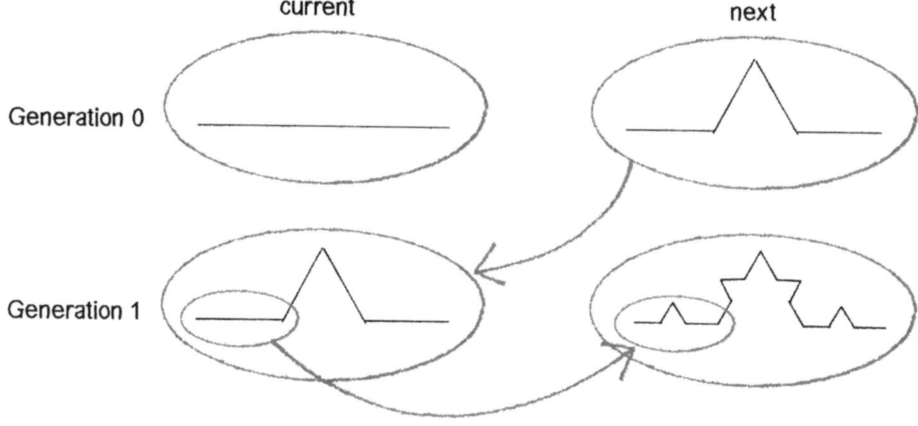

Figure 8.15

Here's how the code will look:

```
void generate() {
  ArrayList next = new ArrayList<KochLine>();    // Create the next ArrayList...

  for (KochLine l : lines) {                     // ...for every current line.

    next.add(new KochLine(???,???));             // Add four new lines. (We need to figure out
    next.add(new KochLine(???,???));             // how to compute the locations of these
    next.add(new KochLine(???,???));             // lines!)
    next.add(new KochLine(???,???));
  }
  lines = next;                                  // The new ArrayList is now the one we care
                                                 // about!
}
```

By calling `generate()` over and over again (for example, each time the mouse is pressed), we recursively apply the Koch curve rules to the existing set of `KochLine` objects. Of course, the above omits the real "work" here, which is figuring out those rules. How do we break one line segment into four as described by the rules? While this can be accomplished with some simple arithmetic and trigonometry, since our `KochLine` object uses `PVector`, this is a nice opportunity for us to practice our vector math. Let's establish how many points we need to compute for each `KochLine` object.

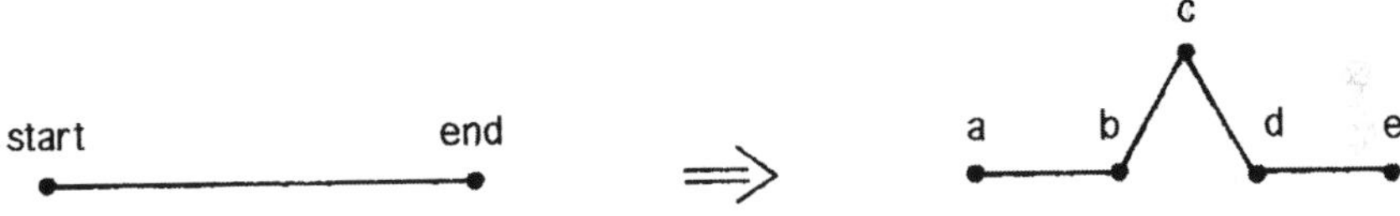

Figure 8.16

As you can see from the above figure, we need five points (a, b, c, d, and e) to generate the new `KochLine` objects and make the new line segments (ab, cb, cd, and de).

```
next.add(new KochLine(a,b));
next.add(new KochLine(b,c));
next.add(new KochLine(c,d));
next.add(new KochLine(d,e));
```

Where do we get these points? Since we have a `KochLine` object, why not ask the `KochLine` object to compute all these points for us?

```
void generate() {
  ArrayList next = new ArrayList<KochLine>();
  for (KochLine l : lines) {
```

```
    PVector a = l.kochA();
    PVector b = l.kochB();
    PVector c = l.kochC();
    PVector d = l.kochD();
    PVector e = l.kochE();
```

The KochLine object has five functions, each of which return a PVector according to the Koch rules.

```
    next.add(new KochLine(a, b));
    next.add(new KochLine(b, c));
    next.add(new KochLine(c, d));
    next.add(new KochLine(d, e));
  }

  lines = next;
}
```

Now we just need to write five new functions in the `KochLine` class, each one returning a `PVector` according to Figure 8.16 (see page 370) above. Let's knock off `kochA()` and `kochE()` first, which are simply the start and end points of the original line.

```
PVector kochA() {
  return start.get();
}

PVector kochE() {
  return end.get();
}
```

Note the use of get(), which returns a copy of the PVector. As was noted in Chapter 6, section 14, we want to avoid making copies whenever possible, but here we will need a new PVector in case we want the segments to move independently of each other.

Now let's move on to points B and D. B is one-third of the way along the line segment and D is two-thirds. Here we can make a `PVector` that points from start to end and shrink it to one-third the length for B and two-thirds the length for D to find these points.

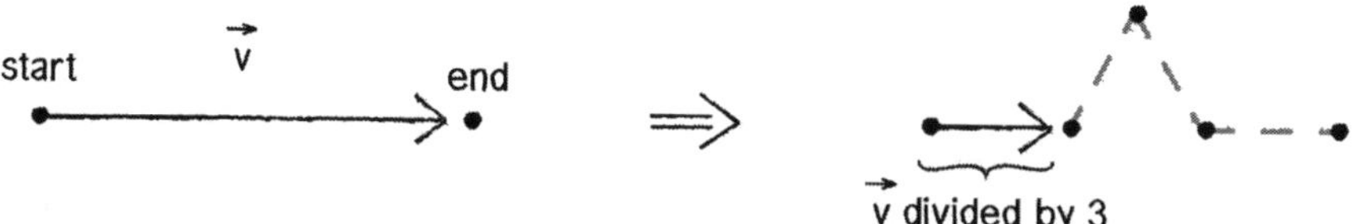

Figure 8.17

```
PVector kochB() {
  PVector v = PVector.sub(end, start);
  v.div(3);
```

PVector from start to end

One-third the length

```
    v.add(start);          // Add that PVector to the beginning of the line to find the new point.

    return v;
  }

  PVector kochD() {
    PVector v = PVector.sub(end, start);
    v.mult(2/3.0);         // Same thing here, only we need to move two-thirds along the line instead of one-third.
    v.add(start);
    return v;
  }
```

The last point, C, is the most difficult one to find. However, if you recall that the angles of an equilateral triangle are all sixty degrees, this makes it a little bit easier. If we know how to find point B with a `PVector` one-third the length of the line, what if we were to rotate that same `PVector` sixty degrees and move along that vector from point B? We'd be at point C!

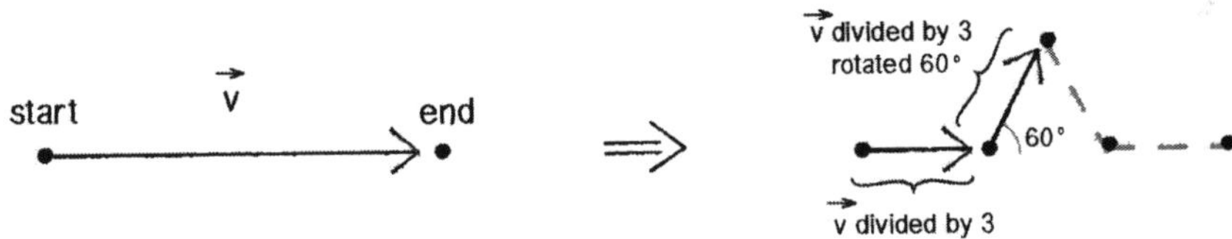

Figure 8.18

```
  PVector kochC() {
    PVector a = start.get();          // Start at the beginning.

    PVector v = PVector.sub(end, start);
    v.div(3);                         // Move 1/3rd of the way to point B.
    a.add(v);

    v.rotate(-radians(60));           // Rotate "above" the line 60 degrees.
    a.add(v);                         // Move along that vector to point C.

    return a;
  }
```

Putting it all together, if we call `generate()` five times in `setup()`, we'll see the following result.

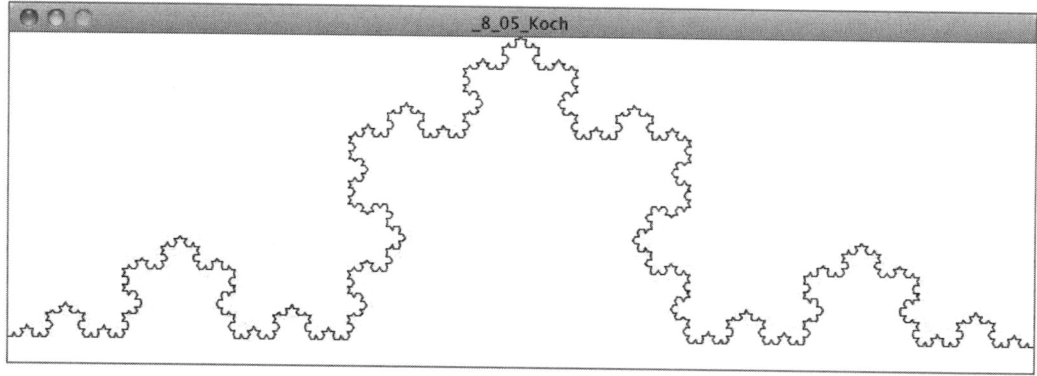

Example 8.5: Koch curve

```
ArrayList<KochLine> lines;

void setup() {
  size(600, 300);
  background(255);
  lines = new ArrayList<KochLine>();
  PVector start = new PVector(0, 200);
  PVector end   = new PVector(width, 200);
  lines.add(new KochLine(start, end));

  for (int i = 0; i < 5; i++) {
    generate();
  }
}
```

Arbitrarily apply the Koch rules five times.

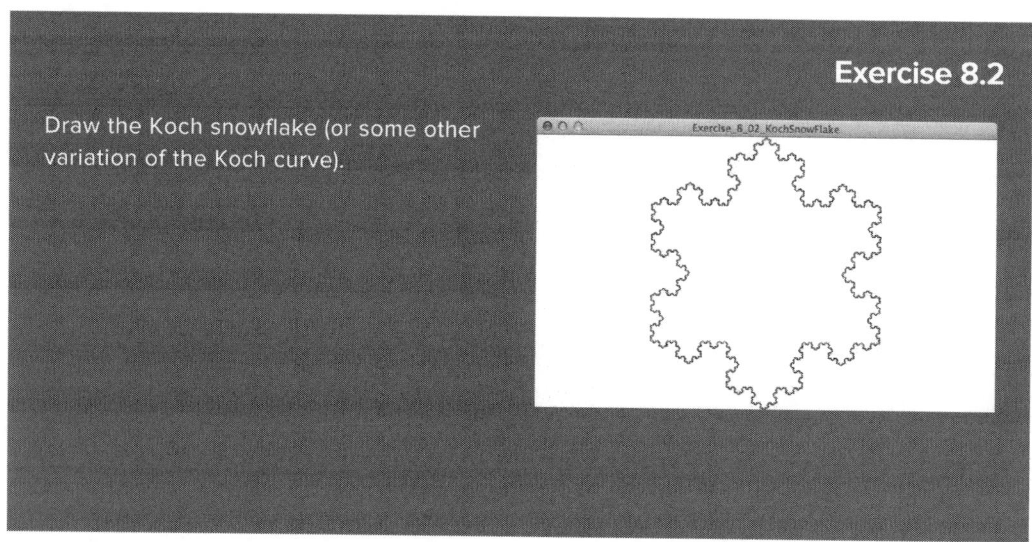

Exercise 8.2

Draw the Koch snowflake (or some other variation of the Koch curve).

Exercise 8.3

Try animating the Koch curve. For example, can you draw it from left to right? Can you vary the visual design of the line segments? Can you move the line segments using techniques from earlier chapters? What if each line segment were made into a spring (toxiclibs) or joint (Box2D)?

Exercise 8.4

Rewrite the Cantor set example using objects and an `ArrayList`.

Exercise 8.5

Draw the Sierpiński triangle (as seen in Wolfram elementary CA) using recursion.

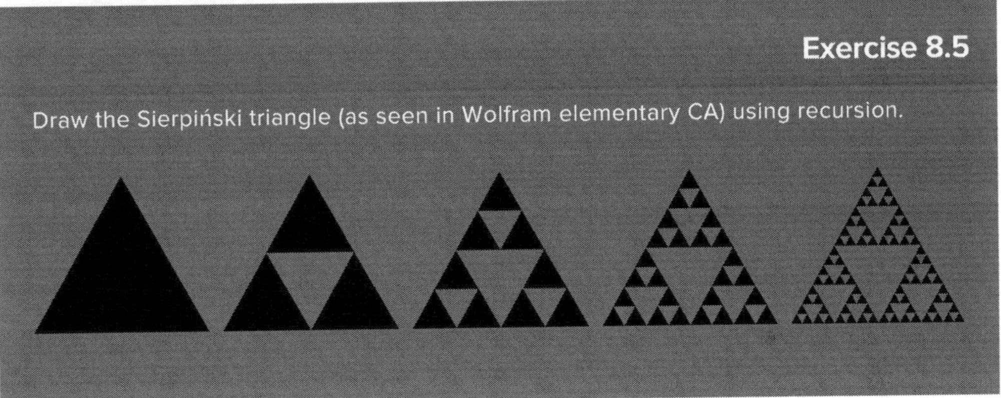

8.5 Trees

The fractals we have examined in this chapter so far are deterministic, meaning they have no randomness and will always produce the identical outcome each time they are run. They are excellent demonstrations of classic fractals and the programming techniques behind drawing them, but are too precise to feel *natural*. In this next part of the chapter, I want to examine some techniques behind generating a stochastic (or non-deterministic) fractal. The example we'll use is a branching tree. Let's first walk through the steps to create a deterministic version. Here are our production rules:

1. Draw a line.
2. At the end of the line, (a) rotate to the left and draw a shorter line and (b) rotate to the right and draw a shorter line.
3. Repeat step 2 for the new lines, again and again and again.

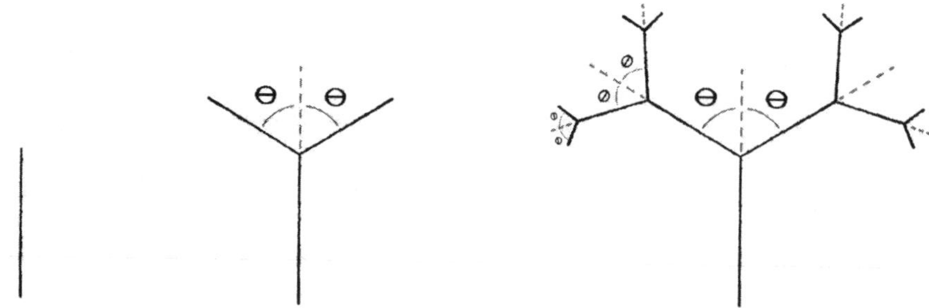

Figure 8.19

Again, we have a nice fractal with a recursive definition: A branch is a line with two branches connected to it.

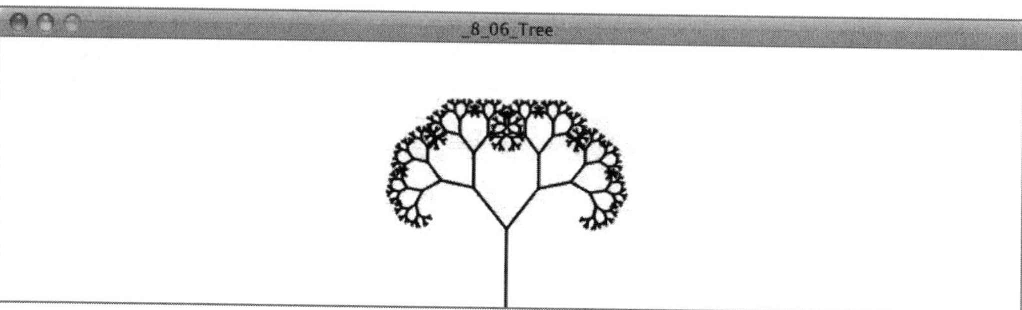

The part that is a bit more difficult than our previous fractals lies in the use of the word *rotate* in the fractal's rules. Each new branch must rotate relative to the previous branch, which is rotated relative to all its previous branches. Luckily for us, Processing has a mechanism to keep track of rotations for us—the ***transformation matrix***. If you aren't familiar with the functions `pushMatrix()` and `popMatrix()`, I suggest you read the online Processing tutorial 2D Transformations (http://processing.org/learning/transform2d/), which will cover the concepts you'll need for this particular example.

Let's begin by drawing a single branch, the trunk of the tree. Since we are going to involve the `rotate()` function, we'll need to make sure we are continuously translating along the branches while we draw the tree. And since the root starts at the bottom of the window (see above), the first step requires translating to that spot:

```
translate(width/2,height);
```

...followed by drawing a line upwards (Figure 8.20):

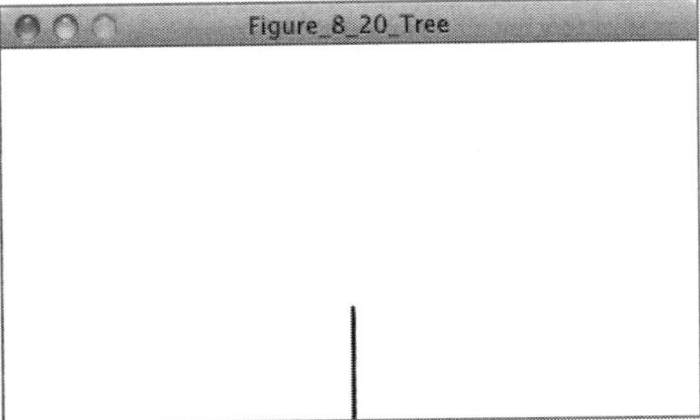

Figure 8.20

```
line(0,0,0,-100);
```

Once we've finished the root, we just need to translate to the end and rotate in order to draw the next branch. (Eventually, we're going to need to package up what we're doing right now into a recursive function, but let's sort out the steps first.)

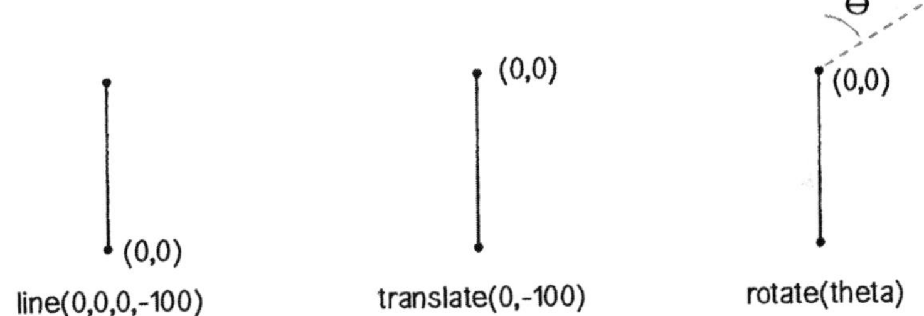

Figure 8.21

Remember, when we rotate in Processing, we are always rotating around the point of origin, so here the point of origin must always be translated to the end of our current branch.

```
translate(0,-100);
rotate(PI/6);
line(0,0,0,-100);
```

Now that we have a branch going to the right, we need one going to the left. We can use `pushMatrix()` to save the transformation state before we rotate, letting us call `popMatrix()` to restore that state and draw the branch to the left. Let's look at all the code together.

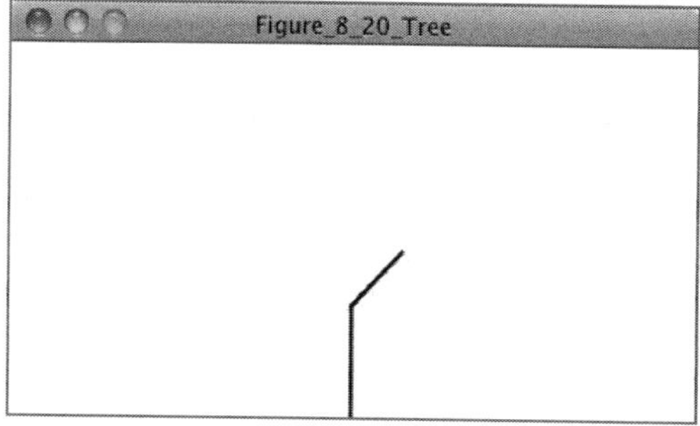

Figure 8.22

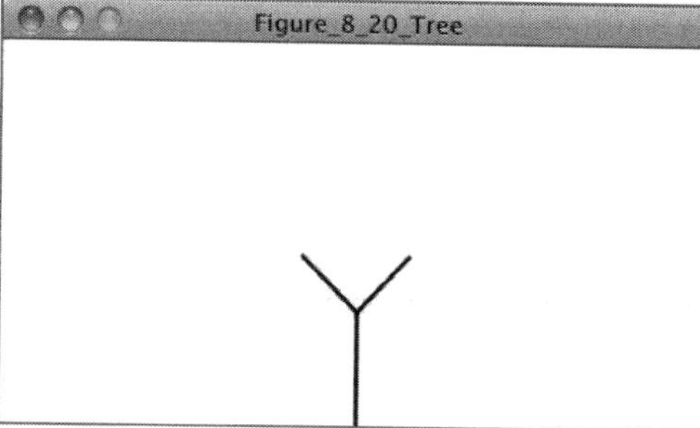

Figure 8.23

```
translate(width/2,height);
line(0,0,0,-100);                    The root
translate(0,-100);

pushMatrix();
rotate(PI/6);
line(0,0,0,-100);                    Branch to the right
popMatrix();

rotate(-PI/6);
line(0,0,0,-100);                    Branch to the left
```

If you think of each call to the function `line()` as a "branch," you can see from the code above that we have implemented our definition of branching as a line that has two lines connected to its end. We could keep adding more and more calls to `line()` for more and more branches, but just as with the Cantor set and Koch curve, our code would become incredibly complicated and unwieldy. Instead, we can use the above logic as our foundation for writing a recursive function, replacing the direct calls to `line()` with our own function called `branch()`. Let's take a look.

Example 8.6: Recursive tree

```
void branch() {
  line(0, 0, 0, -100);               Draw the branch itself.
  translate(0, -100);                Translate to the end.

  pushMatrix();
```

```
  rotate(PI/6);                          Rotate to the right and branch again.
  branch();
  popMatrix();

  pushMatrix();
  rotate(-PI/6);                         Rotate to the left and branch again.
  branch();
  popMatrix();
}
```

Notice how in the above code we use `pushMatrix()` and `popMatrix()` around each subsequent call to `branch()`. This is one of those elegant code solutions that feels almost like magic. Each call to `branch()` takes a moment to remember the location of that particular branch. If you turn yourself into Processing for a moment and try to follow the recursive function with pencil and paper, you'll notice that it draws all of the branches to the right first. When it gets to the end, `popMatrix()` will pop us back along all of the branches we've drawn and start sending branches out to the left.

Exercise 8.6

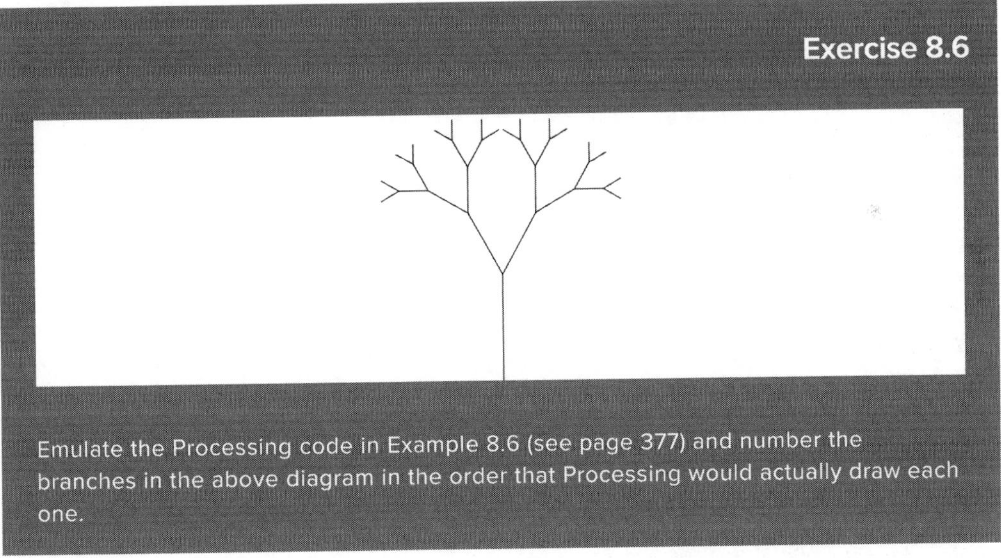

Emulate the Processing code in Example 8.6 (see page 377) and number the branches in the above diagram in the order that Processing would actually draw each one.

You may have noticed that the recursive function we just wrote would not actually draw the above tree. After all, it has no exit condition and would get stuck in infinite recursive calls to itself. You'll also probably notice that the branches of the tree get shorter at each level. Let's look at how we can shrink the length of the lines as the tree is drawn, and stop branching once the lines have become too short.

```
void branch(float len) {

  line(0, 0, 0, -len);
  translate(0, -len);

  len *= 0.66;

  if (len > 2) {
    pushMatrix();
    rotate(theta);
    branch(len);
    popMatrix();

    pushMatrix();
    rotate(-theta);
    branch(len);
    popMatrix();
  }
}
```

Each branch now receives its length as an argument.

Each branch's length shrinks by two-thirds.

Subsequent calls to branch() include the length argument.

We've also included a variable for theta that allows us, when writing the rest of the code in `setup()` and `draw()`, to vary the branching angle according to, say, the `mouseX` location.

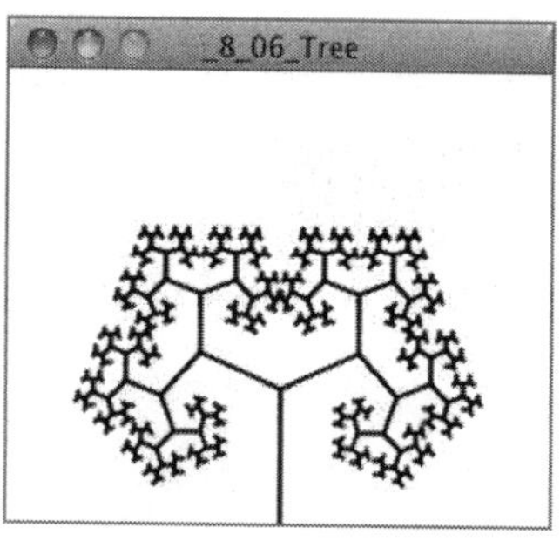

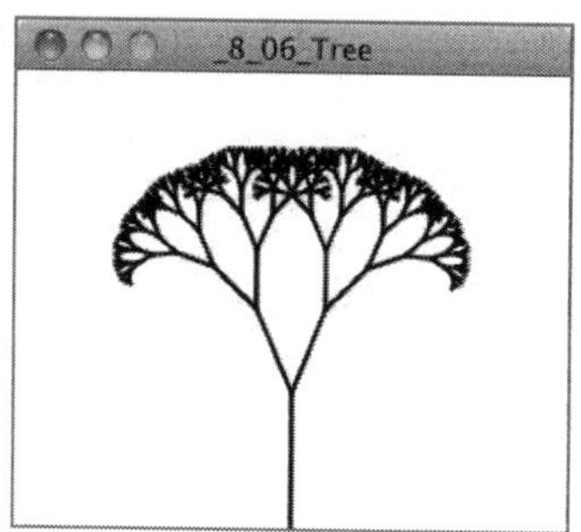

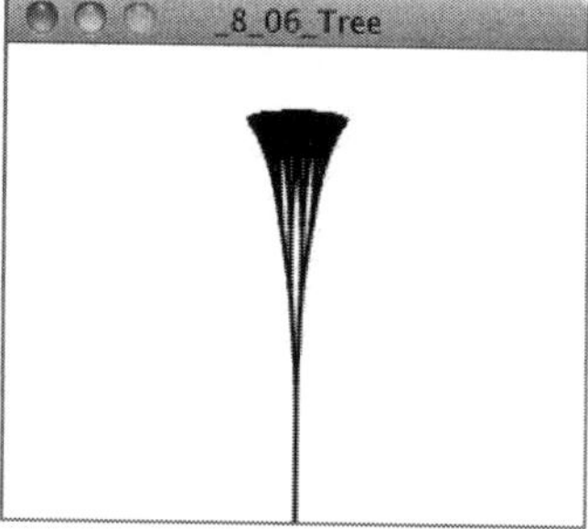

Example 8.7: Recursive tree

```
float theta;

void setup() {
  size(300, 200);
}

void draw() {
  background(255);
```

```
  theta = map(mouseX,0,width,0,PI/2);
```

Pick an angle according to the mouse location.

```
  translate(width/2, height);
```

The first branch starts at the bottom of the window.

```
  stroke(0);
  branch(60);
}
```

Exercise 8.7

Vary the `strokeWeight()` for each branch. Make the root thick and each subsequent branch thinner.

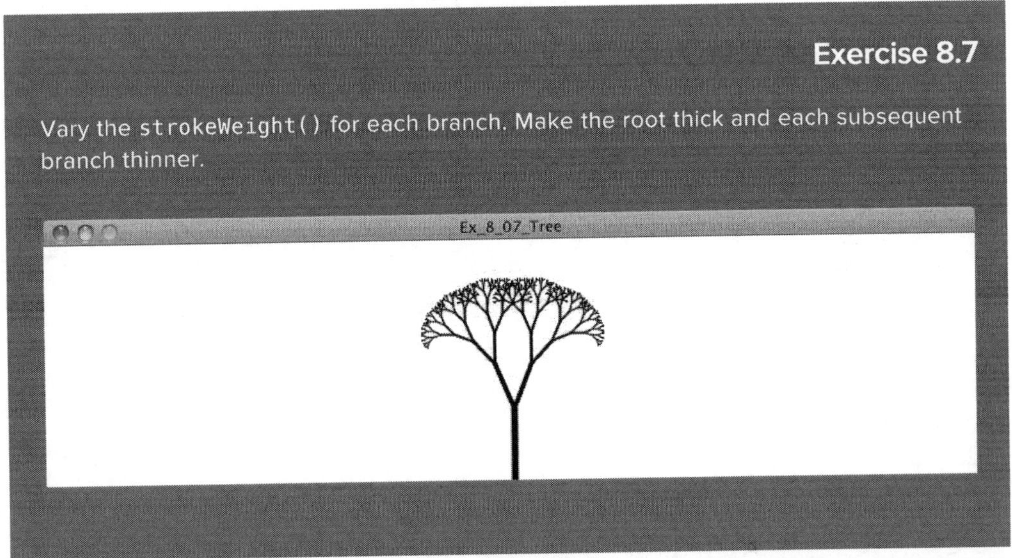

Exercise 8.8

The tree structure can also be generated using the `ArrayList` technique demonstrated with the Koch curve. Recreate the tree using a `Branch` object and an `ArrayList` to keep track of the branches. Hint: you'll want to keep track of the branch directions and lengths using vector math instead of Processing transformations.

Exercise 8.9

Once you have the tree built with an `ArrayList` of `Branch` objects, animate the tree's growth. Can you draw leaves at the end of the branches?

The recursive tree fractal is a nice example of a scenario in which adding a little bit of randomness can make the tree look more natural. Take a look outside and you'll notice that branch lengths and angles vary from branch to branch, not to mention the fact that branches don't all have exactly the same number of smaller branches. First, let's see what happens when we simply vary the angle and length. This is a pretty easy one, given that we can just ask Processing for a random number each time we draw the tree.

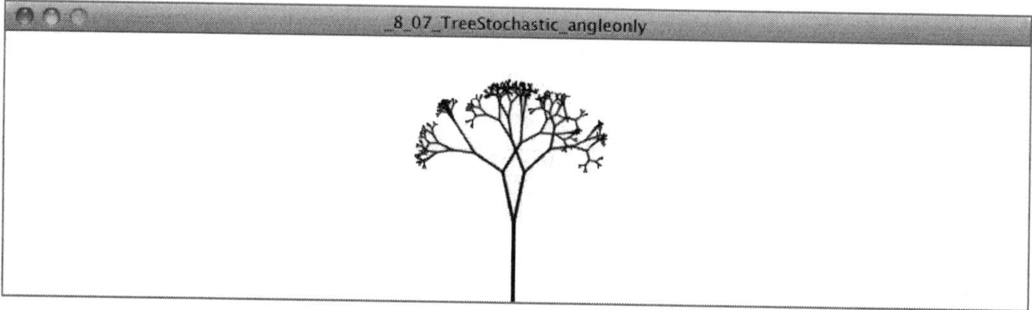


```
void branch(float len) {
  float theta = random(0,PI/3);

  line(0, 0, 0, -len);
  translate(0, -len);
  len *= 0.66;
  if (len > 2) {
    pushMatrix();
    rotate(theta);
    branch(len);
    popMatrix();
    pushMatrix();
    rotate(-theta);
    branch(len);
    popMatrix();
  }
}
```

Start by picking a random angle for each branch.

In the above function, we always call `branch()` twice. But why not pick a random number of branches and call `branch()` that number of times?

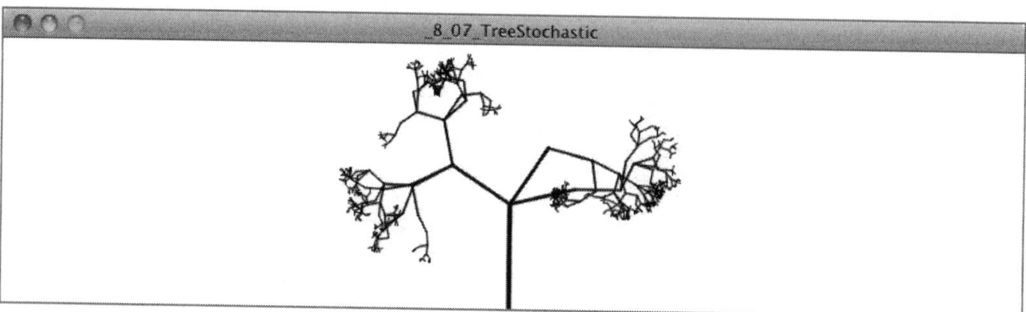

Example 8.8: Stochastic tree

```
void branch(float len) {

  line(0, 0, 0, -len);
  translate(0, -len);

  if (len > 2) {

    int n = int(random(1,4));                    Call branch() a random number of times.

    for (int i = 0; i < n; i++) {

      float theta = random(-PI/2, PI/2);         Each branch gets its own random angle.

      pushMatrix();
      rotate(theta);
      branch(h);
      popMatrix();
    }
  }
```

Exercise 8.10

Set the angles of the branches of the tree according to Perlin noise values. Adjust the noise values over time to animate the tree. See if you can get it to appear as if it is blowing in the wind.

Exercise 8.11

Use toxiclibs to simulate tree physics. Each branch of the tree should be two particles connected with a spring. How can you get the tree to stand up and not fall down?

8.6 L-systems

In 1968, Hungarian botanist Aristid Lindenmayer developed a grammar-based system to model the growth patterns of plants. L-systems (short for Lindenmayer systems) can be used to generate all of the recursive fractal patterns we've seen so far in this chapter. We don't need L-systems to do the kind of work we're doing here; however, they are incredibly useful because they provide a mechanism for keeping track of fractal structures that require complex and multi-faceted production rules.

In order to create an example that implements L-systems in Processing, we are going to have to be comfortable with working with (a) recursion, (b) transformation matrices, and (c) strings. So far we've worked with recursion and transformations, but strings are new here. We will assume the basics, but if that is not comfortable for you, I would suggest taking a look at the Processing tutorial Strings and Drawing Text (http://www.processing.org/learning/text/).

An L-system involves three main components:

- ***Alphabet.*** An L-system's alphabet is comprised of the valid characters that can be included. For example, we could say the alphabet is "ABC," meaning that any valid "sentence" (a string of characters) in an L-system can only include these three characters.
- ***Axiom.*** The axiom is a sentence (made up with characters from the alphabet) that describes the initial state of the system. For example, with the alphabet "ABC," some example axioms are "AAA" or "B" or "ACBAB."
- ***Rules.*** The rules of an L-system are applied to the axiom and then applied recursively, generating new sentences over and over again. An L-system rule includes two sentences, a "predecessor" and a "successor." For example, with the Rule "A —> AB", whenever an "A" is found in a string, it is replaced with "AB."

Let's begin with a very simple L-system. (This is, in fact, Lindenmayer's original L-system for modeling the growth of algae.)

```
Alphabet: A B
Axiom: A
Rules: (A → AB) (B → A)
```

As with our recursive fractal shapes, we can consider each successive application of the L-system rules to be a generation. Generation 0 is, by definition, the axiom.

Let's look at how we might create these generations with code. We'll start by using a `String` object to store the axiom.

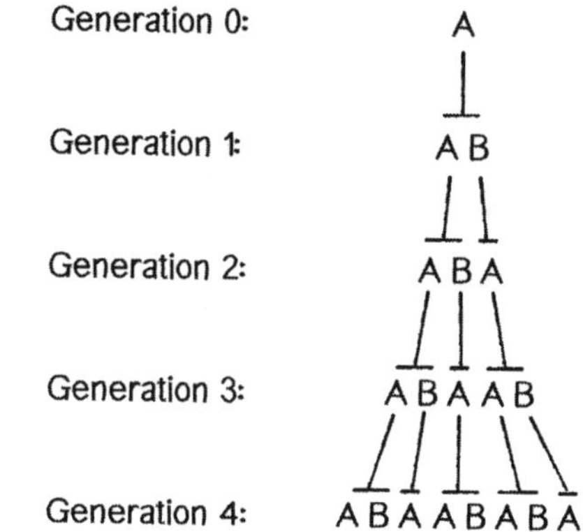

Figure 8.24: And so on and so forth...

```
String current = "A";
```

And once again, just as we did with the Game of Life and the Koch curve `ArrayList` examples, we will need an entirely separate string to keep track of the "next" generation.

```
String next = "";
```

Now it's time to apply the rules to the current generation and place the results in the next.

```
for (int i = 0; i < current.length(); i++) {
  char c = current.charAt(i);
  if (c == 'A') {                        Production rule A --> AB
    next += "AB";
  } else if (c == 'B') {                 Production rule B --> A
    next += "A";
  }
}
```

And when we're done, current can become next.

```
current = next;
```

To be sure this is working, let's package it into a function and and call it every time the mouse is pressed.

```
Generation 0: A
Generation 1: AB
Generation 2: ABA
Generation 3: ABAAB
Generation 4: ABAABABA
Generation 5: ABAABABAABAAB
Generation 6: ABAABABAABAABABAABABA
Generation 7: ABAABABAABAABABAABABAABAABABAABAAB
Generation 8: ABAABABAABAABABAABABAABAABABAABAABABAABABAABAABABAABABA
Generation 9: ABAABABAABAABABAABABAABAABABAABAABABAABABAABAABABAABABAABAABABAABAABABAABABAABAABABAABAAB
Generation 10:
ABAABABAABAABABAABABAABAABABAABAABABAABABAABAABABAABABAABAABABAABAABABAABABAABAABABAABAABABAABABAABAABABAABAABABAABABAABAABABAABAABABAABABAAB
AABABAABABA
```

Example 8.9: Simple L-system sentence generation

```
String current = "A";                    Start with an axiom.
int count = 0;                           Let's keep track of how many generations.

void setup() {
  println("Generation " + count + ": " + current);
}

void draw() {
}

void mousePressed() {
  String next = "";
```

```
  for (int i = 0; i < current.length(); i++) {      // Traverse the current String and make the new one.
    char c = current.charAt(i);
    if (c == 'A') {
      next += "AB";
    }  else if (c == 'B') {
      next += "A";
    }
  }
  current = next;
  count++;
  println("Generation " + count + ": " + current);
}
```

Since the rules are applied recursively to each generation, the length of the string grows exponentially. By generation #11, the sentence is 233 characters long; by generation #22, it is over 46,000 characters long. The Java `String` class, while convenient to use, is a grossly inefficient data structure for concatenating large strings. A `String` object is "immutable," which means once the object is created it can never be changed. Whenever you add on to the end of a `String` object, Java has to make a brand new `String` object (even if you are using the same variable name).

```
String s = "blah";
s += "add some more stuff";
```

In most cases, this is fine, but why duplicate a 46,000-character string if you don't have to? For better efficiency in our L-system examples, we'll use the `StringBuffer` class, which is optimized for this type of task and can easily be converted into a string after concatenation is complete.

```
StringBuffer next = new StringBuffer();      // A StringBuffer for the "next" sentence
for (int i = 0; i < current.length(); i++) {
  char c = current.charAt(i);
  if (c == 'A') {
    next.append("AB");                        // append() instead of +=
  } else if (c == 'B') {
    next.append("A");
  }
}
current = next.toString();                    // StringBuffer can easily be converted back to a String.
```

You may find yourself wondering right about now: what exactly is the point of all this? After all, isn't this a chapter about *drawing* fractal patterns? Yes, the recursive nature of the L-system sentence structure seems relevant to the discussion, but how exactly does this model plant growth in a visual way?

What we've left unsaid until now is that embedded into these L-system sentences are instructions for drawing. Let's see how this works with another example.

```
Alphabet: A B
Axiom: A
Rules: (A → ABA) (B → BBB)
```

To read a sentence, we'll translate it in the following way:

```
A: Draw a line forward.
B: Move forward without drawing.
```

Let's look at the sentence of each generation and its visual output.

```
Generation 0: A
Generation 1: ABA
Generation 2: ABABBBABA
Generation 3: ABABBBABABBBBBBBBBABABBBABA
```

Look familiar? This is the Cantor set generated with an L-system.

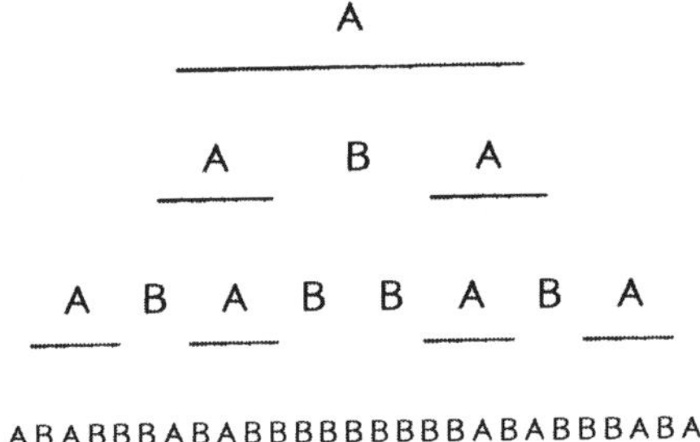

Figure 8.25

The following alphabet is often used with L-systems: "FG+-[]", meaning:

```
F: Draw a line and move forward
G: Move forward (without drawing a line)
+: Turn right
-: Turn left
[: Save current location
]: Restore previous location
```

This type of drawing framework is often referred to as "Turtle graphics" (from the old days of LOGO programming). Imagine a turtle sitting on your computer screen to which you could issue a small set of commands: turn left, turn right, draw a line, etc. Processing isn't set up to operate this way by default, but by using `translate()`, `rotate()`, and `line()`, we can emulate a Turtle graphics engine fairly easily.

Here's how we would translate the above L-system alphabet into Processing code.

```
F: line(0,0,0,len); translate(0,len);
G: translate(0,len);
+: rotate(angle);
-: rotate(-angle);
[: pushMatrix();
]: popMatrix();
```

Assuming we have a sentence generated from the L-system, we can walk through the sentence character by character and call the appropriate function as outlined above.

```
for (int i = 0; i < sentence.length(); i++) {

  char c = sentence.charAt(i);        // Looking at each character one at a time

  if (c == 'F') {                     // Performing the correct task for each
    line(0,0,len,0);                  // character. This could also be written with a
    translate(len,0);                 // "case" statement, which might be nicer to
  } else if (c == 'F') {              // look at, but leaving it as an if/else if
   translate(len,0);                  // structure helps readers not familiar with
  } else if (c == '+') {              // case statements.
    rotate(theta);
  } else if (c == '-') {
    rotate(-theta);
  } else if (c == '[') {
    pushMatrix();
  } else if (c == ']') {
    popMatrix();
  }
}
```

The next example will draw a more elaborate structure with the following L-system.

```
Alphabet: FG+-[]
Axiom: F
Rules: F → FF+[+F-F-F]-[-F+F+F]
```

The example available for download on the book's website takes all of the L-system code provided in this section and organizes it into three classes:

- **`Rule`**: A class that stores the predecessor and successor strings for an L-system rule.
- **`LSystem`**: A class to iterate a new L-system generation (as demonstrated with the `StringBuffer` technique).
- **`Turtle`**: A class to manage reading the L-system sentence and following its instructions to draw on the screen.

We won't write out these classes here since they simply duplicate the code we've already worked out in this chapter. However, let's see how they are put together in the main tab.

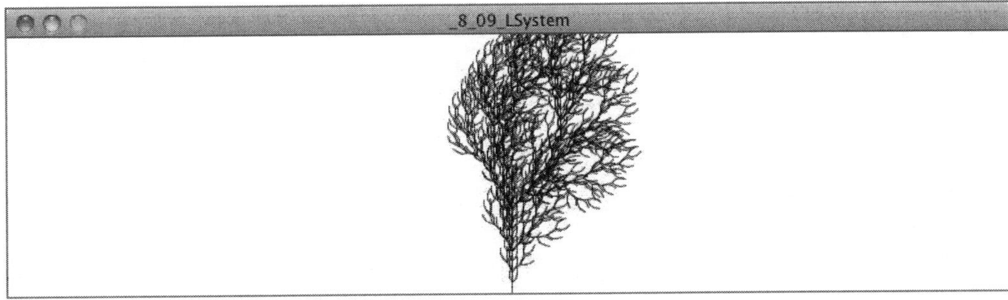

Example 8.10: LSystem

```
LSystem lsys;
Turtle turtle;

void setup() {
  size(600,600);

  Rule[] ruleset = new Rule[1];
  ruleset[0] = new Rule('F',"FF+[+F-F-F]-[-F+F+F]");

  lsys = new LSystem("F",ruleset);

  turtle = new Turtle(lsys.getSentence(),width/4,radians(25));
}

void draw() {
  background(255);
  translate(width/2,height);
  turtle.render();
}

void mousePressed() {
  lsys.generate();
  turtle.setToDo(lsys.getSentence());

  turtle.changeLen(0.5);
}
```

A ruleset is an array of Rule objects.

The L-system is created with an axiom and a ruleset.

The Turtle graphics renderer is given a sentence, a starting length, and an angle for rotations.

Start at the bottom of the window and draw.

Generate a new sentence when the mouse is pressed.

The length shrinks each generation.

Exercise 8.12

Use an L-system as a set of instructions for creating objects stored in an `ArrayList`. Use trigonometry and vector math to perform the rotations instead of matrix transformations (much like we did in the Koch curve example).

Exercise 8.13

The seminal work in L-systems and plant structures, *The Algorithmic Beauty of Plants* by Przemysław Prusinkiewicz and Aristid Lindenmayer, was published in 1990. It is available for free in its entirety online (http://algorithmicbotany.org/papers/#abop). Chapter 1 describes many sophisticated L-systems with additional drawing rules and available alphabet characters. In addition, it describes several methods for generating stochastic L-systems. Expand the L-system example to include one or more additional features described by Prusinkiewicz and Lindenmayer.

Exercise 8.14

In this chapter, we emphasized using fractal algorithms for generating visual patterns. However, fractals can be found in other creative mediums. For example, fractal patterns are evident in Johann Sebastian Bach's Cello Suite no. 3. The structure of David Foster Wallace's novel *Infinite Jest* was inspired by fractals. Consider using the examples in this chapter to generate audio or text.

The Ecosystem Project

Step 8 Exercise:

Incorporate fractals into your ecosystem. Some possibilities:

- **Add plant-like creatures to the ecosystem environment.**
- **Let's say one of your plants is similar to a tree. Can you add leaves or flowers to the end of the branches? What if the leaves can fall off the tree (depending on a wind force)? What if you add fruit that can be picked and eaten by the creatures?**
- **Design a creature with a fractal pattern.**
- **Use an L-system to generate instructions for how a creature should move or behave.**

Chapter 9. The Evolution of Code

"The fact that life evolved out of nearly nothing, some 10 billion years after the universe evolved out of literally nothing, is a fact so staggering that I would be mad to attempt words to do it justice."

— Richard Dawkins

Let's take a moment to think back to a simpler time, when you wrote your first Processing sketches and life was free and easy. What is one of programming's fundamental concepts that you likely used in those first sketches and continue to use over and over again? *Variables*. Variables allow you to save data and reuse that data while a program runs. This, of course, is nothing new to us. In fact, we have moved far beyond a sketch with just one or two variables and on to more complex data structures—variables made from custom types (objects) that include both data and functionality. We've made our own little worlds of movers and particles and vehicles and cells and trees.

In each and every example in this book, the variables of these objects have to be initialized. Perhaps you made a whole bunch of particles with random colors and sizes or a list of vehicles all starting at the same x,y location on screen. But instead of acting as "intelligent designers" and assigning the properties of our objects through randomness or thoughtful consideration, we can let a process found in nature—*evolution*—decide for us.

Can we think of the variables of an object as its DNA? Can objects make other objects and pass down their DNA to a new generation? Can our simulation evolve?

The answer to all these questions is yes. After all, we wouldn't be able to face ourselves in the mirror as nature-of-coders without tackling a simulation of one of the most powerful algorithmic processes found in nature itself. This chapter is dedicated to examining the principles behind biological evolution and finding ways to apply those principles in code.

9.1 Genetic Algorithms: Inspired by Actual Events

It's important for us to clarify the goals of this chapter. We will not go into depth about the science of genetics and evolution as it happens in the real world. We won't be making Punnett squares (sorry to disappoint) and there will be no discussion of nucleotides, protein synthesis, RNA, and other topics related to the actual biological processes of evolution. Instead, we are going to look at the core principles behind Darwinian evolutionary theory and develop a set of algorithms *inspired* by these principles. We don't care so much about an accurate simulation of evolution; rather, we care about methods for applying evolutionary strategies in software.

This is not to say that a project with more scientific depth wouldn't have value, and I encourage readers with a particular interest in this topic to explore possibilities for expanding the examples provided with additional evolutionary features. Nevertheless, for the sake of keeping things manageable, we're going to stick to the basics, which will be plenty complex and exciting.

The term "genetic algorithm" refers to a specific algorithm implemented in a specific way to solve specific sorts of problems. While the formal genetic algorithm itself will serve as the foundation for the examples we create in this chapter, we needn't worry about implementing the algorithm with perfect accuracy, given that we are looking for creative uses of evolutionary theories in our code. This chapter will be broken down into the following three parts (with the majority of the time spent on the first).

1. ***Traditional Genetic Algorithm.*** We'll begin with the traditional computer science genetic algorithm. This algorithm was developed to solve problems in which the solution space is so vast that a "brute force" algorithm would simply take too long. Here's an example: I'm thinking of a number. A number between one and one billion. How long will it take for you to guess it? Solving a problem with "brute force" refers to the process of checking every possible solution. Is it one? Is it two? Is it three? Is it four? And so and and so forth. Though luck does play a factor here, with brute force we would often find ourselves patiently waiting for years while you count to one billion. However, what if I could tell you if an answer you gave was good or bad? Warm or cold? Very warm? Hot? Super, super cold? If you could evaluate how "fit" a guess is, you could pick other numbers closer to that guess and arrive at the answer more quickly. Your answer could evolve.

2. ***Interactive Selection.*** Once we establish the traditional computer science algorithm, we'll look at other applications of genetic algorithms in the visual arts. Interactive selection refers to the process of evolving something (often an computer-generated image) through user interaction. Let's say you walk into a museum gallery and see

ten paintings. With interactive selection, you would pick your favorites and allow an algorithmic process to generate (or "evolve") new paintings based on your preferences.

3. ***Ecosystem Simulation.*** The traditional computer science genetic algorithm and interactive selection technique are what you will likely find if you search online or read a textbook about artificial intelligence. But as we'll soon see, they don't really simulate the process of evolution as it happens in the real world. In this chapter, I want to also explore techniques for simulating the process of evolution in an ecosystem of pseudo-living beings. How can our objects that move about the screen meet each other, mate, and pass their genes on to a new generation? This would apply directly to the Ecosystem Project outlined at the end of each chapter.

9.2 Why Use Genetic Algorithms?

While computer simulations of evolutionary processes date back to the 1950s, much of what we think of as genetic algorithms (also known as "GAs") today was developed by John Holland, a professor at the University of Michigan, whose book *Adaptation in Natural and Artificial Systems* pioneered GA research. Today, more genetic algorithms are part of a wider field of research, often referred to as "Evolutionary Computing."

To help illustrate the traditional genetic algorithm, we are going to start with monkeys. No, not our evolutionary ancestors. We're going to start with some fictional monkeys that bang away on keyboards with the goal of typing out the complete works of Shakespeare.

Figure 9.1

The “infinite monkey theorem” is stated as follows: A monkey hitting keys randomly on a typewriter will eventually type the complete works of Shakespeare (given an infinite amount of time). The problem with this theory is that the probability of said monkey actually typing Shakespeare is so low that even if that monkey started at the Big Bang, it’s unbelievably unlikely we’d even have *Hamlet* at this point.

Let’s consider a monkey named George. George types on a reduced typewriter containing only twenty-seven characters: twenty-six letters and one space bar. So the probability of George hitting any given key is one in twenty-seven.

Let’s consider the phrase “to be or not to be that is the question” (we’re simplifying it from the original “To be, or not to be: that is the question”). The phrase is 39 characters long. If George starts typing, the chance he’ll get the first character right is 1 in 27. Since the probability he’ll get the second character right is also 1 in 27, he has a 1 in 27*27 chance of landing the first two characters in correct order—which follows directly from our discussion of "event probability" in the Introduction (see page 7). Therefore, the probability that George will type the full phrase is:

(1/27) multiplied by itself 39 times, i.e. $(1/27)^{39}$

which equals a 1 in 66,555,937,033,867,822,607,895,549,241,096,482,953,017,615,834,735,226,163 chance of getting it right!

Needless to say, even hitting just this one phrase, not to mention an entire play, is highly unlikely. Even if George is a computer simulation and can type one million random phrases per second, for George to have a 99% probability of eventually getting it right, he would have to type for 9,719,096,182,010,563,073,125,591,133,903,305,625,605,017 years. (Note that the age of the universe is estimated to be a mere 13,750,000,000 years.)

The point of all these unfathomably large numbers is not to give you a headache, but to demonstrate that a brute force algorithm (typing every possible random phrase) is not a reasonable strategy for arriving randomly at “to be or not to be that is the question”. Enter genetic algorithms, which will show that we can still start with random phrases and find the solution through simulated evolution.

Now, it’s worth noting that this problem (*arrive at the phrase “to be or not to be that is the question”*) is a ridiculous one. Since we know the answer, all we need to do is type it. Here’s a Processing sketch that solves the problem.

```
string s = "To be or not to be that is the question";
println(s);
```

Nevertheless, the point here is that solving a problem with a known answer allows us to easily test our code. Once we’ve successfully solved the problem, we can feel more confident in using genetic algorithms to do some actual useful work: solving problems with unknown answers. So this first example serves no real purpose other than to demonstrate how genetic algorithms work. If we test the GA results against the known answer and get "to be or not to be", then we've succeeded in writing our genetic algorithm.

Exercise 9.1

Create a sketch that generates random strings. We'll need to know how to do this in order to implement the genetic algorithm example that will shortly follow. How long does it take for Processing to randomly generate the string "cat"? How could you adapt this to generate a random design using Processing's shape-drawing functions?

9.3 Darwinian Natural Selection

Before we begin walking through the genetic algorithm, let's take a moment to describe three core principles of Darwinian evolution that will be required as we implement our simulation. In order for natural selection to occur as it does in nature, all three of these elements must be present.

1. ***Heredity.*** There must be a process in place by which children receive the properties of their parents. If creatures live long enough to reproduce, then their traits are passed down to their children in the next generation of creatures.

2. ***Variation.*** There must be a variety of traits present in the population or a means with which to introduce variation. For example, let's say there is a population of beetles in which all the beetles are exactly the same: same color, same size, same wingspan, same everything. Without any variety in the population, the children will always be identical to the parents and to each other. New combinations of traits can never occur and nothing can evolve.

3. ***Selection.*** There must be a mechanism by which some members of a population have the opportunity to be parents and pass down their genetic information and some do not. This is typically referred to as "survival of the fittest." For example, let's say a population of gazelles is chased by lions every day. The faster gazelles are more likely to escape the lions and are therefore more likely to live longer and have a chance to reproduce and pass their genes down to their children. The term *fittest*, however, can be a bit misleading. Generally, we think of it as meaning bigger, faster, or stronger. While this may be the case in some instances, natural selection operates on the principle that some traits are better adapted for the creature's environment and therefore produce a greater likelihood of surviving and reproducing. It has nothing to do with a given creature being "better" (after all, this is a subjective term) or more "physically fit." In the case of our typing monkeys, for example, a more "fit" monkey is one that has typed a phrase closer to "to be or not to be".

Next I'd like to walk through the narrative of the genetic algorithm. We'll do this in the context of the typing monkey. The algorithm itself will be divided into two parts: a set of conditions for initialization (i.e. Processing's `setup()`) and the steps that are repeated over and over again (i.e. Processing's `draw()`) until we arrive at the correct answer.

9.4 The Genetic Algorithm, Part I: Creating a Population

In the context of the typing monkey example, we will create a population of phrases. (Note that we are using the term "phrase" rather loosely, meaning a string of characters.) This begs the question: How do we create this population? Here is where the Darwinian principle of ***variation*** applies. Let's say, for simplicity, that we are trying to evolve the phrase "cat" and that we have a population of three phrases.

```
hug
rid
won
```

Sure, there is variety in the three phrases above, but try to mix and match the characters every which way and you will never get *cat*. There is not *enough* variety here to evolve the optimal solution. However, if we had a population of thousands of phrases, all generated randomly, chances are that at least one member of the population will have a *c* as the first character, one will have an *a* as the second, and one a *t* as the third. A large population will most likely give us enough variety to generate the desired phrase (and in Part 2 of the algorithm, we'll have another opportunity to introduce even more variation in case there isn't enough in the first place). So we can be more specific in describing Step 1 and say:

> Create a population of randomly generated elements.

This brings up another important question. What is the element itself? As we move through the examples in this chapter, we'll see several different scenarios; we might have a population of images or a population of vehicles à la Chapter 6 (see page 308). The key, and the part that is new for us in this chapter, is that each member of the population has a virtual "DNA," a set of properties (we can call them "genes") that describe how a given element looks or behaves. In the case of the typing monkey, for example, the DNA is simply a string of characters.

In the field of genetics, there is an important distinction between the concepts *genotype* and *phenotype*. The actual genetic code—in our case, the digital information itself—is an element's ***genotype***. This is what gets passed down from generation to generation. The ***phenotype***, however, is the expression of that data. This distinction is key to how you will use genetic algorithms in your own work. What are the objects in your world? How will you design the genotype for your objects (the data structure to store each object's properties) as well as the phenotype (what are *you* using these variables to express?) We do this all the time in graphics programming. The simplest example is probably color.

Genotype	Phenotype
int c = 255;	
int c = 127;	
int c = 0;	

As we can see, the genotype is the digital information. Each color is a variable that stores an integer and we choose to express that integer as a color. But how we choose to express the data is arbitrary. In a different approach, we could have used the integer to describe the length of a line, the weight of a force, etc.

Same Genotype	Different Phenotype (line length)
int c = 255;	
int c = 127;	
int c = 0;	

The nice thing about our monkey-typing example is that there is no difference between genotype and phenotype. The DNA data itself is a string of characters and the expression of that data is that very string.

So, we can finally end the discussion of this first step and be more specific with its description, saying:

> Create a population of N elements, each with randomly generated DNA.

9.5 The Genetic Algorithm, Part II: Selection

Here is where we apply the Darwinian principle of *selection*. We need to evaluate the population and determine which members are fit to be selected as parents for the next generation. The process of selection can be divided into two steps.

1) Evaluate fitness.

For our genetic algorithm to function properly, we will need to design what is referred to as a ***fitness function***. The function will produce a numeric score to describe the fitness of a given member of the population. This, of course, is not how the real world works at all. Creatures are not given a score; they simply survive or not. But in the case of the traditional genetic algorithm, where we are trying to evolve an optimal solution to a problem, we need to be able to numerically evaluate any given possible solution.

Let's examine our current example, the typing monkey. Again, let's simplify the scenario and say we are attempting to evolve the word "cat". We have three members of the population: *hut*, *car*, and *box*. *Car* is obviously the most fit, given that it has two correct characters, *hut* has only one, and *box* has zero. And there it is, our fitness function:

```
fitness = the number of correct characters
```

DNA	Fitness
hut	1
car	2
box	0

We will eventually want to look at examples with more sophisticated fitness functions, but this is a good place to start.

2) Create a mating pool.

Once the fitness has been calculated for all members of the population, we can then select which members are fit to become parents and place them in a mating pool. There are several different approaches we could take here. For example, we could employ what is known as the ***elitist*** method and say, "Which two members of the population scored the highest? You two will make all the children for the next generation." This is probably one of the easier methods to program; however, it flies in the face of the principle of variation. If two members of the population (out of perhaps thousands) are the only ones available to reproduce, the next generation will have little variety and this may stunt the evolutionary process. We could instead make a mating pool out of a larger number—for example, the top 50% of the population, 500 out of 1,000. This is also just as easy to program, but it will not produce optimal results. In this case, the high-scoring top elements would have the same chance of being selected as a parent as the ones toward the middle. And why should element number 500 have a solid shot of reproducing, while element number 501 has no shot?

A better solution for the mating pool is to use a ***probabilistic*** method, which we'll call the "wheel of fortune" (also known as the "roulette wheel"). To illustrate this method, let's consider a simple example where we have a population of five elements, each with a fitness score.

Element	Fitness
A	3
B	4
C	0.5
D	1.5
E	1

The first thing we'll want to do is ***normalize*** all the scores. Remember normalizing a vector? That involved taking an vector and standardizing its length, setting it to 1. When we normalize a set of fitness scores, we are standardizing their range to between 0 and 1, as a percentage of total fitness. Let's add up all the fitness scores.

total fitness = 3 + 4 + 0.5 + 1.5 + 1 = 10

Then let's divide each score by the total fitness, giving us the normalized fitness.

Element	Fitness	Normalized Fitness	Expressed as a Percentage
A	3	0.3	30%
B	4	0.4	40%
C	0.5	0.05	5%
D	1.5	0.15	15%
E	1	0.1	10%

Now it's time for the wheel of fortune.

Spin the wheel!

Parent	Probability
A	30%
B	40%
C	5%
D	10%
E	15%

Figure 9.2

Spin the wheel and you'll notice that Element B has the highest chance of being selected, followed by A, then D, then E, and finally C. This probability-based selection according to fitness is an excellent approach. One, it guarantees that the highest-scoring elements will be most likely to reproduce. Two, it does not entirely eliminate any variation from the population. Unlike with the elitist method, even the lowest-scoring element (in this case C) has a chance to pass its information down to the next generation. It's quite possible (and often the case) that even low-scoring elements have a tiny nugget of genetic code that is truly useful and should not entirely be eliminated from the population. For example, in the case of evolving "to be or not to be", we might have the following elements.

```
A: to be or not to go
B: to be or not to pi
C: xxxxxxxxxxxxxxxxbe
```

As you can see, elements A and B are clearly the most fit and would have the highest score. But neither contains the correct characters for the end of the phrase. Element C, even though it would receive a very low score, happens to have the genetic data for the end of the phrase. And so while we would want A and B to be picked to generate the majority of the next generation, we would still want C to have a small chance to participate in the reproductive process.

9.6 The Genetic Algorithm, Part III: Reproduction

Now that we have a strategy for picking parents, we need to figure out how to use *reproduction* to make the population's next generation, keeping in mind the Darwinian principle of heredity—that children inherit properties from their parents. Again, there are a number of different techniques we could employ here. For example, one reasonable (and easy to program) strategy is asexual reproduction, meaning we pick just one parent and create a child that is an exact copy of that parent. The standard approach with genetic algorithms, however, is to pick two parents and create a child according to the following steps.

1) Crossover.

Crossover involves creating a child out of the genetic code of two parents. In the case of the monkey-typing example, let's assume we've picked two phrases from the mating pool (as outlined in our selection step).

`Parent A: FORK`
`Parent B: PLAY`

It's now up to us to make a child phrase from these two. Perhaps the most obvious way (let's call this the 50/50 method) would be to take the first two characters from A and the second two from B, leaving us with:

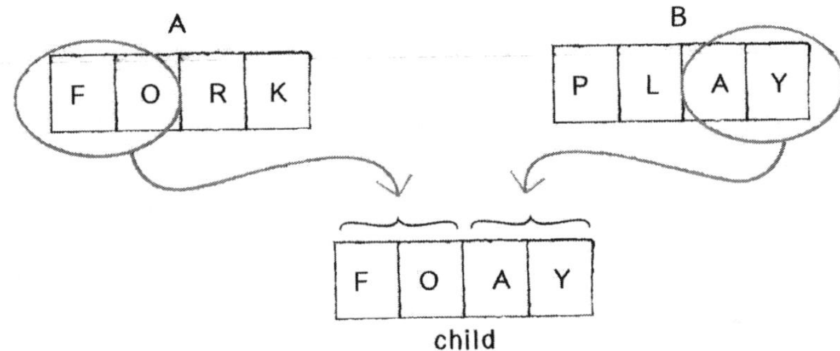

Figure 9.3

A variation of this technique is to pick a random midpoint. In other words, we don't have to pick exactly half of the code from each parent. We could sometimes end up with FLAY, and sometimes with FORY. This is preferable to the 50/50 approach, since we increase the variety of possibilities for the next generation.

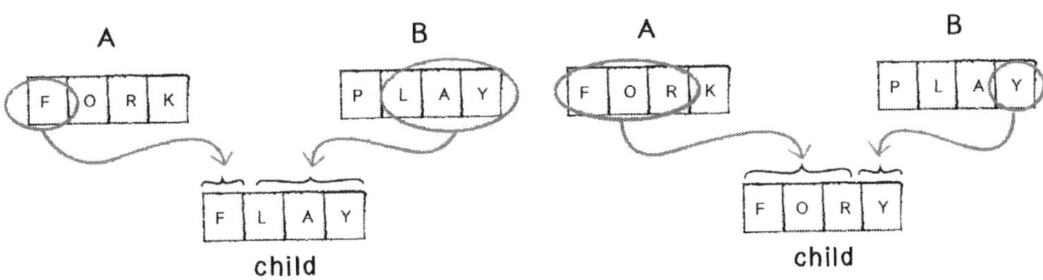

Figure 9.4: Picking a random midpoint

Another possibility is to randomly select a parent for each character in the child string. You can think of this as flipping a coin four times: heads take from parent A, tails from parent B. Here we could end up with many different results such as: PLRY, FLRK, FLRY, FORY, etc.

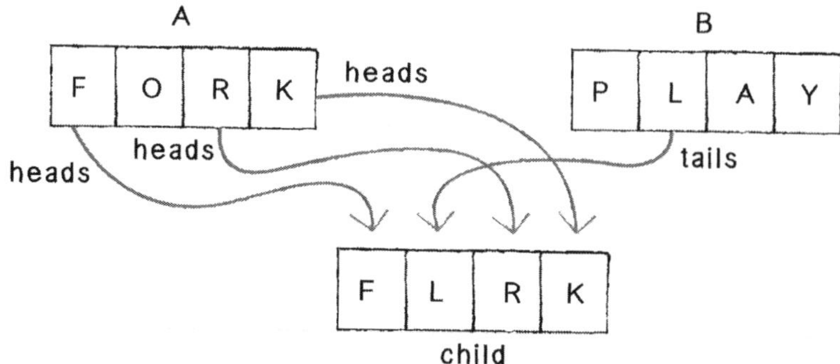

Figure 9.5: Coin-flipping approach

This strategy will produce essentially the same results as the random midpoint method; however, if the order of the genetic information plays some role in expressing the phenotype, you may prefer one solution over the other.

2) Mutation.

Once the child DNA has been created via crossover, we apply one final process before adding the child to the next generation—***mutation***. Mutation is an optional step, as there are some cases in which it is unnecessary. However, it exists because of the Darwinian principle of variation. We created an initial population randomly, making sure that we start with a variety of elements. However, there can only be so much variety when seeding the first generation, and mutation allows us to introduce additional variety throughout the evolutionary process itself.

Mutation is described in terms of a *rate*. A given genetic algorithm might have a mutation rate of 5% or 1% or 0.1%, etc. Let's assume we just finished with crossover and ended up with the child FORY. If we have a mutation rate of 1%, this means that for each character in the phrase generated from crossover, there is a 1% chance that it will mutate. What does it mean for a character to mutate? In this case, we define mutation as picking a new random character. A 1% probability is fairly low, and most of the time mutation will not occur at all in a four-character string (96% of the time to be more precise). However, when it does, the mutated character is replaced with a randomly generated one (see Figure 9.6).

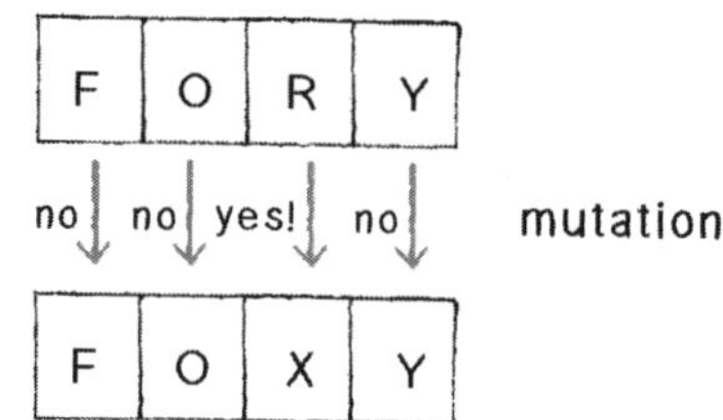

Figure 9.6

As we'll see in some of the examples, the mutation rate can greatly affect the behavior of the system. Certainly, a very high mutation rate (such as, say, 80%) would negate the evolutionary process itself. If the majority of a child's genes are generated randomly, then we cannot guarantee that the more "fit" genes occur with greater frequency with each successive generation.

The process of selection (picking two parents) and reproduction (crossover and mutation) is applied over and over again `N` times until we have a new population of `N` elements. At this point, the new population of children becomes the current population and we loop back to evaluate fitness and perform selection and reproduction again.

Now that we have described all the steps of the genetic algorithm in detail, it's time to translate these steps into Processing code. Because the previous description was a bit longwinded, let's look at an overview of the algorithm first. We'll then cover each of the three steps in its own section, working out the code.

SETUP:

Step 1: ***Initialize***. Create a population of N elements, each with randomly generated DNA.

LOOP:

Step 2: ***Selection***. Evaluate the fitness of each element of the population and build a mating pool.

Step 3: ***Reproduction***. Repeat N times:

a) Pick two parents with probability according to relative fitness.
b) Crossover—create a "child" by combining the DNA of these two parents.
c) Mutation—mutate the child's DNA based on a given probability.
d) Add the new child to a new population.

Step 4. Replace the old population with the new population and return to Step 2.

9.7 Code for Creating the Population

Step 1: Initialize Population

If we're going to create a population, we need a data structure to store a list of members of the population. In most cases (such as our typing-monkey example), the number of elements in the population can be fixed, and so we use an array. (Later we'll see examples that involve a growing/shrinking population and we'll use an `ArrayList`.) But an array of what? We need an object that stores the genetic information for a member of the population. Let's call it ***DNA***.

```
class DNA {

}
```

The population will then be an array of DNA objects.

```
DNA[] population = new DNA[100];
```

A population of 100 DNA objects

But what stuff goes in the DNA class? For a typing monkey, its DNA is the random phrase it types, a string of characters.

```
class DNA {
  String phrase;
}
```

While this is perfectly reasonable for this particular example, we're not going to use an actual String object as the genetic code. Instead, we'll use an array of characters.

```
class DNA {
  char[] genes = new char[18];
}
```

Each "gene" is one element of the array. We need 18 genes because "to be or not to be" is 18 characters long.

By using an array, we'll be able to extend all the code we write into other examples. For example, the DNA of a creature in a physics system might be an array of PVectors—or for an image, an array of integers (RGB colors). We can describe any set of properties in an array, and even though a string is convenient for this particular sketch, an array will serve as a better foundation for future evolutionary examples.

Our genetic algorithm dictates that we create a population of N elements, each with *randomly generated DNA*. Therefore, in the object's constructor, we randomly create each character of the array.

```
class DNA {
  char[] genes = new char[18];

  DNA() {
    for (int i = 0; i < genes.length; i++) {
      genes[i] = (char) random(32,128);
    }
  }
}
```

Picking randomly from a range of characters with ASCII values between 32 and 128. For more about ASCII: http://en.wikipedia.org/wiki/ASCII

Now that we have the constructor, we can return to setup() and initialize each DNA object in the population array.

```
DNA[] population = new DNA[100];

void setup() {
  for (int i = 0; i < population.length; i++) {
    population[i] = new DNA();        // Initializing each member of the population
  }
}
```

Our DNA class is not at all complete. We'll need to add functions to it to perform all the other tasks in our genetic algorithm, which we'll do as we walk through steps 2 and 3.

Step 2: Selection

Step 2 reads, *"Evaluate the fitness of each element of the population and build a mating pool."* Let's first evaluate each object's fitness. Earlier we stated that one possible fitness function for our typed phrases is the total number of correct characters. Let's revise this fitness function a little bit and state it as the percentage of correct characters—i.e., the total number of correct characters divided by the total characters.

`Fitness = Total # Characters Correct/Total # Characters`

Where should we calculate the fitness? Since the DNA class contains the genetic information (the phrase we will test against the target phrase), we can write a function inside the DNA class itself to score its own fitness. Let's assume we have a target phrase:

```
String target = "to be or not to be";
```

We can now compare each "gene" against the corresponding character in the target phrase, incrementing a counter each time we get a correct character.

```
class DNA {
  float fitness;                      // We are adding another variable to the DNA class to track fitness.

  void fitness () {                   // Function to score fitness
    int score = 0;
    for (int i = 0; i < genes.length; i++) {
      if (genes[i] == target.charAt(i)) {   // Is the character correct?
        score++;                      // If so, increment the score.
      }
    }
    fitness = float(score)/target.length();   // Fitness is the percentage correct.
  }
```

In the main tab's `draw()`, the very first step we'll take is to call the fitness function for each member of the population.

```
void draw() {

  for (int i = 0; i < population.length; i++) {
    population[i].fitness();
  }
```

After we have all the fitness scores, we can build the "mating pool" that we'll need for the reproduction step. The mating pool is a data structure from which we'll continuously pick two parents. Recalling our description of the selection process, we want to pick parents with probabilities calculated according to fitness. In other words, the members of the population that have the highest fitness scores should be most likely to be picked; those with the lowest scores, the least likely.

In the Introduction (see page 7), we covered the basics of probability and generating a custom distribution of random numbers. We're going to use those techniques to assign a probability to each member of the population, picking parents by spinning the "wheel of fortune." Let's look at Figure 9.2 again.

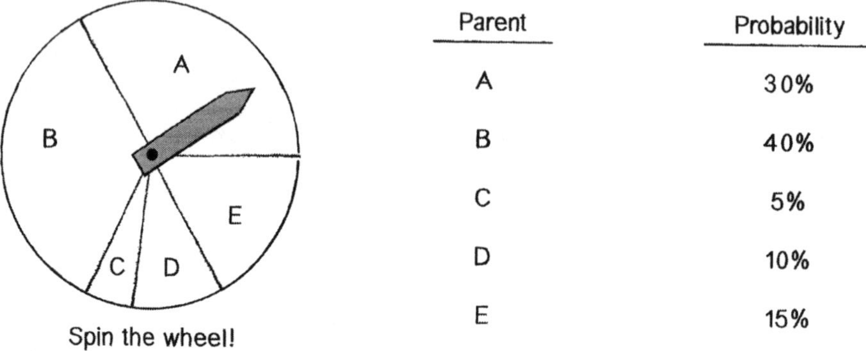

A
B
C
D
E
Spin the wheel!
Parent
Probability
A
30%
B
40%
C
5%
D
10%
E
15%

Figure 9.2 (again)

It might be fun to do something ridiculous and actually program a simulation of a spinning wheel as depicted above. But this is quite unnecessary.

Instead we can pick from the five options (ABCDE) according to their probabilities by filling an `ArrayList` with multiple instances of each parent. In other words, let's say you had a bucket of wooden letters—30 As, 40 Bs, 5 Cs, 15 Ds, and 10 Es.

If you pick a random letter out of that bucket, there's a 30% chance you'll get an A, a 5% chance you'll get a C, and so on. For us, that bucket is an `ArrayList`, and each wooden letter is a potential parent. We add each parent to the `ArrayList` N number of times where N is equal to its percentage score.

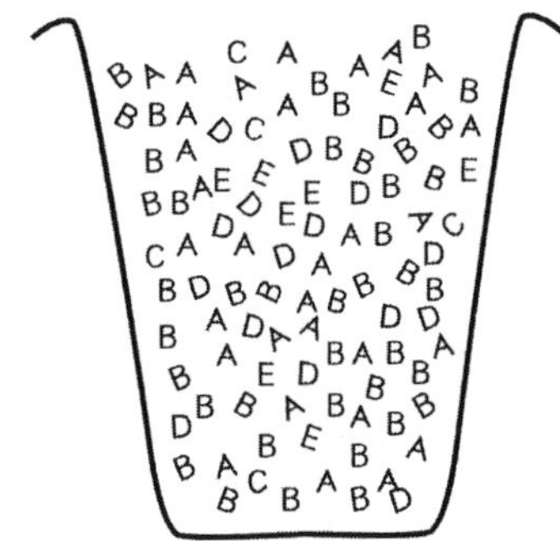

Figure 9.7

```
ArrayList<DNA> matingPool = new ArrayList<DNA>();
```

Start with an empty mating pool.

```
for (int i = 0; i < population.length; i++) {

  int n = int(population[i].fitness * 100);
```

n is equal to fitness times 100, which leaves us with an integer between 0 and 100.

```
  for (int j = 0; j < n; j++) {

    matingPool.add(population[i]);
```

Add each member of the population to the mating pool N times.

```
  }
}
```

Exercise 9.2

One of the other methods we used to generate a custom distribution of random numbers is called the Monte Carlo method. This technique involved picking two random numbers, with the second number acting as a qualifying number and determining if the first random number should be kept or thrown away. Rewrite the above mating pool algorithm to use the Monte Carlo method instead.

Exercise 9.3

In some cases, the wheel of fortune algorithm will have an extraordinarily high preference for some elements over others. Take the following probabilities:

```
A: 98%
B: 1%
C: 1%
```

This is sometimes undesirable given how it will decrease the amount of variety in this system. A solution to this problem is to replace the calculated fitness scores with the ordinals of scoring (meaning their rank).

```
A: 50% (3/6)
B: 33% (2/6)
C: 17% (1/6)
```

Rewrite the mating pool algorithm to use this method instead.

Step 3: Reproduction

With the mating pool ready to go, it's time to make some babies. The first step is to pick two parents. Again, it's somewhat of an arbitrary decision to pick two parents. It certainly mirrors human reproduction and is the standard means in the traditional GA, but in terms of your work, there really aren't any restrictions here. You could choose to perform "asexual" reproduction with one parent, or come up with a scheme for picking three or four parents from which to generate child DNA. For this code demonstration, we'll stick to two parents and call them `parentA` and `parentB`.

First thing we need are two random indices into the mating pool—random numbers between 0 and the size of the `ArrayList`.

```
int a = int(random(matingPool.size()));
int b = int(random(matingPool.size()));
```

We can use these indices to retrieve an actual DNA instance from the mating pool.

```
DNA parentA = matingPool.get(a);
DNA parentB = matingPool.get(b);
```

Because we have multiple instances of the same `DNA` objects in the mating pool (not to mention that we could pick the same random number twice), it's possible that `parentA` and `parentB` could be the same `DNA` object. If we wanted to be strict, we could write some code to ensure that we haven't picked the same parent twice, but we would gain very little efficiency for all that extra code. Still, it's worth trying this as an exercise.

Exercise 9.4

Add code to the above to guarantee that you have picked two unique "parents."

Once we have the two parents, we can perform ***crossover*** to generate the child DNA, followed by ***mutation***.

```
DNA child = parentA.crossover(parentB);    // A function for crossover
child.mutate();                            // A function for mutation
```

Of course, the functions `crossover()` and `mutate()` don't magically exist in our `DNA` class; we have to write them. The way we called `crossover()` above indicates that the function receives an instance of DNA as an argument and returns a new instance of DNA, the child.

```
DNA crossover(DNA partner) {                    // The function receives one argument (DNA) and returns DNA.
  DNA child = new DNA();                        // The child is a new instance of DNA. Note that the DNA is generated randomly in the constructor, but we will overwrite it below with DNA from parents.
  int midpoint = int(random(genes.length));     // Picking a random "midpoint" in the genes array

  for (int i = 0; i < genes.length; i++) {
    if (i > midpoint) child.genes[i] = genes[i];   // Before midpoint copy genes from one parent, after midpoint copy genes from the other parent
    else child.genes[i] = partner.genes[i];
  }

  return child;                                 // Return the new child DNA
}
```

The above crossover function uses the "random midpoint" method of crossover, in which the first section of genes is taken from parent A and the second section from parent B.

Exercise 9.5

Rewrite the crossover function to use the "coin flipping" method instead, in which each gene has a 50% chance of coming from parent A and a 50% chance of coming from parent B.

The mutate() function is even simpler to write than crossover(). All we need to do is loop through the array of genes and for each randomly pick a new character according to the mutation rate. With a mutation rate of 1%, for example, we would pick a new character one time out of a hundred.

```
float mutationRate = 0.01;

if (random(1) < mutationRate) {
                                        // Any code here would be executed 1% of the time.
}
```

The entire function therefore reads:

```
void mutate() {
  for (int i = 0; i < genes.length; i++) {        // Looking at each gene in the array
    if (random(1) < mutationRate) {
      genes[i] = (char) random(32,128);           // Mutation, a new random character
    }
  }
}
```

9.8 Genetic Algorithms: Putting It All Together

You may have noticed that we've essentially walked through the steps of the genetic algorithm twice, once describing it in narrative form and another time with code snippets implementing each of the steps. What I'd like to do in this section is condense the previous two sections into one page, with the algorithm described in just three steps and the corresponding code alongside.

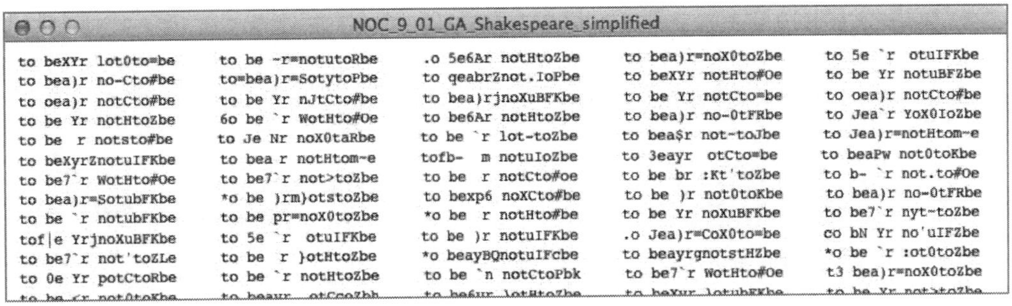

NOC_9_01_GA_Shakespeare_simplified

```
to beXYr lot0to=be      to be ~r=notutoRbe      .o 5e6Ar notHtoZbe      to bea)r=noX0toZbe      to 5e `r  otuIFKbe
to bea)r no-Cto#be      to=bea)r=SotytoPbe      to qeabrZnot.IoPbe      to beXYr notHto#Oe      to be Yr notuBFZbe
to oea)r notCto#be      to be Yr nJtCto#be      to bea)rjnoXuBFKbe      to be Yr notCto=be      to oea)r notCto#be
to be Yr notHtoZbe      6o be `r WotHto#Oe      to be6Ar notHtoZbe      to bea)r no-0tFRbe      to Jea`r YoX0IoZbe
to be  r notsto#be      to Je Nr noX0taRbe      to be `r lot-toZbe      to bea$r not~toJbe      to Jea)r=notHtom~e
to beXyrZnotuIFKbe      to bea r notHtom~e      tofb-  m notuIoZbe      to 3eayr  otCto=be      to beaPw not0toKbe
to be7`r WotHto#Oe      to be7`r not>toZbe      to be  r notCto#oe      to be br :Kt'toZbe      to b- `r not.to#Oe
to bea)r=SotubFKbe      *o be )rm}otstoZbe      to bexp6 noXCto#be      to be )r not0toKbe      to bea)r no-0tFRbe
to be `r notubFKbe      to be pr=noX0toZbe      *o be  r notHto#be      to be Yr noXuBFKbe      to be7`r nyt~toZbe
tof|e YrjnoXuBFKbe      to 5e `r  otuIFKbe      to be )r notuIFKbe      .o Jea)r=CoX0to=be      co bN Yr no'uIFZbe
to be7`r not'toZLe      to be  r }otHtoZbe      *o beayBQnotuIFcbe      to beayrgnotstHZbe      *o be `r :ot0toZbe
to 0e Yr potCtoRbe      to be `r notHtoZbe      to be `n notCtoPbk      to be7`r WotHto#Oe      t3 bea)r=noX0toZbe
```

Example 9.1: Genetic algorithm: Evolving Shakespeare

Variables we need for our GA

Mutation rate

```
float mutationRate;
```

Population total

```
int totalPopulation = 150;
```

Population array

```
DNA[] population;
```

Mating pool ArrayList

```
ArrayList<DNA> matingPool;
```

Target phrase

```
String target;

void setup() {
  size(640, 360);
```

Initializing target phrase and mutation rate

```
  target = "to be or not to be";
  mutationRate = 0.01;
```

Step 1: Initialize Population

```
  population = new DNA[totalPopulation];
  for (int i = 0; i < population.length; i++) {
    population[i] = new DNA();
  }
}

void draw() {
```

Step 2: Selection

Step 2a: Calculate fitness.

```
  for (int i = 0; i < population.length; i++) {
    population[i].fitness();
  }
```

```
ArrayList<DNA> matingPool = new ArrayList<DNA>();    Step 2b: Build mating pool.

for (int i = 0; i < population.length; i++) {
  int n = int(population[i].fitness * 100);         Add each member n times according to its
  for (int j = 0; j < n; j++) {                      fitness score.
    matingPool.add(population[i]);
  }
}

for (int i = 0; i < population.length; i++) {       Step 3: Reproduction
  int a = int(random(matingPool.size()));
  int b = int(random(matingPool.size()));
  DNA partnerA = matingPool.get(a);
  DNA partnerB = matingPool.get(b);
  DNA child = partnerA.crossover(partnerB);          Step 3a: Crossover
  child.mutate(mutationRate);                        Step 3b: Mutation

  population[i] = child;                             Note that we are overwriting the population
  }                                                  with the new children. When draw() loops,
}                                                    we will perform all the same steps with the
                                                     new population of children.
```

The main tab precisely mirrors the steps of the genetic algorithm. However, most of the functionality called upon is actually present in the DNA class itself.

```
class DNA {

  char[] genes;
  float fitness;

  DNA() {                                            Create DNA randomly.
    genes = new char[target.length()];
    for (int i = 0; i < genes.length; i++) {
      genes[i] = (char) random(32,128);
    }
  }

  void fitness() {                                   Calculate fitness.
     int score = 0;
     for (int i = 0; i < genes.length; i++) {
        if (genes[i] == target.charAt(i)) {
          score++;
        }
     }
     fitness = float(score)/target.length();
  }
```

```
DNA crossover(DNA partner) {
  DNA child = new DNA(genes.length);
  int midpoint = int(random(genes.length));
  for (int i = 0; i < genes.length; i++) {
    if (i > midpoint) child.genes[i] = genes[i];
    else              child.genes[i] = partner.genes[i];
  }
  return child;
}
```

Crossover

```
void mutate(float mutationRate) {
  for (int i = 0; i < genes.length; i++) {
    if (random(1) < mutationRate) {
      genes[i] = (char) random(32,128);
    }
  }
}
```

Mutation

```
String getPhrase() {
  return new String(genes);
}
```

Convert to String—PHENOTYPE.

```
}
```

Exercise 9.6

Add features to the above example to report more information about the progress of the genetic algorithm itself. For example, show the phrase closest to the target each generation, as well as report on the number of generations, average fitness, etc. Stop the genetic algorithm once it has solved the phrase. Consider writing a `Population` class to manage the GA, instead of including all the code in draw().

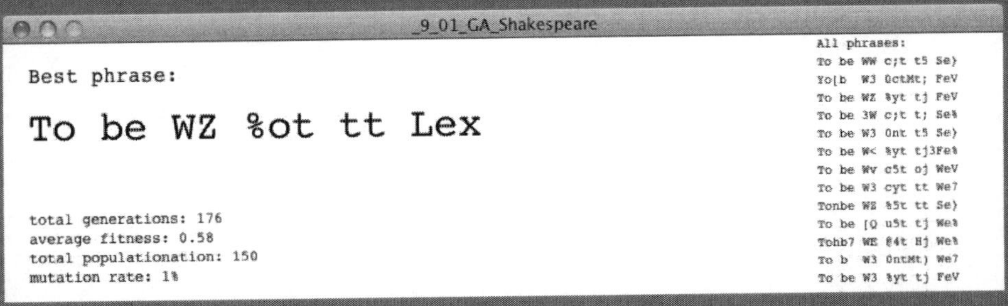

9.9 Genetic Algorithms: Make Them Your Own

The nice thing about using genetic algorithms in a project is that example code can easily be ported from application to application. The core mechanics of selection and reproduction don't need to change. There are, however, three key components to genetic algorithms that you, the developer, will have to customize for each use. This is crucial to moving beyond trivial demonstrations of evolutionary simulations (as in the Shakespeare example) to creative uses in projects that you make in Processing and other creative programming environments.

Key #1: Varying the variables

There aren't a lot of variables to the genetic algorithm itself. In fact, if you look at the previous example's code, you'll see only two global variables (not including the arrays and `ArrayLists` to store the population and mating pool).

```
float mutationRate = 0.01;
int totalPopulation = 150;
```

These two variables can greatly affect the behavior of the system, and it's not such a good idea to arbitrarily assign them values (though tweaking them through trial and error is a perfectly reasonable way to arrive at optimal values).

The values I chose for the Shakespeare demonstration were picked to virtually guarantee that the genetic algorithm would solve for the phrase, but not too quickly (approximately 1,000 generations on average) so as to demonstrate the process over a reasonable period of time. A much larger population, however, would yield faster results (if the goal were algorithmic efficiency rather than demonstration). Here is a table of some results.

Total Population	Mutation Rate	Number of Generations until Phrase Solved	Total Time (in seconds) until Phrase Solved
150	1%	1089	18.8
300	1%	448	8.2
1,000	1%	71	1.8
50,000	1%	27	4.3

Notice how increasing the population size drastically reduces the number of generations needed to solve for the phrase. However, it doesn't necessarily reduce the amount of time. Once our population balloons to fifty thousand elements, the sketch runs slowly, given the amount of time required to process fitness and build a mating pool out of so many elements. (There are, of course, optimizations that could be made should you require such a large population.)

In addition to the population size, the mutation rate can greatly affect performance.

Total Population	Mutation Rate	Number of Generations until Phrase Solved	Total Time (in seconds) until Phrase Solved
1,000	0%	37 or never?	1.2 or never?
1,000	1%	71	1.8
1,000	2%	60	1.6
1,000	10%	never?	never?

Without any mutation at all (0%), you just have to get lucky. If all the correct characters are present somewhere in some member of the initial population, you'll evolve the phrase very quickly. If not, there is no way for the sketch to ever reach the exact phrase. Run it a few times and you'll see both instances. In addition, once the mutation rate gets high enough (10%, for example), there is so much randomness involved (1 out of every 10 letters is random in each new child) that the simulation is pretty much back to a random typing monkey. In theory, it will eventually solve the phrase, but you may be waiting much, much longer than is reasonable.

Key #2: The fitness function

Playing around with the mutation rate or population total is pretty easy and involves little more than typing numbers in your sketch. The real hard work of a developing a genetic algorithm is in writing a fitness function. If you cannot define your problem's goals and evaluate numerically how well those goals have been achieved, then you will not have successful evolution in your simulation.

Before we think about other scenarios with other fitness functions, let's look at flaws in our Shakespearean fitness function. Consider solving for a phrase that is not nineteen characters long, but one thousand. Now, let's say there are two members of the population, one with 800 characters correct and one with 801. Here are their fitness scores:

Phrase A:	800 characters correct	fitness = 80%
Phrase B:	801 characters correct	fitness = 80.1%

There are a couple of problems here. First, we are adding elements to the mating pool N numbers of times, where N equals fitness multiplied by 100. Objects can only be added to an `ArrayList` a whole number of times, and so A and B will both be added 80 times, giving them an equal probability of being selected. Even with an improved solution that takes floating point probabilities into account, 80.1% is only a teeny tiny bit higher than 80%. But getting 801 characters right is a whole lot better than 800 in the evolutionary scenario. We really want to make that additional character count. We want the fitness score for 801 characters to be exponentially better than the score for 800.

To put it another way, let's graph the fitness function.

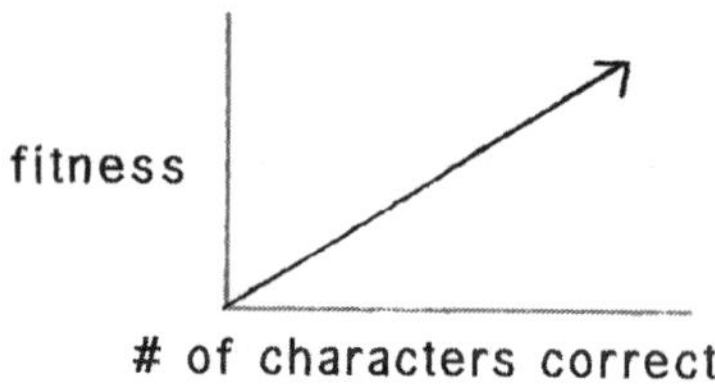

Figure 9.8

This is a linear graph; as the number of characters goes up, so does the fitness score. However, what if the fitness increased exponentially as the number of correct characters increased? Our graph could then look something like:

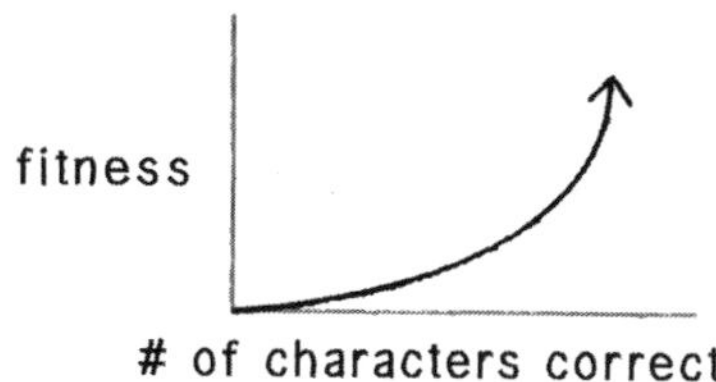

Figure 9.9

The more correct characters, the even greater the fitness. We can achieve this type of result in a number of different ways. For example, we could say:

```
fitness = (number of correct characters) * (number of correct characters)
```

Let's say we have two members of the population, one with five correct characters and one with six. The number 6 is a 20% increase over the number 5. Let's look at the fitness scores squared.

Characters correct	Fitness
5	25
6	36

The fitness scores increase exponentially relative to the number of correct characters. 36 is a 44% increase over 25.

Here's another formula.

$$\texttt{fitness} = 2^{\texttt{(number of correct characters)}}$$

Characters correct	Fitness
1	2
2	4
3	8
4	16

Here, the fitness scores increase at a faster rate, doubling with each additional correct character.

Exercise 9.7

Rewrite the fitness function to increase exponentially according to the number of correct characters. Note that you will also have to normalize the fitness values to a range between 0 and 1 so they can be added to the mating pool a reasonable number of times.

While this rather specific discussion of exponential vs. linear fitness functions is an important detail in the design of a good fitness function, I don't want us to miss the more important point here: *Design your own fitness function!* I seriously doubt that any project you undertake in Processing with genetic algorithms will actually involve counting the correct number of characters in a string. In the context of this book, it's more likely you will be looking to evolve a creature that is part of a physics system. Perhaps you are looking to optimize the weights of steering behaviors so a creature can best escape a predator or avoid an obstacle or make it through a maze. You have to ask yourself what you're hoping to evaluate.

Let's consider a racing simulation in which a vehicle is evolving a design optimized for speed.

```
fitness = total number of frames required for vehicle to reach target
```

How about a cannon that is evolving the optimal way to shoot a target?

```
fitness = cannonball distance to target
```

The design of computer-controlled players in a game is also a common scenario. Let's say you are programming a soccer game in which the user is the goalie. The rest of the players are controlled by your program and have a set of parameters that determine how they kick a ball towards the goal. What would the fitness score for any given player be?

```
fitness = total goals scored
```

This, obviously, is a simplistic take on the game of soccer, but it illustrates the point. The more goals a player scores, the higher its fitness, and the more likely its genetic information will appear in the next game. Even with a fitness function as simple as the one described here, this scenario is demonstrating something very powerful—the adaptability of a system. If the players continue to evolve from game to game to game, when a new *human* user enters the game with a completely different strategy, the system will quickly discover that the fitness scores are going down and evolve a new optimal strategy. It will adapt. (Don't worry, there is very little danger in this resulting in sentient robots that will enslave all humans.)

In the end, if you do not have a fitness function that effectively evaluates the performance of the individual elements of your population, you will not have any evolution. And the fitness function from one example will likely not apply to a totally different project. So this is the part where you get to shine. You have to design a function, sometimes from scratch, that works for your particular project. And where do you do this? All you have to edit are those few lines of code inside the function that computes the fitness variable.

```
void fitness() {
  ????????????
  ????????????
  fitness = ??????????
}
```

Key #3: Genotype and Phenotype

The final key to designing your own genetic algorithm relates to how you choose to encode the properties of your system. What are you trying to express, and how can you translate that expression into a bunch of numbers? What is the genotype and phenotype?

When talking about the fitness function, we happily assumed we could create computer-controlled kickers that each had a "set of parameters that determine how they kick a ball towards the goal." However, what those parameters are and how you choose to encode them is up to you.

We started with the Shakespeare example because of how easy it was to design both the genotype (an array of characters) and its expression, the phenotype (the string drawn in the window).

The good news is—and we hinted at this at the start of this chapter—you've really been doing this all along. Anytime you write a class in Processing, you make a whole bunch of variables.

```
class Vehicle {
  float maxspeed;
  float maxforce;
  float size;
  float separationWeight;
  // etc.
```

All we need to do to evolve those parameters is to turn them into an array, so that the array can be used with all of the functions—`crossover()`, `mutate()`, etc.—found in the `DNA` class. One common solution is to use an array of floating point numbers between 0 and 1.

```
class DNA {

  float[] genes;                          An array of floats

  DNA(int num) {
    genes = new float[num];
    for (int i = 0; i < genes.length; i++) {
      genes[i] = float(1);                Always pick a number between 0 and 1.
    }
  }
```

Notice how we've now put the genetic data (genotype) and its expression (phenotype) into two separate classes. The `DNA` class is the genotype and the `Vehicle` class uses a `DNA` object to drive its behaviors and express that data visually—it is the phenotype. The two can be linked by creating a `DNA` instance inside the `Vehicle` class itself.

```
class Vehicle {
  DNA dna;                                A DNA object embedded into the Vehicle
                                          class

  float maxspeed;
  float maxforce;
  float size;
  float separationWeight;
                                          Etc.

  Vehicle() {
    DNA = new DNA(4);
```

```
    maxspeed = dna.genes[0];                    Using the genes to set variables
    maxforce = dna.genes[1];
    size = dna.genes[2];
    separationWeight = dna.genes[3];
  }                                             Etc.
```

Of course, you most likely don't want all your variables to have a range between 0 and 1. But rather than try to remember how to adjust those ranges in the DNA class itself, it's easier to pull the genetic information from the DNA object and use Processing's `map()` function to change the range. For example, if you want a size variable between 10 and 72, you would say:

```
    size = map(dna.genes[2],0,1,10,72);
```

In other cases, you will want to design a genotype that is an array of objects. Consider the design of a rocket with a series of "thruster" engines. You could describe each thruster with a `PVector` that outlines its direction and relative strength.

```
class DNA {

  PVector[] genes;                              The genotype is an array of PVectors.

  DNA(int num) {
    genes = new float[num];
    for (int i = 0; i < genes.length; i++) {
      genes[i] = PVector.random2D();            A PVector pointing in a random direction
      genes[i].mult(random(10));                And scaled randomly
    }
  }
```

The phenotype would be a `Rocket` class that participates in a physics system.

```
class Rocket {
  DNA dna;
  // etc.
```

What's great about this technique of dividing the genotype and phenotype into separate classes (`DNA` and `Rocket` for example) is that when it comes time to build all of the code, you'll notice that the `DNA` class we developed earlier remains intact. The only thing that changes is the array's data type (`float`, `PVector`, etc.) and the expression of that data in the phenotype class.

In the next section, we'll follow this idea a bit further and walk through the necessary steps for an example that involves moving bodies and an array of `PVectors` as DNA.

9.10 Evolving Forces: Smart Rockets

We picked the rocket idea for a specific reason. In 2009, Jer Thorp (http://blprnt.com) released a genetic algorithms example on his blog entitled "Smart Rockets." Jer points out that NASA uses evolutionary computing techniques to solve all sorts of problems, from satellite antenna design to rocket firing patterns. This inspired him to create a Flash demonstration of evolving rockets. Here is a description of the scenario:

A population of rockets launches from the bottom of the screen with the goal of hitting a target at the top of the screen (with obstacles blocking a straight line path).

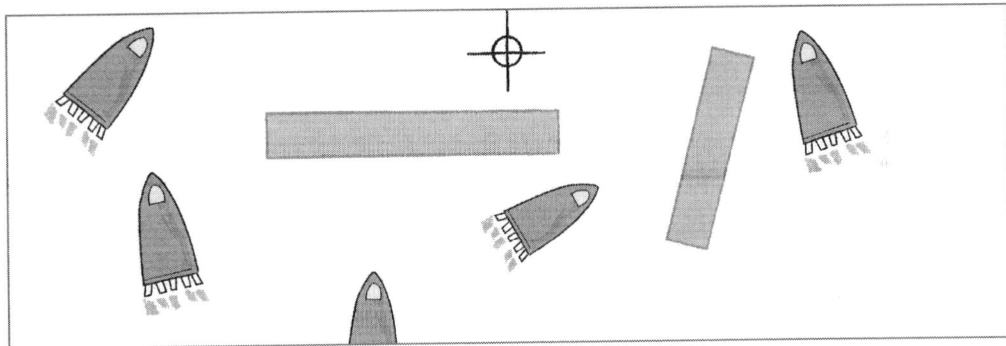

Figure 9.10

Each rocket is equipped with five thrusters of variable strength and direction. The thrusters don't fire all at once and continuously; rather, they fire one at a time in a custom sequence.

Figure 9.11

In this section, we're going to evolve our own simplified Smart Rockets, inspired by Jer Thorp's. When we get to the end of the section, we'll leave implementing some of Jer's additional advanced features as an exercise.

Our rockets will have only one thruster, and this thruster will be able to fire in any direction with any strength for every frame of animation. This isn't particularly realistic, but it will make building out the framework a little easier. (We can always make the rocket and its thrusters more advanced and realistic later.)

Let's start by taking our basic `Mover` class from Chapter 2 examples and renaming it `Rocket`.

```
class Rocket {
```

```
  PVector location;          // A rocket has three vectors: location, velocity, acceleration.
  PVector velocity;
  PVector acceleration;

  void applyForce(PVector f) {          // Accumulating forces into acceleration (Newton's 2nd law)
    acceleration.add(f);
  }

  void update() {          // Our simple physics model (Euler integration)
    velocity.add(acceleration);          // Velocity changes according to acceleration.
    location.add(velocity);          // Location changes according to velocity.
    acceleration.mult(0);
  }
}
```

Using the above framework, we can implement our smart rocket by saying that for every frame of animation, we call `applyForce()` with a new force. The "thruster" applies a single force to the rocket each time through `draw()`.

Considering this example, let's go through the three keys to programming our own custom genetic algorithm example as outlined in the previous section.

Key #1: Population size and mutation rate

We can actually hold off on this first key for the moment. Our strategy will be to pick some reasonable numbers (a population of 100 rockets, mutation rate of 1%) and build out the system, playing with these numbers once we have our sketch up and running.

Key #2: The fitness function

We stated the goal of a rocket reaching a target. In other words, the closer a rocket gets to the target, the higher the fitness. Fitness is inversely proportional to distance: the smaller the distance, the greater the fitness; the greater the distance, the smaller the fitness.

Let's assume we have a `PVector` target.

```
void fitness() {
  float d = PVector.dist(location,target);          // How close did we get?
  fitness = 1/d;          // Fitness is inversely proportional to distance.
}
```

This is perhaps the simplest fitness function we could write. By using one divided by distance, large distances become small numbers and small distances become large.

distance	1 / distance
300	1 / 300 = 0.0033
100	1 / 100 = 0.01
5	1 / 5 = 0.2
1	1 / 1 = 1.0
0.1	1 / 0.1 = 10

And if we wanted to use our exponential trick from the previous section, we could use one divided by distance squared.

distance	1 / distance	$(1 / distance)^2$
300	1 / 400 = 0.0025	0.00000625
100	1 / 100 = 0.01	0.0001
5	1 / 5 = 0.2	0.04
1	1 / 1 = 1.0	1.0
0.1	1 / 0.1 = 10	100

There are several additional improvements we'll want to make to the fitness function, but this simple one is a good start.

```
void fitness() {
  float d = PVector.dist(location,target);
  fitness = pow(1/d,2);                    Squaring 1 divided by distance
}
```

Key #3: Genotype and Phenotype

We stated that each rocket has a thruster that fires in a variable direction with a variable magnitude in each frame. And so we need a `PVector` for each frame of animation. Our genotype, the data required to encode the rocket's behavior, is therefore an array of `PVector`s.

```
class DNA {
  PVector[] genes;
```

The happy news here is that we don't really have to do anything else to the DNA class. All of the functionality we developed for the typing monkey (crossover and mutation) applies here. The one difference we do have to consider is how we initialize the array of genes. With the typing monkey, we had an array of characters and picked a random character for each element of the array. Here we'll do exactly the same thing and initialize a DNA sequence as an array of random PVectors. Now, your instinct in creating a random PVector might be as follows:

```
PVector v = new PVector(random(-1,1),random(-1,1));
```

This is perfectly fine and will likely do the trick. However, if we were to draw every single possible vector we might pick, the result would fill a square (see Figure 9.12). In this case, it probably doesn't matter, but there is a slight bias to diagonals here given that a PVector from the center of a square to a corner is longer than a purely vertical or horizontal one.

Figure 9.12

What would be better here is to pick a random angle and make a PVector of length one from that angle, giving us a circle (see Figure 9.13). This could be easily done with a quick polar to Cartesian conversion (see page 112), but a quicker path to the result is just to use PVector's random2D().

Figure 9.13

```
for (int i = 0; i < genes.length; i++) {
  genes[i] = PVector.random2D();          // Making a PVector from a random angle
}
```

A PVector of length one is actually going to be quite a large force. Remember, forces are applied to acceleration, which accumulates into velocity thirty times per second. So, for this example, we can also add one more variable to the DNA class: a maximum force that scales all the PVectors. This will control the thruster power.

```
class DNA {

  PVector[] genes;                    // The genetic sequence is an array of PVectors.

  float maxforce = 0.1;               // How strong can the thrusters be?

  DNA() {
    genes = new PVector[lifetime];    // We need a PVector for every frame of the rocket's life.
    for (int i = 0; i < genes.length; i++) {
      genes[i] = PVector.random2D();
      genes[i].mult(random(0, maxforce));   // Scaling the PVectors randomly, but no stronger than maximum force
    }
  }
```

Notice also that we created an array of `PVectors` with length lifetime. We need a `PVector` for each frame of the rocket's life, and the above assumes the existence of a global variable lifetime that stores the total number of frames in each generation's life cycle.

The expression of this array of `PVectors`, the phenotype, is a `Rocket` class modeled on our basic `PVector` and forces examples from Chapter 2. All we need to do is add an instance of a DNA object to the class. The fitness variable will also live here. Only the `Rocket` object knows how to compute its distance to the target, and therefore the fitness function will live here in the phenotype as well.

```
class Rocket {

  DNA dna;                            // A Rocket has DNA.

  float fitness;                      // A Rocket has fitness.

  PVector location;
  PVector velocity;
  PVector acceleration;
```

What are we using the DNA for? We are marching through the array of `PVectors` and applying them one at a time as a force to the rocket. To do this, we'll also have to add an integer that acts as a counter to walk through the array.

```
  int geneCounter = 0;

  void run() {
    applyForce(dna.genes[geneCounter]);   // Apply a force from the genes array.
    geneCounter++;                        // Go to the next force in the genes array.
```

```
    update();                              Update the Rocket's physics.
  }
```

9.11 Smart Rockets: Putting It All Together

We now have our DNA class (genotype) and our Rocket class (phenotype). The last piece of the puzzle is a Population class, which manages an array of rockets and has the functionality for selection and reproduction. Again, the happy news here is that we barely have to change anything from the Shakespeare monkey example. The process for building a mating pool and generating a new array of child rockets is exactly the same as what we did with our population of strings.

```
class Population {

  float mutationRate;                  Population has variables to keep track of
  Rocket[] population;                 mutation rate, current population array,
  ArrayList<Rocket> matingPool;        mating pool, and number of generations.
  int generations;

  void fitness() {}                    These functions haven't changed, so no
  void selection() {}                  need to go through the code again.
  void reproduction() {}
```

There is one fairly significant change, however. With typing monkeys, a random phrase was evaluated as soon as it was created. The string of characters had no lifespan; it existed purely for the purpose of calculating its fitness and then we moved on. The rockets, however, need to live for a period of time before they can be evaluated; they need to be given a chance to make their attempt at reaching the target. Therefore, we need to add one more function to the Population class that runs the physics simulation itself. This is identical to what we did in the run() function of a particle system—update all the particle locations and draw them.

```
  void live () {
    for (int i = 0; i < population.length; i++) {
      population[i].run();             The run function takes care of the forces,
    }                                  updating the rocket's location, and
  }                                    displaying it.
```

Finally, we're ready for setup() and draw(). Here in the main tab, our primary responsibility is to implement the steps of the genetic algorithm in the appropriate order by calling the functions in the Population class.

```
population.fitness();
population.selection();
population.reproduction();
```

However, unlike the Shakespeare example, we don't want to do this every frame. Rather, our steps work as follows:

1. Create a population of rockets
2. Let the rockets live for N frames
3. Evolve the next generation
    - Selection
    - Reproduction
4. Return to Step #2

Example 9.2: Simple Smart Rockets

```
int lifetime;
```

How many frames does a generation live for?

```
int lifeCounter;
```

What frame are we on?

```
Population population;
```

The population

```
void setup() {
  size(640, 480);
  lifetime = 500;
  lifeCounter = 0;

  float mutationRate = 0.01;
```

```
  population = new Population(mutationRate, 50);
}

void draw() {
  background(255);
  if (lifeCounter < lifetime) {
    population.live();
    lifeCounter++;
  } else {
    lifeCounter = 0;
    population.fitness();
    population.selection();
    population.reproduction();
  }
}
```

Step 1: Create the population. Here is where we could play with the mutation rate and population size.

The revised genetic algorithm

Step 2: The rockets live their life until lifeCounter reaches lifetime.

When lifetime is reached, reset lifeCounter and evolve the next generation (Steps 3 and 4, selection and reproduction).

The above example works, but it isn't particularly interesting. After all, the rockets simply evolve to having DNA with a bunch of vectors that point straight upwards. In the next example, we're going to talk through two suggested improvements for the example and provide code snippets that implement these improvements.

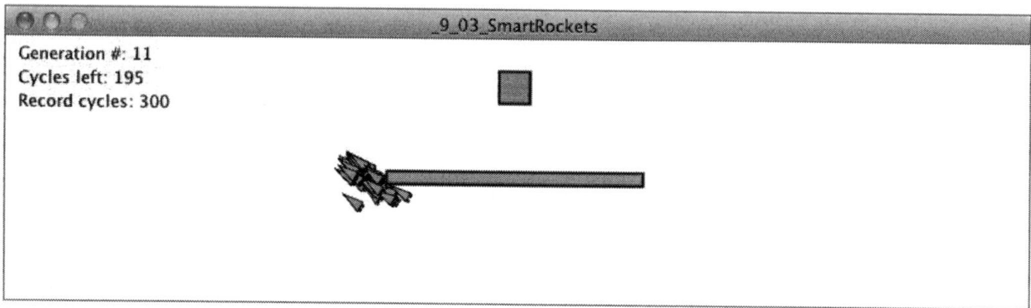

Improvement #1: Obstacles

Adding obstacles that the rockets must avoid will make the system more complex and demonstrate the power of the evolutionary algorithm more effectively. We can make rectangular, stationary obstacles fairly easily by creating a class that stores a location and dimensions.

Example 9.3: Smart Rockets

```
class Obstacle {

  PVector location;
  float w,h;
```

An obstacle is a location (top left corner of rectangle) with a width and height.

We can also write a `contains()` function that will `return true` or `return false` to determine if a rocket has hit the obstacle.

```
  boolean contains(PVector v) {
    if (v.x > location.x && v.x < location.x + w && v.y > location.y && v.y <
location.y + h) {
      return true;
    } else {
      return false;
    }
  }
```

Assuming we make an `ArrayList` of obstacles, we can then have each rocket check to see if it has collided with an obstacle and set a `boolean` flag to be true if it does, adding a function to the rocket class.

```
  void obstacles() {
    for (Obstacle obs : obstacles) {
      if (obs.contains(location)) {
        stopped = true;
      }
    }
  }
```

This new function lives in the rocket class and checks if a rocket has hit an obstacle.

If the rocket hits an obstacle, we choose to stop it from updating its location.

```
  void run() {
    if (!stopped) {
      applyForce(dna.genes[geneCounter]);
      geneCounter = (geneCounter + 1) % dna.genes.length;
      update();
      obstacles();
    }
  }
```

Only run the rocket if it doesn't hit an obstacle.

And we also have an opportunity to adjust the rocket's fitness. We consider it to be pretty terrible if the rocket hits an obstacle, and so its fitness should be greatly reduced.

```
void fitness() {
  float d = dist(location.x, location.y, target.location.x, target.location.y);
  fitness = pow(1/d, 2);
  if (stopped) fitness *= 0.1;
}
```

Improvement #2: Evolve reaching the target faster

If you look closely at our first Smart Rockets example, you'll notice that the rockets are not rewarded for getting to the target faster. The only variable in their fitness calculation is the distance to the target at the end of the generation's life. In fact, in the event that the rockets get very close to the target but overshoot it and fly past, they may actually be penalized for getting to the target faster. Slow and steady wins the race in this case.

We could improve the algorithm to optimize for speed a number of ways. First, instead of using the distance to the target at the end of the generation, we could use the distance that is the closest to the target at any point during the rocket's life. We would call this the rocket's "record" distance. (All of the code snippets in this section live inside the `Rocket` class.)

```
void checkTarget() {
  float d = dist(location.x, location.y, target.location.x, target.location.y);
  if (d < recordDist) recordDist = d;
```

Every frame, we check its distance and see if it's closer than the "record" distance. If it is, we have a new record.

In addition, a rocket should be rewarded according to how quickly it reaches the target. The faster it reaches the target, the higher the fitness. The slower, the lower. To accomplish this, we can increment a counter every cycle of the rocket's life until it reaches the target. At the end of its life, the counter will equal the amount of time the rocket took to reach that target.

```
  if (target.contains(location)) {
    hitTarget = true;
  } else if (!hitTarget) {
    finishTime++;
  }
}
```

If the object reaches the target, set a boolean flag to true.

As long as we haven't yet reached the target, keep incrementing the counter.

Fitness is also inversely proportional to `finishTime`, and so we can improve our fitness function as follows:

```
void fitness() {
  fitness = (1/(finishTime*recordDist));
```

Finish time and record distance!

```
    fitness = pow(fitness, 2);              Make it exponential.

    if (stopped) fitness *= 0.1;            Fitness goes way down if you hit an
                                            obstacle.

    if (hitTarget) fitness *= 2;            You are rewarded for reaching the target.
  }
```

These improvements are both incorporated into the code for Example 9.3: Smart Rockets.

Exercise 9.8

Create a more complex obstacle course. As you make it more difficult for the rockets to reach the target, do you need to improve other aspects of the GA—for example, the fitness function?

Exercise 9.9

Implement the rocket firing pattern of Jer Thorp's Smart Rockets. Each rocket only gets five thrusters (of any direction and strength) that follow a firing sequence (of arbitrary length). Jer's simulation (http://www.blprnt.com/smartrockets/) also gives the rockets a finite amount of fuel.

Exercise 9.10

Visualize the rockets differently. Can you draw a line for the shortest path to the target? Can you add particle systems that act as smoke in the direction of the rocket thrusters?

Exercise 9.11

Another way to achieve a similar result is to evolve a flow field. Can you make the genotype of a rocket a flow field of `PVectors`?

One of the more famous implementations of genetic algorithms in computer graphics is Karl Sims's "Evolved Virtual Creatures." In Sims's work, a population of digital creatures (in a simulated physics environment) is evaluated for the creatures' ability to perform tasks, such as swimming, running, jumping, following, and competing for a green cube.

One of the innovations in Sims's work is a node-based genotype. In other words, the creature's DNA is not a linear list of `PVectors` or numbers, but a map of nodes. (For an example of this, take a look at Exercise 5.15 (see page 256), toxiclibs' Force Directed Graph.) The phenotype is the creature's design itself, a network of limbs connected with muscles.

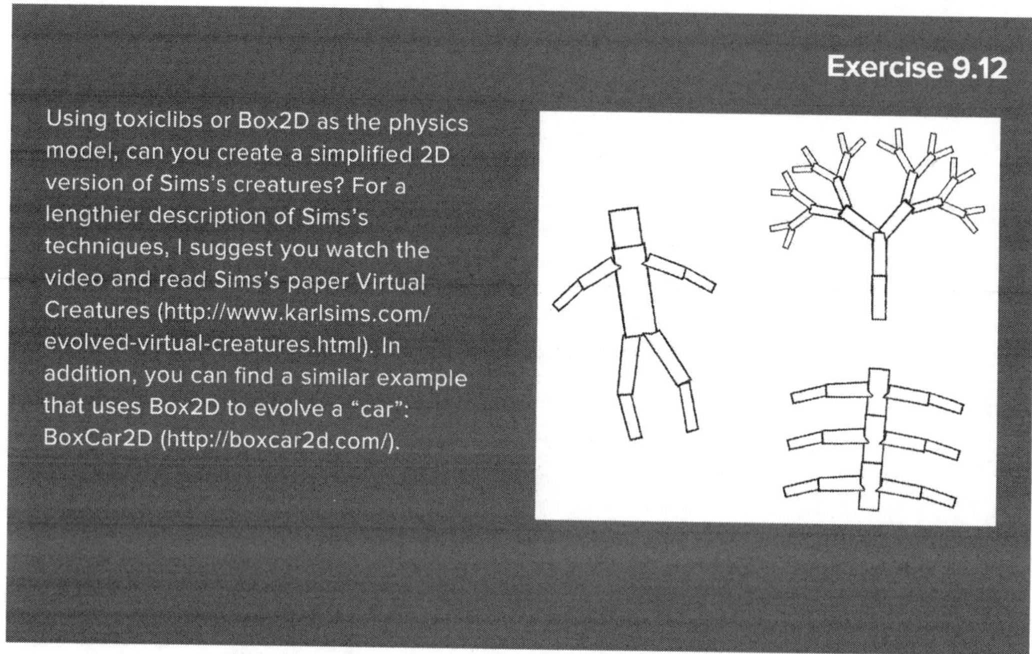

Exercise 9.12

Using toxiclibs or Box2D as the physics model, can you create a simplified 2D version of Sims's creatures? For a lengthier description of Sims's techniques, I suggest you watch the video and read Sims's paper Virtual Creatures (http://www.karlsims.com/evolved-virtual-creatures.html). In addition, you can find a similar example that uses Box2D to evolve a "car": BoxCar2D (http://boxcar2d.com/).

9.12 Interactive Selection

In addition to Evolved Virtual Creatures, Sims is also well known for his museum installation *Galapagos*. Originally installed in the Intercommunication Center in Tokyo in 1997, the installation consists of twelve monitors displaying computer-generated images. These images evolve over time, following the genetic algorithm steps of selection and reproduction. The innovation here is not the use of the genetic algorithm itself, but rather the strategy behind the fitness function. In front of each monitor is a sensor on the floor that can detect the presence of a user viewing the screen. The fitness of an image is tied to the length of time that viewers look at the image. This is known as *interactive selection*, a genetic algorithm with fitness values assigned by users.

Think of all the rating systems you've ever used. Could you evolve the perfect movie by scoring all films according to your Netflix ratings? The perfect singer according to American Idol voting?

To illustrate this technique, we're going to build a population of simple faces. Each face will have a set of properties: head size, head color, eye location, eye size, mouth color, mouth location, mouth width, and mouth height.

The face's DNA (genotype) is an array of floating point numbers between 0 and 1, with a single value for each property.

Figure 9.14

```
class DNA {

  float[] genes;
  int len = 20;                    We need 20 numbers to draw the face.

  DNA() {
    genes = new float[len];
    for (int i = 0; i < genes.length; i++) {
      genes[i] = random(0,1);      Each gene is a random float between 0 and 1.
    }
  }
```

The phenotype is a Face class that includes an instance of a DNA object.

```
class Face {

  DNA dna;
  float fitness;
```

When it comes time to draw the face on screen, we can use Processing's `map()` function to convert any gene value to the appropriate range for pixel dimensions or color values. (In this case, we are also using `colorMode()` to set the RGB ranges between 0 and 1.)

```
void display() {
  float r          = map(dna.genes[0],0,1,0,70);   Using map() to convert the genes to a range for drawing the face.
  color c          = color(dna.genes[1],dna.genes[2],dna.genes[3]);
  float eye_y      = map(dna.genes[4],0,1,0,5);
  float eye_x      = map(dna.genes[5],0,1,0,10);
  float eye_size   = map(dna.genes[5],0,1,0,10);
  color eyecolor   = color(dna.genes[4],dna.genes[5],dna.genes[6]);
  color mouthColor = color(dna.genes[7],dna.genes[8],dna.genes[9]);
  float mouth_y    = map(dna.genes[5],0,1,0,25);
  float mouth_x    = map(dna.genes[5],0,1,-25,25);
  float mouthw     = map(dna.genes[5],0,1,0,50);
  float mouthh     = map(dna.genes[5],0,1,0,10);
```

So far, we're not really doing anything new. This is what we've done in every GA example so far. What's new is that we are not going to write a `fitness()` function in which the score is computed based on a math formula. Instead, we are going to ask the user to assign the fitness.

Now, how best to ask a user to assign fitness is really more of an interaction design problem, and it isn't really within the scope of this book. So we're not going to launch into an elaborate discussion of how to program sliders or build your own hardware dials or build a Web app for users to submit online scores. How you choose to acquire fitness scores is really up to you and the particular application you are developing.

For this simple demonstration, we'll increase fitness whenever a user rolls the mouse over a face. The next generation is created when the user presses a button with an "evolve next generation" label.

Let's look at how the steps of the genetic algorithm are applied in the main tab, noting how fitness is assigned according to mouse interaction and the next generation is created on a button press. The rest of the code for checking mouse locations, button interactions, etc. can be found in the accompanying example code.

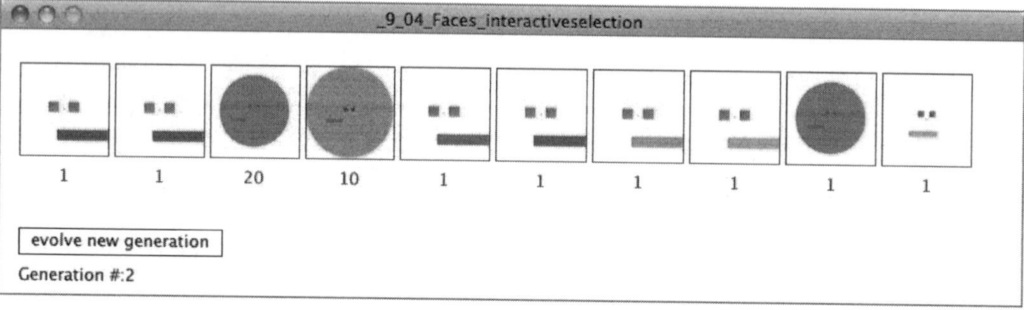

Example 9.4: Interactive selection

```
Population population;
Button button;

void setup() {
  size(780,200);
  float mutationRate = 0.05;
  population = new Population(mutationRate,10);
  button = new Button(15,150,160,20, "evolve new generation");
}

void draw() {

  population.display();
```

```
  population.rollover(mouseX,mouseY);
  button.display();
}

void mousePressed() {
  if (button.clicked(mouseX,mouseY)) {
    population.selection();
    population.reproduction();
  }
}
```

The mouse location is passed to the population, which will score each face according to rollover time.

When a button is pressed, the new generation is created via selection and reproduction.

This example, it should be noted, is really just a demonstration of the idea of interactive selection and does not achieve a particularly meaningful result. For one, we didn't take much care in the visual design of the faces; they are just a few simple shapes with sizes and colors. Sims, for example, used more elaborate mathematical functions as his images' genotype. You might also consider a vector-based approach, in which a design's genotype is a set of points and/or paths.

The more significant problem here, however, is one of time. In the natural world, evolution occurs over millions of years. In the computer simulation world of our previous examples, we were able to evolve behaviors relatively quickly because we were producing new generations algorithmically. In the Shakespeare monkey example, a new generation was born in each frame of animation (approximately sixty per second). Since the fitness values were computed according to a math formula, we could also have had arbitrarily large populations that increased the speed of evolution. In the case of interactive selection, however, we have to sit and wait for a user to rate each and every member of the population before we can get to the next generation. A large population would be unreasonably tedious to deal with—not to mention, how many generations could you stand to sit through?

There are certainly clever solutions around this. Sims's Galapagos exhibit concealed the rating process from the users, as it occurred through the normal behavior of looking at artwork in a museum setting. Building a Web application that would allow many users to rate a population in a distributed fashion is also a good strategy for achieving many ratings for large populations quickly.

In the end, the key to a successful interactive selection system boils down to the same keys we previously established. What is the genotype and phenotype? And how do you calculate fitness, which in this case we can revise to say: "What is your strategy for assigning fitness according to user interaction?"

Exercise 9.14

Build your own interactive selection project. In addition to a visual design, consider evolving sounds—for example, a short sequence of tones. Can you devise a strategy, such as a Web application or physical sensor system, to acquire ratings from many users over time?

9.13 Ecosystem Simulation

You may have noticed something a bit odd about every single evolutionary system we've built so far in this chapter. After all, in the real world, a population of babies isn't born all at the same time. Those babies don't then grow up and all reproduce at exactly the same time, then instantly die to leave the population size perfectly stable. That would be ridiculous. Not to mention the fact that there is certainly no one running around the forest with a calculator crunching numbers and assigning fitness values to all the creatures.

In the real world, we don't really have "survival of the fittest"; we have "survival of the survivors." Things that happen to live longer, for whatever reason, have a greater chance of reproducing. Babies are born, they live for a while, maybe they themselves have babies, maybe they don't, and then they die.

You won't necessarily find simulations of "real-world" evolution in artificial intelligence textbooks. Genetic algorithms are generally used in the more formal manner we outlined in this chapter. However, since we are reading this book to develop simulations of natural systems, it's worth looking at some ways in which we might use a genetic algorithm to build something that resembles a living "ecosystem," much like the one we've described in the exercises at the end of each chapter.

Let's begin by developing a very simple scenario. We'll create a creature called a "bloop," a circle that moves about the screen according to Perlin noise. The creature will have a radius and a maximum speed. The bigger it is, the slower it moves; the smaller, the faster.

```
class Bloop {
  PVector location;                 // A location

  float r;                          // Variables for size and speed
  float maxspeed;
```

```
  float xoff, yoff;                              Some variables for Perlin noise
                                                 calculations

  void update() {
    float vx = map(noise(xoff),0,1,-maxspeed,maxspeed);
    float vy = map(noise(yoff),0,1,-maxspeed,maxspeed);
    PVector velocity = new PVector(vx,vy);       A little Perlin noise algorithm to calculate a
                                                 velocity
    xoff += 0.01;
    yoff += 0.01;

    location.add(velocity);                      The bloop moves.
  }

  void display() {                               A bloop is a circle.
    ellipse(location.x, location.y, r, r);
  }
}
```

The above is missing a few details (such as initializing the variables in the constructor), but you get the idea.

For this example, we'll want to store the population of bloops in an `ArrayList`, rather than an array, as we expect the population to grow and shrink according to how often bloops die or are born. We can store this `ArrayList` in a class called `World`, which will manage all the elements of the bloops' world.

```
class World {

  ArrayList<Bloop> bloops;                       A list of bloops

  World(int num) {
    bloops = new ArrayList<Bloop>();

    for (int i = 0; i < num; i++) {
      bloops.add(new Bloop());                   Making an initial population of bloops
    }
  }
```

So far, what we have is just a rehashing of our particle system example from Chapter 5. We have an entity (`Bloop`) that moves around the window and a class (`World`) that manages a variable quantity of these entities. To turn this into a system that evolves, we need to add two additional features to our world:

- ***Bloops die.***
- ***Bloops are born.***

Bloops dying is our replacement for a fitness function, the process of "selection." If a bloop dies, it cannot be selected to be a parent, because it simply no longer exists! One way we can build a mechanism to ensure bloop deaths in our world is by adding a `health` variable to the `Bloop` class.

```
class Bloop {
  float health = 100;                    A bloop is born with 100 health points.
```

In each frame of animation, a bloop loses some health.

```
void update() {
                                         All that other stuff for movement
  health -= 1;                           Death is always looming!
}
```

If health drops below 0, the bloop dies.

```
boolean dead() {                         We add a function to the Bloop class to test
  if (health < 0.0) {                    if the bloop is alive or dead.
    return true;
  } else {
    return false;
  }
}
```

This is a good first step, but we haven't really achieved anything. After all, if all bloops start with 100 health points and lose 1 point per frame, then all bloops will live for the exact same amount of time and die together. If every single bloop lives the same amount of time, they all have equal chances of reproducing and therefore nothing will evolve.

There are many ways we could achieve variable lifespans with a more sophisticated world. For example, we could introduce predators that eat bloops. Perhaps the faster bloops would be able to escape being eaten more easily, and therefore our world would evolve to have faster and faster bloops. Another option would be to introduce food. When a bloop eats food, it increases its health points, and therefore extends its life.

Let's assume we have an `ArrayList` of `PVector` locations for food, named "food." We could test each bloop's proximity to each food location. If the bloop is close enough, it eats the food (which is then removed from the world) and increases its health.

```
void eat() {
  for (int i = food.size()-1; i >= 0; i--) {
    PVector foodLocation = food.get(i);
    float d = PVector.dist(location, foodLocation);
```

```
      if (d < r/2) {                    Is the Bloop close to the food?

        health += 100;                  If so, it gets 100 more health points.

        food.remove(i);                 The food is no longer available for other
                                        Bloops.
      }
    }
  }
```

Now we have a scenario in which bloops that eat more food live longer and have a greater likelihood of reproducing. Therefore, we expect that our system would evolve bloops with an optimal ability to find and eat food.

Now that we have built our world, it's time to add the components required for evolution. First we should establish our genotype and phenotype.

Genotype and Phenotype

The ability for a bloop to find food is tied to two variables—size and speed. Bigger bloops will find food more easily simply because their size will allow them to intersect with food locations more often. And faster bloops will find more food because they can cover more ground in a shorter period of time.

Since size and speed are inversely related (large bloops are slow, small bloops are fast), we only need a genotype with a single number.

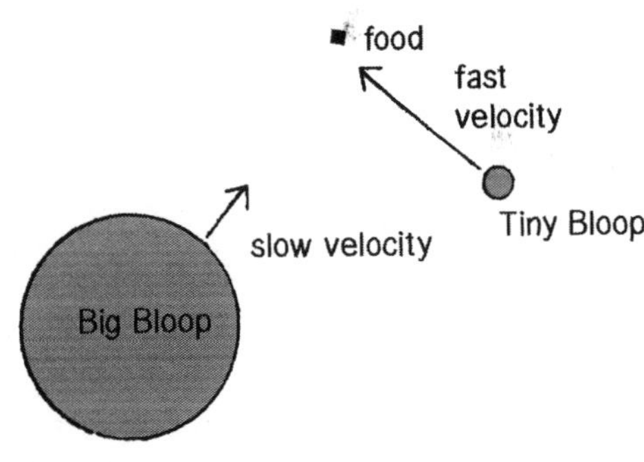

Figure 9.15

```
class DNA {

  float[] genes;

  DNA() {
```

```
    genes = new float[1];
    for (int i = 0; i < genes.length; i++) {
      genes[i] = random(0,1);
    }
  }
```

It may seem absurd to use an array when all we have is a single value, but we stick with an array in case we want to make more sophisticated bloops later.

The phenotype then is the bloop itself, whose size and speed is assigned by adding an instance of a DNA object to the Bloop class.

```
class Bloop {
  PVector location;
  float health;

  DNA dna;

  float r;
  float maxspeed;

  Bloop(DNA dna_) {
    location = new PVector(width/2,height/2);
    health = 200;
    dna = dna_;

    maxspeed = map(dna.genes[0], 0, 1, 15, 0);
    r        = map(dna.genes[0], 0, 1, 0, 50);
  }
```

A bloop now has DNA.

maxspeed and r (radius) are mapped to values according to the DNA.

Notice that with maxspeed, the range is mapped to between 15 and 0, meaning a bloop with a gene value of 0 moves at a speed of 15 and a bloop with a gene value of 1 doesn't move at all (speed of 0).

Selection and Reproduction

Now that we have the genotype and phenotype, we need to move on to devising a means for bloops to be selected as parents. We stated before that the longer a bloop lives, the more chances it has to reproduce. The length of life is the bloop's fitness.

One option would be to say that whenever two bloops come into contact with each other, they make a new bloop. The longer a bloop lives, the more likely it is to come into contact with another bloop. (This would also affect the evolutionary outcome given that, in addition to eating food, their ability to find other bloops is a factor in the likelihood of having a baby.)

A simpler option would be to have "asexual" reproduction, meaning a bloop does not require a partner. It can, at any moment, make a clone of itself, another bloop with the same genetic makeup. If we state this selection algorithm as follows:

At any given moment, a bloop has a 1% chance of reproducing.

...then the longer a bloop lives, the more likely it will make at least one child. This is equivalent to saying the more times you play the lottery, the greater the likelihood you'll win (though I'm sorry to say your chances of that are still essentially zero).

To implement this selection algorithm, we can write a function in the `Bloop` class that picks a random number every frame. If the number is less than 0.01 (1%), a new bloop is born.

```
Bloop reproduce() {                     // This function will return a new bloop, the child.
  if (random(1) < 0.01) {               // A 1% chance of executing the code in this conditional, i.e. a 1% chance of reproducing
    // Make the Bloop baby
  }
}
```

How does a bloop reproduce? In our previous examples, the reproduction process involved calling the `crossover()` function in the `DNA` class and making a new object from the newly made DNA. Here, since we are making a child from a single parent, we'll call a function called `copy()` instead.

```
Bloop reproduce() {
  if (random(1) < 0.0005) {
    DNA childDNA = dna.copy();                  // Make a copy of the DNA.
    childDNA.mutate(0.01);                      // 1% mutation rate
    return new Bloop(location, childDNA);       // Make a new bloop at the same location with the new DNA.
  } else {
    return null;                                // If the bloop does not reproduce, return null.
  }
}
```

Note also that we've reduced the probability of reproducing from 1% to 0.05%. This value makes quite a difference; with a high probability of reproducing, the system will quickly tend towards overpopulation. Too low a probability, and everything will likely quickly die out.

Writing the `copy()` function into the `DNA` class is easy since Processing includes a function `arraycopy()` that copies the contents of one array into another.

```
class DNA {

  DNA copy() {                          // This copy() function replaces crossover() in this example.
```

```
    float[] newgenes = new float[genes.length];
    arraycopy(genes,newgenes);
    return new DNA(newgenes);
  }
}
```

Make a new array the same length and copy its contents.

Now that we have all the pieces in place for selection and reproduction, we can finalize the `World` class that manages the list of all `Bloop` objects (as well as a `Food` object, which itself is a list of `PVector` locations for food).

Before you run the example, take a moment to guess what size and speed of bloops the system will evolve towards. We'll discuss following the code.

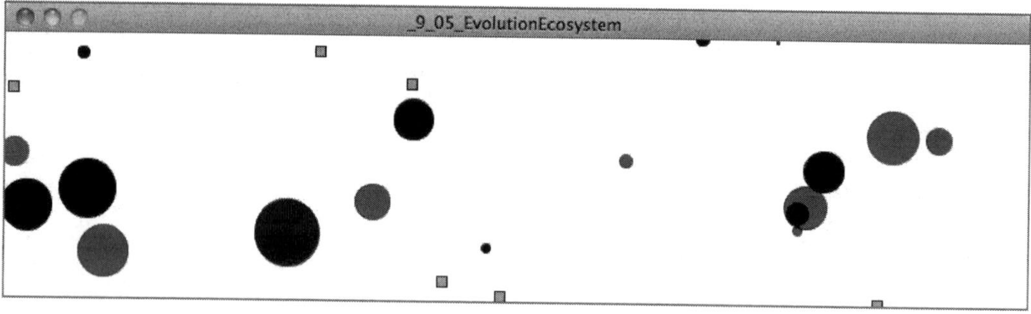

Example 9.5: Evolution ecosystem

```
World world;

void setup() {
  size(600,400);
  world = new World(20);
}

void draw() {
  background(255);
  world.run();
}
```

setup() and draw() do nothing more than create and run a World object.

```
class World {

  ArrayList<Bloop> bloops;
  Food food;

  World(int num) {
    food = new Food(num);
    bloops = new ArrayList<Bloop>();
```

The World object keeps track of the population bloops as well as the food.

```
    for (int i = 0; i < num; i++) {                Creating the population
      PVector location = new PVector(random(width),random(height));
      DNA dna = new DNA();
      bloops.add(new Bloop(l,dna));
    }
  }

  void run() {
    food.run();

    for (int i = bloops.size()-1; i >= 0; i--) {
      Bloop b = bloops.get(i);                     The bloops live their life.
      b.run();
      b.eat(food);
      if (b.dead()) {                              If one dies, it is removed from the
        bloops.remove(i);                          population and food is added at its
        food.add(b.location);                      location.
      }

      Bloop child = b.reproduce();                 Here is where each living bloop has a
      if (child != null) bloops.add(child);        chance to reproduce. As long as a child is
                                                   made (i.e. not null) it is added to the
                                                   population.
    }
  }
}
```

If you guessed medium-sized bloops with medium speed, you were right. With the design of this system, bloops that are large are simply too slow to find food. And bloops that are fast are too small to find food. The ones that are able to live the longest tend to be in the middle, large enough and fast enough to find food (but not too large or too fast). There are also some anomalies. For example, if it so happens that a bunch of large bloops end up in the same location (and barely move because they are so large), they may all die out suddenly, leaving a lot of food for one large bloop who happens to be there to eat and allowing a mini-population of large bloops to sustain themselves for a period of time in one location.

This example is rather simplistic given its single gene and asexual reproduction. Here are some suggestions for how you might apply the bloop example in a more elaborate ecosystem simulation.

The Ecosystem Project

Step 9 Exercise:

Add evolution to your ecosystem, building from the examples in this chapter.

- Add a population of predators to your ecosystem. Biological evolution between predators and prey (or parasites and hosts) is often referred to as an "arms race," in which the creatures continuously adapt and counter-adapt to each other. Can you achieve this behavior in a system of multiple creatures?
- How would you implement crossover and mutation between two parents in an ecosystem modeled after the bloops? Try implementing an algorithm so that two creatures meet and mate when within a certain proximity. Can you make creatures with gender?
- Try using the weights of multiple steering forces as a creature's DNA. Can you create a scenario in which creatures evolve to cooperate with each other?
- One of the greatest challenges in ecosystem simulations is achieving a nice balance. You will likely find that most of your attempts result in either mass overpopulation (followed by mass extinction) or simply mass extinction straight away. What techniques can you employ to achieve balance? Consider using the genetic algorithm itself to evolve optimal parameters for an ecosystem.

Chapter 10. Neural Networks

"You can't process me with a normal brain."
— Charlie Sheen

We're at the end of our story. This is the last official chapter of this book (though I envision additional supplemental material for the website and perhaps new chapters in the future). We began with inanimate objects living in a world of forces and gave those objects desires, autonomy, and the ability to take action according to a system of rules. Next, we allowed those objects to live in a population and evolve over time. Now we ask: What is each object's decision-making process? How can it adjust its choices by learning over time? Can a computational entity process its environment and generate a decision?

The human brain can be described as a biological neural network—an interconnected web of neurons transmitting elaborate patterns of electrical signals. Dendrites receive input signals and, based on those inputs, fire an output signal via an axon. Or something like that. How the human brain actually works is an elaborate and complex mystery, one that we certainly are not going to attempt to tackle in rigorous detail in this chapter.

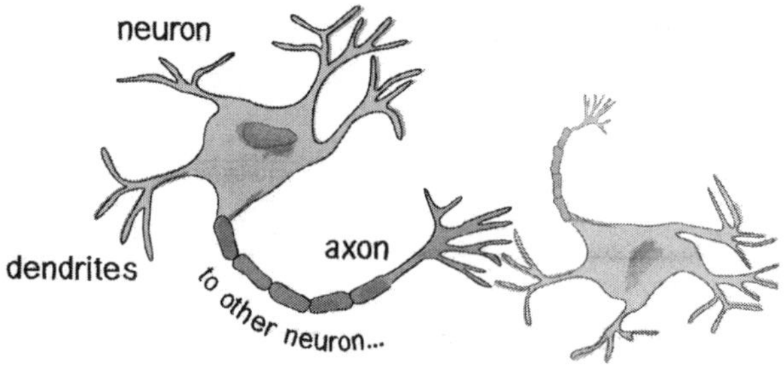

Figure 10.1

The good news is that developing engaging animated systems with code does not require scientific rigor or accuracy, as we've learned throughout this book. We can simply be inspired by the idea of brain function.

In this chapter, we'll begin with a conceptual overview of the properties and features of neural networks and build the simplest possible example of one (a network that consists of a single neuron). Afterwards, we'll examine strategies for creating a "Brain" object that can be inserted into our `Vehicle` class and used to determine steering. Finally, we'll also look at techniques for visualizing and animating a network of neurons.

10.1 Artificial Neural Networks: Introduction and Application

Computer scientists have long been inspired by the human brain. In 1943, Warren S. McCulloch, a neuroscientist, and Walter Pitts, a logician, developed the first conceptual model of an artificial neural network. In their paper, "A logical calculus of the ideas imminent in nervous activity," they describe the concept of a neuron, a single cell living in a network of cells that receives inputs, processes those inputs, and generates an output.

Their work, and the work of many scientists and researchers that followed, was not meant to accurately describe how the biological brain works. Rather, an artificial neural network (which we will now simply refer to as a "neural network") was designed as a computational model based on the brain to solve certain kinds of problems.

It's probably pretty obvious to you that there are problems that are incredibly simple for a computer to solve, but difficult for you. Take the square root of 964,324, for example. A quick line of code produces the value 982, a number Processing computed in less than a millisecond. There are, on the other hand, problems that are incredibly simple for you or me to solve, but not so easy for a computer. Show any toddler a picture of a kitten or puppy and they'll be able to tell you very quickly which one is which. Say hello and shake my hand one morning and you should be able to pick me out of a crowd of people the next day. But need a machine to perform one of these tasks? Scientists have already spent entire careers researching and implementing complex solutions.

The most common application of neural networks in computing today is to perform one of these "easy-for-a-human, difficult-for-a-machine" tasks, often referred to as pattern recognition. Applications range from optical character recognition (turning printed or handwritten scans into digital text) to facial recognition. We don't have the time or need to use some of these more elaborate artificial intelligence algorithms here, but if you are interested in researching neural networks, I'd recommend the books *Artificial Intelligence: A Modern Approach* by Stuart J. Russell and Peter Norvig and *AI for Game Developers* by David M. Bourg and Glenn Seemann.

A neural network is a "connectionist" computational system. The computational systems we write are procedural; a program starts at the first line of code, executes it, and goes on to the next, following instructions in a linear fashion. A true neural network does not follow a linear path. Rather, information is processed collectively, in parallel throughout a network of nodes (the nodes, in this case, being neurons).

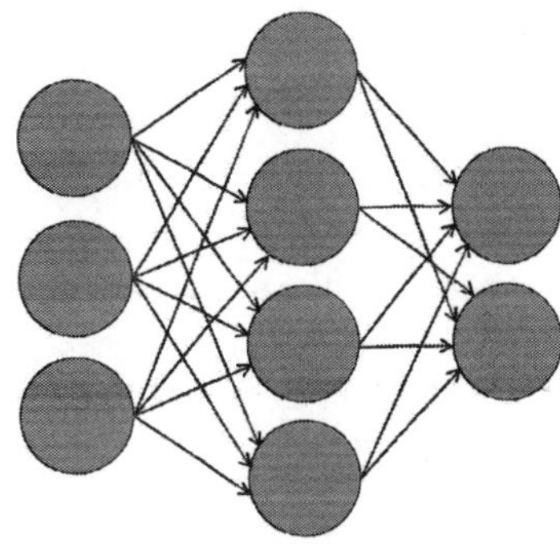

Figure 10.2

Here we have yet another example of a complex system, much like the ones we examined in Chapters 6, 7, and 8. The individual elements of the network, the neurons, are simple. They read an input, process it, and generate an output. A network of many neurons, however, can exhibit incredibly rich and intelligent behaviors.

One of the key elements of a neural network is its ability to *learn*. A neural network is not just a complex system, but a complex ***adaptive*** system, meaning it can change its internal structure based on the information flowing through it. Typically, this is achieved through the adjusting of *weights*. In the diagram above, each line represents a connection between two neurons and indicates the pathway for the flow of information. Each connection has a ***weight***, a number that controls the signal between the two neurons. If the network generates a "good" output (which we'll define later), there is no need to adjust the weights. However, if the network generates a "poor" output—an error, so to speak—then the system adapts, altering the weights in order to improve subsequent results.

There are several strategies for learning, and we'll examine two of them in this chapter.

- ***Supervised Learning*** —Essentially, a strategy that involves a teacher that is smarter than the network itself. For example, let's take the facial recognition example. The teacher shows the network a bunch of faces, and the teacher already knows the name associated with each face. The network makes its guesses, then the teacher provides the network with the answers. The network can then compare its answers to the known "correct" ones and make adjustments according to its errors. Our first neural network in the next section will follow this model.

- ***Unsupervised Learning*** —Required when there isn't an example data set with known answers. Imagine searching for a hidden pattern in a data set. An application of this is clustering, i.e. dividing a set of elements into groups according to some unknown pattern. We won't be looking at any examples of unsupervised learning in this chapter, as this strategy is less relevant for our examples.

- ***Reinforcement Learning*** —A strategy built on observation. Think of a little mouse running through a maze. If it turns left, it gets a piece of cheese; if it turns right, it receives a little shock. (Don't worry, this is just a pretend mouse.) Presumably, the mouse will learn over time to turn left. Its neural network makes a decision with an outcome (turn left or right) and observes its environment (yum or ouch). If the observation is negative, the network can adjust its weights in order to make a different decision the next time. Reinforcement learning is common in robotics. At time `t`, the robot performs a task and observes the results. Did it crash into a wall or fall off a table? Or is it unharmed? We'll look at reinforcement learning in the context of our simulated steering vehicles.

This ability of a neural network to learn, to make adjustments to its structure over time, is what makes it so useful in the field of artificial intelligence. Here are some standard uses of neural networks in software today.

- ***Pattern Recognition*** —We've mentioned this several times already and it's probably the most common application. Examples are facial recognition, optical character recognition, etc.

- ***Time Series Prediction*** —Neural networks can be used to make predictions. Will the stock rise or fall tomorrow? Will it rain or be sunny?

- ***Signal Processing*** —Cochlear implants and hearing aids need to filter out unnecessary noise and amplify the important sounds. Neural networks can be trained to process an audio signal and filter it appropriately.

- ***Control*** —You may have read about recent research advances in self-driving cars. Neural networks are often used to manage steering decisions of physical vehicles (or simulated ones).

- ***Soft Sensors*** —A soft sensor refers to the process of analyzing a collection of many measurements. A thermometer can tell you the temperature of the air, but what if you also knew the humidity, barometric pressure, dewpoint, air quality, air density, etc.? Neural networks can be employed to process the input data from many individual sensors and evaluate them as a whole.

- ***Anomaly Detection*** —Because neural networks are so good at recognizing patterns, they can also be trained to generate an output when something occurs that doesn't fit the pattern. Think of a neural network monitoring your daily routine over a long period of time. After learning the patterns of your behavior, it could alert you when something is amiss.

This is by no means a comprehensive list of applications of neural networks. But hopefully it gives you an overall sense of the features and possibilities. The thing is, neural networks are complicated and difficult. They involve all sorts of fancy mathematics. While this is all fascinating (and incredibly important to scientific research), a lot of the techniques are not very practical in the world of building interactive, animated Processing sketches. Not to mention that in order to cover all this material, we would need another book—or more likely, a series of books.

So instead, we'll begin our last hurrah in the nature of code with the simplest of all neural networks, in an effort to understand how the overall concepts are applied in code. Then we'll look at some Processing sketches that generate visual results inspired by these concepts.

10.2 The Perceptron

Invented in 1957 by Frank Rosenblatt at the Cornell Aeronautical Laboratory, a perceptron is the simplest neural network possible: a computational model of a single neuron. A perceptron consists of one or more inputs, a processor, and a single output.

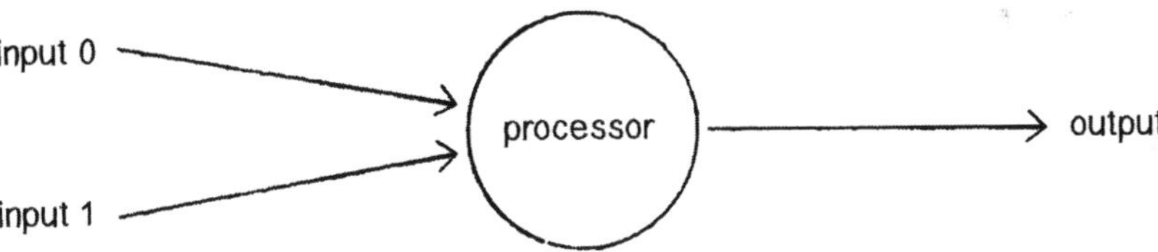

Figure 10.3: The perceptron

A perceptron follows the "feed-forward" model, meaning inputs are sent into the neuron, are processed, and result in an output. In the diagram above, this means the network (one neuron) reads from left to right: inputs come in, output goes out.

Let's follow each of these steps in more detail.

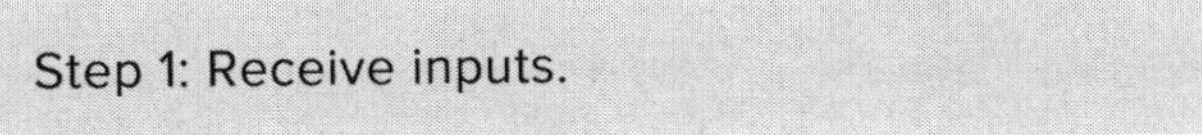

Step 1: Receive inputs.

Say we have a perceptron with two inputs—let's call them *x1* and *x2*.

```
Input 0: x1 = 12
Input 1: x2 = 4
```

Step 2: Weight inputs.

Each input that is sent into the neuron must first be weighted, i.e. multiplied by some value (often a number between -1 and 1). When creating a perceptron, we'll typically begin by assigning random weights. Here, let's give the inputs the following weights:

```
Weight 0: 0.5
Weight 1: -1
```

We take each input and multiply it by its weight.

```
Input 0 * Weight 0 ⇒ 12 * 0.5 = 6

Input 1 * Weight 1 ⇒ 4 * -1 = -4
```

Step 3: Sum inputs.

The weighted inputs are then summed.

```
Sum = 6 + -4 = 2
```

Step 4: Generate output.

The output of a perceptron is generated by passing that sum through an activation function. In the case of a simple binary output, the activation function is what tells the perceptron whether to "fire" or not. You can envision an LED connected to the output signal: if it fires, the light goes on; if not, it stays off.

Activation functions can get a little bit hairy. If you start reading one of those artificial intelligence textbooks looking for more info about activation functions, you may soon find yourself reaching for a calculus textbook. However, with our friend the simple perceptron, we're going to do something really easy. Let's make the activation function the sign of the sum. In other words, if the sum is a positive number, the output is 1; if it is negative, the output is -1.

```
Output = sign(sum) ⇒ sign(2) ⇒ +1
```

Let's review and condense these steps so we can implement them with a code snippet.

The Perceptron Algorithm:

1. For every input, multiply that input by its weight.
2. Sum all of the weighted inputs.
3. Compute the output of the perceptron based on that sum passed through an activation function (the sign of the sum).

Let's assume we have two arrays of numbers, the inputs and the weights. For example:

```
float[] inputs  = {12 , 4};
float[] weights = {0.5,-1};
```

"For every input" implies a loop that multiplies each input by its corresponding weight. Since we need the sum, we can add up the results in that very loop.

```
float sum = 0;
for (int i = 0; i < inputs.length; i++) {
  sum += inputs[i]*weights[i];
}
```

Steps 1 and 2: Add up all the weighted inputs.

Once we have the sum we can compute the output.

```
float output = activate(sum);
```

Step 3: Passing the sum through an activation function

```
int activate(float sum) {
```

The activation function

```
  if (sum > 0) return 1;
  else return -1;
```

Return a 1 if positive, -1 if negative.

```
}
```

10.3 Simple Pattern Recognition Using a Perceptron

Now that we understand the computational process of a perceptron, we can look at an example of one in action. We stated that neural networks are often used for pattern recognition applications, such as facial recognition. Even simple perceptrons can demonstrate the basics of classification, as in the following example.

Consider a line in two-dimensional space. Points in that space can be classified as living on either one side of the line or the other. While this is a somewhat silly example (since there is clearly no need for a neural network; we can determine on which side a point lies with some simple algebra), it shows how a perceptron can be trained to recognize points on one side versus another.

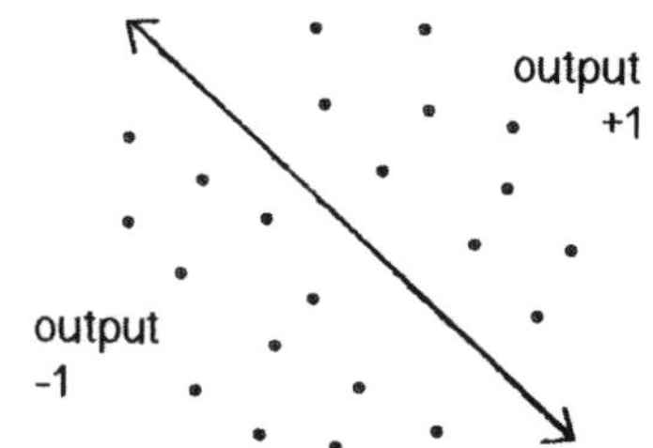

Figure 10.4

Let's say a perceptron has 2 inputs (the x- and y-coordinates of a point). Using a sign activation function, the output will either be -1 or 1—i.e., the input data is classified according to the sign of the output. In the above diagram, we can see how each point is either below the line (-1) or above (+1).

The perceptron itself can be diagrammed as follows:

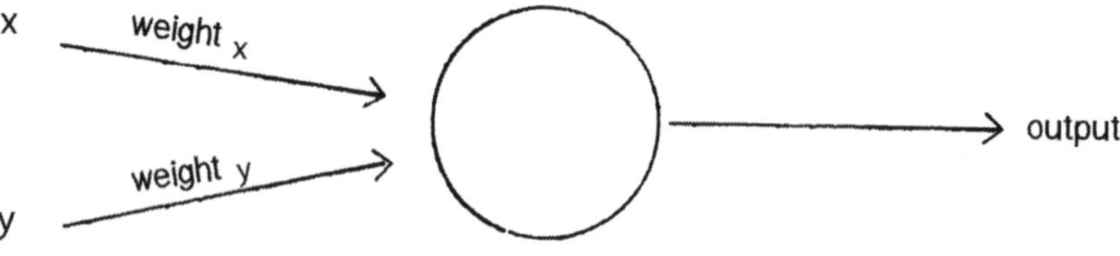

Figure 10.5

We can see how there are two inputs (*x* and *y*), a weight for each input ($weight_x$ and $weight_y$), as well as a processing neuron that generates the output.

There is a pretty significant problem here, however. Let's consider the point (0,0). What if we send this point into the perceptron as its input: x = 0 and y = 0? What will the sum of its weighted inputs be? No matter what the weights are, the sum will always be 0! But this can't be right—after all, the point (0,0) could certainly be above or below various lines in our two-dimensional world.

To avoid this dilemma, our perceptron will require a third input, typically referred to as a ***bias*** input. A bias input always has the value of 1 and is also weighted. Here is our perceptron with the addition of the bias:

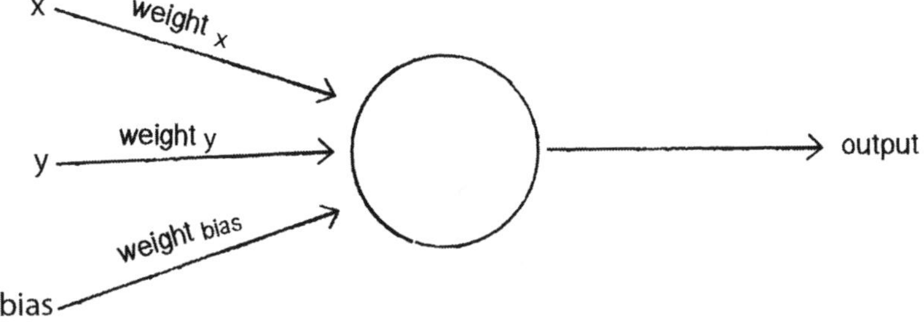

Figure 10.6

Let's go back to the point (0,0). Here are our inputs:

```
0 * weight for x = 0
0 * weight for y = 0
1 * weight for bias = weight for bias
```

The output is the sum of the above three values, 0 plus 0 plus the bias's weight. Therefore, the bias, on its own, answers the question as to where (0,0) is in relation to the line. If the bias's weight is positive, (0,0) is above the line; negative, it is below. It "biases" the perceptron's understanding of the line's position relative to (0,0).

10.4 Coding the Perceptron

We're now ready to assemble the code for a `Perceptron` class. The only data the perceptron needs to track are the input weights, and we could use an array of floats to store these.

```
class Perceptron {
  float[] weights;
```

The constructor could receive an argument indicating the number of inputs (in this case three: x, y, and a bias) and size the array accordingly.

```
  Perceptron(int n) {
    weights = new float[n];
    for (int i = 0; i < weights.length; i++) {
      weights[i] = random(-1,1);          // The weights are picked randomly to start.
    }
  }
```

A perceptron needs to be able to receive inputs and generate an output. We can package these requirements into a function called `feedforward()`. In this example, we'll have the perceptron receive its inputs as an array (which should be the same length as the array of weights) and return the output as an integer.

```
int feedforward(float[] inputs) {
  float sum = 0;
  for (int i = 0; i < weights.length; i++) {
    sum += inputs[i]*weights[i];
  }
  return activate(sum);
}
```

Result is the sign of the sum, -1 or +1. Here the perceptron is making a guess. Is it on one side of the line or the other?

Presumably, we could now create a `Perceptron` object and ask it to make a guess for any given point.

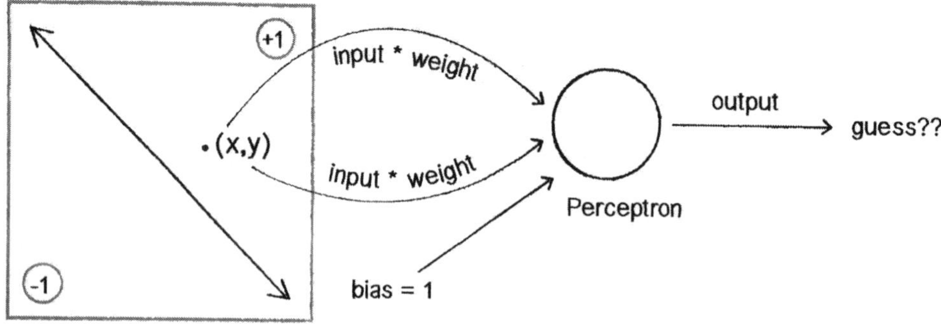

Figure 10.7

```
Perceptron p = new Perceptron(3);
```

Create the Perceptron.

```
float[] point = {50,-12,1};
```

The input is 3 values: x,y and bias.

```
int result = p.feedforward(point);
```

The answer!

Did the perceptron get it right? At this point, the perceptron has no better than a 50/50 chance of arriving at the right answer. Remember, when we created it, we gave each weight a random value. A neural network isn't magic. It's not going to be able to guess anything correctly unless we teach it how to!

To train a neural network to answer correctly, we're going to employ the method of *supervised learning* that we described in section 10.1 (see page 445).

With this method, the network is provided with inputs for which there is a known answer. This way the network can find out if it has made a correct guess. If it's incorrect, the network can learn from its mistake and adjust its weights. The process is as follows:

1. Provide the perceptron with inputs for which there is a known answer.

2. Ask the perceptron to guess an answer.
3. Compute the error. (Did it get the answer right or wrong?)
4. Adjust all the weights according to the error.
5. Return to Step 1 and repeat!

Steps 1 through 4 can be packaged into a function. Before we can write the entire function, however, we need to examine Steps 3 and 4 in more detail. How do we define the perceptron's error? And how should we adjust the weights according to this error?

The perceptron's error can be defined as the difference between the desired answer and its guess.

```
ERROR = DESIRED OUTPUT - GUESS OUTPUT
```

The above formula may look familiar to you. In Chapter 6 (see page 263), we computed a steering force as the difference between our desired velocity and our current velocity.

```
STEERING = DESIRED VELOCITY - CURRENT VELOCITY
```

This was also an error calculation. The current velocity acts as a guess and the error (the steering force) tells us how to adjust the velocity in the right direction. In a moment, we'll see how adjusting the vehicle's velocity to follow a target is just like adjusting the weights of a neural network to arrive at the right answer.

In the case of the perceptron, the output has only two possible values: ***+1*** or ***-1***. This means there are only three possible errors.

If the perceptron guesses the correct answer, then the guess equals the desired output and the error is 0. If the correct answer is -1 and we've guessed +1, then the error is -2. If the correct answer is +1 and we've guessed -1, then the error is +2.

Desired	Guess	Error
-1	-1	0
-1	+1	-2
+1	-1	+2
+1	+1	0

The error is the determining factor in how the perceptron's weights should be adjusted. For any given weight, what we are looking to calculate is the change in weight, often called *Δweight* (or "delta" weight, delta being the Greek letter Δ).

NEW WEIGHT = WEIGHT + ΔWEIGHT

Δweight is calculated as the error multiplied by the input.

ΔWEIGHT = ERROR * INPUT

Therefore:

NEW WEIGHT = WEIGHT + ERROR * INPUT

To understand why this works, we can again return to steering (see page 263). A steering force is essentially an error in velocity. If we apply that force as our acceleration (Δvelocity), then we adjust our velocity to move in the correct direction. This is what we want to do with our neural network's weights. We want to adjust them in the right direction, as defined by the error.

With steering, however, we had an additional variable that controlled the vehicle's ability to steer: the *maximum force*. With a high maximum force, the vehicle was able to accelerate and turn very quickly; with a lower force, the vehicle would take longer to adjust its velocity. The neural network will employ a similar strategy with a variable called the "learning constant." We'll add in the learning constant as follows:

NEW WEIGHT = WEIGHT + ERROR * INPUT * LEARNING CONSTANT

Notice that a high learning constant means the weight will change more drastically. This may help us arrive at a solution more quickly, but with such large changes in weight it's possible we will overshoot the optimal weights. With a small learning constant, the weights will be adjusted slowly, requiring more training time but allowing the network to make very small adjustments that could improve the network's overall accuracy.

Assuming the addition of a variable c for the learning constant, we can now write a training function for the perceptron following the above steps.

```
float c = 0.01;
```

A new variable is introduced to control the learning rate.

```
void train(float[] inputs, int desired) {
```

Step 1: Provide the inputs and known answer. These are passed in as arguments to train().

```
  int guess = feedforward(inputs);
```

Step 2: Guess according to those inputs.

```
  float error = desired - guess;
```

Step 3: Compute the error (difference between answer and guess).

```
    for (int i = 0; i < weights.length; i++) {
      weights[i] += c * error * inputs[i];
    }
  }
```

Step 4: Adjust all the weights according to the error and learning constant.

We can now see the `Perceptron` class as a whole.

```
class Perceptron {
  float[] weights;
  float c = 0.01;
```

The Perceptron stores its weights and learning constants.

```
  Perceptron(int n) {
    weights = new float[n];
    for (int i = 0; i < weights.length; i++) {
      weights[i] = random(-1,1);
    }
  }
```

Weights start off random.

```
  int feedforward(float[] inputs) {
    float sum = 0;
    for (int i = 0; i < weights.length; i++) {
      sum += inputs[i]*weights[i];
    }
    return activate(sum);
  }
```

Return an output based on inputs.

```
  int activate(float sum) {
    if (sum > 0) return 1;
    else return -1;
  }
```

Output is a +1 or -1.

```
  void train(float[] inputs, int desired) {
    int guess = feedforward(inputs);
    float error = desired - guess;
    for (int i = 0; i < weights.length; i++) {
      weights[i] += c * error * inputs[i];
    }
  }
}
```

Train the network against known data.

To train the perceptron, we need a set of inputs with a known answer. We could package this up in a class like so:

```
class Trainer {
```

```
  float[] inputs;
  int answer;

  Trainer(float x, float y, int a) {
    inputs = new float[3];
    inputs[0] = x;
    inputs[1] = y;
    inputs[2] = 1;
    answer = a;
  }
}
```

A "Trainer" object stores the inputs and the correct answer.

Note that the Trainer has the bias input built into its array.

Now the question becomes, how do we pick a point and know whether it is above or below a line? Let's start with the formula for a line, where y is calculated as a function of x:

```
y = f(x)
```

In generic terms, a line can be described as:

```
y = ax + b
```

Here's a specific example:

```
y = 2*x + 1
```

We can then write a Processing function with this in mind.

```
float f(float x) {
  return 2*x+1;
}
```

A function to calculate y based on x along a line

So, if we make up a point:

```
float x = random(width);
float y = random(height);
```

How do we know if this point is above or below the line? The line function `f(x)` gives us the y value on the line for that x position. Let's call that `yline`.

```
float yline = f(x);
```

The y position on the line

If the y value we are examining is above the line, it will be less than `yline`.

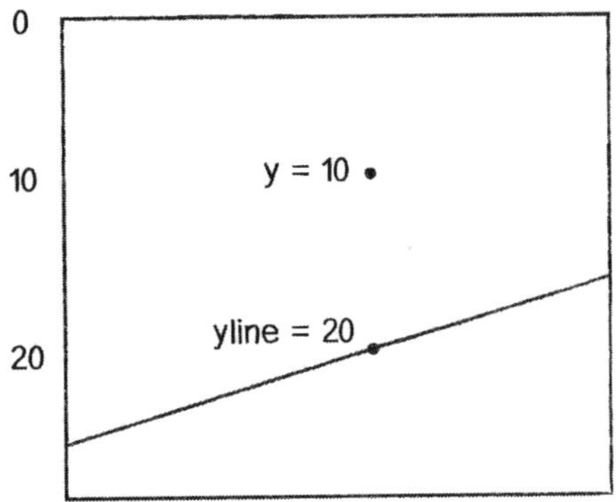

Figure 10.8

```
if (y < yline) {
  answer = -1;                 The answer is -1 if y is above the line.
} else {
  answer = 1;
}
```

We can then make a `Trainer` object with the inputs and the correct answer.

```
Trainer t = new Trainer(x, y, answer);
```

Assuming we had a `Perceptron` object `ptron`, we could then train it by sending the inputs along with the known answer.

```
ptron.train(t.inputs,t.answer);
```

Now, it's important to remember that this is just a demonstration. Remember our Shakespeare-typing monkeys (see page 392)? We asked our genetic algorithm to solve for "to be or not to be"—an answer we already knew. We did this to make sure our genetic algorithm worked properly. The same reasoning applies to this example. We don't need a perceptron to tell us whether a point is above or below a line; we can do that with simple math. We are using this scenario, one that we can easily solve without a perceptron, to demonstrate the perceptron's algorithm as well as easily confirm that it is working properly.

Let's look at how the perceptron works with an array of many training points.

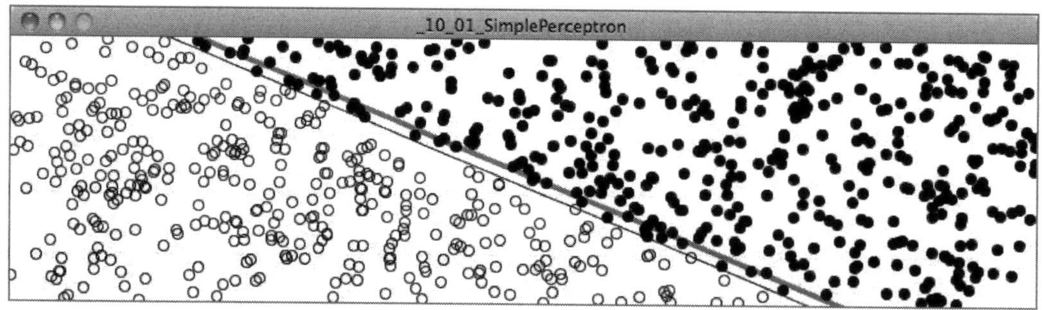

Example 10.1: The Perceptron

```
Perceptron ptron;                                    // The Perceptron

Trainer[] training = new Trainer[2000];              // 2,000 training points
int count = 0;

float f(float x) {                                   // The formula for a line
  return 2*x+1;
}

void setup() {
  size(640, 360);

  ptron = new Perceptron(3);

  for (int i = 0; i < training.length; i++) {        // Make 2,000 training points.
    float x = random(-width/2,width/2);
    float y = random(-height/2,height/2);
    int answer = 1;                                  // Is the correct answer 1 or -1?
    if (y < f(x)) answer = -1;
    training[i] = new Trainer(x, y, answer);
  }
}


void draw() {
  background(255);
  translate(width/2,height/2);

  ptron.train(training[count].inputs, training[count].answer);
  count = (count + 1) % training.length;             // For animation, we are training one point at a time.

  for (int i = 0; i < count; i++) {
    stroke(0);
    int guess = ptron.feedforward(training[i].inputs);
```

```
    if (guess > 0) noFill();            Show the classification—no fill for -1,
    else           fill(0);             black for +1.

    ellipse(training[i].inputs[0], training[i].inputs[1], 8, 8);
  }
}
```

Exercise 10.1

Instead of using the supervised learning model above, can you train the neural network to find the right weights by using a genetic algorithm?

Exercise 10.2

Visualize the perceptron itself. Draw the inputs, the processing node, and the output.

10.5 A Steering Perceptron

While classifying points according to their position above or below a line was a useful demonstration of the perceptron in action, it doesn't have much practical relevance to the other examples throughout this book. In this section, we'll take the concepts of a perceptron (array of inputs, single output), apply it to steering behaviors, and demonstrate reinforcement learning along the way.

We are now going to take significant creative license with the concept of a neural network. This will allow us to stick with the basics and avoid some of the highly complex algorithms associated with more sophisticated neural networks. Here we're not so concerned with following rules outlined in artificial intelligence textbooks—we're just hoping to make something interesting and brain-like.

Remember our good friend the `Vehicle` class? You know, that one for making objects with a location, velocity, and acceleration? That could obey Newton's laws with an `applyForce()` function and move around the window according to a variety of steering rules?

What if we added one more variable to our `Vehicle` class?

```
class Vehicle {
```

```
Perceptron brain;                                    Giving the vehicle a brain!

PVector location;
PVector velocity;
PVector acceleration;
//etc...
```

Here's our scenario. Let's say we have a Processing sketch with an `ArrayList` of targets and a single vehicle.

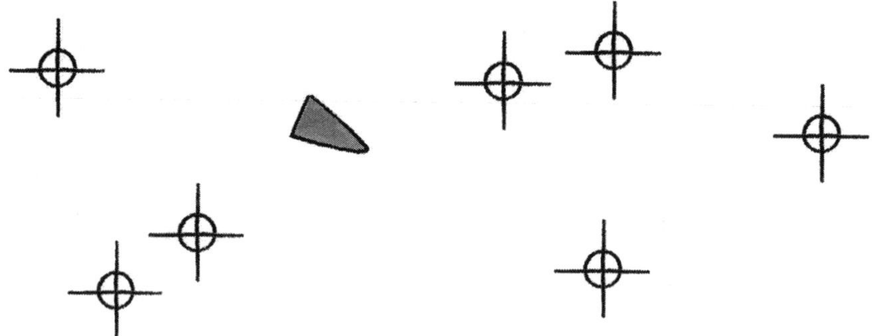

Figure 10.9

Let's say that the vehicle seeks all of the targets. According to the principles of Chapter 6, we would next write a function that calculates a steering force towards each target, applying each force one at a time to the object's acceleration. Assuming the targets are an `ArrayList` of `PVector` objects, it would look something like:

```
void seek(ArrayList<PVector> targets) {
  for (PVector target : targets) {
    PVector force = seek(targets.get(i));    For every target, apply a steering force
                                              towards the target.
    applyForce(force);
  }
}
```

In Chapter 6, we also examined how we could create more dynamic simulations by weighting each steering force according to some rule. For example, we could say that the farther you are from a target, the stronger the force.

```
void seek(ArrayList<PVector> targets) {
  for (PVector target : targets) {
    PVector force = seek(targets.get(i));
    float d = PVector.dist(target,location);
    float weight = map(d,0,width,0,5);
```

```
      force.mult(weight);                          Weighting each steering force individually
      applyForce(force);
    }
  }
```

But what if instead we could ask our brain (i.e. perceptron) to take in all the forces as an input, process them according to weights of the perceptron inputs, and generate an output steering force? What if we could instead say:

```
  void seek(ArrayList<PVector> targets) {

    PVector[] forces = new                         Make an array of inputs for our brain.
PVector[targets.size()];

    for (int i = 0; i < forces.length; i++) {
      forces[i] = seek(targets.get(i));            Fill the array with a steering force for each
                                                   target.
    }

    PVector output = brain.process(forces);        Ask our brain for a result and apply that as
    applyForce(output);                            the force!
  }
```

In other words, instead of weighting and accumulating the forces inside our vehicle, we simply pass an array of forces to the vehicle's "brain" object and allow the brain to weight and sum the forces for us. The output is then applied as a steering force. This opens up a range of possibilities. A vehicle could make decisions as to how to steer on its own, learning from its mistakes and responding to stimuli in its environment. Let's see how this works.

We can use the line classification perceptron as a model, with one important difference—the inputs are not single numbers, but vectors! Let's look at how the `feedforward()` function works in our vehicle's perceptron, alongside the one from our previous example.

Vehicle PVector inputs	**Line float inputs**

<pre>PVector feedforward(PVector[] forces) {
  // Sum is a PVector.
  PVector sum = new PVector();
  for (int i = 0; i < weights.length; i++) {
    // Vector addition and multiplication
    forces[i].mult(weights[i]);
    sum.add(forces[i]);
  }
  // No activation function
  return sum;
}</pre>
	<pre>int feedforward(float[] inputs) {
	  // Sum is a float.
	  float sum = 0;
	  for (int i = 0; i < weights.length; i++) {
	    // Scalar addition and multiplication
	    sum += inputs[i]*weights[i];
	
	  }
	  // Activation function
	  return activate(sum);
	}</pre>

Note how these two functions implement nearly identical algorithms, with two differences:

1. ***Summing PVectors.*** Instead of a series of numbers added together, each input is a `PVector` and must be multiplied by the weight and added to a sum according to the mathematical `PVector` functions.

2. ***No activation function.*** In this case, we're taking the result and applying it directly as a steering force for the vehicle, so we're not asking for a simple boolean value that classifies it in one of two categories. Rather, we're asking for raw output itself, the resulting overall force.

Once the resulting steering force has been applied, it's time to give feedback to the brain, i.e. *reinforcement learning*. Was the decision to steer in that particular direction a good one or a bad one? Presumably if some of the targets were predators (resulting in being eaten) and some of the targets were food (resulting in greater health), the network would adjust its weights in order to steer away from the predators and towards the food.

Let's take a simpler example, where the vehicle simply wants to stay close to the center of the window. We'll train the brain as follows:

```
PVector desired = new PVector(width/2,height/2);
PVector error = PVector.sub(desired, location);
brain.train(forces,error);
```

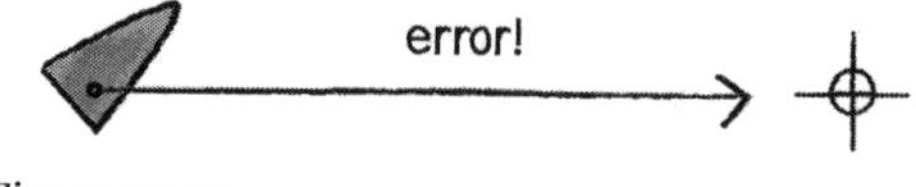

Figure 10.10

Here we are passing the brain a copy of all the inputs (which it will need for error correction) as well as an observation about its environment: a `PVector` that points from its current location to where it desires to be. This `PVector` essentially serves as the error—the longer the `PVector`, the worse the vehicle is performing; the shorter, the better.

The brain can then apply this "error" vector (which has two error values, one for x and one for y) as a means for adjusting the weights, just as we did in the line classification example.

Training the Vehicle	Training the Line Classifier

`void train(PVector[] forces, PVector error) {`
 	
`  for (int i = 0; i < weights.length; i++) {`
`    weights[i] += c*error.x*forces[i].x;`
`    weights[i] += c*error.y*forces[i].y;`
`  }`
`}`
	`void train(float[] inputs, int desired) {`
	
	`  int guess = feedforward(inputs);`
	`  float error = desired - guess;`
	
	`  for (int i = 0; i < weights.length; i++) {`
	`    weights[i] += c * error * inputs[i];`
	
	`  }`
	`}`

Because the vehicle observes its own error, there is no need to calculate one; we can simply receive the error as an argument. Notice how the change in weight is processed twice, once for the error along the x-axis and once for the y-axis.

```
weights[i] += c*error.x*forces[i].x;
weights[i] += c*error.y*forces[i].y;
```

We can now look at the `Vehicle` class and see how the `steer` function uses a perceptron to control the overall steering force. The new content from this chapter is highlighted.

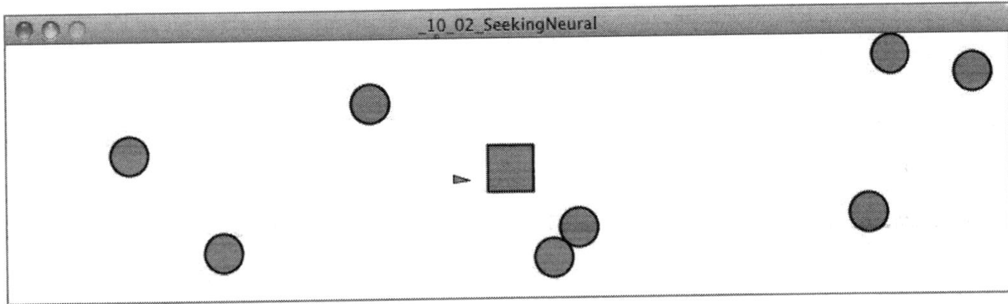

Example 10.2: Perceptron steering

```
class Vehicle {

  Perceptron brain;
```

The Vehicle now has a brain.

```
  PVector location;
  PVector velocity;
  PVector acceleration;
  float maxforce;
  float maxspeed;
```

Same old variables for physics

```
  Vehicle(int n, float x, float y) {
    brain = new Perceptron(n,0.001);
    acceleration = new PVector(0,0);
    velocity = new PVector(0,0);
    location = new PVector(x,y);
    maxspeed = 4;
    maxforce = 0.1;
  }
```

The Vehicle creates a perceptron with n inputs and a learning constant.

```
  void update() {                                       // Same old update() function
    velocity.add(acceleration);
    velocity.limit(maxspeed);
    location.add(velocity);
    acceleration.mult(0);
  }

  void applyForce(PVector force) {                      // Same old applyForce() function
    acceleration.add(force);
  }

  void steer(ArrayList<PVector> targets) {
    PVector[] forces = new PVector[targets.size()];

    for (int i = 0; i < forces.length; i++) {
      forces[i] = seek(targets.get(i));
    }
    PVector result = brain.feedforward(forces);         // All the steering forces are inputs.

    applyForce(result);                                 // The result is applied.

    PVector desired = new PVector(width/2,height/2);
    PVector error = PVector.sub(desired, location);     // The brain is trained according to the
    brain.train(forces,error);                          // distance to the center.

  }

  PVector seek(PVector target) {                        // Same old seek() function
    PVector desired = PVector.sub(target,location);
    desired.normalize();
    desired.mult(maxspeed);
    PVector steer = PVector.sub(desired,velocity);
    steer.limit(maxforce);
    return steer;
  }

}
```

Exercise 10.3

Visualize the weights of the network. Try mapping each target's corresponding weight to its brightness.

Exercise 10.4

Try different rules for reinforcement learning. What if some targets are desirable and some are undesirable?

10.6 It's a "Network," Remember?

Yes, a perceptron can have multiple inputs, but it is still a lonely neuron. The power of neural networks comes in the networking itself. Perceptrons are, sadly, incredibly limited in their abilities. If you read an AI textbook, it will say that a perceptron can only solve ***linearly separable*** problems. What's a linearly separable problem? Let's take a look at our first example, which determined whether points were on one side of a line or the other.

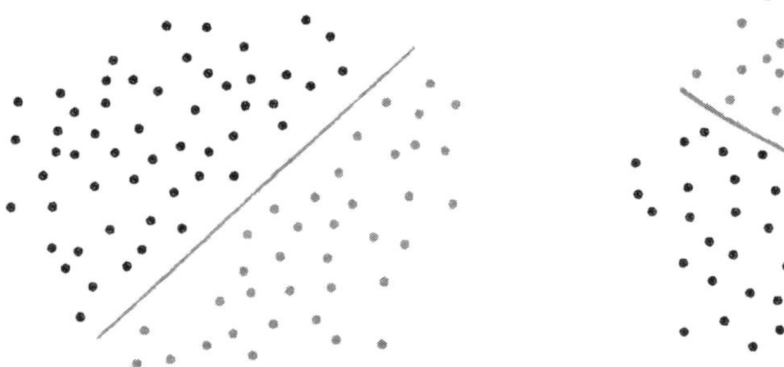

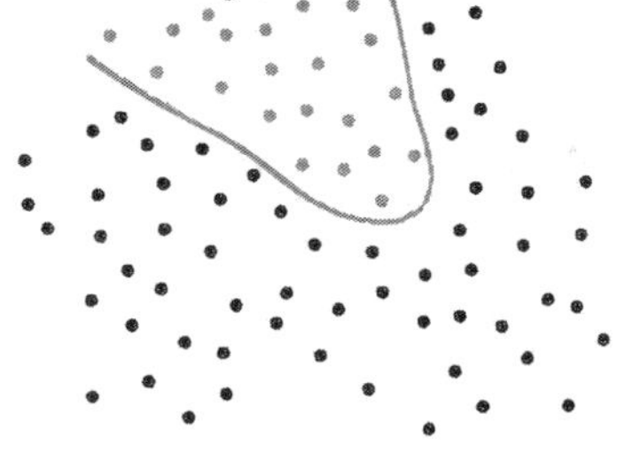

Figure 10.11

On the left of Figure 10.11, we have classic linearly separable data. Graph all of the possibilities; if you can classify the data with a straight line, then it is linearly separable. On the right, however, is non-linearly separable data. You can't draw a straight line to separate the black dots from the gray ones.

One of the simplest examples of a non-linearly separable problem is *XOR*, or "exclusive or." We're all familiar with *AND*. For *A AND B* to be true, both *A* and *B* must be true. With *OR*, either *A* or *B* can be true for *A OR B* to evaluate as true. These are both linearly separable problems. Let's look at the solution space, a "truth table."

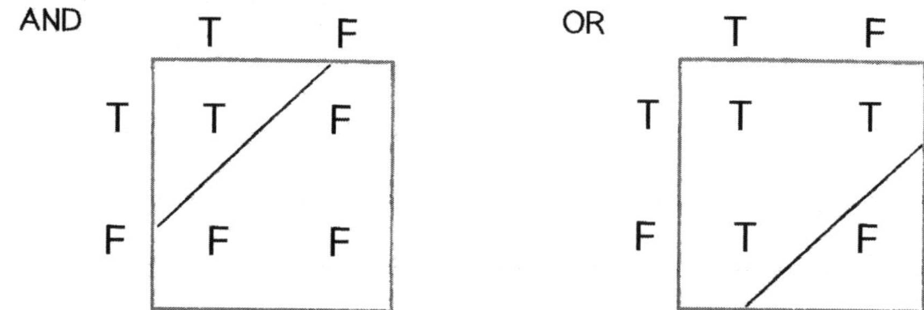

Figure 10.12

See how you can draw a line to separate the true outputs from the false ones?

XOR is the equivalent of *OR* and *NOT AND*. In other words, *A XOR B* only evaluates to true if one of them is true. If both are false or both are true, then we get false. Take a look at the following truth table.

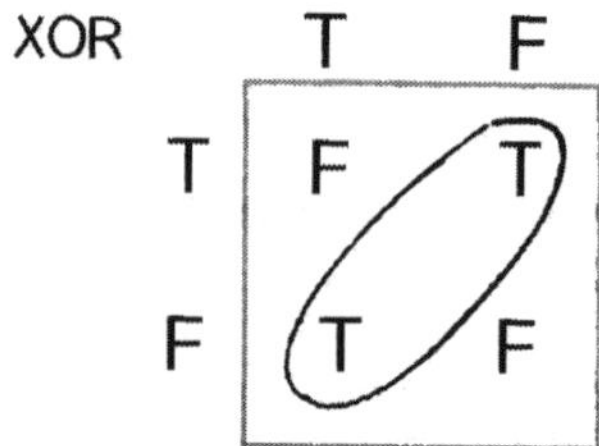

Figure 10.13

This is not linearly separable. Try to draw a straight line to separate the true outputs from the false ones—you can't!

So perceptrons can't even solve something as simple as *XOR*. But what if we made a network out of two perceptrons? If one perceptron can solve *OR* and one perceptron can solve *NOT AND*, then two perceptrons combined can solve *XOR*.

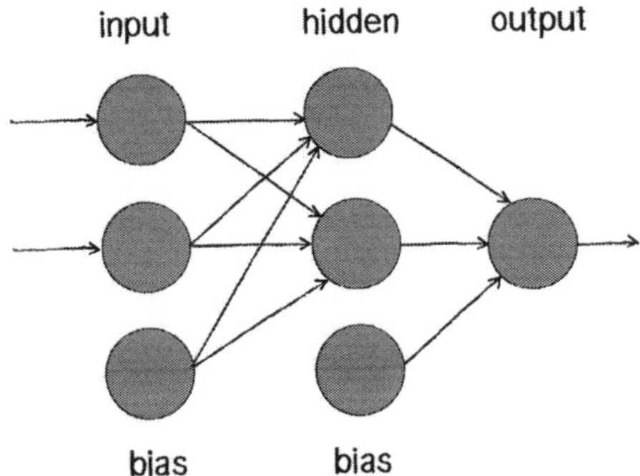

Figure 10.14

The above diagram is known as a *multi-layered perceptron*, a network of many neurons. Some are input neurons and receive the inputs, some are part of what's called a "hidden" layer (as they are connected to neither the inputs nor the outputs of the network directly), and then there are the output neurons, from which we read the results.

Training these networks is much more complicated. With the simple perceptron, we could easily evaluate how to change the weights according to the error. But here there are so many different connections, each in a different layer of the network. How does one know how much each neuron or connection contributed to the overall error of the network?

The solution to optimizing weights of a multi-layered network is known as ***backpropagation***. The output of the network is generated in the same manner as a perceptron. The inputs multiplied by the weights are summed and fed forward through the network. The difference here is that they pass through additional layers of neurons before reaching the output. Training the network (i.e. adjusting the weights) also involves taking the error (desired result - guess). The error, however, must be fed backwards through the network. The final error ultimately adjusts the weights of all the connections.

Backpropagation is a bit beyond the scope of this book and involves a fancier activation function (called the sigmoid function) as well as some basic calculus. If you are interested in how backpropagation works, check the book website (and GitHub repository) for an example that solves *XOR* using a multi-layered feed forward network with backpropagation.

Instead, here we'll focus on a code framework for building the visual architecture of a network. We'll make `Neuron` objects and `Connection` objects from which a `Network` object can be created and animated to show the feed forward process. This will closely resemble some of the force-directed graph examples we examined in Chapter 5 (toxiclibs).

10.7 Neural Network Diagrams

Our goal will be to create the following simple network diagram:

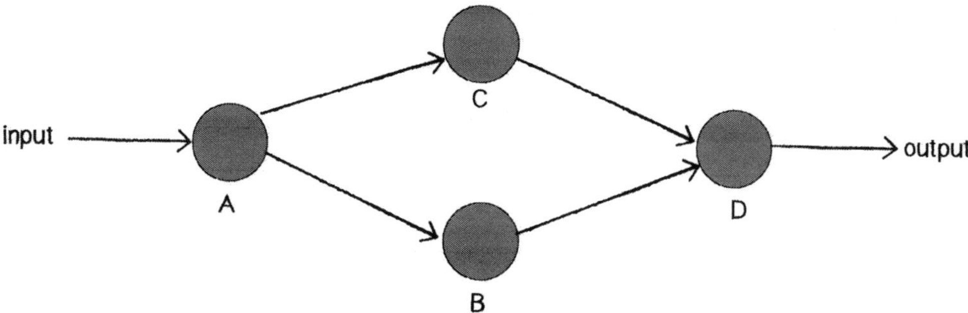

Figure 10.15

The primary building block for this diagram is a neuron. For the purpose of this example, the `Neuron` class describes an entity with an *(x,y)* location.

```
class Neuron {
  PVector location;

  Neuron(float x, float y) {
    location = new PVector(x, y);
  }

  void display() {
    stroke(0);
    fill(0);
    ellipse(location.x, location.y, 16, 16);
  }
}
```

An incredibly simple Neuron class stores and displays the location of a single neuron.

The `Network` class can then manage an `ArrayList` of neurons, as well as have its own location (so that each neuron is drawn relative to the network's center). This is particle systems 101. We have a single element (a neuron) and a network (a "system" of many neurons).

```
class Network {
  ArrayList<Neuron> neurons;
  PVector location;

  Network(float x, float y) {
    location = new PVector(x,y);
    neurons = new ArrayList<Neuron>();
  }

  void addNeuron(Neuron n) {
    neurons.add(n);
  }
```

A Network is a list of neurons.

We can add an neuron to the network.

```
  void display() {                                  // We can draw the entire network.
    pushMatrix();
    translate(location.x, location.y);
    for (Neuron n : neurons) {
      n.display();
    }
    popMatrix();
  }
}
```

Now we can pretty easily make the diagram above.

```
Network network;

void setup() {
  size(640, 360);
  network = new Network(width/2,height/2);          // Make a Network.

  Neuron a = new Neuron(-200,0);                    // Make the Neurons.
  Neuron b = new Neuron(0,100);
  Neuron c = new Neuron(0,-100);
  Neuron d = new Neuron(200,0);

  network.addNeuron(a);                             // Add the Neurons to the network.
  network.addNeuron(b);
  network.addNeuron(c);
  network.addNeuron(d);
}

void draw() {
  background(255);
  network.display();                                // Show the network.
}
```

The above yields:

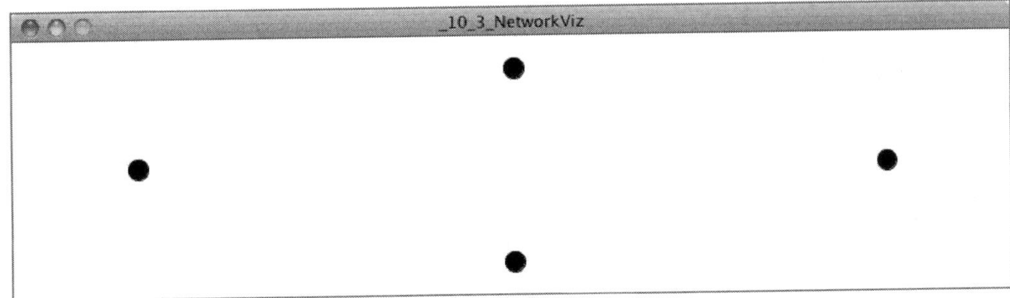

What's missing, of course, is the connection. We can consider a `Connection` object to be made up of three elements, two neurons (from `Neuron` a to `Neuron` b) and a `weight`.

```
class Connection {
  Neuron a;
  Neuron b;                          A connection is between two neurons.

  float weight;                      A connection has a weight.

  Connection(Neuron from, Neuron to,float w) {
    weight = w;
    a = from;
    b = to;
  }

  void display() {                   A connection is drawn as a line.
    stroke(0);
    strokeWeight(weight*4);
    line(a.location.x, a.location.y, b.location.x, b.location.y);
  }
}
```

Once we have the idea of a `Connection` object, we can write a function (let's put it inside the `Network` class) that connects two neurons together—the goal being that in addition to making the neurons in `setup()`, we can also connect them.

```
void setup() {
  size(640, 360);
  network = new Network(width/2,height/2);

  Neuron a = new Neuron(-200,0);
  Neuron b = new Neuron(0,100);
  Neuron c = new Neuron(0,-100);
  Neuron d = new Neuron(200,0);

  network.connect(a,b);              Making connections between the neurons
  network.connect(a,c);
  network.connect(b,d);
  network.connect(c,d);

  network.addNeuron(a);
  network.addNeuron(b);
  network.addNeuron(c);
  network.addNeuron(d);
}
```

The `Network` class therefore needs a new function called `connect()`, which makes a `Connection` object between the two specified neurons.

```
void connect(Neuron a, Neuron b) {
  Connection c = new Connection(a, b,
random(1));
```

Connection has a random weight.

```
  // But what do we do with the Connection object?
}
```

Presumably, we might think that the `Network` should store an `ArrayList` of connections, just like it stores an `ArrayList` of neurons. While useful, in this case such an `ArrayList` is not necessary and is missing an important feature that we need. Ultimately we plan to "feed forward" the neurons through the network, so the `Neuron` objects themselves must know to which neurons they are connected in the "forward" direction. In other words, each neuron should have its own list of `Connection` objects. When `a` connects to `b`, we want `a` to store a reference of that connection so that it can pass its output to `b` when the time comes.

```
void connect(Neuron a, Neuron b) {
  Connection c = new Connection(a, b, random(1));
  a.addConnection(c);
}
```

In some cases, we also might want `Neuron` `b` to know about this connection, but in this particular example we are only going to pass information in one direction.

For this to work, we have to add an `ArrayList` of connections to the `Neuron` class. Then we implement the `addConnection()` function that stores the connection in that `ArrayList`.

```
class Neuron {
  PVector location;

  ArrayList<Connection> connections;
```

The neuron stores its connections.

```
  Neuron(float x, float y) {
    location = new PVector(x, y);
    connections = new ArrayList<Connection>();
  }

  void addConnection(Connection c) {
    connections.add(c);
  }
```

Adding a connection to this neuron

The neuron's `display()` function can draw the connections as well. And finally, we have our network diagram.

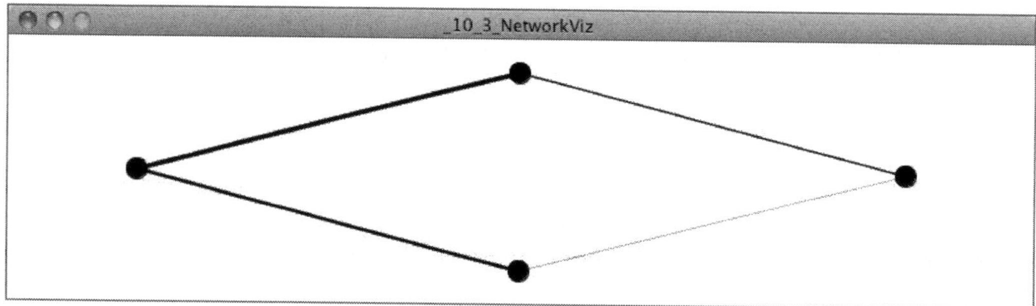

Example 10.3: Neural network diagram

```
  void display() {
    stroke(0);
    strokeWeight(1);
    fill(0);
    ellipse(location.x, location.y, 16, 16);

    for (Connection c : connections) {        // Drawing all the connections
      c.display();
    }
  }
}
```

10.8 Animating Feed Forward

An interesting problem to consider is how to visualize the flow of information as it travels throughout a neural network. Our network is built on the feed forward model, meaning that an input arrives at the first neuron (drawn on the lefthand side of the window) and the output of that neuron flows across the connections to the right until it exits as output from the network itself.

Our first step is to add a function to the network to receive this input, which we'll make a random number between 0 and 1.

```
void setup() {
                                             // All our old network set up code

  network.feedforward(random(1));            // A new function to send in an input
}
```

The network, which manages all the neurons, can choose to which neurons it should apply that input. In this case, we'll do something simple and just feed a single input into the first neuron in the `ArrayList`, which happens to be the left-most one.

```
class Network {

  void feedforward(float input) {          A new function to feed an input into the
    Neuron start = neurons.get(0);         neuron
    start.feedforward(input);
  }
```

What did we do? Well, we made it necessary to add a function called `feedforward()` in the `Neuron` class that will receive the input and process it.

```
class Neuron

  void feedforward(float input) {
                                           What do we do with the input?
  }
```

If you recall from working with our perceptron, the standard task that the processing unit performs is to sum up all of its inputs. So if our `Neuron` class adds a variable called `sum`, it can simply accumulate the inputs as they are received.

```
class Neuron

  int sum = 0;

  void feedforward(float input) {
    sum += input;                          Accumulate the sums.
  }
```

The neuron can then decide whether it should "fire," or pass an output through any of its connections to the next layer in the network. Here we can create a really simple activation function: if the sum is greater than 1, fire!

```
void feedforward(float input) {
  sum += input;
  if (sum > 1) {                           Activate the neuron and fire the outputs?
    fire();
    sum = 0;                               If we've fired off our output, we can reset
                                           our sum to 0.
  }
}
```

Now, what do we do in the `fire()` function? If you recall, each neuron keeps track of its connections to other neurons. So all we need to do is loop through those connections and `feedforward()` the neuron's output. For this simple example, we'll just take the neuron's `sum` variable and make it the output.

```
void fire() {
  for (Connection c : connections) {
    c.feedforward(sum);
  }
}
```

The Neuron sends the sum out through all of its connections

Here's where things get a little tricky. After all, our job here is not to actually make a functioning neural network, but to animate a simulation of one. If the neural network were just continuing its work, it would instantly pass those inputs (multiplied by the connection's weight) along to the connected neurons. We'd say something like:

```
class Connection {

  void feedforward(float val) {
    b.feedforward(val*weight);
  }
```

But this is not what we want. What we want to do is draw something that we can see traveling along the connection from `Neuron` a to `Neuron` b.

Let's first think about how we might do that. We know the location of `Neuron` a; it's the `PVector` `a.location`. `Neuron` b is located at `b.location`. We need to start something moving from `Neuron` a by creating another `PVector` that will store the path of our traveling data.

```
PVector sender = a.location.get();
```

Once we have a copy of that location, we can use any of the motion algorithms that we've studied throughout this book to move along this path. Here—let's pick something very simple and just interpolate from a to b.

```
sender.x = lerp(sender.x, b.location.x, 0.1);
sender.y = lerp(sender.y, b.location.y, 0.1);
```

Along with the connection's line, we can then draw a circle at that location:

```
stroke(0);
line(a.location.x, a.location.y, b.location.x, b.location.y);
fill(0);
ellipse(sender.x, sender.y, 8, 8);
```

This resembles the following:

Figure 10.16

OK, so that's how we might move something along the connection. But how do we know when to do so? We start this process the moment the `Connection` object receives the "feedforward" signal. We can keep track of this process by employing a simple `boolean` to know whether the connection is sending or not. Before, we had:

```
void feedforward(float val) {
  b.feedforward(val*weight);
}
```

Now, instead of sending the value on straight away, we'll trigger an animation:

```
class Connection {

  boolean sending = false;
  PVector sender;
  float output;

  void feedforward(float val) {
    sending = true;                  // Sending is now true.
    sender = a.location.get();       // Start the animation at the location of Neuron A.
    output = val*weight;             // Store the output for when it is actually time to feed it forward.
  }
```

Notice how our `Connection` class now needs three new variables. We need a `boolean` "sending" that starts as false and that will track whether or not the connection is actively sending (i.e. animating). We need a `PVector` "sender" for the location where we'll draw the traveling dot. And since we aren't passing the output along this instant, we'll need to store it in a variable that will do the job later.

The `feedforward()` function is called the moment the connection becomes active. Once it's active, we'll need to call another function continuously (each time through `draw()`), one that will update the location of the traveling data.

```
void update() {
   if (sending) {
     sender.x = lerp(sender.x, b.location.x,
0.1);
     sender.y = lerp(sender.y, b.location.y, 0.1);
                                      // As long as we're sending, interpolate our points.
   }
 }
```

We're missing a key element, however. We need to check if the sender has arrived at location b, and if it has, feed forward that output to the next neuron.

```
void update() {
  if (sending) {
    sender.x = lerp(sender.x, b.location.x, 0.1);
    sender.y = lerp(sender.y, b.location.y, 0.1);

    float d = PVector.dist(sender, b.location);    // How far are we from neuron b?

    if (d < 1) {                                   // If we're close enough (within one pixel) pass
      b.feedforward(output);                       // on the output. Turn off sending.
      sending = false;
    }
  }
}
```

Let's look at the Connection class all together, as well as our new draw() function.

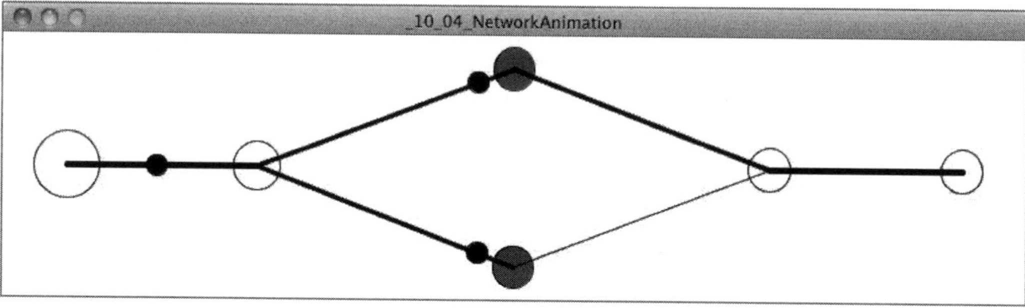

Example 10.4: Animating a neural network diagram

```
void draw() {
  background(255);
  network.update();                              // The Network now has a new update()
  network.display();                             // method that updates all of the Connection
                                                 // objects.
  if (frameCount % 30 == 0) {
    network.feedforward(random(1));              // We are choosing to send in an input every
  }                                              // 30 frames.
}

class Connection {
```

```
  float weight;                                    The Connection's data

  Neuron a;
  Neuron b;

  boolean sending = false;                         Variables to track the animation

  PVector sender;
  float output = 0;

  Connection(Neuron from, Neuron to, float w) {
    weight = w;
    a = from;
    b = to;
  }

  void feedforward(float val) {                    The Connection is active with data
    output = val*weight;                           traveling from a to b.
    sender = a.location.get();
    sending = true;
  }

  void update() {                                  Update the animation if it is sending.
    if (sending) {
      sender.x = lerp(sender.x, b.location.x, 0.1);
      sender.y = lerp(sender.y, b.location.y, 0.1);
      float d = PVector.dist(sender, b.location);
      if (d < 1) {
        b.feedforward(output);
        sending = false;
      }
    }
  }

  void display() {                                 Draw the connection as a line and traveling
    stroke(0);                                     circle.
    strokeWeight(1+weight*4);
    line(a.location.x, a.location.y, b.location.x, b.location.y);

    if (sending) {
      fill(0);
      strokeWeight(1);
      ellipse(sender.x, sender.y, 16, 16);
    }
  }
}
```

Exercise 10.5

The network in the above example was manually configured by setting the location of each neuron and its connections with hard-coded values. Rewrite this example to generate the network's layout via an algorithm. Can you make a circular network diagram? A random one? An example of a multi-layered network is below.

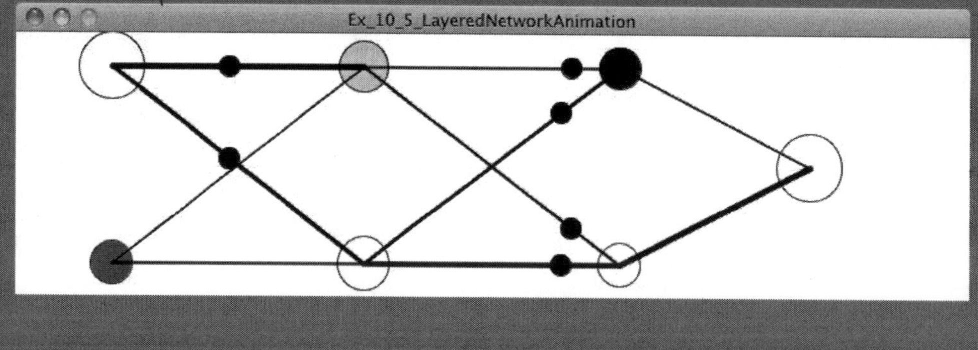

Exercise 10.6

Rewrite the example so that each neuron keeps track of its forward and backward connections. Can you feed inputs through the network in any direction?

Exercise 10.7

Instead of `lerp()`, use moving bodies with steering forces to visualize the flow of information in the network.

The Ecosystem Project

Step 10 Exercise:

Try incorporating the concept of a "brain" into your creatures.

- **Use reinforcement learning in the creatures' decision-making process.**
- **Create a creature that features a visualization of its brain as part of its design (even if the brain itself is not functional).**
- **Can the ecosystem as a whole emulate the brain? Can elements of the environment be neurons and the creatures act as inputs and outputs?**

The end

If you're still reading, thank you! You've reached the end of the book. But for as much material as this book contains, we've barely scratched the surface of the world we inhabit and of techniques for simulating it. It's my intention for this book to live as an ongoing project, and I hope to continue adding new tutorials and examples to the book's website (http://natureofcode.com) as well as expand and update the printed material. Your feedback is truly appreciated, so please get in touch via email at (daniel@shiffman.net) or by contributing to the GitHub repository (http://github.com/shiffman/The-Nature-of-Code/), in keeping with the open-source spirit of the project. Share your work. Keep in touch. Let's be two with nature.

Further Reading

Books

- Alexander, R. McNeill. *Principles of Animal Locomotion* (http://t.co/IQ0iranE). Princeton, NJ: Princeton University Press, 2002.
- Bentley, Peter. *Evolutionary Design by Computers* (http://t.co/XIp7b1zw). San Francisco: Morgan Kaufmann Publishers, 1999.
- Bohnacker, Hartmut, Benedikt Gross, Julia Laub, and Claudius Lazzeroni. *Generative Design: Visualize, Program, and Create with Processing* (http://t.co/8yekmakL). New York: Princeton Architectural Press, 2012.
- Flake, Gary William. *The Computational Beauty of Nature: Computer Explorations of Fractals, Chaos, Complex Systems, and Adaptation* (http://t.co/KdbTo1ZX). Cambridge, MA: MIT Press, 1998.
- Hale, Nathan Cabot. *Abstraction in Art and Nature* (http://t.co/ztbQ1zCL). New York: Dover, 1993.
- Hildebrandt, Stefan, and Anthony J. Tromba. *Mathematics and Optimal Form* (http://t.co/IQ0iranE). New York: Scientific American Library, 1985. Distributed by W. H. Freeman.
- Kline, Morris. *Mathematics and the Physical World* (http://t.co/v84SZnGx). New York: Crowell, [1959].
- Kodicek, Danny. *Mathematics and Physics for Programmers* (http://t.co/ygDdHMak). Hingham, MA: Charles River Media, 2005.

- McMahon, Thomas A., and John Tyler Bonner. *On Size and Life* (http://t.co/EhX3KwZB). New York: Scientific American Library, 1983. Distributed by W. H. Freeman.
- Mandelbrot, Benoit B. *The Fractal Geometry of Nature* (http://t.co/jHRQ5sQC). San Francisco: W. H. Freeman, 1982.
- Pearce, Peter. *Structure in Nature Is a Strategy for Design* (http://t.co/zaGQMOMc). Cambridge, MA: MIT Press, 1980.
- Pearson, Matt. *Generative Art* (http://t.co/bXCWfgOC). Greenwich, CT: Manning Publications, 2011. Distributed by Pearson Education.
- Prusinkiewicz, Przemysław, and Aristid Lindenmayer. *The Algorithmic Beauty of Plants* (http://t.co/koD7FhJQ). New York: Springer-Verlag, 1990.
- Reas, Casey, and Chandler McWilliams. *Form+Code in Design, Art, and Architecture* (http://t.co/1jGgwhvU). Design Briefs. New York: Princeton Architectural Press, 2010.
- Reas, Casey, and Ben Fry. *Processing: A Programming Handbook for Visual Designers and Artists* (http://t.co/dtODdOQp). Cambridge, MA: MIT Press, 2007.
- Thompson, D'Arcy Wentworth. *On Growth and Form: The Complete Revised Edition* (http://t.co/vncWa1uW). New York: Dover, 1992.
- Vogel., Steven. *Life in Moving Fluids* (http://t.co/fyTbVta1). Princeton, NJ: Princeton University Press, 1994.
- Wade, David. *Li: Dynamic Form in Nature* (http://t.co/1QYDIsDH). Wooden Books. New York: Walker & Co., 2003.
- Waterman, Talbot H. *Animal Navigation* (http://t.co/c2otv8LZ). New York: Scientific American Library, 1989. Distributed by W. H. Freeman.
- Whyte, Lancelot Law. *Aspects of Form: A Symposium on Form in Nature and Art* (http://t.co/f7UkVLQM). Midland Books, MB 31. Bloomington: Indiana University Press, 1966.

For other books that use Processing, see Processing Books (http://www.processing.org/learning/books).

Papers and Articles

- Galanter, Philip. "The Problem with Evolutionary Art Is..." (http://bit.ly/S7dhnq) Paper presented at EvoCOMNET'10: The 7th European Event on the Application of

Nature-inspired Techniques for Telecommunication Networks and other Parallel and Distributed Systems, April 7-9, 2010.

- Gardner, Martin. "Mathematical Games: The Fantastic Combinations of John Conway's New Solitaire Game Life." (http://www.ibiblio.org/lifepatterns/october1970.html) *Scientific American* 229 (October 1970): 120-23.
- Reeves, William T. "Particle Systems—A Technique for Modeling a Class of Fuzzy Objects." (http://dl.acm.org/citation.cfm?id=357320) *ACM Transactions on Graphics* 2:2 (April 1983): 91-108.
- Sims, Karl. "Artificial Evolution for Computer Graphics." (http://www.karlsims.com/papers/siggraph91.html) Paper presented at SIGGRAPH '91: The 18th Annual Conference on Computer Graphics and Interactive Techniques, Las Vegas, NV, July 28-August 2, 1991.
- ---. "Evolving Virtual Creatures." (http://www.karlsims.com/papers/siggraph94.pdf) Paper presented at SIGGRAPH '94: The 21st Annual Conference on Computer Graphics and Interactive Techniques, Orlando, FL, July 24-29, 1994.
- ---. "Particle Animation and Rendering Using Data Parallel Computation." (http://www.karlsims.com/papers/ParticlesSiggraph90.pdf) Paper presented at SIGGRAPH '90: The 17th Annual Conference on Computer Graphics and Interactive Techniques, Dallas, TX, August 6-10, 1990.

Index

A

acceleration 49, 50, 67, 69, 104, 127, 131
- Newton's second law 67
- algorithms for 50
- angular, determining 127
- damping 131
- force accumulation and 69
- rotation 104

acceleration algorithms 50, 53, 57
- constant 50
- interactive 57
- random 53

action selection 262
activation functions of neural networks 449
Adaptation in Natural and Artificial Systems (Holland) 392
add() function (PVector class) 33, 34
- implementation of 34

add() function (Vec2 class) 195
addForce() function (toxiclibs) 256
addition operator 33
additive blend mode 185
addLocal() function (Vec2) 195
addParticle() function (toxiclibs) 246
AI for Game Developers (Bourg/Seemann) 445
Algorithmic Beauty of Plants, The (Prusinkiewicz/Lindenmayer) 389
alignment (flocking) 309, 311
- implementing 311

alphabet (L-system component) 383
amplitude 117
angleBetween() function (PVector class) 37
angles 101, 102, 104, 112
- measuring in degrees 101
- measuring in radians 102
- motion 104
- theta (θ) 112

Angry Birds 190
angular acceleration 127
angular velocity, oscillation with 119
anomaly detection 447
ants, modeling for 299
applyForce() function (Box2D) 232
Aristotle 64
ArrayList class (Java) 149, 150, 151, 153, 366
- Iterator class and 153
- fractals and 366
- generics, using 150
- resizability of 151

arrays 8, 15
- Lévy flights, implementing with 15
- custom distributions, creating with 8

arrays (2D) **277**

arriving behavior **270**, **273**

- steering force and **273**

artificial intelligence **444**, **445**

- pattern recognition **445**

Artificial Intelligence: A Modern Approach (Russell/Norvig) **445**

atan() function (Processing) **110**

atan2() function (Processing) **111**

AttractionBehavior class (toxiclibs) **256**

autonomous agents **260**, **261**, **262**, **263**, **270**, **274**, **276**, **282**, **286**, **298**, **306**, **308**, **317**

- action selection **262**
- arriving behavior **270**
- combinations **306**
- complex systems and **298**
- desired velocity **274**
- dot product **282**
- efficiency **317**
- flocking **308**
- flow field following **276**
- key components of **261**
- locomotion **263**
- path following **286**
- steering **262**

axiom (L-system component) **383**

B

backpropagation **468**

beginContact() function (PBox2D) **235**

beginShape() function (Processing) **217**

bell curve **11**

- mean and **11**

bias input, perceptron **450**

Big O Notation **315**

Big O Notation N-Squared **315**

bin-lattice spatial subdivision **316**

blend modes **185**, **186**

- additive **185**
- list of **186**

body (Box2D element) **194**, **198**, **199**, **200**, **202**, **218**

- BodyDef type **198**
- attaching fixture element to **202**
- building **198**
- bullet setting for **200**
- initial settings for **200**
- multiple shapes and **218**
- object, creating **200**
- types of **199**

body lists, maintaining in Processing **203**

BodyDef type (body element) **198**, **199**, **209**

- STATIC type **209**
- configuring **199**

boids model **261**

bouncing ball sketch **28**, **35**

- implementing with vectors **35**

boundaries **209**, **211**

- curvy **211**
- fixed **209**

Bourg, David M. **445**

Box2D **190**, **192**, **194**, **196**, **209**, **215**, **216**, **241**

- Fisica **192**
- JBox2D and **192**
- PBox2D helper class **192**
- PVector vs. **194**
- Processing and **192**
- complex forms in **215**
- concave shapes and **216**
- coordinate system vs. Processing **196**
- core elements **194**
- fixed objects in **209**
- order of vertices **216**
- overhead with **190**
- toxiclibs vs. **241**
- usage **192**

Braitenberg, Valentino **262**

brute force method **392**

C

Cantor set **358**, **363**, **386**

L-systems and **386**
recursion and **363**
Cantor, George **358**
Cartesian coordinates **112**, **113**
polar coordinates, converting from **113**
Catto, Erin **190**
cellular automaton (automata) **324**, **325**, **326**, **328**, **330**, **334**, **340**, **342**, **351**, **352**, **353**
Sierpiński triangle **328**
Wolfram algorithm for **325**
Wolfram classification **340**
characteristics of **324**
continuous **352**
defined **324**
elementary **325**
elementary, implementing **330**
historical **353**
image processing **352**
moving cells **353**
nesting **353**
non-rectangular grids and **351**
probabilistic **352**
rulesets, defining **334**
self-replicating cells **324**
time and **326**
two-dimensional **342**
variations of **351**
ChainShape class **211**
configuring **211**
class (Processing) **2**, **3**, **47**
constructor **3** , **47**
defined **2**
functionality **3**
code duplication, inheritance and **161**
coefficient of friction **80**
mu (μ) **80**
cohesion (flocking) **309**, **312**
implementing **312**
collisions **190**, **234**, **235**, **241**, **301**
Box2D and **234**
avoiding in group behavior **301**
beginContact() function (PBox2D) **235**
toxiclibs and **241**
combinations **306**
complex systems **298**, **299**, **300**, **323**, **342**, **446**
Game of Life as **342**
cellular automata **323**
competition/cooperation component **300**
connectionist computational system **446**
feedback component **300**
group behavior **300**
key principles of **299**
non-linearity component **299**
superorganisms **299**
Complexity class (Wolfram classification) **341**
Computational Beauty of Nature (Flake) **314**
connected systems **249**, **253**
force-directed graphs **253**
strings **249**
connectionist computational system **446**
constrain() function (Processing) **280**
constructor **3**, **47**, **75**
arguments, adding to **75**
Contact objects (PBox2D) **236**
ContactListener class (JBox2D) **234**
continuous (cellular automata) **352**
contract() function (Processing) **149**
control (of physical objects) **447**
Conway's Game of Life (Klise) **345**
Conway, John **342**
coordinate systems **112**, **196**
Box2D vs. Processing **196**
Cartesian **112**
Processing and **112**
polar **112**
coordPixelsToWorld() function (PBox2D) **197**
coordWorldToPixels() function (PBox2D) **198**
Cornell Aeronautical Laboratory **448**
cos() function (Processing) **113**
cosine lookup tables **318**
Crayon Physics **190**
createBody() function (PBox2D) **200**
createFixture() function (PBox2D) **202**
cross() function (PVector class) **37**

crossover (natural selection algorithms) **400**, **408**
- implementing **408**

D

damping **131**
dampingRatio setting (Box2D joint element) **223**
Darwinian natural selection **394**
degrees **101**, **103**
- radians, converting to **103**

delta weight **454**
density **67**
derivatives **238**
Descartes, René **112**
desired velocity **264**, **274**
destroyBody() function (PBox2D) **208**
differentiation **238**
dissipative force **80**
dist() function (PVector class) **37**
distance joints **222**
DistanceJointDef (Box2D joint type) **223**
distributions, custom **14**
distributions, non-uniform **7**, **8**, **14**, **15**, **16**, **17**
- Monte Carlo method **16**
- Perlin noise **17**
- creating with arrays **8**
- custom **14**
- probability and **7**
- qualifying random values **15**

distributions, normal **11**
div() function (PVector class) **41**
dot product (PVector) **282**, **283**, **284**
- defined **283**
- theta **284**

dot syntax **35**
dot() function (PVector class) **37**
drag force **83**
dynamic (body type) **199**

E

ecosystem simulation genetic algorithms **392**, **435**, **437**, **438**, **439**
- genotype **438**
- lifespans, varying **437**
- phenotype **438**
- reproduction **439**
- selection **439**

efficiency **315**, **316**, **317**, **318**, **319**
- Big O Notation **315**
- Big O Notation N-Squared **315**
- bin-lattice spatial subdivision **316**
- magSq() function (PVector class). **318**
- sine/cosine lookup tables **318**
- temporary objects and **319**

elementary cellular automata **325**, **330**, **332**, **333**, **336**
- drawing **336**
- edge cases and **332**
- generations, maintaining integrity of **333**
- implementing **330**

emitter **146**
endContact() function (PBox2D) **235**
endShape() function (Processing) **217**
equilibrium **64**
Euclid **27**, **355**
Euclidean geometry **355**, **358**
- fractals and **358**

Euclidean vector **27**
Euler integration **239**, **240**
- symplectic Euler (Box2D) **240**

Euler, Leonhard **239**
evolution **390**, **391**, **394**
- Darwinian natural selection **394**
- genetic algorithms **391**
- modeling **390**

evolutionary computing **392**
Evolved Virtual Creatures (Sims) **430**
exclusive or (XOR) **466**
exit conditions for recursion **361**
expand() function (Processing) **149**
Exploring Emergence (Resnick/Silverman) **345**
extends keyword (Processing) **164**

F

factorial **359**
feed-forward model (neural networks) **448**, **473**
- animating **473**

Fisica **192**
fitness functions (natural selection algorithms) **397**, **414**, **416**, **417**, **427**, **429**, **436**
- avoidance of obstacles and **427**
- design your own **416**
- ecosystem simulations and **436**
- evolving for specific attributes **429**
- exponential vs. linear **414**
- robotic enslavement of humanity and **417**

fixture (Box2D element) **194**, **201**, **202**
- attaching to body element **202**
- creating **201**

Flake, Gary **314**
flocking **308**, **309**, **315**, **316**
- bin-lattice spatial subdivision **316**
- performance and **315**
- rules of **309**

Flocks, Herds, and Schools: A Distributed Behavioral Model (Reynolds) **308**
flow field following **276**, **277**
- resolution and **277**

fluid resistance, modeling **83**
for loops **150**
- ArrayList objects and **150**
- enhanced **150**

force accumulation **69**
force-directed graphs **253**
forces **63**, **64**, **68**, **71**, **73**, **77**, **78**, **80**, **83**, **89**, **127**, **131**, **134**, **173**, **178**, **232**, **260**, **263**
- Hooke's law **134**
- Newton's laws of motion **63**
- accumulation of **68**
- applyForce() function **232**
- applying to objects **71**
- applying to single objects in a system **178**
- autonomous agents and **260**
- creating **73**
- damping **131**
- defined **63**
- equilibrium **64**
- fluid resistance **83**
- friction, modeling **80**
- gravity, modeling **77**
- models of, building **78**
- particle systems with **173**
- springs **134**
- steering **263**
- terminal velocity **64**
- trigonometry and **127**
- universal gravitational constant **89**

forces, modeling **77**
- real forces **77**

formulae, evaluating in code **79**
Fractal Geometry of Nature, The (Mandelbrot) **356**
fractals **355**, **356**, **357**, **358**, **366**, **374**, **375**, **382**
- Koch curve **366**
- L-systems and **382**
- defined **356**
- fine structure of **358**
- recursion **358**
- self-replicating behavior of **357**
- stochastic **358**
- transformation matrix (Processing) **375**
- trees and **374**

frequency (of oscillations) **119**
frequencyHz setting (Box2D joint element) **223**
friction **79**, **80**, **81**, **83**, **84**, **131**
- applying to an object **84**
- coefficient of friction **80**
- damping **131**
- determining direction/magnitude of **80**
- formula for **79**
- modeling with formulae **80**
- mu (μ) **80**
- normal force **81**
- rho (ρ) **83**

functionality **3**
functions **54**

static vs. non-static 54

G

Galileo 77
Game of Life 324, 342, 343, 344
drawing 344
rules of 343
Gardner, Martin 342
Gauss, Carl Friedrich 11
Gaussian distribution 11
genetic algorithms 391, 392, 394, 395, 397, 409, 413, 414, 420, 435
Darwinian natural selection 394
Smart Rockets (Thorp) 420
building 409
defined 391
ecosystem simulation 392 , 435
fitness algorithms, modifying 414
interactive selection 391
modifying 413
mutation rate, varying 413
population maximum, varying 413
populations, creating 395
purpose of 392
selection, implementing 397
traditional 391
genotype (natural selection algorithms) 395, 417, 438
ecosystem simulation 438
modifying 417
geometric vector 27
getAngle() function (PBox2D) 207
getBodyList() function (World class) 203
getBodyPixelCoord() function (PBox2D) 207
getGroundBody() function (Box2D joint element) 229
gravity 88, 89, 94, 128, 244
GravityBehavior (toxiclibs) 244
implementing model of 89
modeling 88
modeling reality vs. arbitrary values 128
modeling with trigonometry 128
placing limits on model of 94
universal gravitational constant 89
GravityBehavior class (toxiclibs) 244
grid (cellular automata) 324
group behavior 300, 301, 306, 308
collisions, avoiding 301
combinations 306
flocking 308

H

heading() function (PVector class) 37, 112
heredity (natural selection) 394, 399, 400, 401
crossover 400
implementing 399
mutation 401
historical (cellular automata) 353
Hodgin, Robert 185
Holland, John 392
Hooke's law 134, 135
formula for expressing 135
Hooke, Robert 134

I

image processing (cellular automata) 352
image textures 183, 184, 185
PImage objects (Processing) 184
PNG format and 184
blend modes 185
infinite monkey theorem 392
inheritance 144, 160, 163, 164, 165, 166
adding functionality to superclass objects 165
extends keyword (Processing) 164
implementing 166
overriding superclass functions 165
subclass 163
super() function (Processing) 164
superclasses 163
syntax for 163
integration 238, 239, 240

- Euler integration **239**
- Runge-Kutta method **240**

Interaction with Groups of Autonomous Characters (Reynolds)
316

interactive selection genetic algorithms **391**, **431**, **433**, **434**
- time lag and **434**
- user interaction and **433**

interfaces **234**

iterating **152**, **153**
- Iterator class (Java) **153**
- removing elements in for loops **152**

Iterator class (Java) **153**

iTunes visualizer **185**

J

Java **192**

JBox2D **192**, **195**, **234**
- ContactListener class **234**
- full documentation for **195**

joint (Box2D element) **194**, **222**, **225**, **228**
- distance **222**
- mouse type **228**
- revolute type **225**

K

kinematic (body type) **199**, **231**
- MouseJoints and **231**

Klise, Steven **345**

Koch curve **366**, **369**
- implementing **369**

Kutta, M. W. **240**

L

L-systems **382**, **383**, **386**
- components of **383**
- translating into code **386**

Laplace, Pierre-Simon **11**

Laplacian distribution **11**

learning constant **455**

Learning Processing (Shiffman) **160**

lerp() function (PVector class) **37**

limit() function (PVector class) **37**, **51**

Lindenmayer systems **382**

Lindenmayer, Aristid **382**, **389**

linearly separable problems **466**

locations **31**
- as vectors **31**

lock() function (toxiclibs) **247**

locomotion **263**

Logical calculus of the ideas imminent in nervous activity, A (McCulloch/Pitts)
445

Los Alamos National Laboratory **324**

Lucasfilm Ltd. **143**

Lévy flight **14**, **15**
- implementing with arrays **15**
- implementing with qualifying random values **15**

M

m_p variable (Vec2 class) **220**

mag() function (PVector class) **43**, **318**
- magSq() function vs. **318**

Magnetosphere **185**

magnitude (of vectors) **42**, **51**
- limiting **51**

magSq() function (PVector class). **318**

Mandelbrot, Benoit **356**

map() function (Processing) **20**, **117**
- oscillation and **117**

Marxer, Ricard **192**

mass **67**, **70**
- modeling **70**
- units of measurement, defining **70**
- weight vs. **67**

mating pools (natural selection) **397**, **405**
- creating **397**

implementing **405**
McCulloch, Warren S. **445**
mean **11**
methods, static vs. non-static **54**
millis() function (Processing) **117**
Monster curve **367**
Monte Carlo method **16**
motion **45, 104, 112**
angular **104**
heading() function (PVector class) **112**
mouse joint (Box2D joint type) **228**
setTransform() function **228**
mouse joint (Box2D Joint type) **228**
moving cells (cellular automata) **353**
mu (μ) **11, 80**
mult() function (PVector class) **40**
implementation **40**
mutation (natural selection algorithms) **401, 409**
implementing **409**
rate of **401**

N

natural fractals **374**
natural phenomena **2, 7, 17, 67, 70, 73, 77, 78, 80, 83, 88, 89, 127, 128, 184, 260, 299, 300, 308, 324, 355, 374, 382, 383, 390, 391, 394, 435**
Darwinian natural selection **394**
L-systems and **382**
Newton's second law, modeling **67**
Perlin noise and **17**
ants, modeling **299**
autonomous agents **260**
cellular automata **324**
ecosystems, modeling **435**
evolution **390**
flocking **308**
fluid resistance, modeling **83**
forces, modeling **73 , 77**
fractals **355**
friction **80**
genetic algorithms **391**
gravity **77 , 88 , 89**
group behavior **300**
mass, modeling **70**
modeling reality vs. arbitrary values **128**
modeling with random walks **2**
modeling with the random() function **7**
physics (real world), modeling **78**
pivots, modeling **127**
plant growth, modeling **383**
smoke, modeling with particle systems **184**
trees and **374**
natural selection algorithms **394, 395, 397, 398, 399**
fitness functions **397**
mating pools, creating **397**
populations, creating **395**
probability **398**
reproduction **399**
naturally ordered sequence of numbers **17**
neighborhood (cellular automata) **325**
nesting (cellular automata) **353**
neural networks **444, 445, 446, 447, 448, 449, 467, 468, 473, 475**
activation functions of **449**
animating **473**
backpropagation **468**
connectionist computational system **446**
diagramming **468**
learning and **446**
networks of perceptrons **467**
pattern recognition **445**
perceptron **448**
real vs. simulated **475**
reinforcement learning **447**
supervised learning **446**
unsupervised learning **447**
uses of **447**
New Kind of Science, A (Wolfram) **325**
new operator (objects) **4**
Newton's first law **64, 65**
PVector class and **65**
Newton's second law **67**

Newton's third law 65, 66
- PVector class and 66

Newton, Isaac 63
nextGaussian() function (Random class) 13
- default mean/standard deviation settings of 13

noise() function (Processing) 18
- arguments for 18

noiseDetail() function (Processing) 18
non-linearly separable problems 466
non-rectangular grids (cellular automata) 351
non-uniform distributions 7, 8, 14, 15, 16, 17
- Monte Carlo method 16
- Perlin noise 17
- creating with arrays 8
- custom 14
- probability and 7
- qualifying random values 15

normal distribution 11
normal force 81
normal points 291, 295
- series of, for path following 295

normalization 43, 398
- mating pools, creating with 398

normalize() function (PVector class) 44
Norvig, Peter 445

O

object 2, 4, 92, 349
- cells in cellular automata as 349
- defined 2
- interaction between 92
- new operator 4

object-oriented programming 2, 35, 72, 137, 144, 155, 160, 168, 176, 349, 419
- cellular automata and 349
- class 2
- classes of user-defined objects, creating 155
- dot syntax 35
- genotype/phenotype objects and 419
- inheritance 144 , 160
- instances of subclasses, creating 168
- maintaining encapsulation 176
- object 2
- polymorphism 144 , 160 , 168
- references to vs. copies of objects 72
- review of 2
- structures, choosing between 137

optimization 318, 319
- magSq() function (PVector class). 318
- sine/cosine lookup tables 318
- temporary objects and 319

oscillation 116, 117, 119, 120, 122, 124
- amplitude 117
- angular velocity and 119
- frequency of 119
- on two axes 120
- period 117
- simple harmonic motion 117
- simulating with sine curves 116
- varying 124
- waves 122

oversampling 14

P

particle systems 143, 144, 145, 146, 149, 155, 156, 157, 170, 173, 178, 184, 240, 246
- ArrayList, using 149
- Verlet integration and 240
- addParticle() function (toxiclibs) 246
- applying force to single particles in 178
- class for, creating 155
- dead particles, checking for 146
- emitter 146
- forces and 173
- lifespan of particles 146
- multiple systems, organizing 157
- origin point (of particles) 156
- particles in 145
- polymorphism, using 170
- purpose of 144
- smoke, modeling 184

particles **145**, **146**, **147**, **178**, **244**, **245**
- VerletParticle2D object (toxiclibs) **245**
- applying force to single particles in **178**
- death, checking for **146**
- lifespan of **146**
- testing **147**
- toxiclibs implementation of **244**

path **286**

path following **286**, **288**, **291**, **292**, **294**
- current distance from path, finding **288**
- multiple segments **294**
- normal points **291**
- pathfinding vs. **286**
- target, determining **292**

pathfinding **286**

pattern recognition **445**, **450**
- perceptron and **450**

PBox2D helper class **192**, **196**, **197**, **207**
- coordinate systems, converting between **197**
- createWorld() function **196**
- getBodyPixelCoord() function (PBox2D) **207**

perceptron **448**, **450**, **455**, **456**, **460**, **466**, **467**
- bias input **450**
- error calculations and **450**
- implementing **448**
- learning constant **455**
- linearly separable problems and **466**
- networks of **467**
- pattern recognition with **450**
- steering and **460**
- training **456**

performance **315**, **316**, **317**, **318**, **319**
- Big O Notation **315**
- Big O Notation N-Squared **315**
- bin-lattice spatial subdivision **316**
- magSq() function (PVector class). **318**
- sine/cosine lookup tables **318**
- temporary objects and **319**

period **117**, **122**
- defined in pixels rather than frames **122**

Perlin noise **17**, **18**, **20**, **22**, **279**
- flow field following and **279**
- map() function **20**
- natural phenomena, modeling with **17**
- noise() function (Processing) **18**
- two-dimensional **22**

phenotype (natural selection algorithms) **395**, **417**, **438**
- ecosystem simulation **438**

physics **78**, **189**, **190**
- collisions **190**
- modeling **78**
- open-source libraries for **189**

physics libraries **189**, **190**
- Box2D **190**

pi (π) **103**

PI variable (Processing) **103**

PImage objects (Processing) **184**

Pitts, Walter **445**

pivots, modeling **127**

plant growth, modeling **383**

PNG graphic file format **184**

polar coordinates **112**, **113**
- Cartesian coordinates, converting to **113**

PolygonShape class **215**
- as list of vectors **215**

polymorphism **144**, **160**, **168**, **170**
- creating object instances with **170**

popMatrix() function (Processing) **375**

populations (genetic algorithms) **395**, **402**, **435**
- creating **395**
- ecosystem simulations and **435**
- elements of **395**
- implementing **402**

postSolve() function (PBox2D) **235**

preSolve() function (PBox2D) **235**

probabilistic (cellular automata) **352**

probability **7**, **8**, **11**, **352**, **392**, **398**
- cellular automata based on **352**
- infinite monkey theorem **392**
- mean **11**
- natural selection algorithms and **398**
- non-uniform distributions and **7**

normal distributions **11**
standard deviation **11**
probability of the fittest **7**
Processing **2, 12, 18, 30, 46, 54, 102, 103, 110, 111, 112, 117, 163, 183, 184, 192, 196, 203, 205, 241**
Box2D and **192**
Box2D objects, adding to projects **205**
JBox2D **192**
OOP online tutorial **46**
PImage objects **184**
Random class **12**
angles, measuring in **102**
atan() function **110**
atan2() function **111**
body lists, maintaining **203**
class inheritance, syntax for **163**
coordinate systems and **112**
coordinate systems vs. Box2D **196**
incorporating images into projects **183**
measuring time in **117**
noise() function **18**
noiseDetail() function **18**
radians() function **103**
review of object-oriented programming with **2**
rotation tutorial **103**
static vs. non-static methods **54**
toxiclibs and **241**
vectors and **30**
Prusinkiewicz, Przemysław **389**
pseudo-random numbers **7, 17**
Perlin noise and **17**
pushMatrix() function (Processing) **375**
PVector class (Processing) **30, 37, 38, 40, 41, 43, 44, 51, 65, 66, 112, 194**
Box2D vs. **194**
Newton's first law and **65**
Newton's third law and **66**
div() function **41**
function list for **37**
heading() function **112**
limit() function **51**
mag() function **43**
mathematical functions for **37**
mult() function **40**
normalize() function **44**
sub() function **38**
Pythagoras **42**
Pythagorean theorem **42**

Q

qualifying random values **15, 16**
Monte Carlo method **16**

R

radians **102, 103**
converting from degrees **103**
radians() function (Processing) **103**
Random class (Processing) **12, 13**
nextGaussian() function **13**
Random class (Wolfram classification) **341**
random number generators **3, 6, 7, 14**
custom distributions, creating **14**
non-uniform distributions, creating **7**
pseudo-random numbers **7**
random() function **3**
uniform number distributions and **6**
random walks **1, 14**
Gaussian **14**
Lévy flight **14**
oversampling **14**
random() function **3, 7, 8**
natural phenomena, modeling with **7**
non-uniform distributions, creating with **8**
random2D() function (PVector class) **37**
random3D() function (PVector class) **37**
real forces **77**
recursion **358, 359, 361, 366**
ArrayList objects and **366**
exit conditions **361**
factorial **359**

implementing **359**

Reeves, William T. **143**

reinforcement learning (neural networks) **447**

reinforcement learning(neural networks) **463**

remove() function (ArrayList class) **151**

Repetition class (Wolfram classification) **340**

reproduction (natural selection algorithms) **399**, **407**, **439**

ecosystem simulation **439**

implementing **407**

repulsion **302**

group behavior and **302**

Resnick, Mitchel **262**, **345**

resolution, flow field following and **277**

rest length (Box2D joint element) **223**

revolute joint type (Box2D) **225**, **226**

properties, configuring **226**

RevoluteJointDef object (Box2D joint element) **226**

Reynolds, Craig **261**, **286**

path following algorithm **286**

rho (ρ) **83**

Rosenblatt, Frank **448**

rotate() function (PBox2D) **207**

rotate() function (PVector class) **37**

rotation **104**, **109**

pointing towards movement **109**

roulette wheel probability method **398**

rules (L-system component) **383**

rulesets for cellular automata **334**

Runge, C. **240**

Runge-Kutta method **240**

Russell, Stuart J. **445**

S

scalar notation, vs. vector notation **33**

scalar projection **291**

scalarPixelsToWorld() function (PBox2D) **198**

scalarWorldToPixels() function (PBox2D) **198**

Schmidt, Karsten **241**

Seemann, Glenn **445**

selection (natural selection algorithms) **394**, **397**, **404**, **439**

ecosystem simulation **439**

implementing **397** , **404**

self-replicating cells **324**

self-similarity of fractals **357**

separation (flocking) **309**, **310**

implementing **310**

setGravity() function (World class) **196**

setTransform() function (Box2D) **228**

Shape (Box2D element) **200**, **201**, **220**

defining **201**

friction attribute **200**

local position for **220**

restitution attribute **200**

shape (Box2D element) **194**

shapes **104**, **112**, **113**

displaying **112**

moving with polar coordinates **113**

rotating **104**

short range relationships **299**, **310**

complex systems **299**

flocking behavior and **310**

Sierpiński triangle **328**

Sierpiński, Wacław **328**

sigma (σ) **11**

signal processing **447**

Silverman, Brian **345**

simple harmonic motion **117**

Sims, Karl **430**

sin() function (Processing) **113**

sine lookup tables **318**

size() function (ArrayList class) **152**

Smart Rockets (Thorp) **420**

soft sensors **447**

sohcahtoa **108**

splice() function (Processing) **149**

springs **134**, **135**, **136**, **246**, **247**

Hooke's law **134**

VerletConstrainedSpring class (toxiclibs) **246**

VerletMinDistanceSpring class (toxiclibs) **246**

VerletSpring class (toxiclibs) **246**

direction of force, determining **136**
lock() function (toxiclibs) **247**
magnitude of force, determining **135**
rest length **136**
toxiclibs and **246**

standard deviation **11, 12**
calculating **12**
variance **12**

Star Trek II: The Wrath of Khan (1982) **143**
state (cellular automata) **324**
static (body type) **199, 209**
static functions **55**
steering behaviors **274, 276, 302, 460**
flow field following **276**
group behavior and **302**
perceptron for **460**
wandering **274**

Steering Behaviors for Autonomous Characters (Reynolds) **262**
steering force **262, 264, 266, 273**
arriving behavior and **273**
desired velocity **264**
magnitude of **266**

steering perceptron **460, 463**
reinforcement learning(neural networks) **463**

step() function (Box2D) **205**
stochastic fractals **358, 374**
trees as **374**

StringBuffer class **385**
strings **251, 385**
StringBuffer class vs. **385**
hanging from fixed points **251**

sub() function (PVector class) **38**
subclass **163, 165**
adding functionality to superclass objects **165**

subset() function (Processing) **149**
super() function(Processing) **164**
superclasses **163, 165, 169, 170**
adding functionality within subclasses **165**
overriding functions from **165 , 170**
polymorphism and **169**

superorganisms **299**
supervised learning (neural networks) **446**
symplectic Euler (Box2D) **240**

T

tangent **110, 111, 112**
atan() function (arctangent) **110**
atan2() function **111**
heading() function (PVector class) **112**

terminal velocity **64**
theta (θ) **112, 284**
dot product and **284**

Thorp, Jer **420**
time **117, 326**
cellular automata and **326**
millis() function, measuring with **117**

time series prediction **447**
toxiclibs **241, 242, 244, 246, 249, 253, 256**
AttractionBehavior class **256**
Box2D vs. **241**
VerletPhysics class **244**
VerletPhysics2D class **244**
attraction/repulsion behaviors and **256**
connected systems **249**
downloading **242**
force-directed graphs **253**
particles, implementing in **244**
springs **246**
world, building **244**

traditional genetic algorithms **391**
transformation matrix (Processing) **375**
Transformations tutorial (Processing) **375**
translate() function (PBox2D) **207**
trees **374**
trigonometry **108, 110, 113, 127**
atan() function **110**
cos() function (Processing) **113**
forces and **127**
sin() function (Processing) **113**
sohcahtoa **108**
tangent **110**

Tron (1982) **17**
Turtle graphics **386**
Turtles, Termites, and Traffic Jams (Resnick) **262**
two-dimensional cellular automata **342, 345**
  implementing **345**

U

Ulam, Stanisław **324**
uniform number distributions **6**
Uniformity class (Wolfram classification) **340**
unit vectors **43**
universal gravitational constant **89**
unsupervised learning (neural networks) **447**
update() function (toxiclibs) **244**

V

variance **12**
variation (natural selection) **394**
Vec2 (Box2D element) **194, 195**
  adding vectors with **195**
  manitude, finding **195**
  multiplying vectors with **195**
  normalizing vectors **195**
  scaling vectors with **195**
Vec2D (toxiclibs type) **243, 246**
  VerletParticle2D class and **246**
  math functions for **243**
Vec3D (toxiclibs type) **243**
vector notation, vs. scalar notation **33**
vectors **27, 28, 30, 31, 33, 39, 40, 41, 42, 43, 45, 49, 109, 110, 194, 278, 282**
  Processing and **30**
  Vec2 (Box2D element) **194**
  acceleration **49**
  adding **33**
  as right triangles **109**
  associative/distributive rules for multiplication/division of **41**
  bouncing ball sketch **28**
  commutative/associative rules of addition/subtraction with **39**
  defined **27**
  dot product **282**
  flow fields, computing for **278**
  locations and **31**
  magnitude **42**
  motion, implementing with **33**
  multiplying **40**
  normalization **43**
  notation **27**
  scaling **40**
  tangent **110**
  unit vectors **43**
  velocity and **31, 45**
Vehicles: Experiments in Synthetic Psychology (Braitenberg) **262**
velocity **31, 45, 49, 51, 274**
  acceleration **49**
  as vector **31**
  desired, for autonomous agents **274**
  limiting **51**
Verlet integration **240, 241**
  toxiclibs **241**
VerletConstrainedSpring class (toxiclibs) **246**
VerletMinDistanceSpring class (toxiclibs) **246**
VerletParticle2D object (toxiclibs) **245**
VerletPhysics class (toxiclibs) **242, 244**
  core elements of **242**
VerletPhysics2D class (toxiclibs) **244**
VerletSpring class (toxiclibs) **246**
viscous force **83**
von Neumann, John **324**

W

wandering behavior (Reynolds) **274**
waves **122, 124**
  angular velocity, defining with **122**
  varying **124**
weight **67, 446**

- mass vs. **67**
- neural networks and **446**

wheel of fortune probability method **398**
Wolfram classification **340**, **341**
- Complexity class **341**
- Random class **341**
- Repetition class **340**
- Uniformity class **340**

Wolfram, Stephen **325**, **340**
- Wolfram classification **340**
- elementary cellular automata algorithm **325**

World class (Box2D) **194**, **196**, **203**
- createWorld() function (PBox2D) **196**
- getBodyList() function **203**

X

XOR (exclusive or) **466**

22677577R00294

Made in the USA
Middletown, DE
05 August 2015